CAPTAIN JAMES COOK, F.R.S.
From the portrait by Nathaniel Dance, R.A., in the Gallery of
Greenwich Hospital.

AUSTRALIAN DISCOVERY
By Sea

EDITED WITH AN INTRODUCTION BY
ERNEST SCOTT

PROFESSOR OF HISTORY IN THE
UNIVERSITY OF MELBOURNE

ILLUSTRATED WITH FIFTEEN
CONTEMPORARY PORTRAITS & MAPS

LONDON AND TORONTO
J. M. DENT AND SONS, LTD
NEW YORK: E. P. DUTTON & CO. INC.

FIRST PUBLISHED . . 1929

PRINTED IN GREAT BRITAIN

"Dost thou think, though I am caparisoned like a man, I have a doublet and hose in my disposition? One inch of delay more is *a South-sea of Discovery*. . . . I prithee, take the cork out of thy mouth that I may drink thy tidings."

As You Like It, III. ii.

INTRODUCTION

BEFORE any part of the southern regions of the earth was known to Europeans there was speculation, chiefly among men adept in theology and dialectics, whether there could be antipodes. Some declared it positively sinful to believe in the existence of lands situated where the upholders of the contrary theory believed that there probably was a habitable continent. Lactantius, "the Christian Cicero" (b. A.D. 260), asked whether anybody could be so absurd as to believe that there were men whose feet were higher than their heads, places where things hung upwards, where trees grew downwards, and where water fell up instead of down (*Divinarum Institutionum*, III. xxiv.). The greatest figure in the early church was St. Augustine of Hippo, and he, unfortunately, gave the authority of his name to the same argument. "There is no reason," he wrote (*De Civitate Dei*, XVI. 9), "for giving credit to that fabulous hypothesis of men who walk a part of the earth opposite to our own, whose feet are in a position contrary to ours, and where the sun rises when it sets with us." St. Augustine also pointed out that Scripture, the true guide as to what men should believe, said nothing about antipodes, nor was there any historical testimony to the existence of such regions; the belief in them was mere conjecture, wholly unworthy of acceptance.

A lesser man than these, the monk Cosmas Indicopleustes, who wrote a puzzle-headed book on cosmography in the sixth century, denounced the antipodean hypothesis as both a theological and a geographical heresy. Did not the Scriptures say that the rain fell upon the earth? How could it be said to fall at the antipodes if it came up? How ridiculous it was to suppose that there were men whose heads were hanging downward in space, whilst the soles of their feet were opposite the soles of other men in another part of the earth! Such beliefs were not merely old wives' tales handed down from the pagan Greeks; they were blasphemous; they made Christ a liar, and the word of God a heap of errors.

By one of the pleasant ironies of history there are nowadays churches dedicated to St. Augustine in the antipodes, the very existence of which he declared to be incredible; but none, so far as is known, are dedicated to less famous but, on this subject, more dependable ecclesiastics who championed the contrary idea. St. Isidore of Seville saw no objection to a belief in antipodean lands, though it is not clear that he realised the possibility of people living in them. Virgilius, one of the Irish priests who in the eighth century were sent to evangelise Central Europe, appears to have derived a belief in the existence of antipodean lands from the reading of ancient books. In A.D. 748 he was reported to have declared that there was another world, inhabited by other men, "sub terra"; for this heresy he was attacked by St. Boniface and condemned by Pope Zacharias, and was forced to disown his belief. Happily the speculation appears to have done him no harm in the long run, as he became Archbishop of Salzburg and was sainted.

Controversy on this topic was set at rest, however, during the great period of geographical discovery from the last decade of the fifteenth century to about the middle of the sixteenth. The voyages of Bartholomew Diaz (1486) and Vasco da Gama (1497–8) round the Cape of Good Hope, Magellan's voyage through the strait which bears his name, and his discovery of the Pacific Ocean (1519–21), left no room for doubt. Richard Eden, writing in the reign of Edward VI of England, made sport of the "chyldische erroures" of Lactantius and St. Augustine; and a contemporary astronomer, Peter Apian, wrote:

"But do not doubt, gentle readers of this work, that the Apostles of Jesus Christ were antipodal the one to the other, and walked each with his feet against the other's. For if St. James the Greater, brother of St. John the Evangelist and son of Zebedee, preached the word of God in Spain in the kingdom of Galicia (where his body, they say, now lies), and St. Thomas on the Indian mainland, which two regions are antipodal and go directly with men's steps opposed to each other . . . understand that they do not lie *exactly* opposite each other, but, since the inexactitude is very small, they should be called Antipodes. For the Spaniards are antipodes to the Indians and the Indians in like manner to the Spaniards."

What was true of east and west was equally true of north and south. The idea of antipodes was well established, and Marlowe seized upon it for a climax to his pyramid of hyperbole when he made Tamburlaine the Great declare:

> "We mean to travel to the antarctic pole,
>   Conquering the people underneath our feet,
>   And be renowned as never emperors were."

Pigafetta, a companion of Magellan on his voyage, and its historian, relates that the ships departed from the strait on November 28, 1520, and sailed three months and twenty days before any land was seen. *Pacificum* (that is, peaceful) seemed an appropriate name for the newly-found ocean; "in truth it is a peaceful ocean, for in all that time we suffered no storm." The Pacific was gracious and placid for its discoverers, as it can be when a quiet mood lies upon its vast expanse of basking blue, and its coral-fringed islands seem to be set in a region where "it is always afternoon." Magellan's crew did not know it in a rage. Other interesting observations they made: "The Antarctic Pole," wrote Pigafetta, "is not so well supplied with stars as is the Arctic Pole. But one sees many small stars clustered together, which have the appearance of two mist-clouds (*nebulæ*). There is but little distance between them, and they are rather dim." That was the first record made by Europeans (the Arabs had seen them long before) of the star-clouds since known as the Magellanic Clouds. A little later there were other stars to see; "when we were in the midst of that open expanse, we saw a cross with five very bright stars directly westwards, which are placed very exactly with regard to each other" (*i.e.* are equidistant from each other), a description of the Southern Cross sufficient for identification, though not precisely accurate. Magellan himself was killed in a fight with the natives of the Philippines, but one of his ships, the *Victoria*, safely returned to Europe. The speculation that on this voyage the ship came near the western Australian coast is not supported by a careful study of Pigafetta's narrative. He describes Timor, but the voyage from that island to the Cape of Good Hope would not have brought the *Victoria* within a hundred miles of Australia; nor does Galvano's later narrative (*circa* 1555) warrant such an inference.

The discovery of the Pacific, however, with the Portuguese discovery of the Cape route to India, put the antipodes on the map. Further debate on that theme was at an end. New lands, new seas, new stars, came within the world's definite knowledge.

But the endeavour to fit the fresh knowledge into the old

scheme of cosmography occasioned a new and gigantic error. A great southern continent, which nobody had ever seen, but which many assumed must be there, was placed upon a succession of maps of the world; and, as there was no dependable information about it, the name given to it was *Terra Australis Incognita*. The generation of this large geographical fiction can, with a little patience, be traced.

Throughout the Middle Ages much reliance was reposed, in regard to geographical questions, in Claudius Ptolemy of Alexandria. Ptolemy was a mathematician and astronomer who (*circa* A.D. 150–160) set himself to reform the map of the known world. The reform which in his view was needed was to determine the latitude and longitude of features and places shown upon the maps. Working at Alexandria, then the most important seaport in the world, he was in a position to gather information from men who had made voyages to various parts of Europe and to Asia. But his data were incomplete, not merely because the world was inadequately known in his day, but also because even as to some parts which were known his information was inaccurate. He did not know much of Africa below the tropic of Cancer, he was ignorant of the extreme eastern end of Asia, his outline of India was wrong, and of course he did not dream of the existence of another continent westwards across the Atlantic. Being also unaware what the southern regions of the earth were like, Ptolemy drew a line across the bottom of his map, connecting Africa with Further India, and put upon the space below this line the lettering *Terra Incognita*. He did not know anything about it, and candidly said so; it was land unknown, if there were any land there at all.

In the sixteenth century there were published maps of the world which, in respect of southern regions, may be divided into two classes. One series of maps showed no land mass whatever below America and Africa. A beautiful map of this class is the one drawn on vellum which hangs in the Vatican Museum at Rome. It was produced by Diego Ribero at Seville in 1529, and is a correct representation of the world as known at that date. Ribero knew of no southern continent, and showed nothing but open ocean where the continent of Australia lies. Indeed, he has a pretty picture of a Spanish ship, with all her sails bellying before the wind, in the very quarter where Western Australia is. A map published at Paris in 1587 was also without any outline of land to the south of America. These are types of quite truthful maps, wherein imagination does not supply what was deficient in positive geographical knowledge.

But another series of maps indicated an impatience with this
great expanse of emptiness; and the cosmographers who drew
them put in a fanciful *Terra Australis Incognita*. They did not
agree as to the outline of this great land mass, which was supposed to surround the South Pole, and to reach northwards as far
as the tropic of Capricorn. The map of Plancius (Amsterdam,
1594) is unlike that of Hondius (1595), and neither resembled any
land actually existing in that quarter of the globe. It was a *terra
australis imaginaria*.

The most misleading of this group of maps was one, the earliest
example of which is supposed to have been drawn for the son of
Francis I of France, the Dauphin who was afterwards King
Henry II. It was long believed to have been prepared from some
unknown Portuguese original, and to afford proof that Portuguese navigators were acquainted with part at least of the coast
of Australia between 1511 and 1529; but closer examination has
dissipated that belief completely. The maker of the "Dauphin"
map was possibly Pierre Desceliers of Arques. At any rate a map
undoubtedly made by him not more than twenty years later
shows a coastal outline very similar to that of the "Dauphin" map,
and is decorated similarly with human, animal and other figures.
Both maps show men building wooden houses. Camels and deer
are figured; and on the second we find also elephants, a temple,
a castellated building like a fortress, and people wearing clothes
made of some woven fabric. These figures cannot be representa-
tive of anything seen in Australia, where there were no such
animals, and no people who wore fabrics, or who knew the use of
building tools, or who built houses. The figures are very like the
decorations which at this period Catalan map-makers, working in
Barcelona, used to put upon their maps to illustrate the kind of
life led by the people of the countries mapped.

What had happened in this case was that the map-maker,
working probably from a Catalan original not now known to exist,
wanted to illustrate by means of these little figures the life of the
people of Java. He also had before him a copy of Ptolemy's map;
so he connected up Java with Ptolemy's imaginary outline of *Terra
Incognita*, and also with the outline of the land which Magellan
saw to the south of him when he sailed through his strait in 1520.
But in so doing he played tricks with Ptolemy's frank confession
of ignorance. He did not like the look of Ptolemy's plain line, so
he serrated it. He actually attributed names to the teeth of the
saw as if they were real capes, and showed rivers flowing into the
gaps between. He produced a pretty and mysterious-looking map,

which geographically was a hoax. There is no land where Desceliers marked those capes and streams. There is no continent stretching from Java to South America on the one side and to the south of Africa on the other. In joining up Java with Ptolemy's line he necessarily covered the area where the real continent of Australia was, and accidentally produced a certain delusive resemblance to part of the outline of that land. Desceliers' map does not prove that up to this date any navigator had seen any portion of Australia.

Yet these maps, and a lingering sense of the authority of the venerable Ptolemy, induced a general belief in the existence of the great southern continent, which survived until Captain James Cook set out to look for it and did not find it. In 1772, and again in 1775, Cook sailed backwards and forwards over the region where it was supposed to be. He found plenty of fog and ice, but no land; and he told the world confidently that it was not there. After Cook there was no more reason for believing in *Terra Australis Incognita* than in the marvels of the mendacious Sir John Mandeville or the figments of Lucian's exuberant imagination.

The first question of political importance which arose out of South Sea discovery concerned the rival claims of Spain and Portugal to the Moluccas. The bull of partition issued by Pope Alexander VI gave Spain exclusive rights of discovery and exploitation westward of a line drawn down the Atlantic to the west of the Cape Verde Islands, whilst the Portuguese were to enjoy similar rights eastward of the line. But that demarcation assumed a flat surface across which the line was drawn. When the Pacific was discovered, the Spaniards reached the Moluccas by sailing west, the Portuguese by sailing east. Both intended to observe the Papal award, but it had not contemplated the rotundity of the earth and the existence of another ocean. Consequently there was a dispute as to which nation had the better right to the trade of the Moluccas.

The sovereigns of Spain and Portugal appointed "cosmographers and pilots which should determine the controversy." The Spaniards produced a globe upon which the Pope's line was carried round into the Pacific, but the Portuguese refused to accept a decision contrary to their interests. Evidently there was bitter feeling about the issue. Peter Martyr of Seville relates "a merry tale" of "a little boy who stood keeping his mother's clothes which she had washed" by the side of the river Guadiana, when certain Portuguese emissaries walked past. The lad inquired of them whether they were the men who were dividing the world with his sovereign; as they answered yes, "he took up his shirt," revealed his hinder parts, and said, "Come and draw your line here through the midst;" which saying, avers the Spanish chronicler, "was afterwards in everyone's mouth and laughed at in the town of Badajos, yea, even among the commissioners themselves, of whom some were angry and some marvelled at the saying of the child." The king of Spain, however—Charles I (fifth Holy Roman Emperor of that name)—did not desire to prolong the contention with Portugal, and agreed to sell to that country whatever rights he possessed in the Moluccas and neighbouring lands, much to the dissatisfaction of the Spanish trading classes, "who well understood the profit, commodity and richness of that trade."

After the occupation of Central and South America by the Spaniards, it was but natural that they should wish to ascertain whether there were valuable territories across the ocean which washed the western coasts of the American continent. The records which we have of Spanish voyages in the Pacific during the late sixteenth and early seventeenth centuries leave no doubt that those responsible for them implicitly believed in the existence of the great southern continent. Mendaña, the pioneer, set out from Lima in 1567 "for the discovery of certain islands and of a terra firma," by which term was meant a continent. Cortes, the conqueror of Mexico, in his letters, speaks of the mainland of America as "terra firma," and it was a customary expression among the Spaniards of the age of discovery for describing land masses as distinguished from islands. Mendaña was the nephew of Lope Garcia de Castro, Viceroy of Peru, who authorised the expedition on the advice of Pedro Sarmiento, one of the boldest and most enterprising of the Spanish-Americans of this period. Sarmiento sailed with the expedition, and it is clear from the narrative of the voyage that, if his advice had been taken, the eastern shores of Australia would have been discovered. But there was contention on board between him and the pilot, Gallego, who insisted on sailing upon a route which brought the Solomon Islands into view in February 1568.

Both Mendaña and Gallego, who wrote reports on the voyage, agree that it was believed by the Spaniards that they had found the continent. "We thought it must be a continent," said Mendaña. But further examination of the vicinity seems to have convinced them that they had reached an extensive group of islands, for Sarmiento wrote of "the western islands in the South

Ocean commonly called the isles of Solomon." It is from Lopez Vaz, a Portuguese writer whose story of South Sea exploration was translated by Hakluyt, that we learn why the name was chosen: "The discoverer of these Islands named them the Isles of Solomon, to the end that the Spaniards supposing them to be those Isles from whence Solomon fetched gold to adorn the temple at Jerusalem, might be the more desirous to go and inhabit the same." The intention was, of course, that valuable lands, if any were found, should be occupied by the subjects of the Spanish Crown. The Solomons, however, did not offer much that promised to be profitable. The inhabitants were wild and warlike, showing no disposition to receive the messages and ministrations of the Franciscan friars who accompanied Mendaña with the hope of winning fresh conquests for their faith. No precious metals were found. The voyage was fruitless, except for the geographical discovery which added the Solomons to the map.

No satisfactory reasons are available why Mendaña did not make further efforts to explore the Pacific for more than a quarter of a century after his voyage of 1567–8. There is evidence that in 1574 the King of Spain granted him a licence to establish a colony; but either he was prevented by the Viceroy of Peru from making use of it, or was unable to raise the means. Lopez Vaz gives the following explanation: "Now the same time when they thought to have sent colonies unto these islands, Captain Drake entered the South Sea; whereupon commandment was given, that they should not be inhabited, to the end that such Englishmen, and of other nations as passed the Straits of Magellan to go to the Malucos (Moluccas) might have no succour there, but such as they got of the Indian people."

The Spaniards had good reason for regarding Francis Drake and other English voyagers as unwelcome intruders into the South Sea, and it may well be that it was considered undesirable to establish a colony where foreign adventurers might find such "comfortable dew of heaven," together with "some crowns and reasonable booties," as satisfied them. But Drake did not penetrate the Pacific till 1578; if Mendaña had possessed resources for another expedition, he might have been expected to take steps to give effect to the project between 1574 and that date. Drake was, truly, a very-present fear to the Spanish authorities in America, but there is some *post hoc, propter hoc,* confusion in the explanation given by Lopez Vaz.

In 1595, however, Mendaña did make his second attempt, with four ships, which sailed from Callao in April. Colonisation as well as exploration was clearly intended, for there was "a goodly company of married couples" on board. After very slowly crawling over the ocean for three months and twelve days, the ships reached a group of islands which had not been sighted on the previous voyage. Mendaña named them the Marquesas, after the Viceroy of Peru at that time, the Marquis de Mendoza. But he could not find the Solomons again. He was hundreds of miles out in his calculations. The ships sailed on and on across the Pacific, but the earthly paradise that the commander had promised never shone upon the horizon. Crews and passengers became mutinous. "No one knows where we are," they said; and they were right. "The Isles of Solomon had fled away, or the Adelantado had forgotten where they were." On September 7 an island, which Mendaña named Santa Cruz, was sighted and admired for its beauty. But that night one of the four ships, the *Santa Isabel*, disappeared. Probably she struck a coral rock and foundered. Her loss increased the doubt and depression already prevailing. A mutiny arose. Mendaña put the ringleader to death, but a few days later he himself died.

His widow, who had shared the excitements of the voyage, was a woman of remarkable determination. She took command of the expedition, with the title of Governess, and was able to exert sufficient authority to induce the crews to search farther for the lost Solomons. Groping about in the brilliant sunlight of a southern summer for islands which were not where they were supposed to be and a continent which was never anywhere, these quixotic dons of Peru at length gave up the quest and sailed for the Philippines. A second ship foundered, leaving not a wrack behind. After suffering severe privations the survivors reached Manila in February 1596. Mendaña's widow vowed that she would engage priests and people and return to complete the discovery; but she never did, and the Solomons remained in the undisturbed possession of their head-hunting inhabitants for a period of 214 years after Mendaña found them.

The voyages of circumnavigation of Francis Drake (1577–80), and of Thomas Cavendish (1586–8) made the South Seas known to English seamen. Drake evoked a rhapsody from Richard Hakluyt, the ever-watchful historian of the maritime exploits of the Elizabethan age. "What English ships," he wrote, "did heretofore ever anchor in the mighty river of Plate? pass and repass the unpassable (in former opinion) strait of Magellan, range along the coast of Chili, Peru, and all the backside of Nova Hispania, further than any Christian ever passed, traverse the mighty breadth of the South Sea, land upon the Luzones in despite of the enemy, enter into alliance, amity and traffic with the princes of the Moluccas, and the isle of Java, double the famous Cape of Bona Speranza, arrive at the Isle of Santa Helena, and last of all return home most richly laden with the commodities of China, as the subjects of this now flourishing monarchy have done?" Drake's voyage is important not only as an achievement, but also because he for the first time introduced a note of scepticism as to the existence of the supposed *Terra Australis Incognita*. Magellan had apparently supposed the land south of the strait to be part of this continent. But Drake, driven south by a storm, found that below what we now call Cape Horn (which is marked as "Insula Elizabeth" on the map of the region made by Francis Fletcher, "Preacher of the Gospel, adventurer and traveller in the same voyage") there was open sea connecting the Atlantic and the Pacific.

No man in that age had a firmer belief in the existence of the great southern continent than Pedro Fernandez de Quiros. He was Portuguese by birth, but had been a subject of the Spanish Crown since he was fifteen years of age. He had accompanied Mendaña as chief pilot in 1595, and wrote one of the original narratives of that voyage. It was his ambition to take up the research, and to establish the King of Spain as sovereign of these lands, lest the English should find them first, corrupt the natives with their heresies, and dominate the South Seas with their sea-power. He visited Spain and Rome to solicit aid. The Pope gave him audience, blessed his mission, and gave him a piece of the wood of the True Cross. The political advisers of the Spanish Crown were less encouraging. They thought the scheme doubtful, pooh-poohed the competency of Quiros, and suggested that Spain already had more territory in the New World than she could manage. But the Pope's support carried great weight, and the importunity of Quiros survived many rebuffs. He tells us that he submitted "fresh memorials every day." He wore down officials and courtiers who wanted to get rid of him. So the King was advised to give him an order for the Viceroy of Peru to provide him with two ships fitted out for the discovery of the supposed southern "islands and lands."

The Viceroy no more believed in the project than did the officials in Spain. Causes for delay were invented. Quiros was put off from day to day, from week to week. He wrote more memorials, sheaves of them. He brandished his order from the King, reminded everybody of the blessing of the Pope, and showed the precious relic. He wore down opposition at Lima as he had done at Seville. At last they gave him two ships, the *St. Peter and St. Paul* for flagship (*capitana*) and the *St. Peter* to carry his second-in-command (therefore known as the *almirante*), as well as a launch, the *Three Kings*, for a storeship. Six Franciscan friars joined the expedition to emphasise a religious purpose which was near to the heart of Quiros, and he with all his officers wore the Franciscan habit on the day of sailing, December 21, 1605.

On May 1, 1606, Quiros reached the island of Espiritu Santo in the New Hebrides group. He got no farther. He was a sick man, and there was a mutinous spirit on board the flagship. Torres, the commander of the *almirante*, was more resolute. "My temper was diffcrent from that of Captain Fernandez de Quiros," he scornfully wrote. Quiros allowed himself to be overmastered by the people whom he ought to have commanded, and crept back to America, reaching Navidad in Mexico in October. Torres determined to pursue the voyage of discovery by continuing across the Pacific and making for Manila. He passed through the strait to the north of Australia which was afterwards named after him, but it seems doubtful whether he saw the mainland of Australia, *i.e.* the hills of Cape York peninsula. Certain it is, at any rate, that Quiros never saw any part of Australia, and the statements sometimes made that he did so are merely mythical. He believed that Espiritu Santo was part of the great southern continent. Torres was under no such delusion. He assured himself that it was an island, and the description which he gave of the natives and the animals they kept does not fit the facts as a description of Australia. Quiros was a poor leader for an expedition of discovery. He had enthusiasm without knowledge, piety without reasonableness, persistency without balance, and courage without discretion. One of his companions called him a lunatic, a liar and a fraud; but these were the epithets of disillusion. A modern critic compares him with Don Quixote, and that is nearer the mark. He tilted at islands and thought he had speared a continent, and flourished a wisp of seaweed on the end of his lance as a trophy of a new world subdued.

In the year of Quiros' failure the Dutch made the first of their important contributions towards the unveiling of the unknown south, when the yacht *Duyfken*, examining the coasts of New Guinea, entered the Gulf of Carpentaria. There was no romantic guess-work on the part of these practical people. They were not interested in chasing geographical phantoms. They came into

b

the East Indies for business, and, immense as was their conbution to knowledge, they pursued their investigations with the
object of extending their trading opportunities. Having laid the
foundations of their colonial empire at Java in 1598, and established regular communications between that island and Holland,
they were bound, sooner or later, to come upon lands hitherto not
marked on maps of the world.

The *Duyfken*, commanded by Willem Jansz, did not find a
way through Torres Strait in 1606, though there is every reason
to believe that Jansz believed that there was a passage between
New Guinea and the peninsula terminating in the headland
which is now known as Cape York. Seventeen years later
another Dutch skipper, Jan Carstensz, whose Journal gives a
full and precise account of his voyage in command of the two
ships *Pera* and *Arnhem*, tried to find a way through, but was
greatly troubled by coastal shoals, unfavourable winds, scarcity
of fresh water, the desertion of his consort vessel, the *Arnhem*,
the multiplicity of islands, and fights with aboriginals. He was
the first navigator to give an account of Australian blackfellows, whom he described as "the most wretched and poorest
creatures that I have ever seen." What was more discouraging
from the point of view of the commercially-minded managers of
the Dutch East India Company, he reported that he had not
seen one fruit-bearing tree, "or anything that man could make
use of." Carstensz's voyage of 1623, therefore, though important
in the history of Dutch exploration, tended to deter his countrymen from pursuing further investigations in the seas around
southern New Guinea and Northern Australia.

When they forced their way into the Eastern trade, the Dutch
followed Portuguese sailing routes. Their ships, after rounding
the Cape of Good Hope, followed the trend of the African coast
as far as Madagascar, and thence made for Java across the Indian
Ocean. But in 1611 Hendrik Brouwer made a useful discovery.
He found that by sailing due east for about three thousand miles
from the Cape, his ships secured the advantage of favourable
winds and avoided the calms which frequently hindered them in
tropical seas. He therefore recommended to the directors of the
Dutch East India Company that they should instruct their captains to make this easterly run, and then turn northward for Java.
In following Brouwer's route some ships, bowling along before
the wind, ran beyond his recommended three thousand miles,
and came upon the coasts of Western Australia. The first of these
was the *Eendragt*, commanded by Dirk Hartog. On October 25,

1616, this vessel sighted the coast of Western Australia, and erected a post with a pewter plate on it to commemorate the visit. The Company thereupon amended its sailing directions by ordering its captains to sail from the Cape between the latitudes of thirty and forty degrees for about four thousand miles until they sighted the "Land of the *Eendragt*," which was the first name given to any part of Australia on any map. From this date a succession of Dutch ships sighted portions of the west and north of Australia, until there was pieced together a fairly accurate outline of the land which from about 1690 became known as New Holland, and retained that name long after the English had planted Australian colonies. The whole of the important discoveries in the Australian region made between 1606 and the time of James Cook were Dutch. We may dismiss as fabulous the supposition that either the Portuguese or the Spaniards discovered any part of these coasts.

The most distinguished of the Dutch explorers of Australasia was Abel Tasman, the discoverer of New Zealand and of Van Diemen's Land (Tasmania). He was a skipper in the service of the Dutch East India Company, who made many voyages to and from Holland and Java, to China, Japan, India, South America and the islands of the Malay Archipelago. In 1642 the Governor-General of the Dutch East Indies, Anthony Van Diemen, inspired a policy of exploring the unknown southern regions, in the hope that profitable trade might result. Two ships fitted out for the purpose were placed under the command of Tasman, a man "strongly inclined to this discovery." He was accompanied by an experienced pilot and cartographer, Franz Visscher. Sailing from Batavia in August 1642, Tasman ran due south from Mauritius till he entered a very cold latitude and encountered thick fogs and heavy seas. He sailed back into the latitude of 44° S., and on November 24 saw land—the mountains which now bear the names of his ships, Mounts Heemskirck and Zeehaen, on the west coast of Tasmania. In Frederick Henry Bay, named after the Stadtholder of the Dutch Republic, a pole was set up with the Company's mark cut into it, "that those who shall come after us may become aware that we have been here and have taken possession of the said land as our lawful property."

After leaving Tasmania, Tasman's ships ran east for nine days, when land was again sighted. It was the south island of New Zealand. Tasman's Journal gives a very entertaining account of the Maoris, now for the first time seen by Europeans. He believed that the country was part of the supposed great southern conti-

*

nent, and did not explore it sufficiently to find that New Zealand consisted of islands. On his return to Batavia, though he was rewarded for the service (as were all the officers and crew), he was officially blamed because he had been " remiss in investigating the situation, conformation and nature of the lands and peoples discovered, and left the main part of this task to be executed by some more inquisitive successor." It was still more vexing that he had brought back no information whether the lands which he had discovered were of any value for purposes of trade. The Company did not spend its money for the purpose of adding to geographical knowledge, however desirable that might be on scientific grounds, but with a view to increasing its business.

Despite this intimation of dissatisfaction, Tasman was chosen again in 1644 to command an expedition to ascertain whether New Guinea and the Unknown South Land were connected, or whether there was a strait dividing them. If he found a channel, he was to sail through it and pursue the coast southward until he came to the land which he had discovered two years previously. We do not know why Tasman failed in this mission; his Journals have disappeared. But we have the instructions which were furnished to him, and it is clear from these that, if he had carried out the prescribed plan, he would have traversed Torres Strait and discovered the east coast of Australia in 1644. Apparently he got into the Gulf of Carpentaria and drew the inference that it was joined on to New Guinea. The Governor-General was again dissatisfied with Tasman's exploratory work, and wrote that he intended to have the problem "diligently and closely investigated by persons more vigilant and courageous than those who have hitherto been employed on this service." This purpose was never pursued. Anthony Van Diemen died in 1645, and his successors were not so keen about making fresh discoveries as he had been. Much money had been spent, and no profit had ensued. The managers of the Company in Holland discouraged further efforts of the kind. There seemed to be no commercial advantage from sending ships to examine lands inhabited by savages, when there were rich trading grounds to be exploited in Malaya, China, Japan and India.

Tasman, then, left the map of the region south of New Guinea with that island joined to the tip of what is now Cape York; and for more than a century and a quarter maps of the world continued to be published embodying that error. The Dutch made no further effort to clear up the mystery.

Nor did William Dampier, the first English explorer of these southern regions, though he had an excellent opportunity. The early career of Dampier is full of interest, stranger than any novel or film of adventure. Being thrown on his own resources by the death of his father and mother while he was a lad, he went to sea, sailed as an ordinary mariner in a ship of the East India Company, entered the Royal Navy during the Anglo-Dutch war in 1672, was discharged ill after taking part in two battles, and at length drifted to the West Indies to work on a Jamaica plantation. There he formed a connection with piratical gentry, and led a buccaneering life for several years. He first became acquainted with the Australian coasts in the ship *Cygnet*, Captain Swan. The mutinous crew seized the vessel while the skipper was ashore in the Philippines in 1687, and cruised about in the China seas and among the Malay islands, indulging their buccaneering propensities till it became prudent to slip away from trade-routes for a while. So they stood southward towards New Holland, intending, Dampier wrote, "to see what that country would afford us." On January 4, 1688, they fell in with the north-west coast of Australia, and lingered there for more than two months.

On his return to England Dampier published his *Voyage round the Terrestrial Globe*, and by dedicating the book to Charles Montague (afterwards Earl of Halifax), who was at that time President of the Royal Society, secured a humble post in the Customs House. The book was a pronounced success. Dampier was regarded as a man of exceptionally large maritime experience; and, Montague obtaining for him an introduction to the political head of the Admiralty, he was invited to submit a plan for a voyage of exploration.

In these circumstances, Dampier prepared for the consideration of the Admiralty a scheme for the examination of the unexplored coasts of New Holland. Evidently what he had seen of the land which was not yet named Australia had interested him, though no part he had seen from the coast gave promise of being a suitable field for colonisation. But he was well aware of the fact that the Dutch had found and mapped the whole of the western and northern coasts. What more profitable piece of exploration could be pursued than that of the unknown eastern and southern coasts? That was the work which Dampier proposed to the Admiralty. His scheme was perfectly sound. He would, he said, sail first to Madagascar; he would steer "directly from thence to the northernmost part of New Holland"; afterwards he would "range towards New Guinea." From that land he would direct his course southerly, "coasting by the land, and where I found a harbour or river I would land and seek about for men and other Animals, Vegetables, Minerals, etc., and having made what discovery I could I would return home by the way of Terra del Fuego." If he had pursued his investigations according to his programme, he would have discovered the east coast of Australia.

His failure to achieve this purpose was due to several causes. His crew was discontented. There were violent quarrels on board. Dampier put his chief officer in irons and confined him to his cabin in tropical seas—an act for which he was afterwards court-martialled and punished. He altered his plans on account of "the state of my ship's crew rather than my own judgment and experience." When he did at length bring his ship, the *Roebuck*, to the coast of Australia, he was half-hearted in the pursuit of his design. He was, in fact, deficient in the personal qualities requisite for command and exploration. He was a good observer and an interesting writer, but his talents would have been more capably exercised in a subordinate capacity. He blamed his men for negligence and an untoward desire to return home. Everything but his own defects hindered him, according to his own apology, "from prosecuting any further my intended search." But the voyage of 1699–1701 added another delightful narrative to the English literature of the sea, and Dampier's true tale was exploited by Swift for the brilliant fiction of *Gulliver's Travels;* for Captain Gulliver, be it remembered, confessed his connection with "my cousin Dampier," and the land of the Houyhnhnms was placed by Swift to the south of the mysterious land marked on Dampier's map of New Holland.

In the eighteenth century the chief explorers of the South Seas were the French and the English. Bouvet, who was a believer in the existence of a great southern continent, sailed from France in 1738, commanding two vessels of the French East India Company, to search for this supposed land. They reached high latitudes where navigation was impeded by fogs and ice, and sailed (so he said) along a rocky, barren coast from which, it was recorded, "we have reaped no other advantage than being able to affirm its existence, without being able, nevertheless, to decide whether it is part of a continent or an island." Later voyagers were not able to find land where Bouvet said it was, and it was surmised that he miscalculated his position owing to variations in his compass needle due to magnetic influences. It is fairly certain that he was not within sight of the land surrounding the South Pole, and there is no continent where Bouvet supposed himself to be looking at part of one.

In 1740 the English captain George Anson brought all but two of a squadron of ships of the Royal Navy round Cape Horn into the Pacific—the two being unable to weather the storms of the Cape; but he made no discoveries. Commodore John Byron, in H.M.S. *Dolphin*, threaded the Straits of Magellan in 1765, but his Pacific cruise was not important from the discovery point of view —though it was proudly remembered in the lines referring to "my grand-dad's Narrative" in a more celebrated Byron's *Don Juan*. The Englishmen Wallis (1766–8) and Cartaret (1766–9) did useful exploring work among the island groups and the Frenchman Bougainville (1768) rescued the lost Solomons of Mendaña from oblivion and wrote a delightful book about his Pacific voyage.

The two great problems were whether *Terra Australis Incognita* was a myth, and what kind of land lay east and south of the land known to the Dutch as New Holland.

Both French and English writers on geography pressed the importance of discovery in this region upon the Governments and the educated public of their countries. In France Maupertuis drew up a list of some questions which it would be advantageous to science to investigate, among them that of the thorough exploration of the Austral lands. This theme was developed at length in two substantial volumes by de Brosses, in his *Histoire des Navigations aux Terres Australes* (Paris, 1756). It was, this eloquent and learned writer urged, an enterprise much more worthy of the attention of an enlightened monarch, and much more glorious, than war or conquest. A succession of French voyages was due directly to the influence of de Brosses—those of Marion du Fresne (1771–2), who met his death in New Zealand; of Kerguelen (in the same years), who penetrated the antarctic seas and believed that he had found a new land which he called "la France Australe"; of Lapérouse (1785–8), who was despatched on a discovery expedition in the latter part of the reign of Louis XVI; of Dentrecasteaux (1791–3), who was sent out to look for Lapérouse; and of Nicholas Baudin (1800–4), who sailed from France for the South Seas at the beginning of the Consulate of Napoleon Bonaparte. The argument of de Brosses was sustained officially by Fleurieu, Minister of Marine under Louis XVI, and by the Institute of France, the organised promoter of scientific projects. This is the reason why there was a long succession of French South Sea exploratory voyages, extending over more than thirty years, and under Governments which varied from monarchical despotism to revolutionary and military dictatorships. French scientific curiosity thus sustained an impetus which was not diverted from its purpose by some of the most sensational political changes in modern history.

But the two great problems were solved by one man, James Cook. In 1769, after conveying a scientific party to Tahiti to study the transit of Venus, Cook directed his vessel, the *Endeavour*, towards New Zealand, and circumnavigated the country for the first time (Tasman in 1642 had not attempted that task). He found that New Zealand was not a continuous stretch of territory, but consisted of two large islands with a smaller island to the south; he also demonstrated certainly that it was not part of a continent. Cook was by this time convinced that the *Terra Australis Incognita* of the old maps was fictitious. If his ship had been thoroughly seaworthy after the buffeting of the seas round New Zealand he would probably have sailed farther south to satisfy himself that there was no continent nearer than the land mass immediately surrounding the South Pole. As that course would have been imprudent, he determined to sail westward till he fell in with the east coast of New Holland, "and then to follow the direction of that coast northward, or whatever direction it might take us, until we arrive at its northern extremity." In pursuit of that design he sailed from New Zealand at the end of March 1770; and on April 20th (by the calendar date; April 19th by the ship's log; for Cook, having sailed continuously westward since leaving England, was by ship's reckoning a day behind the calendar date) he sighted the south-eastern coast of what was hereafter to be named Australia. Ten days later he discovered and anchored in a bay which, in consequence of the great quantity of plants new to science which his botanists found there, he named Botany Bay. The coast to the northward was carefully explored and mapped, and finally, on Possession Island in Torres Strait, Cook "took possession of the whole eastern coast" by the name of New South Wales.

That, then, was one problem solved. The south coast of New Holland remained to be discovered; but it was now definitely known that this land (which the Dutch had begun to chart at the beginning of the seventeenth century) was not part of a continent. It might be itself an island-continent; it might be a group of large islands, as many at that time supposed; there might be a strait dividing the known west from the east just discovered by Cook; but at all events this land had no connection with any other land that had been dreamt of by Quiros and the believers in the great continent of the south.

There was, however, one man in England who was still a strong believer in *Terra Australis Incognita*. Alexander Dalrymple, who had edited a valuable *Historical Collection of several Voyages and Discoveries in the South Pacific Ocean* (1771), was a great student of the literature of the subject. He had aspired to the command of the expedition of 1769–70, and did not conceal his resentment that Cook was preferred. Dalrymple was not satisfied that *Terra Australis* had been wiped off the map, and still raised doubts. "To put an end to all diversity of opinion about a matter so curious and important" was therefore the main object of Cook's next voyage of 1772–4, when he commanded the *Resolution* and the *Adventure*. Making for New Zealand as a rendezvous, he sailed farther south into the region of cold, where his men were "cased in frozen snow as if clad in armour," and the rigging was coated with ice. He sailed over the ground where the continent ought to have been, if it was anywhere. He took great risks, but his voyage left no room for doubt that there was no land mass between New Zealand and Cape Horn, and that the only large area of land, apart from New Zealand and New Holland, was that which was fringed by the Antarctic ice. The voyage of 1772–4 finally relegated the fondly-imagined *Terra Australis Incognita* to the company of lost Atlantis and the "Land East of the Sun and West of the Moon."

The murder of Cook by Hawaiian natives in 1779 is one of the great tragedies of Pacific history. The object of his voyage in that year was to search for a supposed strait through Canada from the west to Hudson's Bay. A native chief was killed by some of the crew, with the consequence that a thirst for revenge was generated. Cook had done his best to avert trouble. He was ashore with a party of marines, when they were attacked. Stones were thrown; the marines fired a volley. Cook turned to order the men to cease firing, when he was felled by a blow on the head and stabbed. Cook was one of the greatest navigators and discoverers of history, not only by virtue of the magnitude of his discoveries, but also because he cleared the map of the fictitious continent which had been imposed upon it since the sixteenth century. His attention to the health of his men and the cleanliness of his ships was so scrupulously careful that he was able to circumnavigate the globe without having a single case of scurvy on board—an unheard-of achievement up till his time.

A tragedy not less poignant, though different in surrounding circumstances, overtook the gallant French navigator Lapérouse in 1788. He was despatched to the Pacific by command of Louis

XVI, with instructions to visit various groups of islands in the
Pacific, including the Society, Friendly and Navigator groups,
New Caledonia, Tahiti and Easter Island. He was to explore the
Gulf of Carpentaria, run down the western coast of New Holland,
"and take a closer view of the southern, the greater part of which
has never been visited." Then he was to visit Van Diemen's Land
and New Zealand; and afterwards to explore the China Sea,
Japan and the Philippines. His instructions contained no reference to Botany Bay; though in fact his visit to that harbour,
shortly after the arrival of the "First Fleet" which commenced
the settlement of Australia, was to be particularly interesting.
He was, however, to ascertain in New Zealand "whether the English have formed or entertain the project of forming any settlement on those islands, and if he should hear that they have
actually formed a settlement, he will endeavour to repair thither
in order to learn the condition, strength and object of the
settlement."

Lapérouse visited the northern Pacific before coming south,
where his troubles commenced. At one of the islands of the
Navigator group a tragedy occurred. An officer and two boat
parties went ashore to get fresh water, were attacked by natives,
and were all massacred. Lapérouse had already sustained the loss
of several men during the earlier part of the voyage, and feared
that, if he lost any more through collisions with natives, he would
be compelled to beach and burn one of his ships in order to leave
himself with enough men to work the remaining vessel. He knew
of Botany Bay through his study of the writings of Cook, and
resolved to sail thither, so that he might take in wood and fresh
water, and fit together the parts of two new boats which he carried
in the hold. He entered Botany Bay on the morning of January
26, 1788, and was surprised to find there a large fleet of English
vessels. They were the ships under the command of Governor
Arthur Phillip, newly arrived to found the first colony in Australia. Phillip had by this time decided to abandon Botany Bay,
because he had found a better site for the settlement at Port Jackson; but Lapérouse stayed there six weeks, on terms of perfect
friendship with various English officers who visited him from the
new settlement five miles away. He sailed into the Pacific on
March 10; and there is no doubt that his two ships were wrecked
on the coral reefs of Vanicoro Island in the New Hebrides.

Disaster also overtook the expedition under the command of
Bruni Dentrecasteaux which was despatched from France in
1791. The fate of Lapérouse can hardly have been considered

doubtful by this time, but there was an intense desire for definite information. Louis XVI, sorely troubled though he was by the threatening developments of the great Revolution, gave anxious attention to the question, and used such influence as he still possessed to induce the Government to send forth ships to search for tidings. The National Assembly gave an unanimous assent, and two vessels, the *Recherche* and the *Espérance*, were detailed for the task. But the expedition was ruined by the same passionate distractions as were at this time disrupting the French nation. Fierce disputes broke out on board. Dentrecasteaux and his chief officers were royalists, and insisted on the Bourbon flag being flown; their subordinates clamoured for the tricolour, which was the symbol of the Revolution. Both the commander and his principal officer, Huon Kermadec, died at sea from what was officially certified as "une colique bilieuse."

The officer upon whom the command then devolved, D'Auribeau, who was likewise a strong royalist, took the ships to Java. There information was obtained that Louis XVI had been guillotined (January 1793). D'Auribeau maintained that his loyalty was pledged to the monarchy, not to the republicans who were then governing his country. Moreover, he was of opinion that, if he sailed from Java, he and his royalist fellow-officers would be murdered by the crew; he therefore determined to hand the ships over to the Dutch colonial government. He died within a few weeks of taking this step. The survivors of the expedition were conveyed to England as prisoners of war, where one of them, Rossel, who was generously befriended by the hydrographer of the Admiralty, wrote in two volumes a *Voyage de Dentrecasteaux, envoyé à la recherche de Lapérouse*, wherein he discreetly refrained from mention of the troubles which prevented the expedition from fulfilling its purpose. The ships did not even put into Port Jackson or Botany Bay for information which might have assisted their search.

Captain Matthew Flinders ranks next to Cook for the importance of his maritime discoveries in the south, and even before that great navigator for the scientific thoroughness which characterised his work. Flinders, in company with the naval surgeon George Bass, sailed round Van Diemen's Land in the *Norfolk* in 1798, proving it to be an island, and not part of New Holland as represented on Cook's chart. Up to this date the southern coasts of Australia from the south-west corner (King George's Sound) to the south-east corner near Cape Howe were practically unknown. The diligence and skill shown by Flinders in pursuing the exploratory tasks which he set himself in such time as he could snatch, while performing his routine duties as a naval lieutenant on service in Australian waters, induced the Admiralty to entrust him with the command of the ship *Investigator*, with a commission to explore the southern coasts of New Holland. This task was accomplished during February–May, 1802. Spencer's and St. Vincent's Gulfs were discovered, but Flinders was forestalled by a few weeks in the discovery of Port Phillip, the most important harbour on the southern coasts of Australia, this port having been found by Lieutenant John Murray, in H.M.S. *Lady Nelson*, in January of the same year.

In Encounter Bay Flinders met the French vessel *Le Géographe*, commanded by Nicholas Baudin. Baudin had left France in October 1801 with two ships, but the second of these, the *Naturaliste*, had become separated from him during rough weather some weeks before he met Flinders and the *Investigator*. Baudin, who had never been an officer of the French navy, was nominated for this command by the Institute of France, which had requested the Government to send out an expedition having "for its sole object the perfecting of scientific knowledge." Plans for the voyage had been prepared before the end of 1800, when Napoleon Bonaparte became First Consul, and he merely gave his consent to what had been arranged.

Baudin was extremely dilatory in the pursuit of his task; otherwise, having had the advantage of starting from Europe nine months before Flinders sailed from England, he would have discovered the south coast himself. The two captains met in a friendly manner on board the *Géographe*, and afterwards again at Port Jackson, whither Baudin went after spending a few weeks charting the two gulfs and Kangaroo Island, all previously discovered by Flinders. There is no evidence to justify the belief that the French had a colonising purpose in view; but during the Napoleonic wars the Emperor did endeavour to make military use of information gathered by the officers of Baudin's expedition. At a time when the French colony in the Indian Ocean, Ile-de-France (Mauritius), was hard pressed and in need of supplies, Napoleon directed the governor, De Caen, to "take the English colony of Port Jackson, where considerable resources will be found." But De Caen was being closely blockaded by British men-of-war, and, even if the seas had been free to him, was never in a position to attack a port so far away from Mauritius.

The circumnavigation of Australia by Flinders in 1803 may be taken to be the last considerable piece of exploratory work in these seas. There were still some portions of coast-line to be more accurately defined, still some islands in the south Pacific to be more exactly surveyed. But by 1803 the clouds of mystery had been rolled away from the regions of the south, and the map was substantially complete.

This book gives, in the words of the original narrators, the story of the more important phases of the discovery. Here are large extracts from the histories of the voyages of Tasman, Dampier, Cook and Flinders, with some glimpses of the tragedies which pertain to the exploration of the south. More than three centuries ago Shakespeare was much interested in a map which he saw in a copy of Hukluyt's *Voyages*, and, according to his habit of turning everything which he saw in books or in nature into imagery for his plays, adroitly used it when he made Maria in *Twelfth Night* say of Malvolio, "He doth smile his face into more lines than are in the new map with the augmentation of the Indies." "The augmentation of the Indies"—for the new map showed some lands which Shakespeare had not seen upon a map before. This book illustrates that process of augmentation, and shows how an imaginary continent was wiped off to make way for the real world of the south.

Ernest Scott.

Melbourne,
1929.

CONTENTS

LIST OF ILLUSTRATIONS

The maps and prints which illustrate this book have been chosen and arranged by Miss Kathleen Ussher.

PORTRAITS

MAPS

ACKNOWLEDGMENT

THE majority of the maps contained in this volume have been photographed by kind permission of the Trustees of the British Museum, the helpful co-operation of whose Librarians has rendered the work of collecting the illustrations a particularly pleasant one.

The publishers are indebted to the Hakluyt Society for permission to reproduce the Map of the World, London 1598, referred to by Professor Scott in his Introduction in the passage quoted from *Twelfth Night*. This map is generally regarded as the work of Emmeric Mollineux of Lambeth.

The Chart of part of the South Sea [1771], showing the lands discovered by the *Endeavour*, and bearing Cook's own signature, is preserved in the British Museum, as is also the original Map of Pierre Desceliers, made at Arques in the year 1550.

Thevenot's Map of New Holland, Paris 1663, is said to be copied from a map by J. Blaeu, dated Amsterdam 1659. The latter is included in the Mammoth Atlas preserved in the King's Library at the British Museum and entitled, *Archipelagus Orientalis sive Asiaticus*. Because of its enormous bulk—this Atlas is known as "the largest book in the world" and was presented by the Dutch merchants to Charles II—the attempt to photograph Blaeu's original was reluctantly abandoned and the Thevenot map substituted in its place.

Thanks are especially due to Mr. F. P. Sprent, the Superintendent of the Map Room in the British Museum, and his assistants; to Mr. W. G. Perrin, O.B.E., and his deputy at the Admiralty Library; to the Agent-General for New South Wales for permission to reproduce the portrait of George Bass, which appears in Volume V of the *Historical Records* of that State; and to S. Gravenhage Martinus Nijhoff at the Hague for a similar courtesy in connection with the portrait of Van Diemen, which is taken from the magnificent Dutch series, *Onze Mannen Ter Zee in Dicht en Bild*, 1572–1800.

KATHLEEN USSHER.

LIST OF PRINCIPAL DATES

WORKS OF REFERENCE

THE best modern treatises on the subject of this book are Rainaud's *Le Continent Austral* and G. Arnold Wood's *The Discovery of Australia*. G. Collingridge's *Discovery of Australia* is also valuable; many of its main contentions are controverted by Wood. The best biographies of Cook are those by Kitson and Sir Walter Besant. There is a good short life of Dampier by W. Clark Russell. Heeres' *The Part borne by the Dutch in the Discovery of Australia*, and the same author's edition of Tasman's Journal of his voyage of 1642, are invaluable works. See also E. Scott's *Life of Captain Matthew Flinders* and *Life of Lapérouse*.

The following works published by the Hakluyt Society are of first-class importance for the original historical material which they contain : Major, *Early Voyages to Australia*; Lord Amherst and Basil Thompson, *Voyage of Mendaña to the Solomon Islands*; Markham, *The Voyages of Quiros*; Corney, *The Quest and Occupation of Tahiti*; and Corney, *The Voyage of Gonzalez to Easter Island*.

The Voyages of Dampier have been reprinted several times; the most convenient modern edition is that in one volume published by Messrs. Dent & Sons. There are also several editions of Cook's Voyages, but the only authentic edition of Cook's Journal of his famous voyage of 1768–71 is that edited by the Hydrographer to the Admiralty, W. J. L. Wharton. Flinders' *Voyage to Terra Australis* has never been reprinted. *The Logbooks of the " Lady Nelson,"* edited by Ida Lee, contains valuable material, supplementing Grant's *Narrative of a Voyage of Discovery*. The original narratives of the voyages of Bougainville, Lapérouse, Dentrecasteaux and Baudin are available in English translations as well as in the French editions.

J. Callander's *Terra Australis Cognita*, J. Burney's *Discoveries in the South Seas*, and A. Dalrymple's *Historical Collection of the several voyages and discoveries in the South Pacific Ocean*, are still useful; as is also Charles de Brosses' *Histoire des Navigations aux Terres Australes*.

AUSTRALIAN DISCOVERY
BY SEA

I. TERRA AUSTRALIS INCOGNITA

[THE memorial of Dr. Juan Arias, addressed to King Philip III
of Spain, presents an argument for the discovery and occupation
of the supposed great southern continent by the Spanish nation
for the various reasons set forth by the writer; it also supplies a
statement of the ideas which were prevalent at this period as to
the nature of the southern regions. The original document is
in the British Museum, and the translation was published by
R. H. Major in his *Early Voyages to Australia*, Hakluyt Society,
1859.]

SIRE,—The memorial of the Doctor Juan Luis Arias showeth:
That in consideration of the great advantage which will accrue to
the service of Your Majesty, to the entension of the Catholic
Church, and to the increase of our holy faith, from the conversion
of the Gentiles of the southern land, which is the principal obligation to which Your Majesty and your crown are pledged, he now
earnestly begs (great as have been his former importunities) to
solicit Your Majesty's consideration to that which is here set
forth.

For the English and Dutch heretics, whom the devil unites for
this purpose by every means in his power, most diligently continue the exploration, discovery, and colonisation of the principal
ports of this large part of the world in the Pacific Ocean, and sow
in it the most pernicious poisons of their apostasy, which they put
forth with the most pressing anxiety in advance of us, who should
put forth the sovereign light of the gospel. This they are now
perseveringly doing in that great continent in which are the provinces of Florida, and they will afterwards proceed to do the same
with New Spain, and then with New Mexico, the kingdom of
Quivira, the Californias, and other most extensive provinces. For
which purpose, and for other reasons connected with their
machinations against our kingdom, they have already colonised

B

Virginia. To further the same object also, they have fortified and colonised Bermuda, and continue most zealously and rapidly sowing the infernal poison of their heresy, and infecting with it the millions upon millions of excellent people who inhabit those regions. From Virginia also they are advancing most rapidly inland, with the most ardent desire to deprive the Catholic Church of the inestimable treasure of an infinite number of souls; and to found in that land an empire in which they will at length possess much better and richer Indies than our own, and from which position they will be able to lord it absolutely over all our territories, and over all our navigation and commerce with the West Indies. This is a most grievous case for us, and most offensive to our Lord God and His Church, and this kingdom has reason to dread from so mischievous a state of things very great injuries from the hands of these enemies, and no less punishment from the divine indignation for having allowed these basilisks to locate themselves in such a position; from whence, before we of the Catholic Church arrive with the preaching of the gospel with which we are commissioned, they draw to themselves and infect with the depravity of their apostasy that countless number of Gentiles which inhabit the said provinces, and which cover a greater surface of land than all Europe.

In order to understand the question, it must be premised that the whole globe of earth and water is divided into two equal parts or halves by the equinoctial line. The northern hemisphere, which stretches from the equinoctial to the Arctic Pole, contains all which has been hitherto discovered and peopled in Asia, Europe, and the chief part of Africa. The remaining half, or southern hemisphere, which reaches from the equinoctial to the Antarctic Pole, comprises part of what we call America, and the whole of that Austral land the discovery and apostolic conquest of which is now treated of. Now, if we except from this southern hemisphere all that there is of Africa lying between the equinoctial line and the Cape of Good Hope, and all that there is of Peru from the parallel of the said equinoctial line, which passes near Quito, down to the straits of Magellan, and that small portion of land which lies to the south of the strait, all the rest of the firm land of the said southern hemisphere remains to be discovered. Thus of the whole globe, there is little less than one entire half which remains to be discovered, and to have the gospel preached in it; and this discovery and evangelical conquest forms the principal part of the obligation under which these kingdoms lie for the preaching of the gospel to the Gentiles, in conformity with

FERDINAND MAGELLAN.
Drawn by Thomas Derrick, from *The Effigies Regum* of Crespin de Passe.

the agreement made with the Catholic Church and its head, the supreme pontiffs Alexander VI and Paul III.

Some have asked, as already pointed out, whether the southern hemisphere be not all water, forming, as it were, a great part of the ocean, so as to leave but little of the surface of the earth in it uncovered. The reply to this is, that, according to what we are taught by sacred writ and by philosophical reasoning, there is proportionately as great a surface of land uncovered in the southern hemisphere as in the northern. For the fiat of the Creator, that the waters should be collected into certain hollows of the earth, in order that there should remain uncovered the portion that was necessary for the production of vegetation; as where He says in Genesis the 1st: "Let the waters under the heaven be gathered together into one place, and let the dry land appear," supposes this water to have been created an entire orb, which covered and surrounded the whole of the earth, in the same manner as we reckon the positions of the elements; the land the lowest, in the middle of which is the centre of the whole elementary and celestial machine, then the water, and after that the air and igneous substance or the fire, which reaches its culmination or convex part in the concave of the celestial firmament. Then if, when God commanded that the waters should be gathered together, it was to be understood solely with reference to the northern hemisphere, the water in the southern hemisphere would remain as it was, surrounding and covering all, and the whole sphere of water could not be contained beneath one spherical surface equidistant to the centre of gravity, which always seeks to be united with the centre of the whole machine. And thus all the water of the southern hemisphere would be more remote from the said centre than that of the other hemisphere, without being contained in any sinus, and thus would be much higher, and naturally could not contain itself without flowing towards the other hemisphere, until it placed itself in equilibrium with the said centre of gravity; as is plainly gathered from the demonstration of Archimedes, in his work *De Insidentibus Aquæ*, and is manifestly seen in the ebb and flow of the ocean; in which it is observed, that when the water rises above the surface of equidistance from its centre of gravity, it immediately outflows its ordinary limits until it finds its level with that surface; so that the gathering together of the waters was proportional in the two halves of the sphere of earth and water, gathering itself into certain hollows of the earth, which also have their means of correspondence between the two hemispheres. For as the quiet and equilibrium of the parts of the earth and water with respect to the centre of gravity consist in the equal tendencies of the opposite parts towards the same centre, it follows that the sinuses or receptacles of water in the one half are nearly proportioned in their position and other respects to those of the other. From all which it follows, that in the southern hemisphere there is an uncovered surface of land correspondent, or nearly so, to that which has been discovered in the northern hemisphere.

II. TORRES AND QUIROS

[LUIS VAEZ DE TORRES commanded the *Almirante*, one of the two ships despatched from Peru in December 1605 to explore the Pacific. Quiros, the commander of the expedition, was under the delusion that he had discovered the great southern continent when he reached the island of Espiritu Santo, in the New Hebrides group. Torres, after Quiros sailed back to South America, satisfied himself that it was an island. This narrative is contained in a manuscript which was found at Manila in 1762 when the English captured that city during the war against the Family Compact (France and Spain). It was first printed in Burney's *Discoveries and Voyages in the South Sea*.]

We sailed from Callao, in Peru, December 21st, 1605, with two ships and a launch, under the command of Captain Pedro Fernandez de Quiros, and I for his almirante; and without losing company, we stood W.S.W., and went on this course 800 leagues.

Our commander, seeing we wanted water, agreed that we should go to the island Santa Cruz, where he had been with the adelantado Alvaro de Mendaña, saying we might there supply ourselves with water and wood, and then he would determine what was most expedient for Your Majesty's service. The crew of the *Capitana* at this time were mutinous, designing to go directly to Manila: on this account he sent the chief pilot a prisoner on board my ship, without doing anything farther to him or others, though I strongly importuned him to punish them, or give me leave to punish them; but he did not choose to do it, from whence succeeded what Your Majesty knows, since they made him turn from the course (voyage), as will be mentioned and he has probably said at Your Majesty's court.

Sailing thence to the southward towards the large island, we discovered a very large bay, well peopled, and very fertile in yams and fruits, hogs and fowls. They are all black people and naked. They fight with bows, darts, and clubs. They did not choose to have peace with us, though we frequently spoke to them and made presents; and they never, with their good-will, let us set foot on shore.

5

This bay is very refreshing, and in it fall many and large rivers. It is in 15⅔° S. latitude, and in circuit it is twenty-five leagues. We named it the bay de San Felipe y Santiago, and the land del Espiritu Santo.

There we remained fifty days: we took possession in the name of Your Majesty. From within this bay, and from the most sheltered part of it, the *Capitana* departed at one hour past midnight, without any notice given to us, and without making any signal. This happened the 11th of June. And although the next morning we went out to seek for them, and made all proper efforts, it was not possible for us to find them; for they did not sail on the proper course, nor with good intention. So I was obliged to return to the bay, to see if by chance they had returned thither. And on the same account we remained in this bay fifteen days; at the end of which we took Your Majesty's orders, and held a consultation with the officers of the frigate. It was determined that we should fulfil them, although contrary to the inclination of many, I may say, of the greater part; but my condition was different from that of Captain Pedro Fernandez de Quiros.

At length we sailed from this bay, in conformity to the order, although with intention to sail round this island, but the season and the strong currents would not allow this, although I ran along a great part of it. In what I saw there are very large mountains. It has many ports, though some of them are small. All of it is well watered with rivers. We had at this time nothing but bread and water: it was the height of winter, with sea, wind, and ill-will (of his crew) against us. All this did not prevent me from reaching the mentioned latitude, which I passed one degree, and would have gone farther if the weather had permitted; for the ship was good. It was proper to act in this manner, for these are not voyages performed every day, nor could Your Majesty otherwise be properly informed. Going into the said latitude on a S.W. course, we had no signs of land that way.

From hence I stood back to the N.W. to 11½° S. latitude: there we fell in with the beginning of New Guinea, the coast of which runs W. by N. and E. by S. I could not weather the east point, so I coasted along to the westward on the south side.

All this land of New Guinea is peopled with Indians, not very white, and naked, except their waists, which are covered with a cloth made of the bark of trees, and much painted. They fight with darts, targets, and some stone clubs, which are made fine with plumage. Along the coast are many islands and habitations. All the coast has many ports, very large, with very large rivers, and many plains. Without these islands there runs a reef of shoals, and between them (the shoals) and the mainland are the islands. There is a channel within. In these ports I took possession for Your Majesty.

We went along three hundred leagues of coast, as I have mentioned, and diminished the latitude $2\frac{1}{2}°$, which brought us into 9°. From hence we fell in with a bank of from three to nine fathoms, which extends along the coast above 180 leagues. We went over it along the coast to $7\frac{1}{2}°$ S. latitude, and the end of it is in 5°. We could not go farther on for the many shoals and great currents, so we were obliged to sail out S.W. in that depth to 11° S. latitude. There is all over it an archipelago of islands without number, by which we passed, and at the end of the eleventh degree the bank became shoaler. Here were very large islands, and there appeared more to the southward: they were inhabited by black people, very corpulent, and naked: their arms were lances, arrows, and clubs of stone ill-fashioned. We could not get any of their arms. We caught in all this land twenty persons of different nations, that with them we might be able to give a better account to Your Majesty. They give much notice to other people, although as yet they do not make themselves well understood.

We went upon this bank for two months, at the end of which time we found ourselves in twenty-five fathoms, and in 5° S. latitude, and ten leagues from the coast. And having gone 480 leagues, here the coast goes to the N.E. I did not reach it, for the bank became very shallow. So we stood to the north, and in twenty-five fathoms to 4° latitude, where we fell in with a coast, which likewise lay in a direction east and west. We did not see the eastern termination, but from what we understood of it, it joins the other we had left on account of the bank, the sea being very smooth. This land is peopled by blacks, different from all the others; they are better adorned: they use arrows, darts, and large shields, and some sticks of bamboo filled with lime, with which, by throwing it out, they blind their enemies. Finally, we stood to the W.N.W. along the coast, always finding this people, for we landed in many places: also in it we took possession for Your Majesty. In this land also we found iron, china bells, and other things, by which we knew we were near the Malucas; and so we ran along this coast above 130 leagues, where it comes to a termination fifty leagues before you reach the Malucas. There is an infinity of islands to the southward, and very large, which for the want of provisions we did not approach; for I doubt if in ten years could be examined the coasts of all the islands we descried.

We observed the variation in all this land of New Guinea to the Malucas; and in all of it the variation agrees with the meridian of the Ladrone Islands and of the Philippine Islands.

At the termination of this land we found Mahometans, who were clothed, and had fire-arms and swords. They sold us fowls, goats, fruit, and some pepper, and biscuit which they called sagoe, which will keep more than twenty years. The whole they sold us was but little; for they wanted cloth, and we had not any; for all the things that had been given us for traffic were carried away by the *Capitana*, even to tools and medicines, and many other things which I do not mention, as there is no help for it; but, without them, God took care of us.

III. TASMAN'S DISCOVERY OF VAN DIEMEN'S LAND AND NEW ZEALAND

[TASMAN's narrative of his discovery of Van Diemen's Land and New Zealand in 1642 is taken from the translation of his Journal by Dr. J. E. Heeres, published by Muller of Amsterdam.]

Journal or Description drawn up by me, Abel Jansz Tasman, of a voyage made from the town of Batavia in East India, for the discovery of the unknown South-land, in the year of our Lord 1642, the 14th of August. May God Almighty vouchsafe His blessing on this work. Amen.

This day August 14, A.D. 1642, we set sail from the roads of *Batavia* with two ships, to wit: the Yacht Heemskercq and the Flute Zeehaen, the wind being north-east with good weather. On the same day in the evening the Zeehaen ran aground near the island of Rotterdam, but got afloat again in the night without any notable damage, after which we continued our voyage to the Straits of Zunda.

> . . . .

Item the 24th do. (*November*).—Good weather and a clear sky. At noon Latitude observed 42° 25′, Longitude 163° 31′; course kept east by north, sailed 30 miles; the wind south-westerly and afterwards from the south with a light top-gallant breeze. In the afternoon, about 4 o'clock, we saw land, bearing east by north of us, at about 10 miles' distance from us by estimation; the land we sighted was very high; towards evening we also saw, east-south-east of us, three high mountains, and to the north-east two more mountains, but less high than those to southward; we found that here our compass pointed due north. In the evening, in the first glass after the watch had been set, we convened our ship's council with the second mates, and represented to them whether it would not be advisable to run farther out to sea; we also asked their advice as to the time when it would be best to do so; upon which it was unanimously resolved to run out to sea at the expiration of three glasses, to keep doing so for the space of ten glasses, and after this, to make for the land again; all of which may *in extenso* be seen from to-day's resolution, to which we beg leave to refer.

During the night, when three glasses had run out, the wind turned to the south-east; we held off from the shore, and sounded in 100 fathom, fine white sandy bottom with small shells; we sounded once more, and found black coarse sand with pebbles; during the night we had a south-east wind with a light breeze.

Item the 25th do.—In the morning we had a calm; we floated the white flag and pendant from our stern, upon which the officers of the Zeehaen with their steersmen came on board of us; we then convened the ship's council, and resolved together upon what may *in extenso* be seen from to-day's resolution, to which we beg leave to refer. Towards noon the wind turned to the south-east, and afterwards to the south-south-east and the south; upon which we made for the shore; at about 5 o'clock in the evening we got near the coast; three miles off shore we sounded in 60 fathom coral bottom; one mile off the coast we had clean, fine, white sand; we found this coast to bear south by east and north by west; it was a level coast, our ship being in 42° 30′ S. Latitude, and average Longitude 163° 50′. We then put off from shore again, the wind turning to the south-south-east, with a top-gallant gale. If you come from the west, and find your needle to show 4° north-westerly variation, you had better look out for land, seeing that the variation is very abruptly decreasing here. If you should happen to be overtaken by rough weather from the westward, you had best heave to, and not run on. Near the coast here, the needle points due north. We took the average of our several longitudes, and found this land to be in 163° 50′ Longitude.

This land being the first land we have met with in the South Sea, and not known to any European nation, we have conferred on it the name of Anthoony van Diemenslandt, in honour of the Hon. Governor-General, our illustrious master, who sent us to make this discovery; the islands circumjacent, so far as known to us, we have named after the Hon. Councillors of India, as may be seen from the little chart which has been made of them.

Item the 26th do.—We had the wind from eastward with a light breeze and hazy weather, so that we could see no land; according to our estimation we were at 9½ miles' distance from shore. Towards noon we hoisted the top-pendant, upon which the Zeehaen forthwith came astern of us; we called out to her men that we should like Mr. Gilsemans to come on board of us, upon which the said Mr. Gilsemans straightways came on board of us, to whom we imparted the reasons set forth in the subjoined letter, which we

enjoined him to take with him on board the Zeehaen, to be shown
to Skipper Gerrit Jansz, who is to give orders to her steersmen in
accordance with its purport:

The officers of the Flute Zeehaen are hereby enjoined to set
down in their daily journals this land which we saw and came
near to yesterday, in the longitude of 163° 50′, seeing that we have
found this to be its average longitude; and to lay down the said
longitude as an established point of departure for their further
reckonings; he who before this had got the longitude of 160° or
more, will henceforth have to take this land for his starting-point;
we make this arrangement in order to preclude all errors as much
as is at all possible. The officers of the Zeehaen are requested to
give orders in conformity to her steersmen, and to see them acted
up to, because we opine this to be their duty; any charts that
should be drawn up of this part, will have to lay down this land
in the average longitude of 163° 50′, as hereinbefore stated.

Actum Heemskercq datum ut supra

(Signed)

ABEL JANSZ TASMAN.

At noon Latitude estimated 43° 36′ South, Longitude 163° 2′;
course kept south-south-west, sailed 18 miles. We had ½ degree
N.W. variation; in the evening the wind went round to the north-
east, and we changed our course to east-south-east.

Item the 27th do.—In the morning we again saw the coast, our
course still being east-south-east. At noon Latitude estimated
44° 4′ South, Longitude 164° 2′; course kept south-east by east,
sailed 13 miles; the weather was drizzly, foggy, hazy and rainy,
the wind north-east and north-north-east with a light breeze;
at night, when 7 glasses of the first watch had run out, we began
trying under reduced sail, because we dared not run on, owing to
the thick darkness.

Item the 28th do.—In the morning, the weather still being dark,
foggy and rainy, we again made sail, shaped our course to eastward and afterwards north-east by north; we saw land north-east
and north-north-east of us, and made straight for it; the coast
here bears south-east by east and north-west by west; as far as I
can see, the land here falls off to eastward. At noon Latitude
estimated 44° 12′, Longitude 165° 2′; course kept east by south,
sailed 11 miles, with a northwesterly wind and a light breeze. In
the evening we got near the coast; here near the shore there are a
number of islets, of which one in shape resembles a lion; this islet
lies out into the sea at about 3 miles′ distance from the mainland;

in the evening the wind turned to the east; during the night we lay a-trying under reduced sail.

Item the 29th do.—In the morning we were still near the rock which is like a lion's head; we had a westerly wind with a top-gallant gale; we sailed along the coast, which here bears east and west; towards noon we passed two rocks, of which the westernmost was like Pedra Branca off the coast of China; the easternmost was like a *tall, obtuse, square tower*, and is at about 4 miles' distance from the mainland. We passed between these rocks and the mainland; at noon Latitude estimated 43° 53', Longitude 166° 3'; course kept east-north-east, sailed 12 miles, we were still running along the coast. In the evening, about 5 o'clock, we came before a bay which seemed likely to afford a good anchorage; upon which we resolved with our ship's council to run into it, as may be seen from to-day's resolution; we had nearly got into the bay, when there arose so strong a gale that we were obliged to take in sail, and to run out to sea again under reduced sail, seeing that it was impossible to come to anchor in such a storm; in the evening we resolved to stand out to sea during the night under reduced sail, to avoid being thrown on a lee-shore by the violence of the wind; all which may *in extenso* be seen from the resolution aforesaid, to which for briefness' sake we beg leave to refer.

Item the last do.—At daybreak we again made for shore, the wind and the current having driven us so far out to sea, that we could barely see the land; we did our utmost to get near it again, and at noon had the land north-west of us; we now turned the ship's head to westward, with a northerly wind which prevented us from getting close to the land. At noon Latitude observed 43° 41', Longitude 168° 3'; course kept east by north, sailed 20 miles, in a storm and with variable weather. The needle points due north here. Shortly after noon we turned our course to westward with a strong variable gale; we then turned to the north under reduced sail.

Item the first of December.—In the morning, the weather having become somewhat better, we set our top-sails, the wind blowing from the west-south-west, with a top-gallant gale; we now made for the coast. At noon Latitude observed 43° 10', Longitude 167° 55'; course kept north-north-west, sailed 8 miles, it having fallen a calm; in the afternoon we hoisted the white flag, upon which our friends of the Zeehaen came on board of us, with whom we resolved that it would be best and most expedient, wind and weather permitting, to touch at the land the sooner the better; both to get better acquainted with its condition, and to attempt to procure refreshments for our own behoof; all which may be more amply seen from this day's resolution. We then got a breeze from eastward, and made for the coast to ascertain whether it would afford a fitting anchorage; about one hour after sunset we dropped anchor in a good harbour, in 22 fathom, white and grey fine sand, a naturally drying bottom; for all which it behoves us to thank God Almighty with grateful hearts.

Item the 2nd do.—Early in the morning we sent our Pilot-major Francoys Jacobsz in command of our pinnace, manned with 4 musketeers and 6 rowers, all of them furnished with pikes and side-arms, together with the cock-boat of the Zeehaen with one of her second mates and 6 musketeers in it, to a bay, situated north-west of us at upwards of a mile's distance, in order to ascertain what facilities (as regards fresh water, refreshments, timber and the like) may be available there. About three hours before nightfall the boats came back, bringing various samples of vegetables, which they had seen growing there in great abundance, some of them in appearance not unlike a certain plant growing at the Cabo de Bona Esperance, and fit to be used as pot-herbs, and another species with long leaves and a brackish taste, strongly resembling persil de mer or samphire. The Pilot-major and the second mate of the Zeehaen made the following report, to wit:

That they had rowed the space of upwards of a mile round the said point, where they had found high but level land, covered with vegetation (not cultivated, but growing naturally by the will of God), abundance of excellent timber, and a gently sloping water-course in a barren valley, the said water, though of good quality, being difficult to procure, because the water-course was so shallow, that the water could be dipped with bowls only.

That they had heard certain human sounds, and also sounds nearly resembling the music of a trump, or a small gong, not far from them, though they had seen no one.

That they had seen two trees about 2 or 2½ fathom in thickness, measuring from 60 to 65 feet from the ground to the lowermost branches, which trees bore notches made with flint implements, the bark having been removed for the purpose; these notches, forming a kind of steps to enable persons to get up the trees and rob the birds' nests in their tops, were fully 5 feet apart, so that our men concluded that the natives here must be of very tall stature, or must be in possession of some sort of artifice for getting up the said trees; in one of the trees these notched steps were so fresh and new that they seemed to have been cut less than four days ago.

That on the ground they had observed certain footprints of animals, not unlike those of a tiger's claws; they also brought on board certain specimens of animal excrements voided by quadrupeds, so far as they could surmise and observe, together with a small quantity of gum of a seemingly very fine quality, which had exuded from trees, and bore some resemblance to gum-lac.

That round the eastern point of this bay they had sounded 13 or 14 feet at high water, there being about 3 feet at low tide.

That at the extremity of the said point they had seen large numbers of gulls, wild ducks and geese, but had perceived none farther inward, though they had heard their cries; and had found no fish except different kinds of muscles forming small clusters in several places.

That the land is pretty generally covered with trees, standing so far apart that they allow a passage everywhere, and a look-out to a great distance, so that when landing our men could always get sight of natives or wild beasts, unhindered by dense shrubbery or underwood, which would prove a great advantage in exploring the country.

That in the interior they had in several places observed numerous trees which had deep holes burnt into them at the upper end of the foot, while the earth had here and there been dug out with the fist so as to form a fireplace, the surrounding soil having become as hard as flint through the action of the fire.

A short time before we got sight of our boats returning to the ships, we now and then saw clouds of dense smoke rising up from the land, which was nearly west by north of us, and surmised this might be a signal given by our men, because they were so long coming back; for we had ordered them to return speedily, partly in order to be made acquainted with what they had seen, and partly that we might be able to send them to other points, if they should find no profit there, to the end that no precious time might be wasted. When our men had come on board again, we inquired of them whether they had been there and made a fire, to which they returned a negative answer, adding, however, that at various times and points in the wood they also had seen clouds of smoke ascending. So there can be no doubt there must be men here of extraordinary stature. This day we had variable winds from the eastward, but for the greater part of the day a stiff, steady breeze from the south-east.

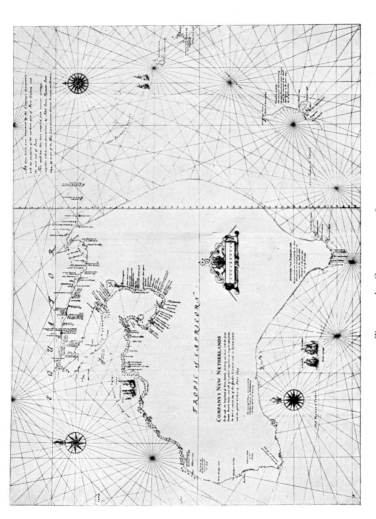

TASMAN'S CHART OF 1644.

From *The Journal of Tasman*, ed. by J. E. Heerse.

Item the 3rd do.—We went to the south-east side of this bay in the same boats as yesterday, with Supercargo Gilsemans and a number of musketeers, the oarsmen furnished with pikes and side-arms; here we found water, it is true, but the land is so low-lying that the fresh water was made salt and brackish by the surf, while the soil is too rocky to allow of wells being dug; we there-fore returned on board and convened the councils of our two ships, with which we have resolved and determined what is set forth *in extenso* in to-day's resolution, to which for briefness' sake we refer. In the afternoon we went to the south-east side of this bay in the boats aforesaid, having with us Pilot-major Francoys Jacobsz, Skipper Gerrit Jansz, Isack Gilsemans, supercargo on board the Zeehaen, sub-cargo Abraham Coomans, and our master carpenter Pieter Jacobsz; we carried with us a pole with the Company's mark carved into it, and a Prince-flag to be set up there, that those who shall come after us may become aware that we have been here, and have taken possession of the said land as our lawful property. When we had rowed about half-way with our boats, it began to blow very stiffly, and the sea ran so high that the cock-boat of the Zeehaen, in which were seated the Pilot-major and Mr. Gilsemans, was compelled to pull back to the ships, while we ran on with our pinnace. When we had come close inshore in a small inlet which bore west-south-west of the ships, the surf ran so high that we could not get near the shore without running the risk of having our pinnace dashed to pieces. We then ordered the carpenter aforesaid to swim to the shore alone, with the pole and the flag, and kept by the wind with our pinnace; we made him plant the said pole with the flag at the top into the earth, about the centre of the bay near four tall trees easily recognisable and standing in the form of a crescent, exactly before the one standing lowest. This tree is burnt in just above the ground, and in reality taller than the other three, but it seems to be shorter because it stands lower on the sloping ground; at top, projecting from the crown, it shows two long dry branches, so symmetrically set with dry sprigs and twigs, that they look like the large antlers of a stag; by the side of these dry branches, slightly lower down, there is another bough which is quite green and leaved all round, whose twigs, owing to their regular proportion, wonderfully embellish the said bough, and make it look like the upper part of a larding-pin. Our master carpenter, having in the sight of myself, Abel Jansz Tasman, Skipper Gerrit Jansz, and Subcargo Abraham Coomans, per-formed the work entrusted to him, we pulled with our pinnace as near the shore as we ventured to do; the carpenter aforesaid thereupon swam back to the pinnace through the surf. This work having been duly executed, we pulled back to the ships, leaving the above mentioned as a memorial for those who shall come after us, and for the natives of this country, who did not show themselves, though we suspect some of them were at no great distance and closely watching our proceedings. We made no arrangements for gathering vegetables, since the high seas prevented our men from getting ashore, except by swimming, so that it was impossible to get anything into the pinnace. During the whole of the day the wind blew chiefly from the north; in the evening we took the sun's azimuth, and found 3° north-easterly variation of the compass; at sunset we got a strong gale from the north, which by and by rose to so violent a storm from the north-north-west, that we were compelled to get both our yards in, and drop our small bower-anchor.

Item the 4th do.—At dawn the storm abated, the weather became less rough, and the land-wind blowing from the west by north, we hove our bower-anchor; when we had weighed the said anchor, and got it above water, we found that both the flukes were broken off so far that we hauled home nothing but the shank; we then weighed the other anchor also, and set sail forthwith, in order to pass to the north to landward of the northernmost islands, and seek a better watering-place. Here we lay at anchor in 43° S. Latitude, Longitude 167½°; in the forenoon the wind was westerly. At noon Latitude observed 42° 40′, Longitude 168°, course kept north-east, sailed 8 miles; in the afternoon the wind turned to the north-west; we had very variable winds all day; in the evening the wind went round to west-north-west again with a strong gale, then to west by north and west-north-west once more; we then tacked to northward, and in the evening saw a round mountain bearing north-north-west of us at about 8 miles' distance; course kept to northward very close to the wind. While sailing out of this bay and all through the day, we saw several columns of smoke ascend along the coast. Here it would be meet to describe the trend of the coast and the islands lying off it, but we request to be excused for briefness' sake, and beg leave to refer to the small chart drawn up of it, which we have appended.

Item the 5th do.—In the morning the wind blowing from the north-west by west, we kept our previous course; the high round mountain, which we had seen the day before, now bore due west of us at 6 miles' distance; at this point the land fell off to the north-west, so that we could no longer steer near the coast here, seeing that the wind was almost ahead. We therefore convened the council and the second mates, with whom after due deliberation we resolved, and subsequently called out to the officers of the Zeehaen, that pursuant to the resolution of the 11th ultimo we should direct our course due east, and on the said course run on to the full longitude of 195° or the Salamonis islands, all which will be found set forth *in extenso* in this day's resolution. At noon Latitude estimated 41° 34', Longitude 169°, course kept northeast by north, sailed 20 miles; we then shaped our course due east for the purpose of making further discoveries, and of avoiding the variable winds between the trade-wind and the anti-trade-wind; the wind from the north-east with a steady breeze; during the night the wind from the west, a brisk steady breeze and good clear weather.

Item the 6th do.—In the morning the wind from the south-west with a light breeze; at noon we were in Latitude 41° 15', Longitude 172° 35'; course kept east, sailed 40 miles; the weather was quite calm and still all the afternoon, the sea running high from all quarters, but especially from the south-west; in the evening, when the watches were setting, we got a steady breeze from the east-north-east and north-east.

Item the 7th do.—The wind still continuing to blow from the north-east, the breeze quite as fresh as during the night. At noon Latitude estimated 42° 13', Longitude 174° 31'; course kept south-east by east, sailed 26 miles. Variation increasing 5° 45' N.E.

Item the 8th do.—During the night we had a calm, the wind going round to the west and north-west. At noon Latitude estimated 42° 29', Longitude 176° 17'; course kept east by south, sailed 20 miles.

Item the 9th do.—We drifted in a calm, so that by estimation we were carried 3 miles to the south-eastward. At noon Latitude observed 42° 37', Longitude 176° 29'. Variation 5°. Towards evening we had a light breeze from the west-north-west.

Item the 10th do.—Occasional squalls of rain mixed with hail, the wind being westerly with a top-gallant gale. At noon Latitude observed 42° 45', Longitude 178° 40'; course kept east, sailed 24 miles.

Item the 11th do.—Good weather with a clear sky and a westerly wind with a top-gallant gale. At noon Latitude observed 42° 48', Longitude 181° 51'; course kept east, sailed 38 miles. Variation increasing 7° N.E.

Item the 12th do.—Good weather, the wind blowing from the

c

south-south-west and south-west with a steady breeze. At noon Latitude observed 42° 38′, Longitude 185° 17′; course kept east, sailed 38 miles. The heavy swells still continuing from the south-west, there is no mainland to be expected here to southward. Variation 7° N.E.

Item the 13th do.—Latitude observed 42° 10′, Longitude 188° 28′; course kept east by north, sailed 36 miles in a south-south-westerly wind with a top-gallant gale. Towards noon we saw a large, high-lying land, bearing south-east of us at about 15 miles' distance; we turned our course to the south-east, making straight for this land, fired a gun and in the afternoon hoisted the white flag, upon which the officers of the Zeehaen came on board of us, with whom we resolved to touch at the said land as quickly as at all possible, for such reasons as are more amply set forth in this day's resolution. In the evening we deemed it best, and gave orders accordingly to our steersmen, to stick to the south-east course while the weather keeps quiet, but should the breeze freshen, to steer due east, in order to avoid running on shore, and to preclude accidents as much as in us lies; since we opine that the land should not be touched at from this side, on account of the high open sea running there in huge hollow waves and heavy swells, unless there should happen to be safe land-locked bays on this side. At the expiration of four glasses of the first watch, we shaped our course due east. Variation 7° 30′ N.E.

Item the 14th do.—At noon Latitude observed 42° 10′, Longitude 189° 3′; course kept east, sailed 12 miles. We were about 2 miles off the coast, which showed as a very high double land, but we could not see the summits of the mountains, owing to thick clouds. We shaped our course to northward along the coast, so near to it that we could constantly see the surf break on the shore. In the afternoon we took soundings at about 2 miles' distance from the coast, in 55 fathom, a sticky sandy soil, after which it fell a calm. Towards evening we saw a low-lying point north-east by north of us, at about 3 miles' distance; the greater part of the time we were drifting in a calm towards the said point; in the middle of the afternoon we took soundings in 45 fathom, a sticky sandy bottom. The whole night we drifted in a calm, the sea running from the west-north-west, so that we got near the land in 28 fathom, good anchoring-ground, where, on account of the calm, and for fear of drifting nearer to the shore, we ran out our kedge-anchor during the day-watch, and are now waiting for the land-wind.

Item the 15th do.—In the morning with a light breeze blowing from the land, we weighed anchor, and did our best to run out to sea a little, our course being north-west by north; we then had the northernmost low-lying point of the day before, north-north-east and north-east by north of us. This land consists of a high double mountain-range, not lower than Ilha Formoza. At noon Latitude observed 41° 40', Longitude 189° 49'; course kept north-north-east, sailed 8 miles; the point we had seen the day before, now lay south-east of us, at 2½ miles' distance; northward from this point extends a large rocky reef; on this reef, projecting from the sea, there are a number of high steep cliffs, resembling steeples or sails; one mile west of this point we could sound no bottom. As we still saw this high land extend to north-north-east of us, we from here held our course due north, with good, dry weather and smooth water. From the said low point with the cliffs, the land makes a large curve to the north-east, trending first due east, and afterwards due north again. The point aforesaid is in Latitude 41° 50' south. The wind was blowing from the west. It was easy to see here that in these parts the land must be very desolate; we saw no human beings nor any smoke rising; nor can the people here have any boats, since we did not see any signs of them; in the evening we found 8° N.E. variation of the compass.

Item the 16th do.—At six glasses before the day we took soundings in 60 fathom good anchoring-ground. The northernmost point we had in sight then bore from us north-east by east, at three miles' distance, and the nearest land lay south-east of us at 1½ miles' distance. We drifted in a calm, with good weather and smooth water; at noon Latitude observed 40° 58', average Longitude 189° 54'; course kept north-north-east, sailed 11 miles; we drifted in a calm the whole afternoon; in the evening at sunset we had 9° 23' increasing N.E. variation; the wind then went round to south-west with a freshening breeze; we found the fartherest point of the land that we could see to bear from us east by north, the land falling off so abruptly there that we did not doubt that this was the farthest extremity. We now convened our council with the second mates, with whom we resolved to run north-east and east-north-east till the end of the first watch, and then to sail near the wind, wind and weather not changing, as may *in extenso* be seen from this day's resolution. During the night in the sixth glass it fell calm again, so that we stuck to the east-north-east course; although in the fifth glass of the dog-watch, we had the point we had seen in the evening, south-east of us, we could not sail higher than east-north-east slightly easterly, owing to the sharpness of the wind; in the first watch we took soundings once, and a second time in the dog-watch, in 60 fathom, clean, grey sand. In the second glass of the day-watch we got a breeze from the south-east, upon which we tacked for the shore again.

Item the 17*th do.*—In the morning at sunrise we were about one mile from the shore; in various places we saw smoke ascending from fires made by the natives; the wind then being south and blowing from the land, we again tacked to eastward. At noon Latitude estimated 40° 32′, Longitude 190° 47′; course kept north-east by east, sailed 12 miles; in the afternoon the wind being west, we held our course east by south, along a low-lying shore with dunes, in good dry weather; we sounded in 30 fathom, black sand, so that by night one had better approach this land aforesaid, sounding; we then made for this sandy point, until we got in 17 fathom, where we cast anchor at sunset owing to a calm, when we had the northern extremity of this dry sandspit west by north of us; also high land extending to east by south; the point of the reef south-east of us; here, inside this point or narrow sandspit, we saw a large open bay upwards of 3 or 4 miles wide; to eastward of this narrow sandspit there is a sandbank upwards of a mile in length, with 6, 7, 8 and 9 feet of water above it, and projecting east-south-east from the said point. In the evening we had 9° N.E. variation.

Item the 18*th do.*—In the morning we weighed anchor in calm weather; at noon Latitude estimated 40° 49′, Longitude 191° 41′; course kept east-south-east, sailed 11 miles. In the morning before weighing anchor, we had resolved with the officers of the Zeehaen, that we should try to get ashore here, and find a good harbour; and that, as we neared it, we should send out the pinnace to reconnoitre; all which may *in extenso* be seen from this day's resolution. In the afternoon our skipper Ide Tiercxz and our pilot-major Francoys Jacobsz, in the pinnace, and Supercargo Gilsemans with one of the second mates of the Zeehaen in the latter's cock-boat, went on before to seek a fitting anchorage and a good watering-place. At sunset, when it fell a calm, we dropped anchor in 15 fathom, good anchoring-ground; in the evening, about an hour after sunset, we saw a number of lights on shore and four boats close inshore, two of which came towards us, upon which our own two boats returned on board; they reported that they had found no less than 13 fathom water, and that when the sun sank behind the high land, they were still about half a mile from shore. When our men had been on board for the space of about one glass, the men in the two prows began to call out to us in a rough, hollow voice, but we could not understand a word of what they said. We, however, called out to them in answer, upon which they repeated their cries several times, but came no nearer than a stone shot; they also blew several times on an instrument of which the sound was like that of a Moorish trumpet; we then ordered one of our sailors (who had some knowledge of trumpet-blowing) to play them some tunes in answer. Those on board the Zeehaen ordered their second mate (who had come out to India as a trumpeter, and had in the Mauritius been appointed second mate by the council of that fortress and the ships) to do the same; after this had been repeated several times on both sides, and as it was getting more and more dark, those in the native prows at last ceased, and paddled off. For more security, and to be on guard against all accidents, we ordered our men to keep double watches, as we are wont to do, when out at sea, and to keep in readiness all necessaries of war, such as muskets, pikes and cutlasses. We cleaned the guns on the upper-orlop, and placed them again, in order to prevent surprises, and be able to defend ourselves, if these people should happen to attempt anything against us. Variation 9° N.E.

Item the 19*th do.*—Early in the morning a boat manned with 13 natives approached to about a stone's cast from our ships; they called out several times, but we did not understand them, their speech not bearing any resemblance to the vocabulary given us by the Hon. Governor-General and Councillors of India, which is hardly to be wondered at, seeing that it contains the language of the Salamonis islands, etc. As far as we could observe, these people were of ordinary height; they had rough voices and strong bones, the colour of their skin being between brown and yellow; they wore tufts of black hair right upon the top of their heads, tied fast in the manner of the Japanese at the back of their heads, but somewhat longer and thicker, and surmounted by a large, thick white feather. Their boats consisted of two long narrow prows side by side, over which a number of planks or other seats were placed in such a way that those above can look through the water underneath the vessel; their paddles are upwards of a fathom in length, narrow and pointed at the end; with these vessels they could make considerable speed. For clothing, as it seemed to us, some of them wore mats, others cotton stuffs; almost all of them were naked from the shoulders to the waist. We repeatedly made signs for them to come on board of us, showing them white linen and some knives that formed part of our cargo. They did not come nearer, however, but at last paddled back to shore. In the meanwhile, at our summons sent the previous evening, the officers of the Zeehaen came on board of us, upon which we convened a council, and resolved to go as near the shore as we could, since there was good anchoring-ground here, and these people apparently sought our friendship. Shortly after we had drawn up this resolution we saw 7 more boats put off from the shore, one of which (high and pointed in front, manned with 17 natives) paddled round behind the Zeehaen, while another with 13 able-bodied men in her, approached to within half a stone's throw of our ship; the men in these two boats now and then called out to each other; we held up and showed to them, as before, white linens, etc., but they remained where they were. The skipper of the Zeehaen now sent out to them his quartermaster with her cock-boat with six paddlers in it, with orders for the second mates, that if these people should offer to come alongside the Zeehaen, they should not allow too many of them on board of her, but use great caution and be well on their guard. While the cock-boat of the Zeehaen was paddling on its way to her, those in the prow nearest to us called out to those who were lying behind the Zeehaen, and waved their paddles to them, but we could not make out what they meant. Just as the cock-boat of the Zeehaen had put off from board again, those in the prow before us, between the two ships, began to paddle so furiously towards it, that, when they were about half-way slightly nearer to our ship, they struck the Zeehaen's cock-boat so violently alongside with the stem of their prow, that it got a violent lurch, upon which the foremost man in this prow of villains with a long, blunt pike thrust the quartermaster Cornelis Joppen in the neck several times with so much force, that the poor man fell overboard. Upon this the other natives, with short thick clubs, which we at first mistook for heavy blunt parangs, and with their paddles, fell upon the men in the cock-boat, and overcame them by main force, in which fray three of our men were killed, and a fourth got mortally wounded through the heavy blows. The quarter-master and two sailors swam to our ship, whence we had sent our pinnace to pick them up, which they got into alive. After this outrageous and detestable crime the murderers sent the cock-boat adrift, having taken one of the dead bodies into their prow and thrown another into the sea. Ourselves and those on board the Zeehaen seeing this, diligently fired our muskets and guns, and though we did not hit any of them, the two prows made haste to the shore, where they were out of the reach of shot. With our fore upper-deck and bow guns we now fired several shots in the direction of their prows, but none of them took effect. Thereupon our skipper Ide Tercxsen Holman in command of our pinnace, well manned and armed, rowed towards the cock-boat of the Zeehaen (which, fortunately for us, these accursed villains had let drift), and forthwith returned with it to our ships, having found in it one of the men killed and one mortally wounded. We now weighed anchor and set sail, since we could not hope to enter into any friendly relations with these people, or to be able to get water or refreshments here. Having weighed anchor and being under sail, we saw 22 prows near the shore, of which eleven, swarming with people, were making for our ships. We kept quiet until some of the foremost were within reach of our guns, and then fired 1 or 2 shots from the gun-room with our pieces, without, however, doing them any harm; those on board the Zeehaen also fired, and in the largest prow hit a man who held a small white flag in his hand, and who fell down. We also heard the canister-shot strike the prows inside and outside, but could not make out what other damage it had done. As soon as they had got this volley, they paddled back to shore with great speed, two of them hoisting a sort of tingang sails. They remained lying near the shore without visiting us any further. About noon skipper Gerrit Jansz and Mr. Gilsemans again came on board of us; we also sent for their first mate, and convened the council, with whom we drew up the resolution following, to wit: Seeing that the detestable deed of these natives against four men of the Zeehaen's crew, perpetrated this morning, must teach us to consider the inhabitants of this country as enemies; that, therefore, it will be best to sail eastward along the coast, following the trend of the land, in order to ascertain whether there are any fitting places, where refreshments and water would be obtainable; all of which will be found set forth *in extenso* in this day's resolution. In this murderous spot (to which we have accordingly given the name of *Moordenaersbay*) we lay at anchor in 40° 50′ S. Latitude, 190° 30′ Longitude. From here we shaped our course east-north-east. At noon Latitude estimated 40° 57′, Longitude 191° 41′; course kept south, sailed 2 miles. In the afternoon we got the wind from the west-north-west, when, by the advice of our steersmen and with our own approval, we turned our course north-east by north. During the night we kept sailing, as the weather was favourable, but about an hour after midnight we sounded in 25 or 26 fathom, a hard, sandy bottom. Soon after, the wind went round to north-west, and we sounded in 15 fathom; we forthwith tacked to await the day, turning our course to westward, exactly contrary to the direction by which we had entered. Variation 9° 30′ N.E.

This is the second land which we have sailed along and discovered. In honour of Their High Mightinesses the States-General we gave to this land the name of *Staten Landt*, since we deemed it quite possible that this land is part of the great Staten Landt, though this is not certain. This land seems to be a very fine country, and we trust that this is the mainland coast of the unknown South-land. To this course we have given the name of *Abel Tasman passagie*, because he has been the first to navigate it.

Item the 13*th do.* (*May* 1643).—In the morning we were at about 2 miles' distance from the western point of Willem Schoutens island, which was almost due south-west by south of us; another islet lying north-west by north of the point just mentioned, at about 3 or 4 miles' distance, bore from us north-west. We kept sailing westward along the coast, until the said point was east of us, and then, in order to get the mainland coast alongside again, we set our course west-south-west. In the forenoon we got the wind from the south with a fair breeze. At noon Latitude estimated 54′, Longitude 152° 6′; course held west, sailed 18 miles with an east wind. Variation 6° 30′ N.E. In the afternoon the wind turned to the south-east with rainy weather. We then sighted land again, south-south-west of us; it was a low-lying coast, forming part of the mainland of Nova Guinea. From here we set our course due west; during the night we had a fair breeze.

Item the 14*th do.*—In the morning we were again close to the mainland coast of Noua Guinea. Here the interior was *very high like Il do Fermoza; but the foreland was almost everywhere low or level*. We kept sailing to westward along the coast towards the cape de Goede Hoope. At noon Latitude observed 48′, Longitude 150° 31′; course held west, sailed 24 miles, with an east wind. In the afternoon there was a light breeze; in the evening it fell a calm; we saw the *cape de Goede Hoope* west and west by south of us at about 6 miles' distance. Eastward of the cape de Goede Hoope the land begins to be *very high* until quite close to the shore, *without having any low foreland; the land is somewhat higher than the island of Fermoza*. We continued on our west by north course to the cape de Hoop, the sea now running from the north-east. During the night we had dark weather with a drizzling rain, the wind being very variable; afterwards we drifted in a calm.

Item the 15*th do.*—At noon we had the cape de Goede Hoop south of us at 3 miles' distance; Latitude estimated 41′, Longitude 149° 53′; course held west by north, sailed 12 miles. Variation 6° N.E.; the wind variable. In the afternoon the wind was east-north-east with calm weather. We set our course to westward to the west side of the bay which Willem Schoutens had sailed into, but had to return from. During the night we drifted in a calm, and made little progress.

Item the 16th do.—In the morning we were still drifting in a calm, and saw the western point of the land at the west-side of the bay aforesaid; this western point lay west of us at about 7 miles' distance. At noon it was calm and we had the western point of the bay south-south-west of us; we set our course west by north. At noon Latitude observed 16′, Longitude 149° 9′; course held west-north-west, sailed 12 miles. Variation 5° 50′; the weather calm; in the afternoon it was calm too, but since the current was carrying us to westward, our progress was greater as measured by the land we passed, than by our advance over the water. This day we saw several small islands near the western point; we steered our course towards them west by south. In the evening at sunset, the westernmost point of the mainland we saw, bore from us slightly southerly, at 3 or 4 miles' distance, and a small islet lying off the said point, west slightly northerly, at 3 or 4 miles' distance. Between the mainland and Nova Guinea and the island last mentioned, we saw the open sea, due west of us. We drifted in a calm; at midnight the land-breeze sprung up, and we set our course west by north, in order to run outside the said islet; during the night we had variable winds alternating with calms.

Item the 17th do.—Early in the morning we were close under the island aforesaid, at about one mile's distance; we then came upon a shoal, and when sailing over it we sounded in the shallowest part 9 fathom, rocky bottom. When we were past the first shoal just mentioned, we got deeper water again; but shortly after, when we had the island south by east of us, we could see the bottom, the sea being only 7 fathom deep here, bottom as before; this shoal runs off to north-west from the land aforesaid. We kept holding our course west by south, and saw still more islands ahead, west of us 5 or 6 of them. At noon the island we had passed, bore from us east at about 3 miles' distance. During these twenty-four hours we had advanced 9 miles, on a west slightly southerly course. Latitude estimated 20′ south of the equator, Longitude 148° 34′; course held west, one third of a point southerly, sailed 9 miles. In the evening at sunset, there lay west-north-west and north-west by west of us, 7 or 8 small islands in a row, bearing from each other west by north and east by south. We then passed a number of rocks all overgrown with brushwood; these we left on our starboard, and four more small islands to larboard, the latter lying very near the mainland coast. The coast of Noua Guinea here is full of small bays and projecting points; but there is almost everywhere deep water, so that we run on a mile only from shore; about 4 glasses in the first watch, off a pretty large bay, we were about ⅔ mile from shore. We took soundings here in 40 fathom, sandy bottom, where we forthwith anchored. Here we had a large island west by south of us at about 6 miles' distance, where in the evening we had seen a passage through between the mainland coast and the said island.

Item the 18th do.—Early in the morning with the land-wind we weighed anchor, and set sail for the narrows between the mainland coast and the island, in order to pass through. Shortly afterwards we drifted in a calm; about noon a light breeze from the west and the current were against us, so that we were carried back, and at length came to anchor in 16 fathom between an island and a rock which lay level with the water, the bottom being small coral. At noon Latitude estimated 26', Longitude *
°　', sailed 6 miles. As we lay here, the current began to run much stronger in the afternoon; we are here in 26' S. Latitude; Variation 5½ degrees N.E. About four o'clock in the afternoon the current began to change, the ebb-tide running here to west, and the flood to east, so that a west-south-west moon makes high water here; but since we cannot be far from the western extremity of Noua Guinea, as the coast begins to trend southward here, it is quite possible that the two tides meet here at the extremity of Nova Guinea, since before we had the flood from the east everywhere along the coast of Noua Guinea. As there was no moon, we remained at anchor during the night for safety. This afternoon several prows came close to our ship; the men in them said they were Ternatans, and spoke the language of Ternate. One of our men who was conversant with the language of Ternate spoke with them a long time, and with kind words tried to get them on board of us, but they pretended to be timid and afraid; from which we concluded that these men must have been Tydorese. They returned to the shore with their prows, the wind being west with good weather. During the night we had a violent current to westward, and frequent whirling currents, so that our anchor quitting its hold, we had to pay out more cable. For the rest it was calm all through the night.

* Longitudes here and subsequently left blank in original journal.

Item the 19*th do.*—In the morning the current again began to set to westward; we weighed anchor and went under sail, the wind being south by west with good weather; we set our course south-east by east over to landward, with good dry weather. In this passage we generally sounded from 25 to 45 and 50 fathom. At this point there was a good deal of broken land, as may be seen in our chart of the same. At noon Latitude observed 35′, Longitude ° ′; course held west-south-west, sailed 7 miles, the wind being south by west and variable; we tacked about to landward, since the wind became south with occasional calms. In the forenoon the current setting from the south-south-west, we anchored in 35 fathom, good sandy bottom. In the afternoon it fell a dead calm. During the night we had variable currents.

Item the 20*th do.*—In the morning the current ran slightly to southwest, and was variable, the wind blowing from the south-east with a light breeze. We did our best to tack to the south, and pass through between the islands. But a contrary wind and calms prevented us from making any considerable progress. We sailed here over a shoal, where we sounded 5 fathom, sandy bottom mixed with shingle, but soon afterwards 25, 30 and 40 fathom, same bottom. In the forenoon the wind blew from the south, so that we went over to eastward; shortly after noon, the wind being south-south-west, we again came upon the shoal aforesaid, and as the current was setting strong to the north-east, we cast anchor in 5 fathom. At this point here the current runs very strangely, so that in my opinion no certain information can be given concerning it. Who comes here immediately sees it, and must shape his course accordingly. This point aforesaid of Noua Guinea mainly consists of *broken land* which would take more time in mapping out than we think necessary to bestow on it. We are satisfied with having discovered a good passage through, which in future may be of great use to the Company's ships coming from Peru or Chili at the time of the eastern monsoon. During the night the wind was southerly with a strong current setting to the south-west, and we remained at anchor.

Item the 21*st do.*—In the morning before daybreak, with the current setting to the south-west and the wind blowing from the south-east, we weighed anchor and went under sail with a steady gale and our course set to the south-west. In the forenoon the wind went about to south by east, so that we made no progress by tacking. About noon we therefore cast anchor under a small island in 25 fathom, pretty good bottom, in Latitude 38′ South, Longitude ° ′; course held south, sailed one mile with a south

by east wind; it being our intention, with the first favourable
wind and current that should offer on the coast of Noua Guinea
or near it, to steer our course for the south, until we shall have
passed the latitude of Cape Wedda in the island of Gilolo, from
where we can cross as far north as possible. We sailed close to
shore here in order to get some firewood, of which there was great
plenty here. When arrived on the said island, we certainly
observed signs of men, but did not see any natives. It would
seem that the only persons landing on this island are fishermen
who dry their fish here at certain seasons of the year, and then
carry the same to other places to be sold there. Near this islet
and round the whole point along and between the islands, there
are everywhere currents as strong (as the old saw has it) as the
tide before Flushing pier-head. In these parts the flood runs
northward and the ebb southward, but almost everywhere here
the tides follow the direction of the coast, of the islands and passages, narrows and straits. In the evening at the end of the first
watch, the wind being south-south-east, we set sail, endeavouring
by tacking to run to the south with a steady breeze.

Item the 22nd do.—In the morning the wind continuing
southerly, we kept endeavouring to run to the south as before,
but about noon were again forced to come to anchor in 35 fathom,
sandy bottom, near a small island, about 2 miles south-east by
east of the island where we had previously been at anchor; so
that in these twenty-four hours we advanced no more than
2 miles south-east by east. At noon Latitude observed 40',
Longitude ° '; course held south-east by east, sailed 12 miles.

Item the 23rd do.—In the morning the wind being south-east
but inclining to a calm, we set sail and endeavoured to run to the
south. In the forenoon the wind was variable, so that at noon we
had progressed about 4 miles to the south by east. At noon Latitude estimated 55', Longitude ° '; course held south by east,
sailed 4 miles, with variable winds. Variation 4° 30'. Here we
again came close under a number of islands, but at first found no
anchorage. The coast of Noua Guinea in these parts is continually running in and out, with so many windings and so many
large and small islands that there is no counting them. During
the greater part of the night we drifted in a calm; in the evening
we had had soundings in 50 fathom.

Item the 24th do.—In the morning we drifted in a calm as
before; in the forenoon the wind blowing from the south by east,
we did our best by tacking to run to the south, but we made little
progress. At noon Latitude observed 1° 6', Longitude ° ';

course held south-west by west, sailed 3 miles, the wind being south inclining to a calm. We convened the council with the second mates of the ships Heemskerck and Zeehaen, in which meeting it was resolved and determined that we should shape our course above the point of Wedde and towards Ceram, and further navigate to Batavia, seeing that at this season of the year there is no other course possible owing to contrary winds and counter-currents; all which is *in extenso* set forth in the resolution this day drawn up touching this matter. In the course of the night we came close to a small islet which we could not weather, so that we were obliged to anchor there for some time in 11 fathom, coarse sandy bottom; as we were lying at anchor, we found that the current was setting pretty strong to westward.

Item the 25th do.—In the morning the wind being east-south-east, we weighed anchor, and set sail; we passed through between the two islets. This day we had many variable winds, alternating with calms and rains; we kept doing our best to run to the south. At noon Latitude observed 1° 15′, Longitude   °   ′; course held south-west by west, sailed 4 miles with variable winds. During the night we set our course due south by west, and passed a large island to larboard of us.

Item the 26th do.—At noon we took no latitude. Latitude estimated 1° 38′, Longitude   °   ′; course held south by west, sailed 11 miles, with variable winds. South-east of us we again saw a large island about 8 miles in length. It extended mainly east-north-east and west-south-west, with many small islands lying off it on the north-west side. We then set our course south-south-west, to run to westward of all these small islands. In the evening before sunset we still saw 2 high islets north-west by west of us at about 7 or 8 miles' distance, for which we set our course. We then saw south-south-west of us the whole extent of the coast of *Ceram;* we steered straight for it in good calm weather, the wind then being north-west. During the first and second quarter of the night we drifted in a calm; in the day-watch we got the wind from the north with rain.

Item the 27th do.—In the morning the wind was chiefly west; the western point of the large island, which we had passed the previous evening, now bore from us north-east by north at about 3 miles' distance; the wind being westerly with good calm weather, we turned our course over to southward close by the wind towards the coast of Ceram, from which at noon we were still 5 miles' distant, to wit from the centre of Ceram. At noon Latitude observed 2° 40′, Longitude   °   ′; course held south-

south-west, sailed 11 miles with variable winds alternating with
calms. At sunset we were still 2 or 2½ miles off the land; the
wind continuing westerly, we endeavoured to run westward,
northward of Ceram. During the night we advanced about 5 or
6 miles with variable winds; in the day-watch it was mostly calm.

Item the 28th do.—In the morning variable winds with rain,
thunder and lightning. Since the land-wind was partly blowing
from the south, we tacked about to westward. We were now right
off the small islands, which lie, 6 together, close to the coast of
Ceram, and had the middle of the said coast south-south-west of
us, at about 3 miles' distance. At noon the westernmost of the
said small islands were south-south-east of us, at about 3 or 2½
miles' distance. To-day in the forenoon we had had rain. At
noon Latitude estimated 2° 48' South, middle longitude 146° 15';
course held west by south, sailed 10 miles; in the afternoon we had
dry weather, the wind being south-south-east with a light variable
breeze.

Item the 29th do.—At noon we had the island of Boona west-
south-west of us at about 5 miles' distance; we set our course close
along the coast with the intention of running southward through
the straits of Nassouw; at noon Latitude estimated 2° 52' South,
Longitude 145° 15'; course held west a quarter of a point southerly, sailed 15 miles, with the wind southerly but variable. In the
afternoon it was calm, and then the wind went round to westward
of the south with a fair breeze, so that in the night we were forced
to run northward of Boona; during the night the wind blew from
the south; we set our course for the island of Boure as close to the
wind as possible.

Item the 30th do.—In the morning we were close under the
mainland coast of Boure, along the north-side of which we sailed
with good weather and a fair breeze from the south. At noon we
had the north-western point of Boure, known by the name of
Tannewary, south by east of us, at 1½ miles' distance. At noon
Latitude estimated 3° 8' South, Longitude 143° 52'; course held
west by south, sailed 21 miles; in the afternoon we drifted to a
calm under the island of Boure, the sea running from different
quarters; the wind going round to westward, we tacked about to
the south in order to be near the land in the evening, as we
expected the land-wind; during the night we got a light land-
breeze; course held west by south along the land.

Item the 31st do.—In the forenoon we had variable winds
alternating with calms. At noon we had the western point of
Boure, known by the name of Tamahoo, south of us about 3

miles' distance. About one o'clock in the afternoon, the wind
becoming south with a steady breeze, we set our course over to
westward. At noon Latitude estimated 3° 15′, Longitude 147°
17′; course held west by south. Towards evening the wind went
round to the south-east; we shaped our course to south-west with
a steady breeze and good dry weather. During the night, at the
end of the first watch, the wind became east-south-east, and we
set our course south-west by west for the entrance of the strait
of Botton, because we intended to pursue our course through the
said strait and then to the Booqueroenis.

Item the first of June.—In the morning the wind kept blowing
from the east-south-east with good dry weather and a fair
breeze; we set our course west-south-west for the northern point
of the island of Botton. At noon Latitude observed 4° 13′, Longitude 141° 5′; course held south-west by west, sailed 26 miles,
with an east-south-east wind. In the afternoon we sighted the
strait of Botton. We sailed in the strait in the evening and during
the night with variable winds, alternating with calms, and
endeavoured to continue our voyage through the strait to the
south.

Item the 2nd do.—In the morning at sunrise we had advanced
into the strait a distance of about 3 miles. In the afternoon we
drifted in a calm, the current being against us. We cast anchor
close to the coast of Boutton in 26 fathom, stiff ground; here we
found two junks at anchor, of which the Anachgoddes forthwith
came on board of us, and showed us their passports which they
had obtained from the Honble Governor Gerrit Demmer, with
which passports they were going to Byma, to return afterwards
to Amboyna or to Batavia. The names of the Anachgoddes of
the junks were Mouna and Jurregan Wanga, besides there was
still a free black, Hendricq Jansz of Solor, ensign of the Groene
Geuszen. From them we learned that the Honble Anthoony Caen
had arrived at Amboyna with a number of vessels, with destina-
tion for Ternate. They also told us that the ship Hollandia was
reported to have been lost on her way from Batavia to Amboyna
but whether this is true we shall learn in time. At noon Latitude
estimated 4° 32′, Longitude 141° 3′; course held west-south-west,
sailed 13 miles, with variable winds. During the night, when
4 glasses in the first watch had run out, and the current began to
set southwards, we set sail; all through the night the wind was
very variable, but chiefly south; we did what we could by tacking.

Item the 3rd do.—We kept tacking as before, the wind being
southerly. At noon we were full in the first narrows with the

wind northerly but with frequent calms. At noon Latitude estimated 4° 54′ South, Longitude 140° 59′; course kept south by west, sailed 6 miles. In the afternoon we had heavy rains; shortly before evening we anchored in a calm one mile past the first narrows in 30 fathom, good stiff ground, the current setting to northward. About midnight with still water we weighed anchor and set sail, but there was hardly any breeze, so that we made little progress.

Item the 4th do.—In the morning we still drifted in a calm. At noon Latitude estimated 5° 10′ South, Longitude 140° 56′; course kept south by west, sailed 4 miles with variable winds. At 4 o'clock in the afternoon we got the wind from the south-east, and set our course south-south-west straight for the narrows lying close to Boutton; this is the narrowest part of the strait of Boutton, where we cast anchor after midnight close to the island in 12 fathom, stiff ground.

Item the 5th do.—Early in the morning we weighed anchor in a calm, but as the ebb-tide had nearly run out, two hours before noon we anchored in the middle of the narrows with our kedge-anchor in 45 fathom, hard bottom. At noon Latitude estimated 5° 5′ South, Longitude 140° 52′; course kept south by west, sailed 3½ miles with variable winds and rain. In the afternoon at early ebb-tide and in a calm, being engaged in weighing our kedge-anchor, we found that it had got under a rock, and were forced to let it go, continuing our voyage to Boutton, so as in the evening to get clear of the straits south of Boutton, with a south-wind alternating with calms. In the evening after the setting of the first watch, the steward's mate Jan Pietersz, of Meldorp, whom we had put on board the fluteship until such time as we should arrive at Batavia, on account of certain charges that had been brought against him, and of misdemeanours of which he was suspected, let himself overboard into the sea by means of a rope and swam to shore at Botton. During the night the wind was northerly, with a light breeze; course held west-south-west.

Item the 6th do.—In the morning the middle of the island of Camboona was north-west of us at about 2½ miles' distance; the wind being easterly, and our course held west by south. At noon we had the western point of Cambona north by west of us, at 3 miles' distance. At noon Latitude estimated 5° 43′, Longitude 140° 11′; course held west-south-west, sailed 11 miles. In the afternoon we had a steady breeze from the east by south. During the night at the end of the second watch we passed the islets known as the Booqueroenis, in good, clear, dry weather.

Item the 7th do.—At noon we had the western point of the high land of Turatte north-north-east of us, at about 3 miles' distance course held west-north-west, along the coast in dry weather and with a steady east wind. At noon Latitude estimated 6° South, Longitude 138° 1'; course held west half a point southerly, the wind being east with a steady breeze. In the evening at sunset we set our course west by south, straight for the great shoal, which we passed over at midnight in 13 fathom, rocky bottom.

Item the 8th do.—In the morning we had a steady south-east wind. About 3 hours before noon we passed over a large rocky reef, sounding 6 fathom in the shallowest part. We quite distinctly saw the bottom, which was strewn with large stones. At noon Latitude observed 6° 2', Longitude 135° 21'; course held west, sailed 40 miles, with a south-east wind; afterwards we set our course west by south in good weather.

Item the 9th do.—South-east monsoon with good, dry weather. At noon the island of Maduere was by estimation at 8 miles' distance, south-south-west of us. At noon Latitude observed 6° 15'; course held west by south, sailed 26 miles; Longitude 133° 49'.

Item the 10th do.—Good dry weather; we took soundings in 35 fathom. At noon Latitude observed 6° 26', Longitude 132° 29'; course held west by south, sailed 20 miles; in the evening we had the western extremity of the island of Lubock north by west of us at 4 miles' distance.

Item the 11th do.—In the morning the wind kept blowing from the south-east; we saw the line of the coast of Java, near Lubuan; at noon it fell a calm; Latitude estimated 6° 26', Longitude 131° 23'; course held west, sailed 16½ miles. We had here both sea- and land-wind; a light, mild breeze; in the afternoon the wind became south with a fair breeze. We set our course west; in the evening the mountain of Lubuan was due south of us; then we also saw the high mountain of Japare, and the islet of Mandelycke, which bore from us due west by south, at about 6 miles' distance.

Item the 12th do.—In the morning we drifted in a calm; towards noon the sea-wind sprang up from the north-east; course held west by south. At noon we had the islet of Mandelycque east by south of us at 4 miles' distance, and the central land of Crymon Java north-north-west of us at 6 miles' distance. At noon Latitude observed 6° 27', Longitude 130° 33'; course held west by south half a point westerly, sailed 12 miles with land- and sea-wind. In the afternoon the wind becoming north-east

D

with a fair breeze, we set our course west by north. In the evening at sunset the island of Crymon Java lay north-east by north and north-north-east of us; we continued sailing on a west by north course as before.

Item the 13th do.—In the morning the wind was south-east; at noon we had the mountain of Cerebon south-east by south of us, and the Boomtjes island west of us at 10 miles' distance by estimation; course held as before in calm weather. At noon Latitude observed 6°, Longitude 129° 3'; course held west by north, sailed 23 miles with land and sea-wind. We then shaped our course west by south in order to make Poulo Rakit and the coast of Java; in the evening at sunset we had Poulo Rakit west by north of us, at about 5 miles' distance; the wind being east-south-east with calm weather, the mountain of Cerabon bearing from us south by west. During the night we kept sailing along the coast with the land-wind in 20 or 21 fathom, stiff ground.

Item the 14th do.—In the morning we passed the point with the grove of trees; we had the land-wind with a fair breeze, and thus sailed along the land in depths of from 18 to 15 fathom, until we got near the shallows of the Schadelycken hoeck. At noon Latitude estimated 6° 3' South, Longitude 127° 59'; course held west, sailed 21 miles. At noon we came upon the shallows of the Schadelycken Hoeck, which we rounded sounding in 7 or 8 fathom. At the end of the shoal we saw an English ship lying, with flags from her main and mizen-tops; on our approach she weighed anchor, and sailed eastward, but for what port we do not know. In the evening at sunset we had the point of Carauan south-west of us, at about 4 miles' distance. We set our course along the coast, having the wind still along shore; during the night we passed through between the islands of Leyden and Enckhuyzen; when we had advanced a quarter of a mile between these islands, we dropped anchor in 11 fathom, stiff ground; Latitude estimated 6° 12', Longitude 127° 18'; course held west by north and west-north-west, sailed 11 miles.

Item the 15th do.—In the morning at daybreak I went to Batavia in the pinnace. God be praised and thanked for this happy voyage. Amen.

Done in the ship Heemskercq, date as above.

Your Worships' obedient and ever obliged servant,

ABEL JANSZ TASMAN.

IV. GOVERNOR-GENERAL VAN DIEMEN'S REPORT ON TASMAN'S VOYAGE

Friday, June XIX, A.D. XVIcXLIII.

INASMUCH as on the 15th instant Commander Abel Janszoon Tasman has again come to anchor on this roadstead (for which God be praised) with the yacht *Heemskerck* and the flute *Zeehaen*, who on the 14th of August of last year had been dispatched from here by way of the island of Mauritius with orders to navigate to and discover the unknown Southern and Eastern lands; as shown by the journals kept on board the said vessels and the reckonings recorded by them, in sailing on an eastern course they found the wind very strong and the seas so high that they did not think it advisable to run farther southward, but thought it better gradually to deviate more to northward of the said course, until they came to 44° Lat. and 167° Long., where on the 24th of November last they sighted and discovered a certain great land surrounded by islands, which land they have christened Antonij van Diemens land, without, however, being aware how far it extends to north-west or north-east, and without communicating with any of the inhabitants, the ships having only sailed along the south-coast of it and onward as far as 189° Long., where in the latitude of from 43 to 35 degrees, on December 13, they sighted and came upon another large land, to which they have given the name of Staten landt, of which latter land they found the natives to be of a malignant and murderous nature, seeing that in a certain large bay these natives came upon them with a number of strongly-manned prows, cut off one of our boats from the ships, and killed four of our men in her with wooden clubs, and wounded another who returned on board swimming; the said land was found to trend to southward in Lat. 35° and Long. 192°, and consequently a passage from the Indian Ocean into the South Seas has been found, it having been ascertained that in this parallel, where the westerly trade-wind is blowing, there is a convenient passage to the gold-bearing coast of Chili; from there running on a north-east course they next in Lat. 21° and Long. 205° came upon certain islands apparently well-peopled by

35

civilised and kindly disposed natives, who allowed them to land and take in fresh water, at the same time providing them with such refreshments as they stood in need of; thence they next turned their course to westward, passed a few more islands and shoals, which they strongly surmise to form part of the Insulis Salomonis, and then went on tacking about as far as between the 5th and 4th degree, where they got the coast of New Guinea along-side; they sailed on north of this coast until they got between the western extremity of it and the island of Gilolo, then ran south towards the north coast of Ceram, and farther in through Buton strait, whence they arrived here as above stated;

And inasmuch as by the instruments handed to Commander Tasman aforesaid and his Council, we had assured and promised them that, in case in the course of this voyage any rich lands or islands profitable to the Company's commerce should be discovered, or serviceable passages for navigation be found, we should on their return award a handsome recompense to the leaders of the undertaking and the common sailors for extra-ordinary pains taken and diligence shown by them;

Therefore, although in point of fact no treasures or matters of great profit have as yet been found, but only the lands aforesaid and the promising passage referred to been discovered, whose real situation and nature will have to be further ascertained by a subsequent investigation set on foot for the express purpose,

Yet we have unanimously resolved for the reasons above cited to award a recompense to the said discoverers on behalf of the Honourable Company and in fulfilment of our promise aforesaid; to wit, to the commander, skippers, super-, and sub-cargoes, steersmen and inclusive of the book-keeper, two months' pay each; and to the common sailors and soldiers one months' pay each; for which they shall each of them be credited in running account to the debit of the Company, and subsequently be debited again for the amount of the said recompenses, which shall be paid to them in cash.

Done and resolved in the Castle of Batavia, date as above,
(Signed) ANTONIO VAN-DIEMEN,
CORNELIS VAN DER LIJN,
JOAN MAETSUIJCKER,
JUSTUS SCHOUTEN,
SALOMON SWEERS, and
PIETER MESTDAGH, Secretary.

ANTONIO · VAN DIEMEN

Gouverneur Generaal · Van Nederlands Indiën.

ANTHONY VAN DIEMEN.

From the engraving in Volume I of *Onze Mannen Ter Zee in Dicht en Bild*, The Hague.

V. TASMAN'S INSTRUCTIONS

[THE instructions furnished to Abel Tasman by the Governor-General and Council of the Dutch East Indies in 1644 are interesting, first because they summarise the discoveries made by the Dutch up to this time, and secondly because they show that Anthony van Diemen and his colleagues had a correct idea of the character of the discoveries remaining to be made in the South Seas. If Tasman had carried out the instructions he would have discovered the east coast of Australia in 1644.]

Instructions for the commodore, Captain Abel Jansz Tasman, the skipper chief-pilot, Franz Jacobsz Visser, and the council of the yachts *Limmen* and *Zeemeuw*, and the tender *de Brak*, destined for a nearer discovery of Nova Guinea, and the unknown coasts of the discovered east and south lands, together with the channels and the islands supposed to be situated between and near them.

The several successive administrations of India, in order to enlarge and extend the trade of the Dutch East India Company, have zealously endeavoured to make an early discovery of the great land of Nova Guinea, and other unknown east and southerly countries, as you know by several discourses, and maps, journals, and papers communicated to you. But hitherto with little success, although several voyages have been undertaken.

1st. By order of the president, John Williamsson Verschoor, who at that time directed the Company's trade at Bantam, which was in the year 1606, with the yacht the *Duyfhen*, who in their passage sailed by the islands Key and Aroum, and discovered the south and west coast of Nova Guinea, for about 220 miles (880) from 5° to 13¾° south latitude: and found this extensive country, for the greatest part desert, but in some places inhabited by wild, cruel, black savages, by whom some of the crew were murdered; for which reason they could not learn anything of the land or waters, as had been desired of them, and, by want of provisions and other necessaries, they were obliged to leave the discovery unfinished: the furtherest point of the land was called in their map Cape Keer-Weer, situated in 13¾° S.

The second voyage was undertaken with a yacht, in the year 1617, by order of the fiscal D'Edel, with little success, of which adventures and discoveries, through the loss of their journals and remarks, nothing certain is to be found.

From this time the further discoveries of the unknown east and south countries were postponed until the year 1623, on account of there being no ships to spare; but in the interim, in the year 1619, a ship named the *Arms of Amsterdam*, destined to Banda, drove past that place and touched at the south coast of Nova Guinea, where some of the crew were murdered by the savage inhabitants, wherefore they acquired no certain knowledge of the country.

But in the meantime, in the years 1616, 1618, 1619, and 1622, the west coast of this great unknown south land, from 35° to 22° south latitude, was discovered by outward bound ships, and among them by the ship *Endraght;* for the nearer discovery of which the Governor-General, Jan Pietersz Coen (of worthy memory), in September 1622, dispatched the yachts *De Haring* and *Harewind;* but this voyage was rendered abortive by meeting the ship *Mauritius*, and searching after the ship *Rotterdam*.

In consequence of which, by order of His Excellency, the third voyage was undertaken in the month of January 1623, with the yachts *Pera* and *Arnhem*, out of Amboina, under the command of Jan Carstens; with order to make a nearer friendship with the inhabitants of the islands Key, Aroum, and Tenimber, and better to discover Nova Guinea and the south lands, when an alliance was made with the said islands and the south coast of Nova Guinea nearer discovered. The skipper, with eight of the crew of the yacht *Arnhem*, was treacherously murdered by the inhabitants; and after a discovery of the great islands Arnhem and the Spult (by an untimely separation) this yacht, with very little success, came back to Amboina.

But the yacht *Pera*, persisting in the voyage, sailed along the south coast of Nova Guinea to a flat cove on this coast, situated in 10° south latitude, and run along the west coast of this land to Cape Keer-Veer, from thence discovered the coast farther southward as far as 17° S. to Staten River (from this place what more of the land could be discerned seemed to stretch westward), and from thence returned to Amboina.

In this discovery were found everywhere shallow water and barren coast; islands altogether thinly peopled by divers cruel, poor, and brutal nations, and of very little use to the Company. The Journal of this voyage is not now to be found; but the discovered countries may be seen in the maps which were made of them.

Through the little success of this third voyage, but mostly because no ships could be spared, the discovery was again omitted until 1636; but in the interim, in the year 1627, the south coast of the great south land was accidentally discovered by the ship the *Gulde Zeepard*, outward bound from Fatherland, for the space of 250 miles (1000); and again accidentally in the year following, 1628, on the north side, in the latitude of 21.° S., by the ship *Vianen*, homeward bound from India; when they coasted about 50 miles (200) without gaining any particular knowledge of this great country, only observing a foul and barren shore, green fields, and very wild, black, barbarous inhabitants; all which, by the loss of the ship *Batavia*, and the cruelties and miseries which followed from that, is fully proved, and was experienced by the crew of the yacht *Sardam*, in their course along this coast.

At last the fourth voyage was undertaken (in our government) in the month of April 1636, from Banda, with the yachts *Clyn Amsterdam* and *Wesel*, under the command of Gerrit Tomasz Pool, for the discovery of the east and south lands; when they first discovered the coast of Nova Guinea in 3½° south latitude, and coasted about 60 miles (240) to the eastward to 5° S.; when the commodore Pool, with three of the crew (by the barbarous inhabitants) was murdered, at the same place where the skipper of the yacht *Arnhem* was killed in the year 1623.

Notwithstanding which the voyage was assiduously continued, under the supercargo Pieter Pietersz, and the islands Key and Aroum visited; by very strong easterly winds they could not reach the west coast of Nova Guinea, but shaping their course very near south, descried the coast of Arnhem or Van Diemen's Land, in 11° south latitude, and sailed along the coast for 30 miles (120), without seeing any people, but many signs of smoke; when, turning towards the north, they visited the unknown islands of Timor Laut, and the known islands of Tenimber, Kauwer, etc., but without ever being able to converse with the inhabitants, who were a very timid people; when, after three months' cruising, they returned in July to Banda, without (in this voyage) having done or discovered anything of consequence; which may be seen by the journals and maps.

After the little success in these voyages, nothing further was attempted on discovery to the eastward; but last year (under your direction) the discovery of the remaining unknown south lands was assiduously re-attempted; and in that remarkable voyage was that great unknown Staten and Van Diemen's Land discovered from 35° to 43° south latitude, and at the same time the (so long wished for) passage to the South Sea; but it is unnecessary to relate more here, as you are perfectly acquainted with all particulars.

But to obtain a thorough knowledge of these extensive countries, the discovery whereof has been begun (in consequence of the intention of the Company and the recommendation of our masters), now only remains for the future to discover whether Nova Guinea is one continent with that great south land, or separated by channels and islands lying between them; and also whether that New Van Diemen's Land is the same continent with these two great countries, or with one of them; or, if separated from them, what islands may be dispersed between Nova Guinea and the unknown south land, when, after more experience and knowledge of all the said known and unknown countries, we shall be better enabled for further undertakings.

After considering well what is above related, and by our estimate of the present strength of the Company's naval forces, it is found that, without prejudice to the ordinary trading and warlike expeditions, two or three yachts could be spared, it is therefore resolved in the Council of India, to equip the yachts *Limmen*, the *Zeemeuw*, and the *Brak* for the further discovery of the east and south lands, to furnish them well with all necessaries, and to commit them to your conduct, in confidence that you will, with courage, vigilance, prudence, good order, and the requisite perseverance, skilfully direct this important voyage, in such a manner as to be capable to give an account, on your return, fully to our contentment.

VI. PELSART AND THE WRECK OF THE *BATAVIA*

[THE Dutch ship *Batavia*, Captain Pelsart, was wrecked on the west coast of New Holland in 1629. This narrative originally appeared in Thevenot's *Recueil de divers Voyages curieux*. It contains the earliest account we have of Australian aborigines.]

The Directors of the East India Company, encouraged by the successful return of the five ships of General Carpenter, richly laden, caused eleven vessels to be equipped the very same year, 1628, for the same voyage: amongst which, there was one ship called the *Batavia*, commanded by Captain Francis Pelsart. He sailed from the Texel on the 28th of October 1628; and, as it would be tedious to the reader to give him a long account of a passage so well known as that to the Cape of Good Hope, I shall pass over in silence that portion of his Journal, and content myself with observing, that on the 4th of June in the following year, 1629, this vessel, the *Batavia*, being separated from the fleet in a storm, was driven on some rocks which lie in the latitude of 28° south, and which are called by the Dutch the Abrolhos of Frederick Houtman. Captain Pelsart, who was sick in bed when this accident happened, perceived at once that his ship had struck. It was night, indeed; but the moon shone very brightly, and the weather was fair. He immediately ran upon deck, and found that all the sails were set; their course was north-east by north; and the sea appeared covered with a white froth as far as the eye could reach. He summoned the master, and charged him with the loss of the ship; who excused himself by saying he had taken all the care he could; and that, having discerned the froth at a distance, he asked his shipmate what he thought of it; who told him that this whiteness was occasioned by the rays of the moon. The captain then asked him what was to be done; and in what part of the world they were. The master replied, that God only knew that, and that the ship was on an unknown reef. They sounded, and found eighteen feet of water abaft, and much less forward. They immediately agreed to throw their cannon overboard, in hopes that, when the ship was lightened, she might be brought to float again. They dropped an anchor, however; but

41

meanwhile there arose a storm of wind and rain, which soon convinced them of the danger they were in; for, being surrounded with rocks and shoals, the ship was perpetually striking.

They then resolved to cut away the mainmast, which they did, but this increased the shock; for though they cut the mast close by the board, they could not get it clear, because it was much entangled with the rigging. They could see no land, except an island, which, as far as they could judge, was at about the distance of three leagues, and two smaller islands, or rather rocks, which lay nearer. The master was sent to examine them. He returned about nine in the morning, and reported that the sea, at high water, did not cover them; but that the coast was so rocky and full of shoals that it would be very difficult to land upon them. They resolved, however, to run the risk, and to send most of their company on shore, to pacify the women, children, sick people, and such as were out of their wits with fear, whose cries and noise served only to disturb them. They put these on board their shallop and skiff; and about ten o'clock in the morning they perceived that their vessel began to break. They redoubled their exertions to get up their bread upon deck, but they did not take the same care of the water, not reflecting, in the extremity of their danger, that they might be much distressed for want of it on shore; but what embarrassed them most of all was the brutal behaviour of some of the crew, who made themselves so drunk with the wine, upon which no check was now kept, that they were able to make only three trips that day, in which they landed one hundred and eighty persons, twenty barrels of bread, and some small casks of water. The master returned on board towards evening, and told the captain that it was of no use to send more provisions on shore, for the crew only wasted those they had already. Pelsart then went in the shallop to put things into some order, and discovered that there was no water to be found upon the island. He endeavoured to return to the ship, in order to bring off a supply, together with the most valuable part of their cargo; but a storm suddenly arising, he was forced to return.

The whole of the fifth day of the month was spent in removing the water, and some of the merchandise, on shore; and afterwards, the captain in the skiff, and the master in the shallop, endeavoured to return to the vessel, but found the sea running so high that it was impossible to get on board. In this extremity the carpenter threw himself out of the ship and swam to them, in order to inform them to what hardships those left in the vessel were reduced; and he was sent back, with orders for them to make rafts, by tying the planks together, and endeavour on these to reach the shallop and skiff; but before this could be done, the weather became so rough that the captain was obliged to return, leaving, with the utmost grief, his lieutenant and seventy men on the very point of perishing on board the vessel. Those who had reached the little island were not in much better condition; for, upon taking an account of their water, they found they had not above eighty pints for forty people; and on the larger island, where there were one hundred and eighty, the stock was still less. Those who were on the little island began to murmur, and to complain of their officers, because they did not go in search of water on the neighbouring islands; and they represented the necessity of this to Captain Pelsart, who yielded to their remonstrances, but told them that before he went, he wished to communicate this resolution to the rest of the people. It was with difficulty that he gained their consent to this, for the master was afraid that the other party would keep the captain with them. At length they consented, but not till the captain had declared, that without the consent of the company on the large island that he should go in search of water, he would, rather than leave them, perish on board his ship. When he got near to the island, he who commanded the boat told the captain, that if he had anything to say, he must call out to the people; for that they would not suffer him to go out of the boat. The captain then attempted to throw himself overboard, in order to swim to the island; but he was prevented, and the order given to pull off from the shore. Thus he was obliged to return, having first left these words written on a leaf of a tablet, that he was gone in the skiff to look for water in the nearest country or islands that he could find.

They first sought along the coasts of the islands, and certainly found water in the holes of the rocks, but the sea had dashed into it and rendered it unfit for use; they therefore determined to seek farther on. They made a deck to their boat, as it would have been impracticable to navigate those seas in an open vessel. A few more of the crew joined themselves to the company for the same purpose and after the captain had obtained the signature of his people to that resolution, they immediately put to sea, having first taken an observation, by which they found themselves in latitude 28°13′ south. A short time afterwards they had sight of the continent, which appeared, according to their estimation, to lie about sixteen miles north by west from the place where they had suffered shipwreck. They found the water about twenty-five or thirty fathoms deep; and, as night drew on, kept out to sea, standing in for the land again after midnight. On the morning of the 9th (of June) they found themselves, according to their reckoning, about three miles from the shore; this day they made four or five miles by many tacks, sailing sometimes north, sometimes west, the coast lying north-quarter-west, the coast appearing low, naked, and excessively rocky, being nearly of the same height as that near Dover. At last they saw a little creek, with sandy bottom, into which they were anxious to enter, but upon approaching it they found that the sea ran high, and the weather becoming more threatening, they were obliged to haul off the coast.

After midnight in the second watch of the 29th, they perceived an island before them, which they left on their starboard or right side, and at daybreak found themselves near the cove which lies upon the west side thereof, from whence they continued their course towards the west-north-west. By pursuing this route one gives a wide berth to the shore at the bottom of this cove, but nears it again before the Trowuen Islands are reached. About midday they found themselves in latitude 6° 48′, and that by reckoning they had made thirty miles, the course lying west-north-west, about three o'clock in the afternoon. They passed between these two islands, and saw upon the more westerly one a great quantity of cocoa-nut trees. About evening they were still distant one mile from the south point of Java, and at the third bell of the second watch found themselves exactly between Java and Prince's Island. On the morning of the thirtieth day they were near the coast of Prince's Island, and made only two miles that day. Towards evening a slight breeze sprung up from the land.

The weather moderated on the 1st of July, and at midday they were still full three leagues distant from the island called Dwaers-inden-wegh, the wind being inconstant. About evening the wind blew from the north-west, so that they gained the island of which I speak. The night was calm, and they were constrained to row.

On the morning of the 2nd, being opposite to the island called Toppers-hoëtien, they were forced to remain at anchor till nigh eleven o'clock, expecting the sea breeze; but it rose so slightly that they were compelled to continue rowing, and found by the evening that they had only advanced two miles. At sunset they perceived a sail astern opposite to the island Dwaers-inden-wegh, whereupon they reached the coast and cast anchor there, resolved to await its coming. When the morning came they boarded this vessel, hoping to obtain assistance and arms for their defence against the Javanese in case they were at war with the Dutch. They found the vessel accompanied by two others of the Company, in one of which was Ramburgh, counsellor to the Company. Pelsart went on board his vessel, and having recounted to him with grief the accident that had befallen him, sailed with him to Batavia.

Whilst Pelsart is soliciting assistance, I will return to those of the crew who remained upon the island; but I should first inform you that the supercargo, named Jerome Cornelis, formerly an apothecary at Harlem, had conspired with the pilot and some others, when off the coast of Africa, to obtain possession of the ship and to take her to Dunkirk, or to avail themselves of her for the purposes of piracy. This supercargo remained upon the wreck ten days after the vessel had struck, having discovered no means of reaching the shore. He even passed two days upon the mainmast, which floated, and having from thence got upon a yard, at length gained the land. In the absence of Pelsart he became commander, and deemed this a suitable occasion for putting his original design into execution, concluding that it would not be difficult to become master of that which remained of the wreck, and to surprise the commander when he should arrive with the assistance which he had gone to Batavia to seek, and afterwards to cruise in these seas with his vessel. To accomplish this it was necessary to get rid of those of the crew who were not of his party; but before embruing his hands with blood, he caused his accomplices to sign a species of compact, by which they promised fidelity one to another. The entire crew was divided between three islands; upon that of Cornelis, which they had named the graveyard of Batavia, was the greatest number of men. One of them, by name Weybehays, had been dispatched to another island to seek for water, and having discovered some after a search of twenty days, he made the preconcerted signal by lighting three fires, but in vain, for they were not seen by the people of Cornelis's company, the conspirators having, during that time, murdered those who were not of their party. Of these they killed thirty or forty; some few saved themselves upon pieces of wood, which they joined together, and going in search of Weybehays informed him of the horrible massacre that had taken place. Having with him forty-five men he resolved to keep upon his guard, and to defend himself from these assassins if they should make an attack upon his company, which, in effect, they designed to do, and to treat the other party in the same manner; for they feared lest their company, or that which remained upon the third island, should inform the commander upon his arrival, and thus prevent the execution of their design. They succeeded easily with the party last mentioned, which was the weakest, killing the whole of them, excepting seven children and some women. They hoped to succeed as easily with Weybehays' company, and in the meanwhile broke open the chests of merchandise which had been saved from the vessel. Jerome Cornelis caused clothing to be made for his company out of the rich stuffs which he found therein, choosing to himself a body-guard, each of whom he clothed in scarlet, embroidered with gold and silver. Regarding the women as part of the spoil, he took one for himself, and gave one of the daughters of the minister to a principal member of his party, abandoning the other three for public use; he drew up also certain rules for the future conduct of his men.

After these horrible proceedings, he caused himself to be elected captain-general by a document which he compelled all his companions to sign. He afterwards sent twenty-two men in two shallops to destroy the company of Weybehays, but they met with a repulse. Taking with him thirty-seven men he went himself against Weybehays, who received him at the water's edge as he disembarked, and forced him to retire, although he had no other weapons but clubs, the ends of which he had armed with spikes. Finding force unavailing he had recourse to other means. He proposed a treaty of peace, the chaplain who remained with Weybehays drawing up the conditions; it was agreed to with this proviso, that Weybehays' company should remain unmolested, who, upon their part, agreed to deliver up a little boat in which one of the sailors had escaped from the island where Cornelis was located to that of Weybehays, receiving in return some stuffs for clothing his people. During the negotiations, Cornelis wrote to certain French soldiers who belonged to the company, offering to each six thousand pounds to corrupt them, with the hope that with this assistance he might easily compass his design. His letters, which were without effect, were shown to Weybehays, and Cornelis, who was ignorant of their disclosure, having arrived the next day with three or four others to find Weybehays and bring him the apparel, the latter caused him to be attacked, killed two or three of his company, and took Cornelis himself prisoner. One of them, by name Wouterlos, who escaped from this rout, returned the following day to renew the attack, but with little success.

Pelsart arrived during these occurrences in the frigate *Sardam;* as he approached the wreck he observed smoke from a distance, rising from one of the islands, a circumstance that afforded him great consolation, since he perceived by it that his people were not all dead. He cast anchor, and threw himself immediately into a skiff with bread and wine, and proceeded to land in one of the islands. Nearly at the same time a boat came alongside armed with four men. Weybehays, who was one of the four, ran to him, informed him of the massacre, and advised him to return as speedily as possible to his vessel, for that the conspirators designed to surprise him—having already murdered twenty-five persons—and to attack him with two shallops; adding, that he himself had that morning been at close quarters with them. Pelsart perceived at the same time the two shallops coming towards him, and had scarcely got on board his own vessel before they came alongside. He was surprised to see the people covered with embroidery of gold and silver, and weapons in their hands, and demanded of them why they approached the vessel armed. They replied that they would inform him when they came on board. He commanded them to cast their arms into the sea, or otherwise he would sink them. Finding themselves compelled to submit, they threw away their weapons, and, being ordered on board, were immediately placed in irons. One of them, named Jan de Bremen, who was the first examined, confessed that he had put to death or assisted in the assassination of twenty-seven persons. The same evening Weybehays brought his prisoner on board.

On the 18th day of September, the captain and the master-pilot, taking with them ten men of Weybehays' company, passed over in boats to the island of Cornelis. Those who still remained thereon lost all courage as soon as they saw them alongside, and allowed themselves to be placed in irons. The captain's first care was to make search for the jewels, which had been distributed here and there. The whole of these were discovered at the first search, with the exception of a chain of gold and a ring, the latter of which was afterwards recovered. The wreck was afterwards visited. The vessel was broken into a hundred pieces; the keel upon one side aground upon a sandbank, the forepart of the vessel resting upon a rock, and other pieces scattered here and there, holding out little hope to Pelsart of saving any part of the Company's merchandise. The steward informed him that about one month previous, upon the only fine day they had had during their residence there, having gone out fishing near the wreck, he had struck against one of the chests filled with silver with the end of a pike.

On the 19th, they conveyed the other accomplices to the island for the purpose of examining them.

On the 20th, they sent various necessaries to Weybehays' company, and brought away water from them; for, after being ten days upon the island without discovering any, they thought of tasting some which was in two wells, but which they had believed to be salt, because it rose and fell with the tide, but they afterwards found it to be good to drink.

On the 21st, they found the tide very low, and the wind so strong from the east-south-east that the boat could not go out this day.

On the 22nd, they again wished to examine the wreck, but the sea broke upon it so roughly that the swimmers themselves did not venture to approach it.

On the 25th, the master and pilot approached it at a favourable moment, and those who remained on shore perceiving that there was something that they were unable to remove therefrom, sent assistance to them, the captain going in person, and they found that they had discovered a chest full of silver. A second chest was afterwards found, and the two were placed on dry land; but they were unable to obtain more that day on account of the bad weather, although the divers of Guzaret assured them they had found six other chests which they could easily remove.

On the 26th, after they had dined, the weather being fine and the tide very low, the master set out for the spot where the chests had been seen and recovered three, placing an anchor and a piece of artillery to mark the spot where a fourth remained, which, after great endeavours, they found themselves unable to move.

On the 27th, the wind blew very cold from the south.

On the 28th, the wind continued from the same quarter, and as it did not suffer them to work near the wreck, the captain assembled a council to advise whether he should bring the prisoners to trial there, or carry them to Batavia, to be there tried by the officers of the Company. The great number of them, and the temptation offered by the great treasures which they had recovered from the wreck, and with which the frigate was loaded, caused the majority to vote for their immediate trial and execution, which was there and then carried into effect.

VII. DUTCH SAILING DIRECTIONS

[DUTCH navigators became acquainted with the west coast of Australia through alterations made in the sailing directions with which they were furnished by the East India Company. Originally they followed the course which their Portuguese predecessors had pursued; that is to say, after rounding the Cape of Good Hope, they ran up the east African coast as far as Madagascar, and then turned east across the Indian Ocean. But in 1611 Hendrik Brouwer discovered that by steering due east after leaving the Cape he had the benefit of favourable winds and avoided the calms of the tropics. He recommended an easterly passage for three thousand miles, and then a northerly course. Dutch captains were ordered to take this course after 1613. One of them, Dirk Hartog, in the ship *Eendracht*, in 1616, ran further east than the sailing directions ordered, and found himself off Shark's Bay, where he set up a post with a plate upon it recording that his ship arrived there on October 25, 1616. The Company then amended its sailing directions, issuing those here printed, indicating that ships should make for the land of the *Eendracht* before setting a course for Java.]

By the instructions for the sailing in the autumn from the Netherlands to Java, amongst other things it is also enjoined: "The Cape of Good Hope being doubled, it is thought good that you sail in the E. direction between 36° and 39° S. lat., until you have reached a point eight hundred miles E. of the Cape of Good Hope; that you then direct your course as much N. as E., in such a manner that, on reaching 30° S. lat., you should find yourself about 950 or 1000 m. from the Cape of Good Hope.

"These 950 or 1000 m. from the Cape being attained, it is advisable—wind and weather permitting—that you bear down upon the land Eendraght at 27° S. lat., or more to the N., so as to take thence such a course as will enable you to clear the Tryals Shoals, lying about 20° S. lat., without danger, and to touch at the south coast of Java with ease, in order to have the weather gauge of the Straits of Sunda, and thus reach these straits without loss of time. It must be understood that this is

E   49

about the time when the east monsoon blows south of the line, and that the said 900 or 1000 miles E. of the Cape may be reached between the beginning of March and the end of September. Observe that the distance between the Cape and the land of Eendraght is, in reality, much shorter than the chart shows; and it may happen, by the aid of currents, that the route may be found even shorter than it really is, so that the land might be reached in much less time than we are led to expect. Remember, also, that the land of Eendraght has, south of 27° lat., many perilous sandbanks, and that the soundings are of sharp rocks. Consequently extreme caution, and the constant use of the lead at night and in stormy weather, is indispensably necessary, as at seven, six, or five miles from the coast the soundings are found to be one hundred, eighty, or seventy fathoms."

VIII. A DUTCH ACCOUNT OF NEW HOLLAND AND VAN DIEMEN'S LAND

[THIS narrative relates the adventures of two ships which sailed from Java in 1705 to New Holland and Van Diemen's Land. The translation was first printed by Major in his volume of *Early Voyages to Australia*, published by the Hakluyt Society.]

MY LORDS,—Before entering into a detail of matters of note occurring on the above-mentioned voyage, it may not perhaps be superfluous to offer a few preliminary observations, in order to throw a clearer light upon the subject; briefly these:—that the above-mentioned vessels having, in accordance with the instructions delivered to their crew by your Excellency on the twentieth of January of this year, weighed anchor from the port of Batavia on the 23rd of the same month, heard on their way, at Rembang on the east coast of Java, how the sloop *Doriados*, which had been destined for this voyage instead of the *Waijer*, had been disabled, but has been helped on its way by friendly vessels to Timor, and thence to New Holland.

They arrived on the twelfth of February before Copang, on the island of Timor, where they were obliged, by bad weather, to remain for twenty days, until the second of March. A month later, namely, on the second of April, they explored the north-west corner of Van Diemen's Land, without having so far observed anything remarkable on this voyage, except that for fifty or sixty miles straight north and south from this point the land is elevated, and along the whole of this coast there was continually found from fifty to twenty and fewer fathoms' water; besides, that on the passage from Timor the compasses were on the sixth of March affected by the thunder and lightning to such a degree that the north end of the needle pointed due south, and was brought home in that position.

This point of Van Diemen's Land having been thus explored, they occupied themselves, from the second of April to the twelfth of July, in visiting the bays, headlands, islands, rivers, etc., to the best of their ability according to their instructions. But not being sufficiently provided with fresh provisions for so long a voyage, many men on board began to suffer and also to die, from severe sickness, principally fever, acute pains in the head and eyes, and above all, dropsy, so that they were compelled to resolve upon returning, and to direct their course to Banda; the patsjallang, however, alone arrived there; the fluit *Vossenbosch*, and the sloop *Waijer*, being forced by unfavourable weather and the weakness of the crew to pass the government, and to hold on towards Macassar, as your nobilities will have already learnt by the papers from Banda and Macassar. The skipper, upper and under steersman, with most of the petty officers and sailors of the *Vossenbosch* being already dead, and their incomplete journals alone having reached us, the new maps, moreover, made by the direction of the skipper Martin van Delft having been improperly detained at Macassar, we are not at present in a position to forward the same complete information on the subject which the arrival of these maps would have enabled us to give, as they contain many new names which could not possibly be found in the limited compass of the Company's former charts. According to their own accounts, they have only been able to visit a strip of land of about sixty miles along the coast E. and W., including merely a very small portion of that great bay which it was recommended to them to sail over and explore as much as possible.

The daily courses, winds, currents, depths, reefs, soundings, variations of the compass, and the like observations, more especially depending upon the art of the steersman, are to be found in the above-mentioned journals, and shall here be passed over as out of place in a compendious report like the present. We shall here principally follow the log-book of the skipper Martin van Delft, of the *Vossenbosch*, and that of the under steersman Andries Roseboom, of the sloop *Waijer*, as the journals of the captain of the patsjallang, Pieter Fredericks of Hamburg, and of the steersman of the *Vossenbosch*, notwithstanding their general usefulness, do not afford any additional information, as they merely describe the same subject.

Besides the journals, some depositions and other papers of the same kind have reached us, referring to the loss of anchors, ropes, sails, the courses and bearings of the ship as recorded on board the *Vossenbosch*, none of them, however, of a nature to call for further observation here. At the same time we cannot omit to mention two papers, written by the captain of the patsjallang, and entered in the register of Banda, under the letters D.E., containing brief notes of the ship's course, the names of, and dates of departure from, the places visited during the voyage, together with the currents encountered, which documents could be forwarded to you, if desired, together with the above-mentioned journals of the skipper of the *Vossenbosch*, and the captain of the *Waijer*, and the new maps, should they arrive here from Macassar, since the maps of the patsjallang have not been drawn up with due regard to the proper soundings, distances, and other requisites, and are, therefore, not to be depended upon.

Continuing our summary of the voyage, we would observe, that from the commencement of the exploration of Van Diemen's Land, they noticed at several points on the strand signs of men, such as smoke and the like. The first inlet within the north point of that land, which was visited by them and called the Roseboom's Bay, runs dead inland, throwing out several branches on both sides. No fresh water is found here. At that time they saw no men, but merely some sign of inhabitants. However, on their leaving the bay, some of the natives were caught sight of, running away with their children and dogs as soon as they perceived our countrymen; and no opportunity was obtained of getting speech of any of them.

The coast here is level. The names Casuaris and Varckenshoek were given to the points E. and W. of this bay; of two other projecting points on the W. side which turned out to be islands, one was named the Goede Hoop, and the other the Kuijle Eijland; they found on the former of them a little water, but brackish, and in small quantity.

Between these two islands or headlands, some natives were met by the men on the thirty-first of April, who did not retire, but ran hastily towards an eminence, and with signs and gestures attempted to drive them away. No one was able to understand their language, which, according to the skipper Martin van Delft, seems to resemble in some respects that of Malabar; but even this is by no means clear. The colour and stature of these men appears from the description given to resemble most that of the Indians of the east; but they go stark naked, without any regard to age or sex, as was constantly observed by our sailors from the above-mentioned date until their departure. The only exception to this rule were the women who had children with them, these alone wearing a slight covering of leaves of such-like over their middle. The whole number of these islanders did not exceed fourteen or fifteen men; seeing that our people could not be induced by their grimaces, violent gestures, yelling and flourishing of assegais, and all kinds of weapons, to retreat from the shore, they were imprudent enough to throw some of their assegais, or rather sharpened sticks, at our men, with the intention of wounding and intimidating them; but their chief, or one who at least appeared to be so, being hit by a ball from the single musket which was fired at them in return, the rest began to run quickly away, being very agile and well made.

The women are tall and slim, with very large mouth and small eyes; the head of both sexes is curly, like that of the Papuan islanders, and a yellow or red ointment, prepared with turtle fat, seems to be used as an ornament. The nature of these tribes is foul and treacherous, as was apparent at the last moment, when our people were on the point of departing. Eight islanders attacked and wounded two sailors, with the hope of seizing upon their clothes, and that after having conversed with these men for weeks, eaten and drunk with them, visited them on board, and being allowed to examine everything to their great admiration, after having received presents, and also on their part regaled our people with fish and crabs. Besides this, their bad disposition came to light in the case of the man who had been previously wounded by our party as before mentioned; when he afterwards was assisted and bandaged, and had every possible attention shown him by our men, he tore the linen to pieces and threw it away into a corner; notwithstanding that at other times these natives appeared particularly greedy after linen, knives, beads, and such toys.

They, however, possess nothing which is of value themselves, and have neither iron nor anything like mineral ore or metal, but only a stone which is ground and made to serve as a hatchet. They have no habitations, either houses or huts; and feed on fish, which they catch with harpoons of wood, and also by means of nets, putting out to sea in small canoes made of the bark of trees, which are in themselves so fragile that it is necessary to strengthen them with cross-beams.

Some of them had marks on their body, apparently cut or carved, which, as it seemed to our people, were looked upon by them as a kind of ornament. They eat sparingly and moderately, whereby they grow up always active and nimble; their diet seems to consist of fish and a few roots and vegetables, but no birds or wild animals of any kind are used as food, for though animal food exists, and was found by our men in abundance, the natives appeared to be indifferent to it.

According to the notes of the captain of the sloop *Waijer*, from the 14th of June, about five hundred people with women and children were met on one occasion about two miles inland; at night also they were descried sitting round several fires among the bushes; nothing, however, was seen in their possession of any value. Our men might also easily have taken and brought to Batavia with them two or three of the natives who daily came on board, but the skipper of the *Vossenbosch*, following out his instructions to the letter, would not allow them to be taken without their full consent, either by falsehood or fraud, and as no one understood their language, nothing was to be done in the matter; consequently they remained in their own country.

The country here is for the most part level, and no mountains are to be seen, except a remarkable eminence which at a distance has the appearance of three mountains, as noted in the journal of the skipper, under date May the 25th. The soil seems productive, if cultivated, but the whole extent of the coast is bordered by sands or downs. In no part were any remarkable trees noticed, much less any of an aromatic and spice kind.

The second bay after the Roseboom's Bay just described, between Tigers and Wolfs-point, visited by our countrymen, has the appearance of a wide river, but is salt; as, however, nothing remarkable was found there, we shall let the journal of the skipper, on the date May 12th, speak for itself, it being described in the account of the commander of the *Waijer* under the name of the Bessia River.

The third inlet visited by the expedition is rather large, its E. point being Kaijmans, and its W., Oranjes-hoek. The tide flows here with great force, and the patsjallang sailed between eight and ten miles inland, without finding any diminution in the saltness of the water. As the bottom and the general aspect still remain the same, it was supposed by our people that this inlet runs right through to the south side of New Holland, and not only this, but also others both E. and W. of the angle of Van Diemen's Land.

From this it seems to follow that the South Land in a great measure consists of islands—a supposition not at all improbable, considering how on its south side, from the point called Leeuwin, or the land visited by the Leeuwin in the year 1622, to Nuytsland, discovered in 1627, it is entirely girt and surrounded by innumerable islands, although these things had better be left to a more accurate examination of the country and a more matured judgment. But there is another consideration in favour of this supposition, namely, the rude and barbarous character and malicious disposition of the above-mentioned islanders, as it has been frequently remarked that such serious defects are much more generally found among islanders than among the inhabitants of continents. However, be this as it may, we shall only further remark, that the patsjallang, owing to the strength of the current, was not able to proceed, but was obliged to return to the *Vossenbosch*, having first discovered within this inlet an island, five miles in circumference, on which was found very good drinking-water, and a tiger was met with; a number of snipes also were seen on another island which lay at the entrance of this strait, and of which more is said in the journal of the sloop *Waijer* under the date of the eighteenth and nineteenth of May. The weather here was observed to become much colder.

The fourth inlet of those visited by the expedition, called Delft Bay, runs five or six miles inland, and demands little further notice than as to its position and depths, both which are to be found clearly stated in the journals and maps, also that it is called on one side of its mouth, Rustenburg, and on the other side in the old maps it is known under the name of Maria's Land, in which district the inhabitants were so stupid that they attempted to tow the patsjallang, while lying at anchor, with three little canoes, but seeing that no progress was made, they tried to effect their object by tugging at the anchor. This also proving ineffectual, they returned to the shore. Our men employed themselves daily in fishing, the fish here being plentiful but of no great size, and attempted to arrest the increasing sickness on board.

The fifth and last inlet E. visited by our people is bounded on one side by the promontory of Lonton, on the other side by the point of Callemore (names given to them by the crew), although the last-mentioned point may rather be called an island than a promontory, since the inlet runs round it and again joins the sea. In front of the point Lonton also an island was found, called by them Schildpads island; nothing remarkable is to be recorded of this place, except that at night, by moonlight, an immense number of black birds, as large as pigeons, were met by the patsjallang *Hollandia Nova*, which flock continued to pass for half an hour; also that the inhabitants became so much accustomed to our people that they assisted them in procuring and carrying water; but afterwards they could not conceal their malicious disposition, as we have already narrated.

This last inlet is called Vossenbosch Bay, and also has before the promontory of Calice a small island, where stands a solitary tree by which it may be recognised.

Thus, thinking we have briefly stated the origin, the adventures, the results, and the return of this expedition, so far as they could be investigated, we shall here conclude.

We are, etc.,

Hk. Swaardecroon,
Cs. Chastelijn,
(S.)   J. S. Craine.

Batavia Castle, Oct. 6, 1705.

IX. DAMPIER'S VOYAGE IN THE CYGNET

[THE following pages contain William Dampier's account of his first visit to the shores of New Holland in the *Cygnet*. The crew had seized the ship and sailed away with it, leaving the captain, Swan, ashore at Mindanao. The description of Australian aboriginals is amongst the most interesting and closely-observed passages in Dampier's writings.]

Being now clear of all the Islands, we stood off South, intending to touch at New Holland, a part of Terra Australis Incognita, to see what that Country would afford us. Indeed as the Winds were we could not now keep our intended Course (which was first westerly, and then northerly) without going to New Holland, unless we had gone back again among the Islands: But this was not a good time of the Year to be among any Islands to the South of the Equator, unless in a good Harbour.

The 31st day we were in Lat. 13 d. 20 m. still standing to the Southward, the Wind bearing commonly very hard at W. we keeping upon it under two Courses, and our Mizen, and sometimes a Main-top-sail Rift. About 10 a Clock at Night we tackt and stood to the Northward, for fear of running on a Shoal, which is laid down in our Drafts in Lat. 13 d. 50 m. or thereabouts: It bearing S. by W. from the East-end of Timor; and so the Island bore from us by our judgments and Reckoning. At 3 a Clock we tackt again, and stood S. by W. and S. S. W.

In the Morning, as soon as it was day, we saw the Shoal right a-head: It lies in 13 d. 50 m. by all our Reckonings. It is a small Spit of Sand, just appearing above the Waters edge, with several Rocks about it, 8 or 10 foot high above water. It lies in a triangular Form; each side being about a League and half. We stemm'd right with the middle of it, and stood within half a Mile of the Rocks, and sounded; but found no ground. Then we went about and stood to the North two Hours; and then tackt and stood to the Southward again, thinking to weather it, but could not. So we bore away on the North-side, till we came to the East-point, giving the Rocks a small birth: Then we trimm'd sharp, and stood to the Southward, passing close by it, and sounded again but found no Ground.

This Shoal is laid down in our Drafts not above 16 or 20 Leagues from New Holland; but we did run afterwards 60 Leagues due South before we fell in with it; and I am very confident, that no part of New Holland hereabouts lies so far Northerly by 40 Leagues, as it is laid down in our Drafts. For if New Holland were laid down true, we must of necessity have been driven near 40 Leagues to the Westward of our Course; but this is very improbable, that the Current should set so strong to the Westward, seeing that we had a constant Westerly Wind. I grant, that when the Monsoon shifts first, the Current does not presently shift, but runs afterwards near a Month; but the Monsoon had been shifted at least two Months now. But of the Monsoons and other Winds, and of the Currents, elsewhere, in their proper place. As to these here, I do rather believe that the Land is not laid down true, than that the Current deceived us; for it was more probable we should have been deceived before we met with a Shoal, than afterwards; for on the Coast of New Holland we found the Tides keeping their constant Course; the Flood running N. by E. and the Ebb S. by W.

The 4th day of January, 1688, we fell in with the Land of New Holland in the Lat. of 16 d. 50 m. having, as I said before, made our Course due South from the Shoal that we past by the 31st day of December. We ran in close by it, and finding no convenient anchoring, because it lies open to the N.W. we ran along shore to the Eastward, steering N. E. by E. for so the Land lies. We steered thus about 12 Leagues; and then came to a Point of Land, from whence the Land trends East and Southerly, for 10 or 12 Leagues; but how afterwards I know not. About 3 Leagues to the Eastward of this Point, there is a pretty deep Bay, with abundance of Islands in it, and a very good place to anchor in, or to hale ashore. About a League to the Eastward of that Point we anchored January the 5th, 1688, 2 Mile from the Shore, in 29 Fathom, good hard Sand, and clean Ground.

New Holland is a very large Tract of Land. It is not yet determined whether it is an Island or a main Continent; but I am certain that it joyns neither to Asia, Africa, nor America. This part of it that we saw is all low even Land, with Sandy Banks against the Sea, only the Points are rocky, and so are some of the Islands in this Bay.

The Land is of a dry sandy Soil, destitute of Water, except you make Wells; yet producing divers sorts of Trees; but the

Woods are not thick, nor the Trees very big. Most of the Trees that we saw are Dragon-trees, as we supposed; and these too are the largest Trees of any there. They are about the bigness of our large Apple-trees, and about the same heighth: and the Rind is blackish, and somewhat rough. The Leaves are of a dark colour; the Gum distils out of the Knots or Cracks that are in the Bodies of the Trees. We compared it with some Gum Dragon, or Dragon's Blood, that was aboard, and it was of the same colour and taste. The other sorts of Trees were not known by any of us. There was pretty long Grass growing under the Trees; but it was very thin. We saw no Trees that bore Fruit or Berries.

We saw no sort of Animal, nor any Track of Beast, but once; and that seemed to be the Tread of a Beast as big as a great Mastiff-Dog. Here are a few small Land-birds, but none bigger than a Blackbird; and but few Sea-fowls. Neither is the Sea very plentifully stored with Fish, unless you reckon the Manatee and Turtle as such. Of these Creatures there is plenty; but they are extraordinary shy; though the Inhabitants cannot trouble them much, having neither Boats nor Iron.

The Inhabitants of this Country are the miserablest People in the world. The Hodmadods of Monomatapa, though a nasty people, yet for Wealth are Gentlemen to these; who have no Houses and skin Garments, Sheep, Poultry, and Fruits of the Earth, Ostrich Eggs, etc., as the Hodmadods have: And setting aside their Humane Shape, they differ but little from Brutes. They are tall, strait-bodied, and thin, with small long Limbs. They have great Heads, round Foreheads, and great Brows. Their Eye-lids are always half closed, to keep the Flies out of their Eyes; they being so troublesome here, that no Fanning will keep them from coming to ones Face; and without the assistance of both Hands to keep them off, they will creep into ones Nostrils, and Mouth too, if the Lips are not shut very close: so that from their Infancy being thus annoyed with these Insects, they do never open their Eyes as other People: And therefore they cannot see far, unless they hold up their Heads, as if they were looking at somewhat over them.

They have great Bottle Noses, pretty full Lips, and wide Mouths. The two Fore-teeth of their Upper jaw are wanting in all of them, Men and Women, Old and Young; whether they draw them out, I know not: Neither have they any Beards. They are long visaged, and of a very unpleasing Aspect, having no one graceful Feature in their Faces. Their Hair is black, short and curl'd, like that of the Negroes; and not long and lank like the common Indians. The colour of their Skins, both of their Faces and the rest of their Body, is coal black, like that of the Negroes of Guinea.

They have no sort of Cloaths, but a piece of the Rind of a Tree ty'd like a Girdle about their Waists, and a handful of long Grass, or 3 or 4 small green Boughs full of Leaves, thrust under their Girdle, to cover their Nakedness.

They have no Houses, but lie in the open Air, without any covering; the Earth being their Bed, and the Heaven their Canopy. Whether they cohabit one Man to one Woman, or promiscuously, I know not: but they do live in Companies, 20 or 30 Men, Women, and Children together. Their only Food is a small sort of Fish, which they get by making Wares of Stone across little Coves or Branches of the Sea; every Tide bringing in the small Fish, and there leaving them for a Prey to these People, who constantly attend there to search for them at Low-water. This small Fry I take to be the top of their Fishery: They have no Instruments to catch great Fish, should they come; and such seldom stay to be left behind at Low-water: Nor could we catch any Fish with our Hooks and Lines all the while we lay there. In other Places at Low-water they seek the Cockles, Muscles and Periwincles: Of these Shell-fish there are fewer still: so that their chiefest dependance is upon what the Sea leaves in their Wares; which, be it much or little they gather up, and march to the Places of their abode. There the old People that are not able to stir abroad by reason of their Age, and the tender Infants, wait their return; and what Providence has bestowed on them, they presently broil on the Coals, and eat it in common. Sometimes they get as many Fish as makes them a plentiful Banquet; and at other times they scarce get every one a taste: But be it little or much that they get, every one has his part, as well the young and tender, the old and feeble, who are not able to go abroad, as the strong and lusty. When they have eaten they lie down till the next Low-water, and then all that are able march out, be it Night or Day, rain or shine, 'tis all one; they must attend the Wares, or else they must fast: For the Earth affords them no Food at all. There is neither Herb, Root, Pulse nor any sort of Grain for them to eat, that we saw; not any sort of Bird or Beast that they can catch, having no Instruments wherewithal to do so.

I did not perceive that they did worship any thing. These poor Creatures have a sort of Weapon to defend their Ware, or fight with their Enemies, if they have any that will interfere with their poor Fishery. They did at first endeavour with their Weapons to frighten us, who lying ashore deterr'd them from one of their Fishing-places. Some of them had wooden swords, others had a sort of Lances. The Sword is a piece of Wood shaped somewhat like a Cutlass. The Lance is a long strait Pole sharp at one end, and hardened afterwards by heat. I saw no Iron, nor any other sort of Metal; therefore it is probable they use Stone-Hatchets, as some Indians in America do, described in Chap. IV.

How they get their Fire I know not; but, probably, as Indians do, out of Wood. I have seen the Indians of Bon-Airy do it, and have my self tryed the Experiment: They take a flat piece of Wood that is pretty soft, and make a small dent in one side of it, then they take another hard round Stick, about the bigness of ones little Finger, and sharpening it at one end like a Pencil, they put that sharp end in the hole or dent of the flat soft piece, and then rubbing or twirling the hard piece between the Palms of their Hands, they drill the soft piece till it smoaks, and at last takes fire.

These People speak somewhat thro' the Throat; but we could not understand one word that they said. We anchored, as I said before, January the 5th, and seeing Men walking on the Shore, we presently sent a Canoa to get some Acquaintance with them: for we were in hopes to get some Provision among them. But the Inhabitants, seeing our Boat coming, run away and hid themselves. We searched afterwards 3 Days in hopes to find their Houses; but found none: yet we saw many places where they had made Fires. At last, being out of hopes to find their Habitations, we searched no farther; but left a great many Toys ashore, in such places where we thought that they would come. In all our search we found no Water, but old Wells on the sandy Bays.

At last we went over to the Islands, and there we found a great many of the Natives: I do believe there were 40 on one Island, Men, Women, and Children. The Men at our first coming ashore, threatened us with their Lances and Swords; but they were frighted by firing one Gun, which we fired purposely to scare them. The Island was so small that they could not hide themselves: but they were much disordered at our Landing, especially the Women and Children: for we went directly to their Camp. The lustiest of the Women snatching up their Infants ran away howling, and the little Children run after squeaking and bawling; but the Men stood still. Some of the Women, and such People as could not go from us, lay still by a Fire, making a doleful noise, as if we had been coming to devour them: but when they saw we did not intend to harm them, they were pretty

quiet, and the rest that fled from us at our first coming, returned
again. This their place of Dwelling was only a Fire, with a few
Boughs before it, set up on that side the Winds was of.

After we had been here a little while, the Men began to be
familiar, and we cloathed some of them, designing to have had
some service of them for it: for we found some Wells of Water
here, and intended to carry 2 or 3 Barrels of it aboard. But it
being somewhat troublesome to carry to the Canoas, we thought
to have made these Men to have carry'd it for us, and therefore
we gave them some old Cloaths; to one an old pair of Breeches,
to another a ragged Shirt, to the third a Jacket that was scarce
worth owning; which yet would have been very acceptable at
some places where we had been, and so we thought they might
have been with these People. We put them on them, thinking
that this finery would have brought them to work heartily for
us; and our Water being filled in small long Barrels, about 6
Gallons in each, which were made purposely to carry Water in,
we brought these our new Servants to the Wells, and put a Barrel
on each of their Shoulders for them to carry to the Canoa. But
all the signs we could make were to no purpose, for they stood
like Statues, without motion, but grinn'd like so many Monkeys,
staring one upon another: For these poor Creatures seem not
accustomed to carry Burthens; and I believe that one of our
Ship-boys of 10 Years old, would carry as much as one of them.
So we were forced to carry our Water our selves, and they very
fairly put the Cloaths off again, and laid them down, as if Cloaths
were only to work in. I did not perceive that they had any great
liking to them at first, neither did they seem to admire any thing
that we had.

At another time our Canoa being among these Islands seeking
for Game, espy'd a drove of these Men swimming from one Island
to another; for they have no Boats, Canoas, or Bark-logs. They
took up Four of them, and brought them aboard; two of them
were middle aged, the other two were young Men about 18 or 20
Years old. To these we gave boiled Rice, and with it Turtle and
Manatee boiled. They did greedily devour what we gave them,
but took no notice of the Ship, or any thing in it, and when they
were set on Land again, they ran away as fast as they could. At
our first coming, before we were acquainted with them, or they
with us, a Company of them who liv'd on the Main, came just
against our Ship, and standing on a pretty high Bank, threatned
us with their Swords and Lances, by shaking them at us; at last
the Captain ordered the Drum to be beaten, which was done of a

sudden with much vigour, purposely to scare the poor Creatures. They hearing the noise, ran away as fast as they could drive, and when they ran away in haste, they would cry "Gurry, Gurry," speaking deep in the Throat. Those Inhabitants also that live on the Main, would always run away from us; yet we took several of them. For, as I have already observed, they had such bad Eyes, that they could not see us till we came close to them. We did always give them Victuals, and let them go again, but the Islanders, after our first time of being among them, did not stir for us.

When we had been here about a week, we hal'd our Ship into a small sandy Cove, at a Spring-tide, as far as she would float; and at low Water she was left dry, and the Sand dry without us near half a mile; for the Sea riseth and falleth here about 5 fathom. The Flood runs North by East, and the Ebb South by West. All the Neep-tides we lay wholly a-ground, for the Sea did not come near us by about a hundred yards. We had therefore time enough to clean our Ships bottom, which we did very well. Most of our Men lay ashore in a Tent, where our Sails were mending; and our Strikers brought home Turtle and Manatee every day, which was our constant Food.

While we lay here, I did endeavour to persuade our Men to go to some English Factory; but was threatened to be turned ashore, and left here for it. This made me desist, and patiently wait for some more convenient place and opportunity to leave them, than here: Which I did hope I should accomplish in a short time; because they did intend, when they went from hence, to bear down towards Cape Comorin. In their way thither they designed also to visit the Island Cocos, which lieth in Lat. 12 d. 12 m. North, by our Drafts; hoping there to find of that Fruit; the Island having its Name from thence.

March the 12th, 1688, we sailed from New Holland, with the Wind at N.N.W. and fair weather. We directed our course to the Northward, intending as I said, to touch at the Island Cocos: But we met with the Winds at N.W.W.N.W. and N.N.W. for several days; which obliged us to keep a more Easterly course than was convenient to find that Island. We had soon after our setting out very bad weather, with much Thunder and Lightning, Rain and high blustring Winds.

It was the 26th day of March before we were in the Lat. of the Island Cocos, which is in 12 d. 12 m. and than, by Judgment, we were 40 or 50 Leagues to the East of it; and the Wind was now at S.W. Therefore we did rather chuse to bear away towards

SIR FRANCIS DRAKE.
From an engraving in the British Museum.

some Islands on the West-side of Sumatra, than to beat against the Wind for the Island Cocos. I was very glad of this; being in hopes to make my escape from them to Sumatra, or to some other Place.

. . . . . .

The 25th day* we crost the Equator, still coasting to the Northward, between the Island Sumatra, and a Range of small Islands, lying 14 or 15 Leagues off it. Amongst all these Islands, Hog Island is the most considerable. It lies in Lat. 3 d. 40 m. North. It is pretty high even Land, cloathed with tall flourishing Trees; we past it by the 28th day.

The 29th we saw a Sail to the North of us, which we chased: but it being little Wind, we did not come up with her till the 30th day. Then, being within a League of her, Captain Read went into a Canoa and took her, and brought her aboard. She was a Proe with four Men in her, belonging to Achin, whither she was bound. She came from one of these Coco-nut Islands that we past by, and was laden with Coco-nuts, and Coco-nut Oil. Captain Read ordered his Men to take aboard all the Nuts, and as much of the Oil as he thought convenient, and then cut a hole in the bottom of the Proe, and turned her loose, keeping the Men Prisoners.

It was not for the lucre of the Cargo, that Captain Read took this Boat, but to hinder me and some others from going ashore; for he knew that we were ready to make our escapes, if an opportunity presented it self; and he thought, that by his abusing and robbing the Natives, we should be afraid to trust our selves among them. But yet this proceeding of his turned to our great advantage, as shall be declared hereafter.

. . . . .

The 5th day of May we ran down on the West side of the Island Nicobar, properly so called and anchored at the N.W. end of it, in a small Bay, in 8 Fathom Water, not half a Mile from the Shore. The body of this Island is in 7 d. 30 m. North Lat. It is about 12 Leagues long, and 3 or 4 broad. The South end of it is pretty high, with steep Cliffs against the Sea; the rest of the Island is low, flat, and even. The Mold of it is black, and deep; and it is very well watered with small running Streams. It produceth abundance of tall Trees, fit for any uses; for the whole bulk of it seems to be but one entire Grove. But that which adds most to its Beauty off at Sea, are the many spots of Coco-nut Trees which grow round it in every small Bay. The Bays are

* Of April.

F

half a Mile, or a Mile long, more or less; and these Bays are intercepted, or divided from each other, with as many little rocky Points of Wood-land.

. . . . . .

I thought now was my time to make my Escape, by getting leave, if possible, to stay here: for it seemed not very feazable to do it by stealth; and I had no reason to despair of getting leave: this being a place where my stay could, probably, do our Crew no harm, should I design it. Indeed one reason that put me on the thoughts of staying at this particular place, besides the present opportunity of leaving Captain Read, which I did always intend to do, as soon as I could, was that I had here also a prospect of advancing a profitable Trade for Ambergrease with these People, and of gaining a considerable Fortune to my self: For in a short time I might have learned their Language, and by accustoming myself to row with them in the Proes or Canoas, especially by conforming my self to their Customs and Manners of Living, I should have seen how they got their Ambergrease, and have known what quantities they get, and the time of the Year when most is found. And then afterwards I thought it would be easie for me to have transported my self from thence, either in some Ship that past this way, whether English, Dutch, or Portuguese; or else to have gotten one of the Young Men of the Island, to have gone with me in one of their Canoas to Achin; and there to have furnished my self with such Commodities, as I found most coveted by them; and therewith, at my return, to have bought their Ambergrease.

I had, till this time, made no open show of going ashore here; but now, the Water being filled, and the Ship in a readiness to sail, I desired Captain Read to set me ashore on this Island. He, supposing that I could not go ashore in a place less frequented by Ships than this, gave me leave: which probably he would have refused to have done, if he thought I should have gotten from hence in any short time; for fear of my giving an account of him to the English or Dutch. I soon got up my Chest and Bedding, and immediately got some to row me ashore; for fear lest his mind should change again.

The Canoa that brought me ashore, landed me on a small sandy Bay, where there were two Houses, but no Person in them. For the Inhabitants were removed to some other House, probably, for fear of us; because the Ship was close by: and yet both Men and Women came aboard the Ship without any sign of fear. When our Ship's Canoa was going aboard again, they met the

Owner of the Houses coming ashore in his Boat. He made a great many signs to them to fetch me off again: but they would not understand him. Then he came to me, and offered his Boat to carry me off: but I refused it. Then he made signs for me to go up into the House, and, according as I did understand him by his signs, and a few Malayan words that he used, he intimated that somewhat would come out of the Woods in the night, when I was asleep, and kill me, meaning probably some wild Beast. Then I carried my Chest and Cloaths up into the House.

I had not been ashore an hour before Captain Teat and one John Damarel, with 3 or 4 armed Men more, came to fetch me aboard again. They need not have sent an armed Posse for me; for had they but sent the Cabbin-boy ashore for me, I would not have denied going aboard. For though I could have hid my self in the Woods, yet then they would have abused, or have killed some of the Natives, purposely to incense them against me. I told them therefore, that I was ready to go with them, and went aboard with all my Things.

When I came aboard I found the Ship in an uproar; for there were 3 Men more, who taking Courage by my example, desired leave also to accompany me. One of them was the Surgeon Mr. Coppinger, the other was Mr. Robert Hall, and one named Ambrose; I have forgot his Sir-name. These Men had always harboured the same Designs as I had. The two last were not much opposed; but Captain Read and his Crew would not part with the Surgeon. At last the Surgeon leapt into the Canoa, and taking up my Gun, swore he would go ashore, and that if any Man did oppose it, he would shoot him: But John Oliver, who was then Quarter-Master, leapt into the Canoa, taking hold of him, took away the Gun, and with the help of two or three more, they dragged him again into the Ship.

Then Mr. Hall and Ambrose and I were again sent ashore; and one of the Men that rowed us ashore stole an Ax, and gave it to us, knowing it was a good Commodity with the Indians. It was now dark, therefore we lighted a Candle, and I being the oldest stander in our new Country, conducted them into one of the Houses, where we did presently hang up our Hammocks. We had scarce done this before the Canoa cam ashore again, and brought the 4 Malayan Men belonging to Achin, (which we took in the Proe we took off of Sumatra) and the Portuguese that came to our Ship out of the Siam Jonk at Pulo Condore: the Crew having no occasion for these, being leaving the Malayan Parts, where the Portuguese Spark served as an Interpreter; and not fearing now that the Achinese could be serviceable to us in bringing us over to their Country, 40 Leagues off; nor imagining that we durst make such an attempt; as indeed it was a bold one. Now we were Men enough to defend our selves against the Natives of this Island, if they should prove our Enemies: though if none of these Men had come ashore to me, I should not have feared any danger. Nay, perhaps less, because I should have been cautious of giving any offence to the Natives: and I am of the Opinion, that there are no People in the World so barbarous as to kill a single Person that falls accidentally into their Hands, or comes to live among them; except they have before been injured, by some outrage, or violence committed against them. Yet even then, or afterwards, if a Man could but preserve his Life from their first rage, and come to treat with them (which is the hardest thing, because their way is usually to abscond, and rushing suddenly upon their Enemy to kill him at unawares) one might, by some slight, insinuate ones self into their Favours again. Especially by shewing some Toy, or Knack that they did never see before: which any European, that has seen the World, might soon contrive to amuse them withal: as might be done, generally even with a little Fire struck with a Flint and Steel.

As for the common Opinion of Anthropophagi, or Maneaters, I did never meet with any such People: All Nations or Families in the World, that I have seen or heard of, having some sort of Food to live on, either Fruit, Grain, Pulse, or Roots, which grow naturally or else planted by them; if not Fish and Land-Animals besides; (yea, even the people of New-Holland, had Fish amidst all their Penury) and would scarce kill a Man purposely to eat him. I know not what barbarous Customs may formerly have been in the World; and to Sacrifice their Enemies to their Gods, is a thing hath been much talked of, with Relation to the Savages of America. I am a Stranger to that also, if it be, or have been customary in any Nation there; and yet, if they Sacrifice their Enemies, it is not necessary they should Eat them too. After all, I will not be peremptory in the Negative, but I speak as to the compass of my own Knowledge, and know some of the Cannibal Stories to be false, and many of them have been disproved since I first went to the West-Indies. At that time, how Barbarous were the poor Florida Indians accounted, which now we find to be civil enough? What strange Stories have we heard of the Indians, whose Islands were called the Isles of Cannibals. Yet we find that they do Trade very civilly with the French and

Spaniards; and have done so with us. I do own that they have formerly endeavoured to destroy our Plantations at Barbadoes, and have since hindred us from settling the Island Santa Lucia by destroying two or three Colonies successively of those that were settled there; and even the Island Tabago has been often annoyed and ravaged by them, when settled by the Dutch, and still lies waste (though a delicate fruitful Island) as being too near the Caribbees on the Continent, who visit it every Year. But this was to preserve their own right, by endeavouring to keep out any that would settle themselves on those Islands, where they had planted themselves; yet even these People would not have hurt a single Person, as I have been told by some that have been Prisoners among them. I could instance also in the Indians of Bocca Toro, and Bocca Drago, and many other Places where they do live as the Spaniards call it, Wild and Savage: yet there they have been familiar with Privateers, but by Abuses have withdrawn their Friendship again. As for these Nicobar People, I found them Affable enough, and therefore I did not fear them, but I did not much care whether I had gotten any more Company or no.

But however, I was very well satisfied, and the rather because we were now Men enough to row ourselves over to the Island Sumatra; and accordingly we presently consulted how to purchase a Canoa of the Natives.

.   .   .   .   .   .

The next Morning . . . we bought a Canoa of him for an Ax, and we did presently put our Chests and Cloaths in it, designing to go to the South-end of the Island, and lye there till the Monsoon shifted, which we expected every day.

When our things were stowed away, we with the Achinese entered with joy into our new Frigot, and launched off from the Shore. We were no sooner off, but our Canoa overset, bottom upwards. We preserved our Lives well enough by Swimming, and dragged also our Chest and Cloaths ashore; but all our things were wet. I had nothing of value but my Journal and some Drafts of Land of my own taking, which I much prized, and which I had hitherto carefully preserved. Mr. Hall had also such another Cargo of Books and Drafts, which were now like to perish. But we presently opened our Chests and took out our Books, which, with much ado, we did afterwards dry; but some of our Drafts that lay loose in our Chests were spoiled.

We lay here afterwards 3 days, making great Fires to dry our Books. The Achinese in the meantime fixt our Canoa, with Outlagers on each side; and they also cut a good Mast for her, and made a substantial Sail with Mats.

The Canoa being now very well fixt, and our Books and Cloaths dry, we launched out the second time, and rowed towards the East-side of the Island, leaving many Islands to the North of us.

. . . . . .

It was the 15th day of May, 1688, about four a Clock in the Afternoon, when we left Nicobar Island, directing our Course towards Achin, being eight Men of us in Company, viz., three English, four Malayans, who were born at Achin, and the Mungrel Portuguese.

Our Vessel, the Nicobar Canoa, was not one of the biggest, nor of the least size: She was much about the Burthen of one of our London Wherries below Bridge, and built sharp at both ends, like the fore part of a Wherry. She was deeper than a Wherry, but not so broad, and was so thin and light, that when empty, four Men could launch her, or hale her ashore on a sandy Bay. We had a good substantial Mast, and a Mat Sail, and good Outlagers lash'd very fast and firm on each side the Vessel, being made of strong Poles. So that while these continued firm the Vessel could not overset, which she would easily have done without them, and with them too had they not been made very strong; and we were therefore much beholding to our Achinese Companions for this Contrivance.

. . . . . .

The Evening of this 18th day was very dismal. The Sky look'd very black, being covered with dark Clouds, the Wind blew hard, and the Seas ran high. The Sea was already roaring in a white Foam about us; a dark Night coming on, and no Land in sight to shelter us, and our little Ark in danger to be swallowed by every Wave; and, what was worst of all, none of us thought our selves prepared for another World. The Reader may better guess than I can express, the Confusion that we were all in. I had been in many eminent Dangers before now, some of which I have already related, but the worst of them all was but a Play-game in comparison with this. I must confess that I was in great Conflicts of Mind at this time. Other Dangers came not upon me with such a leisurely and dreadful Solemnity. A sudden Skirmish or Engagement, or so, was nothing when ones Blood was up, and push'd forwards with eager Expectations. But here I had a lingring view of approaching Death, and little or no hopes of escaping it; and I must confess that my Courage, which I had hitherto kept up, failed me here; and I made very sad Reflections on my former Life, and look'd back with Horror and Detestation, on Actions which before I disliked, but now I trembled at the remembrance of. I had long before this repented me of that roving course of Life, but never with such concern as now. I did also call to mind the many miraculous Acts of God's Providence towards me in the whole course of my Life, of which kind I believe few Men have met with the like. For all these I returned Thanks in a peculiar Manner, and this once more desired God's Assistance, and composed my Mind, as well as I could, in the hopes of it, and as the Event shewed, I was not disappointed of my hopes.

Submitting our selves therefore to God's good Providence, and taking all the Care we could to preserve our Lives, Mr. Hall and I took turns to steer, and the rest took turns to heave out the Water, and thus we provided to spend the most doleful Night I ever was in. About 10 a Clock it began to Thunder, Lighten, and Rain; but the Rain was very welcome to us, having drank up all the Water we brought from the Island.

The Wind at first blew harder than before, but within half an hour it abated, and became more moderate; and the Sea also asswaged of its Fury; and then by a lighted Match, of which we kept a piece burning on purpose, we looked on our Compass, to see how we steered, and found our Course to be still East. We had no occasion to look on the Compass before, for we steered right before the Wind, which if it shifted we had been obliged to have altered our Course accordingly. But now it being abated, we found our Vessel lively enough with that small Sail which was then aboard, to hail to our former Course, S. S. E. which accordingly we did, being now in hopes again to get to the Island Sumatra.

But about 2 a clock in the Morning of the 19th day, we had another Gust of Wind, with much Thunder, Lightning and Rain, which lasted till Day, and obliged us to put before the Wind again, steering thus for several Hours. It was very dark, and the hard Rain soaked us so thoroughly, that we had not one dry Thread upon us. The Rain chill'd us extremely; for any fresh Water is much colder than that of the Sea. For even in the coldest Climates the Sea is warm, and in the hottest Climates the Rain is cold and unwholsome for Man's Body. In this wet starveling plight we spent the tedious Night. Never did poor Mariners on a Lee-shore more earnestly long for the dawning Light then we did now. At length the Day appeared; but with such dark black Clouds near the Horizon, that the first glimpse of the Dawn appeared 30 or 40 degrees high; which was dreadful enough; for it is a common Saying among Seamen, and true, as I have experienced, that a high Dawn will have high Winds, and a low Dawn, small Winds.

We continued our Course still East, before Wind and Sea, till about 8 a Clock in the morning of this 19th day; and then one of our Malayan Friends cried out, Pulo Way. Mr. Hall, and Ambrose and I, thought the Fellow had said Pull away, an Expression usual among English Seamen, when they are Rowing. And we wondered what he meant by it, till we saw him point to his Consorts; and then we looking that way, saw Land appearing, like an Island, and all our Malayans said it was an Island at the N.W. end of Sumatra, called Way; for Pulo Way, is the Island Way. We, who were dropping with Wet, Cold, and Hungry, were all over-joyed at the sight of the Land, and presently marked its bearing. It bore South, and the Wind was still at West, a strong gale; but the Sea did not run so high as in the Night. Therefore we trimmed our small Sail no bigger than an Apron, and steered with it. Now our Outlagers did us a great kindness again, for although we had but a small Sail, yet the Wind was strong, and prest down our Vessel's side very much: But being supported by the Outlagers, we could brook it well enough, which otherwise we could not have done.

About Noon we saw more Land beneath the supposed Pulo Way; and steering towards it, before Night we saw all the Coast of Sumatra, and found the Errors of our Achinese; for the high Land that we first saw, which then appear'd like an Island, was not Pulo Way, but a great high Mountain on the Island Sumatra, called by the English, the Golden Mountain. Our Wind continued till about 7 a Clock at night; then it abated, and at 10 a Clock it died away: And then we stuck to our Oars again, tho all of us quite tired with our former Fatigues and Hardships.

The next Morning, being the 20th day, we saw all the low Land plain, and judged ourselves not above 8 Leagues off. About 8 a Clock in the Morning we had the Wind again at West, a fresh gale, and steering in still for the Shore, at 5 a Clock in the Afternoon we run to the Mouth of a River on the Island Sumatra, called Passange Jonca. It is 34 Leagues to the Eastward of Achin, and 6 Leagues to the West of Diamond Point, which makes with three Angles of a Rhombus, and is low Land.

Our Malayans were very well acquainted here, and carried us to a small Fishing Village, within a Mile of the River's Mouth, called also by the name of the River, Passange Jonca. The Hardships of this Voyage, with the scorching Heat of the Sun, at our first setting out, and the cold Rain, and our continuing Wet for the last two days, cast us all into Fevers, so that now we are not able to help each other, nor so much as to get our Canoa up to the Village; but our Malayans got some of the Townsmen to bring her up.

The News of our Arrival being noised abroad, one of the Oramkai's, or Noblemen of the Island, came in the Night to see us. We were then lying in a small Hut, at the end of the Town, and it being late, this Lord only viewed us, and having spoken with our Malayans, went away again; but he returned to us again the next day, and provided a large House for us to live in, till we should be recovered of our sickness; ordering the Towns-people to let us want for nothing. The Achinese Malayans that came with us, told them all the Circumstances of our Voyage; how they were taken by our Ship, and where, and how we that came with them were Prisoners aboard the Ship, and had been set ashore together at Nicobar, as they were. It was for this reason probably, that the Gentlemen of Sumatra were thus extraordinary kind to us, to provide every thing that we had need of; nay, they would force us to accept of Presents from them, that we knew not what to do with; as young Buffaloes, Goats, etc., for these we would turn loose at Night, after the Gentlemen that gave them to us were gone, for we were prompted by our Achinese Consorts to accept of them, for fear of disobliging by our Refusal. But the Coco-Nuts, Plantains, Fowls, Eggs, Fish, and Rice, we kept for our use. The Malayans that accompanied us from Nicobar, separated themselves from us now, living at one end of the House by themselves, for they were Mahometans, as all those of the Kingdom of Achin are; and though during our Passage by Sea together, we made them be contented to drink their Water out of the same Coco-shell with us; yet being now no longer under that Necessity, they again took up their accustomed Nicety and Reservedness. They all lay sick, and as their sickness increased, one of them threatned us, that if any of them died, the rest would kill us, for having brought them into this Voyage; yet I question whether they would have attempted, or the Country People have suffered it. We made a shift to dress our own Food, for none of these People, though they were very kind in giving us any thing that we wanted, would yet come near us, to assist us in dressing our Victuals: Nay, they would not touch any thing that we used. We had all Fevers, and therefore took turns to dress Victuals, according as we had strength to do it, or Stomachs to eat it. I found my Fever to increase, and my Head so distempered, that I could scarce stand, therefore I whetted and sharpened my Penknife, in order to let my self Blood; but I could not, for my Knife was too blunt.

. . . . . .

It was the beginning of June, 1688, when we left Passange Jonca. We had 4 men to row, one to steer, and a Gentleman of the Country, that went purposely to give an Information to the Government of our Arrival. We were but three days and nights in our Passage, having Sea-breezes by day, and Land-winds by night, and very fair Weather.

When we arrived at Achin, I was carried before the Shabander, the chief Magistrate in the City. One Mr. Dennis Driscal, an Irish-man, and a Resident there, in the Factory which our East India Company had there then, was Interpreter. I being weak, was suffered to stand in the Shabander's Presence: For it is their custom to make Men sit on the Floor, as they do, cross-legg'd like Taylors: But I had not strength then to pluck up my Heels in that manner. The Shabander asked of me several Questions, especially how we durst adventure to come in a Canoa from the Nicobar Islands to Sumatra. I told him, that I had been accustomed to hardships and hazards, therefore I did with much freedom undertake it. He enquired also concerning our Ship, whence she came, etc. I told him, from the South Seas; that she had ranged about the Philippine Islands, etc., and was now gone towards Arabia, and the Red Sea. The Malayans also and Portuguese were afterward examined, and confirmed what I declared, and in less than half an hour, I was dismist with Mr. Driscal, who then lived in the English East India Company's Factory. He provided a Room for us to lie in, and some Victuals.

X. DAMPIER'S VOYAGE IN THE *ROEBUCK*

I SAIL'D from the Downs early on Saturday, Jan. 14, 169$\frac{8}{9}$, with a fair Wind, in his Majesty's Ship the *Roe-buck;* carrying but 12 Guns in this Voyage, and 50 Men and Boys, with 20 Month's Provision. We had several of the King's Ships in Company, bound for Spit-head and Plimouth; and by Noon we were off Dungeness. We parted from them that Night, and stood down the Channel, but found our selves next Morning nearer the French Coast than we expected; C. de Hague bearing S.E. and by E. 6 L. There were many other Ships, some nearer, some farther off the French Coast, who all seem'd to have gone nearer to it than they thought they should. My Master, who was somewhat troubled at it at first, was not displeas'd however to find that he had Company in his Mistake; Which, as I have heard, is a very common one, and fatal to many Ships. The Occasion of it is the not allowing for the Change of the Variation since the making of the Charts; which Captain Hally has observ'd to be very considerable. I shall refer the Reader to his own Account of it which he caus'd to be published in a single Sheet of Paper, purposely for a Caution to such as pass to and fro the English Channel: The Title of it is in the Margin. And my own Experience thus confirming to me the Usefulness of such a Caution, I was willing to take this Occasion of helping towards the making it the more publick.

Not to trouble the Reader with every Day's Run, nor with the Winds or Weather (but only in the remoter Parts, where it may be more particularly useful) standing away from C. la Hague, we made the Start about 5 that Afternoon; which being the last Land we saw of England, we reckon'd our Departure from thence: Tho' we had rather have taken it from the Lizard, if the hazy Weather would have suffer'd us to have seen it.

. . . . . .

It was the 10th day of March, about the Time of the Equinox, when we cross'd the Equator, having had all along from the Lat. of 4 deg. 40 min. N. where the true Trade-wind left us, a great Swell out of the S.E. and but small uncertain Gales, mostly

Southerly, so that we crept to the Southward but slowly. I kept up against these as well as I could to the Southward, and when we had now and then a Flurry of Wind at E. I still went away due South, purposely to get to the Southward as fast as I could; for while near the Line I expected to have but uncertain Winds, frequent Calms, Rains, Tornadoes, &c. which would not only retard my Course, but endanger Sickness also among my Men: especially those who were ill provided with Cloaths, or were too lazy to shift themselves when they were drench'd with the Rains. The Heat of the Weather made them careless of doing this; but taking a Dram of Brandy, which I gave them when wet, with a Charge to shift themselves, they would however lye down in their Hammocks with their wet Cloaths; so that when they turn'd out they caus'd an ill Smell where-ever they came, and their Hammocks would stink sufficiently; that I think the remedying of this is worth the Care of Commanders that cross the Line; especially when they are, it may be, a Month or more e'er they get out of the Rains, at sometimes of the Year, as in June, July or August.

What I have here said about the Currents, Winds, Calms, &c. in this Passage, is chiefly for the farther Illustration of what I have heretofore observ'd in general about these Matters, and especially as to crossing the Line, in my "Discourse of the Winds, &c. in the Torrid Zone." . . . Which Observations I have had very much confirm'd to me in the Course of this Voyage; and I shall particularize in several of the chief of them as they come in my Way. And indeed I think I may say this of the main of the Observations in that Treatise, that the clear Satisfaction I had about them, and how much I might rely upon them, was a great Ease to my Mind during this vexatious Voyage; wherein the Ignorance, and Obstinacy withal, of some under me, occasion'd me a great deal of Trouble: Tho' they found all along, and were often forc'd to acknowledge it, that I was seldom out in my Conjectures, when I told them usually beforehand what Winds, &c. we should meet with at such or such particular Places we should come at.

Pernambuc was the Port that I designed for at my first setting out from St. Jago; it being a Place most proper for my Purpose, by Reason of its Situation, lying near the Extremity of C. St. Augustine, the Easternmost Promontory of Brazil; by which means it not only enjoys the greater Benefit of the Sea-breezes, and is consequently more healthy than other Places to the Southward, but is withal less subject to the Southerly Coasting Trade-winds, that blow half the Year on this Shore; which were now drawing on, and might be troublesome to me: So that I might both hope to reach soonest Pernambuc, as most directly and nearest in my Run; and might thence also more easily get away to the Southward than from Bahia de Todos los Santos, or Ria Janeira.

But notwithstanding these Advantages I propos'd to my self in going to Pernambuc, I was soon put by that Design through the Refractoriness of some under me, and the Discontents and Backwardness of some of my Men. For the Calms and Shiftings of Winds which I met with, as I was to expect, in crossing the Line, made them, who were unacquainted with these Matters, almost heartless as to the Pursuit of the Voyage, as thinking we should never be able to weather Cape St. Augustine: And though I told them that by that Time we should get to about three Degrees South of the Line, we should again have a true brisk general Trade-Wind from the North-East, that would carry us to what part of Brazil we pleas'd, yet they would not believe it till they found it so. This, with some other unforeseen Accidents, not necessary to be mention'd in this Place, meeting with the Aversion of my Men to a long unknown Voyage, made me justly apprehensive of their Revolting, and was a great Trouble and Hindrance to me. So that I was obliged partly to alter my Measures, and met with many difficulties, the Particulars of which I shall not trouble the Reader with: But I mention thus much of it in general for my own necessary Vindication, in my taking such Measures sometimes for prosecuting the Voyage as the State of my Ships Crew, rather than my own Judgment and Experience, determin'd me to. The Disorders of my Ship made me think at present that Pernambuc would not be so fit a Place for me; being told that Ships ride there 2 or 3 Leagues from the Town, under the Command of no Forts; so that whenever I should have been ashore it might have been easy for my discontented Crew to have cut or slipt their Cables, and have gone away from me: Many of them discovering already an Intention to return to England, and some of them declaring openly that they would go no further onwards than Brazil. I alter'd my Course therefore, and stood away for Bahio de todos los Santos, or the Bay of all Saints, where I hop'd to have the Governour's Help, if need should require, for securing my Ship from any such mutinous Attempt; being forced to keep my self all the way upon my Guard, and to lie with my Officers, such as I could trust, and with small Arms upon the Quarter-Deck; it scarce being safe for me to lie in my Cabbin, by Reason of the Discontents among my Men.

.   .   .   .   .

My Stay here at Bahia was about a Month; during which Time the Vice-Roy of Goa came hither from thence in a great Ship, said to be richly laden with all Sorts of India Goods; but she did not break Bulk here, being bound Home for Lisbon; only the Vice-Roy intended to refresh his Men (of whom he had lost many, and most of the rest were very sickly, having been 4 Months in their Voyage hither) and so to take in Water, and depart for Europe, in Company with the other Portugueze Ships thither bound; who had Orders to be ready to sail by the twentieth of May. He desir'd me to carry a Letter for him, directed to his Successor the new Vice-Roy of Goa; which I did, sending it thither afterwards by Captain Hammond, whom I found near the Cape of Good Hope. The refreshing my Men, and taking in Water, was the main also of my Business here; beside the having the better Opportunity to compose the Disorders among my Crew; Which, as I have before related, were grown to so great a Heighth, that they could not without great Difficulty be appeased; However, finding Opportunity, during my Stay in this Place, to allay in some Measure the Ferment that had been raised among my Men, I now set my self to provide for the carrying on of my Voyage with more Heart than before, and put all Hands to work, in order to it, as fast as the Backwardness of my Men would permit; who shew'd continually their Unwillingness to proceed farther. Besides, their Heads were generally fill'd with strange Notions of Southerly Winds that were now setting in (and there had been already some Flurries of them) which, as they surmis'd, would hinder any farther Attempts of going on to the Southward, so long as they should last.

The Winds begin to shift here in April and September, and the Seasons of the Year (the Dry and the Wet) alter with them. In April the Southerly Winds make their Entrance on this Coast, bringing in the wet Season, with violent Tornado's, Thunder and Lightning, and much Rain. In September the other Coasting Trade, at East North-East comes in, and clears the Sky, bringing fair Weather. . . .

.   .   .   .   .

But to return to the Southerly Winds, which came in (as I expected they would) while I was here: These daunted my Ship's Company very much, tho' I had told them they were to look for them: But they being ignorant as to what I told them farther,

that these were only Coasting-Winds, sweeping the Shore to
about 40 or 50 Leagues in Breadth from it, and imagining that
they had blown so all the Sea over, between America and Africa;
and being confirm'd in this their Opinion by the Portugueze
Pilots of the European Ships, with whom several of my Officers
conversed much, and who were themselves as ignorant that these
were only Coasting Trade-Winds (themselves going away before
them, in their Return homewards, till they cross the Line, and
so having no Experience of the Breadth of them) being thus
possess'd with a Conceit that we could not sail from hence till
September; this made them still the more remiss in their Duties,
and very listless to the getting Things in a Readiness for our
Departure. However I was the more diligent my self to have the
Ship scrubb'd, and to send my Water-Casks ashore to get them
trimm'd, my Beer being now out. I went also to the Governour
to get my Water fill'd; for here being but one Watering-place
(and the Water running low, now at the End of the dry Season)
it was always so crouded with the European Ships Boats, who
were preparing to be gone, that my Men could seldom come nigh
it, till the Governour very kindly sent an Officer to clear the
Water-place for my Men, and to stay there till my Water-Casks
were all full, whom I satisfied for his Pains. Here I also got
aboard 9 or 10 Ton of Ballast, and made my Boatswain fit the
Rigging that was amiss: And I enquired also of my particular
Officers whose Business it was, whether they wanted any Stores,
especially Pitch and Tar; for that here I would supply my self
before I proceeded any farther; but they said they had enough,
tho' it did not afterwards prove so.

I commonly went ashore every Day, either upon Business, or
to recreate my self in the Fields, which were very pleasant, and
the more for a Shower of Rain now and then, that ushers in the
wet Season. Several Sorts of good Fruits were also still remaining, especially Oranges, which were in such Plenty, that I and all
my Company stock'd ourselves for our Voyage with them, and
they did us a great Kindness; and we took in also a good Quantity
of Rum and Sugar: But for Fowls they being here lean and dear,
I was glad I had stock'd my self at St. Jago. But by the little
Care my officers took for fresh Provisions, one might conclude,
they did not think of going much farther. Besides, I had like to
have been imbroiled with the Clergy here (of the Inquisition, as
I suppose) and so my Voyage might have been hindred. What
was said to them of me, by some of my Company that went
ashore, I know not; but I was assured by a Merchant there, that

if they got me into their Clutches (and it seems, when I was last ashore they had narrowly watch'd me) the Governor himself could not release me. Besides I might either be murther'd in the Streets, as he sent me Word, or poisoned, if I came ashore any more; and therefore he advised me to stay aboard. Indeed I had now no further Business ashore but to take leave of the Governor, and therefore took his Advice.

Our Stay here was till the 23d of April. I would have gone before if I could sooner have fitted my self; but was now earnest to be gone, because this Harbour lies open to the S. and S.S. W. which are raging Winds here, and now was the Season for them. We had 2 or 3 Touches of them; and one pretty severe, and the Ships ride there so near each other, that if a Cable should fail, or an Anchor start, you are instantly aboard of one Ship or other: And I was more afraid of being disabled here in Harbour by these blustring Winds, than discouraged by them, as my People were, from prosecuting the Voyage; for at present I even wish'd for a brisk Southerly Wind as soon as I should be once well out of the Harbour, to set me the sooner into the true General Trade-Wind.

The Tide of Flood being spent, and having a fine Land-Breeze on the 23d, in the Morning, I went away from the Anchoring place before 'twas light; and then lay by till Day-light that we might see the better how to go out of the Harbour. I had a Pilot belonging to Mr. Cock, who went out with me, to whom I gave 3 Dollars; but I found I could as well have gone out my self, by the Soundings I made at coming in. The Wind was E. by N. and fair Weather. By 10 a Clock I was got past all Danger, and then sent away my Pilot. At 12 Cape Salvadore bore N. distant 6 Leagues, and we had the Winds between the E. by N. and S.E. a considerable Time, so that we kept along near the Shore, commonly in Sight of it. The Southerly blasts had now left us again; for they come at first in short Flurries, and shift to other Points (for 10 or 12 Days sometimes) before they are quite set in: And we had uncertain Winds, between Sea and Land-Breezes, and the Coasting-Trade, which was its self unsettled.

The Easterly-Winds at present made me doubt I should not weather a great Shoal which lies in Lat. between 18 deg. and 19 deg. S. and runs a great Way into the Sea, directly from the Land, Easterly. Indeed the Weather was fair (and continued so a good while) so that I might the better avoid any Danger from it: And if the Wind came to the Southward I knew I could stretch off to Sea; so that I jogg'd on couragiously. The 27th of April we saw a small Brigantine under the Shore plying to the

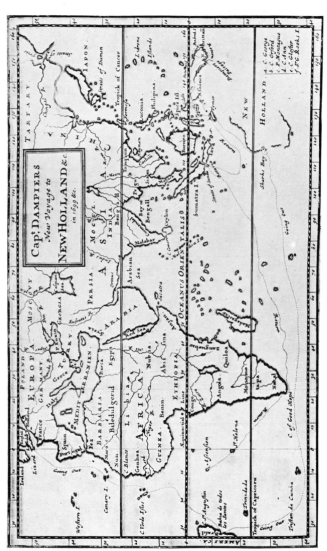

DAMPIER'S MAP OF NEW HOLLAND, 1699.

Southward. We also saw many Men of War-birds and Boobies, and Abundance of Albicore-Fish. Having still fair Weather, small Gales, and some Calms, I had the Opportunity of trying the Current, which I found to set sometimes Northerly and sometimes Southerly: And therefore knew I was still within the Verge of the Tides. Being now in the Lat. of the Abrohlo Shoals, which I expected to meet with, I sounded, and had Water lessening from 40 to 33, and so to 25 Fathom: But then it rose again to 33, 35, 37, &c. all Coral Rocks. Whilst we were on this Shoal (which we cross'd towards the further part of it from Land, where it lay deep, and so was not dangerous) we caught a great many Fish with Hook and Line: and by evening Amplitude we had 6 deg. 38 min. East Variation. This was the 27th of April; we were then in Lat. 18 deg. 13 min. S. and East Longitude from Cape Salvadore 31 min. On the 29th, being then in Lat. 18 deg. 39 min. S. we had small Gales from the W.N.W. to the W.S.W. often shifting. The 30th we had the Winds from W. to S.S.E. Squalls and Rain: And we saw some Dolphins and other Fish about us. We were now out of Sight of Land, and had been so 4 or 5 Days: But the Winds now hanging in the South was an apparent Sign that we were still too nigh the Shore to receive the true General East-Trade; as the Easterly Winds we had before shew'd that we were too far off the Land to have the Benefit of the Coasting South-Trade: and the Faintness of both these Winds, and their often shifting from the S.S.W. to the S.E. with Squalls, Rain and small Gales, were a Confirmation of our being between the Verge of the S. Coasting-Trade, and that of the true Trade; which is here, regularly, S.E.

The 3d of May being in Lat. 20 deg. 00 min. and Merid. distance West from Cape Salvadore 234 Miles, the Variation was 7 deg. 00 min. We saw no Fowl but Shear-waters, as our Sea-men call them, being a small, black Fowl that sweep the Water as they fly, and are much in the Seas that lie without either of the Tropicks: they are not eaten. We caught 3 small Sharks, each 6 Foot 4 Inches long; and they were very good Food for us. The next Day we caught 3 more Sharks of the same Size, and we eat them also, esteeming them as good Fish boil'd and press'd, and then stew'd with Vinegar and Pepper.

We had nothing of Remark from the 3d of May to the 10th, only now and then seeing a small Whale spouting up the Water. We had the Wind Easterly, and we ran with it to the Southward, running in this Time from the Lat. of 20 deg. 00 m. to 29 deg. 5 min. S. and having then 7 d. 3 m. E. Long. from C. Salvadore;

G

the Variation increasing upon us, at present, notwithstanding we
went East. We had all along a great Difference between the
Morning and Evening Amplitudes; usually a Degree or two, and
sometimes more. We were now in the true Trade, and therefore
made good Way to the Southward, to get without the Verge of
the General Trade-Wind into a Westerly Wind's way, that might
carry us towards the Cape of Good Hope. By the 12th of May,
being in Lat. 31 deg. 10 min. we began to meet with Westerly
Winds, which freshned on us, and did not leave us till a little
before we made the Cape. Sometimes it blew so hard that it put
us under a Fore-course; especially in the Night; but in the Day-
time we had commonly our Main Top-sail rift. We met with
nothing of Moment; only we past by a dead Whale, and saw
Millions (as I may say) of Sea-Fowls about the Carcass (and as
far round about it as we could see) some feeding, and the rest
flying about, or sitting on the Water, waiting to take their Turns.
We first discovered the Whale by the Fowls; for Indeed I did
never see so many Fowls at once in my Life before, their Numbers
being inconceivably great: They were of divers Sorts, in Bigness,
Shape and Colour. Some were almost as big as Geese, of a grey
Colour, with white Breasts, and with such Bills, Wings and Tails.
Some were Pintado-Birds, as big as Ducks, and speckled black
and white. Some were Shear-waters; some Petrels; and there
were several Sorts of large Fowls. We saw of these Birds, especially the Pintado-birds, all the Sea over from about 200 Leagues
distant from the Coast of Brazil, to within much the same Distance of New-Holland. The Pintado is a Southern Bird, and of
that temperate Zone; for I never saw of them much to the Northward of 30 deg. S. The Pintado-bird is as big as a Duck; but
appears, as it flies, about the Bigness of a tame Pidgeon, having
a short Tail, but the Wings very long, as most Sea-Fowls have;
especially such as these that fly far from the Shore, and seldom
come nigh it; for their Resting is sitting afloat upon the Water;
but they lay, I suppose, ashore. There are three Sorts of these
Birds, all of the same Make and Bigness, and are only different
in Colour. The first is black all over: The second Sort are grey,
with white Bellies and Breasts. The third Sort, which is the true
Pintado, or Painted-bird, is curiously spotted white and black.
Their Heads, and the Tips of their Wings and Tails, are black
for about an Inch; and their Wings are also edg'd quite round
with such a small black List; only within the black on the Tip
of their Wings there is a white Spot seeming as they fly (for then
their Spots are best seen) as big as a Half-crown. All this is on

the Outside of the Tails and Wings; and as there is a white Spot
in the black Tip of the Wings, so there is in the Middle of the
Wings which is white, a black Spot; but this, towards the Back
of the Bird, turns gradually to a dark grey. The Back it self,
from the Head to the Tip of the Tail, and the Edge of the Wings
next to the Back, are all over-spotted with fine small, round,
white and black Spots, as big as a Silver Two-pence, and as close
as they can stick one by another: The Belly, Thighs, Sides, and
inner-part of the Wings, are of a light grey. These Birds, of all
these Sorts, fly many together, never high, but almost sweeping
the Water. We shot one a while after on the Water in a Calm,
and a Water-Spaniel we had with us brought it in: I have given
a Picture of it . . . but it was so damaged, that the Picture
doth not shew it to Advantage; and its Spots are best seen when
the Feathers are spread as it flies.

The Petrel is a Bird not much unlike a Swallow, but smaller,
and with a shorter Tail. 'Tis all over black, except a white Spot
on the Rump. They fly sweeping like Swallows, and very near
the Water. They are not so often seen in fair Weather; being
Foul-weather Birds, as our Seamen call them, and presaging a
Storm when they come about a Ship; who for that Reason don't
love to see them. In a Storm they will hover close under the
Ship's Stern, in the Wake of the Ship (as 'tis call'd) or the Smooth-
ness which the Ship's passing has made on the Sea: And there as
they fly (gently then) they pat the Water alternately with their
Feet, as if they walk'd upon it; tho' still upon the Wing. And
from hence the Seamen give them the Name of Petrels, in Allusion to St. Peter's walking upon the Lake of Gennesareth.

We also saw many Bunches of Sea-weeds in the Lat. of 39.32
and by Judgment, near the Meridian of the Island Tristian
d'Aconha: And then we had about 2 d. 20 min. East Variation:
which was now again decreasing as we ran to the Eastward, till
near the Meridian of Ascention; where we found little or no
Variation: But from thence, as we ran farther to the East, our
Variation increased Westerly.

Two Days before I made the Cape of G. Hope, my Variation
was 7 deg. 58 min. West. I was then in 43 deg. 27 min. East
Longit. from C. Salvador, being in Lat. 35 deg. 30 min. this was
the first of June. The second of June I saw a large black Fowl,
with a whitish flat Bill, fly by us; and took great Notice of it,
because in the East-India Waggoner, or Pilot-book, there is mention made of large Fowls, as big as Ravens, with white flat Bills
and Black Feathers, that fly not about 30 leagues from the Cape,

and are look'd on as a Sign of ones being near it. My Reckoning made me then think my self above 90 Leagues from the Cape, according to the Longitude which the Cape hath in the common Sea-Charts: So that I was in some doubt, whether these were the right Fowls spoken of in the Waggoner; or whether those Fowls might not fly farther off Shore than is there mentioned; or whether, as it prov'd, I might not be nearer the Cape than I reckoned my self to be; for I found, soon after, that I was not then about 25 or 30 Leagues at most from the Cape. Whether the Fault were in the Charts laying down the Cape too much to the East from Brazil, or were rather in our Reckoning, I could not tell: But out Reckonings are liable to such Uncertainties from Steerage, Log, Currents, Half-Minute-Glasses; and sometimes want of Care, as in so long a Run cause often a Difference of many Leagues in the whole Account.

Most of my Men that kept Journals imputed it to the Half-Minute Glasses: and indeed we had not a good Glass in the Ship beside the Half-watch or Two-Hour-Glasses. As for our Half-Minute-Glasses we tried them all at several Times, and we found those that we had used from Brazil as much too short, as others we had used before were too long: which might well make great Errors in those several Reckonings. A Ship ought therefore to have its Glasses very exact; and besides, an extraordinary Care ought to be used in heaving the Log, for fear of giving too much Stray-Line in a Moderate Gale; and also to stop quickly in a brisk Gale, for when a Ship runs 8, 9 or 10 Knots, half a Knot or a Knot is soon run out, and not heeded: But to prevent Danger, when a Man thinks himself near Land, the best way is to look out betimes, and lye by in the Night, for a Commander may err easily himself; beside the Errors of those under him, tho' never so carefully eyed.

Another Thing that stumbled me here was the Variation, which, at this Time, by the last Amplitude I had I found to be but 7 deg. 58 min. W. whereas the Variation at the Cape (from which I found my self not 30 Leagues distant) was then computed, and truly, about 11 deg. or more: And yet a while after this, when I was got 10 Leagues to the Eastward of the Cape, I found the Variation but 10 deg. 40 min. W. whereas it should have been rather more than at the Cape. These Things, I confess, did puzzle me: Neither was I fully satisfied as to the Exactness of the taking the Variation at Sea: For in a great Sea, which we often met with, the Compass will traverse with the Motion of the Ship; besides the Ship may and will deviate somewhat in steering, even by the best Helmsmen: And then when you come to take an Azimuth, there is often some Difference between him that looks at the Compass, and the Man that takes the Altitude heighth of the Sun; and a small Error in each, if the Error of both should be one way, will make it wide of any great Exactness. But what was most shocking to me, I found that the Variation did not always increase or decrease in Proportion to the Degrees of Longitude East or West; as I had a Notion they might do to a certain Number of Degrees of Variation East or West, at such or such particular Meridians. But finding in this Voyage that the difference of Variation did not bear a regular Proportion to the Difference of Longitude, I was much pleas'd to see it thus observ'd in a Scheme shewn me after my Return home, wherein are represented the several Variations in the Atlantick Sea, on both Sides the Equator; and there, the Line of no Variation in that Sea is not a Meridian Line, but goes very oblique, as do those also which shew the Increase of Variation on each Side of it.

. . . . . .

From my first setting out from England, I did not design to touch at the Cape; and that was one Reason why I touch'd at Brazil, that there I might refresh my Men, and prepare them for a long Run to New Holland. We had not yet seen the Land; but about 2 in the Afternoon we saw the Cape-Land bearing East, at above 16 Leagues distance; And Captain Hammond being also bound to double the Cape, we jog'd on together this Afternoon and the next Day, and had several fair Sights of it; which may be seen.

To proceed: Having still a Westerly Wind, I jog'd on in company with the *Antelope*, till Sunday June the 4th at 4 in the Afternoon, when we parted; they steering away from the East-Indies, and I keeping an E.S.E. Course, the better to make my way for New Holland; For tho' New Holland lies North-Easterly from the Cape, yet all Ships bound towards that Coast, or the Streights of Sundy, ought to keep for a while in the same Parallel, or in a lat. between 35 and 40, at least a little to the S. of the East, that they may continue in a variable Winds way; and not venture too soon to stand so far to the North, as to be within the Verge of the Trade-Wind, which will put them by their Easterly Course. The Wind increased upon us; but we had yet sight of the *Antelope*, and of the Land too, till Tuesday the 6th of June: And then we saw also by us an innumerable Company of Fowls of divers sorts; so that we look'd about to see if there were not another dead Whale, but saw none.

The Night before, the Sun set in a black Cloud, which appeared just like Land; and the Clouds above it were gilded of a dark red Colour. And on the Tuesday, as the Sun drew near the Horizon, the Clouds were gilded very prettily to the Eye, tho' at the same time my Mind dreaded the Consequences of it. When the Sun was now not above 2 deg. high, it entered into a dark Smoaky-coloured Cloud that lay parallel with the Horizon, from whence presently seem'd to issue many dusky blackish Beams. The Sky was at this time covered with small hard Clouds (as we call such as lye scattering about, not likely to Rain) very thick one by another; and such of them as lay next to the Bank of Clouds at the Horizon, were of a pure Gold Colour to 3 or 4 deg. high above the Bank: From these to about 10 deg. high they were redder, and very bright; above them they were of a darker Colour still, to about 60 or 70 deg. high; where the Clouds began to be of their common Colour. I took the more particular Notice of all this, because I have generally observed such colour'd Clouds to appear before an approaching Storm: And this being Winter here, and the time for bad Weather, I expected and provided for a violent blast of Wind, by riffing our Topsails, and giving a strict charge to my Officers to hand them or take them in, if the Wind should grow stronger. The Wind was now at W.N.W. a very brisk Gale. About 12 a Clock at Night we had a pale whitish Glare in the N.W. which was another Sign, and intimated the Storm to be near at hand; and the Wind increasing upon it, we presently handed our Top-sails, furled the Main-sail, and went away only with our Fore-sail. Before 2 in the Morning it came on very fierce, and we kept right before Wind and Sea, the Wind still encreasing: But the Ship was very governable, and steered incomparably well. At 8 in the Morning we settled our Fore-yard, lowering it 4 or 5 Foot, and we ran very swiftly; especially when the Squalls of Rain or Hail, from a black Cloud, came óver Head, for then it blew excessive hard. These, tho' they did not last long, yet came very thick and fast one after another. The Sea also ran very high; But we running so violently before Wind and Sea, we ship'd little or no Water; tho' a little wash'd into our upper Deck-Ports; and with it a Scuttle or Cuttle-Fish was cast upon the Carriage of a Gun.

The Wind blew extraordinary hard all Wednesday, the 7th of June, but abated of its fierceness before Night; Yet it continued a brisk Gale till about the 16th, and still a moderate one till the 19th Day; by which time we had run about 600 Leagues: For the most part of which time the Wind was in some point of the West, viz. from the W.N.W. to the S. by W. It blew hardest when at W. or between the W. and S.W. but after it veered more Southerly the foul Weather broke up: This I observed at other times also in these Seas, that when the Storms at West veered to the Southward they grew less; and that when the Wind came to the E. of the S. we had still smaller Gales, Calms, and fair Weather. As for the Westerly Winds on that side the Cape, we like them never the worse for being violent, for they drive us the faster to the Eastward; and are therefore the only Winds coveted by those who Sail towards such parts of the East-Indies, as lye South of the Equator; as Timor, Java, and Sumatra; and by the Ships bound for China, or any other that are to pass through the Streights of Sundy. Those Ships having once past the Cape, keep commonly pretty far Southerly, on purpose to meet with these West-winds, which in the Winter Season of these Climates they soon meet with; for then the Winds are generally Westerly at the Cape, and especially to the Southward of it: But in their Summer Months they get to the Southward of 40 deg. usually e'er they meet with the Westerly Winds. I was not at this time in a higher Lat. than 36 deg. 40 min. and oftentimes was more Northerly, altering my Latitude often as Winds and Weather required; for in such long Runs 'tis best to shape one's Course according to the Winds. And if in steering to the East, we should be obliged to bear a little to the N. or S. of it, 'tis no great Matter; for 'tis but sailing 2 or 3 Points from the Wind, when 'tis either Northerly or Southerly; and this not only easeth the Ship from straining, but shortens the way more than if a Ship was kept close on a Wind, as some Men are fond of doing.

The 19th of June, we were in Lat. 34 deg. 17 min. S. and Long. from the Cape 39 deg. 24 min. E. and had small Gales and Calms. The Winds were at N.E. by E. and continued in some part of the E. till the 27th Day. When it having been some time at N.N.E. it came about at N. and then to the W. of the N. and continued in the West-board (between the N.N.W. and S.S.W.) till the 4th of July; in which Time we ran 782 Miles; then the Winds came about again to the East, we reckoning our selves to be in a Meridian 1100 L. East of the Cape; and having fair Weather, sounded, but had no Ground.

We met with little of Remark in this Voyage, besides being accompanied with Fowls all the way, especially Pintado-Birds, and seeing now and then a Whale; But as we drew nigher the Coast of New-Holland, we saw frequently 3 or 4 Whales together. When we were about 90 Leagues from the Land we began to see

Sea-weeds, all of one Sort; and as we drew nigher the Shore we saw them more frequently. At about 30 Leagues distance we began to see some Scuttle-bones floating on the Water; and drawing still nigher the Land we saw greater Quantities of them.

July 25, being in Lat. 26 deg. 14 min. S. and Longitude E. from the C. of Good Hope 85 deg. 52 min. we saw a large Gar-fish leap 4 Times by us, which seemed to be as big as a Porpose. It was now very fair Weather, and the Sea was full of a Sort of very small Grass or Moss, which as it floated in the Water seem'd to have been some Spawn of Fish; and there was among it some small Fry. The next Day the Sea was full of small round Things like Pearl, some as big as white Peas; they were very clear and transparent, and upon crushing any of them a Drop of Water would come forth: The Skin that contain'd the Water was so thin that it was but just discernable. Some Weeds swam by us, so that we did not doubt but we should quickly see Land. On the 27th also, some Weeds swam by us, and the Birds that had flown along with us all the way almost from Brazil, now left us, except only 2 or 3 Shear-waters. On the 28th we saw many Weeds swim by us, and some Whales, blowing. On the 29th we had dark cloudy Weather, with much Thunder, Lightning, and violent Rains in the Morning; but in the Evening it grew fair. We saw this Day a Scuttle-bone swim by us, and some of our young Men a Seal, as it should seem by their Description of its Head. I saw also some Boneta's, and some Skipjacks, a Fish about 8 Inches long, broad and sizeable, not much unlike a Roach; which our Seamen call so from their leaping about.

The 30th of July, being still nearer the Land, we saw Abundance of Scuttle-bones and Sea-weed, more Tokens that we were not far from it; and saw also a Sort of Fowls, the like of which we had not seen in the whole Voyage, all the other Fowls having now left us. These were as big as Lapwings; of a grey Colour, black about their Eyes, with red sharp Bills, long Wings, their Tails long and forked like Swallows; and they flew flapping their Wings like Lapwings. In the Afternoon we met with a Ripling like a Tide or Current, or the Water of some Shoal or Overfall; but were past it before we could sound. The Birds last mention'd and this were further Signs of Land. In the Evening we had fair Weather, and a small Gale at West. At 8 a Clock we sounded again; but had no Ground.

We kept on still to the Eastward, with an easy Sail, looking out sharp; For by the many Signs we had, I did expect that we were near the Land. At 12 a Clock in the Night I sounded, and

had 45 Fathom, coarse Sand and small white Shells. I presently
clapt on a Wind and stood to the South, with the Wind at W.
because I thought we were to the South of a Shoal call'd the
Abrohles (an Appellative Name for Shoals, as it seems to me)
which in a Draught I had of that Coast is laid down in 27 deg.
28 min. Lat. stretching about 7 Leagues into the Sea. I was the
day before in 27 deg. 38 min. by Reckoning. And afterwards
steering E. by S. purposely to avoid it, I thought I must have
been to the South of it: But sounding again, at 1 a Clock in the
Morning, Aug. the first, we had but 25 Fathom, Coral Rocks;
and so found the Shoal was to the South of us. We presently
tack'd again, and stood to the North, and then soon deepned
our Water; for at 2 in the Morning we had 26 Fathom Coral still:
At 3 we had 28 Coral-ground: At 4 we had 30 Fathom, coarse
Sand, with some Coral: At 5 we had 45 Fathom, coarse Sand and
Shells; being now off the Shoal, as appear'd by the Sand and
Shells, and by having left the Coral. By all this I knew we had
fallen in to the North of the Shoal, and that it was laid down
wrong in my Sea-Chart: For I found it lye in about 27 deg. Lat.
and by our Run in the next Day, I found that the Outward-edge
of it, which I sounded on, lies 16 Leagues off Shore. When it was
Day we steered in E.N.E. with a fine brisk Gale; but did not see
the Land till 9 in the Morning, when we saw it from our Topmast-
head, and were distant from it about 10 Leagues; having had
40 Fathom-water, and clean Sand. About 3 Hours after we saw
it on our Quarter-Deck, being by Judgment about 6 Leagues off,
and we had then 40 Fathom, clean Sand. As we ran in, this Day
and the next, we took several Sights of it, at different Bearings
and Distances; from which it appear'd as you see it. And here I
would note once for all, that the Latitudes mark'd in the
Draughts, or Sights here given, are not the Latitude of the Land,
but of the Ship when the Sight was taken. This Morning, August
the first, as we were standing in we saw several large Sea-fowls,
like our Gannets on the Coast of England, flying 3 or 4 together;
and a Sort of white Sea-Mews, but black about the Eyes, and,
with forked Tails. We strove to run in near the Shore to seek
for a Harbour to refresh us after our tedious Voyage; having
made one continuous Stretch from Brazil hither of about 114 deg.
designing from hence also to begin the discovery I had a Mind to
make on N. Holland and N. Guinea. The Land was low, and
appear'd even, and as we drew nearer to it, it made with some
red and some white Clifts; these last in Lat. 26, 10 S. where you
will find 54 Fathom, within 4 Miles of the Shore.

About the Lat. of 26 deg. S. we saw an Opening, and ran in, hoping to find a Harbour there: But when we came to its Mouth, which was about 2 Leagues wide, we saw Rocks and foul Ground within, and therefore stood out again: There we had 20 Fathom-water within 2 Mile of the Shore. The Land every where appear'd pretty low, flat and even; but with steep Cliffs to the Sea; and when we came near it there were no Trees, Shrubs or Grass to be seen. The Soundings in the Lat. of 26 deg. S. from about 8 or 9 Leagues off till you come within a League of the Shore, are generally about 40 Fathom; differing but little, seldom above 3 or 4 Fathom. But the Lead brings up very different Sorts of Sand, some coarse, some fine; and of several Colours, as Yellow, White, Grey, Brown, Blueish and Reddish.

When I saw there was no Harbour here, nor good anchoring, I stood off to Sea again, in the Evening of the second of August, fearing a Storm on a Lee-shore, in a Place where there was no Shelter, and desiring at least to have Sea-room: For the Clouds began to grow thick in the Western-board, and the Wind was already there, and began to blow fresh almost upon the Shore; which at this Place lies along N.N.W. and S.S.E. By 9 a Clock at Night we had got a pretty good Offin; but the Wind still increasing, I took in my Main Top-sail, being able to carry no more Sail than two Courses and the Mizen. At 2 in the morning, Aug. 3, it blew very hard, and the Sea was much raised; so that I furled all my Sails but my Main-sail. Tho' the Wind blew so hard, we had pretty clear Weather till Noon: But then the whole Sky was blackned with thick Clouds, and we had some Rain, which would last a Quarter of an Hour at a Time, and then it would blow very fierce while the Squalls of Rain were over our Heads; but as soon as they were gone the Wind was by much abated, the Stress of the Storm being over. We sounded several Times, but had no Ground till 8 a Clock Aug. the 4th in the Evening; and then had 60 Fathom-water, Coral-ground. At 10 we had 56 Fathom fine Sand. At 12 we had 55 Fathom, fine Sand, of a pale Blueish Colour. It was now pretty Moderate Weather; yet I made no Sail till Morning; but then, the Wind veering about to the S.W. I made Sail and stood to the North: And at 11 a Clock the next Day, August 5, we saw Land again, at about 10 Leagues distance. This Noon we were in Lat. 25 deg. 30 min. and in the afternoon our Cook died, an old Man, who had been sick a great while, being infirm before we came out of England.

The 6th of August in the Morning we saw an Opening in the

Land, and we ran into it, and anchored in 7 and a half Fathom-water, 2 Miles from the Shore, clean Sand. It was somewhat difficult getting in here, by Reason of many Shoals we met with: But I sent my Boat sounding before me. The Mouth of this Sound, which I call'd Shark's Bay, lies in about 25 deg. S. Lat. and our Reckoning made its Longitude from the C. of Good Hope to be about 87 Degrees; which is less by 195 Leagues than is usually laid down in our common Draughts, if our Reckoning was right, and our Glasses did not deceive us. As soon as I came to anchor in this Bay (of which I have given a Plan) I sent my Boat ashore to seek for fresh Water: But in the Evening my Men returned, having found none. The next Morning I went ashore myself, carrying Pick-axes and Shovels with me, to dig for Water; and Axes to cut Wood. We tried in several Places for Water, but finding none after several Trials, nor in several Miles Compass, we left any farther Search for it, and spending the rest of the Day in cutting Wood, we went aboard at Night.

The Land is of an indifferent Heighth, so that it may be seen 9 or 10 Leagues off. It appears at a Distance very even; but as you come nigher you find there are many gentle Risings; tho' none steep nor high. 'Tis all a steep Shore against the open Sea: But in this Bay or Sound we were now in, the Land is low by the Sea-side, rising gradually in within the Land. The Mould is Sand by the Sea-side, producing a large Sort of Sampier, which bears a white Flower. Farther in, the Mould is reddish, a Sort of Sand producing some Grass, Plants and Shrubs. The Grass grows in great Tufts, as big as a Bushel, here and there a Tuft: Being intermix'd with much Heath, much of the kind we have growing on our Commons in England. Of Trees or Shrubs here are divers Sorts; but none above 10 Foot high: Their Bodies about 3 Foot about, and 5 or 6 Foot high before you come to the Branches, which are bushy and compos'd of small Twigs there spreading abroad, tho' thick set, and full of Leaves; which were mostly long and narrow. The Colour of the Leaves was on one Side whitish, and on the other green; and the Bark of the Trees was generally of the same Colour with the Leaves, of a pale green. Some of these Trees were sweet-scented, and reddish within the Bark, like Sassafras, but redder. Most of the Trees and Shrubs had at this Time either Blossoms or Berries on them. The Blossoms of the different Sort of Trees were of several Colours, as red, white, yellow, &c. but mostly blue: And these generally smelt very sweet and fragrant, as did some also of the rest. There were also beside some Plants, Herbs, and tall Flowers, some very small Flowers, growing on the Ground, that were sweet and beautiful, and for the most part unlike any I had seen elsewhere.

There were but few Land-Fowls; we saw none but Eagles, of the larger Sort of Birds; but 5 or 6 Sorts of small Birds. The biggest Sort of these were not bigger than Larks; some no bigger than Wrens, all singing with great Variety of fine shrill Notes; and we saw some of their Nests with young Ones in them. The Water-Fowls are Ducks, (which had young Ones now, this being the Beginning of the Spring in these Parts;) Curlews, Galdens, Crab-catchers, Cormorants, Gulls, Pelicans; and some Water-Fowl, such as I have not seen any where besides. I have given the Pictures of 4 several Birds on this Coast.

The Land-Animals that we saw here were only a Sort of Raccoons, different from those of the West-Indies, chiefly as to their Legs; for these have very short Fore-Legs; but go jumping upon them as the others do, (and like them are very good Meat:) And a Sort of Guano's, of the same Shape and Size with other Guano's, describ'd, but differing from them in 3 remarkable Particulars: For these had a larger and uglier Head, and had no Tail: And at the Rump, instead of the Tail there, they had a Stump of a Tail, which appear'd like another Head; but not really such, being without Mouth or Eyes: Yet this Creature seem'd by this Means to have a Head at each End; and, which may be reckon'd a fourth Difference, the Legs also seem'd all 4 of them to be Fore-legs, being all alike in Shape and Length, and seeming by the Joints and Bending to be made as if they were to go indifferently either Head or Tail foremost. They were speckled black and yellow like Toads, and had Scales or Knobs on their Backs like those of Crocodiles, plated on to the Skin, or stuck into it, as part of the Skin. They are very slow in Motion; and when a Man comes nigh them they will stand still and hiss, not endeavouring to get away. Their Livers are also spotted black and yellow: And the Body when opened hath a very unsavory Smell. I did never see such ugly Creatures any where but here. The Guano's I have observ'd to be very good Meat: And I have often eaten of them with Pleasure; but tho' I have eaten of Snakes, Crocodiles and Allegators, and many Creatures that look frightfully enough, and there are but few I should have been afraid to eat of, if prest by Hunger, yet I think my Stomach would scarce have serv'd to venture upon these N. Holland Guano's, both the Looks and the Smell of them being so offensive.

The Sea-fish that we saw here (for here was no River, Land or Pond of fresh Water to be seen) are chiefly Sharks. There are

Abundance of them in this particular Sound, that I therefore give it the Name of Shark's Bay. Here are also Skates, Thornbacks, and other Fish of the Ray-kind; (one Sort especially like the Sea-Devil) and Gar-fish, Boneta's &c. Of Shell-fish we got here Muscles, Periwinkles, Limpits, Oysters, both of the Pearlkind and also Eating-Oysters, as well the common Sort as long Oysters; beside Cockles, &c. The Shore was lined thick with many other sorts of very strange and beautiful Shells, for variety of Colour and Shape, most finely spotted with Red, Black, or Yellow, &c. such as I have not seen any where but at this place. I brought away a great many of them; but lost all, except a very few, and those not of the best.

There are also some green Turtle weighing about 200 lb. Of these we caught 2 which the Water Ebbing had left behind a Ledge of Rock, which they could not creep over. These served all my Company 2 Days; and they were indifferent sweet Meat. Of the Sharks we caught a great many, which our Men eat very savourily. Among them we caught one which was 11 Foot long. The space between its two Eyes was 20 Inches, and 18 Inches from one Corner of his Mouth to the other. Its Maw was like a Leather Sack, very thick, and so tough that a sharp Knife could scarce cut it: In which we found the Head and Boans of a Hippopotamus; the hairy Lips of which were still sound and not putrified, and the Jaw was also firm, out of which we pluckt a great many Teeth, 2 of them 8 Inches long, and as big as a Man's Thumb, small at one end and a little crooked; the rest not above half so long. The Maw was full of Jelly which stank extreamly: However I saved for a while the Teeth and the Sharks Jaw: The Flesh of it was divided among my Men; and they took care that no waste should be made of it.

'Twas the 7th of August when we came into Shark's Bay; in which we Anchor'd at three several Places, and stay'd at the first of them (on the W. side of the Bay) till the 11th. During which time we searched about, as I said, for fresh Water, digging Wells, but to no purpose. However, we cut good store of Fire-wood at this first Anchoring-place; and my Company were all here very well refreshed with Raccoons, Turtle, Shark and other Fish, and some Fowles; so that we were now all much brisker than when we came in hither. Yet still I was for standing farther into the Bay, partly because I had a Mind to increase my stock of fresh Water, which was began to be low; and partly for the sake of Discovering this part of the Coast. I was invited to go further, by seeing from this Anchoring-place all open before me; which therefore I designed to search, before I left the Bay. So on the 11th about Noon, I steer'd farther in, with an easie Sail, because we had but shallow Water: We kept therefore good looking out for fear of Sholes; sometimes shortning, sometimes deepning the Water. About 2 in the Afternoon we saw the Land a Head that makes the S. of the Bay, and before Night we had again Sholdings from that Shore: And therefore shortned Sail and stood off and on all Night, under 2 Topsails, continually sounding, having never more than 10 Fathom, and seldom less than 7. The Water deepned and sholdned so very gently, that in heaving the Lead 5 or 6 times we should scarce have a Foot difference. When we came into 7 Fathom either way, we presently went about. From this S. part of the Bay, we could not see the Land from whence we came in the Afternoon: And this Land we found to be an Island of 3 or 4 Leagues long, as is seen in the Plan, but it appearing barren, I did not strive to go nearer it; and the rather because the Winds would not permit us to do it without much Trouble, and at the Openings the Water was generally Shole. I therefore made no farther attempts in this S.W. and S. part of the Bay, but steered away to the Eastward, to see if there was any Land that way, for as yet we had seen none there. On the 12th in the Morning we pass'd by the N. Point of that Land, and were confirm'd in the Persuasion of its being an Island, by seeing an Opening to the East of it, as we had done on the W. Having fair Weather, a small Gale and smooth Water, we stood further on in the Bay, to see what Land was on the E. of it. Our Soundings at first were 7 Fathom, which held so a great while, but at length it decreas'd to 6. Then we saw the Land right a-head, that in the Plan makes the E. of the Bay. We could not come near it with the Ship, having but Shole water: and it being dangerous lying there, and the Land extraordinarily low, very unlikely to have fresh Water, (though it had a few Trees on it, seemingly Mangroves) and much of it probably covered at High-water, I stood out again that Afternoon, deepning the Water, and before Night anchored in 8 Fathom, clean white Sand, about the middle of the Bay. The next day we got up our Anchor; and that Afternoon came to an Anchor once more near two Islands, and a Shole of Corral Rocks that face the Bay. Here I scrubb'd my Ship: and finding it very improbable I should get any thing further here, I made the best of my way out to Sea again, sounding all the way: but finding by the shallowness of the Water that there was no going out to Sea to the East of the two Islands that face the Bay, nor between them, I return'd to the West Entrance, going out by the same

Way I came in at, only on the East instead of the West-side of the small Shole to be seen in the Plan: in which Channel we had 10, 12, and 13 Fathom-water, still deepning upon us till we were out at Sea. The day before we came out I sent a Boat ashore to the most Northerly of the Two Islands, which is the least of them, catching many small Fish in the mean while with Hook and Line. The Boat's Crew returning, told me, That the Isle produces nothing but a sort of green, short, hard, prickly Grass, affording neither Wood nor fresh Water; and that a Sea broak between the two Islands, a Sign that the Water was shallow. They saw a large Turtle, and many Skates and Thornbacks, but caught none.

It was August the 14th when I sail'd out of this Bay or Sound, the Mouth of which lies, as I said, in 25 deg. 5 min. designing to coast along to the N.E. till I might commodiously put in at some other part of N. Holland. In passing out we saw three Water-Serpents swimming about in the Sea, of a yellow Colour, spotted with dark, brown Spots. They were each about four Foot long, and about the bigness of a Man's Wrist, and were the first I saw on this Coast, which abounds with several sorts of them. . . . We had the Winds at our first coming out at N. and the Land lying North-Easterly. We plied off and on, getting forward but little till the next day: When the Wind coming at S.S.W. and S. we began to Coast it along the Shore to the Northward, keeping at 6 or 7 Leagues off Shore; and sounding often, we had between 40 and 46 Fathom-water, brown Sand, with some white Shells. This 15th of August we were in Lat. 24 deg. 41 min. On the 16th Day at Noon we were in 23 deg. 22 min. The Wind coming at E. by N. we could not keep the Shore aboard, but were forced to go farther off, and lost sight of the Land. Then sounding we had no Ground with 80 Fathom-line; however the Wind shortly after came about again to the Southward, and then we jogg'd on again to the Northward, and saw many small Dolphins and Whales, and abundance of Scuttle-shells swimming on the Sea; and some Water-snakes every day. The 17th we saw the Land again, and took a Sight of it.

The 18th in the Afternoon, being 3 or 4 Leagues off Shore, I saw a Shole-point, stretching from the Land into the Sea, a League or more. The Sea broke high on it; by which I saw plainly there was a Shole there. I stood farther off, and coasted along Shore, to about 7 or 8 Leagues distance: And at 12 a Clock at Night we sounded, and had but 20 Fathom, hard Sand. By this I found I was upon another Shoal, and so presently sterred off W.

half an Hour, and had then 40 Fathom. At One in the Morning
of the 18th Day we had 85 Fathom: By two we could find no
Ground; and then I ventur'd to steer along Shore again, due N.
which is two Points wide of the Coast (that lies N.N.E.) for fear
of another Shoal. I would not be too far off from the Land, being
desirous to search into it where-ever I should find an Opening or
any Convenience of searching about for Water, &c. When we
were off the Shoal-point I mention'd, where we had but 20
Fathom-water, we had in the Night Abundance of Whales about
the Ship, some a-head, others a-stern, and some on each side
blowing and making a very dismal Noise; but when we came out
again into deeper Water they left us. Indeed the Noise that they
made by blowing and dashing of the Sea with their Tails, making
it all of a Breach and Foam, was very dreadful to us, like the
Breach of the Waves in very Shoal-water, or among Rocks. The
Shoal these Whales were upon had Depth of Water sufficient, no
less than 20 Fathom, as I said; and it lies in Lat. 22 deg. 22 min.
The Shore was generally bold all along; we had met with no Shoal
at Sea since the Abrohlo-shoal, when we first fell on the N. Holland Coast in the Lat. of 28, till Yesterday in the Afternoon, and
this Night. This Morning also when we expected by the Draught
we had with us to have been 11 Leagues off Shore, we were but
4; so that either our Draughts were faulty, which yet hitherto and
afterwards we found true enough as to the lying of the Coast, or
else here was a Tide unknown to us that deceived us; tho' we had
found very little of any Tide on this Coast hitherto. As to our
Winds in the Coasting thus far, as we had been within the Verge
of the general Trade (tho' interrupted by the Storm I mention'd)
from the Lat. of 28, when we first fell in with the Coast: And by
that Time we were in the Lat. of 25, we had usually the regular
Trade-wind (which is here S.S.E.) when we were at any Distance
from Shore: But we had often Sea and Land-Breezes, especially
when near Shore, and when in Shark's-bay; and had a particular
N. West Wind, or Storm, that set us in thither. On this 18th of
August we coasted with a brisk Gale of the true Trade-wind at
S.S.E. very fair and clear Weather; but haling off in the Evening
to Sea, were next Morning out of Sight of Land; and the Land
now trending away N. Easterly, and we being to the Norward of
it, and the Wind also shrinking from the S.S.E. to the E.S.E.
(that is, from the true Trade-Wind to the Sea-breeze, as the Land
now lay) we could not get in with the Land again yet a-while, so
as to see it, tho' we trim'd sharp and kept close on a Wind. We
were this 19th day in Lat. 21 deg. 42 min. The 20th we were in

Lat. 19 deg. 37 min. and kept close on a Wind to get Sight of the Land again, but could not yet see it. We had very fair Weather; and tho' we were so far from the Land as to be out of Sight of it, yet we had the Sea- and Land-Breezes. In the Night we had the Land-Breeze at S.S.E. a small gentle Gale; which in the Morning about Sun-rising would shift about gradually (and withal increasing in Strength) till about Noon we should have it at E.S.E. which is the true Sea-breeze here. Then it would blow a brisk Gale, so that we could scarce carry our Top-sails double rift: And it would continue thus till 3 in the Afternoon, when it would decrease again. The Weather was fair all the while, not a Cloud to be seen; but very hazy, especially nigh the Horizon. We sounded several Times this 20th Day, and at first had no Ground; but had afterwards from 52 to 45 Fathom, coarse brown Sand, mixt with small brown and white Stones, with Dints besides in the Tallow.

The 21st Day also we had small Land-breezes in the Night, and Sea-breezes in the Day: And as we saw some Sea-snakes every Day, so this Day we saw a great many, of two different Sorts or Shapes. One Sort was yellow, and about the Bigness of a Man's Wrist, about 4 Foot long, having a flat Tail about 4 Fingers broad. The other Sort was much smaller and shorter, round and spotted black and yellow. This Day we sounded several Times, and had 45 Fathom Sand. We did not make the Land till Noon, and then saw it first from our Topmast-head. It bore S.E. by E. about 9 Leagues distance; and it appeared like a Cape or Head of Land. The Sea-breeze this Day was not so strong as the Day before, and it veered out more; so that we had a fair Wind to run in with to the Shore, and at Sunset anchored in 20 Fathom, clean Sand about 5 Leagues from the bluff Point; which was not a Cape (as it appear'd at a great Distance) but the Easternmost End of an Island, about 5 or 6 Leagues in length, and 1 in breadth. There were 3 or 4 Rocky Islands about a League from us between us and the bluff Point; and we saw many other Islands both to the East and West of it, as far as we could see either way from our Topmast-head: And all within them to the S. there was nothing but Islands of a pretty Heighth, that may be seen 8 or 9 Leagues off. By what we saw of them they must have been a Range of Islands of about 20 Leagues in length, stretching from E.N.E. to W.S.W. and for ought I know, as far as to those of Shark's Bay; and to a considerable Breadth also, (for we could see 9 or 10 Leagues in among them) towards the Continent or main Land of N. Holland, if there be any such Thing hereabouts:

H

And by the great Tides I met with a while afterwards, more to
the N. East, I had a strong Suspicion that here might be a kind
of Archipelago of Islands, and a Passage possibly to the S. of N.
Holland and N. Guinea into the great S. Sea Eastward; which I
had Thoughts also of attempting in my Return from N. Guinea
(had Circumstances permitted) and told my Officers so: But I
would not attempt it at this Time, because we wanted Water,
and could not depend upon finding it there. This place is in the
Lat. of 20 deg. 21 min. but in the Draught that I had of this
Coast, which was Tasman's, it was laid down in 19 deg. 50 min.
and the Shore is laid down as all along joining in one Body or
Continent, with some Openings appearing like Rivers; and not
like Islands, as really they are. This Place lies more Northerly by
40 min, than is laid down in Mr. Tasman's Draught: And beside
its being made a firm, continued Land, only with some Openings
like the Mouths of Rivers, I found the Soundings also different
from what the prick'd Line of his Course shews them, and generally shallower than he makes them; which inclines me to think
that he came not so near the Shore as his Line shews, and so had
deeper Soundings, and could not so well distinguish the Islands.
His Meridian or Difference of Longitude from Shark's Bay agrees
well enough with my Account, which is 232 Leagues, tho' we
differ in Lat. And to confirm my Conjecture that the Line of his
Course is made too near the Shore, at least not far to the East of
this place, the Water is there so shallow that he could not come
there so nigh.

But to proceed; in the Night we had a small Land-breeze, and
in the Morning I weighed Anchor, designing to run in among the
Islands, for they had large Channels between them, of a League
wide at least, and some 2 or 3 Leagues wide. I sent in my Boat
before to sound, and if they found Shoal-water to return again;
but if they found Water enough, to go ashore on one of the
Islands, and stay till the Ship came in: where they might in the
mean Time search for Water. So we followed after with the Ship,
sounding as we went in, and had 20 Fathom, till within 2 Leagues
of the Bluff-head, and then we had shoal Water, and very uncertain Soundings: Yet we ran in still with an easy Sail, sounding
and looking out well, for this was dangerous Work. When we
came abreast of the Bluff-head, and about 2 Mile from it, we had
but 7 Fathom: Then we edg'd away from it, but had no more
Water; and running in a little farther, we had but 4 Fathoms; so
we anchored immediately; and yet when we had veered out a
third of a Cable we had 7 Fathom Water again; so uncertain was

the Water. My Boat came immediately aboard, and told me that the Island was very rocky and dry, and they had little Hopes of finding Water there. I sent them to sound, and bad them, if they found a Channel of 8 or 10 Fathom Water, to keep on, and we would follow with the Ship. We were now about 4 Leagues within the outer small rocky Islands, but still could see nothing but Islands within us; some 5 or 6 Leagues long, others not above a Mile round. The large Islands were pretty high; but all appeared dry, and mostly rocky and barren. The Rocks look'd of a rusty yellow Colour, and therefore I despair'd of getting Water on any of them; but was in some Hopes of finding a Channel to run in beyond all these Islands, could I have spent Time there, and either get to the Main of New Holland, or find out some other Islands that might afford us Water and other Refreshments: Besides, that among so many Islands, we might have found some Sort of rich Mineral, or Ambergreece, it being a good Latitude for both these. But we had not sailed above a League farther before our Water grew shoaler again, and then we anchored in 6 Fathom hard Sand.

We were now on the inner Side of the Island, on whose out-side is the Bluff-point. We rode a League from the Island, and I presently went ashore, and carried Shovels to dig for Water, but found none. There grow here 2 or 3 Sorts of Shrubs, one just like Rosemary; and therefore I call'd this Rosemary Island. It grew in great Plenty here, but had no Smell. Some of the other Shrubs had blue and yellow Flowers; and we found 2 Sorts of Grain like Beans: The one grew on Bushes; the other on a Sort of a creeping Vine that runs along on the Ground, having very thick broad Leaves, and the Blossom like a Bean Blossom, but much larger, and of a deep red Colour, looking very beautiful. We saw here some Cormorants, Gulls, Crabcatchers, &c. a few small Land-Birds, and a Sort of White Parrots, which flew a great many together. We found some Shell-fish, viz: Limpits, Perriwinkles, and Abundance of small Oysters growing on the Rocks, which were very sweet. In the Sea we saw some green Turtle, a pretty many Sharks, and Abundance of Water-Snakes of several Sorts and Sizes. The Stones were all of rusty Colour, and ponderous.

We saw a Smoak on an Island 3 or 4 Leagues off; and here also the Bushes had been burned, but we found no other Sign of Inhabitants: 'Twas probable that on the Island where the Smoak was there were Inhabitants, and fresh Water for them. In the Evening I went aboard, and consulted with my officers whether it was best to send thither, or to search among any other of these

Islands with my Boat; or else go from hence, and coast along Shore with the Ship, till we could find some better Place than this was to ride in, where we had shoal Water, and lay expos'd to Winds and Tides. They all agreed to go from hence; so I gave Orders to weigh in the Morning as soon as it should be light, and to get out with the Land-breeze.

Accordingly, August the 23d, at 5 in the Morning we ran out, having a pretty fresh Land-breeze at S.S.E. By 8 a Clock we were got out, and very seasonably; for before 9 the Sea-breeze came on us very strong, and increasing, we took in our Top-sails and stood off under 2 Courses and a Mizen, this being as much Sail as we could carry. The Sky was clear, there being not one Cloud to be seen; but the Horizon appeared very hazy, and the Sun at setting the Night before, and this Morning at rising, appeared very red. The Wind continued very strong till 12, then it began to abate; I have seldom met with a stronger Breeze. These strong Sea-Breezes lasted thus in their Turns 3 or 4 Days. They sprung up with the Sun-rise; by 9 a Clock they were very strong, and so continued till Noon, when they began to abate; and by Sun-set there was little Wind, or a Calm till the Land-breezes came; which we should certainly have in the Morning about 1 or 2 a Clock. The Land-breezes were between the S.S.W. and S.S.E. The Sea-breezes between the E.N.E. and N.N.E. In the Night while Calm, we fish'd with Hook and Line, and caught good Store of Fish, viz. Snappers, Breams, Old-Wives, and Dog-fish. When these last came we seldom caught any others; for if they did not drive away the other Fish, yet they would be sure to keep them from taking our Hooks, for they would first have them themselves, biting very greedily. We caught also a Monk-fish, of which I brought Home the Picture.

On the 25th of August, we still coasted along Shore, that we might the better see any Opening; kept sounding, and had about 20 Fathom clean Sand. The 26th Day, being about 4 Leagues off Shore, the Water began gradually to sholden from 20 to 14 Fathom. I was edging in a little towards the Land, thinking to have anchored; but presently after the Water decreas'd almost at once, till we had but 5 Fathom. I durst therefore adventure no farther, but steered out the same way that we came in; and in a short Time had 10 Fathom (being then about 4 Leagues and a half from the Shore) and even Soundings. I steer'd away E.N.E. coasting along as the Land lies. This Day the Sea-breezes began to be very moderate again, and we made the best of our way along Shore, only in the Night edging off a little for Fear of

Sholes. Ever since we left Shark's Bay we had fair clear Weather, and so for a great while still.

The 27th Day, we had 20 Fathom Water all Night, yet we could not see Land till 1 in the Afternoon from our Topmast-head. By 3 we could just discern Land from our Quarter-deck; we had then 16 Fathom. The Wind was at N. and we steer'd E. by N. which is but one Point in on the Land; yet we decreas'd our Water very fast; for at 4 we had but 9 Fathom; the next Cast but 7, which frighted us; and we then tackt instantly and stood off: But in a short Time the Wind coming at N.W. and W.N.W. we tackt again, and steer'd N.N.E. and then deepned our Water again, and had all Night from 15 to 20 Fathom.

The 28th Day we had between 20 and 40 Fathom. We saw no Land this Day, but saw a great many Snakes and some Whales. We saw also some Boobies, and Noddy-birds; and in the Night caught one of these last. It was of another Shape and Colour than any I had seen before. It had a small long Bill, as all of them have, flat Feet like Ducks Feet; its Tail forked like a Swallow, but longer and broader, and the Fork deeper than that of the Swallow, with very long Wings; the Top or Crown of the Head of this Noddy was Coal-black, having also small black Streaks round about and close to the Eyes; and round these Streaks on each Side, a pretty broad white Circle. The Breast, Belly, and under part of the Wings of this Noddy were white; and the Back and upper part of its Wings of a faint black or smoak Colour; Noddies are seen in most Places between the Tropicks, as well in the East-Indies, and on the Coast of Brazil, as in the West-Indies. They rest ashore a Nights, and therefore we never see them far at Sea, not above 20 or 30 Leagues, unless driven off in a Storm. When they come about a Ship they commonly perch in the Night, and will sit still till they are taken by the Seamen. They build on Cliffs against the Sea, or Rocks, as I have said.

The 30th day, being in Lat. 18 deg. 21 min. we made the Land again, and saw many great Smokes near the Shore; and having fair Weather and moderate Breezes, I steer'd in towards it. At 4 in the Afternoon I anchor'd in 8 Fathom Water, clear Sand, about 3 Leagues and a half from the Shore. I presently sent my Boat to sound nearer in, and they found 10 Fathom about a Mile farther in; and from thence still farther in the Water decreased gradually to 9, 8, 7, and at 2 Mile distance to 6 Fathom. This Evening we saw an Eclipse of the Moon, but it was abating before the Moon appear'd to us; for the Horizon was very hazy, so that we could not see the Moon till she had been half an Hour above the Horizon. And at 2 hours, 22 min. after Sun-set, by the Reckoning of our Glasses, the Eclipse was quite gone, which was not of many Digits. The Moon's Center was then 33 deg. 40 min. high.

The 31st of August betimes in the Morning I went ashore with 10 or 11 men to search for Water. We went armed with Muskets and Cutlasses for our defence, expecting to see people there; and carried also Shovels and Pick-axes to dig Wells. When we came near the Shore we saw 3 tall black naked Men on the sandy Bay a head of us; But as we row'd in, they went away. When we were landed, I sent the Boat with two Men in her to lie a little from the Shore at an Anchor, to prevent being seiz'd; while the rest of us went after the 3 black Men, who were now got on the top of a small Hill about a quarter of a Mile from us, with 8 or 9 Men more in their Company. They seeing us coming, ran away. When we came on the top of the Hill where they first stood, we saw a plain Savannah, about half a Mile from us, farther in from the Sea. There were several Things like Hay-cocks, standing in the Savannah; which at a distance we thought were Houses, looking just like the Hottentot's Houses at the Cape of G. Hope; but we found them to be so many Rocks. We searched about these for Water, but could find none, nor any Houses; nor People, for they were all gone. Then we turned again to the Place where we landed, and there we dug for Water.

While we were at work there came 9 or 10 of the Natives to a small Hill a little way from us, and stood there menacing and threatning of us, and making a great Noise. At last one of them came towards us, and the rest followed at a distance. I went out to meet him, and came within 50 Yards of him, making to him all the Signs of Peace and Friendship I could; but then he ran away, neither would they any of them stay for us to come nigh them; for we tried two or three Times. At last I took two Men with me, and went in the afternoon along by the Sea-side, purposely to catch one of them, if I could, of whom I might learn where they got their fresh Water. There were 10 or 12 of the Natives a little way off, who seeing us three going away from the rest of our Men, followed us at a distance. I thought they would follow us: But there being for a while a Sand-bank between us and them, that they could not then see us, we made a halt, and hid our selves in a bending of the Sand-bank. They knew we must be thereabouts, and being 3 or 4 times our Number, thought to seize us. So they dispers'd themselves, some going to the Sea-shore, and others beating about the Sand-hills. We knew by what Rencounter we had had with them in the Morning that we could easily out-run them. So a nimble young Man that was with me, seeing some of them near, ran towards them; and they for some time, ran away before him. But he soon overtaking them, they faced about and fought him. He had a Cutlass, and they had wooden Lances; with which, being many of them, they were too hard for him. When he first ran towards them I chas'd two more that were by the Shore: But fearing how it might be with my young Man, I turn'd back quickly, and went up to the top of a Sandhill, whence I saw him near me, closely engag'd with them. Upon their seeing me, one of them threw a Lance at me, that narrowly miss'd me. I discharg'd my Gun to scare them, but avoided shooting any of them; till finding the young Man in great danger from them, and my self in some; and that tho' the Gun had a little frighted them at first, yet they had soon learnt to despise it, tossing up their Hands, and crying Pooh, Pooh, Pooh; and coming on afresh with a great Noise, I thought it high time to charge again, and shoot one of them, which I did. The rest, seeing him fall, made a stand again; and my young Man took the Opportunity to disengage himself, and come off to me; my other Man also was with me, who had done nothing all this while, having come out unarm'd; and I return'd back with my Men, designing to attempt the Natives no farther, being very sorry for what had happened already. They took up their wounded Companion; and my young Man, who had been struck through the Cheek by one of their Lances, was afraid it had been poison'd: But I did not think that likely. His Wound was very painful to him, being made with a blunt Weapon: But he soon recover'd of it.

Among the N. Hollanders, whom we were thus engag'd with, there was one who by his Appearance and Carriage, as well in the Morning as this Afternoon, seem'd to be the Chief of them, and a kind of Prince or Captain among them. He was a young brisk Man, not very tall, nor so personable as some of the rest, tho' more active and couragious: He was painted (which none of the rest were at all) with a Circle of white Paste or Pigment (a sort of Lime, as we thought) about his Eyes, and a white streak down his Nose from his Forehead to the tip of it. And his Breast and some part of his Arms were also made white with the same Paint; not for Beauty or Ornament, one would think, but as some wild Indian Warriors are said to do, he seem'd thereby to design the looking more Terrible; this his Painting adding very much to his natural Deformity; for they all of them have the most unpleasant Looks and the worse Features of any People that ever I saw, though I have seen great variety of Savages. These New-Hollanders were probably the same sort of People as those I met with on this Coast in my "Voyage round the World"; for the Place I then touched at was not above 40 or 50 Leagues to the N.E. of this: And these were much the same blinking Creatures (here being also abundance of the same kind of Flesh-flies teizing them) and with the same black Skins, and Hair frizled, tall and thin, &c. as those were: But we had not the Opportunity to see whether these, as the former, wanted two of their Fore-Teeth.

We saw a great many places where they had made Fires; and where there were commonly 3 or 4 Boughs stuck up to Wind-ward of them; for the Wind (which is the Sea-breeze) in the day-time blows always one way with them; and the Land-breeze is but small. By their Fire-places we should always find great heaps of Fish-shells, of several sorts; and 'tis probable that these poor Creatures here lived chiefly on the Shell-fish, as those I before describ'd did on small Fish, which they caught in Wires or Holes in the Sand at Low-water. These gather'd their Shell-fish on the Rocks at Low-water; but had no Wires (that we saw) whereby to get any other sorts of Fish: As among the former I saw not any heaps of Shells as here, though I know they also gather'd some Shell-fish. The Lances also of those were such as these had; how-ever they being upon an Island, with their Women and Children, and all in our Power, they did not there use them against us, as here on the Continent, where we saw none but some of the Men under Head, who come out purposely to observe us. We saw no Houses at either Place: and I believe they have none, since the former People on the Island had none, tho' they had all their Families with them.

Upon returning to my Men I saw that though they had dug 8 or 9 Foot deep, yet found no Water. So I returned aboard that Evening, and the next day, being September 1st, I sent my Boatswain ashore to dig deeper and sent the Sain with him to catch Fish. While I staid aboard I observed the flowing of the Tide, which runs very swift here, so that our Nun-buoy would not bear above the Water to be seen. It flows here (as on that part of N. Holland I described formerly) about 5 Fathom: And here the Flood runs S.E. by S. till the last Quarter; then it sets right in towards the Shore (which lies here S.S.W. and N.N.E.) and the Ebb runs N.W. by N. When the Tides slackned we fish'd with Hook and Line, as we had already done in several Places on this Coast; on which in this Voyage hitherto, we had found but little Tides; But by the Heighth, and Strength, and Course of them hereabouts, it should seem that if there be such a Passage or Streight going through Eastward to the Great South-Sea, as I said one might suspect, one would expect to find the Mouth of it somewhere between this Place and Rosemary Island, which was the part of New Holland I came last from.

Next Morning my Men came aboard and brought a Rundlet of brackish Water which they got out of another Well that they dug in a Place a mile off, and about half as far from the Shore; but this Water was not fit to drink. However we all concluded that it would serve to boil our Oatmeal, for Burgoo, whereby we might save the Remains of our other Water for drinking, till we should get more; and accordingly the next Day we brought aboard 4 Hogsheads of it: But while we were at work about the Well we were sadly pester'd with the Flies, which were more troublesome to us than the Sun, tho' it shone clear and strong upon us all the while, very hot. All this while we saw no more of the Natives, but saw some of the Smoaks of some of their Fires at 2 or 3 miles distance.

The Land hereabouts was much like the part of New Holland that I formerly described, 'tis low, but seemingly barricado'd with a long Chain of Sandhills to the Sea, that let's nothing be seen of what is farther within land. At high Water the Tides rising so high as they do, the Coast shews very low; but when 'tis low Water it seems to be of an indifferent heighth. At low Watermark the Shore is all Rocky, so that then there is no Landing with a Boat; but at high Water a Boat may come in over those Rocks to the Sandy Bay, which runs all along on this Coast. The Land by the Sea for about 5 or 600 yards is a dry Sandy Soil, bearing only Shrubs and Bushes of divers sorts. Some of these had them at this time of the Year, yellow Flowers or Blossoms, some blue, and some white; most of them of a very fragrant Smell. Some had Fruit like Peascods; in each of which there were just ten small Peas; I opened many of them, and found no more nor less. There are also here some of that sort of Bean which I saw at Rosemary-Island: And another sort of small, red, hard Pulse, growing in Cods also, with little black Eyes like Beans. I know not their Names, but have seen them used often in the East-Indies for weighing Gold; and they make the same use of them at Guinea, as I have heard, where the Women also make Bracelets with them to wear about their Arms. These grow on Bushes; but here are also a Fruit like Beans growing on a creeping sort of Shrub-like Vine. There was a great plenty of all these sorts of Cod-fruit growing on the Sand-hills by the Sea-side, some of them green, some ripe, and some fallen on the Ground: But I could not perceive that any of them had been gathered by the Natives; and might not probably be wholesome Food.

The Land farther in, that is lower than what borders on the Sea, was so much as we saw of it, very plain and even; partly Savannahs, and partly Woodland. The Savannahs bear a sort of thin coarse Grass. The Mould is also a coarser Sand than that by the Sea-side, and in some places 'tis Clay. Here are a great many Rocks in the large Savannah we were in, which are 5 or 6 Foot high, and round at top like a Hay-cock, very remarkable; some red, and some white. The Woodland lies farther in still; where there were divers sorts of small Trees, scarce any three Foot in circumference; their Bodies 12 or 14 Foot high, with a Head of small Knibs or Boughs. By the sides of the Creeks, especially nigh the Sea, there grow a few small black Mangrove-Trees.

There are but few Land-Animals. I saw some Lizards and my Men saw two or three Beasts like hungry Wolves, lean like so many Skeletons, being nothing but Skin and Bones; 'Tis probable that it was the Foot of one of those Beasts that I mention'd as seen by us in N. Holland. We saw a Rackoon or two, and one small speckled Snake.

The Land-fowls that we saw here were Crows (just such as ours in England), small Hawks, and Kites; a few of each sort: But here are plenty of small Turtle-Doves, that are plump, fat and very good Meat. Here are 2 or 3 sorts of smaller Birds, some as big as Larks, some less; but not many of either sort. The Sea-Fowl are Pelicans, Boobies, Noddies, Curlews, See-pies, &c. and but few of these neither.

The Sea is plentifully stock'd with the largest Whales that I ever saw; but not to compare with the vast ones of the Northern Seas. We saw also a great many Green Turtle, but caught none; here being no place to set a Turtle-Net in; here being no Channel for them, and the Tides running so strong. We saw some Sharks, and Parracoots; and with Hooks and Lines we caught some Rock-fish and Old-wives. Of Shell-fish, here were Oysters both of the common kind for Eating, and of the Pearl kind; And also Wilks, Conchs, Muscles, Limpits; Perriwinkles, &c. and I gather'd a few strange Shells; chiefly a sort not large, and thick-set all about with Rays or Spikes growing in Rows.

And thus having ranged about, a considerable time, upon this Coast, without finding any good fresh Water, or any convenient Place to clean the Ship, as I had hop'd for; And it being moreover the heighth of the dry Season, and my Men growing Scorbutick for want of Refreshments, so that I had little incouragement to search further; I resolved to leave this Coast, and accordingly in the beginning of September set sail towards Timor. . . .

    .   .   .   .   .

    I had spent about 5 Weeks in ranging off and on the Coast of New-Holland, a length of about 300 Leagues; and had put in at 3 several Places, to see what there might be thereabouts worth discovering; and at the same Time to recruit my Stock of fresh Water and Provisions for the further Discoveries I purposed to attempt on the Terra Australis. This large and hitherto almost unknown Tract of Land is situated so very advantageously in the richest Climates of the World, the Torrid and Temperate Zones; having in it especially all the Advantages of the Torrid Zone, as being known to reach from the Equator it self (within a Degree) to the Tropick of Capricorn, and beyond it; that in coasting round it, which I design'd by this Voyage, if possible; I could not but hope to meet with some fruitful Lands, Continent or Islands, or both, productive of any of the rich Fruits, Drugs, or Spices, (perhaps Minerals also, &c.) that are in the other Parts of the Torrid Zone, under equal Parallels of Latitude; at least a Soil and Air capable of such, upon transplanting them hither, and Cultivation. I meant, also to make as diligent a Survey as I could, of the several smaller Islands, Shores, Capes, Bays, Creeks, and Harbours, fit as well for Shelter as Defence, upon fortifying them; and of the Rocks and Shoals, the Soundings, Tides, and Currents, Winds and Weather, Variation, &c. Whatever might be beneficial for Navigation, Trade or Settlement; or be of use to any who should prosecute the same Designs hereafter; to whom it might be serviceable to have so much of their Work done to their Hands; which they might advance and perfect by their own repeated Experiences. As there is no Work of this Kind brought to Perfection at once, I intended especially to observe what Inhabitants I should meet with, and to try to win them over to somewhat of Traffick and useful Intercourse, as there might be Commodities among any of them that might be fit for Trade or Manufacture, or any found in which they might be employed. Though as to the New Hollanders hereabouts, by the Experience I had had of their Neighbours formerly, I expected no great Matters from them.

With such Views as these, I set out at first from England; and would, according to the Method I proposed formerly have gone Westward, through the Magellanick Streight, or round Terra del Fuego rather, that I might have begun my Discoveries upon the Eastern and least known Side of the Terra Australis. But that way 'twas not possible for me to go, by Reason of the Time of Year in which I came out; for I must have been compassing the South of America in a very high Latitude, in the Depth of the Winter there. I was therefore necessitated to go Eastward by the Cape of Good Hope; and when I should be past it, 'twas requisite I should keep in a pretty high Latitude, to avoid the general Trade-winds that would be against me, and to have the Benefit of the variable Winds; By all which I was in a Manner unavoidably determin'd to fall in first with those Parts of New Holland I have hitherto been describing, For should it be ask'd why at my first making that Shore, I did not coast it to the Southward, and that way try to get round to the East of New Holland and New Guinea; I confess I was not for spending my Time more than was necessary in the higher Latitudes; as knowing that the Land there could not be so well worth the discovering, as the Parts that lay nearer the Line, and more directly under the Sun. Besides, at the Time when I should come first on New Holland, which was early in the Spring, I must, had I stood Southward, have had for some Time a great deal of Winter-weather, increasing in Severity, though not in Time, and in a Place altogether unknown, which my Men, who were heartless enough to the Voyage at best, would never have born, after so long a Run as from Brazil hither.

For these Reasons therefore I chose to coast along to the Northward, and so to the East, and so thought to come round by the South of Terra Australis in my Return back, which should be in the Summer-season there: And this Passage back also I now thought I might possibly be able to shorten, should it appear, at my getting to the East Coast of New Guinea, that there is a Channel there coming out into these Seas, as I now suspected near Rosemary Island: Unless the high Tides and great Indraught thereabout should be occasion'd by the Mouth of some large River; which hath often low Lands on each Side of its Outlet, and many Islands and Sholes lying at its Entrance. But I rather thought it a Channel or Streight, than a River: And I was afterwards confirmed in this Opinion, when by coasting New Guinea, I found that other Parts of this great Tract of Terra Australia, which had hitherto been represented as the Shore of a Continent, were certainly Islands; and 'tis probably the same with New Holland: Though for Reasons I shall afterwards shew, I could not return by the way I propos'd to my self, to fix the Discovery. All that I had now seen from the Latitude of 27 d. South to 25, which is Shark's Bay; and again from thence to Rosemary

Islands, and about the Latitude of 20; seems to be nothing but Ranges of pretty large Islands against the Sea, whatever might be behind them to the Eastward, whether Sea or Land, Continent or Islands.

But to proceed with my Voyage. Though the Land I had seen as yet, was not very inviting, being but barren towards the Sea, and affording me neither fresh Water, nor any great Store of other Refreshments, nor so much as a fit Place for careening; yet I stood out to Sea again with Thoughts of coasting still along Shore (as near as I could) to the North Eastward, for the further Discovery of it: Perswading my self, that at least the Place I anchor'd at in my Voyage round the world, in the Latitude of 16 deg. 15 min. from which I was not now far distant, would not fail to afford me sweet Water upon digging, as it did then; for the brackish Water I had taken in here, though it serv'd tolerably well for boiling, was yet not very wholesome.

With these Intentions I put to Sea on the 5th of September 1699, with a gentle Gale, sounding all the way; but was quickly induc'd to alter my Design. For I had not been out above a Day, but I found that the Sholes among which I was engag'd all the while on the Coast, and was like to be engag'd in, would make it a very tedious Thing to sail along by the Shore, or to put in where I might have occasion. I therefore edged farther off to Sea, and so deepned the Water from 11 to 32 Fathom. The next Day, being September the 6th, we could but just discern the Land, though we had then no more than about 30 Fathom, uncertain Soundings; For even while we were out of Sight of Land, we had once but 7 Fathom, and had also great and uncertain Tides whirling about, that made me afraid to go near a Coast so shallow, where we might be soon a-ground, and yet have but little Wind to bring us off: For should a Ship be near a Shoal, she might be hurl'd upon it unavoidably by a strong Tide, unless there should be a good Wind to work her and keep her off. Thus also on the 7th Day we saw no Land, though our Water decreas'd again to 26 Fathom: for we had deepned it, as I said, to 30.

This Day we saw two Water-snakes, different in Shape from such as we had formerly seen. The one was very small, though long; the other long and as big as a Man's Leg, having a red Head; which I never saw any have, before or since. We had this Day, Lat. 16 d. 9 m. by Observation.

I was by this Time got to the North of the Place I had thought to have put in at, where I dug Wells in my former Voyage; and though I knew by the Experience I had of it then, that there was a

deep Entrance in thither from the Eastward; yet by the Shoals I
had hitherto found so far stretcht on this Coast, I was afraid I
should have the same Trouble to coast all along afterwards beyond that Place: And besides the Danger of running almost continually amongst Shoals on a strange Shore, and where the Tides
were strong and high; I began to bethink my self, that a great
Part of my Time must have been spent in being about a Shore I
was already almost weary of, which I might employ with greater
Satisfaction to my Mind, and better Hopes of Success in going
forward to New Guinea. Add to this the particular Danger I
should have been in upon a Lee-Shore, such as is here describ'd,
when the North-West Monsoon should once come in; the ordinary
Season of which was not now far off, though this Year it staid
beyond the common Season; and it comes on storming at first,
with Tornadoes, violent Gusts, &c. Wherefore quitting the
Thoughts of putting in again at New Holland, I resolv'd to steer
away for the Island Timor; where, besides getting fresh Water, I
might probably expect to be furnished with Fruits, and other
Refreshments to recruit my Men, who began to droop; some of
them being already to my great Grief, afflicted with the Scurvy,
which was likely to increase upon them and disable them, and was
promoted by the brackish Water they took in last for boiling
their Oatmeal. 'Twas now also towards the latter end of the dry
Season; when I might not probably have found Water so plentifully upon digging at that part of New Holland, as when I was
there before in the wet Season. And then, considering the Time
also that I must necessarily spend in getting in to the Shore,
through such Sholes as I expected to meet with; or in going about
to avoid them; and in digging of Wells when I should come
thither; I might very well hope to get to Timor, and find fresh
Water there, as soon as I could expect to get it at New Holland;
and with less Trouble and Danger.

On the 8th of September therefore, shaping our Course for Timor
we were in Lat. 15 d. 37 m. We had 26 Fathom, coarse Sand;
and we saw one Whale. We found them lying most commonly
near the Shore; or in Shoal Water. This Day we also saw some
small white Clouds; the first that we had seen since we came out of
Shark's Bay. This was one Sign of the Approach of the North-
North-West Monsoon. Another Sign was the shifting of the
Winds; for from the Time of our coming to our last Anchoring
place, the Sea-Breezes which before were Easterly and very
strong, had been whiffling about, and changing gradually from
the East to the North, and thence to the West, blowing but

faintly, and now hanging mostly in some Point of the West. This Day the Winds were at South-West by West, blowing very faint; and the 9th Day we had the Wind at North-West by North, but then pretty fresh; and we saw the Clouds rising more and thicker in the North-West. This Night at 12 we lay by for a small low sandy Island, which I reckoned my self not far from. The next Morning at Sun-rising we saw it from the Top-mast-head, right a-head of us; and at Noon were up within a Mile of it: When, by a good Observation, I found it to lye in 13 d. 55 m. I have mentioned it in my first Vol. pag. 450, but my Account then made it to lye in 13 d. 50 m. We had Abundance of Boobies and Man of War Birds flying about us all the Day; especially when we came near the Island; which had also Abundance of them upon it; though it was but a little Spot of Sand, scarce a Mile round.

I did not anchor here, nor send my Boat ashore; there being no appearance of getting any Thing on that Spot of Sand, besides Birds that were good for little: Though had I not been in haste, I would have taken some of them. So I made the best of my way to Timor; and on the 11th in the Afternoon we saw 10 small Land-birds, about the Bigness of Larks, that flew away North West. The 13th we saw a great many Sea-snakes. One of these, of which I saw great Numbers and Variety in this Voyage, was large, and all black; I never saw such another for his Colour.

We had now had for some Days small Gales, from the South-South-West to the North-North-West, and the Sky still more cloudy especially in the Mornings and Evenings. The 14th it look'd very black in the North-West all the Day; and a little before Sun-set we saw, to our great Joy, the Tops of the high Mountains of Timor, peeping out of the Clouds, which had before covered them, as they did still the lower Parts. . . .

. . . .

The 2d of February, we anchored in St. Helena Road, and set sail again from thence on the 13th.

On the 21st we made the Island of Ascension, and stood in towards it. The 22d between 8 and 9 a-Clock, we sprung a leak, which increased so that the Chain-pump could not keep the Ship free. Whereupon I set the Hand-pump to work also, and by 10 a-Clock suck'd her: Then wore the Ship, and stood to the South-ward, to try if that would ease her: and then the Chain-pump just kept her free. At 5 the next Morning we made Sail and stood in for the Bay; and at 9 anchored in 10 and a half Fathom, sandy Grounds. The South-point bore South-South-West distance 2 Miles, and the North-point of the Bay, North-East half North, distance 2 Miles. As soon as we anchored, I ordered the Gunner to clear his Powder-room, that we might there search for the Leak, and endeavour to stop it within board if possible; for we could not heel the Ship so low, it being within 4 Streaks of the Keel; neither was there any convenient place to haul her ashore. I ordered the Boatswain to assist the Gunner; and by 10 a-Clock the Powder-room was clear. The Carpenter's Mate, Gunner, and Boatswain went down; and soon after I followed them my self, and ask'd them whether they could come at the Leak: They said they believed they might, by cutting the Cieling; I told the Carpenter's Mate (who was the only Person in the ship that understood any Thing of Carpenters-work,) that if he thought he could come at the Leak by cutting the Cieling without weakening the Ship, he might do it; for he had stopp'd one Leak so before; which though not so big as this, yet having seen them both, I thought he might as well do this as the other. Wherefore I left him to do his best. The Cieling being cut, they could not come at the Leak; for it was against one of the Foot-hook-Timbers, which the Carpenter's Mate said he must first cut, before it could be stopp'd. I went down again to see it, and found the Water to come in very violently. I told them I never had known any such thing as cutting Timbers to stop Leaks; but if they who ought to be best Judges in such Cases, thought they could do any good, I bid them use their utmost Care and Diligence, promising the Carpenter's Mate that I would always be a Friend to him if he could and would stop it: He said, by 4 a-Clock in the Afternoon he would make all well, it being then about 11 in the Forenoon. In the Afternoon my Men were all employ'd, pumping with both Pumps; except such as assisted the Carpenter's Mate. About one in the Afternoon I went down again, and the Carpenter's Mate was cutting the After-part of the Timber over the Leak. Some said it was best to cut the Timber away at once; I bid them hold their Tongue, and let the Carpenter's Mate alone; for he knew best, and I hop'd he would do his utmost to stop the Leak. I desir'd him to get everything ready for stopping the violence of the Water, before he cut any further; for fear it should over-power us at once. I had already ordered the Carpenter to bring all the Oakam he had, and the Boatswain to bring all the waste Cloaths, to stuff in upon Occasion; and had for the same purpose sent down my own Bed-cloaths. The Carpenter's Mate said he should want short Stantions, to be placed so that the upper-end should touch the Deck, and the under-part rest in what was laid over the Leak; and presently took a Length for them. I ask'd the Master-

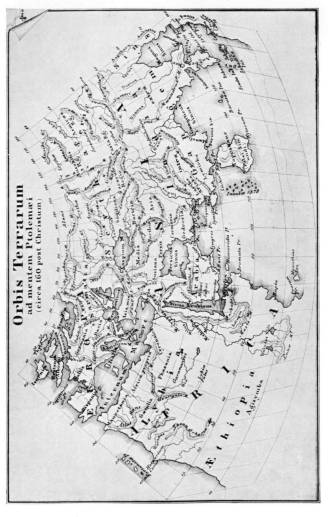

The World according to Ptolemy.
From the *Atlas Antiquus* (Spruner Litglin).

Carpenter what he thought best to be done: He replied till the Leak was all open he could not tell. Then he went to make a Stantion, but it was too long: I ordered him to make many of several Lengths, that we might not want of any Size. So, once more desiring the Carpenter's Mate to use his utmost Endeavours, I went up, leaving the Boatswain and some others there. About 5 a Clock the Boatswain came to me, and told me the Leak was increased, and that it was impossible to keep the Ship above Water; when on the contrary I expected to have had the News of the Leak's being stopt. I presently went down, and found the Timber cut away, but nothing in Readiness to stop the Force of the Water from coming in. I ask'd them why they would cut the Timber, before they had got all Things in Readiness: The Carpenter's Mate answered, they could do nothing till the Timber was cut, that he might take the Dimensions of the Place; and that there was a Chaulk which he had lined out, preparing by the Carpenter's Boy. I ordered them in the mean Time to stop in Oakam, and some Pieces of Beef; which accordingly was done, but all to little Purpose: For now the Water gush'd in with such Violence, notwithstanding all our Endeavours to check it, that it flew in over the Cieling; and for want of Passage out of the Room overflow'd it above 2 Foot deep. I ordered the Bulk-head to be cut open, to give Passage to the Water that it might drain out of the Room; and withal ordered to clear away abaft the Bulk-head, that we might bail: So now we had both Pumps going, and as many bailing as could; and by this Means the Water began to decrease: which gave me some Hope of saving the Ship. I ask'd the Carpenter's Mate, what he thought of it; He said, "Fear not; for by 10 a Clock at Night I'll engage to stop the Leak." I went from him with a heavy Heart; but putting a good Countenance upon the Matter, encouraged my Men, who pump'd and bail'd very briskly; and, when I saw Occasion, I gave them some Drams to comfort them. About 11 a Clock at Night, the Boatswain came to me, and told me, that the Leak still increased; and that the Plank was so rotten, it broke away like Dirt; and that now it was impossible to save the Ship; for they could not come at the Leak, because the Water in the Room was got above it. The rest of the Night we spent in Pumping and Bailing. I worked my self to encourage my Men, who were very diligent; but the Water still encreas'd, and we now thought of nothing but saving our Lives. Wherefore I hoisted out the Boat, that, if the Ship should sink, yet we might be saved: And in the Morning we weighed our Anchor, and warp'd in nearer the Shore; yet did but little good.

I

In the Afternoon, with the Help of a Sea-breeze, I ran into 7 Fathom, and anchored; then carried a small Anchor ashore, and warp'd in till I came into 3 Fathom and a half. Where having fastned her, I made a Raft to carry the Men's Chests and Bedding ashore; and, before 8 at Night, most of them, were ashore. In the Morning I ordered the Sails to be unbent, to make Tents; and then my self and Officers went ashore. I had sent ashore a Puncheon, and a 36 Gallon Cask of Water, with one Bag of Rice for our common use: But great Part of it was stolen away, before I came ashore; and many of my Books and Papers lost.

On the 26th following, we, to our great Comfort, found a Spring of fresh Water, about 8 Miles from our Tents, beyond a very high Mountain, which we must pass over: So that now we were, by God's Providence, in a Condition of subsisting some Time; having Plenty of very good Turtle by our Tents, and Water for the fetching. The next Day I went up to see the Wateringplace, accompanied with most of my Officers. We lay by the way all Night, and next Morning early got thither; where we found a very fine Spring on the South-East-side of the high Mountain, about half a Mile from its Top: But the continual Fogs make it so cold here, that it is very unwholesome living by the Water. Near this Place, are Abundance of Goats and Land-crabs. About 2 Mile South-East from the Spring, we found 3 or 4 shrubby Trees, upon one of which was cut an Anchor and Cable, and the Year 1642. About half a Furlong from these, we found a convenient Place for sheltering Men in any Weather. Hither many of our Men resorted; the hollow Rocks affording convenient Lodging; the Goats, Land-crabs, Men of War Birds, and Boobies, good Food; and the Air was here exceeding wholsome.

About a Week after our coming ashore, our Men that liv'd at this new Habitation, saw 2 Ships making towards the Island. Before Night they brought me the News; and I ordered them to turn about a Score of Turtle, to be in Readiness for these Ships if they should touch here: But before Morning they were out of Sight, and the Turtle were releas'd again. Here we continued without seeing any other Ship till the second of April; when we saw 11 Sail to Windward of the Island; But they likewise past by. The Day after appear'd 4 Sail, which came to anchor in this Bay. They were his Majesty's Ships the *Anglesey*, *Hastings* and *Lizard;* and the *Canterbury* East-India Ship. I went on board the *Anglesey* with about 35 of my Men; and the rest were dispos'd of into the other 2 Men of War.

We sail'd from Ascension, the 8th; and continued aboard till the 8th of May: At which Time the Men of War having miss'd St. Jago, where they design'd to Water, bore away for Barbadoes: But I being desirous to get to England as soon as possible, took my Passage in the Ship *Canterbury*, accompanied with my Master, Purser, Gunner, and 3 of my superiour Officers.

XI. COOK IN NEW ZEALAND

[The following extracts, describing the discoveries of James Cook in New Zealand and on the east coast of Australia, are taken from his own Journal, as edited by the Admiralty hydrographer, Wharton. The story as Cook told it differs from that printed many times in the popular *Voyages*. That book was prepared for publication by Dr. Hawkesworth—that " studious imitator of Dr. Johnson," as Boswell called him—who was employed by Lord Sandwich, the political head of the Navy, to make a readable volume out of the material supplied by Cook and the companions of his voyage. Cook is known to have disapproved of the "literary" editing which his Journal received from Hawkesworth, whose decorative prose was certainly unlike the plain, seamanlike writing of the great navigator. It is more satisfactory to read his own account of these important occurrences than the doctored tale.

The extract begins with the entry for the 9th of October, 1769; and it should be remembered that in Cook's time the nautical day began at noon, so that the day's entries always begin with events of the afternoon. On the other hand, Cook, sailing westwards across the Pacific, had after crossing the 180th meridian gained a day—a gain which he did not in his journal take into account until he reached Batavia. During the whole of his voyaging, therefore, in New Zealand and Australian waters, his entries are a day behind the actual date. The net result of these two divergences from fact is that his entries under, say, "9th Oct." recount first the events of the afternoon of that day and then, under "In the morning," those of the morning of the 10th.]

Monday, 9th Oct.—Gentle breezes and Clear Weather. P.M. stood into the Bay and Anchored on the N.E. side before the Entrance of a small River, in 10 fathoms, a fine sandy bottom. The N.E. point of the Bay bore E. by S. ½ S., and the S.W. point S., distance from the Shore half a League. After this I went ashore with a Party of men in the Pinnace and yawl accompanied by Mr. Banks and Dr. Solander. We landed abreast of the Ship and on the E. side of the River just mentioned; but seeing some of the Natives on the other side of the River of whom I was desirous of speaking with, and finding that we could not ford the River, I order'd the yawl in to carry us over, and the pinnace to lay at the Entrance. In the meantime the Indians made off. However we went as far as their Hutts which lay about 2 or 300 Yards from the water side, leaving 4 boys to take care of the Yawl, which we had no sooner left than 4 Men came out of the woods on the other side the River, and would certainly have cut her off had not the People in the Pinnace discover'd them and called to her to drop down the Stream, which they did, being closely persued by the Indians. The coxswain of the Pinnace, who had the charge of the Boats, seeing this, fir'd 2 Musquets over their Heads; the first made them stop and Look round them, but the 2nd they took no notice of; upon which a third was fir'd and kill'd one of them upon the Spot just as he was going to dart his spear at the Boat. At this the other 3 stood motionless for a Minute or two, seemingly quite surprised; wondering, no doubt, what it was that had thus kill'd their Comrade; but as soon as they recovered themselves they made off, dragging the Dead body a little way and then left it. Upon our hearing the report of the Musquets we immediately repair'd to the Boats, and after viewing the Dead body we return'd on board. In the morning, seeing a number of the Natives at the same place where we saw them last night, I went on shore with the Boats, mann'd and arm'd, and landed on the opposite side of the river. Mr. Banks, Dr. Solander, and myself only landed at first, and went to the side of the river, the natives being got together on the opposite side. We called to them in the George's Island Language, but they answer'd us by flourishing their weapons over their heads and dancing, as we suppos'd, the War Dance; upon this we retir'd until the Marines were landed, which I order'd to be drawn up about 200 yards, behind us. We went again to the river side, having Tupia, Mr. Green, and Dr. Monk-house along with us. Tupia spoke to them in his own Language, and it was an agreeable surprize to us to find that they perfectly understood him. After some little conversation had passed one of them swam over to us, and after him 20 or 30 more; these last brought their Arms, which the first man did not. We made them every one presents, but this did not satisfy them; they wanted everything we had about us, particularly our Arms, and made several attempts to snatch them out of our hands. Tupia told us several times, as soon as they came over, to take care of ourselves for they were not our friends; and this we very soon found, for one of them snatched Mr. Green's hanger from him and would not give it up: this encouraged the rest to be more insolent, and seeing others coming over to join them, I order'd the man who had taken the Hanger to be fir'd at, which was accordingly done, and wounded in such a manner that he died soon after. Upon the first fire, which was only 2 Musquets, the others retir'd to a Rock which lay nearly in the middle of the River; but on seeing the man fall they return'd, probably to carry him off or his Arms, the last of which they accomplished, and this we could not prevent unless we had run our Bayonets into them, for upon their returning from off the Rock, we had discharged off our Peices, which were loaded with small shott, and wounded 3 more; but these got over the River and were carried off by the others, who now thought proper to retire. Finding nothing was to be done with the People on this side, and the water in the river being salt, I embarked with an intent to row round the head of the Bay in search of fresh water, and if possible to surprise some of the Natives and to take them on board, and by good Treatment and Presents endeavour to gain their friendship with this view.

Tuesday, 10th.—P.M., I rowed round the head of the bay, but could find no place to land on account of the Great Surf which beat everywhere upon the Shore. Seeing 2 Boats or Canoes coming in from Sea I rowed to one of them, in order to Seize upon the People; and came so near before they took notice of us that Tupia called to them to come alongside and we would not hurt them; but instead of doing this they endeavour'd to get away, upon which I order'd a Musquet to be fir'd over their Heads, thinking this would either make them surrender, or jump overboard; but here I was mistaken, for they immediately took to their Arms or whatever they had in the Boat, and began to attack us. This obliged us to fire upon them, and unfortunately either 2 or 3 were kill'd and one wounded, and 3 jumped overboard. These last we took up and brought on board, where they was Cloathed and Treated with all imaginable kindness; and to the Surprise of everybody became at once as cheerful and as merry as if they had been with their own Friends. They were all 3 Young, the eldest not above 20 years of Age, and the youngest about 10 or 12. I am aware that most Humane men who have not experienced things of this nature will Censure my Conduct in firing upon the People in their Boat, nor do I myself think that the reason I had for seizing upon her will at all justify me; and had I thought that they would have made the Least Resistance; I would not have come near them; but as they did, I was not to stand still and suffer either myself or those that were with me to be knocked on the head.

In the morning, as I intended to put our 3 Prisoners ashore, and stay here the day to see what effect it might have upon the other Natives, I sent an Officer ashore with the Marines and a party of men to cut wood, and soon after followed myself, accompanied by Mr. Banks, Dr. Solander, and Tupia, taking the 3 Natives with us, whom we landed on the West side of the River before mentioned. They were very unwilling to leave us, pretending that they should fall into the hands of their Enemies, who would kill and Eat them. However, they at last of their own accord left us and hid themselves in some bushes. Soon after this we discover'd several bodys of the Natives marching towards us, upon which we retir'd aCross the River, and joind the wooders; and with us came the 3 Natives we had just parted with, for we could not prevail upon them to go to their own people. We had no sooner got over the River than the others assembled on the other side to the Number of 150 or 200, all Arm'd. Tupia now began to Parly with them, and the 3 we had with us shew'd everything we had given them, part of which they laid and left upon the Body of the Man that was Kill'd the day before. These things seem'd so far to Convince them of our friendly intentions that one man came over to us, while all the others sat down upon the Sand. We everyone made this man a present, and the 3 Natives that were with us likewise presented him with such things as they had got from us, with which, after a short Stay, he retir'd aCross the River. I now thought proper to take everybody on board, to prevent any more Quarrels, and with us came the 3 Natives, whom we could not prevail upon to stay behind; and this appear'd the more strange as the man that came over to us was Uncle to one of them. After we had return'd on board we saw them Carry off the Dead Man; but the one that was Kill'd the first evening we Landed remain'd in the very spot they had left him.

Wednesday, 11th.—In the P.M., as I intended to sail in the Morning, we put the 3 Youths ashore, seemingly very much against their inclination; but whether this was owing to a desire they had to remain with us, or the fear of falling into the hands of their Enemies, as they pretended, I know not. The latter, however, seemed to be ill-founded, for we saw them carried aCross the River in a Catamaran, and walk Leasurely off with the other Natives. At 6 a.m. we weighed and stood out of the Bay, which I have named Poverty Bay, because it afforded us no one thing we

wanted (Lat. 38° 42' S., Long. 181° 36' W.). It is in the form of a
Horse Shoe, and is known by an Island lying close under the
N.E. point. The 2 points which forms the Entrance are high, with
Steap white Cliffs, and lay a League and a half or 2 Leagues from
Each other, N.E. by E. and S.W. by W. The Depth of Water in
this Bay is from 12 to 6 and 5 fathoms, a sandy bottom and good
Anchorage, but you lay open to the winds between the S. and
E. Boats can go in and out of the river above mentioned at any
time of Tide in fine weather; but as there is a Bar at the Entrance,
on which the Sea Sometimes runs so high that no Boat can either
get in or out, which hapned while we laid here; however, I believe
that Boats can generally land on the N.E. side of the river. The
shore of this Bay, from a little within each Entrance, is a low, flat
sand; but this is only a Narrow Slip, for the face of the Country
appears with a variety of hills and Vallies, all cloathed with woods
and Verdure, and to all appearance well inhabited, especially in
the Vallies leading up from the Bay, where we daily saw Smoke
at a great distance inland, and far back in the Country are very
high Mountains. At Noon the S.W. point of Poverty Bay, which
I have named Young Nicks head (after the Boy who first saw this
land), bore N. by W., distance 3 or 4 leagues, being at this time
about 3 Miles from the Shore, and had 25 fathoms Water, the
Main Land extending from N.E. by N. to S. My intention is to
follow the direction of the Coast to the Southward, as far as the
Latitude of 40° or 41°, and then to return to the Northward, in
case we meet with nothing to encourage us to proceed farther.

·   ·   ·   ·   ·   ·   ·

[IN QUEEN CHARLOTTE'S SOUND, JANUARY 1770.]

Wednesday, 31st.—Little wind and Variable. In the P.M. the
Carpenters having prepared the 2 Posts with inscriptions upon
them, setting forth the Ship's Name, Month, and Year, one of
them was set up at the Watering Place, on which was hoisted the
Union flag; and in the Morning I took the other over to the Island
which is known by the name of *Motuouru*, and is the one that lies
nearest to the Sea; but before I attempted to set up the Post I
went first to the Hippa, having Dr. Monkhouse and Tupia along
with me. We here met with the old Man I have before spoke of.
The first thing I did was to inquire after the Man said to be kill'd by
our people, and the one that was wounded at the same time, when
it did not appear to me that any such accidents had happened. I
next (by means of Tupia) explain'd to the old Man and several

others that we were Come to set up a Mark upon the Island, in order to shew to any ship that might put into this place that we had been here before. They not only gave their free Consent to set it up, but promised never to pull it down. I then gave every one a present of one thing or another; to the old man I gave Silver, three penny pieces dated 1763, and Spike Nails with the King's Broad Arrow cut deep in them; things that I thought were most likely to remain long among them. After I had thus prepared the way for setting up the post, we took it up to the highest part of the Island, and after fixing it fast in the ground, hoisted thereon the Union flag, and I dignified this Inlet with the name of Queen Charlotte's Sound, and took formal possession of it and the Adjacent lands in the Name and for the use of his Majesty. We then drank her Majesty's health in a Bottle of wine, and gave the Empty bottle to the old man (who had attended us up the hill), with which he was highly pleased. Whilst the Post was setting up we asked the old man about the Strait or Passage into the Eastern sea, and he very plainly told us there was a Passage, and as I had some Conjectures that the lands to the S.W. of this Strait (which we are now at) was an Island, and not a Continent, we questioned the old Man about it, who said it consisted of two Wannuas, that is 2 lands or Islands that might be circumnavigated in a few days, even in 4. This man spoke of 3 lands, the 2 above mentioned which he called *Tovy-poinammu*, which Signifies green Talk or Stone, such as they make their Tools or ornaments, etc., and for the third he pointed to the land on the East side of the Strait; this, he said, was a large land, and that it would take up a great many Moons to sail round it; this he called *Aeheino Mouwe*, a name many others before had called it by. That part which borders on the strait he called *Teiria Whitte*. After we had done our business upon the Island we returned on board, bringing the old Man along with us, who after dinner went ashore in a Canoe that came to attend upon him.

Thursday, February 1st.—P.M. having compleated the Ship with wood, and filled all our water, the Boatswain was sent ashore with a party of Men to cut and make brooms, while others were Employ'd about the rigging, fishing, etc. In the night and the remainder of the day had a Strong Gale from the N.W., attended with very much rain.

Friday, 2nd.—In the P.M. the Gale increased to a Storm, attended with rain and squalls, which came down in Excessive heavy gusts from off the high land, in one of which the hawser we had fast to the shore broke; this obliged us to let go another

Anchor. Towards midnight the Gale moderated, and in the morning it fell Calm, and we took up the Sheet Anchor, looked at the best bower, and moored the ship again to the Shore. The heavy rain, which both fell and Continues to fall hath caused the Brook we water'd at to overflow its banks, and carry away 10 small Casks we had Standing there full of Water, and notwithstanding we searched the whole Cove, we could not find one of them.

Saturday, 3rd.—Winds Northerly, mostly fair weather. Very early in the A.M. sent the Long boat for Sellery to boil for the Ship's Company's breakfast, and as I intended sailing the first opportunity, I went over to the Hippa, which is on the E. side of the sound, and purchased of the inhabitants a quantity of split and half dry'd fish, and such as I could get. While we were at this Hippa, Tupia made farther enquiry about the Lands and Strait, and these people confirm'd everything the old Man had before told us. About noon we took our leave of them, which some seem'd not sorry for; notwithstanding they sold us their fish very freely, there were some few among them who shew'd evident signs of disapprobation.

Sunday, 4th.—Winds Northerly, a fresh breeze and fair weather. In the P.M. after returning from the Hippa, some of us made an Excursion along shore to the Northward, in order to Traffic with the Natives for fish, in which we had no great Success. In the evening got everything off from the Shore, designing to sail in the Morning, but the wind not permitting, we amused ourselves in fishing, collecting of shells, etc.

Monday, 5th.—Winds and weather as Yesterday. In the A.M. Cast off the Hawser, hove short on the Bower, and carried out the Kedge Anchor, in order to warp the Ship out of the Cove. All the dry fish we have been able to procure from the Natives since we came here were this day divided amongst the Ship's Company.

Tuesday, 6th.—At 2 p.m. hove up the Anchor, warped the Ship out of the Cove, and got under Sail, but it soon after falling little wind, and that very Variable, we anchor'd again a little above Motu-ouru. The old man, seeing us under sail, came on board to take his leave of us. Amongst other conversation that passed between him and Tupia, he was asked if either he or any of his Ancestors had ever seen or heard of any Ship like this being in these parts; to which question he answer'd in the Negative, but said that his Ancestors had told him that there came once to this place a small Vessel from a distant part, wherein were 4 Men that were all kill'd upon their landing; and being asked where this distant land lay, he pointed to the North, intimating that it would take up a great many days to go thither. Something of this land was mentioned by the People of the Bay of Islands, who said that some of their Ancestors had been there, but it is very clear to us that there knowledge of this land is only traditionary. Had it Calm all night until 6 o'clock in the Morning, when a light breeze sprung up at N., and we got again under sail; but as the wind proved very unsteady, we got no farther than just without Motu-ouru by noon, but had a fair prospect of getting clear out of the sound, which I shall next describe.

The entrance of this Sound is situated in the Lat. of 41° S., and Long. 184° 45′ W., and near the middle of the S.W. side of the Strait before mentioned. The land off the S.E. head of the Sound called by the Natives, Koamaroo (off which lies 2 Small Islands and some rocks) makes the Narrowest part of the Strait. There stretcheth out 2 Miles N.E. by N. from the N.W. head a reef of rocks, a part of which is above Water. This account of the 2 Heads will be found sufficient guide to know this sound, which is 3 Leagues broad at the Entrance, and lies in S.W. by S.S.W., and W.S.W. at least 10 Leagues, and is a collection of some of the finest harbours in the world, as will evidently appear from the plan which was taken with all the accuracy that time and Circumstances would admit. The Harbour or Cove in which we lay, called Ship Cove, is not inferior to any in the Sound, both in point of Security and other Conveniences. It lies on the W. side of the Sound, and is the Southermost of 3 Coves lying within Motu-ouru, which Island bears E. from it. You may sail into this Cove either between this last mentioned Island and the Isle Hamote, or Long Island, or between Motuouru and the West shore; in this last Channell are 2 Ledges of Rocks 3 fathoms under water, but they may be known by the Sea Weed which grows upon them. In sailing in or out of this sound with little wind attention must be had to the Tides, which flow 9 or 10 o'Clock full and Change of the Moon, and rises and falls upon a Perpendicular 7 or 8 feet. The flood comes in through the Strait from the S.E., and sets strong over upon the N.W. Head and the reef laying off it; the Ebb sets with great rapidity to the S.E. over upon the Islands and Rocks lying off the S.E. Head. The Variation of the Compass from good observations we found to be 13° 5′ E. The land about this Sound is of such height that we first saw it at the distance of 20 Leagues. It consists wholy of high hills and deep Valleys, well stored with a variety of excellent Timber, fit for all purposes except Ships' Masts, for which use it is too hard and heavy. The

Sea abounds with a variety of fish, and in such plenty that, without going out of the Cove where we lay, we caught daily, what with the Sean, Hook, and Lines, quite sufficient for all hands; and upon our first arrival we found plenty of Shags and some few other Wild Fowls, which to people in our situation was fresh food not to be dispised. The Number of Inhabitants hardly exceeds 300 or 400 People. They live dispers'd along the Shore in search of their daily bread, which is fish and firn roots, for they Cultivate no part of the lands. Upon the appearance of danger they Retire to their Hippas or strongholds, for in this situation we found them, and they remain'd so for some days after. This people are poor when compared to many we have seen, and their Canoes are mean and without ornament. The little Traffick we had with them was wholy for fish, for we saw little else they had to dispose of. They had some knowledge of Iron, for they very readily took Nails in Exchange for fish, and sometimes Prefer'd them to anything else, which was more than the people of any other place would do. They were at first fond of Paper, but when they found it spoile by being wet they would not take it; nor did they set much value upon the cloth we got at George's Island, but shew'd an extraordinary fondness for English broad cloth and red Kersey, which shew'd them to be a more sensible People than many of their Neighbours. Besides the common dress, many of these People wore on their Heads round Caps made of Birds' feathers, which were far from being unbecoming.

Wednesday, 7th.—In the P.M. had a light breeze at N. by W., with which we got out of the Sound and stood over to the Eastward, in order to get the Strait well open before the tide of Ebb Made. At 7 the 2 Small Islands which lies off Cape Koamaroo, or the S.E. head of Queen Charlotte's Sound, bore E., distant 4 miles. At this time we had it nearly Calm, and the tide of Ebb making out, we were Carried by the Rapidity of the Stream in a very short time close upon one of the Islands, where we narrowly escaped being dashed against the Rocks by bringing the Ship to an Anchor in 75 fathoms water, with 150 fathoms of Cable out. Even this would not have saved us had not the Tide, which first set S. by E., by meeting with the Island changed its direction to S.E., and carried us past the first point. When the Ship was brought up she was about 2 Cables' Lengths of the Rocks and in the Strength of the Stream, which set S.E. at least 4 or 5 Knotts or miles per Hour. A little before 12 o'Clock the Tide abated, and we began to heave; by 3 the Anchor was at the bows, and having a light breeze at N.W., we made sail over for the Eastern

Shore; but having the tide against us we made but little way. The wind afterwards freshned, and Came to N. and N.E., with which and the tide of Ebb we were in a short time hurried thro' the narrowest part of the Strait, and then stood away for the Southermost land we had in sight, which bore from us S. by W. Over this land appeared a Prodigious high Mountain, the Summit of which was covered with snow. The narrowest part of the Strait we have passed lies between Cape Koamaroo on Tovy-poinammu and Cape Teerawhitte on Aeheinomouwe; the distance from the one to the other I judged to be between 4 and 5 Leagues. And notwithstanding the strength of the Tides, now that is known, there is no great danger in passing it; in the doing of which I am of opinion that the N.E. Shore is the safest to keep upon, for upon that side there appeared no danger, whereas on the other shore there are not only the Islands and Rocks lying off Cape Koamaroo, for I discover'd from the hill from which I had the Second View of the Strait, a Reef of Rocks stretching from these Islands 6 or 7 Miles to the Southward, and lay about 2 or 3 Miles off from the Shore. I shall not pretend here to assign limits to the length of this Strait; a view of the Chart will best illustrate that. About N. 9 Leagues from Cape Teerawhitte, under the same shore, is a high remarkable Island, that may be distinctly seen from Queen Charlotte Sound, from which it lies N.E. by E. ¼ E., distant 6 or 7 Leagues. I have called it *Entry Isle*, and was taken Notice of when we first past it on Sunday 14th of last Month. On the East side of Cape Teerawhitte the Land Trends away S.E. by E. about 8 Leagues, where it ends in a point, and is the Southermost land on Aeheinomouwe, which I have named Cape Pallisser in Honour of my worthy friend Capt. Pallisser. Lat. 41° 34', Long. 183° 58', it bore from us this day at Noon S. 79° E., distant 12 or 13 Leagues, being then in the Latitude of 41° 27' S.; at the same time Cape Koamaroo bore N. ½ E., distant 7 or 8 Leagues. The Southermost point of land in sight bore S. 16° W., and the snowy Mountain S.W. being about 3 Leagues from the shore and abreast of a Deep Bay or inlet called Cloudy bay, in the bottom of which appear'd low land cover'd with tall Trees.

Thursday, 8th.—In the P.M. had a fresh breeze at N.N.E. and Cloudy weather. At 3 o'Clock was abreast of the Southermost point of land set at Noon, which I named Cape Campbell, Lat. 41° 42' S., Long. 184° 47' W., it lies S. by W., distant 12 or 13 Leagues from Cape Koamaroo, and together with Cape Pallisser forms the Southern Entrance of the Straits; the Distance of the one to the other is 13 or 14 Leagues W. by S. and E. by N. From this cape we steer'd along Shore S.W. by S. until 8 o'Clock, when the wind died away; but an Hour after a fresh breeze sprung up at S.W., and we put the Ship right before it. The reason of my doing this was owing to a notion, which some of the Officers had just started, that Aeheinomouwe was not an Island; founding their opinion on a supposition that the land might extend away to the S.E. from between Cape Turnagain and Cape Pallisser, there being a space of about 12 or 13 Leagues which we had not seen. For my own part, I had seen so far into this Sea the first time I discover'd the Strait, together with many other Concurrent testimonies of its being an Island, that no such supposition ever enter'd my thoughts; but being resolved to clear up every doubt that might Arise on so important an Object, I took the opportunity of the Shifting of the Wind to Stand to the Eastward, and accordingly steer'd N.E. by E. all night. At 9 o'Clock A.M. we were abreast of Cape Pallisser, where we found the Land trend away N.E. towards Cape Turnagain, which I reckon'd to be distant from us about 26 Leagues, but as the weather was hazey so that we could not see above 4 or 5 Leagues ahead, we Still kept standing to the N.E., with a light breeze at S. At Noon Cape Pallisser bore N. 72° W., distant 3 Leagues; our Latitude by account is 41° 30′ S.

Friday, 9th.—Gentle breezes at S. and S.S.E., hazey Cloudy weather. In the P.M. 3 Canoes came off to the Ship, wherein were between 30 and 40 of the Natives, who had been pulling after us sometime. It appeared from the behaviour of these people that they had heard of our being upon the Coast, for they came alongside, and some of them on board the Ship, without shewing the least signs of fear. They were no sooner on board than they asked for Nails, but when Nails was given them they asked Tupia what they were, which was plain that they had never seen any before; yet they not only knowed how to ask for them, but know'd what use to make of them, and therefore must have heard of Nails, which they call *Whow*, the name of a Tool among them made generally of bone, which they use as a Chisel in making Holes, etc. These people asking so readily for Nails proves that their connections must extend as far N. as Cape Kidnapper, which is 45 Leagues, for that was the Southermost place on this side the coast we had any Traffick with the Natives; and it is most probable that the inhabitants of Queen Charlotte's sound got the little knowledge they seem'd to have of Iron by the connections they may have with the Teerawhitteans bordering upon them; for we have no reason to think that the inhabitants of any part of this land had the least knowledge of Iron before we came amongst them. After a short stay these people were dismissed with proper presents, and we continued our Course along shore to the N.E. until 11 o'Clock A.M., when the weather clear'd up, and we saw Cape Turnagain bearing N. by E. ¼ E., distant 7 Leagues. I then called the Officers upon deck, and asked them if they were now satisfied that this land was an Island; to which they answer'd in the Affirmative, and we hauled our wind to the Eastward. At Noon our Latitude by observation was 40° 55′ S., which is 21 Miles to the Southward of Cape Turnagain, it bearing N. by E., and Cape Pallisser by this day's run bears S. 43° W., 19 or 20 Leagues.

[DESCRIPTION OF NEW ZEALAND, under date of 31st March.]

Before I quit this land altogether I shall give a short general discription of the Country, its inhabitants, their manners, Customs, etc., in which it is necessary to observe that many things are founded only on Conjecture, for we were too short a time in any one place to learn much of their interior policy, and therefore could only draw conclusions from what we saw at different times.

Part of the East * Coast of this Country was first discovered by Abel Tasman in 1642, and by him called New Zeland; he, however, never landed upon it; probably he was discouraged from it by the Natives killing 3 or 4 of his People at the first and only place he Anchor'd at. This country, which before now was thought to be a part of the imaginary Southern Continent, consists of 2 large Islands, divided from each other by a Strait or Passage of 4 or 5 Leagues broad. They are situated between the Latitude of 34° and 48° S., and between the Long. of 181° and 194° W. from the Meridian of Greenwich. The situation of few parts of the world are better determin'd than these Islands are, being settled by some hundreds of Observations of the Sun and Moon, and one of the Transit of Mercury made by Mr. Green, who was sent out by the Royal Society to observe the Transit of Venus.

The Northermost of these Islands, as I have before observed, is called by the Natives Aeheinomouwe and the Southermost Tovy-Poenammu. The former name, we were well assured, comprehends the whole of the Northern Island; but we were not so well satisfied with the latter whether it comprehended the whole

* An obvious mistake for "West."

of the Southern Islands or only a part of it. This last, according to the Natives of Queen Charlotte's Sound, ought to consist of 2 Islands, one of which at least we were to have sail'd round in a few days; but this was not verify'd by our own Observations. I am inclinable to think that they know'd no more of this land than what came within the Limits of their sight. The Chart which I have drawn will best point out the figure and Extent of these Islands, the situation of the Bays and Harbours they contain, and the lesser Islands lay about them.

And now I have mentioned the Chart, I shall point out such places as are drawn with sufficient accuracy to be depended upon and such as are not, beginning at Cape Pallisser and proceed round Aeheinomouwe by the E. Cape, etc. The Coast between these 2 Capes I believe to be laid down pretty accurate, both in its figure and the Course and distance from point to point; the opportunities I had and the methods I made use on to obtain these requisites were such as could hardly admit of an Error. From the E. Cape to Cape Maria Van Dieman, altho' it cannot be perfectly true, yet it is without any very Material error; some few places, however, must be excepted, and these are very Doubtfull, and are not only here, but in every other part of the Chart pointed out by a Pricked or broken line. From Cape Maria Van Diemen up as high as the Latitude of 36° 15' we seldom were nearer the Shore than from 5 to 8 Leagues, and therefore the line of the Sea Coast may in some places be erroneous. From the above Lat. to nearly the Length of Entry Island we run along and near the shore all the way, and no circumstance occurd that made me liable to commit any Material error. Excepting Capè Teerawhitte, we never came near the Shore between Entry Island and Cape Pallisser, and therefore this part of the coast may be found to differ something from the truth; in Short, I believe that this Island will never be found to differ Materially from the figure I have given it, and that the Coast Affords few or no Harbours but what are either taken notice of in this Journal or in some Measure pointed out in the Chart; but I cannot say so much for Tovy Poenammu. The Season of the Year and Circumstance of the Voyage would not permit me to spend so much time about this Island as I had done at the other, and the blowing weather we frequently met with made it both dangerous and difficult to keep upon the Coast. However, I shall point out the places that may be Erroneous in this as I have done in the other. From Queen Charlotte's sound to Cape Campbell, and as far to the S.W. as the Lat. 43°, will be found to be pretty Accu-

PART OF DESCELIERS' MAP, 1550.
Preserved in the British Museum.

rate; between this Lat. and the Lat. 44° 20' the coast is very Doubtfully laid down, a part of which we hardly, if at all, saw. From this last mentioned Lat. to Cape Saunders we were generally at too great a distance to be Particular, and the weather at the same time was unfavourable. The Coast, as it is laid down from Cape Saunders to Cape South., and even to Cape West., is no doubt in many places very erroneous, as we hardly were ever able to keep near the Shore, and were sometimes blown off altogether. From the West. Cape down to Cape Farewell, and even to Queen Charlotte's sound, will in most places be found to differ not much from the truth.

Mention is likewise made in the Chart of the appearance or aspect of the face of the Country. With respect to Tovy Poenammu, it is for the most part very Mountainous, and to all appearance a barren Country. The people in Queen Charlotte's sound—those that came off to us from under the Snowy Mountain, and the five we saw to the S.W. of Cape Saunders—were all the inhabitants, or Signs of inhabitants, we saw upon the whole Island; but most part of the Sea Coast of Aeheinomouwe, except the S.W. side, is well inhabited; and although it is a hilly, Mountainous Country, yet the very Hills and Mountains are many of them cover'd with wood, and the Soil of the plains and Valleys appear'd to be very rich and fertile, and such as we had an opportunity to examine we found to be so, and not very much incumber'd with woods.

It was the Opinion of every body on board that all sorts of European grain, fruit, Plants, etc., would thrive here; in short, was this Country settled by an industrious people they would very soon be supplied not only with the necessaries, but many of the Luxuries, of Life. The Sea, Bays, and Rivers abound with a great Variety of Excellent Fish, the most of them unknown in England, besides Lobsters, which were allowed by every one to be the best they ever had eat. Oysters and many other sorts of shell fish all Excellent in their kind. Sea and Water Fowls of all sorts are, however, in no great plenty; those known in Europe are Ducks, Shags, Gannets, and Gulls, all of which were Eat by us, and found exceeding good; indeed, hardly anything came Amiss to us that could be Eat by Man. Land fowl are likewise in no great plenty, and all of them, except Quails, are, I believe, unknown in Europe; these are exactly like those we have in England. The Country is certainly destitute of all sorts of beasts, either wild or tame, except dogs and Rats; the former are tame, and lived with the people, who breed and bring them up for no

K

other purpose than to Eat, and rats are so scarce that not only I, but many others in the Ship, never see one. Altho' we have seen some few Seals, and once a Sea Lion upon this Coast, yet I believe they are not only very scarce, but seldom or ever come ashore; for if they did the Natives would certainly find out some Method of Killing them, the Skins of which they no doubt would preserve for Cloathing, as well as the Skins of Dogs and birds, the only Skins we ever saw among them. But they must sometimes get Whales, because many of the Patta Pattoas are made of the bones of some such fish, and an Ornament they wear at their breast (on which they set great Value), which are supposed to be made of the Tooth of a Whale; and yet we know of no method or instrument they have to kill these Animals.

In the woods are plenty of Excellent Timber, fit for all purposes except Ships' Masts; and perhaps upon a Close Examination some might be found not improper for that purpose. There grows spontainously everywhere a kind of very broad-bladed grass, like flags of the Nature of Hemp, of which might be made the very best of Cordage and Canvas, etc. There are 2 sorts, one finer than the other; of these the Natives make Cloth, rope, Lines, netts, etc. Iron Ore is undoubtedly to be found here, particularly about Mercury Bays, where we found great quantities of Iron sand; however, we met with no Ore of any Sort, neither did we ever see any sort of Metal with the Natives. We met with some stones at Admiralty Bay that appear'd to be Mineral in some degree, but Dr. Solander was of Opinion that they contain'd no Sort of Metal. The white stone we saw near the South Cape and some other parts to the Southward, which I took to be a kind of Marble, such as I had seen on one of the Hills I was upon in Mercury Bay, Mr. Banks—I afterwards found—was of Opinion that they were Mineral to the highest degree; he is certainly a much better Judge of these things than I am, and therefore I might be mistaken in my opinion, which was only founded on what I had before seen not only in this Country, but in other parts where I have been; and at the same time I must observe we were not less than 6 or 8 Leagues from the Land, and nearer it was not possible for us at that time to come without running the Ship into Apparent Danger. However, I am no Judge how far Mineral can be distinguished as such; certain it is that in Southern Parts of this Country there are whole Mountains of Nothing Else but stone, some of which, no doubt, may be found to contain Metal.

Should it ever become an object of settling this Country, the

best place for the first fixing of a Colony would be either in the
River Thames or the Bay of Islands; for at either of these places
they would have the advantage of a good Harbour, and by means
of the former an Easy Communication would be had, and settle-
ments might be extended into the inland parts of the Country.
For a very little trouble and Expence small Vessels might be
built in the River proper for the Navigation thereof. It is too
much for me to assert how little water a Vessel ought to draw to
Navigate this River, even so far up as I was in the Boat; this
depends intirely upon the Depth of Water that is upon the bar
or flat that lay before the narrow part of the River, which I had
not an opportunity of making myself acquainted with, but I am
of Opinion that a Vessel that draws not above 10 or 12 feet may
do it with Ease. So far as I have been able to Judge of the
Genius of these People it does not appear to me to be at all
difficult for Strangers to form a settlement in this Country; they
seem to be too much divided among themselves to unite in opposing, by which means, and kind and Gentle usage, the Colonists
would be able to form strong parties among them.

The Natives of this Country are a Strong, rawboned, well made,
Active People, rather above than under the common size, especially the Men; they are of a very dark brown colour, with black
hair, thin black beards, and white teeth, and such as do not dis-
figure their faces by tattowing, etc., have in general very good
features. The Men generally were their Hair long, Coomb'd up,
and tied upon the Crown of their Heads; some of the women
were it long and loose upon their Shoulders, old women especially;
others again were it crop'd short. Their coombs are made some
of bones, and others of Wood; they sometimes Wear them as an
Ornament stuck upright in their Hair. They seem to enjoy a
good state of Health, and many of them live to a good old Age.
Many of the old and some of the Middle aged Men have their
faces mark'd or tattow'd with black, and some few we have seen
who have had their buttocks, thighs, and other parts of their
bodies marked, but this is less common. The figures they mostly
use are spirals, drawn and connected together with great nicety
and judgment. They are so exact in the application of these
Figures that no difference can be found between the one side of
the face and the other, if the whole is marked, for some have only
one side, and some a little on both sides; hardly any but the old
Men have the whole tattow'd. From this I conclude that it takes
up some time, perhaps Years, to finish the Operation, which all
Who have begun may not have perseverance enough to go

through, as the manner in which it must be done must certainly cause intollerable pain, and may be the reason why so few are Marked at all—at least I know of no other. The Women inlay the Colour of Black under the skins of their lips, and both sexes paint their faces and bodies at times more or less with red Oker, mixed with fish Oil.

Their common Cloathing are very much like square Thrumb'd Matts, that are made of rope Yarns, to lay at the doors or passages into houses to clean ones shoes upon. These they tie round their necks, the Thrumb'd side out, and are generally large enough to cover the body as low as the knee; they are made with very little Preparation of the broad Grass plant before mentioned. Beside the Thrumb'd Matts, as I call them, they have other much finer cloathing, made of the same plant after it is bleached and prepared in such a Manner that it is as white and almost as soft as flax, but much stronger. Of this they make pieces of cloth about 5 feet long and 4 broad; these are wove some pieces close and others very open; the former are as stout as the strongest sail cloth, and not unlike it, and yet it is all work'd or made by hand with no other Instrument than a Needle or Bodkin. To one end of every piece is generally work'd a very neat border of different colours of 4 or 6 inches broad, and they very often Trim them with pieces of Dog Skin or birds' feathers. These pieces of Cloth they wear as they do the other, tying one End round their Necks with a piece of string, to one end of which is fixed a Needle or Bodkin made of Bone, by means of which they can easily fasten, or put the string through any part of the Cloth; they sometimes wear pieces of this kind of Cloth round their Middles, as well as over their Shoulders. But this is not common, especially with the Men, who hardly ever wear anything round their Middles, observing no sort of Decency in that respect; neither is it at all uncommon for them to go quite Naked without any one thing about them besides a belt round their waists, to which is generally fastened a small string, which they tye round the prepuse; in this manner I have seen hundreds of them come off to and on board the Ship, but they generally had their proper Cloathing in the boat along with them to put on if it rain'd, etc. The Women, on the other hand, always wear something round their Middle; generally a short, thrumb'd Matt, which reaches as low as their Knees. Sometimes, indeed, I have seen them with only a Bunch of grass or plants before, tyed on with a piece of fine platting made of sweet-scented grass; they likewise wear a piece of cloth over their shoulders as the Men do; this is generally of the Thrum kind. I hardly ever saw a Woman wear a piece of fine cloth. One day at Talago I saw a strong proof that the Women never appear naked, at least before strangers. Some of us hapned to land upon a small Island where several of them were Naked in the Water, gathering of Lobsters and shell fish; as soon as they saw us some of them hid themselves among the Rocks, and the rest remain'd in the Sea until they had made themselves Aprons of the Sea weed; and even then, when they came out to us, they shew'd Manifest signs of Shame, and those who had no method of hiding their nakedness would by no means appear before us.

The Women have all very soft Voices, and may by that alone be known from the Men. The Making of cloth and all other Domestick work is, I believe, wholy done by them, and the more Labourious work, such as building Boats, Houses, Tilling the ground, etc., by the Men. Both men and women wear ornaments at their Ears and about their Necks; these are made of stone, bone, Shells, etc., and are variously shaped; and some I have seen wear human Teeth and finger Nails, and I think we were told that they did belong to their deceased friends. The men, when they are dressed, generally wear 2 or 3 long white feathers stuck upright in their Hair, and at Queen Charlotte's sound many, both men and women, wore Round Caps made of black feathers.

The old men are much respected by the younger, who seem to be govern'd and directed by them on most Occasions. We at first thought that they were united under one head or Chief, whose Name is Teeratu; we first heard of him in Poverty Bay, and he was own'd as Chief by every one we met with from Cape Kidnappers to the Northward and Westward as far as the Bay of Plenty, which is a great extent of territories for an Indian Prince. When we were upon the East Coast they always pointed inland to the Westward for the place of his residence, which I believe to be in the Bay of Plenty, and that those Hippas or fortified Towns are Barrier Towns either for or against him; but most likely the former, and if so, may be the utmost Extent of his Dominions to the Westwards, for at Mercury bay they did not own him as their Prince, nor no where else either to the Westward or Southward, or any other single person; for at whatever place we put in at, or whatever people we spoke with upon the Coast, they generally told us that those that were at a little distance from them were their Enemies; from which it appear'd to me that they were very much divided into Parties, which make war one with another, and all their Actions and behaviour towards us tended to prove that they are a brave, open, war-like people, and void of Treachery.

Whenever we were Visited by any number of them that had never heard or seen anything of us before they generally came off in the largest Canoe they had, some of which will carry 60, 80, or 100 people. They always brought their best Cloaths along with them, which they put on as soon as they came near the Ship. In each Canoe were generally an old Man, in some 2 or 3; these used always to direct the others, were better Cloathed, and generally carried a Halbard or Battle Axe in their hands, or some such like thing that distinguished them from the others. As soon as they came within about a Stone's throw of the Ship they would there lay, and call out, "Haromoi harenta a patoo ago!" that is, "Come here, come ashore with us, and we will kill you with our patoo patoos!" and at the same time would shake them at us. At times they would dance the War dance, and other times they would trade with and talk to us, and Answer such Questions as were put to them with all the Calmness imaginable, and then again begin the War Dance, shaking their Paddles, Patoo patoos, etc., and make strange contortions at the same time. As soon as they had worked themselves up to a proper pitch they would begin to attack us with Stones and darts, and oblige us, wether we would or no, to fire upon them. Musquetry they never regarded unless they felt the Effect; but great Guns they did, because they threw stones farther than they could Comprehend. After they found that our Arms were so much superior to theirs, and that we took no advantage of that superiority, and a little time given them to reflect upon it, they ever after were our very good friends; and we never had an instance of their attempting to surprize or cut off any of our people when they were ashore; opportunity for so doing they must have had at one time or another.

It is hard to account for what we have every where been told, of their Eating their Enemies killed in Battle, which they most Certainly do; Circumstances enough we have seen to Convince us of the Truth of this. Tupia, who holds this custom in great aversion, hath very often Argued with them against it, but they have always as streniously supported it, and never would own that it was wrong. It is reasonable to suppose that men with whom this custom is found, seldom, if ever, give Quarter to those they overcome in battle; and if so, they must fight desperately to the very last. A strong proof of this supposition we had from the People of Queen Charlotte's sound, who told us, but a few days before we Arrived that they had kill'd and Eat a whole boat's crew. Surely a single boat's crew, or at least a part of them, when they found themselves beset and overpowered by numbers would have surrender'd themselves prisoners was such a thing practised among them. The heads of these unfortunate people they preserved as Trophies; 4 or 5 of them they brought off to shew to us, one of which Mr. Banks bought, or rather forced them to sell, for they parted with it with the utmost reluctancy, and afterwards would not so much as let us see one more for any thing we could offer them.

In the Article of Food these People have no great Variety; Fern roots, Dogs, Fish, and wild fowl is their chief diet, for Cocos, Yams, and Sweet Potatoes is not Cultivated every where. They dress their Victuals in the same Manner as the people in the So. Sea Islands; that is, dogs and Large fish they bake in a hole in the ground, and small fish, birds, and Shell fish, etc., they broil on the fire. Fern roots they likewise heat over the fire, then beat them out flat upon a stone with a wooden Mallet; after this they are fit for Eating, in the doing of which they suck out the Moist and Glutinous part, and Spit out the Fibrous parts. These ferns are much like, if not the same as, the mountain ferns in England.

They catch fish with Seans, Hooks and line, but more commonly with hooped netts very ingeniously made; in the middle of these they tic the bait, such as Sea Ears, fish Gutts, etc., then sink the Nett to the bottom with a stone; after it lays there a little time they haul it Gently up, and hardly ever without fish, and very often a large quantity. All their netts are made of the broad Grass plant before mentioned; generally with no other preparation than by Splitting the blade of the plant into threads. Thier fish hooks are made of Crooked pieces of Wood, bones, and Shells.

The people shew great ingenuity and good workmanship in the building and framing their boats or Canoes. They are long and Narrow, and shaped very much like a New England Whale boat. Their large Canoes are, I believe, built wholy for war, and will carry from 40 to 80 or 100 Men with their Arms, etc. I shall give the Dimensions of one which I measured that lay ashore at Tolago. Length 68½ feet, breadth 5 feet, and Depths 3½; the bottom sharp, inclining to a wedge, and was made of 3 pieces hollow'd out to about 2 Inches or an Inch and a half thick, and well fastned together with strong platting. Each side consisted of one Plank only, which was 63 feet long and 10 or 12 Inches broad, and about 1¼ Inch thick, and these were well fitted and lashed to the bottom part. There were a number of Thwarts laid a Cross and Lashed to each Gunwale as a strengthening to the boat. The head ornament projected 5 or 6 feet without the body of the Boat, and was 4 feet high; the Stern Ornament was 14 feet high, about 2 feet broad, and about 1½ inch thick; it was fixed upon the Stern of the Canoe like the Stern post of a Ship upon her Keel. The Ornaments of both head and Stern and the 2 side boards were of Carved Wood, and, in my opinion, neither ill design'd nor executed. All their Canoes are built after this plan, and few are less than 20 feet long. Some of the small ones we have seen with Outriggers, but this is not Common. In their War Canoes they generally have a quantity of Birds' feathers hung in Strings, and tied about the Head and stern as Additional Ornament. They are as various in the heads of their Canoes as we are in those of our Shipping; but what is most Common is an odd Design'd Figure of a man, with as ugly a face as can be conceived, a very large Tongue sticking out of his Mouth, and Large white Eyes made of the Shells of Sea Ears. Their paddles are small, light, and neatly made; they hardly ever make use of sails, at least that we saw, and those they have are but ill contrived, being generally a piece of netting spread between 2 poles, which serve for both Masts and Yards.

The Houses of these People are better calculated for a Cold than a Hot Climate; they are built low, and in the form of an oblong square. The framing is of wood or small sticks, and the sides and Covering of thatch made of long Grass. The door is generally at one end, and no bigger than to admit of a man to Creep in and out; just within the door is the fire place, and over the door, or on one side, is a small hole to let out the Smoke. These houses are 20 or 30 feet long, others not above half as long; this depends upon the largeness of the Family they are to contain, for I believe few familys are without such a House as these, altho' they do not always live in them, especially in the summer season, when many of them live dispers'd up and down in little Temporary Hutts, that are not sufficient to shelter them from the weather.

The Tools which they work with in building their Canoes, Houses, etc., are adzes or Axes, some made of a hard black stone, and others of green Talk. They have Chiszels made of the same, but these are more commonly made of Human Bones. In working small work and carving I believe they use mostly peices of Jasper, breaking small pieces from a large Lump they have for that purpose; as soon as the small peice is blunted they throw it away and take another. To till or turn up the ground they have wooden spades (if I may so call them), made like stout pickets, with a piece of wood tied a Cross near the lower end, to put the foot upon to force them into the Ground. These Green Talk Axes that are whole and good they set much Value upon, and never would part with them for anything we could offer. I offer'd one day for one, One of the best Axes I had in the Ship, besides a number of Other things, but nothing would induce the owner to part with it; from this I infer'd that good ones were scarce among them.

Diversions and Musical instruments they have but few; the latter Consists of 2 or 3 sorts of Trumpets and a small Pipe or Whistle, and the former in singing and Dancing. Their songs are Harmonious enough, but very doleful to a European ear. In most of their dances they appear like mad men, Jumping and Stamping with their feet, making strange Contorsions with every part of the body, and a hideous noise at the same time; and if they happen to be in their Canoes they flourish with great Agility their Paddles, Pattoo Pattoos, various ways, in the doing of which, if there are ever so many boats and People, they all keep time and Motion together to a surprizing degree. It was in this manner that they work themselves to a proper Pitch of Courage before they used to attack us; and it was only from their after behaviour that we could tell whether they were in jest or in Earnest when they gave these *Heivás*, as they call them, of their own accord, especially at our first coming into a place. Their signs of Friendship is the waving the hand or a piece of Cloth, etc.

We were never able to learn with any degree of certainty in what manner they bury their dead; we were generally told that they put them in the ground; if so it must be in some secret or by place, for we never saw the least signs of a burying place in the whole Country. Their Customs of mourning for a friend or relation is by cutting and Scarifying their bodys, particularly their Arms and breasts, in such a manner that the Scars remain indelible, and, I believe, have some signification such as to shew how near related the deceased was to them.

With respect to religion, I believe these people trouble themselves very little about it; they, however, believe that there is one Supream God, whom they call Tawney, and likewise a number of other inferior deities; but whether or no they worship or Pray to either one or the other we know not with any degree of certainty. It is reasonable to suppose that they do, and I believe it; yet I never saw the least Action or thing among them that tended to prove it. They have the same Notions of the Creation of the World, Mankind, etc., as the people of the South Sea Islands have; indeed, many of their notions and Customs are the very same. But nothing is so great a proof of their all having had one Source as their Language, which differ but in a very few words the one from the other, as will appear from the following Specimens,* which I had from Mr. Banks, who understands their Language as well, or better than, any one on board.

There are some small differance in the Language spoke by the Aeheinomoweans and those of Tovy Poenammu; but this differance seem'd to me to be only in the pronunciation, and is no more than what we find between one part of England and another. What is here inserted as a Specimen is that spoke by the People of Aeheinomouwe. What is meant by the So. Sea Islands are those Islands we ourselves Touched at; but I gave it that title because we have always been told that the same Language is universally spoke by all the Islanders, and that this is a Sufficient proof that both they and the New Zelanders have had one Origin or Source, but where this is even time perhaps may never discover.

It certainly is neither to the Southward nor Eastward, for I cannot perswaide myself that ever they came from America; and as to a Southern Continent, I do not believe any such thing exist, unless in a high Latitude. But as the Contrary opinion hath for many Years prevail'd, and may yet prevail, it is necessary I should say something in support of mine more than what will be directly pointed out by the Track of this Ship in those Seas; for from that alone it will evidently appear that there is a large space extending quite to the Tropick in which we were not, or any other before us that we can ever learn for certain. In our route to the Northward, after doubling Cape Horn, when in the Latitude of 40°, we were in the Longitude of 110°; and in our return to the Southward, after leaving Ulietea, when in the same Latitude, we were in the Longitude of 145°; the differance in this Latitude is 35° of Longitude. In the Latitude of 30° the differance of the 2 Tracks is 21°, and that differance continues as low as 20°; but a view of the Chart will best illustrate this.

Here is now room enough for the North Cape of the Southern Continent to extend to the Northward, even to a pretty low Latitude. But what foundation have we for such a supposition? None, that I know of, but this, that it must either be here or no where. Geographers have indeed laid down part of Quiros' dis-

[* Specimens omitted.]

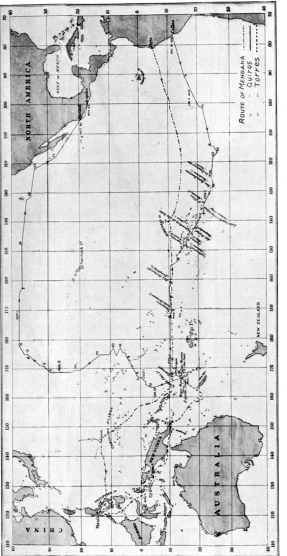

ROUTES OF MENDAÑA 1595, QUIROS 1606, AND TORRES 1606.
Reproduced by permission of the Hakluyt Society.

coveries in this Long., and have told us that he had these signs
of a Continent, a part of which they have Actually laid down in
the Maps; but by what Authority I know not. Quiros, in the
Latitude of 25° or 26° S., discover'd 2 Islands, which, I suppose,
may lay between the Long. of 130° and 140° W. Dalrymple lays
them down in 146° W., and says that Quiros saw to the Southward very large hanging Clouds and a very thick Horizon, with
other known signs of a Continent. Other accounts of their Voyage
says not a word about this; but supposing this to be true, hanging
Clouds and a thick Horizon are certainly no signs of a Continent,
—I have had many proofs to the Contrary in the Course of this
Voyage; neither do I believe that Quiros looked upon such things
as known signs of land, for if he had he certainly would have
stood to the Southward, in order to have satisfied himself before
he had gone to the Northward, for no man seems to have had
discoveries more at heart than he had. Besides this, this was the
ultimate object of his Voyage. If Quiros was in the Latitude of
26° and Longitude 146° W., then I am certain that no part of the
Southern Continent can no where extend so far to the Northward
as the above mentioned Latitude. But the Voyage which seems
to thrust it farthest back in the Long. I am speaking of, viz.,
between 130° and 150° W., is that of Admiral Roggeween, a
Dutchman, made in 1722, who, after leaving Juan Fernandes,
went in search of Davis's Island; but not finding it, he ran 12°
more to the W., and in the Latitude of 28½° discover'd Easter
Island. Dalrymple and some others have laid it down in 27° S.,
and 106° 30' W., and supposes it to be the same as Davis's Isle,
which I think cannot be from the Circumstance of the Voyage;
on the other hand Mr. Pingre, in his Treatise concerning the
Transit of Venus, gives an extract of Roggeween's Voyage and a
map of the So. Seas, wherein he places Easter Island in the Lat.
of 28½° S., and in the Long. of 123° W.; his reason for so doing
may be seen at large in the said Treatise. He likewise lays down
Roggeween's rout through those So. Seas very different from any
other Author I have seen; for after leaving Easter Island he
makes him to steer S.W. to the height of 34° S., and afterwards
W.N.W. If Roggeween really took this rout, then it is not probable that there is any Main land to the Northward of 35° S.
However, Mr. Dalrymple and some Geographers have laid down
Roggeween's track very different from Mr. Pingre. From Easter
Isle they have laid down his Track to the N.W., and afterwards
very little different from that of La Maire; and this I think is not
probable, that a man who, at his own request, was sent to dis-

cover the Southern Continent should take the same rout thro'
these Seas as others had done before who had the same thing in
View; by so doing he must be Morally certain of not finding what
he was in search of, and of course must fail as they had done.
Be this as it may, it is a point that cannot be clear'd up from the
published accounts of the Voyage, which, so far from taking
proper notice of their Longitude, have not even mentioned the
Latitude of several of the Islands they discover'd, so that I find
it impossible to lay down Roggeween's rout with the least degree
of accuracy.

But to return to our own Voyage, which must be allowed to
have set aside the most, if not all, the Arguments and proofs
that have been advanced by different Authors to prove that there
must be a Southern Continent; I mean to the Northward of 40° S.,
for what may lie to the Southward of that Latitude I know not.
Certain it is that we saw no Visible signs of Land, according to
my Opinion, neither in our rout to the Northward, Southward,
or Westward, until a few days before we made the Coast of New
Zeland. It is true we have often seen large flocks of Birds, but
they were generally such as are always seen at a very great distance from land; we likewise saw frequently peices of Sea or Rock
Weed, but how is one to know how far this may drive to Sea.
I am told, and that from undoubted Authority, that there is
Yearly thrown up upon the Coast of Ireland and Scotland a sort
of Beans called Oxe Eyes, which are known to grow no where but
in the Wt. Indies; and yet these 2 places are not less than 1200
Leagues asunder. Was such things found floating upon the Water
in the S. Seas one would hardly be perswaided that one was even
out of sight of Land, so apt are we to Catch at everything that
may at least point out to us the favourite Object we are in persuit
of; and yet experiance shews that we may be as far from it as
ever.

Thus I have given my Opinion freely and without prejudice,
not with any View to discourage any future attempts being made
towards discovering the Southern Continent; on the Contrary, as
I think this Voyage will evidently make it appear that there is
left but a small space to the Northward of 40° where the grand
object can lay. I think it would be a great pity that this thing,
which at times has been the Object of many Ages and Nations,
should not now be wholy be clear'd up; which might very Easily
be done in one Voyage without either much trouble or danger or
fear of Miscarrying, as the Navigator would know where to go to
look for it; but if, after all, no Continent was to be found, then he

might turn his thoughts towards the discovery of those Multitude of Islands which, we are told, lay within the Tropical regions to the South of the Line, and this we have from very good Authority as I have before hinted. This he will always have in his power; for, unless he be directed to search for the Southern lands in a high Latitude, he will not, as we were, be obliged to go farther to the Westward in the Latitude of 40° than 140° or 145° W., and therefore will always have it in his power to go to George's Island, where he will be sure of meeting with refreshments to recruit his people before he sets out upon the discovery of the Islands. But should it be thought proper to send a Ship out upon this Service while Tupia lives, and he to come out in her, in that case she would have a prodidgious Advantage over every ship that hath been upon discoveries in those Seas before; for by means of Tupia, supposing he did not accompany you himself, you would always get people to direct you from Island to Island, and would be sure of meeting with a friendly reception and refreshment at every Island you came to. This would enable the Navigator to make his discoveries the more perfect and Compleat at least it would give him time so to do, for he would not be Obliged to hurry through those Seas thro' any apprehentions of wanting Provisions.

XII. COOK'S DISCOVERY OF EASTERN AUSTRALIA

[SEE Introduction to XI. This extract begins with the Journal entry for the 19th of April, 1770.]

Thursday, 19th.—In the P.M. had fresh Gales at S.S.W. and Cloudy Squally weather, with a large Southerly Sea; at 6 took in the Topsails, and at 1 A.M. brought too and Sounded, but had no ground with 130 fathoms of line. At 5, set the Topsails close reef'd, and 6, saw land extending from N.E. to W., distance 5 or 6 Leagues, having 80 fathoms, fine sandy bottom. We continued standing to the Westward with the Wind at S.S.W. until 8, at which time we got Topgallant Yards a Cross, made all sail, and bore away along shore N.E. for the Eastermost land we had in sight, being at this time in the Latitude of 37° 58' S., and Long. of 210° 39' W. The Southermost point of land we had in sight, which bore from us W. ¼ S., I judged to lay in the Latitude of 38° 0' S. and in the Long. of 211° 7' W. from the Meridian of Greenwich. I have named it Point Hicks, because Lieutenant Hicks was the first who discover'd this Land. To the Southward of this point we could see no land, and yet it was clear in that Quarter, and by our Longitude compared with that of Tasman's, the body of Van Diemen's land ought to have bore due S. from us, and from the soon falling of the Sea after the wind abated I had reason to think it did; but as we did not see it and finding the Coast to trend N.E. and S.W., or rather more to the Westward, makes me Doubtfull whether they are one land or no. However, every one who compares this Journal with that of Tasman's will be as good a judge as I am; but it is necessary to observe that I do not take the Situation of Vandiemen's from the Printed Charts, but from the extract of Tasman's Journal, published by Dirk Rembrantse. At Noon we were in the Latitude of 37° 50' and Long. of 210° 29' W. The extreams of the Land extending from N.W. to E.N.E., a remarkable point, bore N. 20° E., distant 4 Leagues. This point rises to a round hillock very much like the Ramhead going into Plymouth sound, on which account I called it by the same name; Lat. 37° 39', Long. 210° 22' W. The Variation by an Azimuth taken this morning was 8° 7' E. What we have as yet seen of this land appears rather low, and not very hilly, the face of the Country green and Woody, but the Sea shore is all a white Sand.

Friday, 20th.—In the P.M. and most part of the night had a fresh Gale Westerly, with Squalls, attended with Showers of rain. In the A.M. had the Wind at S.W., with Severe weather. At 1 p.m. saw 3 Water Spouts at once; 2 were between us and the Shore, and one at some distance upon our Larboard Quarter. At 6, shortned sail, and brought too for the Night, having 56 fathoms fine sandy bottom. The Northermost land in sight bore N. by E. ½ E., and a small Island lying close to a point on the Main bore W., distant 2 Leagues. This point I have named Cape Howe; it may be known by the Trending of the Coast, which is N. on the one Side and S.W. on the other. Lat. 37° 28' S., Long. 210° 3' W. It may likewise be known by some round hills upon the main just within it. Having brought too with her head off Shore, we at 10 wore, and lay her head in until 4 a.m., at which time we made sail along shore to the Northward. At 6, the Northermost land in sight bore N., being at this time about 4 Leagues from the Land. At Noon we were in the Lat. of 36° 51' S., and Long. of 209° 53' W., and 3 Leagues from the land. Course sail'd along shore since Yesterday at Noon was first N. 52° E., 30 miles, then N. by E. and N. by W., 41 Miles. The weather being clear gave us an opportunity to View the Country, which had a very agreeable and promising aspect, diversified with hills, ridges, plains, and Valleys, with some few small lawns; but for the most part the whole was covered with wood, the hills and ridges rise with a gentle slope; they are not high, neither are there many of them.

Saturday, 21st.—Winds Southerly, a Gentle breeze, and Clear weather, with which we coasted along shore to the Northward. In the P.M. we saw the smoke of fire in several places; a Certain sign that the Country is inhabited. At 6, being about 2 or 3 Leagues from the land, we shortned Sail, and Sounded and found 44 fathoms, a sandy bottom. Stood on under an easey sail until 12 o'Clock, at which time we brought too until 4 A.M., when we made sail, having then 90 fathoms, 5 Leagues from the land. At 6, we were abreast of a pretty high Mountain laying near the shore, which, on account of its figure, I named Mount Dromedary (Lat. 36° 18' S., Long. 209° 55' W.). The shore under the foot of the Mountain forms a point, which I have named Cape Dromedary, over which is a peaked hillock. At this time found the Variation to be 10° 42' E. Between 10 and 11 o'Clock Mr. Green and I took several Observations of the Sun and Moon, the mean result of which gave 209° 17' W. Longitude from the Meridian of Greenwich. By observations made yesterday we were in the Longitude 210° 9′. West 20′ gives 209° 49′ the Longitude of the Ship today at noon per yesterday's observation, the Mean of which and to-day's give 209° 33′ W., by which I fix the Longitude of this Coast. Our Latitude at Noon was 35° 49′ S.; Cape Dromedary bore S. 30° W., distant 12 Leagues. An Open Bay wherein lay 3 or 4 Small Islands, bore N.W. by W., distant 5 or 6 Leagues. This Bay seem'd to be but very little Shelter'd from the Sea Winds, and yet it is the only likely Anchoring place I have yet seen upon the Coast.

Sunday, 22nd.—In the P.M. had a Gentle breeze at S. by W. with which we steer'd along shore N. by E. and N.N.E. at the distance of about 3 Leagues. Saw the smoke of fire in several places near the Sea beach. At 5, we were abreast of a point of land which, on account of its perpendicular Clifts, I call'd Point Upright; Lat. 35° 35′ S.; it bore from us due W., distant 2 Leagues, and in this Situation had 31 fathoms, Sandy bottom. At 6, falling little wind, we hauld off E.N.E.; at this time the Northermost land in sight bore N. by E. ½ E., and at midnight, being in 70 fathoms, we brought too until 4 A.M., at which time we made sail in for the land, and at daylight found ourselves nearly in the same Place we were at 5 o'Clock in the evening, by which it was apparent that we had been drove about 3 Leagues to the Southward by a Tide or Current in the night. After this we steer'd along shore N.N.E., having a Gentle breeze at S.W., and were so near the Shore as to distinguish several people upon the Sea beach. They appeared to be of a very dark or black Colour; but whether this was the real Colour of their skins or the Cloathes they might have on I know not. At Noon we were by Observation in the Latitude of 35° 27′ and Longitude 209° 23′; Cape Dromedary bore S. 28° W., distance 15 Leagues. A remarkable peak'd hill laying inland, the Top of which looked like a Pigeon house, and occasioned my giving it that name, bore N. 32° 33′ W., and a small low Island, laying close under the Shore, bore N.W., distance 2 or 3 Leagues; Variation of the Compass 9° 50′ E. When we first discover'd this Island in the morning I was in hopes, from its appearance, that we should have found Shelter for the Ship behind it; but when we came to approach it near I did not think that there was even security for a Boat to land. But this, I believe, I should have attempted had not the wind come on Shore, after which I did not think it safe to send a Boat from the Ship, as we had a large hollow Sea from the S.E. rowling in upon the land, which beat every where very high upon the

Shore; and this we have had ever since we came upon the Coast. The land near the Sea coast still continues of a moderate height, forming alternately rocky points and Sandy beaches; but inland, between Mount Dromedary and the Pigeon house, are several pretty high Mountains, 2 only of which we saw but what were covered with Trees, and these lay inland behind the Pigeon House, and are remarkably flat a Top, with Steep rocky clifts all round them. As far as we could see the Trees in this Country hath all the appearance of being stout and lofty. For these 2 days past the observed Latitude hath been 12 or 14 Miles to the Southward of the Ship's account given by the Log, which can be owing to nothing but a Current set to the Southward.

Monday, 23rd.—In the P.M. had a Gentle breeze at E., which in the night veer'd to N.E. and N. at ½ past 4 P.M., being about 5 Miles from the Land, we Tack'd and stood off S.E. and E. until 4 A.M., at which time we Tack'd and stood in, being then about 9 or 10 Leagues from the Land. At 8, it fell little wind, and soon after Calm. At Noon we were by Observation in the Latitude of 35° 38′ and about 6 Leagues from the land, Mount Dromedary bearing S. 37° W., distant 17 Leagues, and the Pidgeon house N. 40° W.; in this situation had 74 fathoms.

Tuesday, 24th.—In the P.M. had Variable light Airs and Calms until 6 o'Clock, at which time a breeze sprung up at N. by W.; at this time we had 70 fathoms Water, being about 4 or 5 Leagues from the land, the Pidgeon house bearing N. 40° W., Mount Dromedary S. 30° W., and the Northermost land in sight N. 19° E. Stood to the N.E. until Noon, having a Gentle breeze at N.W., at which time we Tack'd and stood to the Westward, being then, by observation, in the Latitude of 35° 10′ S. and Longitude 208° 51′ W. A point of land which I named Cape St. George, we having discovered it on that Saint's day, bore W., distant 19 Miles, and the Pidgeon house S. 7° W., the Latitude and Longitude of which I found to be 35° 19′ S. and 209° 42′ W. In the morning we found the Variation to be, by the Amplitude, 7° 50′ E., by several Azimuths 7° 54′ E.

Wednesday, 25th.—In the P.M. had a fresh breeze at N.W. until 3 o'Clock, at which time it came to West, and we Tack'd and stood to the Northward. At 5 o'Clock, being about 5 or 6 Leagues from the land, the Pidgeon house bearing W.S.W., distant 9 Leagues, sounded and had 86 fathoms. At 8, being very squally, with lightning, we close reef'd the Topsails and brought too, being then in 120 fathoms. At 3 A.M. made sail again to the Northward, having the advantage of a fresh Gale at S.W. At

L

Noon we were about 3 or 4 Leagues from the land and in the Latitude of 34° 22′ and Longitude 208° 36′ W. Course and distance sail'd since Yesterday noon is N. by E. 49 Miles. In the Course of this day's run we saw the Smoke of fire in several places near the Sea beach. About 2 Leagues to the Northward of Cape St. George the Shore seems to form a bay, which appear'd to be shelter'd from the N.E. winds; but as we had the wind it was not in my power to look into it, and the appearance was not favourable enough to induce me to loose time in beating up to it. The N. point of this bay, on account of its Figure, I nam'd Long Nose. Latitude 45° 4′ S., 8 Leagues to the Northward of this, is a point which I call'd Red Point; some part of the Land about it appeared of that Colour (Latitude 34° 29′ S., Longitude 208° 49′ W.). A little way inland to the N.W. of this point is a round hill, the top of which look'd like the Crown of a Hatt.

Thursday, 26th.—Clear, serene weather. In the P.M. had a light breeze at N.N.W. until 5, at which time it fell Calm, we being then about 3 or 4 Leagues from the land and in 48 fathoms. Variation by Azimuth 8° 48′ E., the extreams of the land from N.E. by N. to S.W. by S. Saw several smokes along shore before dark, and 2 or 3 times a fire. In the Night we lay becalm'd, driving in before the Sea, until one o'Clock A.M., at which time we got a breeze from the land, with which we steer'd N.E., being then in 38 fathoms water. At Noon it fell little Wind, and veer'd to N.E. by N., we being then in the Latitude of 34° 10′ and Longitude 208° 27′ W., and about 5 Leagues from the land, which extended from S. 37° W. to N. ½ E. In this Latitude are some White Clifts, which rise perpendicular from the Sea to a moderate height.

Friday, 27th.—Var'able light Airs between the N.E. and N.W., clear pleasant weather. In the P.M. stood off Shore until 2, then Tackt and Stood in till 6, at which time we tack'd and stood off, being then in 54 fathoms and about 4 or 5 miles from the land, the Extreams of which bore from S., 28° W. to N. 25° 30′ E. At 12 we tack'd and stood in until 4 A.M., then made a Trip off until day light, after which we stood in for the land; in all this time we lost ground, owing a good deal to the Variableness of the winds, for at Noon we were by Observation in the Latitude of 34° 21′ S., Red Point bearing S. 27° W., distant 3 Leagues. In this Situation we were about 4 or 5 Miles from the land, which extended from S. 19° 30′ W. to N. 29° E.

Saturday, 28th.—In the P.M. hoisted out the Pinnace and Yawl in order to attempt a landing, but the Pinnace took in the Water so fast that she was obliged to be hoisted in again to stop her leakes. At this time we saw several people a shore, 4 of whom where carrying a small Boat or Canoe, which we imagin'd they were going to put in to the Water in order to Come off to us; but in this we were mistaken. Being now not above 2 Miles from the Shore Mr. Banks, Dr. Solander, Tupia, and myself put off in the Yawl, and pull'd in for the land to a place where we saw 4 or 5 of the Natives, who took to the Woods as we approached the Shore; which disappointed us in the expectation we had of getting a near View of them, if not to speak to them. But our disappointment was heightened when we found that we no where could effect a landing by reason of the great Surff which beat every where upon the shore. We saw haul'd up upon the beach 3 or 4 small Canoes, which to us appeared not much unlike the Small ones of New Zeland. In the wood were several Trees of the Palm kind, and no under wood; and this was all we were able to observe from the boat, after which we return'd to the Ship about 5 in the evening. At this time it fell Calm, and we were not above a Mile and a half from the Shore, in 11 fathoms, and within some breakers that lay to the Southward of us; but luckily a light breeze came off the Land, which carried us out of danger, and with which we stood to the Northward. At daylight in the morning we discover'd a Bay, which appeared to be tollerably well shelter'd from all winds, into which I resolved to go with the Ship, and with this View sent the Master in the Pinnace to sound the Entrance, while we keept turning up with the Ship, having the wind right out. At noon the Entrance bore N.N.W., distance 1 Mile.

Sunday, *29th*.—In the P.M. wind Southerly and Clear weather, with which we stood into the bay and Anchored under the S. shore about 2 Miles within the Entrance in 5 Fathoms, the S. point bearing S.E. and the N. point E. Saw, as we came in, on both points of the bay, several of the Natives and a few hutts; Men, Women, and Children on the S. Shore abreast of the Ship, to which place I went in the Boats in hopes of speaking with them, accompanied by Mr. Banks, Dr. Solander, and Tupia. As we approached the Shore they all made off, except 2 Men, who seem'd resolved to oppose our landing. As soon as I saw this I order'd the boats to lay upon their Oars, in order to speak to them; but this was to little purpose, for neither us nor Tupia could understand one word they said. We then threw them some nails, beads, etc., a shore, which they took up, and seem'd not ill pleased with, in so much that I thought that they beckon'd to us to come ashore; but in this we were mistaken, for as soon as we put the boat in they again came to oppose us, upon which I fir'd a musquet between the 2, which had no other Effect than to make them retire back, where bundles of their darts lay, and one of them took up a stone and threw at us, which caused my firing a Second Musquet, load with small Shott; and altho' some of the shott struck the man, yet it had no other effect than making him lay hold on a Target. Immediately after this we landed, which we had no sooner done than they throw'd 2 darts at us; this obliged me to fire a third shott, soon after which they both made off, but not in such haste but what we might have taken one; but Mr. Banks being of Opinion that the darts were poisoned, made me cautious how I advanced into the Woods. We found here a few small hutts made of the Bark of Trees, in one of which were 4 or 5 Small Children, with whom we left some strings of beads, etc. A quantity of Darts lay about the Hutts; these we took away with us. 3 Canoes lay upon the beach, the worst I think I ever saw; they were about 12 or 14 feet long, made of one piece of the Bark of a Tree, drawn or tied up at each end, and the middle keept open by means of pieces of Stick by way of Thwarts. After searching for fresh water without success, except a little in a Small hole dug in the Sand, we embarqued, and went over to the N. point of the bay, where in coming in we saw several people; but when we landed now there were nobody to be seen. We found here some fresh Water, which came trinkling down and stood in pools among the rocks; but as this was troublesome to come at I sent a party of men ashore in the morning to the place where we first landed to dig holes in the sand, by which means and a Small stream they found fresh Water sufficient to Water the ship. The String of Beads, etc., we had left with the Children last night were found laying in the Hutts this morning; probably the Natives were afraid to take them away. After breakfast we sent some Empty Casks a shore and a party of men to cut wood, and I went myself in the Pinnace to sound and explore the Bay, in the doing of which I saw some of the Natives; but they all fled at my Approach. I landed in 2 places, one of which the people had just left, as there were small fires and fresh Muscles broiling upon them; here likewise lay Vast heaps of the largest Oyster Shells I ever saw.

Monday, 30th.—As soon as the Wooders and Waterers were come on board to Dinner 10 or 12 of the Natives came to the watering place, and took away their Canoes that lay there, but did not offer to touch any one of our Casks that had been left ashore; and in the afternoon 16 or 18 of them came boldly up to within 100 yards of our people at the watering place, and there made a stand. Mr. Hicks, who was the Officer ashore, did all in his power to intice them to him by offering them presents; but it was to no purpose, all they seem'd to want was for us to be gone. After staying a Short time they went away. They were all Arm'd with Darts and wooden Swords; the darts have each 4 prongs, and pointed with fish bones. Those we have seen seem to be intended more for striking fish than offensive Weapons; neither are they poisoned, as we at first thought. After I had return'd from sounding the Bay I went over to a Cove on the N. side of the Bay, where, in 3 or 4 Hauls with the Sean, we caught about 300 pounds weight of Fish, which I caused to be equally divided among the Ship's Company. In the A.M. I went in the pinnace to sound and explore the N. side of the bay, where I neither met with inhabitants or anything remarkable. Mr. Green took the Sun's Meridian Altitude a little within the S. Entrance of the Bay, which gave the Latitude 34° 0′ S.

Tuesday, May 1st.—Gentle breezes, Northerly. In the P.M. 10 of the Natives again visited the Watering place. I, being on board at this time, went immediately ashore, but before I got there they were going away. I follow'd them alone and unarm'd some distance along shore, but they would not stop until they got farther off than I choose to trust myself. These were armed in the same manner as those that came Yesterday. In the evening I sent some hands to haul the Saine, but they caught but a very few fish. A little after sunrise I found the Variation to be 11° 3′ E. Last night Forby Sutherland, Seaman, departed this Life, and in the A.M. his body was buried ashore at the watering place, which occasioned my calling the south point of this bay after his name. This morning a party of us went ashore to some Hutts, not far from the Watering place, where some of the Natives are daily seen; here we left several articles, such as Cloth, Looking Glasses, Coombs, Beads, Nails, etc.; after this we made an Excursion into the Country, which we found diversified with Woods, Lawns, and Marshes. The woods are free from underwood of every kind, and the trees are at such a distance from one another that the whole Country, or at least great part of it, might be cultivated without being obliged to cut down a single tree. We found the Soil every where, except in the Marshes, to be a light white sand, and produceth a quantity of good Grass, which grows in little Tufts about as big as one can hold in one's hand, and pretty close to one another; in this manner the Surface of the Ground is Coated. In

the woods between the Trees Dr. Solander had a bare sight of a
Small Animal something like a Rabbit, and we found the Dung
of an Animal which must feed upon Grass, and which, we judge,
could not be less than a Deer; we also saw the Track of a Dog, or
some such like Animal. We met with some Hutts and places
where the Natives had been, and at our first setting out one of
them was seen; the others, I suppose, had fled upon our Approach.
I saw some Trees that had been cut down by the Natives with
some sort of a Blunt instrument, and several Trees that were
barqued, the bark of which had been cut by the same instrument;
in many of the Trees, especially the Palms, were cut steps of
about 3 or 4 feet asunder for the conveniency of Climbing them.
We found 2 Sorts of Gum, one sort of which is like Gum Dragon,
and is the same, I suppose, Tasman took for Gum lac; it is
extracted from the largest tree in the Woods.

Wednesday, 2nd.—Between 3 and 4 in the P.M. we return'd out
of the Country, and after Dinner went ashore to the watering
place, where we had not been long before 17 or 18 of the Natives
appeared in sight. In the morning I had sent Mr. Gore, with a
boat, up to the head of the Bay to drudge for Oysters; in his
return to the Ship he and another person came by land, and met
with these people, who followed him at the Distance of 10 or 20
Yards. Whenever Mr. Gore made a stand and faced them they
stood also, and notwithstanding they were all Arm'd, they never
offer'd to Attack him; but after he had parted from them, and
they were met by Dr. Monkhouse and one or 2 more, who, upon
making a Sham retreat, they throw'd 3 darts after them, after
which they began to retire. Dr. Solander, I, and Tupia made all
the haste we could after them, but could not, either by words or
Actions, prevail upon them to come near us. Mr. Gore saw some
up the Bay, who by signs invited him ashore, which he prudently
declined. In the A.M. had the wind in the S.E. with rain, which
prevented me from making an Excursion up the head of the bay
as I intended.

Thursday, 3rd.—Winds at S.E., a Gentle breeze and fair
weather. In the P.M. I made a little excursion along the Sea
Coast to the Southward, accompanied by Mr. Banks and Dr.
Solander. At our first entering the woods we saw 3 of the Natives,
who made off as soon as they saw us; more of them were seen
by others of our people, who likewise made off as soon as they
found they were discover'd. In the A.M. I went in the Pinnace
to the head of the bay, accompanied by Drs. Solander and Monkhouse, in order to Examine the Country, and to try to form some

Connections with the Natives. In our way thither we met with 10 or 12 of them fishing, each in a Small Canoe, who retir'd into Shoald water upon our approach. Others again we saw at the first place we landed at, who took to their Canoes, and fled before we came near them; after this we took Water, and went almost to the head of the inlet, were we landed and Travel'd some distance in land. We found the face of the Country much the same as I have before described, but the land much richer, for instead of sand I found in many places a deep black soil, which we thought was Capable of producing any kind of grain. At present it produceth, besides Timber, as fine Meadow as ever was seen; however, we found it not all like this, some few places were very rocky, but this, I believe, to be uncommon. The stone is sandy, and very proper for building, etc. After we had sufficiently examin'd this part we return'd to the Boat, and seeing some Smoke and Canoes at another part we went thither, in hopes of meeting with the people, but they made off as we approached. There were 6 Canoes and 6 small fires near the Shore, and Muscles roasting upon them, and a few Oysters laying near; from this we conjectured that there had been just 6 people, who had been out each in his Canoe picking up the Shell fish, and come a Shore to eat them, where each had made his fire to dress them by. We tasted of their Cheer, and left them in return Strings of beads, etc. The day being now far spent, we set out on our return to the Ship.

Friday, 4th.—Winds northerly, serene weather. Upon my return to the Ship in the evening I found that none of the Natives had appear'd near the Watering place, but about 20 of them had been fishing in their Canoes at no great distance from us. In the A.M., as the Wind would not permit us to sail, I sent out some parties into the Country to try to form some Connections with the Natives. One of the Midshipmen met with a very old man and Woman and 2 Small Children; they were Close to the Water side, where several more were in their Canoes gathering of Shell fish, and he, being alone, was afraid to make any stay with the 2 old People least he should be discover'd by those in the Canoes. He gave them a bird he had Shott, which they would not Touch; neither did they speak one word, but seem'd to be much frightned. They were quite Naked; even the Woman had nothing to cover her nudities. Dr. Monkhouse and another Man being in the Woods, not far from the watering place, discover'd 6 more of the Natives, who at first seem'd to wait his coming; but as he was going up to them he had a dart thrown at him out of a Tree, which narrowly escaped him. As soon as the fellow had thrown the dart he descended the Tree and made off, and with him all the rest, and these were all that were met with in the Course of this day.

Saturday, 5th.—In the P.M. I went with a party of Men over to the North Shore, and while some hands were hauling the Sean, a party of us made an Excursion of 3 or 4 Miles into the Country, or rather along the Coast. We met with nothing remarkable; great part of the Country for some distance inland from the Sea Coast is mostly a barren heath, diversified with Marshes and Morasses. Upon our return to the Boat we found they had caught a great number of small fish, which the sailors call leather Jackets on account of their having a very thick skin; they are known in the Wt. Indies. I had sent the Yawl in the morning to fish for Sting rays, who returned in the Evening with upwards of four hundred weight; one single one weigh'd 240 lbs. Exclusive of the entrails. In the A.M., as the wind Continued Northerly, I sent the Yawl again a fishing, and I went with a party of Men into the Country, but met with nothing extraordinary.

Sunday, 6th.—In the evening the Yawl return'd from fishing, having Caught 2 Sting rays weighing near 600 lbs. The great quantity of plants Mr. Banks and Dr. Solander found in this place occasioned my giving it the name of Botany Bay.* It is situated in the Lat. of 34° 0′ S., Long. 208° 37′ W. It is capacious, safe, and Commodious; it may be known by the land on the Sea Coast, which is of a pretty even and moderate height, Rather higher than it is inland, with steep rocky Clifts next the Sea, and looks like a long Island lying close under the Shore. The Entrance of the Bay lies about the Middle of this land. In coming from the Southward it is discover'd before you are abreast of it, which you cannot do in coming from the Northward; the entrance is little more than a Quarter of a Mile broad, and lies in W.N.W. To sail into it keep the S. shore on board until within a small bare Island, which lies close under the North Shore. Being within that Island the deepest of Water is on that side, 7, 6, and 5 fathoms a good way up; there is Shoald Water a good way off from the S. shore—from the inner So. Point quite to the head of the harbour; but over towards the N. and N.W. Shore is a Channell of

* In Cook's autograph Journal (now in the Mitchell Library at Sydney) this passage shows several alterations. Cook's original entry was: " The great quantity of this sort of fish [Stingrays] found in this place occasioned my giving it the name of Stingrays Harbour." Then, altering his reason to that given above, he made the name " Botanist Bay "; and on third thoughts altered that to " Botany Bay."

12 or 14 feet at low Water, 3 or 4 Leagues up, to a place where there is 3 or 4 fathoms; but there I found very little fresh Water. We Anchor'd near the South Shore about a Mile within the Entrance for the Conveniency of Sailing with a Southerly wind and the getting of Fresh Water; but I afterwards found a very fine stream of fresh Water on the N. shore in the first sandy Cove within the Island, before which the Ship might lay almost land locked, and wood for fuel may be got everywhere. Although wood is here in great plenty, yet there is very little Variety; the bigest trees are as large or larger than our Oaks in England, and grows a good deal like them, and Yields a reddish Gum; the wood itself is heavy, hard, and black like Lignum Vitae. Another sort that grows tall and Strait something like Pines—the wood of this is hard and Ponderous, and something of the Nature of America live Oak. These 2 are all the Timber trees I met with; there are a few sorts of Shrubs and several Palm Trees and Mangroves about the Head of the Harbour. The Country is woody, low, and flat as far in as we could see, and I believe that the Soil is in general sandy. In the Wood are a variety of very beautiful birds, such as Cocatoos, Lorryquets, Parrots, etc., and crows Exactly like those we have in England. Water fowl is no less plenty about the head of the Harbour, where there is large flats of sand and Mud, on which they seek their food; the most of these were unknown to us, one sort espccially, which was black and white, and as large as a Goose, but most like a Pelican. On the sand and Mud banks are Oysters, Muscles, Cockles, etc., which I believe are the Chief support of the inhabitants, who go into Shoald Water with their little Canoes and peck them out of the sand and Mud with their hands, and sometimes roast and Eat them in the Canoe, having often a fire for that purpose, as I suppose, for I know no other it can be for. The Natives do not appear to be numerous, neither do they seem to live in large bodies, but dispers'd in small parties along by the Water side. Those I saw were about as tall as Europeans, of a very dark brown Colour, but not black, nor had they woolly, frizled hair, but black and lank like ours. No sort of Cloathing or Ornaments were ever seen by any of us upon any of then, or in or about any of their Hutts; from which I conclude that they never wear any. Some that we saw had their faces and bodies painted with a sort of White Paint or Pigment. Altho' I have said that shell fish is their Chief support, yet they catch other sorts of fish, some of which we found roasting on the fire the first time we landed; some of these they strike with Gigs, and others they catch with hook and line; we

have seen them strike fish with gigs, and hooks and lines are found in their Hutts. Sting rays, I believe, they do not eat, because I never saw the least remains of one near any of their Hutts or fire places. However, we could know but very little of their Customs, as we never were able to form any Connections with them; they had not so much as touch'd the things we had left in their Hutts on purpose for them to take away. During our stay in this Harbour I caused the English Colours to be display'd ashore every day, and an inscription to be cut out upon one of the Trees near the Watering place, setting forth the Ship's Name, Date, etc., Having seen everything this place afforded, we, at daylight in the morning, weigh'd with a light breeze at N.W., and put to Sea, and the wind soon after coming to the Southward we steer'd along shore N.N.E., and at Noon we were by observation in the Latitude of 33° 50' S., about 2 or 3 Miles from the Land, and abreast of a Bay, wherein there appear'd to be safe Anchorage, which I called Port Jackson. It lies 3 leagues to the Northward of Botany Bay. I had almost forgot to mention that it is high water in this Bay at the full and change of the Moon about 8 o'Clock, and rises and falls upon a Perpendicular about 4 or 5 feet.

Monday, 7th.—Little wind, Southerly, and Serene pleasant Weather. In the P.M. found the Variation by several Azimuths to be 8° E.; at sunset the Northermost land in sight bore N. 26° E.; and some broken land that appear'd to form a bay bore N. 40° W., distant 4 Leagues. This Bay I named Broken bay, Lat. 33° 36' S. We steer'd along shore N.N.E. all night at the distance of about 3 Leagues from the land, having from 32 to 36 fathoms, hard sandy bottom. A little after sunrise I took several Azimuths with 4 Needles belonging to the Azimuth Compass, the mean result of which gave the Variation of 7° 56' E. At Noon we were by observation in the Lat. of 33° 22' S., and about 3 Leagues from the land, the Northermost part of which in sight bore N. 19° E. Some pretty high land which projected out in 3 bluff Points, and occasioned my calling it Cape 3 Points (Lat. 33° 33' S.), bore S.W., distant 5 Leagues; Long. made from Botany Bay 0° 19' E.

Tuesday, 8th.—Variable Light Airs and Clear weather. In the P.M. saw some smooks upon the Shore, and in the Evening found the Variation to be 8° 25' E.; at this time we were about 2 or 3 Miles from the land, and had 28 fathoms Water. Our situation at Noon was nearly the same as Yesterday, having advanced not one Step to the Northward.

Wednesday, 9th.—Winds northerly; most part a fresh breeze, with which we stood off Shore until 12 at Night. At the distance of 5 Leagues from the land had 70 fathoms, at the distance of 6 Leagues 80 fathoms, which is the Extent of the Soundings, for at the Distance of 10 Leagues off we had no ground with 150 fathoms. Stood in Shore until 8 o'Clock A.M., and hardly fetched Cape Three Points; having a little wind at N.W. by N., we tack'd, and stood off until Noon, at which Time we Tack'd with the wind at N.N.E., being then in the Lat. of 33° 37′ S., Cape Three Points bearing N.W. by W., distance 4 Leagues.

Thursday, 10th.—In the P.M. had the wind at N.E. by N., with which we stood in Shore until near 4 o'Clock, when we Tack'd in 23 fathoms Water, being about a Mile from the land, and as much to the Southward of Cape 3 Points. In the night the wind veer'd to N.W. and W., and in the morning to S.W. Having the advantage of a light Moon, we made the best of our way along shore to the Northward. At Noon we were by observation in the Lat. of 32° 53′ S., and Long. 208° 0′ W., and about 2 Leagues from the land, which extended from N. 41° E. to S. 41° W. A small round rock or Island, laying close under the land, bore S. 82° W., distance 3 or 4 Leagues. At Sunrise in the morning found the Variation to be 8° E. In the Lat. of 33° 2′ S., a little way inland, is a remarkable hill, that is shaped like the Crown of a Hatt, which we past about 9 o'Clock in the forenoon.

Friday, 11th.—Winds Southerly in the day, and in the night Westerly; a Gentle breeze and Clear weather. At 4 P.M. past, at the distance of one Mile, a low rocky point which I named Point Stephens (Lat. 32° 45′); on the N. side of this point is an inlet which I called Port Stephens (Lat. 32° 40′; Long. 207° 51′), that appear'd to me from the Masthead to be shelter'd from all Winds. At the Entrance lay 3 Small Islands, 2 of which are of a Tolerable height, and on the Main, near the shore, are some high hills that make at a distance like Islands. In passing this bay at the distance of 2 or 3 miles from the Shore our soundings were from 33 to 27 fathoms; from which I conjectured that there must be a sufficient depth of Water for Shipping in the bay. We saw several smokes a little way in the Country upon the flat land; by this I did suppose that there were Lagoons which afforded subsistance for the Natives, such as shell-fish, etc., for we as yet know nothing else they have to live upon. At ½ past 5, the Northermost land in sight bore N. 36° E., and Point Stephens S.W., distant 4 Leagues, at which time we took in our Steerings, and run under an Easey sail all night until 4 A.M., when we made all sail; our soundings in the night were from 48 to 62 fathoms, at the distance of between 3 and 4 Leagues from the land. At 8 we were abreast of a high point of Land, which made in 2 Hillocks; this point I called Cape Hawke (Lat. 32° 14' S., Long. 207° 30' W.). It bore from us at this time W. distant 8 Miles, and the same time the Northermost land in sight bore N. 6° E., and appear'd high and like an Island. At Noon this land bore N. 8° E., the Northermost land in sight N. 13° E., and Cape Hawke S. 37° W. Lat. in per Observation 32° 2' S., which was 12 Miles to the Southward of that given by the Log, which I do suppose to be owing to a Current setting that way. Course and distance sail'd since Yesterday at Noon was first N.E. by E., 27 Miles, then N. 10° E., 37 Miles; Long. in 207° 20' W.; Variation per morning Amplitude and Azimuth 9° 10' E.

Saturday, 12*th*.—Winds Southerly, a Gentle breeze in the P.M. As we run along Shore we saw several smokes a little way in land from the Sea, and one upon the Top of a hill, which was the first we have seen upon elevated ground since we have been upon the Coast. At sunset we were in 23 fathoms, and about a League and a half from the land, the Northermost part of which we had in sight bore N. 13° E.; and 3 remarkable large high hills lying Contigious to each other, and not far from the Shore, bore N.N.W. As these Hills bore some resemblance to each other we called them the 3 Brothers. We steer'd N.E. by N. all Night, having from 27 to 67 fathoms, from 2 to 5 and 6 Leagues from the Land, and at day light we steer'd N. for the Northermost land we had in sight. At noon we were 4 Leagues from the Land, and by observation in the Lat. of 31° 18' S., which was 15 miles to the Southward of that given by the Log. Our Course and distance made good since Yesterday noon was N. 24° E., 48 miles. Long. 206° 58' W.; several smokes seen a little way in land.

Sunday, 13*th*.—In the P.M. stood in shore with the Wind at N.E. until 6, at which time we Tack'd, being about 3 or 4 miles from the land, and in 24 fathoms. Stood off shore with a fresh breeze at N. and N.N.W. until midnight, then Tack'd, being in 118 fathoms and 8 Leagues from the Land. At 3 a.m. the wind veer'd to the Westwood, and we Tack'd and stood to the Northward. At noon we were by Observation in the Lat. of 30° 43' S., and Long. 206° 45' W., and about 3 or 4 Leagues from the Land, the Northermost part of which bore from us N. 13° W.; and a point or head land, on which were fires that Caused a great Quantity of smoke, which occasioned my giving it the name of Smokey Cape, bore S.W., distant 4 Leagues; it is moderately high land. Over the pitch of the point is a round hillock; within it 2 others, much higher and larger, and within them very low land (Lat. 30° 51', Long. 206° 5' W.) Besides the smoke seen upon this Cape we saw more in several places along the Coast. The observed Lat. was only 5 Miles to the Southward of the Log.

Monday, 14th.—At the P.M. it fell Calm, and continued so about an hour, when a breeze sprung up at N.E., with which we stood in shore until 6 o'Clock, when, being in 30 fathoms and 3 or 4 Miles from the land, we Tack'd, having the wind at N.N.W. At this time Smoky Cape bore S. ¾° W., distant about 5 Leagues, and the Northermost land in sight N. ¼° E. At 8 we made a Trip in shore for an hour; after this the wind came off Shore, with which we stood along shore to the Northward, having from 30 to 21 fathoms, at the distance of 4 or 5 Miles from the land. At 5 A.M. the Wind veer'd to N., and blow'd a fresh breeze, attended with Squalls and dark cloudy weather. At 8 it began to Thunder and Rain, which lasted about an Hour, and then fell Calm, which gave us an opportunity to sound, and found 86 fathoms, being about 4 or 5 Leagues from the Land; after this we got the wind Southerly, a fresh breeze and fair weather, and we Steer'd N. by W. for the Northermost land we had in sight. At noon we were about 4 Leagues from the Land, and by observation in the Lat. of 30° 22' S., which was 9 Miles to the Southward of that given by the Log. Long. in 206° 39' W., and Course and distance made good since Yesterday Noon N. 16° E., 22 miles; some Tolerable high land near the Shore bore W. As I have not mentioned the aspect of the Country since we left Botany Bay, I shall now describe it as it hath at different times appear'd to us. As we have advanced to the Northward the land hath increased in height, in so much that in this Latitude it may be called a hilly Country; but between this and Botany Bay it is diversified with an agreeable variety of Hills, Ridges, and Valleys, and large plains all Cloathed with wood, which to all appearance is the same as I have before mentioned, as we could discover no Visible alteration in the Soil. Near the shore the land is in general low and Sandy, except the points which are rocky, and over many of them are pretty high hills, which at first rising out of the Water appear like a Island.

Tuesday, 15th.—Fresh Gales at S.W., W. S. W., and S.S.W. In the P.M. had some heavy Squalls, attended with rain and hail, which obliged us to close reef our Topsails. Between 2 and 4 we had some small rocky Islands between us and the land; the Southermost lies in the Lat. of 30° 10', the Northermost in

29° 58′, and about 2 Leagues or more from the land; we sounded, and had 33 fathoms about 12 Miles without this last Island. At 8 we brought too until 10, at which time we made sail under our Topsails. Having the Advantage of the Moon we steer'd along shore N. and N. by E., keeping at the distance of about 3 Leagues from the land having from 30 to 25 fathoms. As soon as it was daylight we made all the sail we could, having the Advantage of a fresh Gale and fair weather. At 9, being about a League from the Land, we saw upon it people and Smoke in Several places. At noon we were by observation in the Lat. of 28° 39′ S., and Long. 206° 27′ W.; Course and distance saild since Yesterday at Noon N. 6° 45′ E., 104 Miles. A Tolerable high point of land bore N.W. by W., distant 3 Miles; this point I named Cape Byron (Lat. 28° 37′ 30″ S., Long. 206° 30′ W.). It may be known by a remarkable sharp peaked Mountain lying in land N.W. by W. from it. From this point the land Trends N. 13° W. Inland it is pretty high and hilly, but near the Shore it is low; to the South-ward of the Point the land is low, and Tolerable level.

Wednesday, 16th.—Winds Southerly, a fresh Gale, with which we steer'd N. along shore until sunset, at which time we dis-cover'd breakers ahead, and on our Larboard bow, being at this time in 20 fathoms, and about 5 miles from the land. Haul'd off E. until 8, at which time we had run 8 Miles, and had increased our Depth of Water to 44 fathoms. We then brought too with her head to the Eastward, and lay on this Tack until 10 o'Clock, when, having increased our Soundings to 78 fathoms, we wore and lay with her head in shore until 5 o'Clock a.m, when we made Sail. At daylight we were surprized by finding ourselves farther to the Southward than we were in the evening, and yet it had blown strong all night Southerly. We now saw the breakers again within us, which we passed at the distance of about 1 League; they lay in the Lat. of 28° 8′ S., and stretch off E. 2 Leagues from a point under which is a small Island; their situa-tion may always be found by the peaked mountain before men-tioned, which bears S.W. by W. from them, and on their account I have named it Mount Warning. It lies 7 or 8 Leagues in land in the Lat. of 28° 22′ S. The land is high and hilly about it, but it is Conspicuous enough to be distinguished from everything else. The point off which these shoals lay I have named Point Danger; to the Northward of it the land, which is low, Trends N.W. by N.; but we soon found that it did not keep that direction long before it turn'd again to the Northward. At Noon we were about 2 Leagues from the land, and by observation in the Lat.

of 27° 46′ ,which was 17 Miles to the Southward of the Log;
Long. 206° 26′ W. Mount Warning bore S. 20° W., distant 14
Leagues; the Northermost land in sight bore N. Our Course and
distance made good since yesterday N. 1° 45′ W., 53 miles.

Thursday, 17th.—Winds Southerly, mostly a fresh breeze, with
which in the P.M. we steer'd along shore N. ¾ E., at the distance
of about 2 Leagues off. Between 4 and 5 we discover'd breakers
on our Larboard bow; our Depth of Water at this time was 37
fathoms. At sunset the Northermost land in sight bore N. by W.,
the breakers N.W. by W., distant 4 Miles, and the Northermost
land set at Noon, which form'd a Point, I named Point Lookout,
bore W., distant 5 or 6 Miles (Lat. 27° 6′). On the North side of
this point the shore forms a wide open bay, which I have named
Morton's Bay, in the Bottom of which the land is so low that I
could but just see it from the Topmast head. The breakers I
have just mentioned lies about 3 or 4 Miles from Point Lookout;
at this time we had a great Sea from the Southward, which broke
prodigious high upon them. Stood on N.N.E. until 8, when, being
past the breakers, and having Deepned our water to 52 fathoms,
we brought too until 12 o'Clock, then made sail to the N.N.E.
At 4 A.M. we sounded, and had 135 fathoms. At daylight I found
that we had in the night got much farther to the Northward and
from the Shore than I expected from the Course we steer'd, for
we were at least 6 or 7 Leagues off, and therefore hauled in N.W.
by W., having the Advantage of a Fresh Gale at S.S.W. The
Northermost land seen last night bore from us at this time S.S.W.,
distant 6 Leagues. This land I named Cape Morton, it being the
North point of the Bay of the same Name (Lat. 26° 56′ S., Long.
206° 28′). From C. Morton the Land Trends away W., further
than we could see, for there is a small space where we could see
no land; some on board where of opinion that there is a River
there because the Sea looked paler than usual. Upon sounding
we found 34 fathoms fine white sandy bottom, which alone is
Sufficient change, the apparent Colour of Sea Water, without the
Assistance of Rivers. The land need only to be low here, as it is
in a Thousand other places upon the Coast, to have made it
impossible for us to have seen it at the distance we were off. Be
this as it may, it was a point that could not be clear'd up as we
had the wind; but should any one be desirous of doing it that
may come after me, this place may always be found by 3 Hills
which lay to the Northward of it in the Lat. of 26° 53′ S. These
hills lay but a little way inland, and not far from Each other;
they are very remarkable on account of their Singular form of

Elivation, which very much resembles Glass Houses, which occasioned my giving them that Name. The Northermost of the 3 is the highest and largest. There are likewise several other peaked hills inland to the Northward of these, but they are not near so remarkable. At Noon we were by Observation in the Lat. of 26° 28′ S., which was 10 Miles to the Northward of the Log; a Circumstance that hath not hapned since we have been upon the Coast before. Our Course and distance run since Yesterday noon was N. by W. 80 Miles, which brought us into the Long. of 206° 46′. At this time we were about 2 or 3 Leagues from the land, and in 24 fathoms Water; a low bluff point, which was the Southern point of an open Sandy bay, bore N. 52° W., distant 3 Leagues, and the Northermost point of land in sight bore N. ¼ E. Several Smokes seen to-day, and some pretty far inland.

Friday, 18*th.*—In steering along shore at the distance of 2 Leagues off our Soundings was from 24 to 32 fathoms Sandy bottom. At 6 P.M. the N. point set at Noon bore N. ¼ W., distant 4 Leagues; at 10 it bore N.W. by W. ½ W., and as we had seen no land to the Northward of it we brought too, not knowing which way to steer, having at this time but little wind, and continued so for the most part of the night. At 2 P.M.* we made sail with the wind at S.W., and at daylight saw the land extending as far as N. ¾ E. The point set last night bore S.W. by W., distant 3 or 4 Leagues; I have named it Double Island Point, on account of its figure (Lat. 25° 58′ S., Long. 206° 48′ W.). The land within this point is of a moderate and pretty equal height, but the point itself is of such an unequal Height that it looks like 2 Small Islands laying under the land; It likewise may be known by the white Clifts on the N. side of it. Here the land trends to the N.W., and forms a large open bay, in the bottom of which the land appear'd to be very low, in so much that we could but just see it from the Deck. In crossing the mouth of this bay our Depth of Water was from 30 to 32 fathoms, a white sandy bottom. At Noon we were about 3 Leagues from the Land, and in the Lat. of 25° 34′ S., Long. 206° 45′ W.; Double Island Point bore S. ¾ W., and the Northermost land in sight N. ¾ E. The land hereabouts, which is of a moderate height, appears more barren than any we have yet seen on this Coast, and the Soil more sandy, there being several large places where nothing else is to be seen; in other places the woods look to be low and Shrubby, nor did we see many signs of inhabitants.

Saturday, 19*th.*—In the P.M. had Variable light Airs, and

* A mistake for A.M.

Calms; in the night had a light breeze from the land, which in the A.M. veer'd to S.W. and S.S.W. In the evening found the Variation to be 8° 36′ E., and in the Morning 8° 20′; as we had but little wind we keept to the Northward all night, having from 23 to 27 fathoms fine sandy bottom, at the Distance of 2 or 3 Leagues from the Land. At Noon we were about 4 Miles from it, and by observation in the Lat. of 25° 4′, and in this situation had but 13 fathoms; the Northermost land in Sight bore N. 21° W., distant 8 Miles; our Course and distance saild since yesterday at Noon was N. 13° 15′ E., 31 Miles.

Sunday, 20th.—Winds Southerly, Gentle breezes. At 10 p.m. we passed, at the distance of 4 Miles, having 17 fathoms, a black bluff head or point of land, on which a number of the Natives were Assembled, which occasioned my naming it Indian Head; Lat. 25° 0′. N. by W., 4 Miles from this head, is another much like it. From this last the land Trends a little more to the Westward, and is low and Sandy next the Sea, for what may be behind it I know not; if land, it must be all low, for we could see no part of it from the Mast head. We saw people in other places besides the one I have mentioned; some Smokes in the day and fires in the Night. Having but little wind all Night, we keept on to the Northward, having from 17 to 34 fathoms, from 4 Miles to 4 Leagues from the Land, the Northermost part of which bore from us at daylight W.S.W., and seem'd to End in a point, from which we discover'd a Reef stretching out to the Northward as far as we could see, being, at this time, in 18 fathoms; for we had, before it was light, hauld our Wind to the Westward, and this course we continued until we had plainly discover'd breakers a long way upon our Lee Bow, which seem'd to Stretch quite home to the land. We then Edged away N.W. and N.N.W., along the E. side of the Shoal, from 2 to 1 Miles off, having regular, even Soundings, from 13 to 7 fathoms; fine sandy bottom. At Noon we were, by Observation, in the Lat. of 24° 26′ S., which was 13 Miles to the Northward of that given by the Log. The extream point of the Shoal we judged to bear about N.W. of us; and the point of land above-mentioned bore S. ¾ W., distant 20 Miles. This point I have named Sandy Cape, on account of 2 very large white Patches of Sand upon it. It is of a height Sufficient to be seen 12 Leagues in Clear weather (Lat. 24° 46′, Long. 206° 51′ W.); from it the Land trends away W.S.W. and S.W. as far as we could see.

Monday, 21st.—In the P.M. we keept along the E. side of the Shoal until 2, when, judging there was water for us over, I sent

M

a Boat a Head to sound, and upon her making the Signal for more than 5 fathoms we hauld our wind and stood over the Tail of it in 6 fathoms. At this time we were in the Lat. of 24° 22′ S., and Sandy Cape bore S. ½ E., distant 8 Leagues; but the Direction of the Shoal is nearest N.N.W. and S.S.E. At this time we had 6 fathoms; the boat which was not above ¼ of a mile to the Southward of us had little more than 5 fathoms. From 6 fathoms we had the next Cast, 13, and then 20 immediately, as fast as the Man could heave the Lead; from this I did suppose that the W. side of the Shoal is pretty steep too, whereas on the other side we had gradual Soundings from 13 to 7 fathoms. This Shoal I called Break Sea Spit, because now we had smooth water, whereas upon the whole Coast to the Southward of it we had always a high Sea or swell from the S.E. At 6, the Land of Sandy Cape extending from S. 17° E. to S. 27° E., distance 8 Leagues; Depth of Water, 23 fathoms, which depth we kept all Night, as we stood to the Westward with light Airs from the Southward; but between 12 and 4 A.M. we had it Calm, after which a Gentle breeze sprung up at S., with which we still kept on upon a Wind to the Westward. At 7 we Saw from the Masthead the Land of Sandy Cape bearing S.E. ½ E., distance 12 or 13 Leagues. At 9, we discover'd from the Mast head land to the Westward, and soon after saw smooke upon it. Our depth of Water was now decreased to 17 fathoms, and by Noon to 13, at which time we were by observation in the Lat. of 24° 28′ S., and about 7 Leagues from the Land, which extended from S. by W. to W.N.W. Long. made from Sandy Cape 0° 45′ W.

For these few days past we have seen at times a sort of Sea fowl we have no where seen before that I remember; they are of the sort called Boobies. Before this day we seldom saw more than 2 or 3 at a time, and only when we were near the land. Last night a small flock of these birds passed the Ship and went away to the N.W., and this morning from ½ an hour before sun rise to half an hour after, flights of them were continually coming from the N.N.W., and flying to the S.S.E., and not one was seen to fly in any other direction. From this we did suppose that there was a Lagoon, River, or Inlet of Shallow Water to the Southward of us, where these birds resorted to in the day to feed, and that not very far to the Northward lay some Island, where they retir'd too in the night.

Tuesday, 22nd.—In the P.M. had a Gentle breeze at S.E., with which we stood in for the land S.W., until 4, when, being in the Lat. of 24° 36′ S., and about 2 Leagues from land, in 9 fathoms, we bore away along shore N.W. by W.; at the same time we could see the land extending to the S.S.E. about 8 Leagues. Near the Sea the land is very low, but inland are some moderately high hills, and the whole appeared to be thickly Cloathed with wood. In running along shore we shoaled our Water from 9 to 7 fathoms, and at one time had but 6 fathoms, which determined me to Anchor for the Night, and accordingly at 8 o'Clock we came too in 8 fathoms, fine gravelly bottom, about 5 miles from the land. This evening we saw a Water Snake, and 2 or 3 evenings ago one lay under the Ship's Stern some time; this was about 1½ Yards in length, and was the first we had seen. At 6 A.M. weighed with a Gentle breeze Southerly, and Steer'd N.W. ¼ W., edging in for the land until we got within 2 Miles of it, having from 7 to 11 fathoms; we then steer'd N.N.W., as the land laid. At Noon we were by Observation in the Lat. of 24° 19′ S.; Long. made from Sandy Cape 1° 14′ W.

Wednesday, 23rd.—Continued our Course alongshore at the distance of about 2 Miles off, having from 12 to 9, 8 and 7 fathoms, until 5 o'Clock, at which time we were abreast of the South point of a Large open Bay, wherein I intended to Anchor. Accordingly we hauld in Close upon a Wind, and sent a boat ahead to sound; after making some Trips we Anchored at 8 o'Clock in 5 fathoms, a Sandy bottom. The South pt. of the bay bore E. ¾ S., distant 2 Miles; the North point N.W. ¼ N., about 2 Miles from the shore, in the bottom of the bay. Last night, some time in the Middle watch, a very extraordinary affair hapned to Mr. Orton, my Clerk. He having been drinking in the evening, some Malicious person or persons in the Ship took Advantage of his being Drunk, and cut off all the Cloaths from off his back; not being satisfied with this, they some time after went into his Cabin and cut off a part of both his Ears as he lay a Sleep in his Bed. The person whom he suspected to have done this was Mr. Magra, one of the Midshipmen; but this did not appear to me. Upon enquiry, however, as I had been told that Magra had once or twice before this in their drunken Frolicks cut off his cloaths, and had been heard to say (as I was told) that if it was not for the Law he would Murder him, these things consider'd, induced me to think that Magra was not Altogether innocent. I therefore for the present dismiss'd him the Quarter deck, and Suspended him from doing any duty in the Ship, he being one of those Gentlemen frequently found on board King's Ships that can very well be spared; besides, it was necessary in me to show my immediate resentment against the person on whom the suspicion fell,

least they should not have stop'd there. With respect to Mr.
Orton, he is a man not without faults; yet from all the inquiry I
could make, it evidently appear'd to me that so far from deserv-
ing such Treatment, he had not designed injuring any person in
the Ship; so that I do—and shall always—look upon him as an
injured man. Some reasons, however, might be given why this
misfortune came upon him, in which he himself was in some
measure to blame; but as this is only conjecture, and would tend
to fix it upon some people in the Ship, whom I would fain believe
would hardly be guilty of such an Action, I shall say nothing
about it, unless I shall hereafter discover the Offenders, which I
shall take every method in my power to do, for I look upon such
proceedings as highly dangerous in such Voyages as this, and the
greatest insult that could be offer'd to my Authority in this Ship,
as I have always been ready to hear and redress every complaint
that have been made against any Person in the Ship.

In the A.M. I went ashore with a party of men in order to
Examine the Country, accompanied by Mr. Banks and the other
Gentlemen; we landed a little within the S. point of the Bay,
where there is a Channel leading into a large Lagoon. The first
thing that I did was to sound and examine the Channell, in which
I found 3 fathoms, until I got about a Mile up it, where I met
with a Shoal, whereon was little more than one fathom; being
over this I had 3 fathoms again. The Entrance into this Channell
lies close to the South point of this Bay, being form'd on the East
by the Shore, and on the West by a large Spit of sand; it is about
a ¼ of a Mile broad, and lies in S. by W.; here is room for a few
Ships to lay very secure, and a small Stream of Fresh Water.
After this I made a little excursion into the Woods while some
hands made 3 or 4 hauls with the Sean, but caught not above a
dozen very small fish. By this time the flood was made, and I
imbarqued in the Boats in order to row up the Lagoon; but in
this I was hindred by meeting everywhere with Shoal Water. As
yet we had seen no people, but saw a great deal of Smook up and
on the West side of the Lagoon, which was all too far off for us to
go by land, excepting one; this we went to and found 10 Small
fires in a very small Compass, and some Cockle Shells laying by
them, but the people were gone. On the windward or S. side of
one of the fires was stuck up a little Bark about a foot and a half
high, and some few pieces lay about in other places; these we
concluded were all the covering they had in the Night, and many
of them, I firmly believe, have not this, but, naked as they are,
sleep in the open air. Tupia, who was with us, observed that they

were Taata Eno's; that is, bad or poor people. The Country is visibly worse than at the last place we were at; the soil is dry and Sandy, and the woods are free from underwoods of every kind; here are of the same sort of Trees as we found in Bottany Harbour, with a few other sorts. One sort, which is by far the most Numerous sort of any in the Woods, grow Something like birch; the Bark at first sight looks like birch bark, but upon examination I found it to be very different, and so I believe is the wood; but this I could not examine, as having no axe or anything with me to cut down a Tree. About the Skirts of the Lagoon grows the true Mangrove, such as are found in the West Indies, and which we have not seen during the Voyage before; here is likewise a sort of a palm Tree, which grows on low, barren, sandy places in the So. Sea Islands. All, or most of the same sort, of Land and Water fowl as we saw at Botany Harbour we saw here; besides these we saw some Bustards, such as we have in England, one of which we kill'd that weighed $17\frac{1}{2}$ pounds, which occasioned my giving this place the Name of Bustard Bay (Lat. 24° 4', Long. 208° 22' W.); we likewise saw some black and white Ducks. Here are plenty of small Oysters sticking to the Rocks, Stones, and Mangrove Trees, and some few other shell fish, such as large Muscles, Pearl Oysters, Cockels, etc. I measured the perpendicular height of the last Tide, and found it to be 8 foot above low water mark, and from the time of low water to-day I found that it must be high Water at the full and Change of the Moon at 8 o'Clock.

Thursday, 24th.—In the P.M. I was employ'd ashore in the Transactions before related; at 4 a.m. we weighed with a Gentle breeze at S., and made sail out of the Bay. In standing out our soundings were from 5 to 15 fathoms; when in this last Depth we were abreast of the North Point, and being daylight we discover'd breakers stretching out from it about N.N.E., 2 or 3 miles; at the Outermost point of them is a Rock just above Water. In passing these rocks at the distance of ½ a mile we had from 15 to 20 fathoms; being past them, we hauld along shore W.N.W. for the farthest land we had in sight. At Noon we were by Observation in the Lat. of 23° 52' S.; the North part of Bustard Bay bore S. 62° E., distance 10 miles, and the Northermost land in sight N. 60° W. Long. in 208° 37' W., distance from the nearest shore 6 Miles; in this situation had 14 fathoms water.

Friday, 25th.—In the P.M. had it calm until 5, when a light breeze sprung up at S.E., and we steer'd N.W. as the land lay until 10, then brought too, having had all along 14 and 15

fathoms. At 5 A.M. we made sail; at daylight the Northermost
point of the Main bore N. 70° W., and soon after we saw more
land making like Islands, bearing N.W. by N.; at 9 we were
abreast of the point, distant from it 1 mile; Depth of Water 14
fathoms. I found this point to lay directly under the Tropic of
Capricorn, and for that reason call it by that Name. Long. 209° 0'
W. It is of a Moderate height, and looks white and barren, and
may be known by some Islands which lie to the N.W. of it, and
some small Rocks one League S.E. from it; on the West side of
the Cape there appeared to be a Lagoon. On the 2 Spits which
form the Entrance were a great Number of Pelicans; at least,
so I call them. The most northermost land we could see bore
from C. Capricorn N. 24° W., and appeared to be an Island; but
the Main land Trended W. by N. ½ N., which Course we steer'd,
having from 15 to 16 fathoms and from 6 to 9, a hard sandy
bottom. At Noon our Lat. by Observation was 23° 24' S.; C.
Capricorn bore S. 60° E., distance 2 Leagues; a small Island N. by
E. 2 Miles. In this Situation had 9 fathoms at the distance of 4
Miles from the Main land, which is here low and Sandy next the
Sea, except the points which are moderately high and rocky; in
land the Country is hilly, and affords but a very indifferent
prospect.

Saturday, 26th.—In the P.M. light breezes at E.S.E., with
which we stood to the N.W. until 4 o'Clock, when it fell calm,
and soon after we Anchored in 12 fathoms. C. Capricorn bearing
S. 54° E., distant 4 Leagues, having the Main land and Islands in
a manner all around us. In the night we found the tide to rise
and fall near 7 feet, and the flood to set to the Westward and Ebb
to the Eastward; which is quite the reverse to what we found it
when at Anchor to the Eastward of Bustard Bay. At 6 a.m. we
weigh'd with the Wind at S., a Gentle breeze, and stood away to
the N.W., between the Outermost range of Islands and the Main
land, leaving several small Islands between us and the Latter,
which we passed Close by. Our soundings was a little irregular,
from 12 to 4 fathoms, which caused me to send a Boat ahead to
sound. At noon we were about 3 Miles from the Main, about the
same distance from the Islands without us; our Lat. by Observation was 23° 7' S. and Long. made from Cape Capricorn 18 Miles
Wt. The Main land in this Lat. is tolerable high and Mountainous; and the Islands which lay off it are the most of them pretty
high and of a Small Circuit, and have more the appearance of
barrenness than fertility. We saw smookes a good way in land,
which makes me think there must be a River, Lagoon, or Inlet

into the Country, and we passed 2 places that had the Appearance of such this morning; but our Depth of Water at that Time was too little to haul in for them, where I might expect to meet with less.

Sunday, 27th.—We had not stood on to the Northward quite an hour before we fell into 3 fathoms, upon which I anchor'd, and Sent away the Master with 2 Boats to sound the Channell, which lay to Leeward of us between the Northermost Island and the Main Land, which appear'd to me to be pretty broad; but I suspected that it was Shoal, and so it was found, for the Master reported to me upon his return that he found in many places only 2½ fathoms, and where we lay at Anchor we had only 16 feet, which was not 2 feet more than the Ship drew. In the Evening the wind veer'd to E.N.E., which gave us an opportunity to stretch 3 or 4 miles back the way we Came before the Wind shifted to S., and obliged us again to Anchor in 6 fathoms. At 5 o'Clock in the A.M. I sent away the Master with 2 Boats to search for a Passage out between the Islands, while the Ship got under sail. As soon as it was light the Signal was made by the Boats of their having found a Passage, upon which we hoisted in the Boats, and made sail to the Northward as the land lay; soundings from 9 to 15 fathoms, having still Some small Islands without us. At noon we were about 2 Leagues from the Main Land, and by observation in the Lat. of 22° 53′ S., Long. made from Cape Capricorn 0° 20′ W. At this time the Northermost point of Land we had in sight bore N.N.W., dist. 10 Miles; this point I named Cape Manyfold, from the Number of high Hills over it; Lat. 22° 43′ S.; it lies N. 20° W., dist. 17 Leagues from C. Capricorn. Between them the shore forms a large Bay, which I call'd Keppel Bay, and the Islands which lay in and Off it are known by the same name; in this Bay is good Anchorage, where there is a sufficient depth of Water; what refreshment it may afford for Shipping I know not. We caught no fish here, withstanding we were at Anchor; it can hardly be doubted but what it afforded fresh Water in several places, as both Mainland and Islands are inhabited. We saw smokes by day and fires in the night upon the Main, and people upon one of the Islands.

Monday, 28th.—Winds at S.S.E., a fresh breeze. At 3 o'Clock in the P.M. we passed Cape Manifold, from which the Land Trends N.N.W. The land of this Cape is tolerable high, and riseth in hills directly from the Sea; it may be known by 3 Islands laying off it, one near the Shore, and the other 2 Eight Miles out at Sea; the one of these is low and flat, and the other high and

round. At 6 o'Clock we shortened sail and brought too; the
Northermost part of the Main we had in sight bore N.W., and
some Islands lying off it bore N. 31° W.; our soundings since Noon
were from 20 to 25 fathoms, and in the Night 30 and 34 fathoms.
At day light we made Sail, Cape Manifold bearing S. by E., distance 8 Leagues, and the Islands set last night in the same directions, distance from us 4 Miles. The farthest point of the Main
bore N. 67° W., distant 22 Miles; but we could see several Islands
to the Northward of this direction. At 9 o'Clock we were abreast
of the above point, which I named Cape Townshend (Lat. 22° 13',
Long. 209° 48' W.); the land of this Cape is of a moderate and
pretty even height, and is more barren than woody. Several
Islands lay to the Northward of it, 4 or 5 Leagues out at Sea.
3 or 4 Leagues to the S.E. the Shore forms a bay, in the bottom
of which there appeared to be an inlet or harbour to the Westward of the Coast, and Trends S.W. ½ S.; and these form a very
large Bay, which turns away to the Eastward, and probably
communicates with the Inlet above mentioned, and by that
Means makes the land of the Cape an Island. As soon as we got
round the Cape we hauld our wind to the Westward in order to
get within the Islands which lay scatter'd up and down in this
bay in great number, and extend out to Sea as far as we could
see from the Masthead; how much farther will hardly be in my
power to determine; they are as Various in their height and Circuit as they are numerous. We had not stood long upon a Wind
before we meet with Shoal Water, and was obliged to Tack about
to avoid it; after which I sent a boat ahead, and we bore away
W. by N., leaving many small Islands, Rocks, and Shoals between
us and the Main, and a number of Large Islands without us;
soundings from 14 to 17 fathoms, Sandy Bottom. A little before
noon the boat made the Signal for meeting with Shoal Water,
upon which we hauld close upon a Wind to the Eastward, but
suddenly fell into 3¼ fathoms water, upon which we immediately
let go an Anchor, and brought the Ship up with all sails standing,
and had then 4 fathoms Coarse sandy bottom. We found here a
strong Tide setting to the N.W. by W. ½ W., at the rate of
between 2 and 3 Miles an Hour, which was what Carried us so
quickly upon the Shoal. Our Latitude by Observation was 22° 8'
S.; C. Townshend bore E. 16° S., distant 13 Miles, and the
Westermost part of the Main Land in sight W. ¾ N., having a
number of Islands in sight all round us.

  Tuesday, 29th.—Fresh gales between the S.S.E. and E.S.E.,
Hazey weather, with some showers of rain. In the P.M., having

sounded about the Ship, and found that their was Sufficient Water for her over the Shoal, we at 3 o'Clock weigh'd and made Sail, and stood to the Westward as the Land lay, having first sent a boat ahead to sound. At 6 we Anchor'd in 10 fathoms, Sandy bottom, about 2 Miles from the Main Land, the Westermost part of which bore W.N.W., having still a Number of Islands in sight a long way without us. At 5 a.m. I sent away the Master with 2 Boats to sound the Entrance of an inlet, which bore from us W., distance about 1 League, into which I intended to go with the Ship to wait a few days, until the Moon increased, and in the meantime to examine the Country. By such time as we had got the Ship under Sail the Boats made the Signal for Anchorage, upon which we stood in with the Ship, and Anchor'd in 5 fathoms, about a League within the Entrance of the inlet, which we judged to be a River running a Good way inland, as I observed the Tides to flow and Ebb something considerable. I had some thoughts of laying the Ship a Shore to Clean her bottom. With this view both the Master and I went to look for a Convenient place for that purpose, and at the same time to look for fresh Water, not one drop of which we could find, but met with several places where a Ship might be laid ashore with safety.

Wednesday, 30th.—In the P.M. I went again in search of Fresh Water, but had no better success than before; wherefore I gave over all thoughts of laying the Ship a Shore, being resolved to spend as little time as possible in a place that was likely to afford us no sort of refreshment. But as I had observed from the Hills the inlet to run a good way in, I thought this a good time to penetrate into the Country to see a little of the inland parts. Accordingly I prepared for making that Excursion in the morning, but the first thing I did was to get upon a pretty high Hill, which is at the N.W. entrance of the inlet, before Sunrise, in order to take a view of the Sea Coast and Islands, etc., that lay off it, and to take their bearings, having the Azimuth Compass with me for that purpose, the Needle of which differ'd from its True position something very considerable, even above 30 degrees, in some places more, and in other less, for I try'd it in several places. I found it differ in itself above 2 points in the space of about 14 feet. The loose stones which lay upon the Ground had no effect upon the Needle; I therefore concluded that it must be owing to Iron Ore upon the Hill, visible signs of which appeared not only here, but in several other places. As soon as I had done here I proceeded up the inlet. I set out with the first of the flood, and long before high water got about 8 Leagues up it; its breadth thus

far was from 2 to 4 or 5 Miles upon a S.W. by S. direction; but
here it spread every way, and formed a Large lake, which communicated with the Sea to the N.W. I not only saw the Sea in
this direction, but found the tide of flood coming strong in from
the N.W. I likewise observ'd an Arm of this Lake extending to
the Eastward, and it is not at all improbable but what it Communicates with the Sea in the bottom of the bay, which lies to the
Westward of Cape Townshend. On the S. side of the Lake is a
ridge of pretty high hills, which I was desirous of going upon; but
as the day was far spent and high water, I was afraid of being be-
wilder'd among the Shoals in the night, which promised to be
none of the best, being already rainy, dirty weather, and therefore I made the best of my way to the Ship. In this little Excursion I saw only 2 people, and those at a distance, and are all that
we have seen in this place, but we have met with several fire
places, and seen smokes at a distance. This inlet, which I have
named Thirsty Sound, by reason we could find no fresh Water,
lies in the Lat. of 22° 05' S., and Long. 210° 24' W.; it may be
known by a Group of small Islands Laying under the shore from
2 to 5 Leagues N.W. from it. There is likewise another Group of
Islands laying right before it between 3 and 4 Leagues out at Sea.
Over each of the Points that form the Entrance is a pretty high,
round Hill; that on the N.W. is a Peninsula, surrounded by the
Sea at high water; the distance from the one to the other is about
2 Miles bold to both Shores. Here is good Anchoring in 7, 6, 5, and
4 fathoms water, and very Convenient places for laying a Ship
ashore, where at Spring Tides the tides doth not rise less than 16
or 18 feet, and flows at full and Change of the Moon about 11
o'Clock. We met with no fresh water, or any other kind of refreshments whatever; we saw 2 Turtle, but caught none, nor no
sort of Fish or wild fowl, except a few small land birds. Here are
the same sort of Water Fowl, as we saw in Botany Bay and like
them, so shy that it is hardly possible to get within shott of them.
No signs of Fertility is to be seen upon the Land; the Soil of the
up lands is mostly a hard, redish Clay, and produceth several sorts
of Trees, such as we have seen before, and some others, and clear
of all underwoods. All the low lands are mostly overrun with
Mangroves, and at Spring tides overflow'd by the Sea; and I believe in the rainy Seasons here are large land floods, as we saw in
many places Gullies, which seem'd to have been made by torrents
of Water coming from the Adjacent hills, besides other Visible
signs of the Water having been a Considerable height above the
Common Spring Tides. Dr. Solander and I was upon a rising

Ground up the inlet, which we thought had at one time or another been overflow'd by the Sea, and if so great part of the Country must at that time been laid under Water. Up in the lakes, or lagoons, I suppose, are shell fish, on which the few Natives subsist. We found Oysters sticking to most of the Rocks upon the Shore, which were so small, as not to be worth the picking off.

Thursday, 31st.—Winds Southerly and S.E.; Dark, Hazey weather, with rain. In the P.M., finding no one inducement to stay longer in this place, we at 6 a.m. Weighed and put to Sea, and stood to the N.W., having the Advantage of a fresh breeze at S.S.E. We keept without the Group of Islands which lay in Shore, and to the N.W. of Thirsty Sound, as there appear'd to be no safe passage between them and the Main; at the same time we had a number of Islands without us extending out to Sea as far as we could see; as we run in this direction our depth of Water was 10, 8 and 9 fathoms. At Noon the N.W. point of Thirsty Sound, which I have named Pier head, bore S. 36° E., distant 5 Leagues; the E. point of the other inlet, which Communicates with the former, as I have before mentioned, bore S. by W., distance 2½ Leagues, the Group of Islands above mentioned laying between us and the point. The farthest part of the Main in sight, on the other side of the inlet, bore N.W.; our Lat. by Observation was 21° 53′ S.

Friday, 1st June.—At ½ an hour After Noon, upon the Boat we had ahead sounding making the Signal for Shoal Water, we hauld our wind to the N.E., having at that time 7 fathoms; the Next cast 5, and then 3, upon which we let go an Anchor, and brought the Ship up. The N.W. point of Thirsty Sound, or Pier Head, bore S.E., distance 6 Leagues, being Midway between the Islands which lies off the E. point of the Western inlet and 3 Small Islands directly without them, it being now the first of the flood which we found to set N.W. by W. ½ W. After having sounded about the Shoal, on which we found not quite 3 fathoms, but without it deep water, we got under Sail, and hauld round the 3 Islands just mentioned, and came to an Anchor under the Lee of them in 15 fathoms, having at this time dark, hazey, rainy weather, which continued until 7 o'Clock a.m., at which time we got again under sail, and stood to the N.W. with a fresh breeze at S.S.E., and fair weather, having the Main land in Sight and a Number of Islands all round us, some of which lay out at Sea as far as we could See. The Western Inlet before mentioned, known in the Chart by the Name of Broad Sound, we had now all open. It is at least 9 or 10 Leagues wide at the Entrance, with several

Islands laying in and before, and I believe Shoals also, for we had very irregular Soundings, from 10 to 5 and 4 fathoms. At Noon we were by Observation in the Lat. of 21° 29′ S., and Long, made from Cape Townshend 59° W. A point of Land, which forms the N.W. Entrance into Broad Sound, bore from us at this Time W., distance 3 Leagues; this Cape I have named Cape Palmerston (Lat. 21° 27′ S., Long. 210° 57′ W.). Between this Cape and Cape Townshend lies the Bay of Inlets, so named from the Number of Inlets, Creeks, etc., in it.

Saturday, 2nd.—Winds at S.S.E. and S.E., a gentle breeze, with which we stood to the N.W. and N.W. by N., as the land lay, under an easey Sail. Having a boat ahead, found our Soundings at first were very irregular, from 9 to 4 fathoms; but afterwards regular, from 9 to 11 fathoms. At 8, being about 2 Leagues from the Main Land, we Anchor'd in 11 fathoms, Sandy bottom. Soon after this we found a Slow Motion of a Tide seting to the Eastward, and rode so until 6, at which time the tide had risen 11 feet; we now got under Sail, and Stood away N.N.W. as the land lay. From the Observations made on the tide last Night it is plain that the flood comes from the N.W.; whereas Yesterday and for Several days before we found it to come from the S.E. This is neither the first nor second time that we have observed the same thing, and in my Opinion easy accounted for; but this I shall do in another place. At sun rise we found the Variation to be 6° 45′ E. In steering along shore between the Island and the Main, at the Distance of 2 Leagues from the Latter, and 3 or 4 from the former, our soundings were Regular, from 12 to 9 fathoms; but about 11 o'Clock we were again embarrassed with Shoal Water, but got clear without letting go an Anchor; we had at one time not quite 3 fathoms. At Noon we were about 2 Leagues from the Main land, and about 4 from the Islands without us; our Lat. by Observation was 20° 56′ S., Long. made from C. Palmerston 16° W.; a pretty high Promontory, which I named Cape Hillsborough, bore W. ½ N., distant 7 Miles. The Main land is here pretty much diversified with Mountains, Hills, plains, and Vallies, and seem'd to be tollerably Cloathed with Wood and Verdure. These Islands, which lay Parrallel with the Coast, and from 5 to 8 or 9 Leagues off, are of Various Extent, both for height and Circuit; hardly any Exceeds 5 Leagues in Circuit, and many again are very small. Besides the Chain of Islands, which lay at a distance from the Coast, there are other Small Ones laying under the Land. Some few smokes were seen on the Main land.

Sunday, 3rd.—Winds between the S. by E. and S.E. A Gentle

breeze and Clear weather. In the P.M. we steer'd along shore N.W. ½ W., at the distance of 2 Leagues from the Main, having 9 and 10 fathoms regular soundings. At sun set the furthest point of the Main Land that we could distinguish as such bore N. 48° W.; to the Northward of this lay some high land, which I took to be an Island, the N.W. point of which bore N. 41° W.; but as I was not sure that there was a passage this way, we at 8 came to an Anchor in 10 fathoms, muddy bottom. 2 hours after this we had a tide setting to the Northward, and at 2 o'clock it had fallen 9 Feet since the time we Anch'd. After this the Tide began to rise, and the flood came from the Northward, which was from the Islands out at Sea, and plainly indicated that there was no passage to the N.W.; but as this did not appear at day light when we got under Sail, and stood away to the N.W. until 8, at this time we discover'd low land, quite a Cross what we took for an Opening between the Main and the Islands, which proved to be a Bay about 5 or 6 Leagues deep. Upon this we hauld our wind to the Eastward round the Northermost point of the Bay, which bore from us at this time N.E. by N., distance 4 Leagues. From this point we found the Main land trend away N. by W. ½ W., and a Strait or Passage between it and a Large Island or Islands laying in a Parrallel direction with the Coast; this passage we Stood into, having the Tide of Ebb in our favour. At Noon we were just within the Entrance, and by observation in the Lat. of 20° 26′ S.; Cape Hillsborough bore S. by E. distant 10 Leagues, and the N. point of the Bay before mentioned bore S. 19° W., distance 4 Miles. This point I have named Cape Conway (Lat. 20° 30′, Long. 211° 28′), and the bay, Repulse Bay, which is formed by these 2 Capes. The greatest and least depth of Water we found in it was 13 and 8 fathoms; every where safe Anchoring, and I believe, was it properly examined, there would be found some good Harbour in it, especially on the N. Side within Cape Conway, for just within the Cape lay 2 or 3 Small Islands, which alone would shelter that side of the Bay from the S.E. and Southerly winds, which seem to be the prevailing or Trade Winds. Among the many Islands that lay upon this Coast there is one more Remarkable than the rest, being of a Small circuit, very high and peaked, and lies E. by S., 10 Miles from Cape Conway at the S. end of the Passage above mention'd.

Monday, 4th.—Winds at S.S.E. and S.E., a Gentle breeze and Clear weather. In the P.M. Steerd thro' the passage, which we found from 3 to 6 or 7 Miles broad, and 8 or 9 Leagues in length, N. by W. ½ W. and S. by E. ½ E. It is form'd by the Main on the

W., and by Islands on the E., one of which is at least 5 Leagues in length. Our Depth of Water in running thro' was between 25 and 20 fathoms; everywhere good Anchorage; indeed the whole passage is one Continued safe Harbour, besides a Number of small Bays and Coves on each side, where ships might lay as it where in a Bason; at least so it appear'd to me, for I did not wait to Examine it, as having been in Port so lately, and being unwilling to loose the benefit of a light Moon. The land, both on the Main and Islands, especially on the former, is Tolerably high, and distinguished by Hills and Vallies, which are diversified with Woods and Lawns that looked green and pleasant. On a Sandy beach upon one of the Islands we saw 2 people and a Canoe, with an outrigger, which appeared to be both Larger and differently built to any we have seen upon the Coast. At 6 we were nearly the length of the N. end of the Passage; the N. Westermost point of the Main in sight bore N. 54° W., and the N. end of the Island N.N.E., having an open Sea between these 2 points. (This passage I have named Whitsundays Passage, as it was discover'd on the day the Church commemorates that Festival, and the Isles which form it Cumberland Isles, in honour of His Royal Highness the Duke of Cumberland). We keept under an Easey sail and the Lead going all Night, having 21, 22, and 23 fathoms, at the distance of 3 Leagues from the land. At daylight A.M. we were abreast of the point above mentioned, which is a lofty promontory; that I named Cape Gloucester (Lat. 19° 57' S., Long. 211° 54' W.). It may be known by an Island which lies out at Sea N. by W. ½ W., 5 or 6 Leagues from it; this I called Holbourn Isle. There are also Islands laying under the Land between it and Whitsundays Passage. On the W. side of the Cape the Land Trends away S.W. and S.S.W., and forms a deep bay. The Sand in the bottom of this bay I could but just see from the Masthead; it is very low, and is a Continuation of the same low land as is at the bottom of Repulse Bay. Without Waiting to look into this bay, which I called Edgcumbe Bay, we continued our Course to the Westward for the Westermost land we had in sight which bore from us W. by N. ¼ N., and appeared very high. At Noon we were about 3 Leagues from the Land, and by observation in the Lat. of 19° 47' S., Cape Gloucester bearing S. 63° E., distant 7½ Leagues.

Tuesday, 5th.—Winds between the South and East, a Gentle breeze, and Serene weather. At 6 a.m. we were abreast of the Western point of Land above mentioned, distant from it 3 Miles, which I have named Cape Upstart, because being surrounded with low land it starts or rises up singley at the first making of it (Lat. 19° 39′ S., Long. 212° 32′ W.); it lies W.N.W. 14 Leagues from Cape Gloucester, and is of a height sufficient to be seen 12 Leagues; but it is not so much of a Promontory as it appears to be, because on each side of it near the Sea is very low land, which is not to be seen unless you are pretty well in with the Shore. Inland are some Tolerable high hills or mountains, which, like the Cape, affords but a very barren prospect. Having past this Cape, we continued standing to the W.N.W. as the land lay, under an easey Sail, having from 16 to 10 fathoms, until 2 o'Clock a.m., when we fell into 7 fathoms, upon which we hauled our wind to the Northward, judging ourselves to be very near the land; as so we found, for at daylight we were little more than 2 Leagues off. What deceived us was the Lowness of the land, which is but very little higher than the Surface of the Sea, but in the Country were some hills. At noon we were in 15 fathoms Water, and about 4 Leagues from the land. Our Lat. by Observation was 19° 12′ S.; Cape Upstart bore 38° 20′ E., distant 12 Leagues. Course and distance sail'd since Yesterday noon N. 48° 45′, 53 Miles. At and before Noon some very large smokes were Seen rise up out of the low land. At sun rise I found the Variation to be 5° 35′ Easterly; at sun set last night the same Needle gave near 9°. This being Close under Cape Upstart, I judged that it was owing to Iron ore or other Magnetical Matter Lodged in the Earth.

Wednesday, 6th.—Light Airs at E.S.E., with which we Steer'd W.N.W. as the Land now lay; Depth of Water 12 and 14 fathoms. At Noon we were by Observation in the Lat. of 19° 1′ S., Long. made from Cape Gloucester 1° 30′ W.; Course and distance saild since Yesterday noon W.N.W., 28 miles. In this situation we had the Mouth of a Bay all open extending from S. ½ E. to S.W. ½ S., distance 2 Leagues. This bay, which I named Cleveland Bay, appeared to be about 5 or 6 Miles in Extent every way. The East point I named Cape Cleveland, and the West, Magnetical Head or Island, as it had much the appearance of an Island; and the Compass did not traverse well when near it. They are both Tolerable high, and so is the Main Land within them, and the whole appeared to have the most rugged, rocky, and barren Surface of any we have yet seen. However, it is not without inhabitants, as we saw smoke in several places in the bottom of the bay. The Northermost land we had in sight at this time bore N.W.; this we took to be an Island or Islands, for we could not trace the Main land farther than W. by N.

Thursday, 7th.—Light Airs between the S. and E., with which we steer'd W.N.W., keeping the Main land on board, the outermost part of which at sun set bore from us W. by N.; but without this lay high land, which we took to be Islands. At daylight A.M. we were the Length of the Eastern part of this Land, which we found to Consist of a Group of Islands laying about 5 Leagues from the Main. We being at this time between the 2, we continued advancing Slowly to the N.W. until noon, at which time we were by observation in the Lat. of 18° 49′, and about 5 Leagues from the Main land, the N.W. part of which bore from us N. by W. ½ W., the Island extending from N. to E.; distance of the nearest 2 Miles. Cape Cleveland bore S. 50° E., distant 18 Leagues. Our Soundings in the Course of this day's Sail were from 14 to 11 fathoms.

Friday, 8th.—Winds at S.S.E. and S.; first part light Airs, the remainder a Gentle breeze. In the P.M. we saw several large smokes upon the Main, some people, Canoes, and, as we thought, Cocoa Nut Trees upon one of the Islands; and, as a few of these Nutts would have been very acceptable to us at this Time, I sent Lieut. Hicks ashore, with whom went Mr. Banks and Dr. Solander, to see what was to be got. In the Meantime we keept Standing in for the Island with the Ship. At 7 they returned on board, having met with Nothing worth Observing. The Trees we saw were a small kind of Cabbage Palms. They heard some of the Natives as they were putting off from the Shore, but saw none. After the Boat was hoisted in we stood away N. by W. for the Northermost land we had in sight, which we were abreast of at 3 o'Clock in the Morning, having passed all the Islands 3 or 4 hours before. This point I have named Point Hillock, on account of its Figure. The Land of this point is Tolerable high, and may be known by a round Hillock or rock that appears to be detached from the point, but I believe it joins to it. Between this Cape and Cape Cleveland the shore forms a Large Bay, which I named Hallifax Bay; before it lay the Groups of Islands before mentioned, and some others nearer the Shore. These Islands shelter the Bay in a manner from all Winds, in which is good Anchorage. The land near the Shore in the bottom of the bay is very low and Woody; but a little way back in the Country is a continued ridge of high land, which appear'd to be barren and rocky. Having passed Point Hillock, we continued standing to the N.N.W. as the land Trended, having the Advantage of a light Moon. At 6 a.m. we were abreast of a point of Land which lies N. by W. ½ W., 11 Miles from Point Hillick; the Land between them is very high, and of a craggy, barren surface. This point I named Cape Sandwich; it may not only be

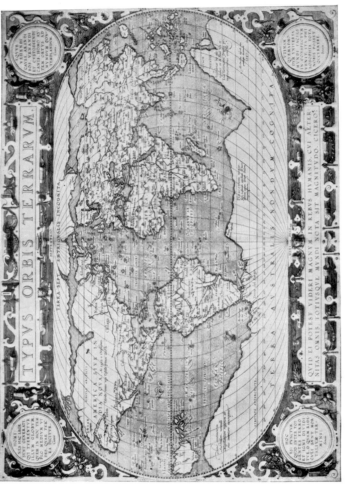

Orbis Terrarum Ortelius.

Chart of 1589, showing the Solomon Islands and Torres Straits 17 years before Torres sailed through them.

known by the high, craggy land over it, but by a small Island which lies E. one Mile from it, and some others about 2 Leagues to the Northward of it. From Cape Sandwich the Land trends W., and afterwards N., and forms a fine, Large Bay, which I called Rockingham Bay; it is well Shelter'd, and affords good Anchorage; at least, so it appear'd to me, for having met with so little encouragement by going ashore that I would not wait to land or examine it further, but continued to range along Shore to the Northward for a parcel of Small Islands laying off the Northern point of the Bay, and, finding a Channel of a Mile broad between the 3 Outermost and those nearer the Shore, we pushed thro'. While we did this we saw on one of the nearest Islands a Number of the Natives collected together, who seem'd to look very attentively upon the Ship; they were quite naked, and of a very Dark Colour, with short hair. At noon we were by observation in the Lat. of 17° 59', and abreast of the N. point of Rockingham Bay, which bore from us W. 2 Miles. This boundry of the Bay is form'd by a Tolerable high Island, known in the Chart by the Name of Dunk Isle; it lays so near the Shore as not to be distinguished from it unless you are well in with the Land. At this time we were in the Long. of 213° 57'. Cape Sandwich bore S. by E. ½ E., distant 19 Miles, and the northermost land in sight N. ¼ W. Our depth of Water in the Course of this day's Sail was not more than 16, nor less than 7, fathoms.

Saturday, 9th.—Winds between the S. and S.E., a Gentle breeze, and Clear weather, with which we steer'd N. by W. as the land lay, the northern extream of which at sunset bore N. 25° W. We keept on our Course under an Easey sail all night, having from 12 to 16 fathoms, at the distance of about 3 or 4 Leagues from the Land. At 6 a.m. we were abreast of Some small Islands, which we called Frankland Isles, that lay about 2 Leagues from the Mainland, the Northern Point of which in sight bore N. by W. ½ W.; but this we afterwards found to be an Island, tolerable high, and about 4 Miles in Circuit. It lies about 2 Miles from the Point on the Main between which we went with the ship, and were in the Middle of the Channell at Noon, and by observation in the Lat. of 16° 55', where we had 20 fathoms of water. The point of land we were now abreast of I called Cape Grafton (Lat. 16° 55′ S., Long. 214° 11′ W.); it is Tolerable high, and so is the whole Coast for 20 Leagues to the southward, and hath a very rocky surface, which is thinly cover'd with wood. In the night we saw several fires along shore, and a little before noon some people.

Sunday, 10th.—After hauling round Cape Grafton we found the

N

land trend away N.W. by W.; 3 Miles to the Westward of the
Cape is a Bay, wherein we Anchor'd, about 2 Miles from the Shore,
in 4 fathoms, owsey bottom. The E. point of the Bay bore S. 74°
E., the West point S. 83° W., and a Low green woody Island laying in the Offing bore N. 35° E. The Island lies N. by E. ½ E., distance 3 or 4 Leagues from Cape Grafton, and is known in the Chart
by the Name of Green Island. As soon as the Ship was brought
to an Anchor I went ashore, accompanied by Mr. Banks and Dr.
Solander; the first thing I did was to look for fresh Water, and
with that View rowed out towards the Cape, because in the bottom of the bay was low Mangrove land, and little probability of
meeting with any there. But the way I went I found 2 Small
streams, which were difficult to get at on account of the Surf and
rocks upon the Shore. As we came round the Cape we saw, in a
sandy Cove, a small stream of Water run over the Beach; but
here I did not go in the boat because I found that it would not be
Easey to land. We hardly advanced anything into the Country,
it being here hilly, which were steep and rocky, and we had not
time to Visit the Low lands, and therefore met with nothing remarkable. My intention was to have stay'd here at least one day,
to have looked into the Country had we met with fresh water convenient, or any other Refreshment; but as we did not, I thought it
would be only spending of time, and loosing as much of a light
Moon to little purpose, and therefore at 12 o'Clock at night we
weighed and stood away to the N.W., having at this time but
little wind, attended with Showers of rain. At 4 the breeze
freshned at S. by E., with fair weather; we continued steering
N.N.W. ½ W. as the Land lay, having 10, 12, and 14 fathoms, at a
distance of 3 Leagues from the Land. At 11 we hauld off N., in
order to get without a Small Low Island which lay about 2
Leagues from the Main; it being about high Water, about the
time we passed it, great part of it lay under water. About 3
Leagues to the N. Westward of this Island close under the Main
land, is another Island, Tolerable high, which bore from us at
Noon N. 55° W., distant 7 or 8 Miles; we being at this time in the
Lat. of 16° 20' S., Cape Grafton bore S. 29° E., distant 40 Miles,
and the Northermost point of Land in Sight N. 20° W., and in this
Situation had 15 fathoms Water. The Shore between Cape Grafton and the above Northern point forms a large but not very deep
Bay, which I named Trinity Bay, after the day on which it was
discover'd; the North point Cape Tribulation, because here began
all our Troubles. Lat. 16° 6' S., Long. 214° 39' W.

Monday, 11*th.*—Wind at E.S.E., with which we steer'd along shore N. by W. at the distance of 3 or 4 Leagues off, having from 14 to 10 and 12 fathoms water. Saw 2 Small Islands in the Offing, which lay in the Lat. of 16° 0′ S., and about 6 or 7 Leagues from the Main. At 6 the Northermost land in sight bore N. by W. ½ W., and 2 low, woody Islands, which some took to be rocks above Water, bore N. ⅓ W. At this time we shortened Sail, and hauld off shore E.N.E. and N.E. by E., close upon a Wind. My intention was to stretch off all Night as well to avoid the danger we saw ahead as to see if any Islands lay in the Offing, especially as we now begun to draw near the Lat. of those discover'd by Quiros, which some Geographers, for what reason I know not, have thought proper to Tack to this land. Having the advantage of a fine breeze of wind, and a Clear Moon light Night in standing off from 6 until near 9 o'Clock, we deepned our Water from 14 to 21 fathoms, when all at once we fell into 12, 10 and 8 fathoms. At this time I had everybody at their Stations to put about and come to an Anchor; but in this I was not so fortunate, for meeting again with Deep Water, I thought there could be no danger in standing on. Before 10 o'Clock we had 20 and 21 fathoms, and Continued in that depth until a few minutes before 11, when we had 17, and before the Man at the Lead could heave another cast, the Ship Struck and stuck fast. Immediately upon this we took in all our Sails, hoisted out the Boats and Sounded round the Ship, and found that we had got upon the S.E. Edge of a reef of Coral Rocks, having in some places round the Ship 3 and 4 fathoms Water, and in other places not quite as many feet, and about a Ship's length from us on the starboard side (the Ship laying with her Head to the N.E.) were 8, 10, and 12 fathoms. As soon as the Long boat was out we struck Yards and Topmast, and carried out the Stream Anchor on our Starboard bow, got the Coasting Anchor and Cable into the Boat, and were going to carry it out in the same way; but upon my sounding the 2nd time round the Ship I found the most water a Stern, and therefore had this Anchor carried out upon the Starboard Quarter, and hove upon it a very great Strain; which was to no purpose, the Ship being quite fast, upon which we went to work to lighten her as fast as possible, which seem'd to be the only means we had left to get her off. As we went ashore about the Top of High Water we not only started water, but threw overboard our Guns, Iron and Stone Ballast, Casks, Hoop Staves, Oil Jarrs, decay'd Stores, etc.; many of these last Articles lay in the way at coming at Heavier. All this time the Ship made little or no Water. At 11 a.m., being high Water as we thought, we try'd to heave her off without

Success, she not being afloat by a foot or more, notwithstanding by this time we had thrown overboard 40 or 50 Tuns weight. As this was not found sufficient we continued to Lighten her by every method we could think off; as the Tide fell the ship began to make Water as much as two pumps could free: at Noon she lay with 3 or 4 Streakes heel to Starboard; Lat. observed 15° 45′ S.

Tuesday, 12th.—Fortunately we had little wind, fine weather, and a smooth Sea, all this 24 Hours, which in the P.M. gave us an Opportunity to carry out the 2 Bower Anchors, one on the Starboard Quarter, and the other right a Stern, got Blocks and Tackles upon the Cables, brought the falls in abaft and hove taught. By this time it was 5 o'Clock p.m.; the tide we observed now begun to rise, and the leak increased upon us, which obliged us to set the 3rd Pump to work, as we should have done the 4th also, but could not make it work. At 9 the Ship righted, and the Leak gain'd upon the Pumps considerably. This was an alarming and, I may say, terrible circumstance, and threatened immediate destruction to us. However, I resolv'd to risque all, and heave her off in case it was practical, and accordingly turn'd as many hands to the Capstan and Windlass as could be spared from the Pumps; and about 20 Minutes past 10 o'Clock the Ship floated, and we hove her into Deep Water, having at this time 3 feet 9 Inches Water in the hold. This done I sent the Long Boat to take up the Stream Anchor, got the Anchor, but lost the Cable among the Rocks; after this turn'd all hands to the Pumps, the Leak increasing upon us.

A mistake soon after hapned, which for the first time caused fear to approach upon every man in the Ship. The man that attended the well took the Depth of water above the Ceiling; he, being relieved by another who did not know in what manner the former had sounded, took the Depth of water from the outside plank, the difference being 16 or 18 inches, and made it appear that the leak had gained this upon the pumps in a short time. This mistake was no sooner cleared up than it acted upon every man like a Charm; they redoubled their vigour, insomuch that before 8 o'clock in the morning they gained considerably upon the leak. We now hove up the Best Bower, but found it impossible to save the small Bower, so cut it away at a whole Cable; got up the Fore topmast and Foreyard, warped the Ship to the S.E., and at 11 got under sail, and stood in for the land, with a light breeze at E.S.E. Some hands employ'd sewing Oakham, Wool, etc., into a Lower Steering Sail to fother the Ship; others employ'd at the Pumps, which still gain'd upon the Leak.

Wednesday, 13th.—In the P.M. had light Airs at E.S.E., with which we keept edging in for the Land. Got up the Maintopmast and Mainyard, and having got the Sail ready for fothering of the Ship, we put it over under the Starboard Fore Chains, where we suspected the Ship had suffer'd most, and soon after the Leak decreased, so as to be keept clear with one Pump with ease; this fortunate circumstance gave new life to every one on board.

It is much easier to conceive than to discribe the satisfaction felt by everybody on this occasion. But a few minutes before our utmost Wishes were to get hold of some place upon the Main, or an island, to run the Ship ashore, where out of her Materials we might build a Vessel to carry us to the East Indies; no sooner were we made sencible that the outward application to the Ship's bottom had taken effect, than the field of every Man's hopes inlarged, so that we thought of nothing but ranging along Shore in search of a Harbour, when we could repair the Damages we had sustained. In justice to the Ship's Company, I must say that no men ever behaved better than they have done on this occasion; animated by the behaviour of every Gentleman on board, every man seem'd to have a just sence of the Danger we were in, and exerted himself to the very utmost. The Ledge of Rocks, or Shoal, we have been upon, lies in the Lat. of 15° 45′, and about 6 or 7 Leagues from the Main land; but this is not the only Shoal that lay upon this part of the Coast, especially to the Northward, and one which we saw to the Southward, the tail of which we passed over when we had the uneven Soundings 2 hours before we Struck. A part of this Shoal is always above Water, and looks to be white Sand; part of the one we were upon was dry at low Water, and in that place consists of Sand and stones, but every where else Coral Rocks. At 6 we Anch'd in 17 fathoms, about 5 or 6 Leagues from the land, and one from the Shoal. At this time the Ship made about 15 Inches Water per hour. At 6 a.m. weigh'd and stood to the N.W., edging in for the land, having a Gentle breeze at S.S.E. At 9 we past close without 2 small low Islands, laying in the Lat. of 15° 41′, and about 4 Leagues from the Main; I have named them Hope Islands, because we were always in hopes of being able to reach these Islands. At Noon we were about 3 Leagues from the Land, and in the Lat. of 15° 37′ S.; the Northermost part of the Main in sight bore N. 30° W., and the above Islands extending from S. 30° E. to S. 40° E. In this situation had 12 fathoms water and several sandbanks without us. The Leak now decreaseth, but for fear it should break out again we got the Sail ready fill'd for fothering; the manner this is done is thus: We Mix Oacham and Wool together (but Oacham alone would do), and chop it up Small, and then stick it loosely by hand-fulls all over the Sail, and throw over it Sheep dung or other filth. Horse Dung for this purpose is the best. The Sail thus prepared is hauld under the Ship's bottom by ropes, and if the place of the Leak is uncertain, it must be hauld from one part of her bottom to another until one finds the place where it takes effect. While the Sail is under the Ship the Oacham, etc., is washed off, and part of it carried along with the water into the Leak, and in part stops up the hole. Mr. Monkhouse, one of my Midshipmen, was once in a Merchant Ship which Sprung a Leak, and made 48 Inches Water per hour; but by this means was brought home from Virginia to London with only her proper crew; to him I gave the direction of this, who executed it very much to my satisfaction.

Thursday, 14th.—P.M., had a Gentle breeze at S.E. by E. Sent the Master, with 2 Boats as well, to sound ahead of the Ship, as to look out for a Harbour where we could repair our defects, and put the Ship on a proper Trim, both of which she now very much wanted. At 3 saw an Opening that had the appearance of a Harbour; stood off and on while the Boats were examining it, who found that there was not a sufficient depth of Water for the Ship. By this time it was almost sun set, and seeing many shoals about us we Anch'd in 4 fathoms about 2 miles from the Shore, the Main land extending from N. ½ E. to S. by E. ½ E. At 8 o'clock the Pinnace, in which was one of the Mates, return'd on board, and reported that they had found a good Harbour about 2 Leagues to leeward. In consequence of this information we, at 6 a.m., weigh'd and run down to it, first sending 2 Boats ahead to lay upon the Shoals that lay in our way; and notwithstanding this precaution, we were once in 3 fathoms with the Ship. Having pass'd these Shoals, the Boats were sent to lay in the Channell leading into the Harbour. By this time it begun to blow in so much that the Ship would not work, having missed stays Twice; and being entangled among Shoals, I was afraid of being drove to Leeward before the Boats could place themselves, and therefore Anch'd in 4 fathoms about a Mile from the Shore, and then made the Signal for the Boats to come on board, after which I went myself and Buoy'd the Channell, which I found very narrow, and the Harbour much smaller than I had been told, but very convenient for our Purpose. At Noon Lat. observed 15° 26' S. (Note.—This day I restor'd Mr. Magra to his Duty, as I did not find him guilty of the crimes laid to his charge.)

Friday, 15th.—A fresh Gale at S.E. and Cloudy weather, attended with Showers of Rain. In the Night, as it blow'd too fresh to break the Ship loose to run into the Harbour, we got down the Topgallant yards, unbent the Mainsail, and some of the Small sails; got down the Fore-topgallent mast, and the Jibb Boom and Spritsailyard in, intending to lighten the Ship Forward as much as possible, in order to lay her ashore to come at the Leak.

Saturday, 16th.—Strong Gales at S.E., and Cloudy, hazey weather, with Showers of Rain. At 6 o'Clock in the A.M. it moderated a little, and we hove short, intending to get under sail, but was obliged to desist, and veer away again; some people were seen ashore to-day.

Sunday, 17th.—Most part strong Gales at S.E., with some heavy showers of rain in the P.M. At 6 a.m., being pretty moderate, we weigh'd and run into the Harbour, in doing of which we run the Ship ashore Twice. The first time she went off without much Trouble, but the Second time she Stuck fast; but this was of no consequence any farther than giving us a little trouble, and was no more than what I expected as we had the wind. While the Ship lay fast we got down the Foreyard, Foretopmast, booms, etc., overboard, and made a raft of them alongside.

Monday, 18th.—Fresh Gales and Cloudy, with Showers of Rain. At 1 p.m. the Ship floated, and we warped her into the Harbour, and moor'd her alongside of a Steep Beach on the S. side; got the Anchors, Cables, and all the Hawsers ashore. In the A.M. made a Stage from the Ship to the Shore, Erected 2 Tents, one for the Sick, and the other for the Stores and Provisions; Landed all the empty Casks and part of the Provisions, and sent a boat to haul the Sean, which return'd without Success.

Tuesday, 19th.—Fresh Gales at S.E. and Cloudy weather, with frequent showers of Rain. P.M., landed all the Provisions and Part of the Stores; got the Sick ashore, which amounted, at this time, to 8 or 9, afflicted with different disorders, but none very dangerously ill. This afternoon I went upon one of the highest Hills over the Harbour, from which I had a perfect View of the inlet or River, and adjacent country, which afforded but a very indifferent prospect. The Low lands near the River is all over run with Mangroves, among which the salt water flows every tide, and the high land appear'd to be barren and Stoney. A.M., got the 4 remaining Guns out of the hold, and mounted them on the Quarter Deck; got a spare Anchor and Stock ashore, and the remaining part of the Stores and ballast that were in the Hold; set up the Forge, and set the Armourer and his Mate to work to make Nails, etc., to repair the ship.

Wednesday, 20th.—Winds at S.E., a fresh breeze, Fore and Middle parts rainy, the Latter fair. This day got out all the Officers' stores and the ground Tier of Water, having now nothing in the Fore and Main Hold But the Coals and a little Stone ballast.

Thursday, 21st.—P.M. landed the Powder, got out the stone ballast, wood, etc., which brought the Ship's Draught of water to 8 ft. 10 in. Forward, and 13 feet abaft. This, I thought, by trimming the Coals aft, would be sufficient, as I find the Tides will rise and fall upon a Perpendicular 8 feet at Spring tides; but after the Coals was trimm'd away from over the Leak we Could hear the Water come Gushing in a little abaft the Foremast about 3 feet from her Keel. This determin'd me to clear the hold intirely; accordingly very early in the Morning we went to work to get out the Coals, which was Employment for all hands.

Friday, 22nd.—Winds at S.E., fair weather. At 4 p.m., having got out most of the coals, cast loose the Ship's moorings, and warped her a little higher up the Harbour to a place I had pitched upon to lay her ashore to stop the Leak; draught of Water Forward 7 ft. 9 in., and abaft 13 ft. 6 in. At 8, being high water, hauld her bow close ashore, but Keept her stern afloat, because I was afraid of Neaping her, and yet it was necessary to lay the whole of her as near the ground as possible. At 2 a.m. the Tide left her, which gave us an Opportunity to Examine the Leak, which we found to be at her Floor Heads, a little before the Starboard Fore Chains; here the Rocks had made their way thro' 4 planks, quite to, and even into the Timbers, and wounded 3 more. The manner these planks were damaged—or cut out, as I may say—is hardly credible; scarce a Splinter was to be seen, but the whole was cut away as if it had been done by the Hands of Man with a blunt-edge Tool. Fortunately for us the Timbers in this place were very close; other wise it would have been impossible to have saved the Ship, and even as it was it appeared very extraordinary that she made no more water than what she did. A large peice of Coral rock was sticking in one Hole, and several peices of the Fothering, small stones, etc., had made its way in, and lodged between the Timbers, which had stopped the Water from forcing its way in in great Quantities. Part of the Sheathing was gone from under the Larboard bow, part of the False Kiel was gone, and the remainder in such a Shatter'd Condition that we should be much better off if it was gone also; her Forefoot and some part of her Main Kiel was also damaged, but not Materially. What damage she may have received abaft we could not see, but believe

not much, as the Ship makes but little water, while the Tide
Keeps below the Leak forward. At 9 the Carpenters went to work
upon the Ship, while the Armourers were buisy making Bolts,
Nails, etc.

Saturday, 23rd.—Winds S. Easterly, a fresh Gale and fair
weather. Carpenters employed Shifting the Damaged planks as
long as the tide would permit them to work. At low water P.M.
we examined the Ship's bottom under the Starboard side, she
being dry as far aft as the After part of the Fore Chains; we could
not find that she had received any other damage on this side but
what has been mentioned. In the morning I sent 3 Men into the
Country to shoot Pidgeons, as some of these birds had been seen
flying about; in the evening they return'd with about ½ a Dozen.
One of the Men saw an Animal something less than a greyhound;
it was of a Mouse Colour, very slender made, and swift of Foot.
A.M., I sent a Boat to haul the Sean, who return'd at noon, having
made 3 Hauls and caught only 3 fish; and yet we see them in
plenty Jumping about the harbour, but can find no method of
catching them.

Sunday, 24th.—Winds and weather as Yesterday. P.M., the
Carpenters finished the Starboard side, and at 9 heeld the Ship
the other way, and hauld her off about 2 feet for fear of Neaping.
In the A.M., they went to work repairing the Sheathing under the
Larboard bow, where we found 2 planks cut about half thro'.
Early in the morning I sent a party of Men into the Country under
the direction of Lt. Gore to seek for refreshments; they return'd
about noon with a few Palm Cabbages and a Bunch or 2 of wild
Plantains; these last were much Smaller than any I had ever seen,
and the Pulp full of small Stones; otherwise they were well tasted.
I saw myself this morning, a little way from the Ship, one of the
Animals before spoke off; it was of a light mouse Colour and the
full size of a Grey Hound, and shaped in every respect like one,
with a long tail, which it carried like a Grey hound; in short, I
should have taken it for a wild dog but for its walking or running,
in which it jump'd like a Hare or Deer. Another of them was
seen to-day by some of our people, who saw the first; they described
them as having very small Legs, and the print of the Feet like
that of a Goat; but this I could not see myself because the ground
the one I saw was upon was too hard, and the length of the Grass
hindered my seeing its legs.

Monday, 25th.—At low water in the P.M. While the Carpenters
were buisey in repairing the Sheathing and plank under the Larboard bow I got people to go under the Ship's bottom, to examine

all her Larboard side, she only being dry Forward, but abaft were 9 feet water. They found part of the Sheathing off abreast of the Mainmast about her floor heads, and a part of one plank a little damaged. There were 3 people who went down, who all agreed in the same Story; the Master was one, who was positive that she had received no Material Damage besides the loss of the Sheathing. This alone will be sufficient to let the worm into her bottom, which may prove of bad consequence. However, we must run all risque, for I know of no method to remedy this but by heaving her down, which would be a work of Emence Labour and time, if not impractical in our present situation.

The Carpenters continued hard at work under her bottom until put off by the Tide in the evening, and the morning Tide did not Ebb out far enough to permit them to work upon her, for here we have only one Tolerable low and high tide in 24 hours. A.M., a party of Men were employ'd ashore filling water, while others were employ'd overhauling the rigging.

Tuesday, 26th.—Fair weather, a S.E. wind, and a fresh Gale; at low Water P.M. the Carpenters finished under the Larboard bow and every other place the tide would permit them to come at. Lashed some Casks under the Ship's bows in order to help to float her, and at high water in the Night attempted to heave her off, but could not, she not being afloat partly owing to some of the Casks not holding that were Lashed under her. A.M., employed getting more Casks ready for the same purpose; but I am much afraid that we shall not be able to float her now the Tides are Taking off.

Wednesday, 27th.—A fresh breeze of Wind at S.E. and Cloudy weather. P.M., lashed 38 empty Butts under the Ship's Bottom in order to float her off, which proved ineffectual, and therefore gave over all hopes of getting her off until the Next spring tides. At daylight we got a Considerable weight of sundry Articles from Aft forward to ease the Ship; the Armourer at work at the Forge repairing Iron work, etc., Carpenters caulking and Stocking one of the Spare Anchors, Seamen employ'd filling of Water and overhauling the rigging, and I went in the pinnace up the Harbour, and made several hauls with the Sean, but caught only between 20 and 30 lb. of fish, which were given to the sick and such as were weak and Ailing.

Thursday, 28th.—Fresh breezes and Cloudy. All hands employ'd as Yesterday.

Friday, 29th.—Wind and weather as Yesterday, and the employment of the People the same, Lieut. Gore having been 4 or 5 miles in the Country, where he met with nothing remarkable. He saw the footsteps of Men, and likewise those of 3 or 4 sorts of wild beasts, but saw neither Man nor beast. Some others of our people who were out Yesterday on the N. side of the River met with a place where the Natives have just been, as their fires was then burning; but they saw nobody, nor have we seen one since we have been in port. In these excursions we found some Wild Yamms or Cocos growing in the Swampy grounds, and this Afternoon I sent a Party of Men to gather some. The Tops we found made good greens, and eat exceedingly well when Boil'd, but the roots were so bad that few besides myself could eat them. This night Mr. Green and I observ'd an Emersion of Jupiter's first Satellite, which hapned at 2 hrs. 58′ 53″ in the A.M.; the same Emersion hapnd at Greenwich, according to Calculation, on the 30th at 5 hrs. 17′ 43″ A.M. The differance is 14 hrs. 18′ 50″, equal to 214° 42′ 30″ of Long., which this place is West of Greenwich, and its Lat. 15° 26′ S. A.M., I sent some hands in a Boat up the River to haul the Sean, while the rest were employ'd about the rigging and sundry other Dutys.

Saturday, 30th.—Moderate breezes at S.E., and clear serene weather. P.M., the Boat returned from hauling the Sean, having caught as much fish as came to a pound and a half a Man. A.M., I sent her again to haul the Sean, and some hands to gather greens, while others were employ'd about the rigging, etc., etc. I likewise sent some of the Young Gentlemen to take a plan of the Harbour, and went myself upon the hill, which is near the South point to take a view of the Sea. At this time it was low water, and I saw what gave me no small uneasiness, which were a Number of Sand Banks and Shoals laying all along the Coast; the innermost lay about 3 or 4 Miles from the Shore, and the outermost extended off to Sea as far as I could see without my glass, some just appeared above water. The only hopes I have of getting clear of them is to the Northward, where there seems to be a Passage, for as the wind blows constantly from the S.E., we shall find it difficult, if not impractical, to return to the Southward.

Sunday, 1st July.—Gentle breezes at S.E., and Cloudy weather, with some Gentle Showers in the morning. P.M., the People return'd from hauling the Sean, having caught as much fish as came to 2½ pound per Man, no one on board having more than another. The few Greens we got I caused to be boil'd among the pease, and makes a very good Mess, which, together with the fish, is a great refreshment to the people. A.M., a party of Men, one from each Mess, went again a fishing, and all the rest I gave leave to go into the Country, knowing that there was no danger from the Natives. To-day at Noon the Thermometer in the Shade rose to 87°, which is 2 or 3 Degrees higher than it hath been on any day before in this place.

Monday, 2nd.—Do. weather. P.M., the fishing-party caught as much fish as came to 2 lbs. a Man. Those that were in the Country met with nothing New. Early in the A.M. I sent the Master in the pinnace out of the Harbour, to sound about the Shoals in the Offing and to look for a Channel to the Northward. At this time we had a breeze of wind from the land, which continued till about 9. What makes me mention this is, that it is the first Land breeze we have had since we have been in this River. At low water lashed empty Casks under the Ship's bows, being in some hopes of floating her the next high Water, and sent some hands a fishing, while others were employ'd in refitting the Ship.

Tuesday, 3rd.—Winds at S.E., Fore and Middle part gentle breeze, the remainder a fresh gale. In the evening the fishing Party return'd, having got as much as came to 2 lbs. a Man. At high water we attempted to heave the Ship off, but did not succeed. At Noon the Master return'd, and reported he had found a passage out to Sea between the Shoals, which passage lies out E.N.E. or E. by N. from the River mouth. He found these Shoals to Consist of Coral Rocks; he landed upon one, which drys at low Water, where he found very large cockles and a Variety of other Shell fish, a quantity of which he brought away with him. He told me that he was 5 Leagues out at Sea, having at that distance 21 fathoms water, and judg'd himself to be without all the Shoals, which I very much doubted. After this he came in Shore, and Stood to the Northward, where he met with a Number of Shoals laying a little distance from the Shore. About 9 in the evening he landed in a Bay about 3 Leagues to the Northward of this Place, where he disturbed some of the Natives, whom he supposed to be at supper: they all fled upon his approach, and Left him some fresh Sea Eggs, and a fire ready lighted behind them; but there was neither House nor Hut near. Although these Shoals lay within sight of the Coast, and abound very much with Shell fish and other small fish, which are to be caught at Low water in holes in the Rocks, yet the Natives never visit them, for if they did we must have seen of these Large shells on shore about their fire places. The reason I do suppose is, that they have no Boats that they dare Venture so far out at Sea in.

Wednesday, 4th.—Strong gales at S.E. and fair weather. P.M., the fishing party return'd with the usual success; at High water hove the ship Afloat. A.M., employ'd trimming her upon an even Kiel, intending to lay her ashore once more, to come at her bottom under the Larboard Main Chains.

Thursday, 5th.—Strong breezes at S.E. and fair weather. P.M. Warped the Ship over, and at high Water laid her ashore on the Sandbank on the S. side of the River, for I was afraid to lay her broad side to the Shore where she lay before, because the ground lies upon too great a decent, and she hath already received some Damage by laying there these last Niep Tides, at least she still makes water.

Friday, 6th.—Do. weather. At low water in the P.M. had hardly 4 feet water under the Ship; yet could not repair the Sheathing that was beat off, the place being all under water. One of the Carpenter's crew, a Man I could trust, went down and Examin'd it, and found 3 Streakes of the Sheathing gone about 7 or 8 feet long, and the Main Plank a little rubbed; this account agrees with the report of the Master and others that were under her bottom before. The Carpenter, who I look upon to be well skill'd in his profession, and a good judge in these matters, was of Opinion that this was of little consequence; and as I found that it would be difficult, if not impractical, for us to get under her bottom to repair it, I resolved to spend no more time about it. Accordingly at high water hove her off, and moor'd her alongside the beach, where the Stores, etc. lay, and in the A.M. got everything in readiness for taking them on board, and at the same time got on board 8 Tuns of water, and stow'd in the ground Tier in the after Hold. In the Morning Mr. Banks and Lt. Gore with 3 Men went in a small Boat up the Harbour, with a View to stay 2 or 3 days to try to kill some of the Animals we have seen about this place.

Saturday, 7th.—Fresh breezes at S.E. and fair weather. Employ'd getting on board Coals, Ballast, etc., and caulking the Ship; a work that could not be done while she lay aground. The Armourer and his Mate are Still employ'd at the Forge making and repairing sundry Articles in the Iron way.

Sunday, 8th.—Gentle breezes and S.E., and clear weather. Early I sent the Master in a Boat out to Sea to sound again about the Shoals, because the account he had given of the Channell before mentioned was to me by no means Satisfactory; likewise sent some hands to haul the Sean, who caught near 80 lbs. of fish; the rest of the people I gave leave to go into the Country.

Monday, 9th.—In the Day Do. Winds, but in the night Calm. P.M. Mr. Gore and Mr. Banks return'd, having met with nothing remarkable; they were about 3 or 4 Leagues up in the Country without finding hardly any Variation either in the Soil or Produce. In the Evening the Master return'd, having been several Leagues out at Sea, and at that Distance off saw Shoals without him, and was of opinion there was no getting out to Sea that way. In his return he touched upon one of the Shoals, the same as he was upon the first time he was out; he here saw a great number of Turtle, 3 of which he Caught weighing 791 lbs. This occasion'd my sending him out again provided with proper gear for Striking them, he having before nothing but a Boat Hook. Carpenters, Smiths, and Coopers at their respective Employments, and the Seamen employed getting on board stones, ballast, etc. This day all hands feasted upon Turtle for the First time.

Tuesday, 10th.—Winds and weather as yesterday. Employ'd hoisting on board and stowing away the ground Tier of Water. P.M. saw 7 or 8 of the Natives on the S. side of the River, and 2 of them came down upon the Sandy point opposite the Ship; but as soon as I put off in a Boat in order to speak with them they run away as fast as they could. At 11 Mr. Banks, who had gone out to Sea with Mr. Molineux, the Master, return'd in his own Small Boat, and gave but a Very bad account of our Turtle-catchers. At the time he left them, which was about 6 o'Clock, they had not got one, nor were they likely to get any; and yet the Master was so obstinate that he would not return, which obliged me to send Mr. Gore out in the Yawl this morning to order the Boat and People in, in Case they could not be employ'd there to some Advantage. In the A.M. 4 of the Natives came down to the Sandy point on the North side of the Harbour, having along with them a small wooden Canoe with Outriggers, in which they seem'd to be employed striking fish, etc. Some were for going over in a Boat to them; but this I would not suffer, but let them alone without seeming to take any Notice of them. At length 2 of them came in the Canoe so near the Ship as to take some things we throw'd them. After this they went away, and brought over the other 2, and came again alongside, nearer than they had done before, and took such Trifles as we gave them; after this they landed close to the Ship, and all 4 went ashore, carrying their Arms with them. But Tupia soon prevailed upon them to lay down their Arms, and come and set down by him, after which most of us went to them, made them again some presents, and stay'd by them until dinner time, when we made them understand that we were going to eat, and asked them by signals to go with us; but this they declined, and as soon as we left them they went away in their Canoe. One of these Men was something above the Middle Age, the other 3 were young; none of them were above 5½ feet high, and all their Limbs proportionately small. They were wholy naked, their skins the Colour of Wood soot, and this seem'd to be their Natural Colour. Their Hair was black, lank, and cropt short, and neither wooly nor Frizled; nor did they want any of their Fore Teeth, as Dampier has mentioned those did he saw on the Western side of this Country. Some parts of their Bodys had been painted with red, and one of them had his upper lip and breast painted with Streakes of white, which he called *Carbanda*. Their features were far from being disagreeable; their Voices were soft and Tunable, and they could easily repeat any word after us, but neither us nor Tupia could understand one word they said.

Wednesday, 11th.—Gentle land and Sea breezes. Employed Airing the Bread, stowing away water, Stores, etc. In the night the Master and Mr. Gore returned with the Long Boat, and brought with them one Turtle and a few Shell fish; the Yawl Mr. Gore left upon the Shoal with 6 Men to endeavour to strike more Turtle. In the morning 4 of the Natives made us another Short Visit; 3 of them had been with us the preceding day, the other was a stranger. One of these men had a hole through the Bridge of his nose, in which he stuck a piece of Bone as thick as my finger. Seeing this we examin'd all their Noses, and found that they had all holes for the same purpose; they had likewise holes in their Ears, but no Ornaments hanging to them; they had bracelets on their Arms made of hair, and like Hoops of small Cord. They sometimes may wear a kind of fillet about their Heads, for one of them had applied some part of an old shirt which I had given them to this use.

Thursday, 12th.—Winds and weather as Yesterday, and the Employment of the People the same. At 2 A.M. the Yawl came on board, and brought 3 Turtle and a large Skeat, and as there was a probability of succeeding in this kind of fishery, I sent her out again after breakfast. About this time 5 of the Natives came over and stay'd with us all the Forenoon. There were 7 in all—5 Men, 1 Woman, and a Boy; these 2 last stay'd on the point of Land on the other side of the River about 200 Yards from us. We could very clearly see with our Glasses that the Woman was as naked as ever she was born; even those parts which I always before now thought Nature would have taught a woman to Conceal were uncovered.

Friday, 13th.—Gentle breezes from the S.E. in day, and Calm or light Airs from the Land in the Night. Employ'd taking on board water, Stores, etc. At Noon the Yawl return'd with one Turtle and a large Sting ray.

Saturday, 14th.—Gentle breezes at S.E. and Hazey weather. In the P.M. compleated out water; got on board all the Bread, and part of our Stores; in the evening sent the Turtlers out again. A.M., employ'd getting on board stone ballast and Airing the spare Sails. Mr. Gore, being in the Country, shott one of the Animals before spoke of; it was a small one of the sort, weighing only 28 pound clear of the entrails; its body was long;* the head, neck, and Shoulders very Small in proportion to the other parts. It was hair lipt, and the Head and Ears were most like a Hare's of any Animal I know; the Tail was nearly as long as the body, thick next the Rump, and Tapering towards the End; the fore Legs were 8 inches long, and the Hind 22. Its progression is by Hopping or Jumping 7 or 8 feet at each hop upon its hind Legs only, for in this it makes no use of the Fore, which seem to be only design'd for Scratching in the ground, etc. The Skin is cover'd with a Short, hairy furr of a dark Mouse or Grey Colour. It bears no sort of resemblance to any European animal I ever saw; it is said to bear much resemblance to the Jerboa, excepting in size, the Jerboa being no larger than a common rat.

Sunday, 15th.—Gentle Breezes at S.E. and E. P.M., got on board the Spare Sails and sundry other Articles. In the A.M., as the people did not work upon the Ship, one of the Petty Officers was desirous of going out to Catch Turtles. I let him have the Pinnace for that purpose, and sent the Long boat to haul the Sean, who caught about 60 fish.

Monday, 16th.—Fore and Latter parts gentle breezes at E.N.E.; in the night had light Airs and Calm. In the evening the Yawl came in with 4 Turtle and a large Sting ray, and soon after went out again; but the Pinnace did not return as I expected. A.M., employ'd getting on board Cables; at the same time I went upon one of the high hills on the N. side of the River, from which I had an extensive view of the inland Country, which consisted of hills, Valleys, and Large plains, agreeably diversified with Woods and Lawns.

Tuesday, 17th.—Wind at S.E., a fresh breeze; people employed as yesterday setting up the rigging. In the evening the Pinnace returned with 3 Turtles, 2 of which the Yawl caught and sent in. At 7 hrs. 41' 17" p.m. observ'd the first Satellite of Jupiter to Emerge, and the same Emersion hapned at Greenwich at 10 hrs. 00' 52" in the a.m.; the difference is 14 hrs. 19' 35" = to 214° 53'

* Blank in MS.

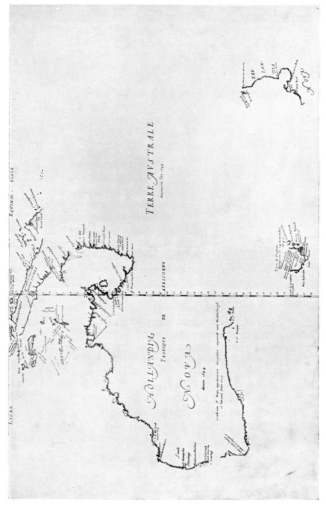

THEVENOT'S MAP OF NEW HOLLAND. PARIS, 1663.

45" of Long. The observation made on the 29th of last Month gave 214° 42′ 30″; the mean is 214° 48′ 7½″, which this place is W. of Greenwich.

Wednesday, 18*th*.—Wind at E.S.E., a Gentle breeze. P.M., I sent the Master and one of the Mates in the Pinnace to the Northward to look for a Channell that way clear of the Shoal. Mr. Banks, Dr. Solander, and myself took a turn into the woods on the other side of the water, where we met with 5 of the Natives; and although we had not seen any of them before, they came to us without showing any signs of fear. 2 of these wore Necklaces made of shells, which they seem'd to Value, as they would not part with them. In the evening the Yawl came in with 3 Turtle, and early in the A.M. she went out again. About 8 we were Visited by several of the Natives, who now became more familiar than ever. Soon after this Mr. Banks and I went over to the S.* side of the River, and Travel'd 6 or 8 miles along shore to the Northward, where we ascended a high hill, from whence I had an extensive view of the Sea Coast; it afforded us a melancholy prospect of the difficulties we are to encounter, for in whatever direction we looked it was cover'd with Shoals as far as the Eye could see; after this we return'd to the Ship without meeting with anything remarkable, and found several of the Natives on board. At this time we had 12 tortoise or Turtle upon our Decks, which they took more Notice of than anything Else in the Ship, as I was told by the Officers, for their Curiosity was Satisfied before I got on board, and they went away soon after.

Thursday, 19*th*.—Gentle breezes and fair weather. Employ'd getting everything in readyness for Sea. A.M., we were Visited by 10 or 11 of the Natives; the most of them came from the other side of the Harbour, where we saw 6 or 7 more, the most of them Women, and, like the men, quite naked. Those that came on board were very desirous of having some of our Turtles, and took the liberty to haul 2 of them to the Gangway to put over the side; being disappointed in this, they grew a little Troublesome, and were for throwing every thing overboard they could lay their hands upon. As we had no Victuals dress'd at this time, I offer'd them some bread to Eat, which they rejected with Scorn, as I believe they would have done anything else excepting Turtle; soon after this they all went ashore, Mr. Banks, myself, and 5 or 6 of our people being their at the same time. Immediately upon their Landing one of them took a Handful of dry grass and lighted it at a fire we had ashore, and before we well know'd what he was going

* This should be "N."

O

about he made a larger Circuit round about us, and set fire to the grass in his way, and in an instant the whole place was in flames. Luckily at this time we had hardly anything ashore, besides the Forge and a Sow with a litter of young Pigs, one of which was scorched to Death in the fire. As soon as they had done this they all went to a place where some of our people were washing, and where all our nets and a good deal of linnen were laid out to dry; here with the greatest obstinacy they again set fire to the grass, which I and some others who were present could not prevent, until I was obliged to fire a Musquet load with small Shott at one of the Ring leaders, which sent them off. As we were apprised of this last Attempt of theirs we got the fire out before it got head, but the first spread like wild fire in the Woods and grass. Notwithstanding my firing, in which one must have been a little hurt, because we saw a few drops of blood on some of the linnen he had gone over, they did not go far from us; for we soon after heard their Voices in the woods, upon which Mr. Banks and I and 3 or 4 more went to look for them, and very soon met them coming toward us. As they had each 4 or 5 Darts, and not knowing their intention, we seized upon 6 or 7 of the first darts we met with. This alarm'd them so much that they all made off, and we follow'd them for near ½ a Mile, and then set down and called to them, and they stop'd also; after some little unintelligible conversation had passed they laid down their darts, and came to us in a very friendly manner. We now return'd the Darts we had taken from them, which reconcil'd everything. There were 4 Strangers among them that we had not seen before, and these were interduced to us by name by the others; the Man which we supposed to have been Struck with small Shott was gone off, but he could not be much hurt as he was at a great distance when I fir'd. They all came along with us abreast of the Ship, where they stay'd a short time, and then went away, and soon after set the woods on fire about a Mile and a half or two Miles from us.

Friday, 20th.—Fresh breezes at S.E. and Cloudy weather. P.M., got everything on board the Ship, new berth'd her, and let her swing with the tide. In the night the Master return'd with the pinnace, and reported that there was no safe Passage for the Ship to the Northward at low water. A.M., I went and Sounded and buoy'd the Bar, being now ready to put to sea the first opportunity.

Saturday, 21st.—Strong breezes at S.E. and Cloudy weather. P.M., sent a Boat to haul the Sean, which return'd with as much fish as came to 1¾ lb. per Man; the Yawl return'd with only one

Turtle, which was caught in the Net, for it blew too hard for the Boat to strike any. In the morning I sent her out again, but she was obliged to return, not being able to get to Windward. The Carpenters employ'd in repairing the Boats and overhauling the Pumps, and as the Wind would not permit us to sail, I sent the Boatswain with some hands ashore to make rope, and a petty Officer with 2 Men to gather Greens for the Ships' Company.

Sunday, 22nd.—Fresh breezes at S.E. and E.S.E. Employ'd as Yesterday. A.M., the weather would not permit us to Sail; sent the Turtlers out again. In opening of one to-day we found sticking thro' both Shoulder bones a wood Harpoon, or Turtle Peg, 15 inches long, bearded at the end, such as we have seen among the Natives; this proves to a Demonstration that they strike Turtle, I suppose at the Time they come ashore to lay their Eggs, for they certainly have no boat fit to do this at Sea, or that will carry a Turtle, and this Harpoon must have been a good while in, as the wound was quite heal'd up.

Monday, 23rd.—Fresh breezes in the S.E. quarter, which so long as it continues will confine us in Port. Yesterday, A.M., I sent some people in the Country to gather greens, one of which stragled from the rest, and met with 4 of the Natives by a fire, on which they were broiling a Fowl, and the hind leg of one of the Animals before spoke of. He had the presence of mind not to run from them (being unarm'd), least they should pursue him, but went and set down by them; and after he had set a little while, and they had felt his hands and other parts of his body, they suffer'd him to go away without offering the least insult, and perceiving that he did not go right for the Ship they directed him which way to go.

Tuesday, 24th.—Winds and weather continues. The Seamen employ'd making ropes, Caulking the Ship, Fishing, etc.

Wednesday, 25th.—Fresh gales at S.E. and fair weather. In the evening the Yawl came in, having not been able to Strike one Turtle on account of the blowing weather, nor can we catch much fish with the Sean in the Harbour.

Thursday, 26th.—Winds and weather as Yesterday. Such people as can be spared from the necessary Dutys of the Ship are employ'd fishing and gathering greens and other refreshments.

Friday, 27th.—Very fresh Gales at S.E. by S. and fair weather. A.M., caught as much fish as served ¾ lb. a man, and Mr. Gore shott one of the Animals before spoke of, which weighed 80 lbs. and 54 lbs., exclusive of the entrails, Skin, and head; this was as large as the most we have seen.

Saturday, 28th.—Winds and weather as above, without the least Variation the whole of the 24 hours. The Carpenters finish'd caulking the Ship.

Sunday, 29th.—Winds at S.E., a fresh breeze until 5 a.m., at which time it fell calm, and soon after had a light breeze from the land. Upon this I sent a Boat to see what water was upon the bar (it being 2 hours Ebb), and hove up the Anchor in order to put to Sea; but upon the return of the Boat came too again, as there were only 13 feet water on the Bar, which was 6 Inches less water than what the Ship Draw'd. After this I sent the Yawl to look for Turtle, as those we had got before were nearly all expended. About 8 the Sea breeze set in again, which put an end to our Sailing this day; after which I sent the Pinnace to haul the Sean; she return'd with only 20 lbs. of Fish.

Monday, 30th.—Winds at S.E., a fresh Gale and fair weather in the P.M., the remainder Hazey, with rain, but the winds, tho more moderate, keept in the S.E. quarter.

Tuesday, 31st.—Fresh Gales at S.E., and hazey with rain all P.M. and most part of the Night. At 2 a.m. I had thoughts of trying to Warp the Ship out of the Harbour, but upon my going first out in a Boat I found it blow too fresh for such an Attempt.

Wednesday, 1st August.—Strong Gales from the S.E., with Squalls attended with Rain. P.M., the Yawl came in with 2 Rays, which together weighed 265 lbs.; it blow'd too hard all the time they were out for striking Turtle. Carpenters employ'd overhauling the Pumps, all of which we find in a state of decay; and this the Carpenter says is owing to the Sap having been left in, which in time has decay'd the sound wood. One of them is quite useless, and was so rotten when hoisted up as to drop to peices. However, I cannot complain of a Leaky Ship, for the most water She makes is not quite an Inch an Hour.

Thursday, 2nd.—Winds and weather as yesterday, or rather more Stormy; we have now no Success in the Sein fishing, hardly getting above 20 or 30 lbs a day.

Friday, 3rd.—Strong breezes, and hazey until 6 a.m., when it moderated, and we unmoor'd, hove up the Anchor, and began to Warp out; but the Ship tailing upon the Sand in the N. side of the River, the Tide of Ebb making out, and a fresh breeze setting in, we were obliged to desist and moor the Ship again just within the Barr.

Saturday, 4th.—In the P.M., having pretty moderate weather, I order'd the Coasting Anchor and Cable to be laid without the barr, to be ready to warp out by, that we might not loose the least opportunity that might Offer; for laying in Port spends time to no purpose, consumes our Provisions, of which we are very Short in many Articles, and we have yet a long Passage to make to the E. Indies through an unknown and perhaps dangerous Sea; these Circumstances consider'd, make me very Anxious of getting to Sea. The wind continued moderate all night, and at 5 a.m. it fell calm; this gave us an opportunity to warp out. About 7 we got under sail, having a light Air from the Land, which soon died away, and was succeeded by the Sea breezes from S.E. by S., with which we stood off to Sea E. by N., having the Pinnace ahead sounding. The Yawl I sent to the Turtle bank, to take up the Net that was left there; but as the wind freshen'd we got out before her, and a little After Noon Anchor'd in 15 fathoms water, Sandy bottom, for I did not think it safe to run in among the Shoals until I had well view'd them at low Water from the Mast head, that I might be better Able to Judge which way to Steer; for as yet I had not resolved whether I should beat back to the Southward round all the Shoals, or seek a Passage to the Eastward or Northward, all of which appeared to be equally difficult and dangerous. When at Anchor the Harbour sail'd from bore S. 70° W., distant 4 or 5 Leagues; the Northermost point of the Main land we have in sight, which I named Cape Bedford (Lat. 15° 17' S., Long. 214° 45' W.), bore N. 20° W., distant 3½ Leagues; but we could see land to the N.E. of this Cape, which made like 2 high Islands; the Turtle banks bore E., distant one Mile. Lat. by Observation 15° 23' S.; our depth of Water, in standing off from the land, was from 3½ to 15 fathoms.

I shall now give a Short description of the Harbour, or River, we have been in, which I named after the Ship, Endeavour River. It is only a small Barr Harbour or Creek, which runs winding 3 or 4 Leagues in land, at the Head of which is a small fresh Water Brook, as I was told, for I was not so high myself; but there is not water for Shipping above a Mile within the barr, and this is on the N. side, where the bank is so steep for nearly a quarter of a Mile that ships may lay afloat at low water so near the Shore as to reach it with a stage, and is extremely Convenient for heaving a Ship down. And this is all the River hath to recommend it, especially for large Shipping, for there is no more than 9 or 10 feet Water upon the Bar at low water, and 17 or 18 feet at high, the Tides rises and falling about 9 feet at spring Tide, and is high on the days of the New and full Moon, between 9 and 10 o'Clock. Besides, this part of the Coast is barrocaded with Shoals, as to make this Harbour more difficult of access; the safest way I know of to come at it is from the South, Keeping the Main land close on board all the way. Its situation may always be found by the Latitude, which hath been before mentioned. Over the S. point is some high Land, but the N. point is formed by a low sandy beach, which extends about 3 Miles to the Northward, then the land is again high.

The refreshments we got there were Chiefly Turtle, but as we had to go 5 Leagues out to Sea for them, and had much blowing weather, we were not over Stocked with this Article; however, what with these and the fish we caught with the Sean we had not much reason to Complain, considering the Country we were in. Whatever refreshment we got that would bear a Division I caused to be equally divided among the whole Company, generally by weight; the meanest person in the Ship had an equal share with myself or any one on board, and this method every commander of a Ship on such a Voyage as this ought ever to Observe. We found in several places on the Sandy beaches and Sand Hills near the Sea, Purslain and beans, which grows on a Creeping kind of a Vine. The first we found very good when boiled, and the latter not to be dispised, and were at first very serviceable to the Sick; but the best greens we found here was the Tarra, or Coco Tops, called in the West Indies Indian Kale, which grows in most Boggy Places; these eat as well as, or better, than Spinnage. The roots, for want of being Transplanted and properly Cultivated, were not good, yet we could have dispensed with them could we have got them in any Tolerable plenty; but having a good way to go for them, it took up too much time and too many hands to gather both root and branch. The few Cabbage Palms we found here were in General small, and yielded so little Cabage that they were not worth the Looking after, and this was the Case with most of the fruit, etc., we found in the woods.

Besides the Animals which I have before mentioned, called by the Natives Kangooroo, or Kanguru, here are Wolves, Possums, an Animal like a ratt, and snakes, both of the Venemous and other sorts. Tame Animals here are none except Dogs, and of these we never saw but one, who frequently came about our Tents to pick up bones, etc. The Kanguru are in the greatest number, for we seldom went into the Country without seeing some. The land Fowls we met here, which far from being numerous, were Crows, Kites, Hawkes, Cockadores of 2 Sorts, the one white, and the other brown, very beautiful Loryquets of 2 or 3 Sorts, Pidgeons, Doves, and a few other sorts of small Birds. The Sea or Water fowl are Herns, Whisling Ducks, which perch and, I believe, roost on Trees; Curlews, etc., and not many of these neither. Some of our Gentlemen who were in the Country heard and saw Wild Geese in the Night.

The Country, as far as I could see, is diversified with Hills and plains, and these with woods and Lawns; the Soil of the Hills is hard, dry, and very Stoney; yet it produceth a thin Coarse grass, and some wood. The Soil of the Plains and Valleys are sandy, and in some places Clay, and in many Parts very Rocky and Stoney, as well as the Hills, but in general the Land is pretty well Cloathed with long grass, wood, Shrubs, etc. The whole Country abounds with an immense number of Ant Hills, some of which are 6 or 8 feet high, and more than twice that in Circuit. Here are but few sorts of Trees besides the Gum tree, which is the most numerous, and is the same that we found on the Southern Part of the Coast, only here they do not grow near so large. On each side of the River, all the way up it, are Mangroves, which Extend in some places a Mile from its banks; the Country in general is not badly water'd, there being several fine Rivulets at no very great distance from one another, but none near to the place where we lay; at least not in the Dry season, which is at this time. However we were very well supply'd with water by springs which were not far off.

Sunday, 5th.—In the P.M. had a Gentle breeze at S.E. and Clear weather. As I did not intend to weigh until the morning I sent all the Boats to the Reef to get what Turtle and Shell fish they could. At low water from the Mast head I took a view of the Shoals, and could see several laying a long way without this one, a part of several of them appearing above water; but as it appear'd pretty clear of Shoals to the N.E. of the Turtle Reef, I came to a Resolution to stretch out that way close upon a wind, because if we found no Passage we could always return back the way we went. In the Evening the Boats return'd with one Turtle, a sting ray, and as many large Clams as came to 1½ lbs. a Man; in each of these Clams were about 20 lbs. of Meat; added to this we Caught in the night several Sharks. Early in the morning I sent the Pinnace and Yawl again to the Reef, as I did not intend to weigh until half Ebb, at which time the Shoals began to appear. Before 8 it came on to blow, and I made the Signal for the Boats to come on Board, which they did, and brought with them one Turtle. We afterwards began to heave, but the wind Freshening obliged us to bear away again and lay fast.

Monday, 6th.—Winds at S.E. At 2 o'Clock p.m. it fell pretty Moderate, and we got under sail, and stood out upon a wind N.E.

by E., leaving the Turtle Reef to windward, having the Pinnace ahead sounding. We had not stood out long before we discovered shoals ahead and on both bows. At half past 4 o'Clock, having run off 8 Miles, the Pinnace made the signal for Shoal water in a place where we little Expected it; upon this we Tack'd and Stood on and off while the Pinnace stretched farther to the Eastward, but as night was approaching I thought it safest to Anchor, which we accordingly did in 20 fathoms water, a Muddy bottom. Endeavour River bore S. 52° W.; Cape Bedford W. by N. ½ N., distant 5 Leagues; the Northermost land in sight, which made like an Island, N.; and a Shoal, a small, sandy part of which appear'd above Water, N.E., distance 2 or 3 Miles. In standing off from this Turtle Reef to this place our Soundings were from 14 to 20 fathoms, but where the Pinnace was, about a Mile farther to the E.N.E., were no more than 4 or 5 feet of water rocky ground; and yet this did not appear to us in the Ship. In the morning we had a strong Gale from the S.E., that, instead of weighing as we intended, we were obliged to bear away more Cable, and to Strike Top Gallant yards.

Tuesday, 7th.—Strong Gales at S.E., S.E. by S., and S.S.E., with cloudy weather at Low water in the P.M. I and several of the Officers kept a look out at the Mast head to see for a Passage between the Shoals; but we could see nothing but breakers all the way from the South round by the East as far as N.W., extending out to Sea as far as we could see. It did not appear to be one continued Shoal, but several laying detached from each other. On the Eastermost that we could see the Sea broke very high, which made one judge it to be the outermost; for on many of those within the Sea did not break high at all, and from about ½ flood to ½ Ebb they are not to be seen, which makes the Sailing among them more dangerous, and requires great care and Circumspection, for, like all other Shoals, or Reefs of Coral Rocks, they are quite steep too. Altho' the most of these Shoals consist of Coral Rocks, yet a part of some of them is sand. The Turtle Reef and some others have a small Patch of Sand generally at the N. end, that is only cover'd at high water. These generally discover themselves before we come near them. Altho' I speak of this as the Turtle Reef, yet it is not to be doubted but what there are Turtle upon the most of them as well as this one. After having well viewed our situation from the Mast Head, I saw that we were surrounded on every side with Dangers, in so much that I was quite at a loss which way to steer when the weather will permit us to get under sail, for to beat back to the S.E. the way we came, as the Master would have had me done, would be an endless peice of work, as the winds blow constantly from that Quarter, and very Strong, without hardly any intermission; on the other hand, if we do not find a passage to the Northward we shall have to come back at last. At 11 the Ship drove, and obliged us to bear away to a Cable and one third, which brought us up again; but in the morning the Gale increasing, she drove again. This made us let go the Small Bower Anchor, and bear away a whole Cable on it and 2 on the other; and even after this she still kept driving slowly, until we had got down Top gallant Masts, struck Yards and Top masts close down, and made all snug; then she rid fast, C. Bedford bearing W.S.W., distant 3½ Leagues. In this situation we had Shoals to the Eastward of us extending from the S.E. by S. to the N.N.W., distant from the nearest part of them about 2 Miles.

Wednesday, 8th.—Strong gales at S.S.E. all this day, in so much that I durst not get up Yards and Topmasts.

Thursday, 9th.—In the P.M., the weather being something moderate, we got up the Top masts, but keept the Lower yards down. At 6 in the morning we began to heave in the Cable, thinking to get under sail; but it blow'd so fresh, together with a head sea, that we could hardly heave the ship a head, and at last was obliged to desist.

Friday, 10th.—Fresh Gales at S.S.E. and S.E. by S. P.M., the wind fell so that we got up the small Bower Anchor, and hove into a whole Cable on the Best Bower. At 3 in the morning we got up the Lower Yards, and at 7 weighed and stood in for the Land (intending to seek for a passage along Shore to the northward), having a Boat ahead sounding; depth of water as we run in from 19 to 12 fathoms. After standing in an hour we edged away for 3 Small Islands that lay N.N.E. ½ E., 3 Leagues from C. Bedford. To these Islands the Master had been in the Pinnace when the Ship was in Port. At 9 we were abreast of them, and between them and the Main, having another Low Island between us and the latter, which lies W.N.W., 4 Miles from the 3 Islands. In this Channell had 14 fathoms water; the Northermost point of the Main we had in sight bore from us N.N.W. ½ W., distant 2 Leagues. 4 or 5 Leagues to the N.E. of this head land appeared 3 high Islands, with some smaller ones near them, and the Shoals and Reefs without, as we could see, extending to the Northward as far as these Islands. We directed our Course between them and the above headland, leaving a small Island to the Eastward of us, which lies N. by E., 4 Miles from the 3 Islands, having all the while a boat ahead sounding. At Noon we were got between the head Land and the 3 high Islands, distant from the former 2, and from the latter 4 Leagues; our Lat. by observation was 14° 51' S. We now judged ourselves to be clear of all Danger, having, as we thought, a Clear, open Sea before us; but this we soon found otherwise, and occasioned my calling the Headland above mentioned Cape Flattery (Lat. 14° 55' S., Long. 214° 43' W.). It is a high Promontory, making in 2 Hills next the sea, and a third behind them, with low sandy land on each side; but it is better known by the 3 high Islands out at Sea, the Northermost of which is the Largest, and lies from the Cape N.N.E., distant 5 Leagues. From this Cape the Main land trends away N.W. and N.W. by W.

Saturday, 11th.—Fresh breezes at S.S.E., and S.E. by S., with which we steer'd along shore N.W. by W. until one o'Clock, when the Petty Officer at the Masthead called out that he saw land ahead, extending quite round to the Islands without, and a large reef between us and them; upon this I went to the Masthead myself. The reef I saw very plain, which was now so far to windward that we could not weather it, but what he took for Main land ahead were only small Islands, for such they appeared to me; but, before I had well got from Mast head the Master and some others went up, who all asserted that it was a Continuation of the Main land, and, to make it still more alarming, they said they saw breakers in a Manner all round us. We immediately hauld upon a wind in for the Land, and made the Signal for the Boat, which was ahead sounding, to come on board; but as she was well to leeward, we were obliged to edge away to take her up, and soon after came to an Anchor under a point of the Main in ¼ less 5 fathoms, about a Mile from the Shore, Cape Flattery bearing S.E., distant 3½ Leagues. After this I landed, and went upon the point, which is pretty high, from which I had a View of the Sea Coast, which trended away N.W. by W., 8 or 10 Leagues, which was as far as I could see, the weather not being very clear. I likewise saw 9 or 10 Small, Low Islands and some Shoals laying off the Coast, and some large Shoals between the Main and the 3 high Islands, without which, I was now well assured, were Islands, and not a part of the Mainland as some had taken them to be. Excepting C. Flattery and the point I am now upon, which I have named point Lookout, the main land next the sea to the Northward of Cape Bedford is low, and Chequer'd with white sand and green Bushes, etc., for 10 or 12 Miles inland, beyond which is high land. To the Northward of Point Lookout the shore appear'd to be shoal and flat some distance off, which was no good sign of meeting with a Channell in with the land, as we have hitherto done. We saw the footsteps of people upon the sand, and smoke and fire up in the Country, and in the evening return'd on board, where I came to a resolution to visit one of the high Islands in the Offing in my Boat, as they lay at least 5 Leagues out at Sea, and seem'd to be of such a height that from the Top of one of them I hoped to see and find a Passage out to sea clear of the Shoals. Accordingly in the Morning I set out in the Pinnace for the Northermost and largest of the 3, accompanied by Mr. Banks. At the same time I sent the Master in the Yawl to Leeward, to sound between the Low Islands and the Main. In my way to the Island I passed over a large reef of Coral Rocks and sand, which lies about 2 Leagues from the Island; I left another to leeward, which lays about 3 Miles from the Island. On the N. part of this is a low, sandy Isle, with Trees upon it; on the reef we pass'd over in the Boat we saw several Turtle, and Chased one or Two, but caught none, it blowing too hard, and I had no time to spare, being otherways employ'd. I did not reach the Island until half an hour after one o'Clock in the P.M. on

Sunday, 12th, when I immediately went upon the highest hill on the Island, where, to my Mortification, I discover'd a Reef of Rocks laying about 2 or 3 Leagues without the Island, extending in a line N.W. and S.E., farther than I could see, on which the sea broke very high. This, however, gave one great hopes that they were the outermost shoals, as I did not doubt but what I should be able to get without them, for there appeared to be several breaks or Partitions in the Reef, and Deep Water between it and the Islands. I stay'd upon the Hill until near sun set, but the weather continued so Hazey all the time that I could not see above 4 or 5 Leagues round me, so that I came down much disappointed in the prospect I expected to have had, but being in hopes the morning might prove Clearer, and give me a better View of the Shoals. With this view I stay'd all night upon the Island, and at 3 in the Morning sent the Pinnace, with one of the Mates I had with me, to sound between the Island and the Reefs, and to Examine one of the breaks or Channels; and in the mean time I went again upon the Hill, where I arrived by Sun Rise, but found it much Hazier than in the Evening. About Noon the pinnace return'd, having been out as far as the Reef, and found from 15 to 28 fathoms water. It blow'd so hard that they durst not venture into one of the Channels, which, the Mate said, seem'd to him to be very narrow; but this did not discourage me, for I thought from the place he was at he must have seen it at disadvantage. Before I quit this Island I shall describe it. It lies, as I have before observed, about 5 Leagues from the Main; it is about 8 Miles in Circuit, and of a height sufficient to be seen 10 or 12 Leagues; it is mostly high land, very rocky and barren, except on the N.W. side, where there are some sandy bays and low land, which last is covered with thin, long grass, Trees, etc., the same as upon the Main. Here is also fresh Water in 2 places; the one is a running stream, the water a little brackish where I tasted it, which was close to the sea; the other is a standing pool, close behind the sandy beach, of good, sweet water, as I daresay the other is a little way from the Sea beach. The only land Animals we saw here were Lizards, and these seem'd to be pretty Plenty, which occasioned my naming the Island Lizard Island. The inhabitants of the Main visit this Island at some Seasons of the Year, for we saw the Ruins of Several of their Hutts and heaps of Shells, etc. S.E., 4 or 5 Miles from this Island, lay the other 2 high Islands, which are very small compared to this; and near them lay 3 others, yet smaller and lower Islands, and several Shoals or reefs, especially to the S.E. There is, however, a clear passage from Cape Flattery to those Islands, and even quite out to the outer Reefs, leaving the above Islands to the S.E. and Lizard Island to the N.W.

Monday, 13th.—At 2 P.M., I left Lizard Island in order to return to the Ship, and in my way landed upon the low sandy Isle mentioned in coming out. We found on this Island a pretty number of Birds, the most of them sea Fowl, except Eagles; 2 of the Latter we shott and some of the others; we likewise saw some Turtles, but got none, for the reasons before mentioned. After leaving Eagle Isle I stood S.W. direct for the Ship, sounding all the way, and had not less than 8 fathoms, nor more than 14. I had the same depth of Water between Lizard and Eagle Isle. After I got on board the Master inform'd me that he had been down to the Islands I had directed him to go too, which he judged to lay about 3 Leagues from the Main, and had sounded the Channel between the 2, found 7 fathoms; this was near the Islands, for in with the Main he had only 9 feet 3 Miles off, but without the Islands he found 10, 12, and 14 fathoms. He found upon the islands piles of turtle shells, and some finns that were so fresh that both he and the boats' crew eat of them. This showed that the natives must have been there lately. After well considering both what I had seen myself and the report of the Master's, I found by experience that by keeping in with the Mainland we should be in continued danger, besides the risk we should run in being lock'd in with Shoals and reefs by not finding a passage out to Leeward. In case we persever'd in keeping the Shore on board an accident of this kind, or any other that might happen to the ship, would infallibly loose our passage to the East India's this Season, and might prove the ruin of both ourselves and the Voyage, as we have now little more than 3 Months' Provisions on board, and that at short allowance. Wherefore, after consulting with the Officers, I resolved to weigh in the morning, and Endeavour to quit the Coast altogether until such time as I found I could approach it with less danger. With this View we got under Sail at daylight in the morning, and stood out N.E. for the N.W. end of Lizard Island, having Eagle Island to windward of us, having the pinnace ahead sounding; and here we found a good Channell, wherein we had from 9 to 14 fathoms. At Noon the N. end of Lizard Island bore E.S.E., distant one Mile; Lat. observed 14° 38′ S.; depth of water 14 fathoms. We now took the pinnace in tow, knowing that there were no dangers until we got out to the Reefs.

Tuesday, 14th.—Winds at S.E., a steady gale. By 2 P.M. we got out to the outermost reefs, and just fetched to Windward of one of the openings I had discover'd from the Island; we tacked and Made a short trip to the S.W., while the Master went in the pinnace to examine the Channell, who soon made the signal for the Ship to follow, which we accordingly did, and in a short time got safe out. This Channel lies N.E. ½ N., 3 Leagues from Lizard Island; it is about one-third of a Mile broad, and 25 or 30 fathoms deep or more. The moment we were without the breakers we had no ground with 100 fathoms of Line, and found a large Sea rowling in from the S.E. By this I was well assured we were got without all the Shoals, which gave us no small joy, after having been intangled among Islands and Shoals, more or less, ever since the 26th of May, in which time we have sail'd above 360 Leagues by the Lead without ever having a Leadsman out of the Chains, when the ship was under sail; a Circumstance that perhaps never hapned to any ship before, and yet it was here absolutely necessary. I should have been very happy to have had it in my power to have keept in with the land, in order to have explor'd the Coast to the Northern extremity of the Country, which I think we were not far off, for I firmly believe this land doth not join to New Guinea. But this I hope soon either to prove or disprove, and the reasons I have before assign'd will, I presume, be thought sufficient for my leaving the Coast at this time; not but what I intend to get in with it again as soon as I can do it with safety. The passage or channel we now came out by, which I have named*   lies

* Blank in MS.

in the Lat. of 14° 32′ S.; it may always be found and known by the 3 high Islands within it, which I have called the Islands of Direction, because by their means a safe passage may be found even by strangers in within the Main reef, and quite into the Main. Lizard Island, which is the Northermost and Largest of the 3, Affords snug Anchorage under the N.W. side of it, fresh water and wood for fuel; and the low Islands and Reefs which lay between it and the Main, abound with Turtle and other fish, which may be caught at all Seasons of the Year (except in such blowing weather as we have lately had). All these things considered there is, perhaps, not a better place on the whole Coast for a Ship to refresh at than this Island. I had forgot to mention in its proper place, that not only on this Island, but on Eagle Island, and on several places of the Sea beach in and about Endeavour River, we found Bamboos, Cocoa Nutts, the seeds of some few other plants, and Pummice-stones, which were not the produce of the Country. From what we have seen of it, it is reasonable to suppose that they are the produce of some lands or Islands laying in the Neighbourhood, most likely to the Eastward, and are brought hither by the Easterly trade winds. The Islands discover'd by Quiros lies in this parrallel, but how far to the Eastward it's hard to say; for altho' we found in most Charts his discoveries placed as far to the West as this country yet from the account of his Voyage, compared with what we ourselves have seen, we are Morally certain that he never was upon any part of this Coast. As soon as we had got without the Reefs we Shortened sail, and hoisted in the pinnace and Long boat, which last we had hung alongside, and then stretched off E.N.E., close upon a wind, as I did not care to stand to the Northward until we had a whole day before us, for which reason we keept making short boards all night. The large hollow sea we have now got into acquaints us with a Circumstance we did not know before, which is that the Ship hath received more Damage than we were aware of, or could perceive when in smooth Water; for now she makes as much water as one pump will free, kept constantly at work. However this was looked upon as trifling to the Danger we had lately made an Escape from. At day light in the morning Lizard Island bore S. by W., distant 10 Leagues. We now made all the sail we could, and stood away N.N.W. ½ W., but at 9 we steer'd N.W. ½ N., having the advantage of a Fresh Gale at S.E.; at Noon we were by observation in the Lat. of 13° 46′ S., the Lizard Island bore S. 15° E., distant 58 Miles, but we had no land in sight.

Wednesday, 15th.—Fresh Trade at S.E. and Clear weather. At

6 in the evening shortned sail and brought too, with her head to
the N.E. By this time we had run near 12 Leagues upon a N.W.
½ N. Course since Noon. At 4 a.m. wore and lay her head to the
S.W., and at 5 made all Sail, and steer'd W., in order to make the
land, being fearful of over shooting the passage, supposing there
to be one, between this land and New Guinea. By noon we had
run 10 Leagues upon this Course, but saw no land. Our Latitude
by Observation was 13° 2′ S., Long. 216° 00′ W., which was 1° 23′
to the W. of Lizard Island.

Thursday, 16th.—Moderate breezes at E.S.E. and fair weather.
A little after Noon saw the Land from the Mast head bearing
W.S.W., making high; at 2 saw more land to the N.W. of the former, making in hills like Islands; but we took it to be a Continuation of the Main land. An hour after this we saw a reef, between
us and the land, extending away to the Southward, and as we
thought, terminated here to the Northward abreast of us; but
this was only on op'ning, for soon after we saw it extend away to
the Northward as far as we could distinguish anything. Upon this
we hauld close upon a Wind, which was now at E.S.E., with all
the sail we could set. We had hardly trimm'd our sails before the
wind came to E. by N., which made our weathering the Reef very
doubtful, the Northern point of which in sight at sun set still bore
from us N. by W., distant about 2 Leagues. However, this being
the best Tack to Clear it, we kept standing to the Northward,
keeping a good look out until 12 at night, when, fearing to run too
far upon one Course, we tack'd and stood to the southward, having run 6 Leagues N. or N. by E. since sun set; we had not stood
above 2 Miles to the S.S.E. before it fell quite Calm. We both
sounded now and several times before, but had not bottom with
140 fathoms of line. A little after 4 o'clock the roaring of the surf
was plainly heard, and at daybreak the Vast foaming breakers
were too plainly to be seen not a mile from us, towards which we
found the ship was carried by the Waves surprisingly fast. We
had at this time not an air of Wind, and the depth of water was
unfathomable, so that there was not a possibility of anchoring.
In this distressed Situation we had nothing but Providence and
the small Assistance the Boats could give us to trust to; the
Pinnace was under repair, and could not immediately be hoisted
out. The Yawl was put in the Water, and the Longboat hoisted
out, and both sent ahead to tow, which, together with the help of
our sweeps abaft, got the Ship's head round to the Northward,
which seemed to be the best way to keep her off the Reef, or at
least to delay time. Before this was effected it was 6 o'clock, and

we were not above 80 or 100 yards from the breakers. The same sea that washed the side of the ship rose in a breaker prodidgiously high the very next time it did rise, so that between us and destruction was only a dismal Valley, the breadth of one wave, and even now no ground could be felt with 120 fathom. The Pinnace was by this time patched up, and hoisted out and sent ahead to Tow. Still we had hardly any hopes of saving the ship, and full as little our lives, as we were full 10 Leagues from the nearest Land, and the boats not sufficient to carry the whole of us; yet in this Truly Terrible Situation not one man ceased to do his utmost, and that with as much Calmness as if no danger had been near. All the dangers we had escaped were little in comparison of being thrown upon this reef, where the Ship must be dashed to pieces in a Moment. A reef such as one speaks of here is Scarcely known in Europe. It is a Wall of Coral Rock rising perpendicular out of the unfathomable Ocean, always overflown at high Water generally 7 or 8 feet, and dry in places at Low Water. The Large Waves of the Vast Ocean meeting with so sudden a resistance makes a most Terrible Surf, breaking Mountains high, especially as in our case, when the General Trade Wind blows directly upon it. At this Critical juncture, when all our endeavours seemed too little, a Small Air of Wind sprung up, but so small that at any other Time in a Calm we should not have observed it. With this, and the Assistance of our Boats, we could observe the Ship to move off from the Reef in a Slanting direction; but in less than 10 minutes we had as flat a Calm as ever, when our fears were again renewed, for as yet we were not above 200 Yards from the Breakers. Soon after our friendly Breeze visited us again, and lasted about as long as before. A Small Opening was now Seen in the Reef about a $\frac{1}{4}$ of a Mile from us, which I sent one of the Mates to Examine. Its breadth was not more than the Length of the Ship, but within was Smooth Water. Into the place it was resolved to Push her if Possible, having no other Probable Views to save her, for we were still in the very Jaws of distruction, and it was a doubt wether or no we could reach this Opening. However, we soon got off it, when to our Surprise we found the Tide of Ebb gushing out like a Mill Stream, so that it was impossible to get in. We however took all the Advantage Possible of it, and it Carried us out about a $\frac{1}{4}$ of a Mile from the breakers; but it was too Narrow for us to keep in long. However, what with the help of this Ebb, and our Boats, we by Noon had got an Offing of $1\frac{1}{2}$ or 2 Miles, yet we could hardly flatter ourselves with hopes of getting Clear, even if a breeze should Spring up, as we were by this time embay'd by the Reef, and the Ship, in Spite of our Endeavours, driving before the Sea into the bight. The Ebb had been in our favour, and we had reason to Suppose the flood which was now made would be against us. The only hopes we had was another Opening we saw about a Mile to the Westwd. of us, which I sent Lieutnt. Hicks in the Small Boat to Examine. Latitude observed 12° 37′ S°., the Main Land in Sight distant about 10 Leagues.

Friday, 17th.—While Mr. Hicks was Examining the opening we struggled hard with the flood, sometime gaining a little and at other times loosing. At 2 o'Clock Mr. Hicks returned with a favourable Account of the Opening. It was immediately resolved to Try to secure the Ship in it. Narrow and dangerous as it was, it seemed to be the only means we had of saving her, as well as ourselves. A light breeze soon after sprung up at E.N.E., with which, the help of our Boats, and a Flood Tide, we soon entered the Opening, and was hurried thro' in a short time by a Rappid Tide like a Mill race, which kept us from driving against either side, though the Channel was not more than a ¼ of a Mile broad, having 2 Boats ahead of us sounding. Our deepth of water was from 30 to 7 fathoms; very irregular soundings and foul ground until we had got quite within the Reef, where we Anchor'd in 19 fathoms, a Coral and Shelly bottom. The Channel we came in by, which I have named Providential Channell, bore E.N.E., distant 10 or 12 Miles, being about 8 or 9 Leagues from the Main land, which extended from N. 66° W. to S.W. by S.

It is but a few days ago that I rejoiced at having got without the Reef; but that joy was nothing when Compared to what I now felt at being safe at an Anchor within it. Such are the Visissitudes attending this kind of Service, and must always attend an unknown Navigation where one steers wholy in the dark without any manner of Guide whatever. Was it not from the pleasure which Naturly results to a man from his being the first discoverer, even was it nothing more than Land or Shoals, this kind of Service would be insupportable, especially in far distant parts like this, Short of Provisions and almost every other necessary. People will hardly admit of an excuse for a Man leaving a Coast unexplored he has once discovered. If dangers are his excuse, he is then charged with Timerousness and want of Perseverance, and at once pronounced to be the most unfit man in the world to be employ'd as a discoverer; if, on the other hand, he boldly encounters all the dangers and Obstacles he meets with, and is unfortunate enough not to succeed, he is then Charged with Temerity, and, perhaps, want of Conduct. The

P

former of these Aspersions, I am confident, can never be laid to my Charge, and if I am fortunate to Surmount all the Dangers we meet with, the latter will never be brought in Question; altho' I must own that I have engaged more among the Islands and Shoals upon this Coast than perhaps in prudence I ought to have done with a single Ship and every other thing considered. But if I had not I should not have been able to give any better account of the one half of it than if I had never seen it; at best, I should not have been able to say wether it was Mainland or Islands; and as to its produce, that we should have been totally ignorant of as being inseparable with the other; and in this case it would have been far more satisfaction to me never to have discover'd it. But it is time I should have done with this Subject, which at best is but disagreeable, and which I was lead into on reflecting on our late Dangers.

In the P.M. as the wind would not permit us to sail out by the same Channel as we came in, neither did I care to move until the pinnace was in better repair, I sent the Master with all the other Boats to the Reef to get such refreshments as he could find, and in the meantime were the Carpenters were repairing the pinnace. Variations by the Amplitude and Azimuth in the morning 4° 9' Easterly; at noon Latitude observed 12° 38' S., Longitude in 216° 45' W. It being now about low water, I and some other of the officers went to the Masthead to see what we could discover. Great part of the reef without us was dry, and we could see an Opening in it about two Leagues farther to the S.E. than the one we came in by; we likewise saw 2 large spots of sand to the Southward within the Reef, but could see nothing to the Northward between it and the Main. On the Mainland within us was a pretty high promontary, which I called Cape Weymouth (Lat. 12° 42' S., Long. 217° 15'); and on the N.W. side of this Cape is a Bay, which I called Weymouth Bay.

Saturday, 18*th*.—Gentle breezes at E. and E.S.E. At 4 P.M. the Boats return'd from the Reef with about 240 lbs. of Shellfish, being the Meat of large Cockles, exclusive of the Shells. Some of these Cockles are as large as 2 Men can move, and contain about 20 pounds of Meat, very good. At 6 in the morning we got under sail, and stood away to the N.W., as we could not expect a wind to get out to Sea by the same Channel as we came in without waiting perhaps a long time for it, nor was it advisable at this time to go without the Shoals, least we should by them be carried so far off the Coast as not to be able to determine wether or no New Guinea joins to or makes a part of this land. This doubtful point I had from my first coming upon the Coast, determined, if Possible, to clear up; I now came to a fix'd resolution to keep the Main land on board, let the Consequence be what it will, and in this all the Officers concur'd. In standing to the N.W. we met with very irregular soundings, from 10 to 27 fathoms, varying 5 or 6 fathoms almost every Cast of the Lead. However, we keept on having a Boat ahead sounding. A little before noon we passed a low, small, sandy Isle, which we left on our Starboard side at the distance of 2 Miles. At the same time we saw others, being part of large Shoals above water, away to the N.E. and between us and the Main land. At Noon we were by observation in the Latitude of 12° 28′ S., and 4 or 5 Leagues from the Main, which extended from S. by W. to N. 71° W., and some Small Islands extending from N 40° W. to N. 54° W., the Main or outer Reef seen from the Masthead away to the N.E.

Sunday, 19*th*.—Gentle breezes at S.E. by E. and Clear wether. At 2 P.M., as we were steering N.W. by N., saw a large shoal right ahead, extending 3 or 4 points on each bow, upon which we hauld up N.N.E. and NE. by N., in order to get round to N. Point of it, which we reached by 4 o'clock, and then Edged away to the westward, and run between the N. end of this Shoal and another, which lays 2 miles to the Northward of it, having a Boat all the time ahead sounding. Our depth of Water was very irregular, from 22 to 8 fathoms. At ½ past 6 we Anchor'd in 13 fathoms; the Northermost of the Small Islands mentioned at Noon bore W. ¼ S., distant 3 Miles. These Islands, which are known in the Chart by the name of Forbes's Isles, lay about 5 Leagues from the Main, which here forms a moderate high point, which we called Bolt head, from which the Land trends more westerly, and is all low, sandy Land, but to the Southward it is high and hilly, even near the Sea. At 6 A.M. we got under sail, and directed our Course for an Island which lay but a little way from the Main, and bore from us at this time N. 40° W., distant 5 Leagues; but we were soon interrupted in our Course by meeting with Shoals, but by the help of 2 Boats ahead and a good lookout at the Mast head we got at last into a fair Channel, which lead us down to the Island, having a very large Shoal on our Starboard side and several smaller ones betwixt us and the Main land. In this Channel we had from 20 to 30 fathoms. Between 11 and 12 o'Clock we hauld round the N.E. side of the Island, leaving it between us and the Main from which it is distant 7 or 8 Miles. This Island is about a League in Circuit and of a moderate height, and is inhabited; to the N.W. of it are several small, low

Islands and Keys, which lay not far from the Main, and to the Northward and Eastward lay several other Islands and Shoals, so that we were now incompassed on every side by one or the other, but so much does a great danger Swallow up lesser ones, that these once so much dreaded spots were now looked at with less concern. The Boats being out of their Stations, we brought too to wait for them. At Noon our Latitude by observation was 12° 0′ S., Longitude in 217° 25′ W.; depth of Water 14 fathoms; Coarse and distance sail'd, reduced to a strait line, since yesterday Noon is N. 29° W., 32 Miles. The Main land within the above Islands forms a point, which I call Cape Grenville (Lat. 11° 58′, Long. 217° 38′); between this Cape and the Bolt head is a Bay, which I named Temple Bay. E. ½ N., 9 Leagues from Cape Grenville, lay some tolerable high Islands, which I called Sir Charles Hardy's Isles; those which lay off the Cape I named Cockburn Isles.

Monday, 20th.—Fresh breezes at E.S.E. About one P.M. the pinnace having got ahead, and the Yawl we took in Tow, we fill'd and Steer'd N. by W., for some small Islands we had in that direction. After approaching them a little nearer we found them join'd or connected together by a large Reef; upon this we Edged away N.W., and left them on our Starboard hand, steering between them and the Island laying off the Main, having a fair and Clear Passage; Depth of Water from 15 to 23 fathoms. At 4 we discover'd some low Islands and Rocks bearing W.N.W., which we stood directly for. At half past 6 we Anchor'd on the N.E. side of the Northermost, in 16 fathoms, distant from the Island one Mile. This Isle lay N.W. 4 Leagues from C. Grenville. On the Isles we saw a good many Birds, which occasioned my calling them Bird Isles. Before and at Sunset we could see the Main land, which appear'd all very low and sandy, Extends as far to the Northward as N.W. by N., and some Shoals, Keys, and low sandy Isles away to the N.E. of us. At 6 A.M. we got again under sail, with a fresh breeze at E., and stood away N.N.W. for some low Islands we saw in that direction; but we had not stood long upon this Course before we were obliged to haul close upon a wind in Order to weather a Shoal which we discover'd on our Larboard bow, having at the same time others to the Eastward of us. By such time as we had weathered the Shoal to Leeward we had brought the Islands well upon our Leebow; but seeing some Shoals spit off from them, and some rocks on our Starboard bow, which we did not discover until we were very near them, made me afraid to go to windward of the Islands; wherefore we brought too, and made the signal for the pinnace, which was a head, to come on board, which done, I sent her to Leeward of the Islands, with Orders to keep along the Edge off the Shoal, which spitted off from the South side of the Southermost Island. The Yawl I sent to run over the Shoals to look for Turtle, and appointed them a Signal to make in case they saw many; if not, she was to meet us on the other side of the Island. As soon as the pinnace had got a proper distance from us we wore, and stood After her, and run to Leeward of the Islands, where we took the Yawl in Tow, she having seen only one small Turtle, and therefore made no Stay upon the Shoal. Upon this Island, which is only a Small Spott of Land, with some Trees upon it, we saw many Hutts and habitations of the Natives, which we supposed come over from the Main to these Islands (from which they are distant about 5 Leagues) to Catch Turtles at the time these Animals come ashore to lay their Eggs. Having got the Yawl in Tow, we stood away after the pinnace N.N.E. and N. by E. to 2 other low Islands, having 2 Shoals, which we could see without and one between us and the Main. At Noon we were about 4 Leagues from the Main land, which we could see Extending to the Northward as far as N.W. by N., all low, flat, and Sandy. Our Lat. by observation was 11° 23′ S., Long, in 217° 46′ W., and Course and distance sail'd since Yesterday at Noon N. 22° W., 40 Miles; soundings from 14 to 23 fathoms. But these are best seen upon the Chart, as likewise the Islands, Shoals, etc., which are too Numerous to be Mentioned singly.

Tuesday, 21st.—Winds at E. by S. and E.S.E., fresh breeze. By one o'Clock we had run nearly the length of the Southermost of the 2 Islands before mentioned, and finding that we could not well go to windward of them without carrying us too far from the Main land, we bore up, and run to Leeward, where we found a fair open passage. This done, we steer'd N. by W., in a parrallel direction with the Main land, leaving a small Island between us and it, and some low sandy Isles and Shoals without us, all of which we lost sight of by 4 o'Clock; neither did we see any more before the sun went down, at which time the farthest part of the Main in sight bore N.N.W. ½ W. Soon after this we Anchor'd in 13 fathoms soft Ground, about five Leagues from the Land, where we lay until day light, when we got again under sail, having first sent the Yawl ahead to sound. We steer'd N.N.W. by Compass from the Northermost land in sight; Variation 3° 6′ E. Seeing no danger in our way we took the Yawl in Tow, and made all the Sail we could until 8 o'Clock, at which time we

discover'd Shoals ahead and on our Larboard bow, and saw that
the Northermost land, which we had taken to be a part of the
Main, was an Island, or Islands, between which and the Main
their appeared to be a good Passage thro' which we might pass
by running to Leeward of the Shoals on our Larboard bow, which
was now pretty near us. Whereupon we wore and brought too,
and sent away the Pinnace and Yawl to direct us clear of the
Shoals, and then stood after them. Having got round the S.E.
point of the Shoal we steer'd N.W. along the S.W., or inside of it,
keeping a good lookout at the Masthead, having another Shoal
on our Larboard side; but we found a good Channel of a Mile
broad between them, wherein were from 10 to 14 fathoms. At 11
o'Clock, being nearly the length of the Islands above mentioned,
and designing to flass between them and the Main, the Yawl,
being thrown a stern by falling in upon a part of the Shoal, She
could not get over. We brought the Ship too, and Sent away the
Long boat (which we had a stern, and rigg'd) to keep in Shore
upon our Larboard bow, and the Pinnace on our Starboard; for
altho' there appear'd nothing in the Passage, yet I thought it
necessary to take this method, because we had a strong flood,
which carried us on end very fast, and it did not want much of
high water. As soon as the Boats were ahead we stood after
them, and got through by noon, at which time we were by
observation in the Lat. of 10° 36′ 30″ S. The nearest part of the
Main, and which we soon after found to be the Northermost,
bore W. southerly, distant 3 or 4 Miles; the Islands which form'd
the passage before mentioned extending from N. to N. 75° E.,
distant 2 or 3 Miles. At the same time we saw Islands at a good
distance off extending from N. by W. to W.N.W., and behind
them another chain of high land, which we likewise judged to be
Islands. The Main land we thought extended as far as N. 71° W.;
but this we found to be Islands. The point of the Main, which
forms one side of the Passage before mentioned, and which is the
Northern Promontory of this Country, I have named York Cape,
in honour of his late Royal Highness, the Duke of York. It lies
in the Long. of 218° 24′ W., the N. point in the Lat. of 10° 37′ S.,
and the E. point in 10° 41′. The land over and to the Southward
of this last point is rather low and very flatt as far inland as the
Eye could reach, and looks barren. To the Southward of the
Cape the Shore forms a large open bay, which I called Newcastle
bay, wherein are some small, low Islands and shoals, and the
land all about it is very low, flatt, and sandy. The land on the
Northern part of the Cape is rather more hilly, and the shore

forms some small bays, wherein there appear'd to be good Anchorage, and the Vallies appear'd to be tolerably well Cloathed with wood. Close to the E. point of the Cape are 3 small Islands, and a small Ledge of rocks spitting off from one of them. There is also an Island laying close to the N. Point. The other Islands before spoke of lay about 4 Miles without these; only two of them are of any extent. The Southermost is the largest, and much higher than any part of the Main land. On the N.W. side of this Island seem'd to be good Anchorage, and Vallies that to all appearance would afford both wood and fresh Water. These Isles are known in the Chart by the name of York Isles. To the Southward and S.E. of them, and even to the Eastward and Northward, are several low Islands, rocks, and Shoals. Our depth of Water in sailing between them and the Main was 12, 13, and 14 fathoms.

Wednesday, 22nd.—Gentle breezes at E. by S. and clear weather. We had not steer'd above 3 or 4 Miles along shore to the westward before we discover'd the land ahead to be Islands detached by several Channels from the main land; upon this we brought too to Wait for the Yawl, and called the other Boats on board, and after giving them proper instructions, sent them away again to lead us thro' the Channell next the Main, and as soon as the Yawl was on board made sail after them with the Ship. Soon after we discover'd rocks and Shoals in this Channell, upon which I made the Signal for the board to lead thro' the next Channel to the Northward laying between the Islands, which they accordingly did, we following with the Ship, and had not less than 5 fathoms; and this in the narrowest part of the Channel, which was about a Mile and a ½ broad from Island to Island. At 4 o'Clock we Anchor'd about a Mile and a ½ or 2 Miles within the Entrance in 6½ fathoms, clear ground, distance from the Islands on each side of us one Mile, the Main land extending away to the S.W.; the farthest point of which we could see bore from us S. 48° W., and the Southermost point of the Islands, on the N.W. side of the Passage, bore S. 76° W. Between these 2 points we could see no land, so that we were in great hopes that we had at last found out a Passage into the Indian seas; but in order to be better informed I landed with a party of men, accompanied by Mr. Banks and Dr. Solander, upon the islands which lies at the S.E. point of the Passage. Before and after we Anchor'd we saw a Number of People upon this Island, Arm'd in the same manner as all the others we have seen, Except one man, who had a bow and a bundle of Arrows, the first we have seen upon this Coast.

From the appearance of the people we expected they would have opposed our landing; but as we approached the shore they all made off, and left us in peaceable possession of as much of the Island as served our purpose. After landing I went upon the highest hill, which, however, was of no great height, yet no less than twice or thrice the height of the Ship's Mastheads; but I could see from it no land between S.W. and W.S.W., so that I did not doubt but there was a passage. I could see plainly that the lands laying to the N.W. of this passage were compos'd of a number of Islands of Various extent, both for height and Circuit, ranged one behind another as far to the Northward and Westward as I could see, which could not be less than 12 or 14 Leagues.

Having satisfied myself of the great Probability of a passage, thro' which I intend going with the Ship, and therefore may land no more upon this Eastern coast of New Holland, and on the Western side I can make no new discovery, the honour of which belongs to the Dutch Navigators, but the Eastern Coast from the Lat. of 38° S. down to this place, I am confident, was never seen or Visited by any European before us; and notwithstanding I had in the Name of his Majesty taken possession of several places upon this Coast, I now once More hoisted English Colours, and in the Name of His Majesty King George the Third took possession of the whole Eastern coast from the above Lat. down to this place by the Name of New Wales, together with all the Bays, Harbours, Rivers, and Islands, situated upon the said Coast; after which we fired 3 Volleys of small Arms, which were answer'd by the like number from the Ship.

This done, we set out for the Ship, but were some time in getting on board on account of a very Rapid Ebb Tide, which set N.E. out of the Passage. Ever since we came in amongst the Shoals this last time we have found a Moderate Tide; the flood setting to the N.W. and Ebb to the S.E; at this place is high water at full and change of the moon, about 1 or 2 o'Clock, and riseth and falleth upon a perpendicular about 10 or 12 feet. We saw upon all the Adjacent Lands and Islands a great number of smokes—a certain sign that they are inhabited—and we have daily seen smokes on every part of the Coast we have lately been upon. Between 7 and 8 o'Clock a.m. we saw several naked people, all or most of them Women, down upon the beach picking up Shells, etc.; they had not a single rag of any kind of Cloathing upon them, and both these and those we saw yesterday were in every respect the same sort of People we have seen everywhere upon the Coast. 2 or 3 of the Men we saw Yesterday had on pretty large breast plates, which we supposed were made of pearl Oyster Shells; this was a thing, as well as the Bow and Arrows, we had not seen before. At low water, which hapned about 10 o'Clock, we got under sail, and stood to the S.W., with a light breeze at East, which afterwards veer'd to N. by E., having the Pinnace ahead; depth of Water from 6 to 10 fathoms, except in one place, were we passed over a Bank of 5 fathoms. At Noon Possession Island, at the S.E. entrance of the Passage, bore N. 53° E., distant 4 Leagues; the Western extream of the Main land in sight S. 43° W., distant 4 or 5 Leagues, being all exceeding low. The S.W. point of the largest Island on the N.W. side of the passage bore N. 71° W., distant 8 Miles; this point I named Cape Cornwall (Lat. 10° 43′ S., Long. 218° 59′ W.), and some low Islands lying about the Middle of the Passage, which I called Wallace's Isles, bore W. by S. ½ S., distance about 2 Leagues. Our Latitude by Observation was 10° 46′ S.

Thursday, 23rd.—In the P.M. had little wind and Variable, with which and the Tide of Flood we keept advancing to the W.N.W.; depth of Water 8, 7, and 5 fathoms. At ½ past 1 the pinnace, which was ahead, made the Signal for Shoal Water, upon which we Tackt and sent away the Yawl to sound also, and then Tack'd again, and stood after them with the Ship; 2 hours after this they both at once made the Signal for having Shoal water. I was afraid to stand on for fear of running aground at that time of the Tide, and therefore came to an Anchor in ¼ less 7 fathoms, sandy ground. Wallice's Islands bore S. by W. ½ W., distant 5 or 6 Miles, the Islands to the Northward extending from N. 73° E. to N. 10° E., and a small Island just in sight bearing N.W. ½ W. Here we found the flood Tide set to the Westward and Ebb to the Contrary. After we had come to Anchor I sent away the Master with the Long boat to sound, who, upon his return in the evening, reported that there was a bank stretching N. and S., upon which were 3 fathoms Water, and behind it 7 fathoms. We had it Calm all Night and until 9 in the Morning, at which time we weigh'd, with a light breeze at S.S.E., and steer'd N.W. by W. for the Small Island above mentioned, having first sent the Boats ahead to sound; depth of Water 8, 7, 6, 5, 4, and 3 fathoms when upon the Bank, it being now the last Quarter Ebb. At this time the most Northermost Islands we had in sight bore N. 9° E.; the S.W. point of the largest Islands on the N.W. side of the Passage, which I named Cape Cornwall, bore E.; distant 3 Leagues. This bank, at least so much as we sounded, extends nearly N. and S., how far I cannot say; its breadth, however, is not more than $\frac{1}{4}$ or at most $\frac{1}{2}$ a Mile. Being over the Bank, we deepned our water to a $\frac{1}{4}$ less 7 fathoms, which depth we carried all the way to the small Island ahead, which we reached by Noon, at which time it bore S., distant near $\frac{1}{2}$ a Mile; depth of Water 5 fathoms. The most northermost land we had in sight (being part of the same Chain of Islands we have had to the Northward of us since we entered the Passage) bore N. 71° E.; Lat. in, by Observation, 10° 33′ S., Long. 219° 22′ W. In this situation we had no part of the Main land in sight. Being now near the Island, and having but little wind, Mr. Banks and I landed upon it, and found it to be mostly a barren rock frequented by Birds, such as Boobies, a few of which we shott, and occasioned my giving it the name of Booby Island. I made but very short stay at this Island before I return'd to the Ship; in the meantime the wind had got to the S.W., and although it blow'd but very faint, yet it was accompanied with a Swell from the same quarter. This, together with other concuring Circumstances, left me no room to doubt but we had got to the Westward of Carpentaria, or the Northern extremity of New Holland, and had now an open Sea to the Westward; which gave me no small satisfaction, not only because the danger and fatigues of the Voyage was drawing near to an end, but by being able to prove that New Holland and New Guinea are 2 separate Lands or Islands, which until this day hath been a doubtful point with Geographers.

The N.E. entrance of this passage or Strait lies in the Latitude of 10° 27′ S., and in the Longitude of 218° 36′ W., from the Meridian of Greenwich. It is form'd by the Main, or the northern extremity of New Holland, on the S.E., and by a Congeries of Islands to N.W., which I named Prince of Wales's Islands. It is very Probable that the Islands extend quite to New Guinea; they are of Various Extent both for height and Circuit, and many of them seem'd to be indifferently well Cloath'd with wood, etc., and, from the smokes we saw, some, if not all of them, must be inhabited. It is also very probable that among these Islands are as good, if not better, passages than the one we have come thro', altho' one need hardly wish for a better, was the access to it from the Eastward less dangerous; but this difficulty will remain until some better way is found out than the one we came, which no doubt may be done was it ever to become an object to be looked for. The northern Extent of the Main or outer Reef, which limit or bounds the Shoals to the Eastward, seems to be the only thing wanting to Clear up this point; and this was a thing I had neither time nor inclination to go about, having been already sufficiently harrass'd with dangers without going to look for more.

This passage, which I have named Endeavour Straits, after the Name of the Ship, is in length N.E. and S.W. 10 Leagues, and about 5 Leagues broad, except at the N.E. entrance, where it is only 2 Miles broad by reason of several small Islands which lay there, one of which, called Possession Island, is of a Moderate height and Circuit; this we left between us and the Main, passing between it and 2 Small round Islands, which lay N.W. 2 Miles from it. There are also 2 Small low Islands, called Wallice's Isles, laying in the Middle of the S.W. entrance, which we left to the southward; the depth of Water we found in the Straits was from 4 to 9 fathoms. Every where good Anchorage, only about 2 Leagues to the Northward of Wallice's Islands is a Bank, whereon is not more than 3 fathoms at low water, but probable there might be found more was it sought for. I have not been particular in describing this Strait, no more than I have been in pointing out the respective Situations of the Islands, Shoals, etc., on the Coast of New Wales; for these I refer to the Chart, where they are deliniated with all the accuracy that Circumstances would admit of.

With respect to the Shoals that lay upon this Coast I must observe, for the benefit of those who may come after me, that I do not believe the one $\frac{1}{2}$ of them are laid down in my Chart; for it would be Absurd to suppose that we Could see or find them all. And the same thing may in some Measure be said of the Islands, especially between the Latitude of 20° and 22°, where we saw Islands out at Sea as far as we could distinguish any thing. However, take the Chart in general, and I believe it will be found to contain as few Errors as most Sea Charts which have not undergone a thorough correction. The Latitude and Longitude of all, or most of, the principal head lands, Bays, etc., may be relied on, for we seldom fail'd of getting an Observation every day to correct our Latitude by, and the Observation for settling the Longitude were no less Numerous, and made as often as the Sun and Moon came in play; so that it was impossible for any Material error to creep into our reckoning in the intermediate times. In justice to Mr. Green, I must say that he was indefatigable in making and calculating these observations, which otherwise must have taken up a great deal of my time, which I could not at all times very well spare; not only this, but by his instructions several of the petty Officers can make and calculate these observations almost as well as himself. It is only by such

Means that this method of finding the Longitude at Sea can be put into universal practice; a Method that we have generally found may be depended upon within ½ a degree, which is a degree of Accuracy more than sufficient for all Nautical purposes. Would Sea Officers once apply themselves to the making and calculating these Observations they would not find them so very difficult as they at first imagine, especially with the Assistance of the Nautical Almanack and Astronomical Ephemeris, by the help of which the Calculation for finding the Longitude takes up but little more time than that of an Azimuth for finding the Variation of the Compass; but unless this Ephemeris is Published for some time to come, more than either one or 2 Years, it can never be of general use in long Voyages, and in short Voyages it's not so much wanted. Without it the Calculations are Laborious and discouraging to beginners, and such as are not well vers'd in these kind of Calculations.

SOME ACCOUNT OF NEW WALES

In the Course of this Journal I have at different times made mention of the Appearance or Aspect of the face of the Country, the Nature of the Soil, its produce, etc. By the first it will appear that to the Southward of 33° or 34° the land in general is low and level, with very few Hills or Mountains; further to the Northward it may in some places be called a Hilly, but hardly anywhere can be called a Mountainous, Country, for the Hills and Mountains put together take up but a small part of the Surface in Comparison to what the Planes and Valleys do which intersect or divide these Hills and Mountains. It is indifferently well water'd, even in the dry Seasons, with small brooks and Springs, but no great Rivers, unless it be in the Wet season, when the low lands and Vallies near the Sea, I do suppose, are mostly laid under Water. The Small Brooks may then become large Rivers; but this can only happen with the Tropick. It was only in Thirsty Sound that we could find no fresh Water, and that no doubt was owing to the Country being there very much intersected with Salt Creeks and Mangrove land.

The low land by the Sea, and even as far in land as we were, is for the most part friable, loose, sandy Soil yet indifferently fertile and Cloathed with woods, long grass, shrubs, plants, etc. The Mountains or Hills are checquer'd with woods and Lawns; some of the Hills are wholy cover'd with Flourishing Trees; others but thinly, and the few that are upon them are small, and the spot of Lawns or Savannahs are rocky and barren, especially to the Northward, where the Country did not afford or produce near the Vegetation that it does to the Southward, nor were the Trees in the Woods half so tall and stout. The Woods do not produce any great variety of Trees; there are only 2 or 3 sorts that can be called Timber. The largest is the gum Tree, which grows all over the country; the wood of this Tree is too hard and ponderous for most common uses. The Tree which resembles our Pines I saw nowhere in perfection but in Botany Bay; this wood, as I have before observed, is something of the same Nature as American Live Oak; in short, most of the large Trees in this Country are of a hard and ponderous nature, and could not be applied to many purposes. Here are several sorts of the Palm kind, Mangrove, and several other sorts of small Trees and Shrubs quite unknown to me, besides a very great number of Plants hitherto unknown; but these things are wholy out of my way to describe, nor will this be of any loss, since not only plants, but every thing that can be of use to the Learned World will be very accurately described by Mr. Banks and Dr. Solander. The Land naturally produces hardly anything fit for Man to eat and the Natives know nothing of Cultivation. There are, indeed, growing wild in the wood a few sorts of Fruit (the most of them unknown to us), which when ripe do not eat amiss, one sort especially, which we called Apples, being about the size of a Crab Apple; it is black and pulpey when ripe, and tastes like a Damson; it hath a large hard stone or Kernel, and grows on Trees or Shrubs.

In the Northern parts of the Country, as about Endeavour River, and probably in many other places, the Boggy or watery Lands produce Taara or Cocos, which, when properly cultivated, are very good roots, without which they are hardly eatable; the Tops, however, make very good greens.

Land Animals are scarce, so far as we know confin'd to a very few species; all that we saw I have before mentioned. The sort which is in the greatest Plenty is the Kangooroo or Kanguru, so called by the Natives; we saw a good many of them about Endeavour River, but kill'd only 3, which we found very good Eating. Here are likewise Lizards, Snakes, Scorpions, Centapees, etc., but not in any plenty. Tame Animals they have none but Dogs, and of these we saw but one, and therefore must be very scarce, probably they eat them faster than they breed them; we should not have seen this one had he not made us frequent Visits while we lay in Endeavour River.

The land Fowls are Bustards, Eagles, Hawks, Crows, such as

we have in England, Cockatoes of 2 sorts, White and Brown, very beautiful Birds of the Parrot kind, such as Lorryquets, etc., Pidgeons, Doves, Quails, and several sorts of smaller birds. The Sea and Water Fowls are Herons, Boobies, Noddies, Guls, Curlews, Ducks, Pelicans, etc., and when Mr. Banks and Mr. Gore where in the Country, at the head of Endeavour River, they saw and heard in the Night great numbers of Geese. The Sea is indifferently well stocked with fish of Various sorts, such as Sharks, Dog-fish, Rock-fish, Mullets, Breams, Cavallies, Mack'rel, old wives, Leather Jackets, Five Fingers, Sting rays, Whip rays, etc., all excellent in their kind. The Shell fish are Oysters of 3 or 4 sorts, viz., Rock Oysters, and Mangrove Oysters, which are small, Pearl Oysters and Mud Oysters; these last are the best and Largest I ever saw. Cockles and Clams of several sorts, many of those that are found upon the Reefs are of a prodigious size, Craw fish, Crabs, Muscles, and a variety of other sorts. Here are also upon the Shoals and Reefs great Numbers of the finest Green Turtle in the world, and in the River and Salt Creeks are some Aligators.

The Natives of this Country are of a middle Stature, streight Bodied and Slender limb'd; their Skins the Colour of Wood soot, their Hair mostly black, some Lank and others curled; they all wear it Cropt Short; their Beards, which are generally black, they likewise crop short, or Singe off. There features are far from being disagreeable, and their Voices are soft and Tunable. They go quite Naked, both Men and Women, without any manner of Cloathing whatever; even the Women do not so much as cover their privities, altho' none of us was ever very near any of their Women, one Gentleman excepted, yet we are all of us as well satisfied of this as if we had lived among them. Notwithstanding we had several interviews with the Men while we lay in Endeavour River, yet, wether through Jealousy or disregard, they never brought any of their women along with them to the Ship, but always left them on the Opposite side of the River, where we had frequent Opportunities viewing them thro' our Glasses. They wear as Ornaments, Nacklaces made of Shells, Bracelets, or Hoops, about their Arms, made mostly of Hair Twisted and made like a Cord Hoop; these they wear tight about the upper parts of their Arms, and some have Girdles made in the same manner. The Men wear a bone, about 3 or 4 Inches long and a finger's thick, run thro' the Bridge of their Nose; they likewise have holes in their Ears for Ear Rings, but we never saw them wear any; neither are all the other Ornaments wore in

Common, for we have seen as many without as with them. Some of these we saw on Possession Island wore breast plates, which we supposed were made of Mother of Pearl Shells. Many of them paint their Bodies and faces with a Sort of White paste or pigment; this they apply different ways, each according to his fancy.

Their offensive weapons are Darts; some are only pointed at one end, others are barb'd, some with wood, others with Stings of rays, and some with Sharks' Teeth, etc.; these last are stuck fast on with Gum. They throw the Darts with only one hand, in the doing of which they make use of a piece of wood about 3 feet long, made thin like the blade of a Cutlass, with a little hook at one End to take hold of the End of the dart, and at the other end is fix'd a thin piece of bone about 3 or 4 Inches long; the use of this is, I believe, to keep the dart steady, and to make it quit the hand in a proper direction. By the helps of these throwing sticks, as we call them, they will hit a mark at the Distance of 40 or 50 yards, with almost, if not as much, Certainty as we can do with a Musquet, and much more so than with a ball. These throwing sticks we at first took for wooden swords, and perhaps on some occasions they may use them as such; that is, when all their darts are expended. Be this as it may, they never Travel without both them and their Darts, not for fear of Enemies, but for killing of Game, etc., as I shall show hereafter. There defensive weapons are Targets, made of wood; but these we never saw used but once in Botany Bay.

I do not look upon them to be a warlike people; on the contrary, I think them a Timerous and inoffensive race, no ways inclined to Cruelty, as appear'd from their behaviour to one of our People in Endeavour River, which I have before mentioned, neither are they very numerous. They live in small parties along by the Sea Coast, the banks of Lakes, Rivers, Creeks, etc. They seem to have no fixed habitation, but move about from place to place like wild beasts in search of Food, and, I believe, depend wholy upon the Success of the present day for their Subsistance. They have wooden fish Gigs, with 2, 3, or 4 prongs, each very ingeniously made, with which they strike fish. We have also seen them strike their fish and birds with their Darts. With these they likewise kill other Animals; they have also wooden Harpoons for striking Turtle, but of these I believe they get but few, except at the seasons they come ashore to lay. In short, these people live wholy by fishing and hunting, but mostly by the former, for we never saw one Inch of Cultivated land in the whole Country. They know, however, the use of Taara, and sometimes eat them;

we do not know that they Eat anything raw, but roast or broil all they eat on slow small fires. Their Houses are mean, small Hovels, not much bigger than an Oven, made of Peices of Sticks, Bark, Grass, etc., and even these are seldom used but in the Wet seasons, for in the daytimes we know they as often sleep in the Open Air as anywhere else. We have seen many of their Sleeping places, where there has been only some branches or peices of Bark, grass, etc., about a foot high on the Windward side.

Their Canoes are as mean as can be conceived, especially to the Southward, where all we saw were made of one peice of the Bark of Trees about 12 or 14 feet long, drawn or Tied together at one end. As I have before made mention, these Canoes will not carry above 2 People, in general there is never more than one in them; but, bad as they are, they do very well for the purpose they apply them to, better than if they were larger, for as they draw but little water they go in them upon the Mud bands, and pick up Sheel fish, etc., without going out of the Canoe. The few Canoes we saw to the Northward were made out of a Log of wood hollow'd out, about 14 feet long and very narrow, with outriggers; these will carry 4 people. During our whole stay in Endeavour River we saw but one Canoe, and had great reason to think that the few people that resided about that place had no more; this one served them to cross the River and to go a Fishing in, etc. They attend the Shoals, and flatts, one where or another, every day at low water to gather Shell fish, or whatever they can find to eat, and have each a little bag to put what they get in; this bag is made of net work. They have not the least knowledge of Iron or any other Metal that we know of; their working Tools must be made of Stone, bone, and Shells; those made of the former are very bad, if I may judge from one of their Adzes I have seen.

Bad and mean as their Canoes are, they at Certain seasons of the Year (so far as we know) go in them to the most distant Islands which lay upon the Coast, for we never landed upon one but what we saw signs of People having been there before. We were surprized to find Houses, etc., upon Lizard Island, which lies 5 Leagues from the nearest part of the Main; a distance we before thought they could not have gone in their Canoes.

The Coast of this Country, at least so much of it as lays to the Northward of 25° of Latitude, abounds with a great Number of fine bays and Harbours, which are Shelter'd from all winds; but the Country itself, so far as we know, doth not produce any one thing that can become an Article in Trade to invite Europeans to fix a settlement upon it. However, this Eastern side is not that barren and miserable country that Dampier and others have described the Western side to be. We are to consider that we see this country in the pure state of nature; the Industry of Man has had nothing to do with any part of it, and yet we find all such things as nature hath bestow'd upon it in a flourishing state. In this Extensive Country it can never be doubted but what most sorts of Grain, Fruit, roots, etc., of every kind would flourish here were they once brought hither, planted and Cultivated by the hands of Industry; and here are Provender for more Cattle, at all seasons of the Year, than ever can be brought into the Country. When one considers the Proximity of this Country with New Guinea, New Britain, and several other Islands which produce Cocoa Nutts and many other fruits proper for the support of man, it seems strange that they should not long ago be Transplanted here; by its not being done it should seem that the Natives of this Country have no commerce with their Neighbours, the New Guineans. It is very probable that they are a different people, and speak a different Language. For the advantage of such as want to Clear up this point I shall add a small Vocabulary of a few Words in the New Holland Language which we learnt when in Endeavour River.

English	*New Holland*
The Head	Whageegee
„ Hair of the head	Morye or Moré
„ Eyes	Meul
„ Ears	Melea
„ Lips	Yembe or Jembi
„ Teeth	Mulere or Moile
„ Chinn	Jæal
„ Beard	Waller
„ Tongue	Unjar
„ Nose	Bonjoo
„ Naval	Toolpoor or Julpur
„ Penis	Keveil or Kerrial
„ Scrotum	Coonal or Kunnol
„ Arms	Aw or Awl
„ Hand	Marigal
„ Thumb	Eboorbalga
„ Fore, Middle and Ring fingers	Egalbaiga
Little Finger	Nakil or Eboonakil

Q

English	*New Holland*
The Thighs	Coman
,, Knees	Ponga
,, Legs	Peegoorgo
,, Feet	Edamal
,, Nails	Kolke or Kulke
A Stone	Walba
Sand	Joo'wal, Yowall, or Joralba
A Rope or Line	Goorgo or Gurka
Fire	Maianang or Meanang
The Sun	Galan or Gallan
,, Sky	Kere or Kearre
A Father	Dunjo
,, Son	Jumurre
,, Man	Bamma or Bā ma
,, Dog	Cotta or Kota
,, Lorryquet	Perpere or Pier-pier
,, Cocatoo	Wanda
Male Turtle	Poonja or Poinja
Female	Mamingo
A great Cockle	Moenjo or Moingo
Cocos Yams	Maracotu (?)
A Canoe	Maragan

From what I have said of the Natives of New Holland they may appear to some to be the most wretched People upon Earth; but in reality they are far more happier than we Europeans, being wholy unacquainted not only with the Superfluous, but with the necessary Conveniences so much sought after in Europe; they are happy in not knowing the use of them. They live in a Tranquility which is not disturbed by the Inequality of Condition. The earth and Sea of their own accord furnishes them with all things necessary for Life. They covet not Magnificient Houses, Household-stuff, etc.; they live in a Warm and fine Climate, and enjoy every wholesome Air, so that they have very little need of Cloathing; and this they seem to be fully sencible of, for many to whom we gave Cloth, etc., left it carelessly upon the Sea beach and in the Woods, as a thing they had no manner of use for; in short, they seem'd to set no Value upon anything we gave them, nor would they ever part with anything of their own for any one Article we could offer them. This, in my opinion, Argues that they think themselves provided with all the necessarys of Life, and that they have no Superfluities.

I shall conclude the account of this Country with a few observations on the Currents and Tides upon the Coast, because I have mentioned in the Course of this Journal that the latter hath sometimes set one way and sometimes another, which I shall Endeavour to account for in the best manner I can. From the Lat. of 32°, or above downwards to Sandy Cape in the Lat. of 24° 46′, we constantly found a Current setting to the Southward at the rate of 10 or 15 Miles per Day, more or less, according to the distance we were from the land, for it runs stronger in shore than in the Offing. All this time I had not been able to satisfy myself whether the flood-tide came from the Southward, Eastward, or Northward, but judged it to come from the S.E.; but the first time we anchor'd upon the coast, which was in the Lat. of 24° 30′, and about 10 Leagues to the S.E. of Bustard Bay, we found there the flood to come from the N.W. On the Contrary, 30 Leagues further to the N.W., on the S. side of Keppel Bay, we found the Flood to come from the East, and at the Northern part of the said Bay we found it come from the Northward, but with a much Slower Motion than the Easterly Tide. Again, on the East side of the Bay of Inlets we found the flood to set strong to the Westward as far as the Op'ning of Broad sound, but on the N. side of that sound the flood come with a Slow motion from the N.W.; and when at Anchor before Repulse bay we found the flood to come from the northward. We need only admit the flood tide to come from the East or S.E., and then all these seeming Contradictions will be found to be conformable to reason and experience. It is well known that where there are deep Inlets, large Creeks, etc., into low lands, that it is not occasioned by fresh water Rivers; there is a very great indraught of the Flood Tide, the direction of which will be determin'd according to the possition or direction of the Coast which forms the Entrance into such Inlets; and this direction the Tide must follow, let it be ever so contrary to their general Course out at Sea, and where the Tides are weak, as they are in general upon this Coast, a large Inlet will, if I may so call it, attract the Flood tide for many Leagues. Any one need only cast an Eye over the Chart to be made sencible of what I have advanced. To the Northward of Whitsundays Passage there are few or no large Inlets, and consequently the Flood sets to the Northward or N.W., according to the direction of the Coast, and Ebb the Contrary; but this is to be understood at a little distance from land, or where there is no Creeks or Inlets, for where such are, be they ever so small, the draw the flood from the Southward, Eastward, and Northward, and, as I found by experience, while we lay in Endeavour River. Another thing I have observed upon the Tides which ought to be remarked, which is that there is only one high Tide in 24 Hours, and that is the night Tide. On the Spring Tides the difference between the perpendicular rise of the night and day Tides is not less than 3 feet, which is a great deal where the Tides are so inconsiderable, as they are here. This inequality of the Tide I did not observe till we run ashore; perhaps it is much more so to the Northward than to the Southward. After we had got within the Reefs the second time we found the Tides more considerable than at any time before, except in the Bay of Inlets. It may be owing to the water being confin'd in Channels between the Shoals, but the flood always set to the N.W. to the extremity of New Wales, from thence W. and S.W. into the India Seas.

. . . . . .

Cook at Batavia, October 1770.

Friday, 12*th.*—At 5 o'Clock P.M. I was introduced to the Governor-General, who received me very politely and told me that I should have everything I wanted, and that in the Morning my request should be laid before the Council where I was desir'd to attend.

About 9 o'clock in the Evening we had much rain, with some very heavy Claps of Thunder, one of which carried away a Dutch Indiaman's Main Mast by the Deck, and split it, the Maintopmast and Topgallantmast all to shivers. She had had an Iron Spindle at the Maintopgallant Mast head which had first attracted the Lightning. The ship lay about 2 Cable lengths from us, and we were struck with the Thunder at the same time, and in all probability we should have shared the same fate as the Dutchman, had it not been for the Electrical Chain which we had but just before got up; this carried the Lightning or Electrical matter over the side clear of the Ship. The Shock was so great as to shake the whole Ship very sencibly. This instance alone is sufficient to recommend these Chains to all Ships whatever, and that of the Dutchman ought to Caution people from having Iron Spindles at their Mast heads.

In the morning I went on shore to the Council Chamber and laid my request before the Governour and Council, who gave me for answer that I should have every thing I wanted.

Saturday, 13*th.*—Received on board a Cask of Arrack and some Greens for the Ship's Company.

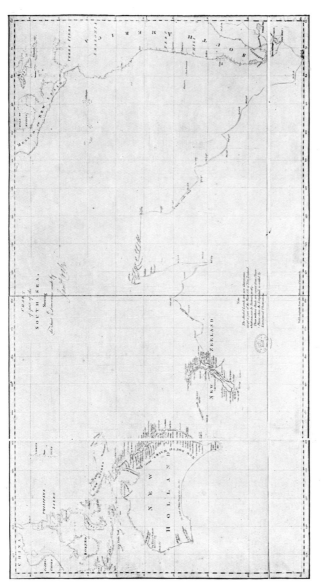

CHART OF PART OF THE SOUTH SEA, SIGNED BY JAMES COOK.

The pricked line shows the track of the *Endeavour*.

Sunday, 14th.—Early this morning a ship sail'd from hence for Holland by which I had just time to write 2 or 3 lines to Mr. Stephens, Secretary of the Admiralty, to acquaint him of our Arrival, after which I went on shore and waited upon the Sha-bander, who has the direction of the Town, Port, etc., to get an order to the Superintendent at Onrust to receive us at that Island, but this, I was told, would not be ready before Tuesday next. Received from the Shore Fresh Beef and Greens for the Ship's Company.

Monday, 15th.—Fresh Sea and land breezes and fair weather. I had forgot to mention, that upon our arrival here I had not one man upon the Sick List; Lieut. Hicks, Mr. Green, and Tupia were the only people that had any complaints occasioned by a long continuance at Sea.

Cook's Report.

[Cook arrived in England on July 13th, 1771; but before he left Batavia he wrote a letter to the Secretary of the Admiralty, covering a copy of his Journal, and summarizing his estimate of the results of the voyage. It is evident that he had no real conception of the magnitude of what he had done, for he said that the discoveries made in the voyage were not great. The letter is also interesting as showing that Cook believed that he had shattered the legend about *Terra Australis Incognita;* and his claim that he had brought his crew through their long traverse of the oceans without the loss of a single man from sickness was made with proper pride in an unparalleled achievement for that age, when scurvy was the scourge of seafaring people. An extract from the letter runs as follows]:*

" In this Journal, I have with undisguised truth and without gloss, inserted the whole transactions of the Voyage, and made such remarks and have given such descriptions of things as I thought was necessary, in the best manner I was capable of. Although the discoverys made in the Voyage are not great, I flatter myself they are such as may merit the Attention of their Lordships, and altho' I have failed in discovering the so much talked of Southern Continent (which perhaps do not exist) and which I myself had much at heart, yet I am confident that no part of the failure of such discovery can be laid to my charge. Had we been so fortunate not to have run ashore, much more would have been done in the latter part of the Voyage than what

* This is Kitson's version; Wharton's differs slightly in spelling, etc.

was, but as it is, I presume this Voyage will be found as compleat as any before made to the St Seas on the same acc^t.

The plans I have drawn of the places I have been at, were made with all the care and accuracy that Time and Circumstances would admit of. Thus far I am certain that the Latitude and Longitude of few parts of the World are better settled than these, in this I was much assisted by Mr. Green, who let slip no opportunity for making observations for settling the Long$^{dc.}$ during the whole course of the Voyage, and the many valuable discoverys made by Mr Banks and Dr Solander in Natural History and other things useful to the learned world, cannot fail of contributing very much to the success of the Voyage. In justice to the officers and the whole of the crew, I must say, they have gone through the fatigues and dangers of the Whole Voyage with that cheerfulness and alertness that will always do honour to the British Seamen, and I have the satisfaction to say that I have not lost one man by Sickness during the whole Voyage. I hope that the repairs wanting to the Ship will not be so great as to detain us any length of time; You may be assured that I shall make no unnecessary delay either here or at any other place, but shall make the best of my way home."

XIII. BLIGH'S ACCOUNT OF THE *BOUNTY* MUTINY

[THE following is the account given by Captain William Bligh himself of the celebrated Mutiny of the *Bounty*, and of his boat voyage from Tahiti to Timor, one of the most remarkable maritime adventures on record.]

1787.—The King having been graciously pleased to comply with a request from the merchants and planters interested in His Majesty's West India possessions, that the bread-fruit tree might be introduced into those islands, a vessel, proper for the undertaking, was bought, and taken into dock at Deptford, to be provided with the necessary fixtures and preparations for executing the object of the voyage. These were completed according to a plan of my much-honoured friend, Sir Joseph Banks, which, in the event, proved the most advantageous that could have been adopted for the intended purpose.

August 16th.—The ship was named the *Bounty*: I was appointed to command her on the 16th of August, 1787. Her burden was nearly two hundred and fifteen tons; her extreme length on deck, ninety feet ten inches; extreme breadth, twenty-four feet three inches; and height in the hold under the beams, at the main hatchway, ten feet three inches. In the cockpit were the cabins of the surgeon, gunner, botanist, and clerk, with a stewart-room and store-rooms. The between decks was divided in the following manner:—the great cabin was appropriated for the preservation of the plants, and extended as far forward as the after hatchway. It had two large skylights, and on each side three scuttles for air, and was fitted with a false floor cut full of holes to contain the garden-pots in which the plants were to be brought home. The deck was covered with lead, and at the foremost corners of the cabin were fixed pipes to carry off the water that drained from the plants, into tubs placed below to save it for future use. I had a small cabin on one side to sleep in, adjoining to the great cabin, and a place near the middle of the ship to eat in. The bulkhead of this apartment was at the after-part of the main hatchway, and on each side of it were the births of the mates and midshipmen; between these births the arm-chest was placed. The cabin of the master, in which was always kept the key of the arms, was opposite to mine. This particular description of the interior parts of the ship is rendered necessary by the event of the expedition. . . .

On Sunday, the 26th October, 1788, at four o'clock in the morning, having run twenty-five leagues from Maitea, we brought to till daylight, when we saw Point Venus bearing S.W. by W., distant about four leagues. As we drew near, a great number of canoes came off to us. Their first inquiries were, if we were *Tyos*, which signifies friends; and whether we came from *Pretanie* (their pronunciation of Britain), or from Lima: they were no sooner satisfied in this than they crowded on board in vast numbers, notwithstanding our endeavours to prevent it, as we were working the ship in; and in less than ten minutes the deck was so full that I could scarce find my own people. At nine in the forenoon we were obliged to anchor in the outer part of Matavai Bay, in thirteen fathoms, being prevented by light variable winds from placing the ship in a proper birth. In this station the west part of One-tree-hill bore S. by E. ½ E. one mile distant.

This passage of fifty-two days from Van Diemen's Land may be rated as moderate sailing. We passed New Zealand with the spring equinox, and the winds, though strong, were at no time violent. To the southward of 40° 0′ S. they were variable; between the latitudes of 40 and 33° S. the wind kept in the N.W. quarter; afterwards, till we got into the trade, the winds were variable, mostly from the eastward, but light, and inclinable to calms. The ship was 3° 22′ in longitude to the eastward of the dead reckoning, which the time-keeper almost invariably proved to be owing to a current giving us more easting than the log. Our track was as distant from any course of former ships as I could conveniently make it; and though we made no new discoveries, except the small cluster of islands near New Zealand, yet in other parts of the track, as has been noticed, we met with signs of being in the neighbourhood of land.

It may not be unworthy of remark, that the whole distance which the ship had run by the log, in direct and contrary courses, from leaving England to our anchoring at Otaheite, was twenty-seven thousand and eighty-six miles, which, on an average, is at the rate of an hundred and eight miles each twenty-four hours.

Sunday, 26th October, 1788.—The ship being anchored, our number of visitors continued to increase; but as yet we saw no person that we could recollect to have been of much consequence. Some inferior chiefs made me presents of a few hogs, and I made them presents in return. We were supplied with cocoanuts in great abundance, but bread-fruit was scarce.

Many inquiries were made after Captain Cook, Sir Joseph Banks, and many of their former friends. They said a ship had been here from which they had learnt that Captain Cook was dead; but the circumstances of his death they did not appear to be acquainted with; and I had given particular directions to my officers and ship's company that they should not be mentioned. The ship spoken of, they informed me, staid at Otaheite one month, and had been gone four months, by some of their accounts; according to others, only three months. The captain they called Tonah. I understood likewise from them that Lieutenant Watts was in the ship; who, having been here in the *Resolution* with Captain Cook, was well known to them. One of my first inquiries, as will naturally be imagined, was after our friend Omai; and it was a sensible mortification and disappointment to me to hear that not only Omai, but both the New Zealand boys who had been left with him were dead. Everyone agreed in their information that they died a natural death. Otoo, who was the chief of Matavai when Captain Cook was here the last time, was absent at another part of the island; they told me messengers were sent to inform him of our arrival, and that he was expected to return soon. There appeared among the natives in general great good-will towards us, and they seemed to be much rejoiced at our arrival. This whole day we experienced no instance of dishonesty. We were so much crowded that I could not undertake to remove to a more proper station without danger of disobliging our visitors, by desiring them to leave the ship: this business was, therefore, deferred till the next morning. . . .

Tuesday, the 28th April, 1789.—Just before sun-rising, while I was yet asleep, Mr. Christian, with the master-at-arms, gunner's mate, and Thomas Burkett, seaman, came into my cabin, and seizing me, tied my hands with a cord behind my back, threatening me with instant death if I spoke or made the least noise: I, however, called as loud as I could, in hopes of assistance; but they had already secured the officers who were not of their party, by placing centinels at their doors. There were three men at my cabin door, besides the four within; Christian had only a cutlass in his hand, the others had muskets and bayonets. I was hauled out of bed and forced on deck in my shirt, suffering great pain from the tightness with which they had tied my hands. I demanded the reason of such violence, but received no other answer than abuse for not holding my tongue. The master, the gunner, the surgeon, Mr. Elphinstone, master's mate, and Nelson were kept confined below; and the fore hatchway was guarded by centinels. The boatswain and carpenter, and also the clerk, Mr. Samuel, were allowed to come upon deck, where they saw me standing abaft the mizen-mast, with my hands tied behind my back, under a guard, with Christian at their head. The boatswain was ordered to hoist the launch out, with a threat, if he did not do it instantly, *to take care of himself.*

When the boat was out, Mr. Hayward and Mr. Hallet, two of the midshipmen, and Mr. Samuel were ordered into it. I demanded what their intention was in giving this order, and endeavoured to persuade the people near me not to persist in such acts of violence; but it was to no effect: "Hold your tongue, Sir, or you are dead this instant," was constantly repeated to me.

The master, by this time, had sent to request that he might come on deck, which was permitted; but he was soon ordered back again to his cabin.

I continued my endeavours to turn the tide of affairs, when Christian changed the cutlass which he had in his hand for a bayonet that was brought to him, and holding me with a strong grip by the cord that tied my hands, he with many oaths threatened to kill me immediately if I would not be quiet: the villains round me had their pieces cocked and bayonets fixed. Particular people were called on to go into the boat, and were hurried over the side; whence I concluded that with these people I was to be set adrift: I therefore made another effort to bring about a change, but with no other effect than to be threatened with having my brains blown out.

The boatswain and seamen, who were to go in the boat, were allowed to collect twine, canvas, lines, sails, cordage, an eight-and-twenty-gallon cask of water, and Mr. Samuel got 150 lbs. of bread, with a small quantity of rum and wine, also a quadrant and compass; but he was forbidden on pain of death to touch either map, ephemeris, book of astronomical observations, sextant, time-keeper, or any of my surveys or drawings.

The mutineers having forced those of the seamen whom they meant to get rid of into the boat, Christian directed a dram to be served to each of his own crew. I then unhappily saw that nothing could be done to effect the recovery of the ship: there was no one to assist me, and every endeavour on my part was answered with threats of death.

The officers were next called upon deck, and forced over the

side into the boat, while I was kept apart from everyone, abaft
the mizen-mast; Christian, armed with a bayonet, holding me by
the bandage that secured my hands. The guard round me had
their pieces cocked, but on my daring the ungrateful wretches to
fire, they uncocked them.

Isaac Martin, one of the guard over me, I saw had an inclination to assist me, and as he fed me with shaddock (my lips being
quite parched), we explained our wishes to each other by our
looks; but this being observed, Martin was removed from me.
He then attempted to leave the ship, for which purpose he
got into the boat; but with many threats they obliged him to
return.

The armourer, Joseph Coleman, and two of the carpenters,
McIntosh and Norman, were also kept contrary to their inclination; and they begged of me, after I was astern in the boat, to
remember that they declared they had no hand in the transaction. Michael Byrne, I am told, likewise wanted to leave the
ship.

It is of no moment for me to recount my endeavours to bring
back the offenders to a sense of their duty; all I could do was by
speaking to them in general; but it was to no purpose, for I was
kept securely bound, and no one except the guard suffered to
come near me.

To Mr. Samuel I am indebted for securing my journals and
commission, with some material ship papers. Without these I had
nothing to certify what I had done, and my honour and character
might have been suspected, without my possessing a proper document to have defended them. All this he did with great resolution, though guarded and strictly watched. He attempted to
save the time-keeper, and a box with my surveys, drawings, and
remarks for fifteen years past, which were numerous; when he
was hurried away with " Damn your eyes, you are well off to get
what you have."

It appeared to me that Christian was some time in doubt
whether he should keep the carpenter or his mates; at length he
determined on the latter, and the carpenter was ordered into the
boat. He was permitted, but not without some opposition, to take
his tool chest.

Much altercation took place among the mutinous crew during
the whole business: some swore "I'll be damned if he does not find
his way home, if he gets anything with him" (meaning me);
and, when the carpenter's chest was carrying away, "Damn
my eyes, he will have a vessel built in a month." While others

laughed at the helpless situation of the boat, being very deep, and so little room for those who were in her. As for Christian, he seemed as if meditating destruction on himself and everyone else.

I asked for arms, but they laughed at me, and said I was well acquainted with the people among whom I was going, and therefore did not want them; four cutlasses, however, were thrown into the boat after we were veered astern.

The officers and men being in the boat, they only waited for me, of which the master at arms informed Christian; who then said, "Come, Captain Bligh, your officers and men are now in the boat, and you must go with them; if you attempt to make the least resistance you will instantly be put to death;" and, without further ceremony, with a tribe of armed ruffians about me, I was forced over the side, where they untied my hands. Being in the boat, we were veered astern by a rope. A few pieces of pork were thrown to us, and some clothes, also the cutlasses I have already mentioned; and it was then that the armourer and carpenters called out to me to remember that they had no hand in the transaction. After having undergone a great deal of ridicule, and being kept some time to make sport for these unfeeling wretches, we were at length cast adrift in the open ocean.

I had with me in the boat the following persons:

Names.	Stations.
John Fryer,	Master.
Thomas Ledward,	Acting Surgeon.
David Nelson,	Botanist.
William Peckover,	Gunner.
William Cole,	Boatswain.
William Purcell,	Carpenter.
William Elphinston,	Master's Mate.
Thomas Haywood ⎰ John Hallet ⎱	Midshipmen.
John Norton ⎰ Peter Linkletter ⎱	Quartermasters.
Lawrence Lebogue,	Sailmaker.
John Smith ⎰ Thomas Hall ⎱	Cooks.
George Simpson,	Quartermaster's Mate.
Robert Tinkler,	A boy.
Robert Lamb,	Butcher.
Mr. Samuel,	Clerk.

There remained on board the *Bounty*:

Names.	Stations.
Fletcher Christian,	Master's Mate.
Peter Haywood	
Edward Young	Midshipmen.
George Stewart	
Charles Churchill,	Master-at-Arms.
John Mills,	Gunner's Mate.
James Morrison,	Boatswain's Mate.
Thomas Burkitt,	Able Seaman.
Matthew Quintal,	Ditto.
John Sumner,	Ditto.
John Milward,	Ditto.
William McKoy,	Ditto.
Henry Hilbrant,	Ditto.
Michael Byrne,	Ditto.
William Musprat,	Ditto.
Alexander Smith,	Ditto.
John Williams,	Ditto.
Thomas Ellison,	Ditto.
Isaac Martin,	Ditto.
Richard Skinner,	Ditto.
Matthew Thompson,	Ditto.
William Brown,	Gardener.
Jospeh Coleman,	Armourer.
Charles Norman,	Carpenter's Mate.
Thomas McIntosh,	Carpenter's Crew.

In all 25 hands, and the most able men of the ship's company.

Having little or no wind, we rowed pretty fast towards Tofoa, which bore N.E. about 10 leagues from us. While the ship was in sight she steered to the W.N.W., but I considered this only as a feint; for, when we were sent away, "Huzza for Otaheite" was frequently heard among the mutineers.

Christian, the chief of the mutineers, is of a respectable family in the north of England. This was the third voyage he had made with me; and, as I found it necessary to keep my ship's company at three watches, I had given him an order to take charge of the third, his abilities being thoroughly equal to the task; and by this means the master and gunner were not at watch and watch.

Haywood is also of a respectable family in the north of England and a young man of abilities, as well as Christian. These two had been objects of my particular regard and attention, and I had taken great pains to instruct them, having entertained hopes that, as professional men, they would have become a credit to their country.

Young was well recommended, and had the look of an able stout seaman: he, however, fell short of what his appearance promised.

Stewart was a young man of creditable parents, in the Orkneys; at which place, on the return of the *Resolution* from the South Seas, in 1780, we received so many civilities that, on that account only, I should gladly have taken him with me; but, independent of this recommendation, he was a seaman, and had always borne a good character.

Notwithstanding the roughness with which I was treated, the remembrance of past kindnesses produced some signs of remorse in Christian. When they were forcing me out of the ship, I asked him if this treatment was a proper return for the many instances he had received of my friendship? He appeared disturbed at my question, and answered with much emotion, "That, Captain Bligh, that is the thing; I am in hell—I am in hell."

As soon as I had time to reflect, I felt an inward satisfaction which prevented any depression of my spirits: conscious of my integrity and anxious solicitude for the good of the service in which I had been engaged, I found my mind wonderfully supported, and I began to conceive hopes, notwithstanding so heavy a calamity, that I should one day be able to account to my King and country for the misfortune.—A few hours before, my situation had been peculiarly flattering. I had a ship in the most perfect order, and well stored with every necessary both for service and health : by early attention to those particulars I had, as much as lay in my power, provided against any accident, in case I could not get through Endeavour Straits, as well as against what might befal me in them; add to this, the plants had been successfully preserved in the most flourishing state; so that, upon the whole, the voyage was two-thirds completed, and the remaining part, to all appearance, in a very promising way; every person on board being in perfect health, to establish which was ever amongst the principal objects of my attention.

It will very naturally be asked, what could be the reason for such a revolt? in answer to which I can only conjecture, that the mutineers had flattered themselves with the hopes of a more happy life among the Otaheiteans than they could possibly enjoy in England; and this, joined to some female connections, most probably occasioned the whole transaction.

The women at Otaheite are handsome, mild and cheerful in their manners and conversation, possessed of great sensibility, and have sufficient delicacy to make them admired and beloved. The chiefs were so much attached to our people that they rather encouraged their stay among them than otherwise, and even made them promises of large possessions. Under these and many other attendant circumstances, equally desirable, it is now perhaps not so much to be wondered at, though scarcely possible to have been foreseen, that a set of sailors, most of them void of connections, should be led away; especially when, in addition to such powerful inducements, they imagined it in their power to fix themselves in the midst of plenty, on one of the finest islands in the world, where they need not labour, and where the allurements of dissipation are beyond anything that can be conceived. The utmost, however, that any commander could have supposed to have happened is, that some of the people would have been tempted to desert. But if it should be asserted that a commander is to guard against an act of mutiny and piracy in his own ship, more than by the common rules of service, it is as much as to say that he must sleep locked up, and when awake be girded with pistols.

Desertions have happened, more or less, from most of the ships that have been at the Society Islands: but it has always been in the commanders' power to make the chiefs return their people: the knowledge, therefore, that it was unsafe to desert, perhaps, first led mine to consider with what ease so small a ship might be surprised, and that so favourable an opportunity would never offer to them again.

The secrecy of this mutiny is beyond all conception. Thirteen of the party, who were with me, had always lived forward among the seamen; yet neither they nor the messmates of Christian, Stewart, Haywood, and Young had ever observed any circumstance that made them in the least suspect what was going on. To such a close-planned act of villainy, my mind being entirely free from any suspicion, it is not wonderful that I fell a sacrifice. Perhaps, if there had been marines on board, a centinel at my cabin-door might have prevented it; for I slept with the door always open, that the officer of the watch might have access to me on all occasions, the possibility of such a conspiracy being ever the farthest from my thoughts. Had their mutiny been occasioned by any grievances, either real or imaginary, I must have discovered symptoms of their discontent which would have put me on my guard; but the case was far otherwise. Christian, in particular, I was on the most friendly terms with: that very day he was engaged to have dined with me; and the preceding night he excused himself from supping with me on pretence of being unwell; for which I felt concerned, having no suspicions of his integrity and honour. . . .

The quantity of provisions I found in the boat was 150 lb. of bread, 16 pieces of pork, each piece weighing 2 lb., 6 quarts of rum, 6 bottles of wine, with 28 gallons of water, and four empty barrecoes.

Fortunately it was calm all the afternoon, till about four o'clock, when we were so far to windward that, with a moderate easterly breeze which sprung up, we were able to sail. It was nevertheless dark when we got to Tofoa, where I expected to land; but the shore proved to be so steep and rocky that we were obliged to give up all thoughts of it, and keep the boat under the lee of the island with two oars; for there was no anchorage. Having fixed on this mode of proceeding for the night, I served to every person half a pint of grog, and each took to his rest as well as our unhappy situation would allow.

Wednesday, 29th.—In the morning, at dawn of day, we rowed along shore in search of a landing-place, and about ten o'clock we discovered a cove with a stone beach, at the N.W. part of the island, where I dropt the grapnel within twenty yards of the rocks. A great surf ran on the shore; but, as I was unwilling to diminish our stock of provisions, I landed Mr. Samuel, and some others, who climbed the cliffs, and got into the country to search for supplies. The rest of us remained at the cove, not discovering any other way into the country than that by which Mr. Samuel had proceeded. It was great consolation to me to find that the spirits of my people did not sink, notwithstanding our miserable and almost hopeless situation. Towards noon, Mr. Samuel returned with a few quarts of water, which he had found in holes; but he had met with no spring, or any prospect of a sufficient supply in that particular, and had seen only the signs of inhabitants. As it was uncertain what might be our future necessities, I only issued a morsel of bread and a glass of wine to each person for dinner.

I observed the latitude of this cove to be 19° 41′ S. This is the N.W. part of Tofoa, the north-westernmost of the Friendly Islands.

The weather was fair, but the wind blew so strong from the E.S.E. that we could not venture to sea. Our detention made it absolutely necessary to endeavour to obtain something towards our support; for I determined, if possible, to keep our first stock entire. We therefore weighed, and rowed along shore to see if anything could be got; and at last discovered some cocoa-nut trees; but they were on the top of high precipices, and the surf made it dangerous landing: both one and the other we, however, got the better of. Some of the people, with much difficulty, climbed the cliffs, and got about twenty cocoa-nuts, and others slung them to ropes, by which we hauled them through the surf into the boat. This was all that could be done here; and, as I found no place so safe as the one we had left to spend the night at, I returned to the cove, and, having served a cocoa-nut to each person, we went to rest again in the boat.

At daylight (Thursday, 30th) we attempted to put to sea; but the wind and weather proved so bad that I was glad to return to our former station; where, after issuing a morsel of bread and a spoonful of rum to each person, we landed, and I went off with Mr. Nelson, Mr. Samuel, and some others into the country, having hauled ourselves up the precipice by long vines, which were fixed there by the natives for that purpose; this being the only way into the country.

We found a few deserted huts and a small plantain walk, but little taken care of; from which we could only collect three small bunches of plantains. After passing this place we came to a deep gully that led towards a mountain near a volcano; and, as I conceived that in the rainy season very great torrents of water must pass through it, we hoped to find sufficient for our use remaining in some holes of the rocks, but, after all our search, the whole that we collected was only nine gallons. We advanced within two miles of the foot of the highest mountain in the island, on which is the volcano that is almost constantly burning. The country near it is covered with lava, and has a most dreary appearance. As we had not been fortunate in our discoveries, and saw nothing to alleviate our distresses, except the plantains and water above mentioned, we returned to the boat, exceedingly fatigued and faint. When I came to the precipice whence we were to descend into the cove, I was seized with such a dizziness in my head that I thought it scarce possible to effect it: however, by the assistance of Nelson and others, they at last got me down in a weak condition. Every person being returned by noon, I gave about an ounce of pork and two plantains to each, with half a glass of wine. I again observed the latitude of this place, 19° 41′ south. The people who remained by the boat I had directed to look for fish, or what they could pick up about the rocks; but nothing eatable

R

could be found: so that, upon the whole, we considered ourselves on as miserable a spot of land as could well be imagined.

I could not say positively, from the former knowledge I had of this island, whether it was inhabited or not; but I knew it was considered inferior to the other islands, and I was not certain but that the Indians only resorted to it at particular times. I was very anxious to ascertain this point; for, in case there had been only a few people here, and those could have furnished us with but very moderate supplies, the remaining in this spot to have made preparations for our voyage would have been preferable to the risk of going amongst multitudes, where perhaps we might lose everything. A party, therefore, sufficiently strong, I determined should go another route as soon as the sun became lower; and they cheerfully undertook it.

. About two o'clock in the afternoon the party set out, but, after suffering much fatigue, they returned in the evening without any kind of success.

At the head of the cove, about 150 yards from the water-side, there was a cave; the distance across the stony beach was about 100 yards, and from the country into the cove there was no other way than that which I have already described. The situation secured us from the danger of being surprised, and I determined to remain on shore for the night, with a part of my people, that the others might have more room to rest in the boat with the master; whom I directed to lie at a grapnel, and be watchful, in case we should be attacked. I ordered one plantain for each person to be boiled; and, having supped on this scanty allowance with a quarter of a pint of grog, and fixed the watches for the night, those whose turn it was laid down to sleep in the cave, before which we kept up a good fire; yet notwithstanding we were much troubled with flies and musquitoes.

Friday, May the 1st.—At dawn of day the party set out again in a different route, to see what they could find; in the course of which they suffered greatly for want of water: they, however, met with two men, a woman, and a child: the men came with them to the cove, and brought two cocoa-nut shells of water. I endeavoured to make friends of these people, and sent them away for bread-fruit, plantains, and water. Soon after, other natives came to us; and by noon there were thirty about us, from whom we obtained a small supply; but I could only afford one ounce of pork and a quarter of a bread-fruit to each man for dinner, with half a pint of water; for I was fixed in my resolution not to use any of the bread or water in the boat.

No particular chief was yet among the natives: they were, notwithstanding, tractable, and behaved honestly, exchanging the provisions they brought for a few buttons and beads. The party who had been out informed me of their having seen several neat plantations; so that it remained no longer a doubt of there being settled inhabitants on the island; for which reason I determined to get what I could, and to sail the first moment that the wind and weather would allow us to put to sea.

I was much puzzled in what manner to account to the natives for the loss of my ship: I knew they had too much sense to be amused with a story that the ship was to join me, when she was not in sight from the hills. I was at first doubtful whether I should tell the real fact, or say that the ship had overset and sunk, and that we only were saved: the latter appeared to be the most proper and advantageous for us, and I accordingly instructed my people, that we might all agree in one story. As I expected, inquiries were made about the ship, and they seemed readily satisfied with our account; but there did not appear the least symptom of joy or sorrow in their faces, although I fancied I discovered some marks of surprise. Some of the natives were coming and going the whole afternoon, and we got enough of bread-fruit, plantains, and cocoa-nuts for another day; but of water they only brought us about five pints. A canoe also came in with four men, and brought a few cocoa-nuts and bread-fruit, which I bought as I had done the rest. Nails were much inquired after, but I would not suffer any to be shown, as they were wanted for the use of the boat.

Towards evening I had the satisfaction to find our stock of provisions somewhat increased; but the natives did not appear to have much to spare. What they brought was in such small quantities that I had no reason to hope we should be able to procure from them sufficient to stock us for our voyage. At sunset all the natives left us in quiet possession of the cove. I thought this a good sign, and made no doubt that they would come again the next day with a better supply of food and water, with which I hoped to sail without farther delay; for if, in attempting to get to Tongataboo, we should be driven to leeward of the islands, there would be a larger quantity of provisions to support us against such a misfortune.

At night I served a quarter of a bread-fruit, and a cocoa-nut to each person for supper; and, a good fire being made, all but the watch went to sleep.

At daybreak the next morning I was pleased to find everyone's spirits a little revived, and that they no longer regarded me with those anxious looks which had constantly been directed towards me since we lost sight of the ship: every countenance appeared to have a degree of cheerfulness, and they all seemed determined to do their best.

As there was no certainty of our being supplied with water by the natives, I sent a party among the gullies in the mountains, with empty shells, to see what could be found. In their absence the natives came about us, as I expected, and in greater numbers; two canoes also came in from round the north side of the island. In one of them was an elderly chief, called Macca-ackavow. Soon after, some of our foraging party returned, and with them came a good-looking chief, called Egijeefow, or perhaps more properly Eefow, Egij or Eghee, signifying a chief. To each of these men I made a present of an old shirt and a knife, and I soon found they either had seen me or had heard of my being at Annamooka. They knew I had been with Captain Cook, who they inquired after, and also Captain Clerk. They were very inquisitive to know in what manner I had lost my ship. During this conversation, a young man, named Nageete, appeared, whom I remembered to have seen at Annamooka : he expressed much pleasure at our meeting. I inquired after Poulaho and Feenow, who, they said, were at Tongataboo; and Eefow agreed to accompany me thither if I would wait till the weather moderated. The readiness and affability of this man gave me much satisfaction.

This, however, was but of short duration, for the natives began to increase in number, and I observed some symptoms of a design against us. Soon after they attempted to haul the boat on shore, on which I brandished my cutlass in a threatening manner, and spoke to Eefow to desire them to desist; which they did, and everything became quiet again. My people, who had been in the mountains, now returned with about three gallons of water. I kept buying up the little bread-fruit that was brought to us, and likewise some spears to arm my men with, having only four cutlasses, two of which were in the boat. As we had no means of improving our situation, I told our people I would wait till sunset, by which time, perhaps, something might happen in our favour: for if we attempted to go at present, we must fight our way through, which we could do more advantageously at night; and that in the meantime we would endeavour to get off to the boat what we had bought. The beach was lined with the natives, and we heard nothing but the knocking of stones together, which they had in each hand. I knew very well this was the sign of an attack. At noon I served a cocoa-nut and a bread-fruit to each person for dinner, and gave some to the chiefs, with whom I continued to appear intimate and friendly. They frequently importuned me to sit down, but I as constantly refused: for it occurred both to Nelson and myself that they intended to seize hold of me if I gave them such an opportunity. Keeping, therefore, constantly on our guard, we were suffered to eat our uncomfortable meal in some quietness.

After dinner we began by little and little to get our things into the boat, which was a troublesome business on account of the surf, I carefully watched the motions of the natives, who continued to increase in number; and found that, instead of their intention being to leave us, fires were made and places fixed on for their stay during the night. Consultations were also held among them, and everything assured me we should be attacked. I sent orders to the master, that when he saw us coming down, he should keep the boat close to the shore, that we might the more readily embark.

I had my journal on shore with me, writing the occurrences in the cave, and in sending it down to the boat, it was nearly snatched away but for the timely assistance of the gunner.

The sun was near setting when I gave the word, on which every person who was on shore with me boldly took up his proportion of things, and carried them to the boat. The chiefs asked me if I would stay with them all night, I said, "No, I never sleep out of my boat; but in the morning we will again trade with you, and I shall remain till the weather is moderate, that we may go, as we have agreed, to see Poulaho at Tongataboo." Macca-ackavow then got up and said, "You will not sleep on shore? then Mattie" (which directly signifies "we will kill you"), and he left me. The onset was now preparing; everyone, as I have described before, kept knocking stones together, and Eefow quitted me. All but two or three things were in the boat, when I took Nageete by the hand, and we walked down the beach, everyone in a silent kind of horror.

While I was seeing the people embark, Nageete wanted me to stay to speak to Eefow; but I found he was encouraging them to the attack, and it was my determination, if they had then began, to have killed him for his treacherous behaviour. I ordered the carpenter not to quit me till the other people were in the boat. Nageete, finding I would not stay, loosed himself from my hold and went off, and we all got into the boat except one man, who, while I was getting on board, quitted it and ran up the beach to cast the stern fast off, notwithstanding the master and others called to him to return while they were hauling me out of the water.

I was no sooner in the boat than the attack began by about 200 men; the unfortunate poor man who had run up the beach was knocked down, and the stones flew like a shower of shot. Many Indians got hold of the stern rope, and were hauling the boat on shore; which they would certainly have effected if I had not had a knife in my pocket, with which I cut the rope. We then hauled off to the grapnel, everyone being more or less hurt. At this time I saw five of the natives about the poor man they had killed, and two of them were beating him about the head with stones in their hands.

We had no time to reflect, for, to my surprise, they filled their canoes with stones, and twelve men came off after us to renew the attack, which they did so effectually as nearly to disable us all. Our grapnel was foul, but Providence here assisted us; the fluke broke, and we got to our oars and pulled to sea. They, however, could paddle round us, so that we were obliged to sustain the attack without being able to return it, except with such stones as lodged in the boat, and in this I found we were very inferior to them. We could not close, because our boat was lumbered and heavy, of which they well knew how to take advantage: I therefore adopted the expedient of throwing overboard some clothes, which, as I expected, they stopped to pick up; and, as it was by this time almost dark, they gave over the attack and returned towards the shore, leaving us to reflect on our unhappy situation.

The poor man killed by the natives was John Norton; this was his second voyage with me as a quartermaster, and his worthy character, made me lament his loss very much. He has left an aged parent, I am told, whom he supported.

I once before sustained an attack of a similar nature, with a smaller number of Europeans, against a multitude of Indians: it was after the death of Captain Cook, on the Morai at Owhyhee, where I was left by Lieutenant King. Yet, notwithstanding this experience, I had not an idea that the power of a man's arm could throw stones, from two to eight pounds weight, with such force and exactness as these people did. Here unhappily we were without fire-arms, which the Indians knew; and it was a fortunate circumstance that they did not begin to attack us in the cave; for in that case our destruction must have been inevitable, and we should have had nothing left for it but to sell our lives as dearly as we could; in which I found everyone cheerfully disposed to concur. This appearance of resolution deterred them, supposing that they could effect their purpose without risk after we were in the boat.

Taking this as a sample of the disposition of the natives, there was but little reason to expect much benefit by persevering in the intention of visiting Poulaho; for I considered their good behaviour formerly to have proceeded from a dread of our firearms, and which, therefore, was likely to cease, as they knew we were now destitute of them; and, even supposing our lives not in danger, the boat and everything we had would most probably be taken from us, and thereby all hopes precluded of ever being able to return to our native country.

We set our sails and steered along shore by the west side of the island Tofoa; the wind blowing fresh from the eastward. My mind was employed in considering what was best to be done, when I was solicited by all hands to take them towards home; and, when I told them that no hopes of relief for us remained (except what might be found at New Holland) till I came to Timor, a distance of full 1200 leagues, where there was a Dutch settlement, but in what part of the island I knew not, they all agreed to live on one ounce of bread and a quarter of a pint of water per day. Therefore, after examining our stock of provisions, and recommending to them, in the most solemn manner, not to depart from their promise, we bore away across a sea where the navigation is but little known, in a small boat, twenty-three feet long from stem to stern, deep laden with eighteen men. I was happy, however, to see that everyone seemed better satisfied with our situation than myself.

Our stock of provisions consisted of about one hundred and fifty pounds of bread, twenty-eight gallons of water, twenty pounds of pork, three bottles of wine, and five quarts of rum. The difference between this and the quantity we had on leaving the ship was principally owing to our loss in the bustle and confusion of the attack. A few cocoa-nuts were in the boat, and some bread-fruit, but the latter was trampled to pieces.

It was about eight o'clock at night when we bore away under a reefed lug fore-sail; and, having divided the people into watches, and got the boat in a little order, we returned God thanks for our miraculous preservation, and, fully confident of His gracious support, I found my mind more at ease than it had been for some time past.

At daybreak the gale increased; the sun rose very fiery and red, a sure indication of a severe gale of wind. At eight it blew a violent storm, and the sea ran very high, so that between the seas the sail was becalmed, and when on the top of the sea it was too much to have set; but we could not venture to take in the sail, for we were in very imminent danger and distress, the sea curling over the stern of the boat, which obliged us to bale with all our might. A situation more distressing has, perhaps, seldom been experienced.

Our bread was in bags, and in danger of being spoiled by the wet: to be starved to death was inevitable if this could not be prevented: I therefore began to examine what clothes there were in the boat, and what other things could be spared; and, having determined that only two suits should be kept for each person, the rest was thrown overboard, with some rope and spare sails, which lightened the boat considerably, and we had more room to bale the water out. Fortunately the carpenter had a good chest in the boat, in which we secured the bread the first favourable moment. His tool chest also was cleared, and the tools stowed in the bottom of the boat, so that this became a second convenience.

I served a tea-spoonful of rum to each person (for we were very wet and cold), with a quarter of a bread-fruit which was scarcely eatable, for dinner: our engagement was now strictly to be carried into execution, and I was fully determined to make our provisions last eight weeks, let the daily proportion be ever so small.

At noon I considered our course and distance from Tofoa to be W.N.W. ¾ W. 86 miles, latitude 19° 27′ S. I directed the course to the W.N.W. that we might get a sight of the islands called Feejee, if they lay in the direction the natives had pointed out to me.

The weather continued very severe, the wind veering from N.E. to E.S.E. The sea ran higher than in the forenoon, and the fatigue of baling, to keep the boat from filling, was exceedingly great. We could no nothing more than keep before the sea; in the course of which the boat performed so well that I no longer dreaded any danger in that respect. But among the hardships we were to undergo, that of being constantly wet was not the least: the night was very cold, and at daylight our limbs were so benumbed that we could scarce find the use of them. At this time I served a tea-spoonful of rum to each person, from which we all found great benefit.

As I have mentioned before, I determined to keep to the W.N.W. till I got more to the northward; for I not only expected to have better weather, but to see the Feejee Islands, as I have often understood from the natives of Annamooka that they lie in that direction. Captain Cook likewise considered them to be N.W.

by W. from Tongataboo. Just before noon we discovered a small flat island, of a moderate height, bearing W.S.W. four or five leagues. I observed our latitude to be 18° 58′ S.; our longitude was, by account, 3° 4′ W. from the island Tofoa, having made a N. 72° W. course, distance 95 miles, since yesterday noon. I divided five small cocoa-nuts for our dinner, and everyone was satisfied.

A little after noon, other islands appeared, and at a quarter past three o'clock we could count eight, bearing from S. round by the W. to N.W. by N.; those to the south, which were the nearest, being four leagues distant from us.

I kept my course to the N.W. by W. between the islands, the gale having considerably abated. At six o'clock we discovered three other small islands to the N.W., the westernmost of them bore N.W. ½ W. seven leagues. I steered to the southward of these islands, a W.N.W. course for the night, under a reefed sail.

Served a few broken pieces of bread-fruit for supper, and performed prayers.

The night turned out fair, and, having had tolerable rest, everyone seemed considerably better in the morning, and contentedly breakfasted on a few pieces of yams that were found in the boat. After breakfast we examined our bread, a great deal of which was damaged and rotten; this nevertheless we were glad to keep for use.

I had hitherto been scarcely able to keep any account of our run; but we now equipped ourselves a little better, by getting a log-line marked, and, having practised at counting seconds, several could do it with some degree of exactness.

The islands we had passed lie between the latitude of 19° 5′ S. and 18° 19′ S., and, according to my reckoning, from 3° 17′ to 3° 46′ W. longitude from the island Tofoa: the largest may be about six leagues in circuit; but it is impossible for me to be very correct. To show where they are to be found again is the most my situation enabled me to do. The sketch I have made will give a comparative view of their extent. I believe all the larger islands are inhabited, as they appeared very fertile.

At noon I observed, in latitude 18° 10′ S., and considered my course and distance from yesterday noon, N.W. by W. ½ W., 94 miles; longitude, by account, from Tofoa 4° 29′ W.

For dinner I served some of the damaged bread, and a quarter of a pint of water.

About six o'clock in the afternoon we discovered two islands, one bearing W. by S. six leagues; and the other N.W. by N. eight leagues; I kept to windward of the northernmost, and passing it by ten o'clock, I resumed our course to the N.W. and W.N.W. for the night.

Wednesday, the 6th.—The weather was fair and the wind moderate all day from the E.N.E. At daylight a number of other islands were in sight from S.S.E. to the W. and round to N.E. by E.; between those in the N.W. I determined to pass. At noon a small sandy island or key, two miles distant from me, bore from E. to S. ¾ W. I had passed ten islands, the largest of which I judged to be six or eight leagues in circuit. Much larger lands appeared in the S.W. and N.N.W., between which I directed my course. Latitude observed 17° 17′ S.; course since yesterday noon N. 50° W.; distance 84 miles longitude made, by account, 5° 37′ W.

Our allowance for the day was a quarter of a pint of cocoa-nut milk, and the meat, which did not exceed two ounces to each person: it was received very contentedly, but we suffered great drought. I durst not venture to land, as we had no arms, and were less capable of defending ourselves than we were at Tofoa.

To keep an account of the boat's run was rendered difficult from being constantly wet with the sea breaking over us; but, as we advanced towards the land, the sea became smoother, and I was enabled to form a sketch of the islands, which will serve to give a general knowledge of their extent and position. Those we were near appeared fruitful and hilly, some very mountainous, and all of a good height. To our great joy we hooked a fish, but we were miserably disappointed by its being lost in trying to get it into the boat.

We continued steering to the N.W. between the islands, which by the evening, appeared of considerable extent, woody and mountainous. At sunset the southernmost bore from S. to S.W. by W., and the northernmost from N. by W. ½ W. to N.E. ½ E. At six o'clock we were nearly midway between them, and about six leagues distant from each shore, when we fell in with a coral bank, on which we had only four feet water, without the least break on it, or ruffle of the sea to give us warning. I could see that it extended about a mile on each side of us; but, as it is probable that it may extend much farther, I have laid it down so in my sketch.

I directed the course W. by N. for the night, and served to each person an ounce of the damaged bread, and a quarter of a pint of water, for supper.

As our lodgings were very miserable and confined for want of

room, I endeavoured to remedy the latter defect by putting ourselves at watch and watch; so that one half always sat up while
the other lay down on the boat's bottom, or upon a chest, with
nothing to cover us but the heavens. Our limbs were dreadfully
cramped, for we could not stretch them out; and the nights were
so cold, and we so constantly wet, that, after a few hours' sleep,
we could scarce move.

At dawn of Day (Thursday, 7th) we again discovered land from
W.S.W. to W.N.W., and another island N.N.W., the latter a high
round lump of but little extent; the southern land that we had
passed in the night was still in sight. Being very wet and cold, I
served a spoonful of rum and a morsel of bread for breakfast.

The land in the west was distinguished by some extraordinary
high rocks, which, as we approached them, assumed a variety of
forms. The country appeared to be agreeably interspersed with
high and low land, and in some places covered with wood. Off
the N.E. part lay some small rocky islands, between which and
an island four leagues to the N.E. I directed my course; but a lee
current very unexpectedly set us very near to the rocky isles, and we
could only get clear of it by rowing, passing close to the reef that
surrounded them. At this time we observed two large sailing
canoes coming swiftly after us along shore, and being apprehensive of their intentions, we rowed with some anxiety, fully
sensible of our weak and defenceless state. At noon it was calm
and the weather cloudy; my latitude is therefore doubtful to
three or four miles. Our course since yesterday noon N.W. by W.,
distance 79 miles; latitude by account, 16° 29' S., and longitude
by account, from Tofoa, 6° 46' W. Being constantly wet, it was
with the utmost difficulty I could open a book to write, and I am
sensible that what I have done can only serve to point out where
these lands are to be found again, and give an idea of their extent.

All the afternoon we had light winds at N.N.E.: the weather
was very rainy, attended with thunder and lightning. Only one
of the canoes gained upon us, which by three o'clock in the afternoon was not more than two miles off, when she gave over chase.

If I may judge from the sail of these vessels, they are of a
similar construction with those at the Friendly islands, which,
with the nearness of their situation, gives reason to believe that
they are the same kind of people. Whether these canoes had any
hostile intention against us must remain a doubt: perhaps we
might be benefited by an intercourse with them; but in our defenceless situation, to have made the experiment would have been
risking too much.

I imagine these to be the islands called Feejee, as their extent, direction, and distance from the Friendly Islands answers to the description given of them by those islanders. Heavy rain came on at four o'clock, when every person did their utmost to catch some water, and we increased our stock to 34 gallons, besides quenching our thirst for the first time since we had been at sea; but an attendant consequence made us pass the night very miserably, for, being extremely wet, and having no dry things to shift or cover us, we experienced cold and shiverings scarcely to be conceived. Most fortunately for us the forenoon turned out fair, and we stripped and dried our clothes. The allowance I issued to-day was an ounce and a half of pork, a tea-spoonful of rum, half a pint of cocoa-nut milk, and an ounce of bread. The rum, though so small in quantity, was of the greatest service. A fishing line was generally towing from the stern of the boat, but though we saw great numbers of fish, we could never catch one.

At noon I observed, in latitude 16° 4' S., and found we had made a course from yesterday noon, N. 62° W., distance 62 miles; longitude, by account, from Tofoa, 7° 42' W.

The land passed yesterday, and the day before, is a group of islands, fourteen or sixteen in number, lying between the latitude of 16° 26' S. and 17° 57' S., and in longitude, by my account, 4° 47' to 7° 17' W. from Tofoa. Three of these islands are very large, having from 30 to 40 leagues of sea-coast.

In the afternoon we cleaned out the boat, and it employed us till sunset to get everything dry and in order. Hitherto I had issued the allowance by guess, but I now made a pair of scales with two cocoa-nut shells; and, having accidentally some pistol-balls in the boat, 25 of which weighed one pounds, or 16 ounces, I adopted one as the proportion of weight that each person should receive of bread at the times I served it. I also amused all hands with describing the situation of New Guinea and New Holland, and gave them every information in my power, that in case any accident happened to me, those who survived might have some idea of what they were about, and be able to find their way to Timor, which at present they knew nothing of, more than the name, and some not even that. At night I served a quarter of a pint of water, and half an ounce of bread, for supper.

Saturday, May the 9th.—In the morning a quarter of a pint of cocoa-nut milk, and some of the decayed bread, was served for breakfast; and for dinner I divided the meat of four cocoa-nuts, with the remainder of the rotten bread, which was only eatable by such distressed people.

At noon I observed the latitude to be 15° 47' S.; course since yesterday N. 75' W., distance 64 miles; longitude made, by account, 8° 45' W.

In the afternoon I fitted a pair of shrouds for each mast, and contrived a canvas weather cloth round the boat, and raised the quarters about nine inches, by nailing on the seats of the stern sheets, which proved of great benefit to us.

The wind had been moderate all day, in the S.E. quarter, with fine weather; but, about nine in the evening, the clouds began to gather, and we had a prodigious fall of rain, with severe thunder and lightning. By midnight we caught about 20 gallons of water. Being miserably wet and cold, I served to the people a tea-spoonful of rum each, to enable them to bear with their distressed situation. The weather continued extremely bad, and the wind increased; we spent a very miserable night, without sleep, except such as could be got in the midst of rain. The day brought no relief but its light. The sea broke over us so much that two men were constantly baling; and we had no choice how to steer, being obliged to keep before the waves for fear of the boat filling.

The allowance now regularly served to each person was one-25th of a pound of bread, and a quarter of a pint of water, at eight in the morning, at noon, and at sunset. To-day I gave about half an ounce of pork for dinner, which, though any moderate person would have considered only as a mouthful, was divided into three or four.

The rain abated towards noon, and I observed the latitude to be 15° 17' S.; course N. 67° W., distance 78 miles; longitude made 10° W.

The wind continued strong from S.S.E. to S.E., with very squally weather and a high breaking sea, so that we were miserably wet, and suffered great cold in the night.

Monday, the 11th.—In the morning at daybreak I served to every person a tea-spoonful of rum, our limbs being so cramped that we could scarce move them. Our situation was now extremely dangerous, the sea frequently running over our stern, which kept us baling with all our strength.

At noon the sun appeared, which gave us as much pleasure as in a winter's day in England. I issued the 25th of a pound of bread, and a quarter of a pint of water, as yesterday. Latitude observed 14° 50' S.; course N. 71° W., distance 102 miles; and longitude, by account, 11° 39' W. from Tofoa.

In the evening it rained hard, and we again experienced a dreadful night. At length the day came, and showed to me a miserable set of beings, full of wants, without any thing to relieve them. Some complained of great pain in their bowels, and every-one of having almost lost the use of his limbs. The little sleep we got was no ways refreshing, as we were covered with sea and rain. I served a spoonful of rum at day-dawn, and the usual allowance of bread and water, for breakfast, dinner, and supper.

At noon it was almost calm, no sun to be seen, and some of us shivering with cold. Course since yesterday W. by N., distance 89 miles; latitude, by account, 14° 33′ S.; longitude made 13° 9′ W. The direction of our course was to pass to the northward of the New Hebrides.

The wet weather continued, and in the afternoon the wind came from the southward, blowing fresh in squalls. As there was no prospect of getting our clothes dried, I recommended to every-one to strip, and wring them through the salt water, by which means they received a warmth that, while wet with rain, they could not have.

This afternoon we saw a kind of fruit on the water which Nelson told me was the Barringtonia of Forster; and, as I saw the same again in the morning, and some men-of-war birds, I was led to believe that we were not far from land.

We continued constantly shipping seas, and baling, and were very wet and cold in the night; but I could not afford the allow-ance of rum at daybreak.

Wednesday, the 13th.—At noon I had a sight of the sun, latitude 14° 17′ S.; course W. by N. 79 miles; longitude made 14° 28′ W. All this day we were constantly shipping water, and suffered much cold and shiverings in the night.

Thursday, the 14th.—Fresh gales at S.E. and gloomy weather, with rain and a high sea. At six in the morning we saw land, from S.W. by S. eight leagues, to N.W. by W. ¾ W. six leagues, which soon after appeared to be four islands, one of them much larger than the others, and all of them high and remarkable. At noon we discovered a small island and some rocks, bearing N.W. by N. four leagues, and another island W. eight leagues, so that the whole were six in number; the four I had first seen bearing from S. ½ E. to S.W. by S.; our distance three leagues from the nearest island. My latitude observed was 13° 29′ S., and longi-tude, by account, from Tofoa, 15° 49′ W.; course since yesterday noon N. 63° W., distance 89 miles. At four in the afternoon we passed the westernmost island.

Friday, the 15th.—At one in the morning another island was discovered, bearing W.N.W., five leagues distance, and at eight o'clock we saw it for the last time, bearing N.E. seven leagues. A number of gannets, boobies, and men-of-war birds were seen.

These islands lie between the latitude of 13° 16′ and 14° 10′ S.: their longitude, according to my reckoning, 15° 51′ to 17° 6′ W. from the island Tofoa. The largest island I judged to be about twenty leagues in circuit, the others five or six. The easternmost is the smallest island, and most remarkable, having a high sugar-loaf hill.

The sight of these islands served only to increase the misery of our situation. We were very little better than starving, with plenty in view; yet to attempt procuring any relief was attended with so much danger, that prolonging of life, even in the midst of misery, was thought preferable while there remained hopes of being able to surmount our hardships. For my own part, I consider the general run of cloudy and wet weather to be a blessing of Providence. Hot weather would have caused us to have died with thirst; and probably being so constantly covered with rain or sea protected us from that dreadful calamity.

As I had nothing to assist my memory, I could not then determine whether these islands were a part of the New Hebrides or not: I believed them to be a new discovery, which I have since found true; but, though they were not seen either by Monsieur Bougainville or Captain Cook, they are so nearly in the neighbourhood of the New Hebrides that they must be considered as part of the same group. They are fertile, and inhabited, as I saw smoke in several places.

The wind was at S.E. with rainy weather all day. The night was very dark, not a star could be seen to steer by, and the sea broke continually over us. I found it necessary to counteract as much as possible the effect of the southerly winds, to prevent being driven too near New Guinea; for in general we were forced to keep so much before the sea, that if we had not, at intervals of moderate weather, steered a more southerly course, we should inevitably, from a continuance of the gales, have been thrown in sight of that coast: in which case there would most probably have been an end to our voyage.

Saturday, the 16th.—In addition to our miserable allowance of one-25th of a pound of bread, and a quarter of a pint of water, I issued for dinner about an ounce of salt pork to each person. I was often solicited for this pork, but I considered it more proper to issue it in small quantities than to suffer it to be all used at once or twice, which would have been done if I had allowed it.

At noon I observed, in 13° 33′ S.; longitude made from Tofoa,

19° 27' W.; course N. 82° W., distance 101 miles. The sun breaking out through the clouds gave us hopes of drying our wet
clothes; but the sunshine was of short duration. We had strong
breezes at S.E. by S., and dark gloomy weather, with storms of
thunder, lightning, and rain. The night was truly horrible, and
not a star to be seen; so that our steerage was uncertain.

Sunday, the 17*th.*—At dawn of day I found every person com-
plaining, and some of them solicited extra allowance; which I
positively refused. Our situation was miserable; always wet, and
suffering extreme cold in the night, without the least shelter from
the weather. Being constantly obliged to bale, to keep the boat
from filling, was, perhaps, not to be reckoned an evil, as it gave
us exercise.

The little rum we had was of great service; when our nights
were particularly distressing, I generally served a tea-spoonful
or two to each person: and it was always joyful tidings when they
heard of my intentions.

At noon a waterspout was very near on board of us. I issued
an ounce of pork, in addition to the allowance of bread and water;
but before we began to eat, every person stript, and having wrung
their clothes through the sea-water, found much warmth and
refreshment. Course since yesterday noon W.S.W., distance 100
miles; latitude, by account, 14° 11' S., and longitude made
21° 3' W.

The night was dark and dismal; the sea constantly breaking
over us, and nothing but the wind and waves to direct our
steerage. It was my intention, if possible, to make New Holland,
to the southward of Endeavour Straits, being sensible that it was
necessary to preserve such a situation as would make a southerly
wind a fair one; that we might range along the reefs till an opening should be found into smooth water, and we the sooner be able
to pick up some refreshments.

Monday, May the 18*th.*—In the morning the rain abated, when
we stripped and wrung our clothes through the sea-water as
usual, which refreshed us greatly. Every person complained of
violent pain in their bones: I was only surprised that no one was
yet laid up. The customary allowance of one-25th of a pound of
bread, and a quarter of a pint of water, was served at breakfast,
dinner, and supper.

At noon I deduced my situation, by account, for we had no
glimpse of the sun, to be in latitude 14° 52' S.; course since
yesterday noon W.S.W. 106 miles; longitude made from Tofoa
22° 45' W. Saw many boobies and noddies, a sign of being in the

neighbourhood of land. In the night we had very severe lightning, with heavy rain, and were obliged to keep baling without
intermission.

Tuesday, the 19*th.*—Very bad weather and constant rain. At
noon, latitude, by account, 14° 37' S.; course since yesterday N.
81° W., distance 100 miles; longitude made 24° 30' W. With the
allowance of bread and water, served half an ounce of pork to
each person for dinner.

Wednesday, May the 20*th.*—Fresh breezes E.N.E. with constant
rain; at times a deluge. Always baling.

At dawn of day some of my people seemed half dead: our
appearances were horrible; and I could look no way but I caught
the eye of someone in distress. Extreme hunger was now too
evident, but no one suffered from thirst, nor had we much inclination to drink, that desire, perhaps, being satisfied through
the skin. The little sleep we got was in the midst of water, and
we constantly awoke with severe cramps and pains in our bones.
This morning I served about two tea-spoonfuls of rum to each
person, and the allowance of bread and water as usual. At noon
the sun broke out, and revived everyone. I found we were in
latitude 14° 49' S.; longitude made 25° 46' W.; course S. 88° W.,
distance 75 miles.

All the afternoon we were so covered with rain and salt water
that we could scarcely see. We suffered extreme cold, and everyone dreaded the approach of night. Sleep, though we longed for
it, afforded no comfort: for my own part, I almost lived without
it. About two o'clock in the morning we were overwhelmed with
a deluge of rain. It fell so heavy that we were afraid it would fill
the boat, and were obliged to bale with all our might. At dawn
of day I served a larger allowance of rum. Towards noon the rain
abated and the sun shone, but we were miserably cold and wet,
the sea breaking constantly over us; so that, notwithstanding the
heavy rain, we had not been able to add to our stock of fresh
water. Latitude, by observation, 14° 29' S., and longitude made,
by account, from Tofoa, 27° 25' W.; course since yesterday noon
N. 78° W., 99 miles. I now considered myself nearly on a meridian with the east part of New Guinea.

Friday, May the 22*nd.*—Strong gales from E.S.E. to S.S.E., a
high sea, and dark dismal night.

Our situation this day was extremely calamitous. We were
obliged to take the course of the sea, running right before it, and
watching with the utmost care, as the least error in the helm
would in a moment have been our destruction.

S

At noon it blew very hard, and the foam of the sea kept running over our stern and quarters; I however got propped up, and made an observation of the latitude in 14° 17′ S.; course N. 85° W., distance 130 miles; longitude made 29° 38′ W.

The misery we suffered this night exceeded the preceding. The sea flew over us with great force, and kept us baling with horror and anxiety. At dawn of day I found everyone in a most distressed condition, and I began to fear that another such night would put an end to the lives of several, who seemed no longer able to support their sufferings. I served an allowance of two teaspoonfuls of rum; after drinking which, having wrung our clothes, and taken our breakfast of bread and water, we became a little refreshed.

Towards noon the weather became fair, but with very little abatement of the gale, and the sea remained equally high. With some difficulty I observed the latitude to be 13° 44′ S.: course since yesterday noon N. 74° W., distance 116 miles; longitude made 31° 32′ W. from Tofoa.

The wind moderated in the evening, and the weather looked much better, which rejoiced all hands, so that they eat their scanty allowance with more satisfaction than for some time past. The night also was fair; but being always wet with the sea, we suffered much from the cold. A fine morning, I had the pleasure to see, produce some cheerful countenances; and, the first time for 15 days past, we experienced comfort from the warmth of the sun. We stripped, and hung our clothes up to dry, which were by this time become so threadbare that they would not keep out either wet or cold.

At noon I observed in latitude 13° 33′ S.; longitude, by account, from Tofoa, 33° 28′ W.; course N. 84° W., distance 114 miles. With the usual allowance of bread and water for dinner I served an ounce of pork to each person. This afternoon we had many birds about us, which are never seen far from land, such as boobies and noddies.

As the sea began to run fair, and we shipped but little water, I took the opportunity to examine into the state of our bread, and found, that according to the present mode of issuing, there was a sufficient quantity remaining for 29 days' allowance; by which time I hoped we should be able to reach Timor. But as this was very uncertain, and it was possible that, after all, we might be obliged to go to Java, I determined to proportion the allowance so as to make our stock hold out six weeks. I was apprehensive that this would be ill received, and that it would require my utmost resolution to enforce it; for, small as the quantity was which I intended to take away for our future good, yet it might appear to my people like robbing them of life: and some, who were less patient than their companions, I expected would very ill brook it. However, on my representing the necessity of guarding against delays that might be occasioned in our voyage by contrary winds, or other causes, and promising to enlarge upon the allowance as we got on, they cheerfully agreed to my proposal. It was accordingly settled, that every person should receive one-25th of a pound of bread for breakfast, and the same quantity for dinner; so that, by omitting the proportion for supper, we had 43 days' allowance.

Monday, the 25th.—At noon some noddies came so near to us that one of them was caught by hand. This bird was about the size of a small pigeon. I divided it, with its entrails, into 18 portions, and by a well-known method at sea, of, *Who shall have this?* it was distributed, with the allowance of bread and water for dinner, and eat up bones and all, with salt water for sauce. I observed the latitude 13° 32′ S.; longitude made 35° 19′ W.; course N. 89° W., distance 108 miles.

In the evening, several boobies flying very near to us, we had the good fortune to catch one of them. This bird is as large as a duck: like the noddy, it has received its name from seamen for suffering itself to be caught on the masts and yards of ships. They are the most presumptive proofs of being in the neighbourhood of land of any sea-fowl we are acquainted with. I directed the bird to be killed for supper, and the blood to be given to three of the people who were the most distressed for want of food. The body, with the entrails, beak, and feet, I divided into 18 shares, and with an allowance of bread, which I made a merit of granting, we made a good supper compared with our usual fare.

Tuesday, the 26th.—Fresh breezes from the S.E., with fine weather. In the morning we caught another booby, so that Providence appeared to be relieving our wants in an extraordinary manner. Towards noon we passed a great many pieces of the branches of trees, some of which appeared to have been no long time in the water. I had a good observation for the latitude, and found our situation to be in 13° 41′ S.; longitude, by account, from Tofoa, 37° 13′ W.; course S. 85° W., 112 miles. The people were overjoyed at the addition to their dinner, which was distributed in the same manner as on the preceding evening; giving the blood to those who were the most in want of food.

To make the bread a little savoury, most of the people frequently dipped it in salt water; but I generally broke mine into small pieces, and eat it in my allowance of water, out of a cocoanut shell, with a spoon; economically avoiding to take too large a piece at a time, so that I was as long at dinner as if it had been a much more plentiful meal.

The weather was now serene, which, nevertheless, was not without its inconveniences, for we began to feel distress of a different kind from that which we had lately been accustomed to suffer. The heat of the sun was so powerful that several of the people were seized with a languor and faintness which made life indifferent. We were so fortunate as to catch two boobies in the evening: their stomachs contained several flying-fish and small cuttle-fish, all of which I saved to be divided for dinner the next day.

Wednesday, the 27th.—A fresh breeze at E.S.E., with fair weather. We passed much driftwood this forenoon, and saw many birds; I therefore did not hesitate to pronounce that we were near the reefs of New Holland. From my recollection of Captain Cook's survey of this coast, I considered the direction of it to be N.W., and I was therefore satisfied that, with the wind to the southward of E., I could always clear any dangers.

At noon I observed in latitude 13° 26' S.; course since yesterday N. 82° W., distance 109 miles; longitude made 39° 4' W. After writing my account I divided the two birds with their entrails, and the contents of their maws, into 18 portions, and, as the prize was a very valuable one, it was divided as before, by calling out *Who shall have this?* so that to-day, with the allowance of a 25th of a pound of bread at breakfast, and another at dinner, with the proportion of water, I was happy to see that every person thought he had feasted.

In the evening we saw a gannet; and the clouds remained so fixed in the west that I had little doubt of our being near the land. The people, after taking their allowance of water for supper, amused themselves with conversing on the probability of what we should find.

Thursday, the 28th.—At one in the morning the person at the helm heard the sound of breakers, and I no sooner lifted up my head than I saw them close under our lee, not more than a quarter of a mile distant from us. I immediately hauled on a wind to the N.N.E., and in ten minutes' time we could neither see nor hear them.

I have already mentioned my reason for making New Holland so far to the southward; for I never doubted of numerous openings in the reef through which I could have access to the shore; and, knowing the inclination of the coast to be to the N.W., and the wind mostly to the southward of E., I could with ease range such a barrier of reefs till I should find a passage, which now became absolutely necessary, without a moment's loss of time. The idea of getting into smooth water, and finding refreshments, kept my people's spirits up: their joy was very great after we had got clear of the breakers, to which we had approached much nearer than I thought was possible without first discovering them.

In the morning, at daylight, we could see nothing of the land or of the reefs. We bore away again, and at nine o'clock saw the reefs. The sea broke furiously over every part, and we had no sooner got near to them than the wind came at E., so that we could only lie along the line of the breakers; within which we saw the water so smooth, that every person already anticipated the heart-felt satisfaction he should receive as soon as we could get within them. I now found we were embayed, for we could not lie clear with the sails, the wind having backed against us; and the sea set in so heavy towards the reef that our situation was become unsafe. We could effect but little with the oars, having scarce strength to pull them; and I began to apprehend that we should be obliged to attempt pushing over the reef. Even this I did not despair of effecting with success, when happily we discovered a break in the reef, about one mile from us, and at the same time an island of a moderate height within it, nearly in the same direction, bearing W. ½ N. I entered the passage with a strong stream running to the westward, and found it about a quarter of a mile broad, with every appearance of deep water.

On the outside the reef inclined to the N.E. for a few miles, and from thence to the N.W.: on the south side of the entrance it inclined to the S.S.W. as far as I could see it; and I conjecture that a similar passage to this which we know entered may be found near the breakers that I first discovered, which are 23 miles S. of this channel.

I did not recollect what latitude Providential channel lies in, but I considered it to be within a few miles of this, which is situate in 12° 51′ S. latitude.

Being now happily within the reefs, and in smooth water, I endeavoured to keep near them to try for fish; but the tide set us to the N.W.; I therefore bore away in that direction, and, having promised to land on the first convenient spot we could find, all our past hardships seemed already to be forgotten.

At noon I had a good observation, by which our latitude was

12° 46′ S., whence the foregoing situations may be considered as determined with some exactness. The island first seen bore W.S.W. five leagues. This, which I have called the island Direction, will in fair weather always show the channel, from which it bears due W., and may be seen as soon as the reefs from a ship's mast-head: it lies in the latitude of 12° 51′ S. These, however, are marks too small for a ship to hit, unless it can hereafter be ascertained that passages through the reef are numerous along the coast, which I am inclined to think they are, in which case there would be little risk even if the wind was directly on the shore.

My longitude, made by dead reckoning, from the island Tofoa to our passage through the reef is 40° 10′ W. Providential channel, I imagine, must lie very nearly under the same meridian with our passage; by which it appears we had out-run our reckoning 1° 9′.

We now returned God thanks for His gracious protection, and with much content took our miserable allowance of a 25th of a pound of bread, and a quarter of a pint of water, for dinner. . . .

Friday, the 12th June (1789).—At three in the morning, with an excess of joy, we discovered Timor bearing from W.S.W. to W.N.W., and I hauled on a wind to the N.N.E. till daylight, when the land bore from S.W. by S. to N.E. by N. Our distance from the shore, two leagues.

It is not possible for me to describe the pleasure which the blessing of the sight of this land diffused among us. It appeared scarce credible to ourselves that in an open boat, and so poorly provided, we should have been able to reach the coast of Timor in forty-one days after leaving Tofoa, having in that time run, by our log, a distance of 3618 miles; and that, notwithstanding our extreme distress, no one should have perished in the voyage.

I have already mentioned that I knew not where the Dutch settlement was situated; but I had a faint idea that it was at the S.W. part of the island. I therefore, after daylight, bore away along shore to the S.S.W., which I was the more readily induced to do as the wind would not suffer us to go towards the N.E. without great loss of time.

The day gave us a most agreeable prospect of the land, which was interspersed with woods and lawns; the interior part mountainous, but the shore low. Towards noon the coast became higher, with some remarkable headlands. We were greatly delighted with the general look of the country, which exhibited many cultivated spots and beautiful situations; but we could only

see a few small huts, whence I concluded that no European resided in this part of the island. Much sea ran on the shore, which
made landing impracticable. At noon we were abreast of a high
headland; the extremes of the land bore S.W. ½ W. and N.N.E. ½
E.; our distance off shore being three miles; latitude, by observation, 9° 59′ S.; and my longitude, by dead reckoning from the
north part of New Holland, 15° 6′ W.

With the usual allowance of bread and water for dinner, I
divided the bird we had caught the night before, and to the surgeon and Lebogue I gave a little wine.

The wind blew fresh at E. and E.S.E., with very hazy weather.
During the afternoon we continued our course along a low shore
covered with innumerable palm trees, called the Fan Palm from
the leaf spreading like a fan; but here we saw no signs of cultivation, nor had the country so fine an appearance as to the east
ward. This, however, was only a small tract, for by sunset it
improved again, and I saw several great smokes where the inhabitants were clearing and cultivating their grounds. . . . We
had now ran 25 miles to the W.S.W. since noon, and were W. five
miles from a low point which, in the afternoon, I imagined had
been the southernmost land; and here the coast formed a deep
bend, with low land in the bight that appeared like islands. The
west shore was high; but from this part of the coast to the high
cape which we were abreast of at noon the shore is low, and I
believe shoal. I particularly remark this situation, because here
the very high ridge of mountains, that run from the east end of
the island, terminate, and the appearance of the country changes
for the worse.

That we might not run past any settlement in the night, I
determined to preserve my station till the morning, and therefore
brought to under a close-reefed fore-sail. We were here in shoal
water, our distance from the shore being half a league, the
westernmost land in sight bearing W.S.W. ½ W. Served bread and
water for supper, and the boat lying to very well, all but the
officer of the watch endeavoured to get a little sleep.

Saturday, the 13th.—At two in the morning we wore, and stood
in shore till daylight, when I found we had drifted, during the
night, about three leagues to the W.S.W., the southernmost land
in sight bearing W. On examining the coast, and not seeing any
sign of a settlement, we bore away to the westward, having a
strong gale against a weather current, which occasioned much sea.
The shore was high and covered with wood; but we did not run
far before low land again formed the coast, the points of which

opening at west, I once more fancied we were on the south part of the island; but at ten o'clock we found the coast again inclining towards the south, part of it bearing W.S.W. ½ W. At the same time, high land appeared in the S.W.; but the weather was so hazy that it was doubtful whether the two lands were separated, the opening only extending one point of the compass. For this reason I stood towards the outer land, and found it to be the island Roti.

I returned to the shore we had left and brought to a grapnel in a sandy bay, that I might more conveniently calculate my situation. In this place we saw several smokes, where the natives were clearing their grounds. During the little time we remained here, the master and carpenter very much importuned me to let them go in search of supplies; to which, at length, I assented; but, not finding any other person willing to be of their party, they did not choose to quit the boat. I stopped here no longer than for the purpose just mentioned, and we continued steering along shore. We had a view of a beautiful-looking country, as if formed by art into lawns and parks. The coast is low, and covered with woods, in which are innumerable fan-palm trees that look like cocoa-nut walks. The interior part is high land, but very different from the more eastern parts of the island, where it is exceedingly mountainous, and to appearance the soil better.

At noon the island Roti bore S.W. by W. seven leagues. I had no observation for the latitude, but by account we were in 10° 12′ S.; our course since yesterday noon being S. 77° W., 54 miles. The usual allowance of bread and water was served for breakfast and dinner, and to the surgeon and Lebogue I continued to give wine.

We had a strong breeze at E.S.E., with hazy weather, all the afternoon. At two o'clock, having run through a very dangerous breaking sea, the cause of which I attributed to be a strong tide setting to windward, and shoal water, we discovered a spacious bay or sound, with a fair entrance about two or three miles wide. I now conceived hopes that our voyage was nearly at an end, as no place could appear more eligible for shipping, or more likely to be chosen for an European settlement; I therefore came to a grapnel near the east side of the entrance, in a small sandy bay, where we saw a hut, a dog, and some cattle; and I immediately sent the boatswain and gunner away to the hut to discover the inhabitants.

The S.W. point of the entrance bore W. ½ S. three miles; the

S.E. point S. by W. three-quarters of a mile; and the island Roti from S. by W. ¼ W. to S.W. ¼ W. about five leagues.

While we lay here I found the ebb came from the northward, and before our departure the falling of the tide discovered to us a reef of rocks about two cables length from the shore: the whole being covered at high-water, renders it dangerous. On the opposite shore also appeared very high breakers; but there is nevertheless plenty of room, and certainly a safe channel for a first-rate man-of-war.

The bay or sound within seemed to be of a considerable extent; the northern part being about five leagues distant. Here the land made in moderate risings joined by lower grounds. But the island Roti to the southward is the best mark by which to know this place.

I had just time to make these remarks when I saw the boatswain and gunner returning with some of the natives: I therefore no longer doubted of our success, and that our expectations would be fully gratified. They brought five Indians, and informed me that they had found two families, where the women treated them with European politeness. From these people I learned that the governor resided at a place called Coupang, which was some distance to the N.E. I made signs for one of them to go in the boat and show us the way to Coupang, intimating that I would pay him for his trouble; the man readily complied, and came into the boat.

These people were of a dark tawny colour, had long black hair, and chewed a great deal of beetle. Their dress was a square piece of cloth round the hips, in the folds of which was stuck a large knife; a handkerchief wrapped round the head; and another hanging by the four corners from the shoulders, which served as a bag for their beetle equipage. They brought us a few pieces of dried turtle and some ears of Indian corn. This last was the most welcome; for the turtle was so hard that it could not be eaten without being first soaked in hot water. They offered to bring us some other refreshments if I would wait; but, as the pilot was willing, I determined to push on. It was about half an hour past four when we sailed.

By direction of the pilot we kept close to the east shore under all our sail; but as night came on the wind died away, and we were obliged to try at the oars, which I was surprised to see we could use with some effect. At ten o'clock, finding we advanced but slowly, I came to a grapnel, and for the first time I issued double allowance of bread and a little wine to each person.

Sunday, the 14*th.*—At one o'clock, in the morning after the most happy and sweet sleep that ever men enjoyed, we weighed, and continued to keep the east shore on board in very smooth water, when at last I found we were again open to the sea; the whole of the land to the westward, that we had passed, being an island, which the pilot called Pulo Samow. The northern entrance of this channel is about a mile and a half or two miles wide, and I had no ground at ten fathoms.

The report of two cannon that were fired gave new life to everyone; and soon after we discovered two square-rigged vessels and a cutter at anchor to the eastward. We endeavoured to work to windward, but were obliged to take to our oars again, having lost ground on each tack. We kept close to the shore, and continued rowing till four o'clock, when I brought to a grapnel, and gave another allowance of bread and wine to all hands. As soon as we had rested a little we weighed again, and rowed till near daylight, when we came to a grapnel off a small fort and town which the pilot told me was Coupang.

Among the things which the boatswain had thrown into the boat before we left the ship was a bundle of signal flags that had been used by the boats to show the depth of water in sounding: with these we had, in the course of the passage, made a small jack, which I now hoisted in the main shrouds as a signal of distress; for I did not think proper to land without leave.

Soon after daybreak a soldier hailed us to land, which I immediately did, among a crowd of Indians, and was agreeably surprised to meet with an English sailor who belonged to one of the vessels in the road. His captain, he told me, was the second person in the town; I therefore desired to be conducted to him, as I was informed the governor was ill, and could not then be spoken with.

Captain Spikerman received me with great humanity. I informed him of our distressed situation; and requested that care might be taken of those who were with me without delay. On which he gave directions for their immediate reception at his own house, and went himself to the governor, to know at what time I could be permitted to see him; which was fixed to be at eleven o'clock.

I now desired my people to come on shore, which was as much as some of them could do, being scarce able to walk: they, however, were helped to the house, and found tea with bread and butter provided for their breakfast.

The abilities of a painter, perhaps, could seldom have been

displayed to more advantage than in the delineation of the two groups of figures which at this time presented themselves to each other. An indifferent spectator would have been at a loss which most to admire; the eyes of famine sparkling at immediate relief, or the horror of their preservers at the sight of so many spectres, whose ghastly countenances, if the cause had been unknown, would rather have excited terror than pity. Our bodies were nothing but skin and bones, our limbs were full of sores, and we were clothed in rags: in this condition, with the tears of joy and gratitude flowing down our cheeks, the people of Timor beheld us with a mixture of horror, surprise, and pity.

The governor, Mr. William Adrian Van Este, notwithstanding extreme ill-health, became so anxious about us that I saw him before the appointed time. He received me with great affection, and gave me the fullest proofs that he was possessed of every feeling of a humane and good man. Sorry as he was, he said, that such a calamity could ever have happened to us, yet he considered it as the greatest blessing of his life that we had fallen under his protection; and, though his infirmity was so great that he could not do the office of a friend himself, he would give such orders as I might be certain would procure us every supply we wanted. A house should be immediately prepared for me, and, with respect to my people, he said that I might have room for them either at the hospital or on board of Captain Spikerman's ship, which lay in the road; and he expressed much uneasiness that Coupang could not afford them better accommodations, the house assigned to me being the only one uninhabited, and the situation of the few families that lived at this place such that they could not conveniently receive strangers. For the present, till matters could be properly regulated, he gave directions that victuals for my people should be dressed at his own house.

On returning to Captain Spikerman's house I found that every kind of relief had been given to my people. The surgeon had dressed their sores, and the cleaning of their persons had not been less attended to, several friendly gifts of apparel having been presented to them.

I desired to be shown to the house that was intended for me, which I found ready with servants to attend. It consisted of a hall, with a room at each end, and a loft overhead; and was surrounded by a piazza, with an outer apartment in one corner, and a communication from the back part of the house to the street. I therefore determined, instead of separating from my people, to lodge them all with me; and I divided the house as follows: One room I took to myself, the other I allotted to the master, surgeon, Mr. Nelson, and the gunner; the loft to the other officers; and the outer apartment to the men. The hall was common to the officers, and the men had the back piazza. Of this disposition I informed the governor, and he sent down chairs, tables, and benches, with bedding and other necessaries for the use of everyone.

The governor, when I took my leave, had desired me to acquaint him with everything of which I stood in need; but it was only at particular times that he had a few moments of ease, or could attend to anything; being in a dying state, with an incurable disease. On this account I transacted whatever business I had with Mr. Timotheus Wanjon, the second of this place, who was the governor's son-in-law; and who also contributed everything in his power to make our situation comfortable. I had been, therefore, misinformed by the seamen, who told me that Captain Spikerman was the next person in command to the governor.

At noon a dinner was brought to the house, sufficiently good to make persons more accustomed to plenty eat too much. Yet I believe few in such a situation would have observed more moderation than my people did. My greatest apprehension was, that they would eat too much fruit, of which there was great variety in season at this time.

Having seen everyone enjoy this meal of plenty, I dined myself with Mr. Wanjon; but I felt no extraordinary inclination to eat or drink. Rest and quiet, I considered, as more necessary to the re-establishment of my health, and therefore retired soon to my room, which I found furnished with every convenience. But, instead of rest, my mind was disposed to reflect on our late sufferings, and on the failure of the expedition; but, above all, on the thanks due to Almighty God, who had given us power to support and bear such heavy calamities, and had enabled me at last to be the means of saving eighteen lives.

XIV. LAPÉROUSE IN THE PACIFIC

[Louis XVI of France was greatly interested in the discovery voyages of Captain Cook, as he was in all matters relating to exploration and navigation. He desired that the French should participate in the pursuit of further discoveries in the South Seas, and for this purpose he instigated the voyage of Lapérouse, who sailed from France in 1785. His instructions contained no reference to Botany Bay, and it had not been his intention originally to make a call at that place, of which, however, he had read an account in Cook's *Voyages*. The reason why he determined to visit Botany Bay is made clear in the following extract from his own narrative of his experiences in the Pacific. The massacre of Captain de Langle and part of his crew at the Navigator Islands, and the destruction of his long-boats determined Lapérouse to sail to some place where he would not be in danger of quarrels with natives while his men were engaged in putting together two new long-boats, the parts of which he carried in the hold. His vessels arrived at Botany Bay on January 26th, 1788. Captain Arthur Phillip and the "First Fleet" for the English settlement had arrived on January 18th; but Phillip speedily came to the conclusion that Botany Bay was an unsuitable site for the settlement, and chose Port Jackson, where the town of Sydney was built. The statement frequently made that "England won Australia by six days" has no foundation. Lapérouse had no thought of settlement; he merely wanted a quiet place for effecting his repairs. These pages give his own story of the tragedy at the Society Islands, and of his experiences at Botany Bay.]

On the first of November (1787), being in 26° 27′ north latitude, and 175° 38′ east longitude, we saw a great number of birds; among others, curlews and plovers, two species which never fly far from land. The weather was thick and squally; but all the parts of the horizon successively cleared up, except towards the south, where some large clouds remained constantly fixed; which made me think it likely that there was land in that point of the compass. I steered my course accordingly, and for two or three days we continued to see birds. By degrees, however, the signs of land left us; but it is probable that we passed by some island or flat rock of which we did not get sight, but which chance will perhaps present to future navigators. We now began to enjoy a serene sky, and it became at last possible to find the longitude by lunar observations, which we had not been able to do since our departure from Kamtschatka. The longitude by observation was a degree farther west than that which was given by our time-keeper No. 19.

We caught several doradoes and two sharks, and found them delicious eating, because we were all reduced to salt pork, which began to suffer from the influence of a burning clime. We repeated our lunar observations, and the difference was constantly the same. Having at length reached the tropic, the sky became clearer, and our horizon was of great extent; but we perceived no land, though we every day saw birds, which are never met with at a great distance from the shore. On the 4th of November, being in 23° 40′ north latitude, and in 175° 58′ 47″ of west longitude, according to a series of observations made that very day, we caught a golden plover, which was still moderately fat, and which could not have been wandering long at sea. The 5th we crossed our own tract from Monterey to Macao; the 6th that of Captain Clerke from the Sandwich Islands to Kamtschatka, by which time the birds had entirely disappeared. Our ships laboured exceedingly by reason of a heavy swell from the east, which, like that from the west in the Atlantic Ocean, constantly pervails in this vast sea. Neither bonetas nor doradoes came in our way, nor anything, indeed, but a few flying fish; a grievous circumstance, as our fresh provision was entirely consumed in consequence of our depending rather too much upon the salt element for the improvement of our unpalatable fare. The 9th we passed by the south point of the shoal, or flat of Villa Lobos, according at least to the position assigned to it in the charts presented to me by M. Fleurieu. I proportioned my canvas in such a way as to cross its latitude in the day-time; but as we perceived neither birds nor weeds, I am inclined to think that, if such a shoal exist, it must be in a more western position, the Spaniards having always placed their discoveries in the great Pacific Ocean too near to the American coast. At this time the sea became somewhat smoother, and the breezes more moderate; but the sky was covered with thick clouds, and scarcely had we reached the 10th degree of north latitude, when it began to rain almost incessantly, at least during the day; for the nights were tolerably fine. The heat was suffocating, and the hygrometer had never indicated more humidity since our departure from Europe. We were breathing an air destitute of elasticity, which, joined to unwholesome aliments, diminished our strength, and would have rendered us almost incapable of exertion if circumstances had required it. I redoubled my care to preserve the health of the crew during this crisis, produced by too sudden a passage from cold to heat and humidity. I had coffee served out every day for breakfast; and I ordered the ship to be dried and ventilated between decks; while the rain-water served to wash the sailors' shirts. Thus did we turn to account even the unfavourable temperature of the climate which we were obliged to cross, and of which I dreaded the influence more than that of all the high latitudes that had occurred in the course of our voyage. On the 6th of November, for the first time we caught eight bonetas, which furnished a good repast to the whole crew, and to the officers, who, as well as myself, had no longer any provision but that of the hold. The rain and storms ceased, and the heavy sea subsided about the 15th, when we had reached the 5° of north latitude. We then enjoyed a clear sky; a very extensive horizon made us easy about the night's run; and the air was so pure, the heavens so serene, and the light thence resulting so strong, that we could have perceived any danger as plainly as in open day. This fine weather accompanied us beyond the equator, which we crossed on the 21st of November, for the third time since we took our departure from Brest. We had been three times at the distance of about 60° from it to the north or south; and, according to the further plan of our voyage, we were not to revisit the northern hemisphere till we should enter the Atlantic Ocean in our way back to Europe. Nothing interrupted the monotony of this long run. We were steering a course nearly parallel to that which we had steered the preceding year in our passage from Easter Island to those that bear the name of Sandwich. During that passage we had been constantly surrounded with birds and bonetas, which afforded us wholesome and abundant food: in the present one, on the contrary, a vast solitude reigned around us, both the air and water of this quarter of the globe being nearly destitute of inhabitants. On the 23rd, however, we caught two sharks, which afforded two meals to the crew, and we shot on the same day a very lean curlew, apparently much fatigued. We supposed that it came from the Duke of York's island, from which we were about 100 leagues distant. It was hashed up and eaten at my table, and was scarcely better than the sharks. In propor-

tion as we advanced in the southern hemisphere, the noddies,
man-of-war birds, terns, and tropic birds flew more frequently
round the ships. We took them for the harbingers of some island,
which we were exceedingly impatient to fall in with; and mur-
mured much at the fatality that had prevented our making the
smallest discovery in the long line we had run down since our
departure from Kamtschatka. These birds, which became innumerable when we had reached the fourth degree of south
latitude, inspired us every moment with the hopes of making
land; but, although the horizon was of prodigious extent, none
could we see. We made, it is true, but little way. While we were
under the second degree of south latitude, the breeze abandoned
us, and was succeeded by light airs of wind from N. to W.N.W.,
of which I availed myself to gain a little easting, being afraid of
falling to leeward of the Friendly Islands. During these calms we
caught several sharks, which we preferred to salt meat, and shot
sea-birds, which we hashed. Though very lean, and smelling
and tasting of fish to a degree that was insupportable, they
appeared to us, in our present want of fresh provisions, almost as
good as woodcocks. Black *goelettes*, and others entirely white,
which I believe peculiar to the South Sea, as I never saw any in
the Atlantic Ocean, were so plenty that we killed more of them
than of noddies or man-of-war birds. And yet the latter flew
round the ships in such numbers, especially during the night,
that we were stunned by the noise they made, and could with
difficulty hear each other speak upon the quarter-deck. Our
sport, which was tolerably successful, punished their insults, and
afforded us tolerable food; but when we had passed the 6° they
entirely disappeared. The light winds from N.W. to W., which
had set in about the 3rd degree of south latitude, then gathered
strength, and did not give over blowing till we had reached the
12th. A heavy swell from the west rendered our navigation
exceedingly fatiguing; our cordage, rotted by the constantly wet
weather we had experienced while exploring the coast of Tartary,
kept breaking every moment; and, as we were fearful of exhaust-
ing our stock, was not replaced till the last extremity. Till the
2nd of December, when we reached 10° 50′, squalls, storms, and
rain constantly accompanied our course. The wind, though still
blowing from the west, then grew more moderate; and as the
weather cleared up, we were enabled to make lunar observations,
in order to rectify the error of our time-keepers. Since our departure from Kamtschatka, they appeared to have lost five
minutes of time, or, in other words, to indicate the longitude

1° 15′ too far east. According to the above astronomical observations, of which the result was 170° 7′ of longitude west, we passed exactly over the spot where Byron's islands of Danger are laid down; for we were exactly in their latitude; but as we neither saw land, nor the smallest sign of there being any near us, it is evident that their longitude has been mistaken; which was the more easy, as Byron regulated his navigation by the defective method of a dead-reckoning. The following day, December the 2nd, we were in 11° 34′ 47″ south latitude, and 170° 7′ 1″ longitude west, according to astronomical observation, precisely in the same parallel of latitude as Quiros's Island of the Handsome Nation, and one degree farther east. I would willingly have run a few degrees westward in order to fall in with it; but the wind blew directly from that quarter; and the island is laid down in too uncertain a manner to be sought for by working to windward. I therefore thought it better to avail myself of the western gale in order to reach the parallel of Bougainville's Navigators Islands, a discovery due to the French, where we might hope to procure fresh provision, of which we were in the greatest want.

On the 6th of December, at three in the afternoon, we got sight of the most easterly island of that Archipelago; stood towards it till eleven in the evening, and then stood on and off during the rest of the night. As I purposed anchoring, in case I met with a proper place, I passed through the channel between the great and the little islands that Bougainville left to the south. It is scarcely a league wide; but it appeared entirely free from danger. We were in mid-channel at noon, and at a mile's distance from the shore found the latitude by observation to be 14° 7′ south, the southern point of one of the islands bearing south 36° west. That point is consequently situated in 14° 8′ south latitude.

Though we did not perceive any canoes till we were in the channel, we had seen habitations on the windward side of the island, and a considerable group of Indians sitting in a circle under cocoanut trees, and appearing quietly to enjoy the sight afforded them by our frigates. They did not then launch a single canoe, or did they follow us along shore. This island, of about two hundred toifes elevation, is very steep, and covered to the top with large trees, among which we distinguished a great number of the cocoa-nut kind. The houses are built about half-way down the declivity, a situation in which the islanders breathe a cooler air than alongshore. Near them we remarked several spots of cultivated ground, planted probably with sweet potatoes or yams; but, upon the whole, the island appeared far

T

from fertile, and in any other part of the South Sea I should have thought it uninhabited. My mistake would have been the greater, as even two little islands, that form the western side of the channel through which we passed, have their inhabitants. We saw five canoes set out from them, and join eleven others that came from the eastern island. After having paddled several times round the two ships with an air of distrust, they at last ventured to approach, and make some exchanges with us, but of so trifling a kind that we only obtained about twenty cocoa-nuts and two blue gallinules. These islanders, like all those of the South Sea, were dishonest in their dealings; and after receiving the price of their cocoa-nuts beforehand, seldom failed to paddle away without fulfilling their part of the agreement. The amount of their thefts was, it is true, of little importance, a few bead necklaces with some scraps of red cloth, being hardly worth asking for again. We sounded several times in the channel with a line of a hundred fathoms, but got no ground, though at less than a mile's distance from the shore. We continued our course in order to double a point behind which we hoped to meet with shelter; but found that the island was not of the breadth indicated by M. de Bougainville's plan. It terminates, on the contrary, in a point, its greatest diameter being at most a league. We found that the east wind raised a surf upon the coast, which is surrounded with reefs; and saw plainly that it would be vain to seek an anchorage there. We then stood out of the channel, with the intention of running along the two islands to the west, which are both together nearly equal in extent to the more eastern one. A canal less than a hundred toifes wide separates them, and at their western extremity is a small island, which I should have called a large rock had it not been covered with trees. Before we doubled the two southern points it fell dead calm, and we were tossed about by a heavy swell, which made me fearful of running foul of the *Astrolabe*. Luckily some little puffs of air soon extricated us from that disagreeable situation, which had not permitted us to attend to the harangue of an old Indian, who held a branch of *kava* in his hand and delivered a discourse of considerable length. We knew, by reading a variety of voyages, that it was a sign of peace; and, while throwing him a few pieces of cloth, answered him by the word *tayo*, which, in the language of several nations inhabiting the islands of the South Sea, means *friend;* but we had not as yet had sufficient practice to understand and pronounce distinctly the words of the vocabularies that we had extracted from Cook's *Voyages.*

At length, when the breeze reached us, we made sail, in order to stand away from the coast and get out of the region of calms. All the canoes then came up alongside. In general they sail pretty well, but row very indifferently; and, as they overset at every moment, would be useless to anybody but such excellent swimmers as these islanders are. *They* are no more surprised or uneasy at such an accident than we are at the fall of a hat. Taking up the canoe on their shoulders, they empty the water out of it, and then get in again, with the certainty of having the same operation to perform half an hour after, it being almost as difficult to preserve an equilibrium in such ticklish vessels as upon the tight-rope. These islanders are in general tall, their mean height appearing to me to be five feet seven or eight inches. The colour of their skin nearly resembles that of the Algerines, or other nations of the coast of Barbary: their hair is long, and tied up on the top of their heads: their cast of countenance far from agreeable. I saw no more than two women; and even *their* features did not appear to be more delicately formed. The younger, who might be about eighteen years of age, had a dreadful and disgusting ulcer upon her leg. Several of the men also had large sores about their persons, possibly a beginning of leprosy; for I remarked two among them whose legs, covered with ulcers, and swelled to the size of their bodies, did not admit of a doubt as to the nature of their disease. They approached us with fear and without arms, every thing bespeaking them as peaceable as the inhabitants of the Society and Friendly Islands. At one time we thought they had entirely taken leave of us, and their apparent poverty easily reconciled us to their absence; but the wind having fallen in the afternoon, the same canoes, accompanied by several others, came two leagues into the offing to traffick with us anew. After quitting us they had gone ashore, and now returned rather more richly laden than before. We obtained from them at different times several curious articles of dress, five fowls, ten gallinules, a small hog, and the most beautiful turtle-dove we had ever seen. Its body was white, its head of the finest purple, its wings green, and its breast checkered with red and black spots, like the leaves of the anemony. This charming bird was tame, and ate out of the hand and mouth; but it was not probable that we could convey it to Europe alive. And so it proved, its death only permitting us to preserve its feathers, which soon lost all their splendour. As the *Astrolabe* was constantly ahead in this day's run, all the canoes began their traffick with M. de Langle, who purchased two dogs, which we found excellent eating.

Although the canoes of these islanders are well constructed, and furnish a good proof of the skill with which they work in wood, we could never prevail on them to accept our hatchets or any other instrument of iron. They preferred a few glass beads, that could be of no use to them, to all the hardware and stuffs we offered them; and gave us in return, among other things, a wooden vessel filled with cocoa-nut oil, exactly of the shape of our earthen pots, and such as no European workman would undertake to fashion by any other means than a turning lathe. Their ropes are round, and twisted like our watch-chains: their mats are very fine; but their stuffs are inferior to those of the Easter and Sandwich Islands. It seems also that they are very scarce; for all the islanders were absolutely naked, and only sold us two pieces. As we were sure of meeting with a much more considerable island farther west, where we flattered ourselves we should at least find shelter, if not a port, we deferred making more extensive observations till after our arrival at that island, which, according to M. Bougainville's plan, is only separated from the last island we had upon our beam at nightfall by a channel eight leagues wide. I ran only three or four leagues to the west-ward after sunset, and passed the rest of the night in standing off and on under easy sail. At break of day I was very much surprised not to see the land to leeward, nor did I get sight of it till six o'clock in the morning, because the channel is infinitely wider than that laid down in the plan that served me as a guide. It is a great pity that the charts of a voyage which yields to none but that of Captain Cook in accuracy of observation, and in extent and importance of discoveries, should not have been drawn up with greater care and upon a larger scale.

We did not find ourselves opposite the north-east point of the island of Maouna till five o'clock in the evening. Intending to seek an anchorage there, I made a signal to the *Astrolabe* to haul her wind, that we might stretch backward and forward to wind-ward of the island during the night, and have the whole of the next day before us to explore it in every part. Though we were three leagues from the land, two or three canoes came alongside the same evening, bringing with them hogs and fruit, which they exchanged for beads. Hence we conceived a high opinion of the riches of the island.

The next morning I approached the land, and stretched along it at the distance of half a league. It is surrounded by a reef of coral, on which the sea broke with great fury; but that reef was almost close inshore, and in the creeks formed by several small projections of the coast there was room for canoes, and probably for our barges and long-boats to enter. We discovered a number of villages at the bottom on each creek, whence came innumerable canoes, laden with hogs, cocoa-nuts, and other fruit, which we purchased with glass ware. Such great abundance increased my desire to anchor, especially as we saw water falling in cascades from the tops of the mountains to the bottom of the villages. So many advantages made me little scrupulous as to an anchorage. We hauled closer inshore, and having found at four o'clock, at a mile from land, and in thirty fathoms water, a band composed of rotten shells and a very little coral, we let go our anchors; but we were tost about by a very heavy swell that set inshore, although the wind blew from the land. We immediately hoisted out our boats; and the same day, M. de Langle and several officers, with three boats manned and armed by the two frigates, landed at a village, where they were received by the inhabitants in the most friendly manner. As night was coming on when they went ashore, the Indians made a great fire to light the place of debarkation; and brought down birds, hogs, and fruit. After an hour's stay, our boats returned on board. Everyone seemed satisfied with this reception, our only concern being to see our frigates anchored in so bad a roadstead, where they rolled as if in the open sea. Though we were sheltered from the easterly winds, the calm thence resulting sufficed to expose us to the greatest danger in case our cables should part, while the impossibility of getting out left us no resource against a strong breeze from the north-west. We knew by the relations of preceding navigators that the trade winds are very uncertain in these seas, and that it is almost as easy to sail east as west, a circumstance which favours the natives in their long excursions to leeward. We had ourselves experienced this inconstancy of the wind, the western breeze having only left us in the latitude of 12°. These reflections made me pass a very bad night, especially as a storm was gathering to the northward, whence the wind was blowing fresh, but fortunately, however, the land breeze prevailed.

The next morning, as the rising of the sun announced a fair day, I resolved to avail myself of it, in order to reconnoitre the country, observe the inhabitants at their own homes, fill water, and then get under way, prudence forbidding me to pass a second night at that anchorage, which M. de Langle had also found too dangerous for a longer stay. It was therefore agreed upon that we should sail in the afternoon, and that the morning, which was very fine, should be in part employed in trading for hogs

and fruit. As early as the dawn of day the islanders had surrounded the two frigates with two hundred canoes full of different kinds of provision, which they would only exchange for beads
—in their estimation diamonds of the first water. Our axes, our
cloth, and all our other articles of commerce they disdained.
While a part of the crew was occupied in keeping them in order,
and in trading with them, the rest filled the boats with empty
casks, in order to go ashore to water. Our two boats, armed,
and commanded by Messrs. de Clonard and Colinet, and those of
the *Astrolabe* commanded by Messrs. de Monti and Bellegarde,
set out with that intention at five o'clock in the morning for a
bay about a league distant, and a little way to windward; a convenient situation, as it enabled them, when loaded with water, to
come back with the wind large. I followed close after Messrs.
Clonard and Monti in my pinnace (*biscayenne*), and landed at the
same time as they did. Unfortunately M. de Langle resolved to
make an excursion in his jolly-boat to another creek, about a
league distant from our watering-place. This excursion, whence
he returned delighted with the beauty of the village he had
visited, was, as will be seen hereafter, the cause of our misfortune. The creek, towards which the long-boats steered, was
large and commodious; both they and the other boats remained
afloat at low water, within half a pistol-shot of the beach; and
the water was both fine and easily procured. Messrs. de Clonard
and de Monti preserved the best order possible. A line of soldiers
was posted between the beach and the Indians, who amounted to
about two hundred, including a great many women and children.
We prevailed upon them all to sit down under cocoa trees, that
were not more than eight toifes distant from our boats. Each
of them had by him fowls, hogs, parrots, pigeons, or fruit,
and all wished to sell them at once, which occasioned some
confusion.

The women, some of whom were very pretty, offered their
favours, as well as their fowls and fruit, to all those who had
beads to give them; and soon tried to pass through the line of
soldiers, who opposed but a feeble resistance to their attempts.
Europeans who have made a voyage round the world, especially
Frenchmen, have no arms to ward off similar attacks. Accordingly the fair savages found little difficulty in breaking the ranks;
the men then approached; and the confusion was growing general,
when Indians, whom we took for chiefs, made their appearance
with sticks in their hands, and restored order, everyone returning
to his post, and our traffick beginning anew, to the great satis-

faction of both buyers and sellers. In the meantime a scene had passed in our long-boat which was a real act of hostility, and which I was desirous of repressing without effusion of blood. An Indian had gotten upon the stern of the boat, had laid hold of a mallet, and had aimed several blows at the arms and back of one of our sailors. I ordered four of the strongest seamen to lay hold of him, and to throw him into the sea, which was immediately done. The other islanders appearing to disapprove of the conduct of their countryman, this squabble was attended with no bad consequences. Perhaps an example of severity would have been necessary to awe these people still more, by letting them know how much the force of our fire-arms was beyond their individual strength; for their height of about five feet ten inches, and their muscular limbs of colossal proportions, gave them an idea of their own superiority, which rendered us by no means formidable in their eyes; but having very little time to remain among them, I thought it right not to inflict a severer penalty upon him who had offended us; and, by the way of giving them some idea of our power, contented myself with buying three pigeons, which were thrown up into the air, and shot in the presence of the whole assembly.

While all this was passing with the greatest tranquillity, and our casks were filling with water, I thought I might venture to the distance of two hundred yards to visit a charming village, situated in the midst of a wood, or rather of an orchard, all the trees of which were loaded with fruit. The houses were placed upon the circumference of a circle, of about a hundred and fifty toifes in diameter, the interior forming a vast open space, covered with the most beautiful verdure, and shaded by trees, which kept the air delightfully cool. Women, children, and old men accompanied me, and invited me into their houses. They spread the finest and freshest mats upon a floor formed of little chosen pebbles, and raised about two feet above the ground in order to guard against the humidity. I went into the handsomest of these huts, which probably belonged to a chief; and great was my surprise to see a large cabinet of lattice-work, as well executed as any of those in the environs of Paris. The best architect could not have given a more elegant curve to the extremities of the ellipsis that terminated the building; while a row of pillars at five feet distance from each other formed a complete colonnade round the whole. The pillars were made of trunks of trees very neatly wrought, and between them were fine mats laid over one another with great art, like the scales of a fish, and

drawing up and down with cords like our Venetian blinds. The
rest of the house was covered with leaves of the cocoa-palm.

This charming country combines the advantages of a soil fruitful without culture, and of a climate which renders clothing
unnecessary. The trees that produce the bread-fruit, the cocoa-
nut, the banana, the guava, and the orange hold out to these
fortunate people an abundance of wholesome food; while the
fowls, hogs, and dogs, which live upon the surplus of these
fruits, afford them an agreeable variety of viands. They were so
rich, and had so few wants, that they disdained our instruments
of iron and our cloth and asked only for beads. Abounding in
real blessings, they were desirous of obtaining superfluities alone.

They had sold at our market more than two hundred wood-
pigeons, which would only eat out of the hand; and a number of
the most beautiful turtle-doves and perroquets, equally tame.
What cold imagination could separate the idea of happiness from
so enchanting a place? These islanders, said we a hundred times
over, are, without doubt, the happiest beings on earth. Surrounded by their wives and children, they pass their peaceful
days in innocence and repose: no care disturbs them but that of
bringing up their birds, and, like the first man, of gathering,
without labour, the fruit that grows over their heads. We were
deceived. This delightful country was not the abode of innocence. We perceived, indeed, no arms; but the bodies of the
Indians, covered over with scars, proved that they were often at
war, or else quarrelling among themselves; while their features
announced a ferocity that was not perceptible in the countenances of the women. Nature had, no doubt, stamped this character on their faces by way of showing that the half-savage, living
in a state of anarchy, is a more mischievous being than the most
ferocious of the brute creation.

The first visit passed without any dispute capable of leading to
disagreeable consequences. I learned, however, that there had
been quarrels between individuals, but that they had been very
prudently appeased. Stones had been thrown at M. Rollin, our
surgeon-major; and an Indian, while pretending to admire
M. de Monernon's sabre, had attempted to snatch it from him;
but finding the scabbard alone left in his hand, he had run off in a
great fright at the sight of the naked weapon. I perceived that
in general these islanders were very turbulent, and in bad sub-
jection to their chiefs; but as I intended to leave them in the
afternoon, I congratulated myself on not having attached any
importance to the little instances of molestation we had met with.

Towards noon I returned to the ship in my barge, and was very closely followed by the long-boats. I found it difficult to get alongside, both frigates being surrounded by canoes, and our market being as much crowded as ever. When I went ashore I had given the command of the *Bouffole* to M. Boutin, and had left him at liberty to establish such police as he might think proper, either by permitting a few of the islanders to come on board, or by positively opposing their entry, according to the turn circumstances might take. Upon the quarter-deck I found seven or eight Indians, the oldest of whom was presented to me as a chief. M. Boutin told me that he could not have prevented their coming on board unless by firing upon them; that when they compared their bodily strength to ours they laughed at our threats, and made a jest of our sentinels; and that my well-known principles of moderation had made him unwilling to recur to violent measures, which, however, were the only ones capable of keeping them in awe. He added, that, since the chief was present, those had come on board before were grown more quiet and less insolent.

I made the chief a number of presents, and showed him every mark of kindness; but wishing at the same time to inspire him with a high opinion of our power, I ordered several experiments on the use of our weapons to be made in his presence. But their effect impressed him so little that he seemed to think them only fit for the destruction of birds.

Our boats now arrived loaded with water, and I made every preparation to get under way, and profit by a light land breeze which gave us hopes of having time to make a little offing. M. de Langle returned at the same moment from his excursion, and related that he had landed in a noble harbour for boats, situated at the foot of a delightful village, and near a cascade of the most pellucid water. On going on board his own ship he had given orders to get under way, of which he felt the necessity as well as myself; but he insisted in the most urgent manner upon our remaining, standing off and on, at a league from the coast, and upon our getting on board a few long-boat loads of water before we should entirely abandon the island. In vain did I represent to him that we were not in the smallest want of it.—He had adopted Captain Cook's system, and thought water recently shipped a thousand times preferable to that which we had in the hold; and as a few individuals of his crew had slight symptoms of scurvy, he thought, with reason, that we owed them every relief in our power. Besides, no island could be compared with this for abundance of provision : the two frigates had already taken on board more than five hundred hogs, a great number of fowls and pigeons, and a great quantity of fruit; and yet all these valuable acquisitions had only cost us a few glass beads.

I felt the truth of these reflections; but a secret presentiment prevented my immediate acquiescence. I told him that I thought the islanders too turbulent for us to trust our boats on shore when they could not be supported by the fire of the ships; and observed to him that our moderation had only served to embolden men who calculated upon nothing but our personal strength, which was certainly very much inferior to theirs. Nothing, however, could shake M. de Langle's resolution. He told me that my resistance would make me responsible for the progress of the scurvy, which already began to show itself in an alarming manner, and that, besides, the harbour he was speaking of was infinitely more commodious than that of our watering-place. Finally, he begged me to permit him to put himself at the head of the first party, assuring me that in three hours he would return on board with all the boats full of water. M. de Langle was a man of so sound a judgment, and so much capacity, that these considerations, more than any other motive, determined me to give my consent, or rather made my will give way to his. I promised him then that we would stand off and on all night, and that in the morning we would dispatch our two long-boats, and two barges, armed in any way he should think proper, and that the whole should be under his command. The event fully justified our opinion that it was time to get under way. On heaving up the anchor we found one strand of the cable cut by the coral; and in two hours more the whole cable would have been cut through. As we were not under sail till four in the afternoon, which was too late an hour to think of sending our boats on shore, we postponed their departure till next day. The night was stormy, and the wind, which shifted every moment, made me come to a resolution of standing off about three leagues from the coast. At break of day a flat calm did not permit me to approach it; and it was not till nine o'clock that a small breeze sprang up from the north-west, and enabled me to near the island, from which at eleven o'clock we were scarcely a league distant. I then dispatched my long boat and barge, commanded by Messieurs Boutin and Mouton, on board the *Astrolabe*, to take M. de Langle's orders. All those who had any slight symptoms of the scurvy were put into them, as well as six soldiers armed, with the master at arms at their head. The two boats contained in all twenty-eight men, and carried twenty empty casks, which were meant to be filled at the watering-place. Messieurs de Lamanon and Colinet, though sick, were of the number of those that set off from the *Bouffole*. M. de Langle, on the other hand, set off in his barge, accompanied by M. Vaujuas, a convalescent. M. le Gobien, a midshipman, commanded the long-boat, and Messrs. de la Martiniere, Lavaux, and Father Receveur made part of the thirty-three persons sent by the *Astrolabe*. Among the sixty-one individuals, of which the whole party consisted, were the choicest men of both crews. M. de Langle armed all his people with muskets and cutlasses, and ordered six swivels to be mounted upon the long-boats. I had left him perfectly at liberty to provide everything he might think conducive to his safety. The certitude we were in of having had no dispute with the natives, of which they could retain any resentment; the immense number of canoes that crowded round us in the offing; the air of gaiety and confidence that prevailed in our markets; everything, in short, tended to increase his security, and I confess that mine could not well be greater than it was. But it was contrary to my principles to send boats on shore without the greatest necessity, especially in the midst of an immense number of people, when they could not be supported or even perceived by the ships.

The boats put off from the *Astrolabe* at half-past twelve, and in three-quarters of an hour arrived at the watering-place. What was the surprise of all the officers, and of M. de Langle himself, to find, instead of a vast and commodious bay, a creek full of coral, through which there was no passage but a winding channel less than twenty-five feet wide, and on which the swell broke as upon a bar! When within, they had only three feet water; the long boats grounded, and the barges only continued afloat because they were hauled to the entrance of the channel at a considerable distance from the beach. Unfortunately M. de Langle had examined the bay at high-water only, never imagining that the tide at these islands rose five or six feet. He could not believe his eyes. The first movement of his mind was to quit the creek and repair to that where we had already filled water, which combined every advantage. But the air of tranquillity and good-humour of the crowds waiting for him upon the beach with an immense quantity of fruit and hogs and the women and children he saw among the Indians, who take care to send them out of the way when they have hostile intentions; all these circumstances concurred to banish his first prudent idea, which an inconceivable fatality forbad him to pursue. He put the casks on shore from the four boats with the greatest tranquillity; while his soldiers preserved the best order possible upon the beach, being drawn up in two lines with a space left open for the working party. But this calm was not of long duration. Several of the canoes, which had parted with their provision to the ships, had returned to the island, and had all landed in the bay of the watering-place, so that in a short time it was entirely full. Instead of two hundred natives, including women and children, whom M. de Langle had found there on his arrival at half-past one, there were at three o'clock from a thousand to twelve hundred. The number of canoes, which had traded with us in the morning, was so considerable that we scarcely perceived its diminution in the afternoon; and I gave myself credit for keeping them employed on board in hopes that our boats would be so much the quieter on shore. Great was my mistake! M. de Langle's situation became every moment more and more embarrassing. He found means, however, with the assistance of Messieurs de Vaujuas, Boutin, Colinet, and Gobien, to ship his water; but the bay was almost dry, and he could not hope to get the long-boats off before four in the afternoon. He stepped into them, however, as well as his detachment, and took post in the bow with his musket and musketeers, forbidding anyone to fire before he should give the word. He began, however, to be sensible that he should soon be forced to do so. Already the stones began to fly, and the Indians, who were only up to their knees in water, surrounded the long-boats at less than six feet distance, the soldiers, who were embarked, making vain efforts to keep them off. If the fear of commencing hostilities, and of being accused of barbarity, had not withheld M. de Langle, he would doubtless have given orders to fire a volley of musketry and swivels, which would not have failed to put the multitude to flight; but he flattered himself that he should be able to keep them in check without effusion of blood, and fell the victim of his humanity. In a very short time a shower of stones, thrown from a small distance with as much force as from a sling, struck almost everyone of those who were in the long-boat. M. de Langle had only time to fire his two shots, when he was knocked down, and unfortunately fell over the larboard side of the boat, where more than two hundred Indians immediately massacred him with clubs and stones. When he was dead they tied him by the arm to one of the rowlocks of the long-boat, in order, no doubt, to make surer of spoil. The long-boat of the *Bouffole*, commanded by M. Boutin, was aground at two toifes from that of the *Astrolabe*, leaving in a parallel line between them a little channel unoccupied by the Indians. It was by that channel that all the wounded, who had the good fortune not to fall on the other side, saved themselves by swimming. They got on board the barges, which, having most fortunately been kept afloat, were the means of saving forty-nine persons out of the sixty-one of which the party consisted. M. Boutin had imitated all the movements, and followed every step of M. de Langle: at the same time, and placed in the same manner, and he occupied the same post in the bow of the boat. Although afraid of the bad consequences of M. de Langle's moderation, he did not take upon him to order his detachment to fire till after M. de Langle had begun. It may be supposed that, at the distance of four or five yards, every shot must have killed an Indian, but there was no time to reload. M. Boutin was likewise knocked down by a stone, and by good fortune fell between the two long-boats, on board of which not a single man remained in less than five minutes. Those who saved themselves by swimming to the two barges had received several wounds each, almost all on the head: those, on the contrary, who were unfortunate enough to fall over on the side of the Indians were instantly dispatched by their clubs. But the rage for plunder was such that the islanders hastened to get possession of the long-boats, and jumped on board to the number of three or four hundred, tearing up the seats and breaking the inside to pieces in order to seek for our supposed riches. While this was going on they no longer paid much attention to the barges; which gave time to Messieurs de Vaujuas and Mouton to save the rest of our people, and to ascertain that nobody remained in the hands of the Indians but those who had been massacred and killed in the water by the blows of their *patows*.

The crews of the barges, who till then had fired upon the islanders and killed a good many, now began to throw their water-casks overboard in order that everybody might find room. They had, besides, almost exhausted their ammunition; and their retreat was become a matter of some difficulty, with such a number of persons dangerously wounded, who lay stretched out upon the thwarts and hindered the working of the oars. To the prudence of M. Vaujuas, to the good order which he established, and to the strict discipline kept up by M. Mouton, who commanded the *Bouffole's* barge, we were indebted for the preservation of the forty-nine persons of both crews who escaped. M. Boutin, who had five wounds on the head and one in the breast, was kept above water by the cockswain of the long-boat, who was himself wounded. M. Colinet was found lying in a state of insensibility upon the grapnel-rope of the barge, having an arm fractured, a finger broken, and two wounds on the head. M. Lavaux, surgeon-major of the *Astrolabe*, was so grievously wounded that he was obliged to suffer the operation of the trepan. He had, however, swum to the barges, as well as M. de la Martiniere, and Father Receveur, who had received a violent contusion on the eye. M. de Lamanon and M. de Langle were massacred with unexampled barbarity, with Talin, master at arms of the *Bouffole*, and nine other persons belonging to the two crews. The savage Indians, after having killed them, still continued to wreak their fury upon the inanimate bodies with their clubs. M. le Gobien, who commanded the *Astrolabe's* long-boat under the orders of M. de Langle, did not abandon his post till he found himself entirely alone. After having exhausted his ammunition, he leaped into the water on the side of the little channel left between the two boats, which, as I have said above, was unoccupied by the Indians; and notwithstanding his wounds, found means to save himself on board one of the barges. That of the *Astrolabe* was so deeply laden that it grounded. This even inspired the natives with the idea of disturbing the wounded in their retreat. They came down accordingly in great numbers towards the reefs at the entrance, within ten feet of which the barges were necessarily obliged to pass. The little ammunition that remained was exhausted upon the infuriated crowd; and at length the boats extricated themselves from a place, more dreadful on account of its deceitful situation and the cruelty of its inhabitants than the dens of wild beasts.

At five o'clock they came on board, and informed us of this disastrous event. We had round us at that moment not less than a hundred canoes, in which the natives were selling their provisions with a security which sufficiently proved their innocence. But they were the brothers, the children, the countrymen of the barbarous assassins; and I confess that it was necessary to call up all my reason to repress the anger that transported me, and to hinder the crew from putting them to death. The soldiers were already casting loose the guns and laying hold of their muskets. I stopped these movements, which were, however, pardonable enough; and ordered a single gun loaded with powder to be fired as a warning to the canoes to depart. A small boat that came from the coast informed them, without doubt, of what had just passed; for in less than an hour not a canoe remained in sight. An Indian who was upon the quarter-deck when our barge came on board was arrested by my orders and put in irons. The next day, having approached the coast, I permitted him to jump overboard, the confidence with which he had remained on board being an unequivocal proof of his innocence.

My first project was to send another party on shore to revenge the death of our unfortunate companions and to recover the wrecks of our boats. With that intention I stood on the westward in search of an anchorage; but I found nothing but the same bottom of coral, with a swell that set inshore and broke upon the reefs. The creek in which the massacre took place was, besides, very deeply indented in the side of the island, and it did not appear possible to approach it within cannon shot. M. Boutin, whose wound confined him to his bed, but who retained the full command of his mind, represented to me also that the situation of the bay was such, that if our boats should unfortunately run aground (a thing very possible), not a single man would return alive; for the trees, which are close to the sea-side, while protecting the Indians against our musketry, would leave the men whom we might debark exposed to a shower of stones, so much the more difficult to avoid as, being thrown with uncommon force and address, they produced almost the same effect as our bullets, and had the advantage of succeeding one another with greater rapidity. M. de Vaujuas was of the same opinion. I would not, however, accede to it till I had fully ascertained the impossibility of anchoring within gun-shot of the village. I passed two days in working to windward opposite the bay, and could perceive the wrecks of our long-boats aground upon the sand, and round them an immense number of Indians. What will no doubt appear incredible is, that during this time five or six canoes came off from the shore with hogs, pigeons, and cocoa-nuts to offer us in exchange. I was obliged every moment to curb my anger lest I should give orders to send them to the bottom. The Indians, not knowing that we had any arms of longer range than our muskets, remained without the least apprehension at fifty toises distance from the ships, and offered us their provisions with great apparent security. Our gestures gave them no encouragement to approach, and in this way they passed a whole hour in the afternoon of the 12th of December. Their offers of barter were succeeded by raillery, and ere long I perceived several other canoes quit the beach in order to join them. As they had no suspicion of the range of our guns, and as everything indicated that I should soon be forced to depart from my principles of moderation, I ordered a shot to be fired into the midst of them. My orders were executed with the utmost precision. The ball dashed the water into the canoes, and they instantly made the best of their way to the shore, being joined in their flight by those that had left the beach a little while before.

It was with difficulty that I could tear myself from this fatal spot and leave the dead bodies of our murdered companions. In M. de Langle I lost an old friend, a man of sense, judgment, and information, and one of the best officers in the French navy. His humanity was the cause of his death. Had he allowed himself to fire upon the first Indians who came into the water in order to surround his boats, he would have saved his own life and those of M. de Lamanon and ten other victims of Indian ferocity. There were, besides, twenty persons belonging to the two frigates grievously wounded; this event deprived us for the moment of thirty-two hands, and two long-boats, the only ones we had capable of containing a sufficient number of armed men to attempt a descent. These considerations were the guide of my future conduct. The smallest check would have forced me to burn one of the two frigates to man the other. I had indeed the frame of a long-boat on board; but I could not put it together without going into port. If, to satisfy my revenge, I had only wished for the massacre of a few Indians, I had an opportunity of destroying, sinking, blowing to pieces a hundred canoes, containing more than five hundred persons; but I was afraid of being mistaken in the choice of my victims, and the voice of conscience saved their lives. Those whom this narrative may remind of the catastrophe of Captain Cook should bear in mind that his ships were anchored in the bay of Karakakooa; that their guns rendered them masters of the beach and that they could give the law to the Indians by threatening to destroy the canoes that remained at the water-side, as well as the villages that skirted the coast. We, on the contrary, were at sea, out of gun-shot, and obliged to keep off the coast, where a calm might have been attended with the greatest danger. A heavy swell drifted us constantly towards the reefs, outside of which we might, without doubt, have anchored with iron chains; but still we should have been out of gun-shot of the village, besides that the swell was sufficient to cut our cable at the hawse-holes, and thereby to expose us to the most imminent hazard. I exhausted every calculation of probability before I left this fatal island; being at length convinced that anchoring was impracticable, and that a descent unsupported by the frigates would be rashness in the extreme. Even success would have been useless, since it was certain that not a single man remained alive in the hands of the Indians, and that our boats, which we had the means of replacing, were broken to pieces and aground. I steered, in consequence, on the 14th, for a third island which was in sight, bearing W. by N., and which M. de Bougainville had only seen from the mast-head, being driven off by bad weather. This island is separated from that of Maouna by a channel only nine leagues wide. The Indians had given us the names of ten islands that composed their archipelago, and had rudely traced their situation upon a sheet of paper. Although no great dependence is to be placed upon the plan they drew, yet to me it appears probable that the people of these different islands are in a kind of confederacy with one another, and that they keep up a frequent intercourse. The farther discoveries we have made leave no doubt of this archi-pelago being more considerable than the Society Islands, while it is equally well-peopled, and abounds in provision no less than they. It is even probable that very good harbours might be found there; but having no boat, and knowing the exasperated state of mind of my crew, I resolved not to anchor till I came to Botany Bay, in New Holland, where I purposed putting together the frame of the new long-boat that I had on board. It was my inten-tion, nevertheless, for the sake of advancing the science of geography, to explore the different islands I might meet with, and to determine their latitude and longitude with precision. I hoped also to be able to traffick with the inhabitants by lying to at a small distance from the coast. I willingly abandon to others the care of writing the uninteresting history of such barbarous nations. A stay of twenty-four hours, and the relation of our misfortunes, suffice to show their atrocious manners, and their arts, as well as the productions of one of the finest countries of the universe.

The 13th December we got sight of Norfolk Island and of the two islets at its south point. The sea was very high, and had so long continued so that I had little hope of meeting with shelter on the north-east coast. On approaching it, however, I found smoother water, and determined to let go the anchor at a mile from the land, in twenty-four fathoms water, over a bottom of hard sand mixed with a little coral. I had no other object than to obtain a knowledge of the soil and productions of this island by means of our naturalists and botanists, who, since our departure from Kamtschatka, had had very few opportunities of entering any new observations in their journals. We, however, saw the sea break with fury round the island; but I flattered myself that

U

our boats would find a shelter behind the large rocks that skirt the coast. As we had learned, however, to our cost, never to depart from the rules of prudence, I charged M. de Clonard, a post-captain, and the second officer in the expedition, with the command of four small boats dispatched by the frigates, and I strictly enjoined him not to risk a landing, under any pretence whatever, should there be the smallest risk of our pinnaces being overset by the surf. His punctuality and prudence left me without fear or apprehension. No one indeed could better deserve my confidence than that officer, whom I destined to the command of the *Astrolabe* as soon as we should arrive at Botany Bay. Our frigates were anchored abreast of two points situated at the northern extremity of the north-east coast of the island, and opposite to the place where we supposed that Captain Cook had debarked. Our boats stood towards this kind of inlet; but they found a surf breaking upon the rocks with a fury which rendered all approach impossible. . . . They coasted along shore within half musket-shot, pulling up to the south-east, and went half a league in that direction without finding a single spot where it was possible to land. They perceived that the island was surrounded by a wall formed of the lava which had flowed from the summit of the mountain, and which, having cooled in its descent, had formed in a number of places a kind of roof projecting several feet over the coast of the island. Even if landing had been practicable, it would still have been impossible to penetrate into the interior, unless by stemming for the space of fifteen or twenty toifes the rapid course of some torrents that had formed ravines. Beyond these natural barriers the island was covered with pines and carpeted with the most beautiful verdure. We should probably have found there several culinary plants; and that hope added still to our desire of visiting an island where Captain Cook had debarked with the greatest facility. It is true that he was there in fine weather that had lasted several days, while we had constantly navigated in so high a sea that for eight days we had not dared to open our ports or cabin windows. From the ship I followed with my telescope the motions of the boats; and seeing that at the fall of night they had not found a convenient place of debarkation, I made a signal to recall them, and soon after gave orders to get under way. I should perhaps have lost a great deal of time in waiting for a more favourable moment, and the survey of the island was not worth such a sacrifice. While I was preparing to make sail, a signal from the *Astrolabe*, indicating that she was on fire, threw me into a state of the utmost anxiety.

I immediately dispatched a boat in all haste to her assistance, but by the time it had gotten half-way, another signal informed me that the fire was extinguished; and shortly after M. de Monti hailed me with a speaking trumpet, and told me that a box of acids and other chemical liquors, belonging to Father Receveur, and deposited under the quarter-deck, had taken fire of itself, and spread so thick a smoke below that it had been difficult to discover whence it proceeded. At length means were found to throw the box overboard, and the accident was attended with no farther consequences. It is probable that a bottle of acid, having burst in the inside of the box, occasioned the fire, which afterwards extended itself to bottles of spirits of wine either broken or ill-corked. I now gave myself credit for having, at the very beginning of the voyage, ordered a similar box, belonging to the Abbé Monges, to be placed in the open air upon the forecastle of the ship, where danger from fire was not much to be apprehended.

Norfolk Island, though very steep, is scarcely more than seventy or eighty toifes above the level of the sea. The pines with which it is covered are probably of the same species as those of New Caledonia or New Zealand. Captain Cook says that he met with a great many cabbage trees; and the hope of procuring some contributed not a little to our desire of landing. It is probable that the palm which bears these cabbages is very small, for we could not perceive a single tree of that species. As this island is not inhabited, it is covered with sea-fowl, particularly tropic birds, none of which are without their long red feathers. There were also a great many boobies and gulls, but not a single man-of-war bird. A bank of sand, over which there are twenty or thirty fathoms water, extends three or four leagues to the north-ward and eastward of the island, and perhaps all round it; but we did not sound on the western side. While we lay at anchor we caught some red fish upon the bank of the kind called *capitaine* at the Isle of France, or *farde*, which afforded us an excellent repast. At eight o'clock in the evening we were under way. I first stood west-north-west, and then bore away by degrees to south-west by west, under easy sail, and sounding continually upon the bank, where it was possible we might meet with shoals; but the bottom was, on the contrary, exceedingly even, and the water deepened foot by foot in proportion as we left the land. At eleven o'clock in the evening we got no ground with a line of sixty fathoms, being then ten miles west-north-west of the most northerly point of Norfolk Island. The wind had settled at east-

south-east, with rather thick squalls; but in the intervals between
them the weather was very clear. At daybreak I crowded sail
towards Botany Bay, which was now at no more than three
hundred leagues distance. The 14th, in the evening, after the
sun was beneath the horizon, I made the signal to bring to, and
to sound with two hundred fathoms of line. The flat bank of
Norfolk Island had made me imagine that bottom might be found
all the way to New Holland; but this conjecture proved false, and
I continued my course with an error the less in my mind; for I
had been strongly persuaded of the truth of my opinion. The
wind from east-south-east to north-east continued to blow till we
came within sight of New Holland. We made a great deal of way
by day and very little by night, because no navigator had pre-
ceded us in the track along which we were running.

On the 17th, being in 31° 28' south latitude, and 159° 15' east
longitude, we were surrounded by innumerable gulls, which
made us suspect that we were passing near some island or rock;
and several bets were laid on the discovery of new land before
our arrival at Botany Bay, from which we were only a hundred
and eighty leagues distant: these birds followed us till within
eighty leagues of New Holland, and it is probable enough that
we had left some islet or rock behind us which serves them as an
asylum, for they are much less numerous near an inhabited
country. From Norfolk Island till we got sight of Botany Bay
we sounded every evening, with two hundred fathoms of line,
and did not find bottom till within eight leagues of the coast in
ninety fathoms water. We got sight of it on the 23rd of January.
The land is of very moderate elevation, and can hardly be seen
at more than twelve leagues distance. The wind then became
very variable, and, like Captain Cook, we met with currents which
drifted us every day fifteen miles to the southward of our reckoning; so that we passed the whole day of the 24th in plying to
windward in sight of Botany Bay without being able to double
Point Solander, which bore north distant one league. The wind
blew strong from that quarter, and our ships sailed too badly to
be able to overcome the force of both wind and currents. We
had this day a sight entirely new to us since our departure from
Manilla. It was an English fleet at anchor in Botany Bay, of
which we could distinguish the colours and pendants.

Europeans are all fellow-countrymen at such a distance from
home, and we felt the greatest impatience to get into an anchorage; but the weather was so hazy the following day that it was
impossible to distinguish the land; and we did not get in till the

26th, at nine in the morning, when I let go the anchor at a mile from the north coast in seven fathoms water, over a bottom of fine grey sand, abreast of the second bay. At the moment I was at the mouth of the channel, an English lieutenant and a midshipman were sent on board my ship by Captain Hunter, commander of the English frigate the *Sirius*. They offered me in his name all the services in his power, adding, however, that as he was on the point of getting under way in order to run to the northward, circumstances would not permit him to furnish us either with provision, ammunition, or sails; so that his services were confined to wishes for the farther success of our voyage. I sent an officer to return my thanks to Captain Hunter, who was already apeak, with his top-sails hoisted. I intimated to him that my wants did not extend beyond wood and water, of which we should find plenty in the bay; and that I was sensible that ships destined to establish a colony at so great a distance from Europe could afford no succour to navigators. We learned from the lieutenant that the English fleet was commanded by Commodore Phillips, who had gotten under way the evening before in the *Spy* sloop, accompanied by four transports, in order to seek farther to the northward for a more convenient place for his settlement. The English lieutenant appeared to make a great mystery of Commodore Phillips's plan, and we did not take the liberty of asking him any question on the subject; but we could have no doubt of the projected establishment being very near Botany Bay; for several boats and launches were under sail in their way thither; and the passage must needs have been short indeed to render it unnecessary to hoist them into the ships. Soon after the crew of the English boat, who were less cautious than their officers, told our sailors that they were only going to Port Jackson, sixteen miles to the north of Cape Banks, where Commodore Phillips had himself found out a very good harbour, running in ten miles to the south-west, and allowing vessels to anchor within pistol-shot of the land, in water as smooth as that of a basin. We had, in the sequel, but too many opportunities of hearing news of the English settlement from deserters, to whom we were indebted for a great deal of trouble and embarrassment.

XV. THE DISCOVERY OF BASS STRAIT

[CAPTAIN COOK'S map of New Holland represented that country and Van Diemen's Land as one. Cook had the idea that there was a strait dividing them, and intended to investigate the matter, but was misled by Captain Furneaux of the *Adventure*, the companion vessel to Cook's *Resolution* during his voyage of 1772–4. Furneaux had become separated from Cook during rough weather, and had actually sailed into the eastern entrance to the strait. He reported his conviction that he had merely been in a deep gulf, and Cook accepted his estimate, though with some doubt. It was left for the naval surgeon George Bass, in a whaleboat with a crew of six bluejackets, to discover the strait which now bears his name, in 1798. The narrative which follows, though not written in the first person, was Bass's story, written afresh by Flinders, in his *Voyage to Terra Australis*. Flinders undoubtedly had access to Bass's papers, which, unfortunately, have disappeared.]

In December 1797, Mr. George Bass obtained leave to make an expedition to the southward; and he was furnished with a fine whale-boat and six weeks' provisions by the governor, and a crew of six seamen from the ships. He sailed Dec. 3, in the evening; but foul and strong winds forced him into *Port Hacking* and *Watta-Mowlee*. On the 5th, in latitude 34° 38', he was obliged to stop in a small bight of the coast, a little south of *Alowrie*. The points of land there are basaltic; and on looking round amongst the burnt rocks scattered over a hollowed circular space behind the shore, Mr. Bass found a hole of twenty-five or thirty feet in diameter, into which the sea washed up by a subterraneous passage.

Dec. 6 he passed a long sloping projection which I have called *Point Bass*, lying about three leagues south of Alowrie. Beyond this point the coast forms a sandy bay of four or five leagues in length, containing two small inlets; and the southernmost being accessible to the boat, Mr. Bass went in and stopped three days. This little place was found to deserve no better name than *Shoals Haven*. The entrance is mostly choaked up by sand, and the

GEORGE BASS.
From Volume V of *The Historical Records of New South Wales*.

inner part with banks of sand and mud; there is, however, a small channel sufficiently deep for boats. The latitude was made to be 34° 52′ south; the sloping Point Bass, to the northward, bore N. 12° E., and a steep head at the southern extremity of the bay, S. 35° E. The tide was found to rise seven or eight feet, and the time of high water to be about eight hours and a half after the moon passed over the meridian.

The great chain of high land, called the Blue Mountains, by which the colony at Port Jackson is prevented from extending itself to the west, appeared to Mr. Bass to terminate here, near the sea-coast. The base of this southern extremity of the chain he judged to extend twenty-five or thirty miles in a south-western direction from Point Bass; after which it turns north-westward. In the direction of west from Shoals Haven, and in all the space to the south of that line, was an extensive, flat country, where a party desirous of penetrating into the interior might reasonably hope to avoid those impediments which, at the back of Port Jackson, have constantly proved insurmountable.

In an excursion from the boat towards the southern end of the mountains, Mr. Bass fell in with a considerable stream, which he traced down to the shore, about three miles north of Shoals Haven: this is the first inlet of the long bay, which had been observed from the sea, with a bar running across the entrance. The soil on the southern bank of this stream he compared, for richness, to the banks of the Hawkesbury; and attributes this unusual fertility to the same cause—repeated inundations. In fact the stream has since been found to descend from the mountains at twelve or fifteen miles from the coast, and to run along their southern extremity to the sea; so that it performs the same office here that the Hawkesbury does further north—that of being a channel for the waters which descend from the high back land; but as, in the heavy rains, it is also unequal to the task, the banks are overflowed, and the low country to the south and west is inundated and fertilised. There are, however, at the back of Shoals Haven, many thousand acres of open ground, whose soil is a rich vegetable mould, and now beyond the reach of the floods.

Dec. 10.—The boat left Shoals Haven and entered *Jervis Bay*, a large open place of very unpromising appearance. On the north side of the entrance, between Point Perpendicular and Long Nose, there is a small cove, where a ship's boat might lie at half tide; and with a hose fill water from the back of the beach, at two pits which appeared to be always full. The best anchorage for ships seemed to be on the east side of the bay, between Long

Nose and the northern beach, though they would not, even there, be entirely landlocked. *Bowen's Island* lies a quarter of a mile from the south side of the entrance, but the passage between does not admit anything larger than boats. There is a small beach at the back of the island, off which ships might anchor in 8 fathoms sandy bottom, and be sheltered as far round as south-east; but with the wind nearer to east they would be exposed.

The east shore of Jervis Bay runs, for twelve or fifteen miles, so near to north from the entrance that it is not, at the head, more than four hundred yards across to the shore of the long outer bay. The piece of land, which is thus made a narrow peninsula, is rather high, with a face of steep cliffs toward the sea. The rocks on the inner side bear strong marks of volcanic fire; and being disposed in parallel layers, their inclination to the west is very evident: quantities of pumice stone were scattered along the shores.

The country round the bay is mostly barren. On the eastern side it is rocky, with heath and brushwood; the west is low, swampy, and sandy, with some partial exceptions; but on the south side there are grassy spaces amongst the brush-wood which might afford pasturage for cattle.

Jervis Bay was quitted Dec. 13, and at noon the Pigeon House bore W. by N. In the evening Mr. Bass stopped in a cove which Point Upright shelters from northern winds; and he employed the next day in looking round the country. The vallies and slopes of the hills were found to be generally fertile; but there being nothing of particular interest in this place, it was quitted on the 15th. Some small islands lying close under the shore (in Bateman Bay) bore west at noon; and the night was passed at anchor under a point, in latitude 36° 00', where, the wind being foul on the 16th, Mr. Bass laid the boat on shore, and proceeded to examine the surrounding country.

At eight or nine miles from the coast is a ridge of hummocky hills, extending to the southward; but the space between these hills and the sea is low, and in great part occupied by salt swamps. The sea was found to have an entrance at the back of the point, and to form a considerable lagoon, which communicated with the swamps by means of several branching arms. The soil, as may be supposed, was generally bad, the sloping sides of some of the hills being alone capable of any utility. In a round of twelve or fourteen miles Mr. Bass could not find a drop of fresh water or see a native. There were, however, many huts, and he traced the paths from them down to holes dug in the lowest grounds; but these were then all dried up, and the country in general seemed to be suffering from drought.

Dec. 17.—The wind having veered to N.N.W., the boat was launched, and proceeded to the southward. Mount Dromedary was passed at eleven; and an island of about two miles in circuit was seen lying off it, a few miles to the eastward: the latitude at noon was 36° 23'. At four the fair breeze died away, and a strong wind, which burst forth from the south, obliged Mr. Bass to run for a gap in the land which had just before been noticed. Here, on a little beach at the mouth of an inlet, across which the sea was breaking, the boat was hauled up for the night. Next morning, the inlet being free of breakers, he entered the prettiest little model of a harbour he had ever seen. Unfortunately it is but a model; for although the shelter within be complete for small craft, yet the depth over the bar is too small even for boats, except at high water, when there is eight or nine feet. This little place was named *Barmouth Creek*, and lies, according to Mr. Bass's computation, in 36° 47' south. The country round, so far as was examined, is rocky and barren near the sea; and towards the head of the creek it is low and penetrated by the salt swamps.

Dec. 19.—At daylight Mr. Bass continued his course to the southward, with a fair breeze. At seven he discovered Two-fold Bay; but unwilling to lose a fair wind, reserved the examination of it for his return. At five in the evening the wind came at S.S.W.; and he anchored under the lee of a point, but could not land. A sea breeze from E.N.E. next day enabled him to continue onward; and at eleven he bore away west, round *Cape Howe*, whose latitude was observed to be 37° 30'. In the evening he landed at the entrance of a lagoon, one mile north of the Ram Head, in order to take in as much fresh water as possible; for it was to be feared that a want of this necessary article might oblige him to discontinue his pursuit at a time when, from the coast being unexplored, it would become more than ever interesting.

Dec. 21.—A gale set in at W.S.W., and continued for nine days without intermission. This time was employed in examining the country, which, though hilly in external appearance, was found to be mostly low, sandy, and wet. The hills have a slight covering of green upon them, but consist of little else than sand; and from what could be seen of the back country, the soil there is scarcely better. The vallies are overgrown with long grass, ferns, brushwood, and climbing plants, so as to be almost impenetrable; yet even there the soil is good for nothing.

At every land place, from Jervis Bay to Barmouth Creek, the fresh water had been observed to diminish both in quantity and quality; and upon this coast of sand the difficulty of procuring it was expected to be very great. It was, on the contrary, plentiful; there being many little runs which drained out from the sand-hills, and either trickled over the rocky spots at their feet or sank through the beaches into the sea.

The western gale being at length succeeded by a breeze at E.N.E., Mr. Bass left the Ram Head early on the 31st. His course was W. by S., close to a low, sandy coast; the beach being interrupted by small, rocky points not oftener than once in ten or fifteen miles. The back land consisted of short ridges of irregular hills, lying at no great distance from the sea. At noon the latitude was 37° 42′; and the distance run from the Ram Head, by computation, was thirty or thirty-five miles.

The furthest land seen by captain Cook is marked at fifteen leagues from the Ram Head, and called *Point Hicks;* but at dusk Mr. Bass had run much more than that distance close along the shore, and could perceive no point or projection which would be distinguishable from a ship; the coast continued to be straight, low, and sandy, similar to what had been passed in the morning. There arose many large smokes from behind the beach; probably from the sides of lagoons, with which there was reason to think the back country abounded.

The breeze continuing to be fresh and favourable, Mr. Bass ventured to steer onward in the night, and kept the shore close aboard. At two in the morning the increased hollowness of the waves made him suspect the water was becoming shallow; and he hauled off for an hour until there was sufficient daylight to distinguish the land. It was still low, level, and sandy, and trended S.W. by W., nearly as the boat was steering. At seven o'clock high land appeared at a considerable distance in the south-west; and the beach then trended in the same direction. It, however, changed soon afterward to run nearly west; and Mr. Bass quitted it to keep on his course for the high land. The latitude at noon was 38° 41′; and the difference made from the noon before, upon the average course of S.W. by W., makes the distance run 107 miles; which, added to the preceding thirty or thirty-five, gives the length of the beach from the Ram Head to be about 140 miles.

The high land extended from the bearing of S.W. by S. to W.N.W., and was distant in the latter direction two or three leagues. North of it there was a deep bight; and further eastward, two or three places in the Long Beach which had the appearance of inlets. To the south there were several rocky islets; and great numbers of petrels, and other sea-birds, were flying about the boat.

From the latitude of the high land, Mr. Bass considered it to be that seen by captain Furneaux (or supposed to have been seen) in 39°; and consequently that he had traced the unknown space between Point Hicks and *Furneaux's Land.* His course was now steered to pass round this land; but on coming abreast of the rocky islets, a hummock appeared above the horizon in the S.E. by S., and presently a larger one at S. ½ W.; and being unable to fetch the first, he steered for the latter, which proved to be an island; and at six in the evening he anchored under its lee. Vast numbers of gulls and other birds were roosting upon it, and on the rocks were many seals; but the surf would not admit of landing. This island was judged to be thirty miles, S. by W., from the situation at noon.

Jan. 2.—The wind was strong at E.N.E.; and Mr. Bass being apprehensive that the boat could not fetch the high main land determined to steer southward for the islands, in the hope of procuring some rice from the wreck of the ship Sydney Cove to eke out his provisions. The wind, however, became unfavourable to him, veering to E.S.E.; so that with the sea which drove the boat to leeward, the course to noon was scarcely so good as S.S.W. The latitude observed was then 39° 51′; and no land being in sight, the prospect of reaching Furneaux's Islands became very faint. At four o'clock an accident caused it to be totally given up: water was observed to rush in fast through the boat's side, and made it absolutely necessary to go upon the other tack. The latitude to which Mr. Bass supposed himself arrived was something to the south of 40°; and the weather was clear enough for land of moderate height to have been seen five leagues further had there been any within that distance.

The boat was then kept north-eastward, towards Furneaux's Land. At nine in the evening the wind blew hard at S.E. by E., accompanied by a hollow, irregular sea, which put our enterprising discoverer and his boat's crew into the greatest danger; but the good qualities of his little bark, with careful steerage, carried him through this perilous night. On the 3rd, at six o'clock, the land was seen; and in the afternoon, whilst standing in to look for a place of shelter, a smoke and several people were observed upon a small island not far from the main coast. On rowing up, they proved to be, not natives, to Mr. Bass's great surprise, but Europeans. They were convicts who, with others, had run away with a boat from Port Jackson, in the intention of plundering the wreck of the Sydney Cove; and not being able to find it, their companions, thinking their number too great, had treacherously left them upon this island whilst asleep. These people were seven in number; and during the five weeks they had been on this desert spot had subsisted on petrels, to which a seal was occasionally added. Mr. Bass promised to call at the island on his return; and in the meantime proceeded to the west side of the high main land, where he anchored, but could not get on shore.

Jan. 4.—The wind being at north-east, he continued his course onward, steering W.N.W. round an open bay; and afterwards N.W. by W., as the coast generally trended. The shore consisted of long, shallow bights in which the land was low and sandy; but the intermediate rocky points were generally steep, with a ridge of hills extending from them into the interior as far as could be distinguished. In the evening an inlet was discovered, with many shoals at the entrance; and the deep channel being not found till a strong tide made it unattainable, Mr. Bass waited for high water; he then entered a spacious harbour which, from its relative position to the hitherto known parts of the coast, was named Western Port. It lies, according to the boat's run, about sixty miles N.W. by W. ½ W. from Furneaux's Land; and its latitude is somewhere about 38° 25′ south. The time of high water is near half an hour after the moon's passage over the meridian, and the rise of tide from ten to fourteen feet.

The examination of this new and important discovery, the repairs of the boat, and the continuance of strong winds kept Mr. Bass thirteen days in Western Port. His sketch of it has since been superseded by the more regular examination of ensign Barralier, copied into the chart, where its form, situation, and extent will be best seen. The land upon its borders is, generally, low and level; but the hills rise as they recede into the country, and afford an agreeable prospect from the port. Wherever Mr. Bass landed he found the soil to be a light, brown mould, which becomes peaty in the lowest grounds. Grass and ferns grow luxuriantly, and yet the country is but thinly timbered. Patches of brush wood are frequent, particularly on the eastern shore, where they are some miles in extent; and there the soil is a rich, vegetable mould. The island (since called *Phillip Island*) which shelters the port is mostly barren, but is covered with shrubs and some diminutive trees.

Mr. Bass had great difficulty in procuring good water, arising, as he judged, from unusual dryness in the season; and the head of the winding creek on the east side of the port was the sole place where it had not a brackish taste. The mud banks at the entrance of the creek may be passed at half tide by the largest boats; and within it there is at all times a sufficient depth of water.

No more than four natives were seen, and their shyness prevented communication; the borders of the port, however, bore marks of having been much frequented, but the want of water seemed to have occasioned a migration to the higher lands. Kangaroos did not appear to be numerous; but black swans went by hundreds in a flight, and ducks, a small, but excellent kind, by thousands; and the usual wild-fowl were in abundance.

The seventh week of absence from Port Jackson had expired by the time Mr. Bass was ready to sail from Western Port; and the reduced state of his provisions forced him, very reluctantly, to turn the boat's head homeward.

Jan. 18.—At daylight he sailed with a fresh wind at west, which increased to a gale in the afternoon, with a heavy swell from the south-west; and he sought shelter behind a cape since named *Cape Liptrap*. Next morning he ran over to the islands on the west side of Furneaux's Land; but was obliged to return to his former place of shelter, where a succession of gales kept him until the 26th. A quantity of petrels had been taken on the islands, and this week of detention was mostly employed in salting them for the homeward bound voyage.

At length Mr. Bass was able to execute the project he had formed for the seven convicts. It was impossible to take them all into the boat; therefore to five, whom he set upon the main land, he gave a musket, half his ammunition, some hooks and lines, a light cooking kettle, and directions how to proceed in their course toward Port Jackson. The remaining two, one of whom was old and the other diseased, he took into the boat with the consent of the crew, who readily agreed to divide the daily bannock into nine with them. He then bore away, with a fresh wind at west, round Furneaux's Land.

From Jan. 26 to Feb. 1, Mr. Bass was detained by eastern gales from proceeding on his return. The boat lay in *Sealers Cove*, whilst he occupied the time in examining Wilson's Promontory. The height of this vast cape, though not such as would be considered extraordinary by seamen, is yet strikingly so from being contrasted with the low, sandy land behind it; and the firmness and durability of its structure make it worthy of being, what there was reason to believe it, the boundary point of a large strait, and a corner-stone to the new continent. It is a lofty mass of hard granite, of about twenty miles long, by from six to fourteen in breadth. The soil upon it is shallow and barren; though the brush wood, dwarf gum trees, and some smaller vegetation, which mostly cover the rocks, give it a deceitful appearance to the eye of a distant observer.

Looking from the top of the promontory to the northward, there is seen a single ridge of mountains, which comes down, out of the interior country, in a southern direction for the promontory; but sloping off gradually to a termination, it leaves a space of twelve or sixteen miles of low, sandy land between them. This low land is nearly intersected by a considerable lagoon on the west, and a large shoal bay, named *Corner Inlet*, on the east side; and it seemed probable that this insulated mass of granite has been entirely surrounded by the sea at no very distant period of time.

There were no inhabitants on Wilson's Promontory; but, upon the sandy neck, some were seen near the borders of the inlets. The few birds were thought to have a sweeter note than those of Port Jackson.

Four small, barren islands lie seven or eight miles to the north-east from Sealers Cove. The northernmost of them was visited, and found to be about one mile and a half in circuit, ascending gradually from the shore to a hill of moderate elevation in the centre. There was neither tree nor shrub upon it; but the surface was mostly covered with tufts of coarse grass, amongst which the seals had everywhere made paths and the petrels their burrows. Mr. Bass was of opinion that upon these islands, and those lying scattered round the promontory, which are all more or less frequented by seals, a commercial speculation on a small scale might be made with advantage. The place of shelter for the vessel would be Sealers Cove, on the main land; which, though small, and apparently exposed to east winds, would be found convenient and tolerably secure: fresh water is there abundant, and a sufficiency of wood at hand to boil down any quantity of blubber likely to be procured.

The observed latitude of the cove was 38° 50'; and the rise of tide found to be ten or eleven feet, ten hours and a quarter after the moon passed over the meridian. The flood, after sweeping south-westward along the great eastern beach, strikes off for the Seal Islands and the promontory, and then runs westward, past it, at the rate of two or three miles an hour: the ebb tide sets to the eastward. "Whenever it shall be decided," says Mr. Bass in his journal, "that the opening between this and Van Diemen's Land is a strait, this rapidity of tide, and the long south-west swell that seems to be continually rolling in upon the coast to the westward, will then be accounted for."

Feb. 2.—Mr. Bass sailed to Corner Inlet; and next day fell in with the five convicts, whom he put across to the long beach, but was himself unable to proceed until the 9th in consequence of foul winds. Corner Inlet is little else than a large flat, the greater part of it being dry at low water. There is a long shoal on the outside of the entrance, which is to be avoided by keeping close to the shore of the promontory; but when the tide is out the depth, except in holes, nowhere exceeds 2½ fathoms. A vessel drawing twelve or thirteen feet may lie safely under the high land from which there are some large runs of most excellent water. The tide rises a foot less here than in Sealers Cove, and flows a hour later; arising, probably, from the flood leaving it in an eddy, by setting past and not into the inlet.

Feb. 9.—Corner Inlet was quitted with a strong south-west wind, and Mr. Bass steered E. by N. along the shore. At the distance of five miles he passed the mouth of a shallow opening in the low sandy beach, from which a half-moon shoal stretches three miles to the south-eastward. Four or five miles further a lesser opening of the same kind was passed; and by noon, when the latitude was 38° 43′ (probably 38° 46′), he had arrived at the point of the long beach which, in going out, had been quitted to steer for the promontory. His general course from thence was N.E. by E. along the shore until nine o'clock, when, judging the coast must begin to trend more easterly, he again steered E. by N.; the wind blowing a fresh gale at W.S.W., with a following sea. At daylight, Feb. 10, the beach was distant two miles, and trending parallel to the boat's course.

The western gale died away in the morning, and was succeeded by one from the eastward. The boat was in no condition to struggle against a foul wind; and Mr. Bass, being unwilling to return to Corner Inlet, ventured through a heavy surf and took refuge upon the beach, having first observed the latitude to be 37° 47′ south.

The country at the back of the beach consisted of dried-up swamps and barren sand-hills. Some natives came down with very little hesitation, and conducted themselves amicably: they appeared never to have seen or heard of white people before.

Feb. 11.—The foul wind had ceased to blow, and the clouds threatened another gale from the south-west. So soon as there was sufficient daylight the boat was launched, and at four the same afternoon anchored under the Ram Head. Mr. Bass was kept there till the 14th in the evening, when a strong breeze sprung up suddenly at south-west, and he sailed immediately, passing Cape Howe at ten o'clock. By noon of the 15th he had reached Two-fold Bay, where the latitude was observed to be 36° 53' south; and having ascertained that *Snug Cove*, on its north-west side, afforded shelter for shipping, he steered north-ward, and passed Mount Dromedary soon after midnight. At noon, Feb. 16, Mr. Bass landed upon a small island lying under the shore to the south-east of the Pigeon House, to examine a pole which he had before observed, and supposed might have been set up as a signal by shipwrecked people; but it proved to be nothing more than the dead stump of a tree, much taller and more straight than the others. He sailed next morning; but the wind hung so much in the north and east quarters that he was forced successively into Jervis Bay, Shoals Haven, and Port Hacking; and it was not until the 24th at night that our adven-turous discoverer terminated his dangerous and fatiguing voyage by entering within the heads of Port Jackson.

It should be remembered that Mr. Bass sailed with only six weeks' provisions; but with the assistance of occasional supplies of petrels, fish, seal's flesh, and a few geese and black swans, and by abstinence, he had been enabled to prolong his voyage beyond eleven weeks. His ardour and perseverance were crowned, in despite of the foul winds which so much opposed him, with a degree of success not to have been anticipated from such feeble means. In three hundred miles of coast, from Port Jackson to the Ram Head, he added a number of particulars which had escaped captain Cook; and will always escape any navigator in a first discovery unless he have the time and means of joining a close examination by boats to what may be seen from the ship.

Our previous knowledge of the coast scarcely extended beyond the Ram Head; and there began the harvest in which Mr. Bass was ambitious to place the first reaping-hook. The new coast was traced three hundred miles; and instead of trending south-ward to join itself to Van Diemen's Land, as captain Furneaux had supposed, he found it, beyond a certain point, to take a direc-tion nearly opposite, and to assume the appearance of being exposed to the buffetings of an open sea. Mr. Bass, himself, entertained no doubt of the existence of a wide strait, separating

Van Diemen's Land from New South Wales; and he yielded with the greatest reluctance to the necessity of returning before it was so fully ascertained as to admit of no doubt in the minds of others. But he had the satisfaction of placing at the end of his new coast an extensive and useful harbour, surrounded with a country superior to any other known in the southern parts of New South Wales.

A voyage expressly undertaken for discovery in an open boat, and in which six hundred miles of coast, mostly in a boisterous climate, was explored, has not, perhaps, its equal in the annals of maritime history. The public will award to its high-spirited and able conductor, alas! now no more, an honourable place in the list of those whose ardour stands most conspicuous for the promotion of useful knowledge.

XVI. FLINDERS' DISCOVERY OF SOUTHERN AUSTRALIA

[FLINDERS' account of his discovery of southern Australia was contained in his book, *A Voyage to "Terra Australis,"* published in 1814. He had wished to adopt the name "Australia" for the island-continent for two good reasons. First, he pointed out that the Dutch, who had given the name New Holland to the western half, had known nothing of the eastern, whilst Cook's name for the eastern coast, New South Wales, was inappropriate for the whole country. Secondly, the name Australia would, he considered, be "more agreeable to the ear, and an assimilation to the names of the other great portions of the earth." But Sir Joseph Banks, whose influence counted for very much, was not favourable to the change, and Arrowsmith, the publisher of Admiralty charts, "did not like the change," because "New Holland" had always been the name used in charts. As Flinders' book was published at the instance of the Admiralty, he could not insist upon the name "Australia" being used in the teeth of official opposition, though he fought hard for it, and enlisted as much support as he could.—The voyage of the *Investigator*, in which the discovery of southern Australia was made, commenced in May 1801. Two years later Flinders circumnavigated Australia in the same ship, after which she was condemned as unseaworthy.]

On the 6th of December, 1801, our latitude was 35° 10', and longitude 114° 19'; which placed us about S.W. ½ S. twenty-two leagues from the westernmost isles lying off the south-west cape of New Holland, according to their position by the French rear-admiral D'Entrecasteaux; a traced copy of whose general chart of this coast had been furnished to me from the hydrographical office at the Admiralty. There were no names applied in this copy; but in the charts of the French voyage, lately published, these islets are called *Iles St. Alouarn.*

Notwithstanding the nearness of the land there were no signs of such proximity: no discolouring in the water, no sea weed, no new birds, and but few of the species before seen. The current had, indeed, somewhat changed; for while, during the three preceding days, it had set N. 12° W. twenty-seven miles per day, on an average, it was found this day to have run N. 47° E. twenty-two miles. This change, however, could scarcely be thought a sign of land, since equal or greater differences had occurred during the passage, and might arise, in part, from errors in the log.

At two in the afternoon, the wind being north-westward, we hauled up to make the south-western point of Leeuwin's Land, and bent the cables. At seven, land was seen right ahead, bearing N. 14° E., at the supposed distance of ten leagues; and on sounding there was 85 fathoms, coral sand. We stood for it until eleven at night, and then veered to the south-west, in 65 fathoms, same bottom.

The examination of Nuyts' and of Leeuwin's Lands was not prescribed in my instructions to be made at this time; but the difference of sailing along the coast at a distance, or in keeping near it and making a running survey, was likely to be so little that I judged it advisable to do all that circumstances would allow whilst the opportunity offered; and I had the pleasure to find this slight deviation approved at the Admiralty.

Monday, 7.—At two in the morning we had 80 fathoms, and veered towards the land. It was seen from the mast head at five; and the highest part, the same which had been set in the evening, bore N. 12° W. This is the largest of the before-mentioned Isles of St. Alouarn; but at half past seven we saw hills extending from behind, and, to all appearance, joining it to the main land. This supposed isle is, therefore, what I denominate Cape Leeuwin, as being the south-western and most projecting part of Leeuwin's Land. The highest hill lies nearly in latitude 34° 19′ south, and longitude 115° 6′ east; it is a sloping piece of land of about six hundred feet in elevation, and appeared to be rocky, with a slight covering of trees and shrubs. A piece of lower land was seen to the north-west, probably a continuation of the coast, and there are some rocky islets scattered on the south side of the cape. The largest of these islets, lying about four miles off, was passed before eight o'clock, at the distance of seven or eight miles, and seen to be surrounded with high and extensive breakers.

On the east side of Cape Leeuwin the land falls back north-eastward three or four leagues, and afterwards curves to the south-east, forming a large bight which appeared to be wholly exposed to the southern winds. The coast-line round the upper part of this bight was not distinguishable; but the hills at the

back showed more of bare sand than of vegetable covering. At
ten o'clock a low, black projection, forming the eastern point of
the bight, bore east three miles; and the depth was 15 fathoms
upon a coarse sandy bottom. We then veered round to the south-
eastward, following the direction of the coast, with the wind at
west-south-west and weather somewhat squally.

The shore abreast was seven or eight miles distant; and behind
it ran a continuation of the same ridge of sandy hillocks which
surrounds the bight, and it extended to the southern extreme.
Over this ridge were perceived, here and there, the tops of some
higher and less sandy hills, standing a few miles inland; but the
general aspect of the country was that of great sterility; nor was
there, as yet, any appearance of its being inhabited.

Tuesday, 8.—The wind was at south-west, and we stretched
onward until one in the morning, before tacking to the north-
west for the land. At daylight the ship was found to have been
carried to the eastward, and neither Point D'Entrecasteaux nor
the two white rocks were in sight; but in the N. 19° E., about
eight miles, was a head not far from the extreme set in the evening. It afterwards proved to be a smooth, steep rock, lying one
mile from the main, and is the land first made upon this coast by
captain Vancouver, who called it Cape Chatham.

At seven o'clock we got sight of the two white rocks, which
enabled me to take up the survey of the preceding evening; and
we then bore away along the coast at the distance of four or five
miles, with a pleasant breeze and fine weather.

Some parts of the shore between Point D'Entrecasteaux and
Cape Chatham were not distinctly seen. That which is nearest to
the cape lies in the line of N. 38° W. from its outer part, and
presents an intermixture of steep cliffs and small sandy beaches,
with a back land moderately high, and better covered with
wood than that before described. On the east side of Cape
Chatham the shore falls back to the northward, and makes a
bight in which is a small reef of rocks. It then projects in a cliffy
head, which lies S. 75° E. seven miles from the cape, and is
called Point Nuyts in the French chart; upon the supposition,
probably, that this was the first land seen by Nuyts in 1627.
Beyond this point the coast trends very nearly east; but forms
several projections, some of which are steep and others low; and
between them are sandy bights where small vessels might obtain
shelter from all northern winds. The hills lying at the back of
the shore seemed to be barren, though trees grew thickly on their
eastern sides; they are not high, but it was rare to perceive any
thing of the interior country above them.

At noon the nearest parts of the coast were a steep and a more eastern low point, both distant about four miles; and from the bight between them was rising the first smoke seen upon this coast.

Soon after two o'clock we passed at the distance of five miles from a steep point which has a broad rock lying near it. This point, being unnamed and somewhat remarkable, I call *Point Hillier;* it lies in 35° 4' south and 117° 9' east. The coast extends from thence nearly east-by-south, without any considerable projection except at the furthest extreme then visible; and on coming up with it, at half-past five, it proved to be the Cape Howe of Vancouver. There is another Cape Howe upon this same coast, named by Captain Cook, which makes it necessary to distinguish this by a descriptive adjunct, and I shall therefore call it *West* Cape Howe. The situation of this projecting cliffy cape is in 35° 8½' south and 117° 40' east. Beyond it the land trends north-by-east, four miles, into a sandy bight, in which there is a small islet; and further along the shore, which then stretches eastward and again becomes cliffy, there are two others. When the cape bore N. 10° W. four miles, the highest of the Eclipse Isles was in sight, bearing E. 4° N.; but "the small detached islet," which Captain Vancouver says "lies from Cape Howe S. 68° E., three leagues," could not be seen; though it should have lain nearly in our track.

The wind blew fresh at this time, and a current of more than one mile an hour ran with us, so that, by carrying all sail, I hoped to get sight of King George's Sound before dark. At seven we passed close on the south side of the Eclipse Isles; but Bald Head at the entrance of the sound had so different an appearance from what I had been led to expect, being a slope in this point of view, that the steep east end of Break-sea Island was at first taken for it. The error was fortunately perceived in time; and at eight o'clock we hauled up round the head, with the wind at west, and made a stretch into the sound. It was then dark; but the night being fine, I did not hesitate to work up by the guidance of captain Vancouver's chart; and having reached nearly into a line between Seal Island and the first beach round Bald Head, we anchored at eleven o'clock in 8 fathoms, sandy bottom.

Wednesday, 9.—King George's Sound had been chosen as the proper place in which to prepare ourselves for the examination of the south coast of Terra Australis, and I sought to make the best use of the advantages it might furnish. The first essential requisite was a place of secure shelter, where the masts could be stripped, the rigging and sails put into order, and communication had with the shore without interruption from the elements; but this, from captain Vancouver's chart and description, I did not expect the outer sound to afford. The facility of quitting Princess-Royal Harbour, with such a wind as would be favourable for prosecuting the investigation of the coast, induced me so far to prefer it to Oyster Harbour as to make it the first object of examination; and in the morning, after we had sounded round the ship and found her so placed as to require no immediate movement, I went in a boat for the purpose, accompanied by the master and landscape painter; the naturalist and some other gentlemen landing at the same time, to botanise in the vicinity of Bald Head.

Seal Island, where we stopped in passing, is a mass of granite, which is accessible only at its western end, as represented in Mr. Westall's sketch. After killing a few seals upon the shore, we ascended the hill to search for the bottle and parchment left by captain Vancouver in 1791; but could find no vestiges either of it or of the staff or pile of stones; and since there was no appearance of the natives having crossed over from the main, I was led to suspect that a second ship had been here before us.

At Point Possession, on the south side of the entrance to Princess-Royal Harbour, we had a good view of that extensive piece of water. Wood seemed not to be abundant near the shores; and therefore a projection two or three miles to the south-west, which was covered with trees, first attracted my notice. The depth of water in going to it was, however, too little for the ship; nor was there any fresh stream in the neighbourhood. Some person, but not captain Vancouver, had nevertheless been cutting wood there; for several trees had been felled with axe and saw. Not far from thence stood a number of bark sheds, like the huts of the natives who live in the forests behind Port Jackson, and forming what might be called a small village; but it had been long deserted. Going across from the woody point to the north side of the harbour, we there found 3 fathoms within less than half a mile of the shore; and an increasing depth from thence out to the entrance. The soundings in the entrance were from 5 to 7 fathoms; but the channel was too narrow to admit of getting in without a leading wind and much caution.

Thursday, 10.—On Thursday morning the master was sent to examine the north side of the harbour for water and wood; and we got the ship under way to beat up to the entrance, the wind blowing still from the westward. At eleven o'clock the anchor was dropped in 6 fathoms, half a mile from Point Possession; and as I was doubtful of the master's success, I went in a boat, accompanied by lieutenant Flinders, to examine Oyster Harbour. We carried 7 and 6 fathoms from the ship towards the entrance until Michaelmas and Break-sea Islands were closing on with each other; after which the depth diminished to 5, 4, 3, and 2¾ fathoms. On hauling westward we got into six feet; but steering the other way, it deepened to seventeen, the east side of the opening behind then in a line with the middle of some high, flat-topped land, at the back of the harbour. Keeping in that direction, we carried 3, 4, and 5 fathoms; and had 6 in the narrowest part of the entrance. Within side the deep water turned on the starboard hand, but in many parts there was not more than 3 fathoms.

As I proposed to make a new survey of King George's Sound, we landed to take a set of angles upon the small central island; the same which captain Vancouver describes as covered with luxuriant grass and other vegetables, and where he planted vine cuttings, water-cresses, and the seeds of various fruits. There were no remains of these valuable gifts, although nothing indicated the island to have been visited since his time; and, to our disappointment, the vegetation upon it now consisted of tufts of wiry grass and a few stunted shrubs, supported by a thin layer of sandy soil, which was every where perforated with rat-holes.

From the island we rowed in various directions, sounding the harbour; but the boat could seldom approach the shore within a cable's length, or the eighth part of a mile. On the south-west side there were two small streams, in one of which the water was fresh, though high-coloured. Returning to the entrance, we landed on the east side, and found a spot of ground six or eight feet square, dug up and trimmed like a garden; and upon it was lying a piece of sheet copper, bearing this inscription: "August 27, 1800. Chr. Dixson—ship Elligood"; which solved the difficulty of the felled trees and the disappearance of captain Vancouver's bottle. On digging in this place I found that fresh water of a high colour, but well tasted, might be obtained; wood was abundant, and the depth of the entrance admitted of the ship being made fast to the shore; so that this was a situation adapted to our purpose of refitment, provided the ship could be got over the bar. This point I was desirous to ascertain in my way on board, but the strength of the wind prevented it.

The report of the master from Princess-Royal Harbour was, that water could be obtained at the north side by digging near the shore, at the foot of the highest hill; but that there was no wood at a convenient distance. I therefore sent him, next morning, to land the naturalists at the entrance of Oyster Harbour, and then to sound the bar; and not being satisfied with his report, that there was not so much as fourteen feet, which the ship drew when captain Vancouver had marked seventeen, I went to the nearest head, with a theodolite and signal flags, to direct his movements. No more, however, than thirteen feet could now be found upon the shallowest part of the bar; and, consequently, the idea of refitting in Oyster Harbour was abandoned. The boat which brought off Mr. Brown and his party in the evening collected a good quantity of oysters, and of the large fan muscles, from the shoals.

Saturday, 12.—The wind continuing foul for going into Princess-Royal Harbour, a wooding party was sent next morning to a bight round the north side of the entrance, where the wood was found to split better than at some other places. Another party went to the same place with the launch, to haul the seine; but the wind coming round to the eastward, the boat was recalled and a kedge anchor and hawser put into it. We then weighed and ran into the harbour under the top-sails; and at eleven anchored in seventeen feet upon muddy ground, at one-third of a mile from the shore under the highest hill. When the ship was moored Michaelmas Island was on with the north, and Break-sea Island with the south point of the entrance, and the highest hill bore N.E. by N. by compass. The least depth of water we had in passing the entrance was 4 fathoms; but to those who may wish to go in, the plan in Plate II of the Atlas, and a good look-out from the masthead, will be of more service than any written directions.

So soon as the ship was secured, I landed with the naturalists; and after fixing upon a place for our tents, ascended the highest hill to take angles. Amongst other objects I perceived in the bearing of N. 87° 20' W. two distant pieces of water, at the back of the bight near West Cape Howe; but whether they were lakes or an inlet of the sea could not be distinguished. Our tents, under the guard of a party of marines, were set up this evening; and in the morning the observatory and instruments were sent on shore, under the care of lieutenant Flinders, who had undertaken to assist me in performing the office of astronomer.

Marks of the country being inhabited were found every where, but as yet there was nothing to indicate the presence of the natives in our neighbourhood; I therefore allowed a part of the ship's company to divert themselves on shore this afternoon; and the same was done every Sunday during our stay in this harbour. On Monday the topmasts were struck, and our various duties commenced; the naturalists ranged the country in all directions, being landed at such places as they desired; whilst my own time was divided betwixt the observatory and the survey of the Sound.

Some smokes being perceived at the head of the harbour, Mr. Brown and other gentlemen directed their excursion that way and met with several of the natives, who were shy but not afraid. One man with whom they had communication was admired for his manly behaviour, and they gave him a bird which had been shot, and a pocket-handkerchief; but, like the generality of people hitherto seen in this country, these men did not seem to be desirous of communication with strangers; and they very early made signs to our gentlemen to return from whence they came. Next morning, however, we were agreeably surprised by the appearance of two Indians, and afterwards of others, upon the side of the hill behind our tents. They approached with much caution, one coming first with poised spear, and making many gestures, accompanied with much vociferous parleying, in which he sometimes seemed to threaten us if we did not be gone, and at others to admit of our stay. On Mr. Purdie, the assistant-surgeon, going up to him unarmed, a communication was brought about, and they received some articles of iron and toys, giving in exchange some of their implements; and after a short stay, left us, apparently on very good terms.

Thursday, 17.—On the 17th one of our former visitors brought two strangers with him; and after this time, they and others came almost every day, and frequently stopped a whole morning at the tents. We always made them presents of such things as seemed to be most agreeable, but they very rarely brought us anything in return; nor was it uncommon to find small mirrors and other things left about the shore, so that at length our presents were discontinued.

Wednesday, 23.—I formed a party on the 23rd, consisting of the officers of the ship, the scientific gentlemen, and others, amounting to thirteen, well armed and provided for two days, in order to visit the lakes behind West Cape Howe. We walked along the shore to the north-western extremity of Princess-Royal Harbour, where several small runs of fresh water were found to drain in from peaty swamps. Striking from thence into the country in a western direction, we had not advanced far when a native was seen running before us; and soon afterward an old man, who had been several times at the tents, came up, unarmed as usual. He was very anxious that we should not go further; and acted with a good deal of resolution in first stopping one and then another of those who were foremost. He was not able to prevail; but we accommodated him so far as to make a circuit round the wood, where it seemed probable his family and female friends were placed. The old man followed us, hallooing frequently to give information of our movements; and when a paroquet was shot, he expressed neither fear nor surprise, but received the bird with gladness and attended with some curiosity to the reloading of the gun.

Our course for the lakes led us through swamps and thick brushwoods, in which our new acquaintance followed for some time; but at length, growing tired of people who persevered in keeping a bad road in opposition to his recommendation of a better, which, indeed, had nothing objectionable in it but that it led directly contrary to where our object lay, he fell behind and left us. We afterwards took to the skirts of the sea-coast hills and made better progress; but were obliged to recross the swamps and force our way through a thick brush before reaching the eastern lake.

This piece of water was found to be one mile and a half east and west, and one mile in breadth, and appeared to receive the drainings from the numerous swamps round about. In coasting round the north side, to reach the south-western lake, we were stopped by a serpentine stream, upon which were two black swans; but they took to flight before we could get near to shoot them. After following the windings of this riverlet some distance to the north-west, without being able to pass over, we struck inland towards the skirt of some rising hills, and crossed the stream early enough to walk a mile to the south-west before sunset, when the convenience of dry ground, with wood and water at hand, induced us to halt for the night.

Thursday, 24.—On Thursday morning we reached the south-western lake, and found it to be larger than the first. Its water was brackish, which bespoke a communication with the sea; and as there was no certainty that this communication might not be too deep to be passed, it was thought prudent to give up the intention of proceeding to the sea side, and our steps were retraced across the riverlet and round the northern lake. We then struck southward and ascended the hills to the top of the cliffs facing the sea; from whence I had an opportunity of seeing the bight near Cape Howe, and the form of the lakes; but no water communication was visible between them.

Our course homeward was pursued along the sandy ridge at the back of the cliffs, where the want of water was as great as the superabundance had been in the low land going out. Towards sunset, when Princess-Royal Harbour was still some miles distant, the natural-history painter became unable to proceed further, being overcome with the labour of the walk, with the excessive heat, and with thirst. To have detained the whole party in a state of sufferance would have been imprudent; and Mr. Brown and two others having volunteered to stay, we left them the scanty remains of our provision, and pushed forward to the tents, which we reached at eight o'clock. At midnight we had the pleasure to see our friends arrive, and the preparation made for sending to their assistance, at daybreak, became unnecessary.

The country through which we passed in this excursion has but little to recommend it. The stony hills of the sea coast were, indeed, generally covered with shrubs; but there was rarely any depth of vegetable soil, and no wood. The land slopes down gradually behind these hills; and at the bottom water drains out and forms a chain of swamps extending from Princess-Royal Harbour to the lakes. Here the country is covered with grass and brushwood, and in the parts a little elevated there are forest trees; nevertheless the soil is shallow and unfit for cultivation.

Wednesday, 30.—On the 30th, our wooding and the watering of the ship were completed, the rigging was refitted, the sails repaired and bent, and the ship unmoored. Our friends the natives continued to visit us; and the old man with several others being at the tents this morning, I ordered the party of marines on shore to be exercised in their presence. The red coats and white crossed belts were greatly admired, having some resemblance to their own manner of ornamenting themselves; and the drum, but particularly the fife, excited their astonishment; but when they saw these beautiful red-and-white men, with their bright muskets, drawn up in a line, they absolutely screamed with delight; nor were their wild gestures and vociferation to be silenced but by commencing the exercise, to which they paid the most earnest and silent attention. Several of them moved their hands involuntarily, according to the motions; and the old man placed himself at the end of the rank, with a short staff in his hand, which he shouldered, presented, grounded as did the marines their muskets, without, I believe, knowing what he did. Before firing, the Indians were made acquainted with what was going to take place; so that the vollies did not excite much terror.

The tents and observatory were already struck; and everything being sent on board, we took leave of the natives, and embarked with the intention of running into the Sound this evening; but a change in the wind, to south-by-east, prevented it. This wind veered to east and north-east, and for a short time blew strong;

so that it was the 3rd of January in the afternoon before we steered out of Princess-Royal Harbour. It was not my intention to proceed immediately to sea; and I therefore took the opportunity of standing backward and forward in the Sound, with the dredge and trawl overboard; and a variety of small fish were brought up. These were of little use as food; but with the shells, sea weeds, and corals they furnished amusement and occupation to the naturalist and draughtsman, and a pretty kind of hippocampus, which was not scarce, was generally admired.

In the evening the anchor was dropped in 7 fathoms, abreast of the second sandy beach near a flat rock on the south side of the Sound, almost in the same spot where captain Vancouver had anchored in 1791. I think the Sound does not afford a more secure place, the sole points of exposition being between Bald Head and Break-sea Island, making an angle of no more than 10°; and as both wood and water are procurable here, though neither very good, a ship proposing to stay only a few days is under no necessity of having recourse to the harbours.

Monday, 4.—On the 4th a fresh gale blew from the westward and prevented me from moving the ship. A bottle, containing a parchment to inform future visitors of our arrival and intention to sail on the morrow, was left upon the top of Seal Island; and the wind having moderated next day, and the weather become finer, though still squally, we then made sail out of King George's Sound to prosecute the further examination of the coast.

The refreshments we had procured were fish and oysters. The seine was frequently hauled upon the different beaches; but although it was done in the evening, round fires which had been previously kindled, little success was obtained in this way. With hook and line we were more fortunate, both alongside and from boats stationed off the rocky points; and the whole ship's company had generally a fresh meal once in three or four days. Of oysters, as many were taken from the shoals in both harbours as we chose to spare time for gathering. Our fire wood was procured from the north point of entrance to Princess-Royal Harbour, at the inner end of the long middle beach; but the trees best calculated for sawing into planks were obtained at the easternmost of the two woody projections on the south side of the harbour. A good number of planks and logs were taken on board for making garden boxes to contain the most curious plants collected by the naturalist, and for a variety of other purposes. The fresh water, procured by digging near the tents, was a little discoloured, but good; and it was sufficiently abundant for every purpose: its specific gravity was 1·003 at the temperature of 69°.

Captain Vancouver has described the country in the neighbourhood of King George's Sound, and therefore a few observations upon it will suffice. The basis stone is granite, which frequently shows itself at the surface in the form of smooth, bare rock; but upon the seacoast hills, and the shores on the south sides of the Sound and Princess-Royal Harbour, the granite is generally covered with a crust of calcareous stone; as it is, also, upon Michaelmas Island. Captain Vancouver mentions having found upon the top of Bald Head, branches of coral protruding through the sand, exactly like those seen in the coral beds beneath the surface of the sea; a circumstance which should seem to bespeak this country to have emerged from the ocean at no very distant period of time. This curious fact I was desirous to verify; and his description was proved to be correct. I found, also, two broken columns of stone three or four feet high, formed like stumps of trees and of a thickness superior to the body of a man; but whether they were of coral or of wood now petrified, or whether they might not have been calcareous rocks worn into that particular form by the weather, I cannot determine. Their elevation above the present level of the sea could not have been less than four hundred feet.

But little calcareous matter was found elsewhere than on the southern shores. In Oyster Harbour a rather strongly impregnated ironstone prevails, but mixed with quartz and granite; and in some parts of both harbours a brown argillaceous earth was not uncommon.

The soil of the hills is very barren, though, except near the seacoast, generally covered with wood; and that of the plains at the head of Princess-Royal Harbour has been described as shallow, and incapable of cultivation. In the neighbourhood of Oyster Harbour the land was said to be better, especially near the rivulet which falls into the northern corner; and on the borders of a small lake, at the back of the long beach between the two harbours, the country was represented to be pleasing to the eye and tolerably fertile.

The timber trees of the woods consist principally of different species of that extensive class called *gum tree* by the colonists at Port Jackson, by botanists *eucalyptus*. They do not grow very large here, and the wood is heavy and seldom fit for other than common purposes. Amongst the plants collected by Mr. Brown and his associates was a small one of a novel kind which we commonly called the pitcher plant. Around the root leaves are several little vases lined with spiny hairs, and there were generally found to contain a sweetish water, and also a number of dead ants. It cannot be asserted that the ants were attracted by the water, and prevented by the spiny hairs from making their escape; but it seemed not improbable that this was a contrivance of nature to obtain the means necessary either to the nourishment or preservation of the plant.

Amongst the animal productions the kanguroo and cassowary hold the first ranks. The kanguroo appeared to be numerous, and of more than one species; but none were caught. Three of them seen by me bore a resemblance to the large kind which inhabits the forests of Port Jackson; and the cassowary showed nothing distinguishable at a distance from the same animal at that place: both were shy; as were the ducks, swans, and all the birds.

Near Point Possession were found two nests of extraordinary magnitude. They were built upon the ground, from which they rose about two feet; and were of vast circumference and great interior capacity, the branches of trees and other matter, of which each nest was composed, being enough to fill a small cart. Captain Cook found one of these enormous nests upon Eagle Island, on the East Coast; and if the magnitude of the constructor be proportionate to the size of the nest, Terra Australis must be inhabited by a species of bird little inferior to the condor of the Andes.

Amongst the reptiles was a variety of lizards; one of which, of the larger size, was met with by Dampier on the West Coast, and is described by him "as a sort of guano, but differing from others in three remarkable particulars: for these had a larger and uglier head, and had no tail: and at the rump, instead of the tail there, they had a stump of a tail, which appeared like another head; but not really such, being without mouth or eyes. Yet this creature seemed, by this means, to have a head at each end; and, which may be reckoned a fourth difference, the legs, also, seemed all four of them to be fore legs, being all alike in shape and length, and seeming by the joints and bendings to be made as if they were to go indifferently either head or tail foremost. They were speckled black and yellow like toads, and had scales or knobs on their backs like those of crocodiles. They are very slow in motion and when a man comes nigh them they will stand and hiss, not endeavouring to get away. Their livers are also spotted black and yellow; and the body when opened hath a very unsavoury smell. The guano's I have observed to be very good meat, and I have often eaten of them with pleasure; but though I have eaten of snakes, crocodiles, and alligators, and many creatures that look frightfully enough, and there are but few I should have been afraid to eat of, if pressed by hunger, yet I think my stomach would scarce have served to venture upon these New Holland guano's, both the looks and the smell of them being so offensive." The animal is certainly of a singular form; but it is scarcely necessary to say that the merit of Dampier's description does not consist in being strictly accurate.

The fish caught with hook and line were principally small mullet, and an excellent kind of snapper, nearly the same as that called *wollamai* by the natives of Port Jackson; but these were larger, weighing sometimes as much as twenty pounds.

Our frequent and amicable communication with the natives of this country has been mentioned. The women were, however, kept out of sight with seeming jealousy; and the men appeared to suspect the same conduct in us, after they had satisfied themselves that the most beardless of those they saw at the tents were of the same sex with the rest. The belief that there must be women in the ship induced two of them to comply with our persuasion of getting into the boat, one morning, to go on board; but their courage failing, they desired to be relanded, and made signs that the ship must go on shore to them.

It was with some surprise that I saw the natives of the east coast of New South Wales so nearly pourtrayed in those of the south-western extremity of New Holland. These do not, indeed, extract one of the upper front teeth at the age of puberty, as is generally practised at Port Jackson, nor do they make use of the *womerah*, or throwing stick; but their colour, the texture of the hair, and personal appearance are the same; their songs run in the same cadence; the manner of painting themselves is similar; their belts and fillets of hair are made in the same way, and worn in the same manner. The short, skin cloak, which is of kanguroo, and worn over the shoulders, leaving the rest of the body naked, is more in the manner of the wood natives living at the back of Port Jackson than of those who inhabit the sea coast; and everything we saw confirmed the supposition of captain Vancouver, that they live more by hunting than fishing. None of the small islands had been visited, no canoes were seen, nor was any tree found in the woods from which the bark had been taken for making one. They were fearful of trusting themselves upon the water; and we could never succeed in making them understand the use of the fish hook, although they were intelligent in comprehending our signs upon other subjects.

The manners of these people are quick and vehement, and their conversation vociferous, like that of most uncivilised people. They seemed to have no idea of any superiority we possessed over them; on the contrary, they left us, after the first interview, with some appearance of contempt for our pusillanimity; which was probably inferred from the desire we showed to be friendly with them. This opinion, however, seemed to be corrected in their future visits.

Notwithstanding the similarity of person and manner to the inhabitants of Port Jackson, the language of these people is very different. We found their pronunciation difficult to be imitated; more so, indeed, than our language was to them. Several English words they pronounced perfectly; whilst of such where an *f* or an *s* entered they could make but little: Finger, was pronounced *bing-gah*, ship, *yip;* and of King George they make *Ken Jag-ger.* In the difficulty of pronouncing the *f* and *s* they resemble the Port Jackson natives; and the word used by them in calling to a distance, *cau-wah!* (come here) is nearly similar to *cow-ee!* The word also to express *eye* is nearly the same. But in the following table, which contains all the words that, with any certainty, I was able to collect, the most essential differences will be found both from the Port Jackson language and from that of the south end of Van Diemen's Land; and the words collected by Captain Cook at Endeavour River bear no resemblance to any of them.

English.	K. George's Sound.	Port Jackson.	Van Diemen's Land.
Head	Kaāt	Ca-ber-ra	
Hair	Kaat-joū	De-war-ra	Pélilogueni
Nose	Mo-il	No-gro	Mugui (Muidge, Cook)
Cheek, or beard	Ny-a-nūk	Yar-rin	Canguiné
Teeth	Yea-al	Da-ra	Pégui or Canan (Kamy, C.)
Ear	Du-ong	Go-ray	Vaigui (Koygee, Cook)
Lips	Ur-luk	Wil-ling	Mogudé lia
Throat	Wurt	Cad-le-an	
Nipple	Bpep	Na-bung	
Belly	Ko-būl	Bar-rong	Lomangui
Posteriors	Wa-la-kah	Boong	Nuné
Thigh	Dtou-al		
Knee	Wo-nat	Go-rook	Ronga
Leg	Maāt	Dar-ra	Lerai
Foot	Jaān	Ma-no-e	Peré
The sun	Djaāt	Co-ing	Panuberé

The following anatomical admeasurement of one of the best proportioned of our visitors was furnished by the surgeon, Mr. Hugh Bell:

	Ft.	in.	l.
Full height	5	7	6
Circumference of the head	1	11	0
From the transverse nasal suture to the posterior ridge of the occiput	1	3	0
From the small rim of each ear across the forehead .	1	0	0
From the nasal suture, over the nose, to the tip of the chin	0	5	2
From ditto to the tip of the nose	0	1	0
From the tip of the nose to the edge of the upper lip .	0	1	0
From the edge of the under lip to the tip of the chin .	0	1	5
Extent of the mouth	0	2	1
————————nostrils	0	1	6
———————— lower jaw from each angle . .	0	8	6
Length of the arm	1	1	6
——————— fore arm	1	0	0
——————— middle metacarpal bone . .	0	4	0
——————— middle finger . . .	0	4	3
——————— femur, from the great trochanter to its lower end	1	5	6
——————— tibia	1	4	6
——————— foot	0	10	0
Length from the protuberance of the inner ancle to the tip of the heel	0	3	9
Ditto to the end of the great toe . . .	0	8	6
Circumference of the neck	1	0	6
————————— chest	2	8	9
————————— pelvis	2	4	9
————————— arm	0	10	6
————————— elbow joint . . .	0	9	6
————————— fore arm	0	9	9
————————— wrist	0	6	0
————————— thigh	1	7	6
Circumference just above the knee joint . . .	1	1	0
————————— of the knee joint . . .	1	1	0
————————— leg, immediately below the knee joint	0	11	0
————————— leg	1	0	0
————————— small	0	7	6
————————— foot	0	10	6

No set of *tide* was perceived on board, either whilst the ship was in the Sound or in Princess-Royal Harbour; nevertheless it was sometimes found to run with considerable strength in the narrow entrances of both harbours. According to lieutenant Flinders' observations on shore during sixteen days there was only one high water in twenty-four hours, which always took place between six and twelve at night; for after, by gradually becoming later, it had been high water at twelve, the next night it took place soon after six o'clock; and then happened later by three-quarters of an hour each night as before. The greatest rise observed was three feet two inches, and the least two feet eight inches. The accumulation was made in this manner: After low water it rose for several hours; then ceased, and became stationary, or perhaps fell back a little. In a few hours it began to rise again; and in about twelve hours from the first commencement was high water. It was observed by Captain Cook upon the east coast of this country, and since by many others, including myself, that the night tide rose considerably higher than that of the day; which is conformable to our observations in King George's Sound; but with this difference, that in the day we had scarcely any tide at all.

The base line for my survey of the Sound was of 2·46 geographic miles, measured round the curve of the long beach between the two harbours. The other stations whence bearings were taken with the theodolite were—in the Sound, four; at the entrance of and within Princess-Royal Harbour, three; and in Oyster Harbour, four; at each of which a point with a circle is marked in the plan. The soundings were either taken in the ship, with simultaneous cross bearings, or in boats, generally accompanied with notices of known objects in a line, or the angles between them taken with a sextant.

There are many small but no very essential differences between my plan and that of captain Vancouver. The most important to navigation is that in the soundings going into Oyster Harbour; I could find only thirteen feet over the bar, whereas he marked seventeen; a difference, however, which may not improbably have taken place between 1791 and 1801.

In running along that part of the South Coast which lies to the west of King George's Sound, I had endeavoured to keep so close in with the land that the breaking water on the shore should be visible from the ship's deck; by which means our supposed distance would be little subject to error, and no river or opening could escape being seen. This close proximity could not, however, be obtained in every part, especially where the coast retreated far back; but it was always attempted where practicable and unattended with much danger or loss of time; and when it could not be done, I was commonly at the mast head with a glass. All the bearings were laid down so soon as taken whilst the land was in sight, and before retiring to rest I made it a practice to finish up the rough chart for the day, as also my journals of astronomical observations, of bearings, and of remarks. When we hauled off from the coast at night, every precaution was taken to come in with the same point in the morning, as soon after daylight as practicable; and when the situation of the ship relatively to the land of the preceding evening was ascertained, our route along the coast was resumed. This plan, to see and lay down everything myself, required constant attention and much labour, but was absolutely necessary to obtaining that accuracy of which I was desirous; and now, on recommencing the survey from King George's Sound to the eastward, I persevered in the same system; and it was adhered to, although not particularly mentioned, in all the succeeding part of the voyage.

On the 5th of January, in the morning, we got under way from the Sound, having a fresh wind from the westward and squally weather. I steered between Michaelmas Island and the main, in order to explore better that part of the Sound, and ascertain the extent of a shoal running off from the north-west end of the island. It was found to run out not further than half a mile, at which distance we passed in 5 fathoms water; and at noon, when the east end of Break-sea Island bore S. 30° W., we had 33 fathoms.

Mount Gardner is a high, conic-shaped hill, apparently of granite, very well delineated in captain Vancouver's atlas. It stands upon a projecting cape, round which the shore falls back to the northward, forming a sandy bight where there appeared to be shelter from western winds; indeed, as the coast-line was not distinctly seen round the south-west corner of the bight, it is possible there may be some small inlet in that part.

The south end of an island, called Ile Pelée (Bald Island) by D'Entrecasteaux, opened round the cape of Mount Gardner at N. 69° E. The French navigator having passed without side of this island, I steered within, through a passage of a short mile wide; and had 17 fathoms for the shoalest water, on a sandy bottom. Bald Island is of moderate elevation, and barren, as its name implies; it is about two-and-half miles in length, and the south end lies in 34° 55′ south and 118° 29′ east. It lies off a rocky projection of the mainland, at which terminates a ridge of mountain extending three leagues along the shore from the bight behind Mount Gardner. There are a number of small peaks upon the top of this ridge which induced me to give it the name *Mount Manypeak*.

After clearing the passage of Bald Island I found the shore to trend north-eastward, and to be low and sandy; but at the distance of eight leagues inland there was a chain of rugged mountains, of which the eastern and highest peak, called *Mount Rugged*, lies N. 11½° W. from the passage. At six we came up with a steep rock, one mile from the main, and then hauled to the wind, offshore, for the night. This lump, which appeared to be of granite, I called *Haul-off Rock;* it lies in 31° 43′ south and

118° 39′ east, and two leagues to the south-west of a cliffy point which bears the name of Cape Riche in the French chart.

Wednesday, 6.—At one in the morning, being seven or eight leagues from the coast and in 45 fathoms, we tacked ship towards the land, having a fresh breeze at west-south-west, with fine weather. Haul-off Rock bore N. 77° W., three or four miles, at six, and we then bore away along the coast. Beyond Cape Riche the shore forms a sandy bight, in which is a small island; and on the north side of another cliffy projection, four leagues further, there is a similar falling back of the coast, where it is probable there is also good shelter for boats, if not a small inlet. At noon a projecting head two miles long, which, from the lumps of rock at the top, I called *Cape Knob*, was three miles distant.

At four o'clock we had passed the Point Hood of Vancouver; and seeing a channel of nearly a mile in width between it and the two outer of his Doubtful Islands, steered through it with soundings from 20 to 24 fathoms. I then hauled up south-westward, along the inner island and point, and sent away the master to sound between them; it being my intention to anchor, if a sufficient depth should be found for the ship to escape in case the wind came to blow from the eastward; it was then light at south-east-by-south. Mr. Thistle found the opening to be very narrow, and no more than 2 fathoms in the shoalest part; we therefore stood out, repassing within a small black islet, upon which were some seals. At eight, tacked to the southward and weathered the Doubtful Islands.

On the north side of the isles and of Point Hood the shore falls back five or six miles to the west-south-west before it curves northward, and affords good shelter against all winds which do not blow strong from between north-east and east. At the time we stood out of the bay the ship was three miles within the outermost islands, and not more than a cable's length from the shore of Point Hood, and we had 7½ fathoms, sandy bottom. The point and islands are steep and rocky, but the western shores of this great bay are mostly sandy beaches. On the north-western and north sides there are some masses of tolerably high land which appeared to be granitic; and for distinction in the survey they are called *West, Middle*, and *East Mount Barren*.

Thursday, 7.—The wind was variable between east and north-by-east during the night. At daybreak the three mounts were in sight, and the north end of the Doubtful Isles bore N. 74° W. three leagues. As the wind veered round to the west and southward, we steered more in for the north side of Doubtful Island Bay.

Our course was directed to the northward, with the wind at

south-east-by-south; but seeing the appearance of an opening in the north-west corner of the bay, with smokes rising there, we steered north-west for it. In an hour the low land was seen from the mast head to extend across the supposed opening, and we then hauled up east-by-north, to the wind, at the distance of five or six miles from the high, rocky shore between the Middle and East Mount Barren. At seven in the evening the eastern mount bore N. 44° W., three leagues, and the coast, which from thence becomes sandy, was seen as far as N. 76° E. A small reef, one of two before laid down both by Vancouver and D'Entrecasteaux, was then observed three or four miles to seaward. It was important to get sight of this reef before dark, for we should otherwise have been at great uncertainty during the night, more especially as the surf upon it broke only at times.

The wind being at south-by-east, we tacked and stood westward, nearly in our afternoon's track, until midnight; and the breeze having then veered to south-west, we were able to stretch off south-south-east to windward of the breakers. At half-past five in the morning, East Mount Barren was four leagues distant to the northward, and our course was resumed along the shore. The breakers were passed at the distance of two miles, and the mount was set over them, bearing N. 38° W. at seven o'clock. The second small reef lies nearly east-north-east from the first, and was left three miles to the northward.

On the preceding evening a small rocky island had been seen indistinctly from the mast head, and it now again came in sight to the eastward. The French ships had passed without side of this island, and I therefore steered to go between it and the mainland; but breaking water was seen to extend so far to the north that the uncertainty of finding a passage made the attempt too dangerous with the wind right aft. We accordingly hauled up to windward of the island, and had 38 fathoms between it and a small reef lying S. 72° W., between two and three miles from it. The island is low, smooth, and sterile, and is frequented by seals; its latitude is 34° 6' and longitude 120° 28', and it lies eight or nine miles from the mainland.

At noon the rocky island was near ten miles astern, and a cluster of four small islets appeared in the offing at the distance of four leagues. The nearest part of the main land, seven or eight miles distant, was low and sandy, as it had been all the way from East Mount Barren, and continued to be to the furthest extreme visible from the masthead; there were, however, a few scattered sandy hillocks on the shore, but nothing could be seen of the back country.

We passed at nearly an equal distance between the four rocky islets and the mainland, that is to say, at six or eight miles from each; and at five o'clock were abreast of a projecting part of the coast where the sandy hills seemed to form white cliffs. This is called Cap des Basses (Shoal Cape) in the French chart; and we saw, in fact, an islet under the land, surrounded with much broken water, and the soundings decreased from 35 to 25 fathoms soon after passing it at the distance of five or six miles. There was an appearance of small inlets on each side of Shoal Cape, but as admiral D'Entrecasteaux passed within three miles and does not mark any, it was probably a deception, caused by the land being very low between the sand-hills.

Before sunset the westernmost isle of D'Entrecasteaux's *Archipel de la Recherche* was in sight to the eastward, and at half-past seven our distance from it was about six miles. The French admiral had mostly skirted round the archipelago, a sufficient reason for me to attempt passing through the middle, if the weather did not make the experiment too dangerous. It was fine at this time, and the breeze moderate at south-south-west; and I therefore took measures to be in with the western group as early on the following morning as possible, to have the whole day for getting through.

Saturday, 9.—At a quarter-past five we bore away for the south end of the westernmost island, passed in within a mile and a half at seven, and steered eastward for the clusters rising ahead and on both bows. At noon the number of rocks above water, the patches of breakers, and the islands with which we were surrounded made it necessary to heave to, in order to take the angles of so many objects with some degree of accuracy. This last peak had been visible from daybreak, and appears to be the top of the imperfectly formed *Ile de Remarque* of D'Entrecasteaux's chart; and from it I measured with a sextant the angles of most of the other objects. The long reef of rocks called *La Chaussée* (The Causeway) was four or five miles distant to the southward; and a sunken rock, upon which the sea broke at times, was three miles off to the north-east. The islands were more particularly numerous to the east-south-east, where our course lay; but as they were generally high, with bold rocky shores, and we had hitherto found deep water, I bore away for them so soon as all the bearings were obtained.

The chart alone can give any adequate idea of this labyrinth of islands and rocks, or of our track amongst them until half past five in the evening. We were then abreast of the *Ile du Mondrain*, and the view from the mast head was almost as crowded as before; but with this difference, that the islands were smaller, and the low rocks and patches of breakers more numerous. Seeing no probability of reaching a space of clear water in which to stand off and on during the night, and no prospect of shelter under any of the islands, I found myself under the necessity of adopting a hazardous measure; and with the concurrence of the master's opinion, we steered directly before the wind for the main coast, where the appearance of some beaches, behind other islands, gave a hope of finding anchorage. At seven in the evening we entered a small sandy bay; and finding it sheltered everywhere except to the south-westward, in which direction there were many islands and rocks in the offing to break off the sea, the anchor was dropped in 7 fathoms, sandy bottom. The master sounded round the ship, but nothing was found to injure the cables; and except the water being shallow in the north-west corner of the bay, there was no danger to be apprehended, unless from strong south-west winds. The critical circumstance under which this place was discovered induced me to give it the name of Lucky Bay.

Sunday, 10.—I had intended to pursue our route through the archipelago in the morning; but the scientific gentlemen having expressed a desire for the ship to remain two or three days, to give them an opportunity of examining the productions of the country, it was complied with; and they landed soon after day-light. I went on shore also, to make observations upon the rates of the time-keepers; and afterwards ascended a hill at the back of the bay to take angles with a theodolite. A party of the gentle-men were upon the top, eating a fruit not much unlike green walnuts in external appearance, and invited me to partake; but having breakfasted, and not much liking their flavour, I did but taste them. Mr. Thistle and some others who had eaten liberally were taken sick, and remained unwell all the day afterward. The plant which produced these nuts was a species of *zamia* (*Zamia spiralis* of Brown's *Prodr. flor. Nov. Holl.*, I. 348); a class of plants nearly allied to the third kind of palm found by captain Cook on the East Coast, the fruit of which produced the same deleterious effects on board the Endeavour.

The weather, unfortunately for my bearings, was so hazy that unless objects were eminently conspicuous they could not be dis-tinguished beyond four or five leagues. My list, however, con-tained forty-five islands and clusters of rocks, independently of many patches of breakers where nothing above water appeared; yet most of those in the western part of the archipelago were in-visible, either from their distance or from being hidden by other lands.

In turning from the view of these complicated dangers to that of the interior country the prospect was but little improved. Sand and stone, with the slightest covering of vegetation, every where presented themselves on the lower lands; and the many shining parts of the sides of the hills showed them to be still more bare. The vegetation, indeed, consisted of an abundant variety of shrubs and small plants, and yielded a delightful harvest to the botanists; but to the herdsmen and cultivator it promised nothing: not a blade of grass, nor a square yard of soil from which the seed delivered to it could be expected back, was perceivable by the eye in its course over these arid plains.

Upon a rock on the side of the hill I found a large nest, very similar to those seen in King George's Sound. There were in it several masses resembling those which contain the hair and bones of mice, and are disgorged by the owls in England after the flesh is digested. These masses were larger, and consisted of the hair of seals and of land animals, of the scaly feathers of pinguins, and the bones of birds and small quadrupeds. Possibly the constructor of the nest might be an enormous owl; and if so, the cause of the bird being never seen, whilst the nests were not scarce, would be from its not going out until dark; but from the very open and exposed situations in which the nests were found, I should rather judge it to be of the eagle kind, and that its powers are such as to render it heedless of any attempts from the natives upon its young.

Monday, 11.—On the following morning I sent the master to examine a small bay or cove lying two miles to the westward of Lucky Bay. He found it to be capable of receiving one ship, which might be placed in perfect security in the western corner, with anchors out on the off bow and quarter, and hawsers on the other side fast to the shore. She would thus lie in from 3 to 5 fathoms, almost near enough to lay a stage to the beach. There was wood for fuel; and at less than a hundred yards from the shore, a lake of fresh water, one mile in circumference, from which a small stream runs into the cove; but another stream, descending from the hills nearer into the western corner, would better suit the purposes of a ship. This account was from the master, after whom this little but useful discovery was named *Thistle's Cove.* It seems to be much superior to Lucky Bay, where neither wood nor water can be procured without much time and trouble, nor is the shelter so complete.

Tuesday, 12.—Next day Mr. Thistle was sent to examine the coast and islands to the eastward, when he found the archipelago to be full as dangerous in that direction as to the west. He landed upon an island three leagues distant, and brought me from thence a list of other islands and rocks further on, whose bearings had been taken. Several seals were procured on this and the preceding day, and some fish were caught alongside the ship; but our success was much impeded by three monstrous sharks, in whose presence no other fish dared to appear. After some attempts we succeeded in taking one of them; but to get it on board required as much preparation as for hoisting in the launch. The length of it, however, was no more than twelve feet three inches, but the circumference of the body was eight feet. Amongst the vast quantity of substances contained in the stomach was a tolerably large seal, bitten in two, and swallowed with half of the spear sticking in it with which it had probably been killed by the natives. The stench of this ravenous monster was great even before it was dead; and when the stomach was opened it became intolerable.

On the 13th the wind blew fresh from the eastward; and as we could not sail with the ship, lieutenant Fowler and Mr. Thistle went over to Mondrain Island, the largest we had yet seen in the archipelago. An observation of the latitude and a set of angles were there taken, and they brought back some seals of a reddish fur, and a few small kanguroos of a species different from any I had before seen. The island was covered with brush wood; but some of the party, either from accident or design, set it on fire; and the wind being fresh, there was a general blaze in the evening all over the island.

Very little other stone was seen about Lucky Bay than granite; and all the surrounding hills, as well as the islands visited, were composed of varieties of the same substance; and some specimens from Mondrain Island contained garnets. In many places the surface of the rocks was scaling off in layers, and in the steep parts great lumps had fallen off, and some caverns were formed in the cliffs. This propensity to decomposition was more remarkable in the high peak of Cape Le Grand, about five miles to the westward, to which Mr. Brown made an excursion. He found a perforation at the top forming an arch of great width and height, and above it, at the very summit of the peak, were loose pieces of granite of considerable size.

There did not appear to be any Indians at this time in the neighbourhood of Lucky Bay; but from their fire places, it was judged that they had not quitted it long since. Geese and ducks were found here, and not being very shy, some of them were killed by the shore parties. The goose was also found upon the islands; and is the same bird spoken of in the Introduction as resembling the *bernacle* goose, and frequenting Furneaux's Islands in Bass Strait.

The rise of *tide* in Lucky Bay was so trifling that under the circumstances of our stay no attention was paid to it.

In the morning of the 14th, the wind being then light from the northward, we got under way and steered for Mondrain Island. In our route eastward from thence, several low rocks and patches of breakers were left on each side, besides small islands whose bearings had been taken from the hill behind Lucky Bay; the depth of water, however, was between 20 and 30 fathoms. The wind was then moderate from the south-westward, but the weather so hazy that there was much difficulty, and some uncertainty, in recognising the different islands.

At half-past ten we steered more towards the main land, that no opening in it might escape unseen; and at noon, hove to for the purpose of taking bearings. The latitude observed to the north was 34° 2′, and longitude 122° 36′. A chain of islands and breakers lay about two miles to the northward; and amongst the cluster to the east were two islands with peaks upon them, which, from their similarity, were named the *Twins:* the southernmost and nearest bore E. 7° N., three leagues. The nearest part of the main land was a projection with hills upon it which had been set from Lucky Bay, whence it is nearly five leagues distant; the intermediate space being a large bight with a low, sandy coast at the back, and containing many small islands and breakers. To the eastward of the hilly projection the coast seemed again to be sandy; but although our distance from it was not more than six or seven miles, it was scarcely visible through the haze.

After the bearings were obtained we bore away along the south side of the chain of islands and rocks; and at half-past one steered north-east to look for a place of shelter, either amongst the cluster near the Twins or in the opposite main land. The water shoaled amongst the small islands, from 30 to 10 fathoms, and suddenly to 3, when the bottom was distinctly seen under the ship. The next cast was 7 fathoms, and we steered on eastward for two islets three-quarters of a mile asunder, between which the master was sent to sound. On his making the signal we followed through, having 20 fathoms, and afterwards hauled the wind to the south-east, seeing no hope of shelter either amongst the islands or near the main land. The coast stretched eastward with little sinuosity, and was sandy, but not so low as before.

At six o'clock we had some larger, flat islands to windward, and in the east-south-east was one much higher and of greater extent, which proved to be the *I. du Milieu* (Middle Island) of

D'Entrecasteaux. Betwixt this island and his *Cap Aride* on the main there were many small isles and apparently passages; and we therefore bore away in the hope of finding anchorage against the approaching night. Many patches of breakers were passed; and seeing a small bay in the north side of Middle Island, we stood in for it under shortened sail, and came to an anchor in 7 fathoms, sandy bottom, off the first of three small beaches. The island sheltered us from east-north-east, round by the south to west-by-north; and to the northward there was, besides the main land, a number of reefs and small isles, of which the nearest and largest was a quarter of a mile distant, as Middle Island was on the other side. The master was immediately sent to examine the passage through to the eastward, that we might know whether there were a possibility of escape in case the anchor should not hold; for the wind blew fresh at west-south-west, and threw some swell into the bay; he found 3 fathoms in the shallow part of the opening.

Friday, 15.—The botanists landed in the morning upon Middle Island; for I had determined to stop a day or two, as well for their accommodation as to improve my chart of the archipelago. I went to the northern island, which is one mile long and near half a mile in breadth, and found it to be covered with tufts of wiry grass intermixed with a few shrubs. Some of the little, blue pinguins, like those of Bass Strait, harboured under the bushes; and amongst the grass and upon the shores were a number of the bernacle geese, of which we killed nine, mostly with sticks; and sixteen more were procured in the course of the day.

After taking bearings from the uppermost of the small elevations of *Goose Island*, as it was now named, I ascended the high north-western hill of Middle Island, which afforded a more extensive view. The furthest visible part of the main land was a projecting cape, with a broad-topped hill upon it bearing N. 58° E., six or seven leagues. This projection not having been seen by D'Entrecasteaux, was named after the late admiral Sir Thomas Pasley, under whom I had the honour of entering the naval service. The shore betwixt Cape Pasley and Cape Arid is low and sandy, and falls back in a large bight, nearly similar to what is formed on the west side of Cape Arid. Behind that cape was a high bank of sand, which stretched from one bight nearly to the other, and had the appearance of having been the sea shore not very long since.

The mount upon which I stood is the highest part of a ridge of almost bare granite, extending along, or rather forming the west side of Middle Island. The other parts of the island are low, and thickly covered with brush wood and some trees, where a small species of kanguroo seemed to be numerous, though none were caught. In the north-eastern part was a small lake of a rose colour, the water of which, as I was informed by Mr. Thistle who visited it, was so satuated with salt that sufficient quantities were crystallised near the shores to load a ship. The specimen he brought on board was of a good quality, and required no other process than drying to be fit for use. This lake is at the back of the easternmost of three small beaches on the north side of the island, and it might be concluded that the salt was formed by the evaporation of the water oozing through the bank which separates it from the sea; but as, in the small drainings from the hills, the water was too salt to be drinkable, this may admit of a doubt.

Saturday, 16.—On Saturday morning a part of the people were employed cutting a boat load of fire wood, and the master was again sent to sound the passage out to the eastward, and amongst the rocks lying beyond it. The shallowest depth he found was 3 fathoms, after which the water deepened to 7 and 10, past the north-east point and out to sea. He landed upon some of the rocky islets, and brought from thence twenty-seven more geese, some of them alive. The botanical gentlemen employed the day in going round Middle Island, but they found very little to reward their labour. A piece of fir plank, with nails in it, which seemed to have been part of a ship's deck, was picked up on the shore; but no trace of the island having been visited, either by Europeans or the natives of the main land, was any where seen.

The basis stone of this, as it appears to be of all the islands as well as of the coast of the archipelago, is granitic; but at the south side of Middle Island there is a thick crust of calcareous rock over it, as there is at the south end of Goose Island. It was also on the south side of King George's Sound that the calcareous rock covered the granite; a coincidence which may perhaps afford some light to the geologist.

Goose-Island Bay may be useful as a place of refreshment, but the geese were not found to be so numerous at a different season of the year: a few hair seals may be procured, probably at all times. The wood is a species of *eucalyptus*, neither abundant nor large; but two or three ships may be supplied with fuel. Fresh water was not to be obtained upon either of the islands; but upon the opposite Cape Arid, five miles to the north, I judged there might be small streams running down from the hills. The lake of salt will be the greatest inducement for vessels to stop in this bay; they must not, however, come to it in the winter season, as there will be occasion to show hereafter.

On the 17th in the morning the anchor was weighed and we steered out eastward. The shallowest water was seventeen feet, between the south-east point of Goose Island and the opposite west point of the middle beach; after which it deepened; and abreast of the middle rock there was 7 fathoms. Having cleared the islets lying off the north-east point of Middle Island, we steered for Cape Pasley, leaving the *South-East Isles* of the archipelago far distant on the starbord hand. A low islet and some rocks lie three miles to the south of the Cape, and the soundings we had in passing between them were 28 and 34 fathoms.

The wind at this time was moderate at south-west, with fine weather. Middle Island and Cape Arid were still visible at noon, and the *Eastern Group*, which, according to D'Entrecasteaux, terminated the archipelago, was coming in sight.

At half-past one we passed within three miles of the point which had been the furthest extreme at noon; it is low and sandy, and a ledge of rocks extends from it to the north-east. I named it *Point Malcolm*, in honour of Captain Pultney Malcolm of the navy. The depth diminished from 20 to 10 fathoms, in passing near a sunken rock two miles to the south-east of the point, and upon which the sea breaks only at times. The coast from thence trended rapidly to the northward; and in following its direction at from three to five miles distance, we left eight islands of the Eastern Group on the starbord and two on the larbord hand. These, with the exception of the southernmost, which has a hill at each end and some vegetation, are little better than low sterile rocks.

From Cape Pasley to the northern extreme the coast is sandy and low, presenting, with trifling exceptions, a continued beach. On the north side of Point Malcolm it stretches north, and then eastward, forming a bight five miles within the land; after which the general trending is north-north-east, with very little sinuosity, Four or five miles behind the shore, and running parallel with it, is a bank of moderately high and level land, over which the tops of some barren-looking mountains were occasionally seen. The most remarkable of these is Mount Ragged, lying N. 8° N. nine or ten leagues from Cape Pasley.

We had now altogether lost sight of the Archipelago of the Recherche. The chart which I have constructed of this extensive mass of dangers is much more full, and in many parts should be more accurate than that of D'Entrecasteaux; but I dare by no means assert that the very great number of islands, rocks, and reefs therein contained are the whole that exist; nor that every individual one is correctly placed, although the greatest care was taken to obtain correctness. All the islands seem to be more or less frequented by seals; but I think not in numbers sufficient to make a speculation from Europe advisable on their account; certainly not for the China market, the seals being mostly of the hair kind, and the fur of such others as were seen was red and coarse. There is, besides, a risk of being caught in the archipelago with strong south or western winds, in which case destruction would be almost inevitable, for I know of no place where a ship might take refuge in a gale. The shelter in Thistle's Cove is, indeed, complete, when a vessel is once placed; but the cove is too small to be entered except under favourable circumstances, and the shelter in the western corner could not be attained with winds blowing strong out of it. The archipelago should not, therefore, be entered without the assurance of carrying fine weather to the proposed anchorage.

During the night of the 17th there was no current or set of tide past the ship. Every thing was kept prepared for getting under way at a moment's notice; but the wind blew gently off the land, and the people of the watch occupied themselves successfully in catching dog-fish. At daybreak we made all sail to the north-eastward, along the same low and, if possible, more sandy coast. The wind was light, and at nine it fell calm. This was succeeded by a sea breeze at east-south-east, and we trimmed close to it, keeping on our former course until four in the afternoon; when the land being one mile and a half distant, we tacked in 12 fathoms, and stretched to the southward.

The shore curved round here, and took a more eastern direction; and the bank of level land, which continued to run along behind it, approached very near to the water side. Three leagues further on it formed cliffs upon the coast; and a projecting part of them, which I called Point Culver, bore N. 77° E. four leagues: this was the furthest land in sight.

This afternoon we passed a number of pale red medusas, such as I had usually seen on the East Coast at the entrances of rivers, and which, on being touched, produced a sensation like the stinging of a nettle. There was also a red scum on the water, and some of it was taken up to be examined by Mr. Brown in a microscope. It consisted of minute particles not more than half a line in length, and each appeared to be composed of several cohering fibres which were jointed; the joints being of an uniform thickness, and nearly as broad as long. These fibres were generally of unequal length, and the extremities of the compound particle thence appeared somewhat torn. The particles exhibited no motion when in salt water; and the sole effect produced by immersing them in spirit of wine was the separation of each into its component fibres.

Until daybreak next morning the wind was unfavourable; but it then veered round to the south, and enabled us to pass Point Culver. Our course along the shore was so favoured by the wind that at seven in the evening we had passed another projecting part of the cliffs, named Point Dover, distant from Point Culver fifty miles; and the extreme in sight ahead was twenty miles further, and still cliffy. The nearest part was two for three leagues distant; and the wind being still at south, we hauled up to it, and at nine o'clock stood back to the westward.

The elevation of these cliffs appeared to be about five hundred feet, and nothing of the back country was seen above them. In the upper part they are brown, in the lower part nearly white, and the two *strata*, as also the small layers of which each is composed, are nearly horizontal. They were judged to be calcareous, as was the white, grey, and brown sand which the lead brought up when the bottom was not of coral.

A surveyor finds almost no object here whose bearing can be set a second time. Each small projection presents the appearance of a steep cape as it opens out in sailing along; but before the ship arrives abreast of it, it is lost in the general uniformity of the coast, and the latitude, longitude, and distance of the nearest cliffs are all the documents that remain for the construction of a chart. Point Culver and Point Dover are exceptions to the general uniformity; but it requires a ship to be near the land before even these are distinguishable. The latter point was somewhat whiter than the cliffs on each side, which probably arose from the front having lately fallen off into the water.

In the night of the 19th the wind shifted round to the eastward, and continued there for three days; and during this time we beat to windward without making much progress. Several observations were taken here for the variation of the compass: with the ship's head east-by-north, azimuths gave 7° 15' west, and at south, 4° 26'; five leagues further eastward they gave 6° 13' with the head north-east, and eight leagues further, an amplitude 4° 18' at south-by-east. These being corrected would be 4° 13', 4° 26', 4° 2', and 3° 42' west; so that the variation had now reassumed a tolerably regular course of diminution. The mean of the whole is 4° 6' west variation in the longitude of 125° 51' east.

Friday, 22.—At the end of three days beating our latitude in the evening of the 22nd was 32° 22', and longitude 126° 23', the depth in that situation was 7 fathoms at two miles from the land, and the furthest extremes visible through the haze bore west-half-north and east, the latter being distant four or five miles. The bank which before formed the cliffs had retired to a little distance from the coast, and left a front screed of low, sandy shore. Several smokes arose from behind the bank, and were the first seen after quitting the archipelago.

The barometer had kept up nearly to 30 inches during the east and south-east winds, but it now fell to 29.65; and we stretched off for the night in the expectation of a change of wind, and probably of blowing weather. At ten the sails were taken aback by a breeze from the westward; but at daylight it had veered to south-by-west, and the mercury was rising. We then bore away for the land; and having reached in with the low, sandy point which had borne east in the evening, steered along the coast at three or four miles distance in from 7 to 11 fathoms water. The latitude at noon from very indifferent observations was 32° 22½′, and longitude 127° 2′; the coast, four miles distant to the northward, was low and sandy, but rose quickly to the level bank, upon which there were some shrubs and small trees. Nothing of the interior country could be seen above the bank; but this might possibly have been owing to the haze, which was so thick that no extremes of the land could be defined. The wind was fresh at south-south-west, and by seven in the evening our longitude was augmented 55′; the land was then distant six or seven miles, trending east-north-eastward; and we hauled to the wind, which had increased in strength though the barometer was fast rising.

Having stood to the south-east till midnight, we then tacked to the westward; and at five next morning bore away north for the land, the wind being then at south-by-east, and the barometer announcing by its elevation a return of foul winds. At six we steered eastward, along the same kind of shore as seen on the preceding day; but the wind coming more unfavourable, and depth diminishing to 5 fathoms soon after eight o'clock, made it necessary to stretch off to sea. The coast in latitude 32° 1′ and longitude 128° 12′ was three miles distant to the north. A league further on it took a more northern direction, but without much changing its aspect; it continued to be the same sandy beach, with a bank behind it of level land topped with small trees and shrubs as before described.

The rest of the day and the whole of the 25th were taken up in beating fruitlessly against an eastern wind. Azimuths observed when the ship's head was east-by-north gave variation 6° 4′; and ten miles to the south a little eastward they gave 3° 8′ west,

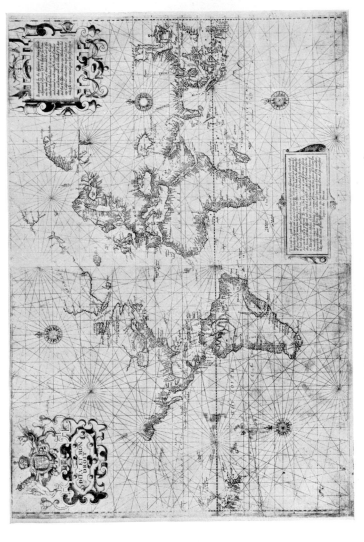

A Map of the World. London, 1598.

From Volume I of the second edition of Hakluyt's *Principal Navigations*.

at south-by-east; corrected 3° 2′ and 2° 32′, and the mean 2° 47′ for the true variation, showing a decrease since the last of 1° 19′ for 2° 11′ of longitude.

At ten in the evening our situation was less advanced than on the morning of the 24th, when we tacked off shore; but the mercury was again descending, and during the night the wind veered to north-east, to north, and at eight in the morning to west-by-north, when we steered in for the land. At ten the shore was eight or nine miles distant, and our course was north-east, nearly as it trended. The latitude at noon, from observations to the north and south, was 31° 51′ 34″, and longitude by time-keepers 128° 41′; the beach was distant three or four miles in the north-north-west, and the bank behind it lay two or three miles inland and was somewhat higher, but had less wood upon it than further westward. The wind was fresh at south-west, and the mercury was rising; but the haziness of the weather was such that no extremes of the land could be set.

Our course from noon was nearly east at the distance of five or six miles from the shore; and we ran at the rate of between seven and eight knots, under double-reefed top-sails and fore-sail. Abreast of our situation at half-past two the level bank again closed in upon the shore, and formed cliffs very similar to those along which we had before run thirty leagues. Their elevation appeared to be from four to six hundred feet, the upper part was brown, and the lower two-thirds white; but as we advanced, the upper brown *stratum* was observed to augment in proportional quantity. We could not distinguish, as before, the smaller layers in the two *strata;* and from the number of excavations in the white part, apparently from pieces having fallen down, I was led to think the lower portion of these cliffs to be grit stone rather than calcareous rock. The bank was not covered with shrubs, as before it came to the water side, but was nearly destitute of vegetation, and almost as level as the horizon of the sea.

Wednesday, 27.—At dusk we hauled up south-east-by-south to the wind, at one in the morning tacked to the westward, and at four bore away north for the land. Having reached within six miles of the cliffs, we steered eastward again, with a fair breeze; and at noon were in latitude 31° 40′ 52″ and longitude 130° 59′; the cliffs were then distant seven miles to the northward, and at N. 9° E. was their termination.

The length of these cliffs, from their second commencement, is thirty-three leagues; and that of the level bank, from near Cape Pasley where it was first seen from the sea, is no less than one

z

hundred and forty-five leagues. The height of this extraordinary bank is nearly the same throughout, being no where less, by estimation, than four hundred, nor any where more than six hundred feet. In the first twenty leagues the ragged tops of some inland mountains were visible over it; but during the remainder of its long course the bank was the limit of our view.

This equality of elevation for so great an extent, and the evidently calcareous nature of the bank, at least in the upper two hundred feet, would bespeak it to have been the exterior line of a vast coral reef, which is always more elevated than the interior parts, and commonly level with high-water mark. From the gradual subsiding of the sea, or perhaps by a sudden convulsion of nature, this bank may have attained its present height above the surface; and however extraordinary such a change may appear, yet, when it is recollected that branches of coral still exist upon Bald Head, at the elevation of four hundred or more feet, this supposition assumes a great degree of probability; and it would further seem that the subsiding of the waters has not been at a period very remote, since these frail branches have yet neither been all beaten down nor mouldered away by the wind and weather.

If this supposition be well founded, it may, with the fact of no hill or other object having been perceived above the bank in the greater part of its course, assist in forming some conjecture of what may be within it; which cannot, as I judge in such case, be other than flat, sandy plains, or water. The bank may even be a narrow barrier between an interior and the exterior sea, and much do I regret the not having formed an idea of this probability at the time; for notwithstanding the great difficulty and risk, I should certainly have attempted a landing upon some part of the coast to ascertain a fact of so much importance.

At the termination of the bank and of the second range of cliffs the coast became sandy, and trended north-eastward about three leagues; after which it turned south-east-by-east, and formed the head of the *Great Australian Bight*, whose latitude I make to be 31° 29′ south, and longitude 131° 10′ east. In the chart of admiral D'Entrecasteaux the head of the Great Bight is placed in 31° 36′ and 131° 27′; but I think there is an error at least in the latitude, for the admiral says, " At daybreak I steered to get in with the land; and the wind having returned to south-east, we hauled our starbord tacks on board, being then four or five leagues from the coast. At *eleven o'clock* the land was seen ahead and we veered ship in 32 fathoms, fine sand." The

latitude observed at noon, as appears by the route table, was
31° 38′ 58″; and if we suppose the ship, lying up south-south-
west, to have made 2′ of southing in the hour, as marked in the
chart, she must have been in 31° 37′ at eleven o'clock; which is
within one mile of the latitude assigned to the head of the bight,
where the shore curves to the south-east-by-east. This does not
accord with the land being only then seen ahead, since the
weather appears to have admitted the sight of it at the distance
of four or five leagues. If we suppose the admiral, when he
veered, to have been eight, instead of one mile from the head of
the Great Bight, and the account strongly favours the supposition,
it will then agree with my latitude. I had only 27 fathoms in
crossing the head; and although it is possible there may be 30
closer in, yet in such a place as this the probability is, that the
ship having the greatest depth of water was the furthest from
the land.

After steering east-north-east, east, and east-south-east, and
having seen the beach all round the head of the Great Bight, we
hauled up parallel to the new direction of the coast, at the distance of six miles; and at five o'clock were abreast of the furthest
part seen by the French admiral when he quitted the examination. The coast is a sandy beach in front; but the land rises
gradually from thence, and at three or four miles back is of
moderate elevation, but still sandy and barren. According to the
chart of Nuyts, an extensive reef lay a little beyond this part.
It was not seen by D'Entrecasteaux, but we were anxiously
looking out for it when, at six o'clock, breakers were seen from
the mast head bearing S. 43° E. some distance open from the
land. We kept on our course for them, with the wind at south-
south-west, until eight o'clock, and then tacked to the westward
in 27 fathoms; and the ship's way being stopped by a head swell,
we did not veer towards the land until three in the morning, at
which time it fell calm.

Thursday, 28.—On a light breeze springing up from the northward we steered in for the coast. The breakers lie five or six miles
from the land, and did not appear to have any connection with it,
nor with two other sets of small reefs which came in sight to the
east and east-south-east, soon afterward. At two o'clock our
situation was betwixt these last reefs. The southernmost patches
are two or three miles in length, and there are large rocks upon
them, standing above water; the northern patches extend eight
miles along the coast, from which they are distant three miles,
and on the eastern parts there are also some rocks above water;
but there were none upon the western reef first seen. It may be

doubted whether the western reef were known to Nuyts, but there can be no doubt concerning these last; and I call the whole Nuyts' Reefs.

The aspect of the shore to the northward was nearly the same as that seen the preceding afternoon, but behind the second reefs it began to assume a more rocky appearance. A high cliffy cape is formed a little further eastward; it has a pyramidal rock near it, and the coast there takes a direction somewhat on the north side of east. This remarkable projection, being within a few leagues of the furthest part of the main coast discovered by the Dutch, I have called Cape Nuyts: its latitude is 32° 2' south, and longitude 132° 18' east.

After clearing Nuyts' Reefs we steered east-north-east, past the cape, to look for anchorage in two bights; but there were rocks in both, and they were open to the southward. Beyond them was a low, cliffy point, lying E. 3° N. seven or eight miles from Cape Nuyts; and seeing a bay behind it which promised shelter from south-west and south winds, we hauled round the point at half-past five. The water shoaled gradually from 11 to 3 fathoms, on which I hove the sails aback and sent the master ahead to sound; and as he did not make the signal for deeper water, as we were already in tolerable shelter, the anchor was dropped in 3¼ fathoms, sandy bottom.

Being arrived at the extremity of that part of the south coast of Terra Australis which had been previously explored, it may be useful, before entering on the unknown part, to compare my examination of it with what was contained in former charts. It will thence appear that the employment of fifteen days in running along the coast, more than would probably have been required had I kept at a distance, was not without some advantage to geography and navigation.

At Cape Leeuwin, the largest *Ile St. Alouarn* of D'Entrecasteaux was seen to be joined to the main, and to form the south-western extremity of Leeuwin's Land, and of Terra Australis. The coast from thence to King George's Sound was more accurately investigated than the French admiral had an opportunity of doing and his omission of soundings supplied. Captain Vancouver's chart is superior to that of the French from Cape Chatham to the Sound; but that officer's distance from some parts prevented him from seeing them correctly. In the Sound, no particular advantage will be derived from the new survey, the plan given by Vancouver being sufficiently correct for nautical purposes, with the exception of the bar to Oyster Harbour, over which he had marked seventeen feet, but where thirteen now appeared to be the greatest depth. From King George's Sound to Point Hood the coast had been very indistinctly, and sometimes not at all seen by Vancouver; but I found it, speaking generally, to be laid down by D'Entrecasteaux with accuracy, though the bights in the land are marked somewhat too deep, from his distance not allowing the low beaches to be always distinguished. These trifling inaccuracies were remedied, the passages between Bald and Doubtful Islands and the main land opposite to them ascertained to be safe, and the omission of soundings along the coast remedied.

In Doubtful Island Bay the French chart does not give the north-western part sufficiently deep; but the coast from thence to the Archipelago of the Recherche, as also the reefs and rocks, were well distinguished, better perhaps than by me; but the usual want of soundings, with the exception of some distant ones by Vancouver, still continued. D'Entrecasteaux's chart appeared to be excellent in the western part of the archipelago, and good in the positions of the islands on the outskirts; so that I have, in some cases, borrowed from it. With respect to the inner islands and the main coast, it was necessarily defective, from the French ships having sailed round the archipelago, and not through the middle of it as I did in the Investigator. Here, my survey, though far from complete in the details, will afford much new information and useful also, since it has brought to light a well-sheltered cove affording wood and water, and two other tolerable anchorages at which some refreshments may be procured, and at one, quantities of salt in the summer season.

From the archipelago eastward the examination of the coast was prosecuted by D'Entrecasteaux with much care, and with some trifling exceptions very closely; but as far as the 127th degree of longitude from Greenwich no soundings were given. These have been supplied, and a more minute description given of the coast. At the 129th degree the French ships seem to have been closer in with the land than was the Investigator; and it would appear by the track that they were also closer at the 130th, and at the head of the Great Bight, but these last are not corroborated by the soundings. From thence to the bay in which we anchored on the 28th, the Dutch chart of 1627 was the sole authority; and making allowances for the state of navigation at that time, it is as correct in form as could reasonably have been expected.

The latitudes and longitudes of the points and islands along the coast have been either verified or corrected, for there are commonly some differences between any longitudes and those of

Vancouver and D'Entrecasteaux. The observations by which certain places, taken as fixed points, are settled in longitude, are mentioned at those places, as also are the corrections applied to the time-keepers for laying down the intermediate parts.

Monsieur *Beautemps Beaupré*, geographical engineer on board La Recherche, was the constructor of the French charts; and they must be allowed to do him great credit. Perhaps no chart of a coast so little known as this was will bear a comparison with its original better than those of M. Beaupré. That the Plates II and III* are offered as being more full and somewhat more correct, does neither arise from a wish to depreciate those of my predecessor in the investigation, nor from an assumption of superior merit; there is, indeed, very little due to any superiority they may be found to possess; but there would be room for reproach if, after having followed with an outline of his chart in my hand, improvements should not have been made in all or some of those parts where circumstances had not before admitted a close examination.

The bay in which we anchored on the evening of January 28, 1802, at the extremity of the before known south coast of Terra Australis, was named Fowler's Bay, after my first lieutenant; and the low, cliffy point which shelters it from southern winds and, not improbably, is the furthest point (marked B) in the Dutch chart, was called *Point Fowler*. The botanical gentlemen landed early on the following morning to examine the productions of the country, and I went on shore to take observations and bearings, and to search for fresh water.

The cliffs and rocks of Point Fowler are calcareous, and connected with the main land by a low, sandy isthmus of half a mile broad. Many traces of inhabitants were found, and amongst others, some decayed spears; but no huts were seen, nor anything to indicate that men had been here lately. Upon the beach were the foot marks of dogs, and some of the emu or cassowary. I found in a hole of the low cliffs one of those large nests which have before been mentioned, but it contained nothing, and had been long abandoned.

No fresh water was discovered round the shores of the bay, nor was there any wood large enough for fuel nearer than the brow of a hill two or three miles off. Two teal were shot on the beach, whence it seemed probable that some lake or pond of fresh water was not far distant; a sea-pie and a gull were also shot, and a few small fish caught alongside. These constituted everything like refreshment obtained here, and the botanists found the scantiness

* Plates omitted.

of plants equal to that of the other productions; so that there was no inducement to remain longer.

Fowler's Bay, however, may be useful to a ship in want of a place of shelter. It is open to the three points of the compass between south-east-by-south and east-south-east; and it was evident, from plants growing close to the water side, that a swell capable of injuring a vessel at anchor was seldom if ever thrown into it.

The wind was at south-east-by-south at one in the afternoon, when the anchor was weighed to beat out of the bay. At half-past five we were three miles from a cliffy head which had been taken for an island at the anchorage, and set at N. 77° E. The shore forms a small bight on the east side of this head, and then stretches south-south-eastward in a sandy beach, with a ridge of barren land behind. At sunset we passed to windward of Point Fowler, and stood off to sea for the night.

Saturday, 30.—Cape Nuyts bore north, two or three leagues, soon after daylight, and the wind was then at east; but as the day advanced it veered to the south-east, and permitted us to make a stretch toward the furthest land. At five in the evening we tacked near some low, whitish cliffs, which had been seen from the mast head when in Fowler's Bay; they were two or three miles off, and the furthest land visible from the deck bore S. 63° E. at no great distance. The coast here is broken into sandy beaches and small, cliffy points, and the same ridge of barren land runs behind it, but the elevation is not great.

Sunday, 31.—At three in the afternoon of the 31st we reached in again with the coast, about four leagues beyond our situation on the preceding day. The depth at two miles off shore was 7 fathoms on a coral bottom; the northern extreme bore N. 58° W., and a low point on the other side, named *Point Bell,* S. 45° E., seven miles. To seaward a flat rock bore W. 3° S., one mile and a half; it is the largest of four which were called *Sinclair's Rocks,* and lie scattered at the distance of two or three miles off the coast. We stood off at this time; but so little could be gained upon the south-east winds that when we came in next morning it was almost exactly in the same spot, and Point Bell was not passed until late in the afternoon; the weather, also, was adverse to the examination, being so hazy that the highest land could not be seen beyond three or four leagues.

At half-past six in the evening, when we tacked to stand off for the night, Point Bell bore N. 68° W. four miles. It lies in 32° 16½' south and 133° 5' east; and there is a broad, flat rock, surrounded with breakers, one mile to the westward. The main coast beyond the point forms some bights, and is divided betwixt sand and rock, as before described: its general trending is nearly east. A small island, somewhat elevated, lies six miles to the south-east of Point Bell, and has a ledge of rocks and islets extending from it a league to the north-eastward, and a separate islet one or two miles to the east: these obtained the name of *Purdie's Isles*. After we had tacked in 9 fathoms, a wave was perceived to break upon a sunken rock within less than half a mile of the ship; and I think it would be dangerous to pass between Point Bell and Purdie's Isles.

At noon of the 2nd February no land was in sight. The weather was still hazy, and the wind at south-east; but in the afternoon it favoured us two points, and we got sight of a higher and larger island than any before seen on this part of the coast. At half-past four, being then near a smaller isle and several rocks, we tacked towards the large island which was six or seven miles to the southward; and soon after eight in the evening got to an anchor in a little sandy bay on its north side. The depth was 6 fathoms in passing the north-west point of the bay, but 10 within side, on a fine sandy bottom, where the anchor was dropped. At daylight we found ourselves half a mile from the shore, and the extremes bearing from N. 32° W., round by the west and south, to S. 77° E.; and at the distance of two miles we were sheltered by four small islands, extending from N. 41° to 88° E. The master was sent to sound in the bay; but the bottom was everywhere good, and nothing found to injure the cables. The scientific gentlemen landed upon their respective pursuits; and I followed them to take angles for my survey, and see what could be procured for the ship's company.

The island is nearly three miles long, north-west and south-east, and is moderately high and cliffy at the ends; the middle part is a sandy isthmus, not more than half a mile broad, but the breadth of the higher ends is from one-and-half to two miles. This island is the central one of a group; for besides the four small isles to the north-east, there are two close to the west end, and two others, something larger, lying off to the southward. I call these the Isles of St. Francis; in the persuasion that the central one is that named St. Francis by Nuyts. Independently of the eight isles and a rock, surrounding this Isle St. Francis, I set from the north-east point three other islands. The first, named *Lacy's Isle*, bore N. 28° E., seven miles; and two miles from it to the north-west there is an islet and a separate rock above water surrounded with breakers, the same near which we had tacked at

half-past four on the preceding evening. The second was called
Evans' Isle, and bore N. 49° E. eleven miles; and the third, to
which the name of *Franklin* was given, bore N. 81° E. sixteen
miles. All these are much inferior in magnitude to the central
island of St. Francis.

For several days before anchoring here we had observed large
flocks of sooty petrels; and I found the surface of the island,
where it was sandy and produced small shrubs, to be full of their
burrows. Pinguins, similar to those of Furneaux's Islands, had
their burrows nearer to the water-side. A small species of kanguroo, was also found, and at some preceding season the island
had been frequented by geese; but at this time, the vegetation
being almost burnt up, they seemed to have quitted it from want
of food. The heat was, indeed, such as to make walking a great
fatigue; and this was augmented by frequently sinking into the
bird holes and falling upon the sand. The thermometer stood at
98° in the shade, whilst it was at 78° on board the ship.

Where the surface is not of sand it consists of calcareous rock,
mostly in loose pieces; but the stone which forms the basis of the
island is heavy and of a close grain, and was judged to be por
phyry. In the crevices of a low calcareous cliff, at the south-east
side of the bay, I found some thin cakes of good salt, incrusted
upon a stone containing *laminæ* of quartz.

A party was sent on shore at dusk to collect petrels, and in less
than two hours returned with sufficient to give four birds to
every man in the ship. Early in the morning the boats were
again sent upon the same errand, and to haul the seine; but the
birds were gone off to sea for the day, and no fish were caught.
A small kanguroo was brought off, as also a yellow snake, which
was the second killed on this island. The great heat deterred the
naturalists from going on shore this morning, for the very little
variety in the vegetable productions presented no inducement
to a repetition of their fatigue. I landed to see what further could
be discovered of the neighbouring islands; and we then prepared
to get under way so soon as the breeze set in from the south-
eastward, which it usually did about noon, after a few hours of
calm or of light airs.

The small bay in the Isle St. Francis, which I call *Petrel Bay*,
affords excellent shelter for two or three ships; but no fresh
water, not even to rince our mouths, could be found at this time;
and a few scattered bushes were the nearest approach to wood
upon the island. Petrels, pinguins, and a few hair seals may be
procured, and probably some geese in the wet season.

I had hitherto observed upon this coast that the south-east and east winds produced the same effect upon the barometer as at the Cape of Good Hope, in keeping the mercury high, commonly at or above 30 inches; and the more fresh was the wind, the higher it stood; but within the last few days the barometer was much lower with the same winds, and at this time was at 29·74. The dense haze which prevailed might possibly have caused the change, but I suspected another reason for it. Winds coming off the land, I had remarked, had a tendency to depress the mercury, and sea winds to make it rise, though no change took place in the weather; and it therefore seemed probable, as the trending of the coast beyond these islands was unknown, that the south-east and east winds came off the land, and not from the sea, as before; in which case the unknown coast would be found trending to the southward, a conjecture which, it will be seen, was verified. That there was no entrance to a strait, nor any large inlet near these islands, was almost demonstrated by the insignificance of the tides; for neither in Fowler's Bay nor at this Isle St. Francis could any set be perceived; nor was there any rise by the shore worthy of notice.

At half-past one we left Petrel Bay; and having passed between the small isles to the north-east, steered for Evans' Island, and toward the Isles of St. Peter, which were expected to lie beyond it. At five o'clock, we passed between Evans' Island and some rocks above water, with breakers round them, lying three miles to the eastward. An island, equally high with that of St. Francis, was then seen to the north, and low land extended from it to N. 45° E., which had some appearance of being part of the main. We steered for these lands; and seeing an opening between them at sunset, I attempted it in the hope of getting anchorage for the night; but the water shoaled suddenly, from 4 fathoms to sixteen feet upon rocks, and obliged me to veer on the instant. We then stood back to the southward till eight o'clock, and nothing being perceived in the way of the ship's drift, hove to for the night.

Friday, 5.—The wind was north-east in the morning; and at half-past four o'clock we filled the sails and steered eastward until eight, when the central island of St. Francis bore N. 71° W., and Franklin's Isles, for there are two, besides rocks, were distant four leagues, the small opening between them bearing N. 28° W. To the south-eastward of these islands, at the distance of eleven miles, is a low projection of the main land, to which the name of *Point Brown* was given, in compliment to the naturalist; and four leagues further, in the same line, was a cliffy head, called *Cape Bauer* after the painter of natural history. Between these projections there was a wide space where no land was visible, and for which we accordingly steered on the wind veering more to the northward. The atmosphere was still hazy, more especially about the horizon, and no observations worthy of confidence could be taken for either latitude or longitude. No land was yet visible ahead; and there being much refuse from the shore, as well as seaweed floating about, some hopes of finding a river were entertained. At half-past two, however, low, sandy land was seen from the mast head, nearly all round, the depth had diminished from 19 to 7 fathoms, and the water was much discoloured in streaks at less than a mile from the ship. Smokes were rising in three different places; but as the wind was unfavourable, and there was no prospect of any opening sufficiently large to admit the *Investigator*, I gave up the further examination of this place, and called it Streaky Bay.

There remained nearly forty miles of space between Point Bell and Point Brown, in which the main coast had not been seen. This it was necessary to explore; but the wind being then at north-north-east, I steered to the southward, to gain some further knowledge of the coast in that direction before dark.

West of Cape Bauer, and distant four miles, there is a low island, extensively surrounded with rocks and breakers, which I called *Olive's Island*. We passed between it and the cape, and observed the cliffs of the latter to be stratified, and apparently calcareous. Another cliffy and somewhat higher projection opened from it at S. 1° W., distant seven miles, the intermediate low land forming a bight four or five miles deep, which is mostly skirted by a sandy beach. This projection I named *Point Westall*, in compliment to the landscape painter; and at six in the evening, when it bore north-east-by-east two or three miles, we veered round to the northward. Beyond Point Westall the coast takes a more eastern direction, the first land which opened out from it being at S. 43° E.: this was a third cliffy projection, terminating another sandy bight in the coast. No hill nor anything behind the shore could be perceived, but it does not certainly follow that there are no hills in the back country, for the haze was too thick to admit of the sight extending beyond four or five leagues.

All sail was made to fetch between Franklin's Isles and Point Brown, in order to follow the course of the main land and as close as possible; but finding, after several tacks, the impossibility of weathering the isles, we bore away; and at noon hauled up north-north-east round them. The wind was light at east, and the weather fine over head; but there was so dense a haze below that the true horizon could not be distinguished from several false ones, and we had six or seven different latitudes from as many observers: those taken by me to the north and south differed 19 minutes. This dense haze, from its great refractive power, altered the appearance of objects in a surprising manner: a sandy beach seemed to be a chalky cliff, and the lowest islands to have steep shores. The thermometer stood, at this time, at 82°, and the barometer at 29·60 inches.

On the north side of Point Brown the shore formed a large open bay, into which we hauled up as much as the wind would permit, passing near to a reef of rocks and breakers, two miles to the north-north-east of Franklin's Isles. At half-past two the water had shoaled to 5 fathoms; and not being able to distinguish any inlet, we then bore away westward along the land. The number of smokes rising from the shores of this wide, open place induced me to give it the name of Smoky Bay.

At four o'clock we passed the small opening which had been unsuccessfully attempted in the evening of the 4th, and hauled up northward under the lee of the island forming its western side. The mainland then came in sight ahead; but between it and the islands was a space five or six miles wide, which had the appearance of being the entrance to a river. No land was visible to the north-east; and besides quantities of grass and branches of trees or bushes floating in the water, there was a number of long, gauze-winged insects topping about the surface, such as frequent fresh-water lakes and swamps. In order to form a judgment of how much fresh was mixed with the salt water, or whether any, I had some taken up for the purpose of ascertaining its specific gravity; but before the experiment could be made, the depth diminished to 3 fathoms, and low land was distinguished nearly all round. We then veered ship; and at seven o'clock came to an anchor in 6 fathoms, off a small beach on the north side of the western and smallest island, being sheltered at all points except between S. 58° and N. 80° W.

The specific gravity of the water taken up proved to be 1·034, or ·008 greater than the water of the Southern Indian Ocean, westward of the Island Amsterdam, although the temperature in which it was weighed was higher by 14°. This circumstance, with the shallowness of the inlet and the land having been seen to close round so nearly, made me give up the intention of attempting to proceed any higher up, since no river of importance was to be expected.

Great flocks of sooty petrels were observed coming in from sea to the island, and at the first dawn next morning a boat was sent to collect a quantity of them, and to kill seals; but the birds were already moving off, and no more than four seals, of the hair kind, were procured. The botanists preferred going on shore to the more eastern land, which, though low, was much more extensive than the island nearer to the ship; and in fact it was not yet ascertained whether it were not a part of the main. I went to the higher island with a theodolite to take bearings; and as the survey had shown that no dependence was to be placed in any observations taken on board the ship during the last five days, I took with me the necessary instruments for determining the latitude and longitude.

Granite was found to compose the rocks of the shore, and seemed to be the basis of the island; but it was covered with a crust of calcareous stone, in some places fifty feet thick. The soil at the top was little better than sand, but was overspread with shrubs, mostly of one kind, a whitish velvety plant (*artriplex reniformis* of Brown), nearly similar to what is called at Port Jackson, Botany Bay greens. Amongst these the petrels had everywhere undermined; and from the excessive heat of the sun, the reflexion from the sand, and frequently stepping up to the mid-leg in the burrows, my strength was scarcely equal to reaching the highest hill near the middle of the island. I had no thermometer, but judged the temperature could scarcely be less than 120°; and there was not a breath of air stirring. My fatigue was, however, rewarded by an extensive set of bearings, and I overlooked the lower and larger island to the eastward, and saw the water behind it communicating with Smoky Bay. That low land and the island upon which I stood, being the north-easternmost of this archipelago, must, I conceive, be the Isles of St. Peter in Nuyts' chart, notwithstanding their relatively small distance from those of St. Francis. The bay to the northward, between these islands and the mainland, I named Denial Bay, as well in allusion to St. Peter as to the deceptive hope we had formed of penetrating by it some distance into the interior country.

On returning to the shore to complete my observations, a flock of teal presented themselves, and four were shot. There were also pied shags, and gulls of three species; and in the island were seen many crows, a green paroquet, and two smaller birds. A black snake, of the common size, was killed, but its form did not bespeak it to be venomous. After observing the sun's altitude at noon, I returned on board with the intention of getting the ship under way, to examine more closely a bight in the coast near Point Bell; and then of returning to Petrel Bay in the Isle

St. Francis, in order to obtain better observations for a base to my chart of this archipelago. At two o'clock, Mr. Brown and his party returned from the eastern island, bringing four kanguroos, of a different species to any before seen. Their size was not superior to that of a hare, and they were miserably thin, and infested with insects. No other than calcareous rock was seen upon the eastern island. It seemed to afford neither wood nor water, nor were there any marks of its having been visited by the natives of the continent; in which respect it resembled the western island, as it also did in its vegetation, and in being frequented by the sooty petrel. Mr. Brown's pocket thermometer stood at 125° when placed on the sand, and 89° in the shade; whilst on board the ship the height was only 83°.

The sun was too high at noon for its altitude to be taken from an artificial horizon with a sextant; but by laying down upon the beach I obtained it from the sea horizon tolerably free from the refractive errors caused by the haze. The *latitude* of the north side of the western Isle of St. Peter, thus observed, was 32° 21¼' south, and the *longitude* by time-keepers, corrected as usual, 133° 29' east. There was no set of *tide* past the ship; but from eight o'clock to noon the water had risen about a foot by the shore.

The anchor was weighed on the return of the botanists, and we steered westward past the small island named *Lound's*, and as far as Purdie's Isles; when, having seen the whole line of the coast behind them, we hauled to the southward at six o'clock for Petrel Bay; and at one in the morning came to, in 13 fathoms, near our former anchorage.

It was here confirmed by satisfactory observations on shore that our former latitudes and longitudes taken on board the ship were erroneous; and the consequent necessity of reconstructing my chart of these islands induced me to remain at anchor the rest of the day. A boat was sent to fish with hook and line, and had some success; and at dusk a sufficient number of sooty petrels were taken from the burrows to give nine to every man, making, with those before caught, more than twelve hundred birds. These were inferior to the teal shot at the western Isle of St. Peter, and by most persons would not be thought eatable on account of their fishy taste; but they made a very acceptable supply to men who had been many months confined to an allowance of salt meat.

The *latitude* of our anchorage in Petrel Bay proved to be 32° 33⅓' south, and corrected *longitude*, by time-keepers, 133° 15½' east. The *variation* of the compass on the binnacle, with the ship's head south-eastwardly, but the exact point not noted, was 2° 23' west. Other azimuths, taken five leagues to the north-westward, with the head south-half-west, gave 0° 19' east; and six leagues to the eastward, the head being north half-west, we had 0° 16' east. All these observations, being corrected, and supposing the ship's head in the first case to have been south-east-half-east, as is probable, would agree in showing that the true and magnetic meridians exactly coincided at the Isles of St. Francis in 1802.

Being about to quit this archipelago, it may be expected that I should make some general remarks upon it. The basis stone of the islands where we landed, and that of the others, as also of the projecting parts of the main, appeared to be similar, was either porphyry or granite; but this was generally covered with a *stratum*, more or less thick, of calcareous rock. The arid sterility of the two largest islands has been already mentioned; and yet they appeared superior to any of the smaller isles, where there was no probability that the small kanguroos could exist in the dry season. The surface of the continent seemed to be almost equally destitute of vegetable soil to cover the sand and rock; and from the hot winds off the land, which we felt in Streaky and Smoky Bays, it would seem that this aridity prevails to a considerable distance in the interior. There are, however, some grounds to believe that a lake or run of fresh water exists not far from Denial Bay: the flock of teal seen upon the western Isle of St. Peter, and the number of winged, fresh-water insects skimming the surface of that bay, are the grounds to which I allude.

My examination of this group of islands was tolerably minute to be done wholly in a ship; but much still remained, which boats would best accomplish, to make the survey complete, especially in the bays of the main land. No more than a general examination was prescribed by my instructions at this time, and I therefore left the minute parts for a second visit, when the ship would be accompanied by the *Lady Nelson* tender.

Upon the identity of the particular islands composing this group, as compared with the chart of Nuyts' discovery, there may possibly be some difference of opinion, but there can be no doubt that the group generally is the same with that laid down by the Dutch navigator; and I therefore distinguish it from others upon this coast by the title of Nuyts' Archipelago. Besides the nine Isles of St. Francis and two of St. Peter, and several distinct rocks and patches of reef, it contains Sinclair's four Rocks, Purdie's Isles, Lound's Isle, Lacy's and Evans' Islands, Franklin's Isles, and Olive's Island ; all of which are named after young officers of the *Investigator*. The state of navigation in 1627 does not permit the expectation of any exact coincidence between the islands laid down by the Dutch and those in my chart.

At daybreak in the morning of February 9, 1802, when the anchor was weighed from Petrel Bay to prosecute the examination of the unknown coast, we were unexpectedly favoured with a refreshing breeze from the westward; and our course was directed for Cape Bauer. At noon, the latitude from mean of observations to the north and south, which differed only 1', was 32° 43' 17"; but although our distance from the land could not be more than three leagues, no part of it was distinguishable; the haze was very thick, but it was of a different nature, and had none of that extraordinary refractive power which the atmosphere possessed during the prevalence of the eastern winds. At one o'clock, Olive's Island was indistinctly perceived; and at two we came in with Point Westall, and then steered south-south-eastward along the coast at the distance of four or five miles. At six, a bold cliffy head, which I named Cape Radstock, in honour of Admiral Lord Radstock, bore N. 75° E., six or seven miles; and the land seemed there to take another direction, for nothing beyond it could be perceived. The wind was at west-south-west; and we kept on the starboard tack till eight o'clock, and then stood off for the night.

At five in the morning we steered for the land; and soon afterward Cape Radstock was in sight, bearing N. 57° E., five leagues. The latitude of this cape is 33° 12' south, and longitude 134° 15' east. Other cliffy heads came in sight as we advanced eastward; and at seven, the appearance of an opening induced me to steer close in; but it proved to be a bight full of rocks, with low land behind. The line of the projecting parts of the coast is nearly east from Cape Radstock for four leagues; and at the end of them is a cliffy point which received the name of *Point Weyland*. Round this point an opening was seen of so promising an appearance that I bore away north and north-east for it, although land was in sight as far as east-south-east. Before noon the greater part of the open space was found to be occupied by low land; and no more of the opening remained than a small inlet through the beach, leading, apparently, into a lagoon, the water of which was distinguished from the mast head. This inlet was fit only to receive boats; and therefore we hauled the wind to the southward, when the sandy shore near it was distant two-and-half miles on one side, and Point Weyland one mile and a half on the other. The latitude of this point is 33° 14' south, and longitude 134° 32' east. As the day advanced the wind veered

Captain Matthew Flinders, R.N.

Aged 27.　From the engraving in the *Naval Chronicle*, 1814.

to south-west, and there being a swell from the same quarter, we could do no more than make a south-east-by-south course, parallel with the shore. At three o'clock the mainland was seen to extend out beyond what the ship could fetch; there were besides two islands lying still further out, and a third was perceived in the offing, almost directly to windward. The two first received the name of *Waldegrave's Isles*, and the latter with some rocks near it were called *Top-gallant Isles*. Our distance from the sandy shore was then barely a league; and coming into 7 fathoms water soon afterward, we tacked, hoping to weather Cape Radstock; but finding this to be impossible, were constrained to pass the night in working to windward in the bay. The weather was squally with rain, but our situation made it necessary to carry all possible sail; and we had the satisfaction, at daylight, to find the ship had gained considerably. It then blew a strong breeze at south-west-by-south, and we stretched in under Waldegrave's Isles; and finding the water become smooth, the anchor was let go in 7 fathoms, on a bottom of calcareous sand, at half a mile from the north-east end of the inner and largest island. We were here sheltered from the present wind, but exposed from west-by-south to north-north-west; the master was therefore immediately sent to sound the opening of one mile wide between the island and the main, by which alone we could hope to escape, should the wind shift to the north-westward and blow strong; but the opening proved to be full of rocks and breakers.

The press of sail carried in the night had so much stretched the rigging that it required to be set up, fore and aft. Whilst this was doing on board, the naturalists landed upon the island; where I also went to take bearings with a theodolite, and observations for the latitude and longitude. The island is about two miles long, and connected by rocks with the small, outer isle; and they extend four or five miles from a projecting part of the main, in a west direction. These islands form the southern boundary, as Cape Radstock does the north point of a great open bay, which, from the night we passed in it, obtained the name of Anxious Bay.

I found the island to bear a great resemblance to the western Isle of St. Peter, in its cliffy shores, granitic basis and *superstratum* of calcareous stone; in its vegetable productions, and in its surface being much excavated by the burrows of the sooty petrels. It had also been frequented by geese at some preceding season of the year, and there were marks of its having been a breeding place for them; but at this time the vegetation was too much dried up to afford any subsistence. Crows of a shining

A A

black colour were numerous; and in two which I shot the bill was surrounded at the base with small feathers, extending one-fourth of the length towards the extremity. There were no appearances of the island having been before visited either by Europeans or Indians, and a single rat was the sole quadruped seen; but a few hair seals were killed upon the shore. Mr. Brown remarked that this was the first island where not a single novelty in natural history had presented itself to his observation.

There were strong squalls during the night, with rain, but the wind being off the land, the ship rode easy with a whole cable. At daylight the weather was more moderate, and we stretched out for the distant piece of land in the offing. At noon it was seven miles to windward, and seen to be an island of about five miles in length; and being near enough at dusk to observe that it afforded shelter, and that there were no apparent dangers, we continued to beat up, and got to anchor at half-past nine, in 7 fathoms, fine sand; the nearest beach being distant half a mile, and the island extending from S. 85° E. to 67° W.

Saturday, 13.—In the morning we were surprised to see breaking water about one mile from the ship, and as much from the shore. It was not far from the place where the last tack had been made in the evening, and the master found no more than six feet water close to it; so that we were fortunate in having escaped. The botanical gentlemen landed early; and I followed them to make the usual observations for the survey.

From my first station, at the north-east end of the island, the largest of the Top-gallant Isles bore S. 67° E., four or five miles. It is of little extent, but high and cliffy; and there are three rocks on its south side resembling ships under sail, from which circumstance this small cluster obtained its present name. To the south-west I distinguished several small islands, of which the northernmost and largest is remarkable from two high and sharp-pointed peaks upon it, lying in latitude 33° 57′ and longitude 134° 13′. This cluster, as it appeared to be, received the name of *Pearson's Isles*; but it is possible that what seemed at a distance to be divided into several may form two or three larger islands, or even be one connected land. Another island, about one mile long and of moderate height, was discovered bearing S. 72° W., about four leagues. It was surrounded with high breakers, as was a smaller isle near it; and the two were called *Ward's Isles*. These three small clusters, with Waldegrave's Isles, and this larger island, which was named *Flinders*, after the second lieutenant, form a group distinct from Nuyts' Archipelago; and I gave it the name of the Investigator's Group.

The form of Flinders' Island is nearly a square, of which each side is from three to five miles in length. Bights are formed in the four sides; but that to the north seems alone to afford good anchorage. In its composition this island is nearly the same as that of Waldegrave's largest isle; but between the granitic basis and the calcareous top there is a *stratum* of sand stone, in some places twenty feet thick. The vegetation differed from that of other islands before visited, in that the lower lands were covered with large bushes; and there was very little either of the white, velvety shrub (*atriplex*) or of the tufted, wiry grass. A small species of kanguroo, not bigger than a cat, was rather numerous. I shot five of them, and some others were killed by the botanists and their attendants, and found to be in tolerably good condition. We were now beginning to want a supply of water, and the northern part of the island was sought over carefully for it; but the nearest approach to success was in finding dried-up swamps in which the growing plants were tinged red, as if the water had been brackish. No other trees than a few small *casuarinas*, at a distance from the anchorage, were seen upon the island; but wood for fuel might with some difficulty be picked out from the larger bushes growing near the shore. The beaches were frequented by seals of the hair kind. A family of them consisting of a male, four or five females, and as many cubs was lying asleep at every two or three hundred yards. Their security was such that I approached several of these families very closely; and retired without disturbing their domestic tranquillity or being perceived by them.

At six o'clock, a very projecting point of calcareous cliffs, distant five miles, was the southernmost visible extreme. It was named *Point Drummond*, in compliment to captain Adam Drummond of the navy; and lies in 34° 10′ south and 135° 13′ east.

The coast from Waldegrave's Isles to Point Drummond runs waving in a south-eastern direction, and forms bights and broad, cliffy heads. It appeared to be of moderate elevation, and barren; but the further parts of it could not be well distinguished on account of the haze.

Tuesday, 16.—At daylight, Point Drummond was seven miles distant to the north-by-east. The shore, after falling back four or five miles from it, trended northward; but there was other land further out, and we steered for the opening between them, passing a rocky islet five miles from Point Drummond and nearly as much from the eastern shore. At eight o'clock we found ourselves in a bay whose width, from the outer western point of entrance, named *Point Sir Isaac*, to the shore on the east side, was near three leagues. It extended also far into the south-south-east but the depth diminished, in less than half an hour, to 4 fathoms, although the head of the bay was still six or seven miles distant. We were then two miles from the eastern shore, with Point Sir Isaac bearing N. 67° W.; and hoping to find deeper water in that direction, hauled to the westward; but coming into 3 fathoms, were obliged to tack, and the wind veering round from the sea, we worked to windward in the entrance of the bay.

The situation of Point Sir Isaac is 34° 27′ south, and from observations of the moon with stars on each side, in 135° 13′ east; but by the time-keepers corrected, which I prefer, the longitude is 135° 10′ east. The basis of the point seemed to be granitic, with an upper stratum of calcareous rock, much similar to the neighbouring isles of the Investigator's Group. Its elevation is inconsiderable, and the surface is sandy and barren, as is all the land near it on the same side. The large piece of water which it shelters from western winds I named *Coffin's Bay*, in compliment to the present vice-admiral Sir Isaac Coffin, Bart.; who, when resident commissioner at Sheerness, had taken so zealous a part in the outfit of the Investigator. Coffin's Bay extends four or five leagues to the south-eastward from Point Sir Isaac; but I do not think that any stream more considerable than perhaps a small rill from the back land falls into it, since sandy cliffs and beach were seen nearly all round. On the east side of the entrance the shore rises quickly from the beach to hills of considerable height, well covered with wood. The highest of these hills I call *Mount Greenly;* its elevation is between six and eight hundred feet, and it stands very near the water-side.

Many smokes were seen round Coffin's Bay, and also two parties of natives, one on each side; these shores were therefore better inhabited than the more western parts of the South Coast; indeed it has usually been found in this country that the borders of shallow bays and lagoons, and at the entrances of rivers, are by far the most numerously peopled. These natives were black and naked, differing in nothing that we could perceive from those of King George's Sound before described.

In the evening the wind veered to the southward; and at sunset we passed Point Sir Isaac at the distance of half a mile. Our course was then directed to the south-west, towards two high pieces of land which appeared in the offing, and obtained the name of *Greenly's Isles*. The ship was hove to at midnight; but on seeing the islands to leeward at two in the morning, we filled; and at three, tacked towards the main land. At daylight a rocky point which lies ten or eleven miles to the south-south-west of

Point Sir Isaac, and is called *Point Whidbey*, was distant two miles; and the peak upon the southernmost of Greenly's Isles bore S. 66° W., four or five leagues. At S. 18° E., seven or eight miles from Point Whidbey, lies an island one mile in length, the middlemost and largest of seven, which I named Whidbey's Isles, after my worthy friend the former master-attendant at Sheerness. The basis of these isles appeared to be granitic, but the more elevated are covered with a thick crust of calcareous rock; and in the middlemost this upper stratum is perforated, admitting the light through the island.

The two easternmost of Whidbey's Isles are close to a low projection of the main land which was named *Point Avoid*. It lies eleven or twelve miles to the east-south-east of Point Whidbey; and the shore between them forms so deep a bight that the peninsula between it and Coffin's Bay seems to be there not more than two or three miles broad. At the head of this bight is a low, rocky island, and there are rocks and breakers on each side of the entrance; on which account, and from its being exposed to the dangerous southern winds, I named it Avoid Bay.

At dusk in the evening, having weathered Whidbey's Isles, we tacked near Point Avoid and stretched off to sea; but on coming in with the land at daylight of the 18th, it appeared that nothing was gained, our situation being then in the same bight to the eastward of the point.

The shore of the bight is sandy and low, and trends from Point Avoid about five miles to the east; after which it takes a more southern direction and becomes higher, and the projecting parts of the waving coast-line are cliffy. Behind the shore the land rises to a moderate height, is destitute of vegetation, and of a yellow colour, but whether from the surface being of bare rock, or of sand, could not be distinguished.

In stretching off again, with the wind at east-south-east, we passed near to a small circular reef, lying nine miles from Point Avoid and six from the nearest shore. Azimuths taken at this time with three compasses on the binnacle, and the ship's head at south (magnetic), gave the mean variation 1° 12′ east; but with the surveying compass alone it was 1° 39′ east, which is what I allowed in the survey. On the preceding day the two guns upon the quarter-deck, nearest to the binnacle, had been struck down into the after-hold, from a persuasion that the differences so often found in the variations and bearings when on different tacks must arise from some iron placed too near the compasses. Strict search had been repeatedly made for sail needles, marline-spikes, or other implements of iron which might have been left in or about the binnacle, but I could fix on nothing unless it were the guns; for it is to be observed that, notwithstanding the constancy of the differences, the idea of any regularly acting cause to derange the needle had not yet fixed itself in my mind. The perfection to which naval science had arrived did not allow me to suppose, that if a constant and unavoidable attraction existed in ships, it would not have been found out, and its laws ascertained; yet no longer than three days before, differences had been observed sufficient, one would think, to have convinced any man that they were produced by some regular cause. Off Point Drummond, about fifteen leagues to the north of where the variation 1° 39' east was observed with the ship's head at south, both azimuths and an amplitude had been taken with the same compass. The first gave 1° 33' *west*, the head being south-east-by-east; and after we had tacked, and the head was south-west-by-west, the amplitude gave 3° 56' *east!* I did not yet see that as the ship's head was as much on the east side of the magnetic meridian in one case as it was to the west in the other, so was the variation as much too far west then as it was too far east afterward. Differences like this, of 5½°, which had frequently occurred, seemed to make accuracy in my survey unattainable from not knowing what variation to allow on the several bearings. The guns were removed in the hope to do away the differences, but they still continued to exist, nearly in the same proportion as before; and almost in despair, I at length set about a close examination of all the circumstances connected with them, in order to ascertain the cause, and if possible to apply a remedy; but it was long, and not without an accumulation of facts, before I could arrive at conclusions.

In the afternoon of the 19th, when the wind had returned to the south, we passed to windward of Liguanea Island, and saw it surrounded with many breakers on its south and west sides. The sloping low point was also visible; and three miles further eastward there was a steep head, with two high rocks and one lower near it, of which Mr. Westall made a sketch. This projection I named Cape Wiles, after a worthy friend at Liguanea, in Jamaica; it lies in latitude 34° 57' south and longitude 135° 38½' east. Before dark we got sight of a hill situate upon a projecting cape, thirteen miles to the east-south-east of Cape Wiles, and observed the intermediate coast to form a large bight or bay, which I proposed to examine in the morning; and for that purpose we stood off and on during the night, with the wind from the southward.

At daylight of the 20th the hill on the east side of the bight bore N. 68° E. five or six miles, and an island, named *Isle*

Williams, was seen to lie two miles from it to the south-east. We steered north-west soon afterward, up the bight; but in an hour were able to see the land all round, and that this place, which I called Sleaford Bay, was dangerous with the wind at south-east, as it was then blowing. We therefore braced up, to work out.

In the afternoon the wind favoured us by veering to south-by-west, and the passage between the projection of the hill and Isle Williams seeming to be clear, we steered through it with good soundings, the least being 12 fathoms upon rippling water. Three miles further the main land formed a point, and took the uncommon direction of N. 15° W.; but to the eastward, there was a large piece of land, whether island or main we could not tell, and several small islands lay between. The opening was four miles wide; and we steered into it, passing through ripplings of tide with irregular soundings. No land could be seen to the north-east, but the night was coming on; and as the eastern land sheltered us from the present wind, we ran within half a mile of the shore and anchored in 3½ fathoms. The master was sent to sound about the ship; and finding we had not a sufficient depth for swinging toward the shore, the anchor was tripped and let go further out, in 7 fathoms, on a sandy bottom. No part of the eastern land was visible beyond the bearing of N. 76° E., distant one mile and a half; and the furthest extreme of what we could be certain was main land bore N. 17° W.

A tide from the north-eastward, apparently the ebb, ran more than one mile an hour; which was the more remarkable from no set of tide, worthy to be noticed, having hitherto been observed upon this coast. No land could be seen in the direction from whence it came; and these circumstances, with the trending of the coast to the north, did not fail to excite many conjectures. Large rivers, deep inlets, inland seas, and passages into the Gulph of Carpentaria, were terms frequently used in our conversations of this evening; and the prospect of making an interesting discovery seemed to have infused new life and vigour into every man in the ship.

Early in the morning I went on shore to the eastern land, anxious to ascertain its connexion with or separation from the main. There were seals upon the beach, and further on, number-less traces of the kanguroo. Signs of extinguished fire existed every-where; but they bespoke a conflagration of the woods, of remote date, rather than the habitual presence of men, and might have arisen from lightning, or from the friction of two trees in a strong wind. Upon the whole I satisfied myself of the insularity of this land; and gave to it, shortly after, the name of Thistle's Island, from the master who accompanied me. In our way up the hills, to take a commanding station for the survey, a speckled, yellow snake lay asleep before us. By pressing the buttend of a musket upon his neck I kept him down whilst Mr. Thistle, with a sail needle and twine, sewed up his mouth; and he was taken on board alive for the naturalist to examine; but two others of the same species had already been killed, and one of them was seven feet nine inches in length. We were proceeding onward with our prize when a white eagle, with fierce aspect and outspread wing, was seen bounding towards us; but stopping short at twenty yards off, he flew up into a tree. Another bird of the same kind discovered himself by making a motion to pounce down upon us as we passed underneath; and it seemed evident that they took us for kanguroos, having probably never seen an upright animal in the island of any other species. These birds sit watching in the trees, and should a kanguroo come out to feed in the day-time, it is seized and torn to pieces by these voracious creatures. This accounted for why so few kanguroos were seen, when traces of them were met with at every step; and for their keeping so much under thick bushes that it was impossible to shoot them. Their size was superior to any of those found upon the more western islands, but much inferior to the forest kanguroo of the continent.

From a clear spot upon the north-western head of the island I traced the main coast to a cape bearing N. 18° W., where it was lost, but reappeared at a further distance, and extended to N. 2½° W. More to the right were three small islands, which I named *Sibsey, Stickney,* and *Spilsby Islands,* but no other land in a north-east, and none in an eastern direction. On the opposite side, six leagues out at sea, there was a small cluster of low islands, and some rocks and breakers at a less distance; these were called *Neptune's* Isles, for they seemed to be inaccessible to men. In the opening between Thistle's Island and the main are several small isles; and the two southernmost so much contract the entrance of the passage that one mile and a half of its breadth, between the main land and western isle, are alone safe for ships; I gave to this the name of Thorny Passage.

Thistle's Island is about twelve miles long, and from one to two or three in breadth, and in the middle part is high enough to be seen ten or twelve leagues from a ship's deck. The stone of the north-east end was found to be calcareous; but at the top of the north-west head, not less than two hundred feet high, there were many small pieces of granite, rounded to all appearance by attrition in the water. Some of the cliffs on the western side are white, as if composed of chalk, and the soil in general seemed to be sandy; yet the island was pretty well covered with wood, principally *eucalyptus* and *casuarina*. No water could be found; and as the ship's hold was becoming very empty, I returned on board, after observing the latitude, with the intention of running over to the main in search of it. But on comparing the longitude observed by lieutenant Flinders with that resulting from my bearings, a difference was found which made it necessary to repeat the observation on shore; and as this would prolong the time too near dusk for moving the ship, Mr. Thistle was sent over with a cutter to the mainland in search of an anchoring place where water might be procured.

The *latitude* of a small beach on the north end of Thistle's Island was found to be 34° 56′; and *longitude*, by the time-keepers corrected, 136° 3½′, agreeing with thirty sets of lunar observations reduced to a place connected with this by land bearings. The strongest *tides* set past the ship at the rate of two miles an hour, from the north-north-east and south-south-west; the latter, which appeared to be the flood, ceasing to run at the time of the moon's passage over the meridian. It rose seven feet and a half by the lead line in the night of the 20th; and there were two tides in the twenty-four hours.

At dusk in the evening the cutter was seen under sail, returning from the main land; but not arriving in half an hour, and the sight of it having been lost rather suddenly, a light was shown and lieutenant Fowler went in a boat, with a lanthorn, to see what might have happened. Two hours passed without receiving any tidings. A gun was then fired, and Mr. Fowler returned soon afterward, but alone. Near the situation where the cutter had been last seen he met with so strong a rippling of tide that he himself narrowly escaped being upset; and there was reason to fear that it had actually happened to Mr. Thistle. Had there been daylight, it is probable that some or all of the people might have been picked up; but it was too dark to see anything, and no answer could be heard to the hallooing or to the firing of muskets. The tide was setting to the southward and ran an hour and a half after the missing boat had been last seen, so that it would be carried to seaward in the first instance; and no more than two out of the eight people being at all expert in swimming, it was much to be feared that most of them would be lost.

Monday, 22.—At daybreak I got the ship under way and steered across Thorny Passage, over to the main land, in the direction where the cutter had been seen; keeping an officer at the mast-head, with a glass, to look out for her. There were many strong ripplings, and some uncommonly smooth places where a boat, which was sent to sound, had 12 fathoms. We passed to the northward of all these; and seeing a small cove with a sandy beach, steered in and anchored in 10 fathoms, sandy bottom; the main land extending from north-half-west, round by the west and south to east-south-east, and the open space being partly sheltered by the northern islands of the passage.

A boat was despatched in search of the lost cutter, and presently returned towing in the wreck, bottom upward; it was stove in every part, having to all appearance been dashed against the rocks. One of the oars was afterwards found, but nothing could be seen of our unfortunate shipmates. The boat was again sent away in search; and a midshipman was stationed upon a headland, without-side of the cove, to observe everything which might drift past with the tide. Mr. Brown and a party landed to walk along the shore to the northward, whilst I proceeded to the southern extremity of the mainland, which was now named Cape Catastrophe. On landing at the head of the cove I found several footmarks of our people, made on the preceding afternoon when looking for water; and in my way up the valley I prosecuted the same research, but ineffectually, although there were many huts and other signs that natives had resided there lately.

From the heights near the extremity of Cape Catastrophe I examined with a glass the islands lying off, and all the neighbouring shores, for any appearance of our people, but in vain; I therefore took a set of angles for the survey and returned on board; and on comparing notes with the different parties, it appeared that no further information had been obtained of our unfortunate companions.

Next morning I went in a boat ten miles along the shore to the northward, in the double view of continuing the search and carrying on the survey. All the little sinuosities of the coast were followed, and in one place I picked up a small keg which had belonged to Mr. Thistle, and also some broken pieces of the boat but these were all that could be discovered. After taking angles at three stations on the main land, I crossed over to the northernmost and largest of the six small islands lying within Thorny passage. It is a mile and a half long, with a small islet off the north, and another off its south end. These I called *Taylor's Isles*, in memory of the young gentleman who was in the cutter with Mr. Thistle. They lie near two miles from the main, and the depth between is from 7 to 10 fathoms, on a sandy bottom. A ship might anchor and be sheltered here, off a small beach at the north end of the largest island; but I did not find any fresh water, either there or on the opposite parts of the main land.

On returning to the ship I learned from some of the gentlemen who had been at the top of the highest hills at the back of the cove, that they had seen an inlet, going in westward, a little beyond where my excursion had terminated. Next day I went up with instruments; and having climbed upon a high lump of granite, saw the water extending 40° behind the coast, and forming, apparently, an extensive port. The view taken from near the same spot by Mr. Westall shows what was visible of this fine piece of water, and the appearance of the neighbouring land. In addition to this interesting discovery, I obtained bearings of Cape Wiles, of the furthest extremity of Thistle's Island, and of a group of four islands and two rocks, five leagues beyond it to the east-south-east. The largest of these was named *Wedge Island*, from its shape, and the group Gambier's Isles, in honour of the worthy admiral (now lord Gambier) who had a seat at the Admiralty board when the Investigator was ordered to be fitted.

This morning lieutenant Fowler had been sent to search the southern islands in Thorny Passage for any remains of our people; but he was not able to land, nor in rowing round them to see any indication of the objects of his pursuit. The recovery of their bodies was now the furthest to which our hopes extended; but the number of sharks seen in the cove and at the last anchorage rendered even this prospect of melancholy satisfaction extremely doubtful; and our want of water becoming every day more pressing, we prepared to depart for the examination of the new opening to the northward. I caused an inscription to be engraven upon a sheet of copper, and set up on a stout post at the head of the cove, which I named *Memory Cove;* and further to commemorate our loss, I gave to each of the six islands nearest to Cape Catastrophe the name of one of the seamen: Thistle's and Taylor's Islands have been already mentioned.

The reader will pardon me the observation that Mr. Thistle was truly a valuable man, as a seaman, an officer, and a good member of society. I had known him, and we had mostly served together, from the year 1794. He had been with Mr. Bass in his perilous expedition in the whale-boat, and with me in the voyage round Van Diemen's Land, and in the succeeding expedition to Glass-house and Hervey's Bays. From his merit and prudent conduct he was promoted from before the mast to be a midshipman, and afterwards a master in his Majesty's service. His zeal for discovery had induced him to join the Investigator when at Spithead and ready to sail, although he had returned to England only three weeks before, after an absence of six years. Besides performing assiduously the duties of his situation, Mr. Thistle had made himself well acquainted with the practice of nautical astronomy, and began to be very useful in the surveying department. His loss was severely felt by me; and he was lamented by all on board, more especially by his messmates, who knew more intimately the goodness and stability of his disposition.

Mr. William Taylor, the midshipman of the boat, was a young officer who promised fair to become an ornament to the service, as he was to society by the amiability of his manners and temper. The six seamen had all volunteered for the voyage. They were active and useful young men; and in a small and incomplete ship's company, which had so many duties to perform, this diminution of our force was heavily felt.

The soil of the land round Memory Cove, and of Cape Catastrophe in general, is barren; though the vallies and eastern sides of the hills are covered with brushwood, and in the least barren parts there are small trees of the genus *eucalyptus*. The basis stone is granite, mostly covered with calcareous rock, sometimes lying in loose pieces; but the highest tops of the hills are huge blocks of granite. Four kanguroos, not larger than those of Thistle's Island, were seen amongst the brushwood; and traces of natives were found so recent, that although none of the inhabitants were seen, they must have been there not longer than a day before. Water does consequently exist somewhere in the neighbourhood, but all our researches could not discover it.

Before quitting Memory Cove a boat was sent to haul a seine upon the beach, which was done with such success that every man had two meals of fish and some to spare for salting. In the morning we sailed for the new discovered inlet, and at two o'clock passed round the projection which had been set at N. 18° W. from Thistle's Island. It formed the south side of the entrance to the new opening, and is named Cape Donington. Our soundings in passing it were from 7 to 9 fathoms, and in steering south-westward we left an island four miles long, named *Boston Island*, on the starboard hand, and passed two islets on the other side, called *Bicker Isles*, which lie off *Surfleet Point*. On the depth of water diminishing to 5 fathoms we tacked, and presently came to an anchor on the west side of this point in 4½ fathoms, soft grey sand. We were then three miles within the entrance, and the nearest shore was a beach half a mile distant, lying under a hill which had been seen from Thistle's Island. This is a ridge of moderately high land about two miles long, but when seen to the north or south it assumes a conical form. I named it *Stamford Hill;* and

menced; and the gunner was installed in the command of a watering party, and furnished with axes to cut wood at such times as the pits might require to be left for replenishing.

The necessary duties being all set forward under the superintendance of proper officers, I employed the following days in surveying and sounding. The direction of the port was too remote from the meridian to obtain a base line from differences of latitude, which, when observed in an artificial horizon, and at stations wide apart, I consider to be the best; nor was there any convenient beach or open place where a base line could be measured. It was therefore attempted in the following manner:— Having left orders on board the ship to fire three guns at given times, I went to the south-east end of Boston Island with a pendulum made to swing half-seconds. It was a musket ball slung with twine, and measured 9·8 inches from the fixed end of the twine to the centre of the ball. From the instant that the flash of the first gun was perceived to the time of hearing the report I counted eighty-five vibrations of the pendulum, and the same with two succeeding guns; whence the length of the base was deduced to be 8·01 geographic miles. A principal station in the survey of Port Lincoln was a hill on the north side called *Northside Hill*, which afforded a view extending to Sleaford Mere and Bay and as far as Cape Wiles on one side, and to the hills at the beak of Coffin's Bay on the other. A great part of the bearings taken from hence crossed those from Stamford Hill very advantageously.

Amongst the various excursions made by the scientific gentlemen, one was directed to Sleaford Mere, of which they made the circuit. The two southern branches were found to terminate within a hundred yards of the head of Sleaford Bay, with which the mere had been suspected to have a communication from its water being not quite fresh; but they are separated by a stony bank too high for the surf ever to pass over it. At the head of the bay a boat's sail and yard were seen floating, and no doubt had belonged to our unfortunate cutter: after being set out to sea by the tide, it had been driven up there by the late south-east winds.

The refitment of the ship being nearly completed on the 3rd of March, lieutenant Fowler was sent round to Memory Cove in a boat, to make a final search along the shores and round the islands in Thorny Passage for the bodies of our late shipmates, which the sea might have thrown up. On the 4th the last turn of water was received, and completed our stock up to sixty tons; and the removal of our establishment from the shore waited only for the observation of a solar eclipse, announced in the nautical ephemeris for this day. The morning was cloudy, with rain; but towards noon the weather cleared up, and I had the satisfaction to observe the eclipse with a refracting telescope of forty-six inches focus, and a power of about two hundred. The beginning took place at 1^h $12'$ $37''\cdot8$ of apparent time, and the end at 3^h $36'$ $11''\cdot8$. So soon as the observation was concluded, the tents and astronomical instruments were carried on board, the launch was hoisted in, and everything prepared for going down the port on the following morning.

Many straggling bark huts, similar to those on other parts of the coast were seen upon the shores of Port Lincoln, and the paths near our tents had been long and deeply trodden; but neither in my excursions nor in those of the botanists had any of the natives been discovered. This morning, however, three or four were heard calling to a boat, as was supposed, which had just landed; but they presently walked away, or perhaps retired into the wood to observe our movements. No attempt was made to follow them, for I had always found the natives of this country to avoid those who seemed anxious for communication; whereas, when left entirely alone, they would usually come down after having watched us for a few days. Nor does this conduct seem to be unnatural; for what, in such case, would be the conduct of any people, ourselves for instance, were we living in a state of nature, frequently at war with our neighbours, and ignorant of the existence of any other nation? On the arrival of strangers, so different in complexion and appearance to ourselves, having power to transport themselves over, and even living upon an element which to us was impassable, the first sensation would probably be terror, and the first movement flight. We should watch these extraordinary people from our retreats in the woods and rocks, and if we found ourselves sought and pursued by them, should conclude their designs to be inimical; but if, on the contrary, we saw them quietly employed in occupations which had no reference to us, curiosity would get the better of fear; and after observing them more closely, we should ourselves seek a communication. Such seemed to have been the conduct of these Australians; and I am persuaded that their appearance on the morning when the tents were struck was a prelude to their coming down, and that had we remained a few days longer, a friendly communication would have ensued. The way was, however, prepared for the next ship which may enter this port, as it was to us in King George's Sound by captain Vancouver and the ship Elligood, to whose previous visits and peaceable conduct we were most probably indebted for our early intercourse with the inhabitants of that place. So far as could be perceived with a glass, the natives of this port were the same in personal appearance as those of King George's Sound and Port Jackson. In the hope of conciliating their good will to succeeding visitors, some hatchets and various other articles were left in their paths, or fastened to stumps of the trees which had been cut down near our watering pits.

In expressing an opinion that these people have no means of passing the water, it must be understood to be a deduction from our having met with no canoe, or the remains of any about the port; nor with any tree in the woods from which a sufficient size of bark had been taken to make one. Upon Boston Island, however, there were abundant marks of fire; but they had the appearance, as at Thistle's Island, of having been caused by some conflagration of the woods several years before, rather than of being the small fire-places of the natives.

There are kanguroos on the main land but none were caught; our efforts, both in hunting and fishing, were indeed very confined, and almost wholly unsuccessful. What has been said of the neck of land between the head of the port and Sleaford Mere may be taken as a description of the country in general; it is rocky and barren, but has a sufficient covering of grass, bushes, and small trees not to look desolate. The basis stone is granitic, with a *super-stratum* of calcareous rock, generally in loose pieces; but in some parts, as at Boston Island, the granite is found at the surface or immediately under the soil. Behind the beach, near our watering pits, the calcareous stone was so imperfectly formed that small shells and bits of coral might be picked out of it. This fact, with the saltness of Sleaford Mere and of a small lake on the south side of the port, accords with the coral found upon Bald Head and various other indications before mentioned to show that this part, at least, of Terra Australis cannot have emerged very many centuries from the sea, the salt imbibed by the rocks having not yet been all washed away by the rains. In the mountains behind Port Jackson, on the East Coast, at a vastly superior elevation, salt is formed in some places by the exhalation of the water which drips from the grit-stone cliffs.

Port Lincoln is certainly a fine harbour; and it is much to be regretted that it possesses no constant run of fresh water, unless it should be in Spalding Cove, which we did not examine. Our pits at the head of the port will, however, supply ships at all times; and though discoloured by whitish clay, the water has no pernicious quality, nor is it ill tasted. This and wood, which was easily procured, were all that we found of use to ships; and

B B

for the establishment of a colony, which the excellence of the port might seem to invite, the little fertility of the soil offers no inducement. The wood consists principally of the *eucalyptus* and *casuarina*.

Of the climate we had no reason to speak but in praise; nor were we incommoded by noxious insects. The range of the thermometer on board the ship was from 66° to 78°, and that of the barometer from 29·4 to 30·20 inches. The weather was generally clouded, the winds light, coming from the eastward in the mornings and southward after noon. On shore the average height of the thermometer at noon was 76°.

On the 5th of March in the morning we ran down the harbour, and anchored under Cape Donington at the entrance of Spalding Cove in 7 fathoms, soft mud; the north-western extremity of the point bearing N. 16° E., one mile, and partly hiding Point Bolingbroke. In the evening, lieutenant Fowler returned from his search. He had rowed and walked along the shore as far as Memory Cove, revisited Thistle's Island, and examined the shores of the isles in Thorny Passage, but could find neither any traces of our lost people nor fragments of the wreck. He had killed two or three kanguroos upon Thistle's Island.

Saturday, 6.—On the following morning I landed at Cape Donington to take some further bearings, and Mr. Evans, the acting master, was sent to sound across the entrance of Spalding Cove, and between Bicker Isles and Surfleet Point, where a small ship-passage was found. The boat was afterwards hoisted up; and our operations in Port Lincoln being completed, we prepared to follow the unknown coast to the northward, or as it might be found to trend.

At ten in the morning of March 6 we sailed out of Port Lincoln, and skirted along the east side of Boston Island and the entrance of Louth Bay. In the afternoon we passed within two miles of Point Bolingbroke, and at six in the evening came to an anchor in 10 fathoms, off the north side of Kirkby Island, which is the nearest to the point of any of Sir Joseph Banks' Group, and had been seen from Stamford Hill. A boat was lowered down to sound about the ship, and I went on shore to take bearings of the different islands; but they proved to be so numerous that the whole could not be completed before dark.

Sunday, 7.—I landed again in the morning with the botanical gentlemen, taking Arnold's watch and the necessary instruments for ascertaining the latitude and longitude. Twelve other isles of the group were counted, and three rocks above water; and it is possible that some others may exist to the eastward, beyond the boundary of my horizon, for it was not extensive. The largest island seen is four or five miles long, and is low and sandy, except at the north-east and south ends; it was called *Reevesby Island*, and names were applied in the chart to each of the other isles composing this group. The main coast extended northward from Point Bolingbroke, but the furthest part visible from the top of Kirkby Island was not more than four or five leagues distant.

Granite forms the basis of Kirkby Island, as it does of the neighbouring parts of the continent before examined; and it is in the same manner covered with a stratum of calcareous rock. The island was destitute of wood, and almost of shrubs; and although there were marks of its having been frequented by geese, none of the birds were seen, nor any other species of animal except a few hair seals upon the shore. This description, unfavourable as it is, seemed applicable to all the group, with the exception of Reevesby and Spilsby Islands, which are higher and of greater extent, and probably somewhat more productive.

The *latitude* of the north side of Kirkby Island, observed from an artificial horizon, was 34° 33′ 1″ south, and longitude by time-keepers, 136° 10′ 0″ east. The *variation* from azimuths taken on board the ship at anchor, with the head south-by-west (magnetic as usual), was 2° 40′ east; which corrected to the meridian would be 2° 2′ east, the same nearly as was observed in Memory Cove and at the entrance of Port Lincoln; but an amplitude taken on shore with the surveying theodolite gave 3° 57′ east. This seemed extraordinary when, except at Point Donington, no local attraction of importance had been found in the shores of Port Lincoln, where the stone is the same. It was, however, corroborated by the bearings; for that of Stamford Hill, with 3° 57′ allowed, differed only 2′ from the back bearing with the allowance of 1° 39′; which is a nearer conicidence than I have generally been able to obtain.

At two in the afternoon the anchor was weighed, and leaving most of Sir Joseph Banks' Group to the right, we steered northward, following the direction of the main land. The coast is very low and commonly sandy, from Boston Bay to the furthest extreme seen from Kirkby Island; but a ridge of hills, commencing at North-side Hill in Port Lincoln, runs a few miles behind it. In latitude 34° 20′ this ridge approaches the water side, and in its course northward keeps nearly parallel at the distance of two or three miles. It is moderately elevated, level, destitute of vegetation, and appeared to be granitic. At half-past six, when we hauled off for the night, the shore was five or six miles distant;

the furthest part bore N.N.E. ½ E., and a bluff inland mountain was set at N. 71° W., over the top of the front ridge.

The wind was moderate from the south-eastward; and at seven on the following morning, when the bluff inland mountain was bearing W. 2° N., we resumed our north-eastern course along the shore; which was distant seven miles, and had not changed its appearance. Towards noon the water shoaled to 6 fathoms at three miles from a sandy beach; a lagoon was visible from the mast head, over the beach, and a small inlet, apparently connected with it, was perceived soon afterward. A few miles short of this the ridge of hills turns suddenly from the shore, and sweeps round at the back of the lagoon, into which the waters running off the ridge appeared to be received. The corner hill, where the direction of the ridge is changed, was called *Elbow Hill;* and since losing sight of the bluff inland mount, it was the first distinguishable mark which had presented itself for the survey; it lies in latitude 33° 43′ and longitude 136° 42′. The coast there trends nearly east-by-north, and obliged us to haul close to the wind, in soundings of 7 to 9 fathoms.

We had then advanced more than twenty-five leagues to the north-north-east from Cape Catastrope; but although nothing had been seen to destroy the hopes formed from the tides and direction of the coast near that cape, they were yet considerably damped by the want of boldness in the shores and the shallowness of the water; neither of which seemed to belong to a channel capable of leading us into the Gulph of Carpentaria, nor yet to any very great distance inland.

At two o'clock the shore again took a northern direction, but it was still very low in front, and the depth did not materially increase. Land was presently distinguished on the starbord bow and beam; and before four, an elevated part, called *Barn Hill* from the form of its top, bore E. 4° N. We continued to follow the line of the western shore, steering north-north-east and north; and the wind being at south, we hauled north-westward at six o'clock, intending to anchor under the shelter of the land. From 7 fathoms the depth diminished to 5, and quickly to seventeen feet; upon which we veered round, ran back into 5 fathoms, and came to an anchor three or four miles off the shore on a sandy bottom. The wind blew fresh, with rainy squalls; but a whole cable being veered out, we rode smoothly all night. The furthest land visible to the northward consisted of detached hummocks of which the highest was called *Mount Young* in honour of the admiral. Abreast of the ship the land rose gradually from the beach to the ridge of hills which still continued to run behind it;

but at this place some back hills were visible over the ridge; and the highest of several hummocks upon the top, which served as a mark in the survey, was named *Middle Mount*.

Our prospect of a channel or strait, cutting off some considerable portion of Terra Australis, was lost, for it now appeared that the ship was entered into a gulph; but the width of the opening round Point Lowly left us a consolatory hope that it would terminate in a river of some importance. In steering for the point we came into 4 fathoms, but on hauling to the eastward found 8, although a dry sand-bank, was seen in that direction. The depth afterwards diminished to 6, on which the course for Point Lowly was resumed; and we passed it at the distance of a mile and a half, in 9 fathoms water. Here the gulph was found to take a river-like form, but the eastern half of it was occupied by a dry, sandy spit and shoal water. We continued to steer upwards, before the wind; but as the width contracted rapidly, and there was much shoal water, it was under very easy sail, and with an anchor ready to be let go. At four o'clock, in attempting to steer close over to the western side, we came suddenly into $2\frac{1}{2}$ fathoms; the ship was instantly veered to the eastward, and on the water deepening to 7, we let go the anchor and veered out a whole cable; for the wind blew a fresh gale right up the gulph, and between S. 4° W. and 30° E. there was no shelter from the land. At sunset a second anchor was dropped under foot.

We had reached near five leagues above Point Lowly, at the entrance of the narrow part of the gulph; but the shores were low on both sides, and abreast of the ship not so much as four miles asunder. At the back of the eastern shore was the ridge of mountains before mentioned, of which Mr. Westall made the sketch given in the Atlas; and the highest peak toward their northern extremity, afterwards called *Mount Brown*, bore N. 32° E. On the western side, upwards, there was moderately high, flat-topped land, whose eastern bluff bore N. 36° W., about three leagues, and there the head of the gulph had the appearance of terminating; but as the tide ran one mile an hour past the ship, we still flattered ourselves with the prospect of a longer course, and that it would end in a fresh-water river.

Wednesday, 10.—Early on the following morning, Messrs. Brown, Bauer and Westall, with attendants, set off upon an excursion to the eastern mountains, intending, if possible, to ascend to the top of Mount Brown; and I went away in a cutter, accompanied by the surgeon, to explore the head of the gulph, taking with me Arnold's pocket time-keeper. After crossing the middle shoal, upon which we had $2\frac{1}{2}$ fathoms in the ship, the water deepened to 10, but afterwards diminished to 2, on approaching the mangroves of the western side. Keeping then upwards, I had from 7 to 10 fathoms in the mid-channel, but found shoal water extending a mile, and sometimes more, from the shore, and no possibility of landing until we came near the broad, flat-topped hill. From the eastern bluff of this hill, Mount Brown bore N. 62° 20′ E., and *Mount Arden*, a peak nearly at the furthest extreme of the ridge, N. 18° 40′ E.; and the inlet was seen to run in a serpentine form to the northward, between low banks covered with mangroves. After taking the bearings we returned to the boat and pursued our course upward along the western shore, having from 4 to 7 fathoms past the bluff; but the inlet was there less than two miles wide, and a league further on it was contracted to one mile, half of which, besides, was occupied by mud flats. These banks were frequented by ducks and other water fowl; and some time being occupied in chasing them, our distance above the ship was not so much as five leagues in a straight line, when the setting sun reminded us of looking out for a place of rest. A landing was effected with some difficulty amongst the mangroves on the eastern shore; and from a small eminence of red earth I set the ship's mast heads at S. 14° E., and Mount Brown N. 85° E.

Thursday, 11.—Next morning we continued the examination upwards, carrying 4, 3, and 2 fathoms in mid-channel; but at ten o'clock our oars touched the mud on each side, and it was not possible to proceed further. I then landed and took observations in an artificial horizon for the time-keeper, which gave 4′ 34″ of longitude to the west of the ship, or only two seconds more than was deduced from the bearings. Mount Brown bore S. 72° E., Mount Arden N. 26° E., and my last station on the eminence of red earth S. 6° E. The inlet wholly terminated at one mile and a half to the N. 16° W.

It seemed remarkable, and was very mortifying, to find the water at the head of the gulph as salt nearly as at the ship; nevertheless it was evident that much fresh water was thrown into it in wet seasons, especially from the eastern mountains. The summits of the ridge lie from three to four leagues back from the water-side, but the greater part of that space seemed to be low, marshy land. To the northward no hill was visible, and to the westward but one small elevation of flat-topped land; all else in those directions was mangroves and salt swamps, and they seemed to be very extensive.

Two miles below the place where the observations for the time-keeper were taken was a small cliff of reddish clay on the western shore; and being near it on our return, when the sun was approaching the meridian, I landed to observe the latitude. It was 32° 27′ 56″ south, so that the termination of the gulph may be called in 32° 24½′ without making a greater error than half a mile. Mount Brown bore from thence S. 80½° E., and its latitude will therefore be 32° 30¼′ south; the longitude deduced from bearings and the time-keepers on board is 138° 0¾′ east.

Our return to the ship was a good deal retarded by going after the black swans and ducks amongst the flats. The swans were all able to fly, and would not allow themselves to be approached; but some ducks of two or three different species were shot, and also several sea-pies or red-bills. Another set of bearings was taken on the western shore, and at ten in the evening we reached the ship, where Mr. Brown and his party had not been long arrived. The ascent of Mount Brown had proved to be very difficult, besides having to walk fifteen miles on a winding course before reaching the foot; by perseverance, however, they gained the top at five on the first evening, but were reduced to passing the night without water; nor was any found until they had descended some distance on the following day. The view from the top of Mount Brown was very extensive, its elevation being not less than three thousand feet; but neither rivers nor lakes could be perceived, nor anything of the sea to the south-eastward. In almost every direction the eye traversed over an uninterruptedly flat, woody country; the sole exceptions being the ridge of mountains extending north and south, and the water of the gulph to the south-westward.

Mr. Brown found the stone of this ridge of craggy mountains to be argillaceous, similar to that of the flat-topped land where I had taken bearings on the west side of the inlet. It is reddish, smooth, close-grained, and rather heavy. Bushes and some small trees grown in the hollows of the rising hills; and between their feet and the mangrove swamps near the water there was some tolerably good though shallow soil.

We had seen fires upon the eastern shore opposite to Point Lowly on first entering the head of the gulph, and wherever I had landed there were traces of natives; Mr. Brown found them even to a considerable height up the side of the mountain; and it should therefore seem that the country here is as well inhabited as most parts of Terra Australis, but we had not the good fortune to meet with any of the people.

We had two flood *tides* in the day setting past the ship, and they ran at the strongest one mile and a half per hour; the rise appeared to be from six to eight feet, and high water to take place at two hours and a half after the moon passed the meridian. Except in the time of high water, which is considerably later than at Thorny Passage, the tides at the head have a near affinity to those at the entrance of the gulph; whence the great differences at Port Lincoln, intermediately situate, become so much the more extraordinary.

Saturday, 13.—Nothing of particular interest having presented itself to detain us at the head of the gulph, we got under way in the morning of the 13th, having a light breeze from the north-westward. The western shore had been followed in going up, and for that reason I proposed to keep close to the east side in returning; but before eight o'clock the water shoaled suddenly from 4 to 2 fathoms, and the ship hung upon a mud bank covered with grass, two or three miles from the shore. A kedge anchor was carried out astern; and in half an hour we again made sail downward, in soundings from 5 to 10 fathoms near the edge of the shoal.

Sunday, 14.—In the morning we followed the line of the great eastern shoal, and its direction permitted us to approach nearer to the land, with soundings between 8 and 4 fathoms. A little before noon, after running half an hour in less than 4 fathoms and getting within about six miles of the land, we were obliged to tack and stretch off, the wind having veered to the south-west. We beat to windward all the afternoon, and at sunset anchored in 3½ fathoms near the edge of the great bank and seven or eight miles from the land. The shore was low and sandy, but there was a ridge of hills behind it nearly similar to that on the west side of the gulph. Barn Hill lies at the back of this ridge and about twelve miles from the water; and towards the southern end of the ridge was another hill, also some distance inland, of which I shall have occasion to speak hereafter. A middle mount on the west side of the gulph, higher and further back than the one before set, was in sight from this anchorage.

Monday, 15.—On the morning of the 15th the wind had shifted to south-east; and the great bank then trending south-westward, we followed it with variable soundings between 3 and 10 fathoms. At ten o'clock the water had deepened to 15; and being then nearer to the west than to the east side of the gulph, and the wind having come more ahead, we tacked to the east-south-east; but in fifty minutes were obliged to steer westward again, having fallen into 3 fathoms on the edge of the bank. This is the narrowest part of the gulph below Point Lowly, the two shores being scarcely more than twenty miles asunder; and of this space, the great eastern bank, if the part where we last had 3 fathoms be

connected with it, occupies about eleven, and the shallow water
of the west side one or two miles. The soundings we had in
stretching westward across the deep channel were, from the
shoal, 3, 5, 7, 10, 12, 12, 12, 10, 9, 8, 7, 6, 7, 6, 5 fathoms, at
nearly equal distances asunder, and the last at six miles from
the western land.

After sounding across the channel we stood back, lying up
south-east, and reached within five miles of the eastern shore,
where the anchor was dropped in 4½ fathoms; Barn Hill bearing
N. 69° E., and a cliffy projection, named *Point Riley* after the
gentleman of that name in the Admiralty, S. 14° W., two or
three leagues. This point was the furthest visible part of the
eastern shore; and so low and uniform had the coast been from
the head of the gulph, that this was the first mark I had found
upon it for the survey. The great eastern bank, which we had
already followed about sixty miles, seemed to terminate at
Point Riley; and from thence southward the gulph greatly
enlarges its breadth. The situation of the point is about 33° 53'
south and 137° 30' E.

We got under way at six in the morning, and the wind being
from the south-eastward made a good stretch along the coast
until noon. A patch of breakers then then lay five miles to the south-
east; but the land was ten miles distant, and some white sandy
cliffs, four or five leagues from Point Riley, bore S. 52° E. The
intermediate coast, as also that which extends several leagues
to the north of the point, is low and sandy; but at a few miles
back it rises to a level land of moderate elevation, and is not ill
clothed with small trees. In the afternoon we had to beat against
a southern wind; and the coast in that part being too open for
anchorage, this was continued all night and the next morning;
but with so little profit that the same land was still in sight at
noon. At six in the evening the reddish cliffs were brought to
bear N. 44° E., and a long point, or an island lying off a point,
bore S. 43° W. two leagues. Our distance from a cliffy islet, close
under the shore, was two or three miles, but the breakers from
it were only half a mile off, and the depth was 4 fathoms.

On the 18th, in the morning, we fetched to windward of the
island-like point, to which I gave the name of *Point Pearce*, in
compliment to Mr. Pearce of the Admiralty. Its latitude is
34° 28½' south and longitude 137° 21' east. On the south side of
this point or island, for I could not fully ascertain its connection,
the shore falls back seven or eight miles to the east, and then
trends southward. It is low and very sandy, but rises gradually
to a level country of the same description as that near Point

Riley. At sunset the land was seen as far as south-west-by-south; and the wind favouring us a little, we made a stretch for it. A fire upon the shore served as a mark to steer by; and on approaching it at ten o'clock, the anchor was let go in 6 fathoms, upon a bottom of coarse sand and small stones, the weather being fine, and wind moderate off the land.

The howling of dogs was heard during the night, and at daylight the shore was found to be distant two or three miles, and was woody, rising land, but not of much elevation. A remarkable point, which I named *Corny Point*, bearing S. 73° W. three miles, was the furthest land visible to the westward; its latitude, from meridian observations of Jupiter and the moon, is 34° 52′ south, and longitude from the time-keepers 137° 6½′ east. Between this point and Point Pearce, twenty-eight miles to the north-north-east, is a large bay, well sheltered from all southern winds, and none others seem to blow with much strength here. The land trends eastward about seven leagues, from Corny Point to the head of the bay; but what the depth of water may be there, or whether any fresh stream fall into it, I am not able to state; the land, however, was better wooded, and had a more fertile appearance than any before seen in the neighbourhood. I called this Hardwicke Bay, in honour of the noble earl of that title.

Although the continuation of the main coast was not to be distinguished beyond the cape, yet there was land in sight at the distance of seven or eight leagues, from about south to S. 18½° W. Whether this land were an island or a part of the continent, and the wide opening to the eastward a strait or a new inlet, was uncertain; but in either case, the investigation of the gulph was terminated; and in honour of the respectable nobleman who presided at the Board of Admiralty when the voyage was planned and ship put into commission, I named it Spencer's Gulph. The cliffy-pointed cape which forms the east side of the entrance, and lies in 35° 18′ south and 136° 55′ east, was named Cape Spencer; and the three isles lying off it, with their rocks, *Althorp Isles*.

A line drawn from the nearest part of Cape Catastrophe to Cape Spencer will be forty-eight miles long, and so much is the entrance of the gulph in width. Gambier's Isles lie not far from the middle of the line; and if we measure upward from them, the gulph will be found, without regard to the small windings, to extend one hundred and eighty-five miles into the interior of the country. For the general exactness of its form in the chart I can answer with tolerable confidence, having seen all that is laid down, and, as usual, taken every angle which enters into the construction. Throughout the whole extent of the shores the

water line was almost every where distinguished; the only exceptions being small portions at the head of Hardwicke and Louth
Bays, of a bight near Point Lowly, and of the low land at the
back of the great Eastern Shoal.

At noon, when off Cape Spencer, the wind became variable and
light, with very hazy, cloudy weather; and the mercury in my
marine barometer had fallen two-tenths of an inch. At six in the
evening a breeze sprung up at west-north-west; and as I expected
a gale would come on, and that as usual it would veer to the
south-west, we ceased to follow the coast beyond Cape Spencer,
and steered for the land seen in the southern quarter. The
Althorp Isles were passed at eight o'clock, at the distance of
eight or nine miles; and the wind being fresh at west, we made
short trips during the night between the two lands, not knowing
what might be in the space to leeward. At daylight the ship was
nearly in mid-channel, between the southern land and Cape
Spencer, and nothing was seen to the eastward. It then blew a
fresh gale at south-west, with much sea running; we stretched
south-west under close-reefed top-sails, to get under the lee of
the southern land; and at eight o'clock, when the largest Althorp
Isle bore N. 32° W., it was distant six or seven miles to the south,
and extended from S. 61° W. to 79° E. as far as the eye could
reach. It was rather high and cliffy; but there was nothing by
which to judge of its connection with the main.

At ten o'clock we were close under the land; and finding the
water tolerably smooth, had shortened sail with the intention of
anchoring near a small, sandy beach; but the situation proving
to be too much exposed, we steered eastward along the shore
under two close-reefed topsails and fore-sail, the wind blowing-
strong in squalls from the south-west. The furthest land seen
ahead at noon was a projecting point, lower than the other cliffs;
it bore E. 7° S., four leagues, and lies in 35° 33' south and
137° 41' east. It was named *Point Marsden*, in compliment to
the second secretary of the Admiralty; and beyond it the coast
was found to trend southward into a large bay containing three
coves, any one of which promised good shelter from the gale. This
was called Nepean Bay, in compliment to the first secretary (now
sir Evan Nepean, Bart.), and we hauled up for it; but the strength
of the wind was such that a head land forming the east side of
the bay was fetched with difficulty. At six in the evening we
came to anchor in 9 fathoms, sandy bottom, within a mile of
the shore; the east extreme bearing S. 76° E., and the land near
Point Marsden, on the west side of Nepean Bay, N. 61° W., six
leagues. A piece of high land, seemingly unconnected, bore from

N. 45° to 78° E.; but no land could be distinguished to the northward.

Neither smokes nor other marks of inhabitants had as yet been perceived upon the southern land, although we had passed along seventy miles of its coast. It was too late to go on shore this evening; but every glass in the ship was pointed there, to see what could be discovered. Several black lumps, like rocks, were pretended to have been seen in motion by some of the young gentlemen, which caused the force of their imaginations to be much admired; next morning, however, on going toward the shore, a number of dark-brown kanguroos were seen feeding upon a grass-plat by the side of the wood and our landing gave them no disturbance. I had with me a double-barrelled gun, fitted with a bayonet, and the gentlemen my companions had muskets. It would be difficult to guess how many kanguroos were seen; but I killed ten, and the rest of the party made up the number to thirty-one, taken on board in the course of the day ; the least of them weighing sixty-nine, and the largest one hundred and twenty-five pounds. These kanguroos had much resemblance to the large species found in the forest lands of New South Wales, except that their colour was darker, and they were not wholly destitute of fat.

After this butchery, for the poor animals suffered themselves to be shot in the eyes with small shot, and in some cases to be knocked on the head with sticks, I scrambled with difficulty through the brushwood, and over fallen trees, to reach the higher land with the surveying instruments; but the thickness and height of the wood prevented anything else from being distinguished. There was little doubt, however, that this extensive piece of land was separated from the continent; for the extraordinary tameness of the kanguroos and the presence of seals upon the shore concurred with the absence of all traces of men to show that it was not inhabited.

The whole ship's company was employed this afternoon in skinning and cleaning the kanguroos; and a delightful regale they afforded, after four months' privation from almost any fresh provisions. Half a hundred weight of heads, fore-quarters and tails were stewed down into soup for dinner on this and the succeeding days; and as much steaks given, moreover, to both officers and men as they could consume by day and by night. In gratitude for so seasonable a supply I named this southern land Kanguroo Island.

Tuesday, 23.—Next day was employed in shifting the topmasts on account of some rents found in the heels. The scientific gentlemen landed again to examine the natural productions of the island, and in the evening eleven more kanguroos were brought on board; but most of these were smaller, and seemed to be of a different species to those of the preceding day. Some of the party saw several large running birds; which, according to their description, seemed to have been the emu or cassowary.

Not being able to obtain a distinct view from any elevated situation, I took a set of angles from a small projection near the ship, named *Kanguroo Head;* but nothing could be seen to the north, and the sole bearing of importance, more than had been taken on board, was that of a high hill at the extremity of the apparently unconnected land to the eastward: it bore N. 39° 10′ E., and was named *Mount Lofty.* The nearest part of that land was a low point bearing N. 60° E. nine or ten miles; but the land immediately at the back was high, and its northern and southern extremes were cliffy. I named it Cape Jervis, and it was afterwards sketched by Mr. Westall.

All the cliffs of Kanguroo Island seen to the west of the anchorage had the appearance of being calcareous, and the loose stones scattered over the surface of Kanguroo Head and the vicinity were of that substance; but the basis in this part seemed to be a brown slate, lying in *strata* nearly horizontal, and *laminæ* of quartz were sometimes seen in the interstices. In some places the slate was split into pieces of a foot long, or more, like iron bars, and had a shining, ore-like appearance; and the *strata* were then further from the horizontal line than I observed them to be elsewhere.

A thick wood covered almost all that part of the island visible from the ship; but the trees in a vegetating state were not equal in size to the generality of those lying on the ground, nor to the dead trees standing upright. Those on the ground were so abundant that in ascending the higher land a considerable part of the walk was made upon them. They lay in all directions, and were nearly of the same size and in the same progress towards decay; from whence it would seem that they had not fallen from age, nor yet been thrown down in a gale of wind. Some general conflagration, and there were marks apparently of fire on many of them, is perhaps the sole cause which can be reasonably assigned; but whence came the woods on fire? That there were no inhabitants upon the island, and that the natives of the continent did not visit it, was demonstrated, if not by the want of all signs of such visit, yet by the tameness of the kanguroo, an animal which, on the continent, resembles the wild deer in timidity. Perhaps lightning might have been the cause, or possibly the friction of two dead trees in a strong wind; but it would be somewhat extraordinary that the same thing should have happened at Thistle's Island, Boston Island and at this place, and apparently about the same time. Can this part of Terra Australis have been visited before, unknown to the world? The French navigator, *La Pérouse*, was ordered to explore it, but there seems little probability that he ever passed Torres' Strait.

Some judgment may be formed of the epoch when these conflagrations happened from the magnitude of the growing trees; for they must have sprung up since that period. They were a species of *eucalyptus*, and being less than the fallen trees, had most probably not arrived at maturity; but the wood is hard and solid, and it may thence be supposed to grow slowly. With these considerations I should be inclined to fix the period at not less than ten, nor more than twenty years before our arrival. This brings us back to La Pérouse. He was in Botany Bay in the beginning of 1788; and if he did pass through Torres' Strait, and come round to this coast, as was his intention, it would probably be about the middle or latter end of that year, or between thirteen and fourteen years before the Investigator. My opinion is not favourable to this conjecture; but I have furnished all the *data* to enable the reader to form his own judgment upon the cause which might have prostrated the woods of these islands.

The soil of that part of Kanguroo Island examined by us was judged to be much superior to any before seen, either upon the south coast of the continent or upon the islands near it, with the exception of some portions behind the harbours of King George's Sound. The depth of the soil was not particularly ascertained; but from the thickness of the wood it cannot be very shallow. Some sand is mixed with the vegetable earth, but not in any great proportion; and I thought the soil superior to some of the land cultivated at Port Jackson, and to much of that in our stony counties in England.

Never perhaps had the dominion possessed here by the kanguroo been invaded before this time. The seal shared with it upon the shores, but they seemed to dwell amicably together. It not unfrequently happened that the report of a gun fired at a kanguroo near the beach brought out two or three bellowing seals from under bushes considerably further from the water-side. The seal, indeed, seemed to be much the most discerning animal of the two; for its actions bespoke a knowledge of our not being kanguroos, whereas the kanguroo not unfrequently appeared to consider us to be seals.

March 24, in the morning, we got under way from Kanguroo Island in order to take up the examination of the main coast at Cape Spencer, where it had been quitted in the evening of the 20th, when the late gale commenced. The wind had continued to blow fresh from the southward, but had now moderated, and was at south-west. We steered north-westward from ten o'clock till six in the evening, and then had sight of land extending from N. 62° W. to a low part terminating at N. 17° E. distant three leagues. A hummock upon this low part was named *Troubridge Hill*, and at first it makes like an island. Nothing was visible to the eastward of the low land; whence I judged there to be another inlet or a strait between it and Cape Jervis. Soon after dusk the wind veered to south-by-east, on which we steered south-westward, and continued the same course until four in the morning; when the largest Althorp Isle being seen to the north-west, the ship was hove to, with her head eastward.

The wind fixed itself at south-east, and it took us two days to work back against it as far as Troubridge Hill. The shore is generally low and sandy; but with the exception of one very low point, it may be approached within two miles. Many tacks were made in these two days from the northern land across to Kanguroo Island, and gave opportunities of sounding the intermediate strait. From 45 fathoms, in the middle of the western entrance, the depth diminished quickly to 25, then more slowly to 20; after which it is irregular between 12 and 20 fathoms as far as the mouth of the second inlet. Of the two sides, that of Kanguroo Island is much the deepest; but there is no danger in any part to prevent a ship passing through the strait with perfect confidence, and the average width is twenty-three miles. It was named Investigator's Strait, after the ship. The bottom is mostly broken shells, mixed with sand, gravel or coral, and appeared to hold well.

Monday, 29.—In the morning, land was seen to the westward, and also a hummocky mountain, capped with clouds, apparently near the head of the inlet. There being almost no wind in the morning, we remained at anchor until nine o'clock, to set up afresh the rigging of the new topmasts; and I took a boat to sound upon a rippling near the ship, but found the same depth of 5 fathoms. Very little progress was made until noon, at which time shoal water obliged us to steer westward. At three the soundings had increased from 3½ to 10 fathoms, which was the deepest water to be found; for it became shallower on approaching the western shore. After steering various northwardly courses, we anchored at sunset in 5 fathoms, sand, shells and broken coral; the shores then appeared to close round at the distance of seven or eight miles; and the absence of tide gave no prospect of finding any river at the head of the inlet.

Tuesday, 30.—Early in the morning I went in a boat, accompanied by the naturalist, to examine more closely the head of the gulph. We carried from 4 to 3 fathoms water four miles above the ship, when it shoaled to fifteen and eight feet, which brought us to mud flats, nearly dry; but by means of a small channel amongst them we got within half a mile of the shore, and walked to it upon a bank of mud and sand.

It was then ten o'clock, and the tide was out; so that I judged the time of high water to be about seven hours after the moon's passage, or three hours later than at Kanguroo Island; and the ordinary rise appeared to be six or eight feet. An observation of the sun's meridian altitude from the artificial horizon showed the landing-place to be in latitude 34° 8′ 52″, and the uppermost water might be 30″ less; whence the extent of this inlet, from Cape Jervis on the east side of the entrance, is 1° 30′ of latitude.

Microscopic shells of various kinds, not larger than grains of wheat, were heaped up in ridges at high-water mark; further back the shore was sandy, but soon rose, in an undulating manner, to hills covered with grass; and several clumps of trees scattered over them gave the land a pleasing appearance from the water side. We set off in the afternoon for the Hummock Mount, which stands upon a northern prolongation of the hills on the west side of the inlet, and about eight miles from the water; but finding it could not be reached in time to admit of returning on board the same evening, I ascended a nearer part of the range to inspect the head of the inlet. It was almost wholly occupied by flats, which seemed to be sandy in the eastern part and muddy to the westward. These flats abounded with rays; and had we been provided with a harpoon, a boat load might have been caught. One black swan and several shags and gulls were seen.

I found the grass upon these pleasant-looking hills to be thinly set, the trees small, and the land poor in vegetable soil. The mountainous ridge on the east side of the inlet passes within a few miles of Hummock Mount, and appeared to be more sandy; but the wood upon it was abundant, and of a larger growth. Between the two ranges is a broad valley, swampy at the bottom; and into it the water runs down from both sides in rainy weather, and is discharged into the gulph, which may be considered as the lower and wider part of the valley.

This eastern ridge is the same which rises at Cape Jervis; from whence it extends northward towards Barn Hill and the ridge of mountains on the east side of Spencer's Gulph. If it joins that ridge, as I strongly suspect, its length, taking it only from Cape Jervis to Mount Arden, will be more than seventy leagues in a straight line. There are some considerable elevations on the southern part; Mount Lofty is one of them, and its height appeared nearly equal to that of Mount Brown to the north, or about three thousand feet. Another lies six or seven miles to the north-by-east of the Hummock Mount, near the head of this inlet, and seems to have been the hill set from Spencer's Gulph, at the anchorage of March 14, in the evening, when it was distant ten or eleven leagues and appeared above the lower range in front of Barn Hill.

From my station on the western hills of the new inlet, across to Spencer's Gulph, the distance was not more than thirty miles; but as I did not ascend the highest part of the range, the water to the westward could not be seen. Had the Hummock Mount been within my reach, its elevation of near fifteen hundred feet would probably have afforded an extensive view, both across the peninsula and of the country to the northward.

In honour of the noble admiral who presided at the Board of Admiralty when I sailed from England, and had continued to the voyage that countenance and protection of which Earl Spencer had set the example, I named this new inlet the Gulph of St. Vincent. To the peninsula which separates it from Spencer's Gulph I have affixed the name of Yorke's Peninsula, in honour of the Right Honourable Charles Philip Yorke, who followed the steps of his above-mentioned predecessors at the Admiralty.

On the 31st at daylight we got under way to proceed down the gulph, and having followed the eastern shore in going up, I wished to trace the coast of the peninsula in returning; but the wind being nearly at south, it could only be done partially. At two in the afternoon we tacked in 3 fathoms from the eastern shoals, and at sunset in the same depth one mile from the western side; our distance from the head of the gulph being then about ten leagues, and the furthest land of the peninsula bearing S. 3° E. The western hills come down nearly to the water-side here, and have the same pleasant appearance as at the head of the gulph, being grassy, with clumps of wood scattered over them; the coast-line is somewhat cliffy, and not so low as the eastern shore.

C C

April 1.—During the night the wind veered round to east, and at three in the morning to north-east; and a fire being seen on the eastern shore, the fore top sail was laid to the mast. At daybreak we made sail west for the land of the peninsula; and at half-past nine it was less than five miles distant, being very low and sandy. The northern extreme then in sight appeared to be the same land set in the evening at S. 3° E.; the other extreme was not far from Troubridge Hill, on the west side of the entrance to the gulph; and near it was an extensive bank, part of it dry, which I called *Troubridge Shoal*.

Our examination of the gulph of St. Vincent was now finished; and the country round it had appeared to be generally superior to that on the borders of Spencer's Gulph. Yorke's Peninsula between them is singular in its form, bearing some resemblance to a very ill-shaped leg and foot. The length of the southern part, from Cape Spencer to the sandy point near Troubridge Shoal, is about forty-five miles; and from thence northward, to where the peninsula joins the main land, about sixty miles. Its least breadth is from the head of Hardwicke Bay to the Investigator's Strait, where it appears to be not more than three leagues.

Having now made myself acquainted with the shores of the continent up to Cape Jervis, it remained to pursue the discovery further eastward; but I wished to ascertain previously whether any error had crept into the time-keepers' rates since leaving Kanguroo Island, and also to procure there a few more fresh meals for my ship's company. Our course was in consequence directed for the island, which was visible from aloft; but the winds being very feeble, we did not pass Kanguroo Head until eleven at night. I purposed to have run up into the eastern cove of Nepean Bay, but finding the water to shoal from 12 to 7 fathoms, did not think it safe to go further in the dark, and therefore dropped the anchor about three-quarters of a mile from the shore, and two miles to the south-west-by-west of our former anchorage.

Friday, 2.—Early on the following morning a party was sent to shoot kanguroos, another to cut wood, and the naturalists went to pursue their researches. The observations taken by lieutenant Flinders, compared with those of March 24th, showed the time-keepers to have erred 2′ 10″ of longitude to the west in the nine days we had been absent; and they had not, consequently, lost quite so much upon a medium as the Port Lincoln rates supposed. This small error, which principally affected the Gulph of St. Vincent, has been corrected in the longitudes there specified and in the chart by an equal proportion.

The kanguroos were found to be less numerous than at the first anchoring place, and they had become shy, so that very few were killed. Those few being brought off, with a boat load of wood, we got under way at daylight next morning to prosecute the examination of the coast beyond Cape Jervis; but the time-keepers had stopped, from having been neglected to be wound up on the preceding day. We therefore came to an anchor again; and as some time would be required to fix new rates, the ship was moored so soon as the flood tide made. I landed immediately, to commence the necessary observations, and a party was established on shore, abreast of the ship, to cut more wood for the holds. Lieutenant Fowler was sent in the launch to the eastward, with a shooting party and such of the scientific gentlemen as chose to accompany him; and there being skins wanted for the service of the rigging, he was directed to kill some seals.

On the 4th I was accompanied by the naturalist in a boat expedition to the head of the large eastern cove of Nepean Bay, intending if possible to ascend a sandy eminence behind it, from which alone there was any hope of obtaining a view into the interior of the island, all the other hills being thickly covered with wood. On approaching the south-west corner of the cove, a small opening was found leading into a considerable piece of water; and by one of its branches we reached within little more than a mile of the desired sandy eminence. After I had observed the latitude 35° 50′ 2″ from an artificial horizon, we got through the wood without much difficulty, and at one o'clock reached the top of the eminence, to which was given the name of *Prospect Hill*. Instead of a view into the interior of the island, I was surprised to find the sea at not more than one and half or two miles to the southward. Two points of the coast towards the east end of the island bore S. 77° E., and the furthest part on the other side, a low point with breakers round it, bore S. 33° W., at the supposed distance of four or five leagues. Between these extremes a large bight in the south coast was formed; but it is entirely exposed to southern winds, and the shores are mostly cliffy. Mount Lofty, on the east side of the Gulph of St. Vincent, was visible from Prospect Hill at the distance of sixty-nine miles, and bore N. 40° 40′ E.

The entrance of the piece of water at the head of Nepean Bay is less than half a mile in width, and mostly shallow; but there is a channel sufficiently deep for all boats near the western shore. After turning two low islets near the east point the water opens out, becomes deeper, and divides into two branches, each of two or three miles long. Boats can go to the head of the southern branch only at high water; the east branch appeared to be accessible at all times; but as a lead and line were neglected to be put into the boat, I had no opportunity of sounding. There are four small islands in the eastern branch; one of them is moderately high and woody, the others are grassy and lower; and upon two of these we found many young pelicans, unable to fly. Flocks of the old birds were sitting upon the beaches of the lagoon, and it appeared that the islands were their breeding-places; not only so, but from the number of skeletons and bones there scattered, it should seem that they had for ages been selected for the closing scene of their existence. Certainly none more likely to be free from disturbance of every kind could have been chosen than these islets in a hidden lagoon of an uninhabited island, situate upon an unknown coast near the antipodes of Europe; nor can anything be more consonant to the feelings, if pelicans have any, than quietly to resign their breath whilst surrounded by their progeny, and in the same spot where they first drew it. Alas for the pelicans! Their golden age is past; but it has much exceeded in duration that of man.

I named this piece of water *Pelican Lagoon*. It is also frequented by flocks of the pied shag, and by some ducks and gulls; and the shoals supplied us with a few oysters. The surrounding country is almost everywhere thickly covered with brushwood; and the soil appeared to be generally of a good quality, though not deep. Prospect Hill and the parts around it are more sandy; and there seemed to be swamps at the head of both branches of the lagoon. The isthmus which separates the southern branch from the sea is low, but rises gradually up the cliffs of the coast.

Not being able to return on board the same night, we slept near the entrance of the lagoon. It was high water by the shore, on the morning of the 5th, at six o'clock; but on comparing this with the swinging of the ship, it appeared that the tide had then been running more than an hour from the westward. The rise in the lagoon seemed to be from four to eight feet.

A few kanguroos had been obtained during my absence, as also some seal skins; but one of the sailors having attacked a large seal incautiously, received a very severe bite in the leg and was laid up. After all the researches now made in the island, it appeared that the kanguroos were much more numerous at our first landing-place, near Kanguroo Head, than elsewhere in the neighbourhood. That part of the island was clearer of wood than most others; and there were some small grass-plats which seemed to be particularly attractive and were kept very bare. Not less than thirty emus or cassowaries were seen at different times; but it so happened that they were fired at only once, and that ineffectually. They were most commonly found near the longest of the small beaches to the eastward of Kanguroo Head, where some little drainings of water oozed from the rocks. It is possible that with much time and labour employed in digging, water might be procured there to supply a ship; and I am sorry to say that it was the sole place found by us where the hope of procuring fresh water could be entertained.

Having received on board a good stock of wood, the launch was hoisted in and every thing prepared for going to sea. Next morning, so soon as the sun was sufficiently elevated to be observed in the artificial horizon, I landed to take the last set of observations for the time-keepers; after which the anchor was weighed, and we steered out of Nepean Bay with a light breeze from the south-west. Towards noon it fell calm, and finding by the land that the ship was set westward, an anchor was dropped nearly in our first place off Kanguroo Head.

The approach of the winter season, and an apprehension that the discovery of the remaining unknown part of the South Coast might not be completed before a want of provisions would make it necessary to run for Port Jackson, prevented me from stopping a day longer at Kanguroo Island than was necessary to obtaining rates for the time-keepers, and consequently from examining the south and west parts of that island. The direction of the main coast and the inlets it might form were the most important points to be now ascertained; and the details of particular parts, which it would interfere too much with those objects to examine, were best referred to the second visit, directed by my instructions to be made to this coast. When, therefore, the rising of a breeze made it advisable to get under way from Kanguroo Head, which was not until two in the afternoon, we proceeded for the eastern outlet of the Investigator's Strait, in order to prosecute the discovery beyond Cape Jervis.

This part of the Investigator's Strait is not more, in the narrowest part, than seven miles across. It forms a private entrance, as it were, to the two gulphs; and I named it *Back-stairs Passage*. The small bay where we had anchored is called the *Ante-chamber*; and the cape which forms the eastern head of the bay and of Kanguroo Island, and lies in 35° 48' south and 138° 13' east, received the appellation of Cape Willoughby. Without side of the passage, and almost equidistant from both shores, there are three small, rocky islets near together, called the *Pages*, whose situation is in latitude 35° 46½' south and longitude 138° 21' east; these are the sole dangers in Backstairs Passage, and two of them are conspicuous. Our soundings in beating through were from 8 to 23 fathoms; and in a strong rippling of tide like breakers there was from 10 to 12, upon a bottom of stones and shells.

At eight in the evening we tacked from Cape Willoughby; and having passed to windward of the Pages, stretched on east and north-eastward until four in the morning. Land was then seen under the lee, and a tack made off shore till daylight, when we stood in with the wind at east-south-east. At nine the land was distant five miles, and of a very different aspect to that of Cape Jervis. As far as six leagues from the cliffy southern extremity of the Cape the land is high, rocky and much cut by gullies or ravines; a short, scrubby brush-wood covers the seaward side, and the stone appeared to be slaty, like the opposite cliffs of Kanguroo Island. But here the hills fall back from the sea, and the shore becomes very low with some hummocks of sand upon it; and the same description of coast prevailed as far as could be seen to the eastward.

Before two in the afternoon we stretched eastward again, and at four a white rock was reported from aloft to be seen ahead. On approaching nearer it proved to be a ship standing towards us; and we cleared for action, in case of being attacked. The stranger was a heavy-looking ship, without any top-gallant masts up; and our colours being hoisted, she showed a French ensign, and afterwards an English jack forward, as we did a white flag. At half-past five, the land being then five miles distant to the north-eastward, I hove to, and learned, as the stranger passed to leeward with a free wind, that it was the French national ship *Le Geographe*, under the command of captain Nicolas Baudin. We veered round as *Le Geographe* was passing, so as to keep our broadside to her, lest the flag of truce should be a deception; and having come to the wind on the other tack, a boat was hoisted out, and I went on board the French ship, which had also hove to.

As I did not understand French, Mr. Brown, the naturalist, went with me in the boat. We were received by an officer who pointed out the commander, and by him were conducted into the cabin. I requested captain Baudin to show me his passport from the Admiralty; and when it was found and I had perused it, offered mine from the French marine minister, but he put it back without inspection. He then informed me that he had spent some time in examining the south and east parts of Van Diemen's Land, where his geographical engineer, with the largest boat and a boat's crew, had been left, and probably lost. In Bass Strait captain Baudin had encountered a heavy gale, the same we had experienced in a less degree on March 21 in the Investigator's Strait. He was then separated from his consort, *Le Naturaliste;* but having since had fair winds and fine weather, he had explored the South Coast from Western Port to the place of our meeting without finding any river, inlet or other shelter which afforded anchorage. I inquired concerning a large island said to lie in the western entrance of Bass Strait; but he had not seen it, and seemed to doubt much of its existence.

Captain Baudin was communicative of his discoveries about Van Diemen's land; as also of his criticisms upon an English chart of Bass Strait published in 1800. He found great fault with the north side of the strait, but commended the form given to the south side and to the islands near it. On my pointing out a note upon the chart, explaining that the north side of the strait was seen only in an open boat by Mr. Bass, who had no good means of fixing either latitude or longitude, he appeared surprised, not having before paid attention to it. I told him that some other and more particular charts of the Strait and its neighbourhood had been since published; and that if he would keep company until next morning, I would bring him a copy, with a small memoir belonging to them. This was agreed to, and I returned with Mr. Brown to the *Investigator.*

It somewhat surprised me that captain Baudin made no enquiries concerning my business upon this unknown coast, but as he seemed more desirous of communicating information, I was happy to receive it; next morning, however, he had become inquisitive, some of his officers having learned from my boat's crew that our object was also discovery. I then told him, generally, what our operations had been, particularly in the two gulphs, and the latitude to which I had ascended in the largest; explained the situation of Port Lincoln, where fresh water might be procured; showed him Cape Jervis, which was still in sight; and as a proof of the refreshments to be obtained at the large island opposite to it, pointed out the kanguroo-skin caps worn by my boat's crew, and told him the name I had affixed to the island in consequence. At parting the captain requested me to take care of his boat and people in case of meeting with them; and to say to *Le Naturaliste* that he should go to Port Jackson so soon as the bad weather set in. On my asking the name of the captain of *Le Naturaliste,* he bethought himself to ask mine; and finding it to be the same as the author of the chart which he had been criticising, expressed not a little surprise, but had the politeness to congratulate himself on meeting me.

The situation of the Investigator, when I hove to for the purpose of speaking captain Baudin, was 35° 40′ south and 138° 58′ east. No person was present at our conversations except Mr. Brown; and they were mostly carried on in English, which the captain spoke so as to be understood. He gave me, besides what is related above, some information of his losses in men, separations from his consort, and of the improper season at which he was directed to explore this coast; as also a memorandum of some rocks he had met with, lying two leagues from the shore, in latitude 37° 1′, and he spoke of them as being very dangerous.

I have been the more particular in detailing all that passed at this interview from a circumstance which it seems proper to explain and discuss in this place.

At the above situation of 35° 40′ south and 138° 58′ east, the *discoveries* made by captain Baudin upon the South Coast have their termination to the west; as mine in the Investigator have to the eastward. Yet Mons. Peron, naturalist in the French expedition, has laid a claim for his nation to the discovery of all the parts between *Western Port* in Bass Strait, and *Nuyts' Archipelago;* and this part of New South Wales is called *Terre Napoleon.* My Kanguroo Island, a name which they openly adopted in the expedition, has been converted at Paris into *L'Isle Decres;* Spencer's Gulph is named *Golfe Bonaparte;* the Gulph of St. Vincent, *Golfe Josephine;* and so on along the whole coast to Cape Nuyts, not even the smallest island being left without some similar stamp of French discovery. It is said by M. Peron, and upon my authority too, that the Investigator had not been able to penetrate behind the Isles of St. Peter and St. Francis; and though he doth not say directly that no part of the before unknown coast was discovered by me, yet the whole tenor of his Chap. XV induces the reader to believe that I had done nothing which could interfere with the prior claim of the French.

Yet M. Peron was present afterwards at Port Jackson when I showed one of my charts of this coast to captain Baudin, and pointed out the limits of his discovery; and so far from any prior title being set up at that time to Kanguroo Island and the parts westward, the officers of the Geographe always spoke of them as belonging to the Investigator. The first lieutenant, Mons. Freycinet, even made use of the following odd expression, addressing himself to me in the house of governor King, and in the presence of one of his companions, I think Mons. Bonnefoy: "Captain, if we had not been kept so long picking up shells and catching butterflies at Van Diemen's Land, you would not have discovered the South Coast before us."

The English officers and respectable inhabitants then at Port Jackson can say if the prior discovery of these parts were not generally acknowledged; nay, I appeal to the French officers themselves, generally and individually, if such were not the case. How then came M. Peron to advance what was so contrary to truth? Was he a man destitute of all principle? My answer is, that I believe his candour to have been equal to his acknowledged abilities; and that what he wrote was from over-ruling authority, and smote him to the heart; he did not live to finish the second volume.

The motive for this aggression I do not pretend to explain. It may have originated in the desire to rival the British nation in the honour of completing the discovery of the globe; or be intended as the forerunner of a claim to the possession of the countries so said to have been first discovered by French navigators. Whatever may have been the object in view, the question, so far as I am concerned, must be left to the judgment of the world; and if succeeding French writers can see and admit the claims of other navigators as clearly and readily as a late most able man of that nation has pointed out their own in some other instances, I shall not fear to leave it even to their decision.

I returned with Mr. Brown on board the Investigator at half-past eight in the morning, and we then separated from Le Geographe; captain Baudin's course being directed to the north-west, and ours to the south-ward. We had lost ground during the night, and the wind was very feeble at east, so that the French ship was in sight at noon

At the place where we tacked from the shore on the morning of the 8th, the high land of Cape Jervis had retreated from the water-side, the coast was become low and sandy, and its trending was north-east; but after running four or five leagues in that direction it curved round to the south-eastward, and thus formed a large bight or bay. The head of this bay was probably seen by captain Baudin in the afternoon; and in consequence of our meeting here, I distinguished it by the name of Encounter Bay. The succeeding part of the coast having been first discovered by the French navigator, I shall make use of the names in describing it which he or his country men have thought proper to apply; that

is, so far as the volume published enables me to make them out;
but this volume being unaccompanied with charts, and containing few latitudes and longitudes by which the capes and bays can
be identified, I must be excused should any errors be committed
in the nomenclature.

There was no wind from noon to two o'clock; and it appeared
by the lead that the ship was drifted to the west-north-west,
probably by a flood tide. On a breeze springing up from the
southward we stretched in for the shore; and at six in the evening
it was four miles distant, being sandy and generally very low;
but there were several hillocks upon it high enough to be seen
four or five leagues from a ship's deck, and one of them, more
bluff than the rest, and nearly destitute of vegetation, bore
N. 17° E. Next day at noon our situation was within three miles
of the land, but very little advanced beyond that of the preceding
day, our latitude being 35° 49⅜', and the bluff hummock in sight
bearing N. 22° W.

At one o'clock we bore away along the coast with a light breeze
from the north-eastward; and having run five leagues, tacked to
seaward soon after dark. Next morning we again followed the
coast at the distance of from five to three miles; and at noon a
somewhat projecting part, which appears to be the *Cape Bernouilli* of the French navigators, was three or four miles distant
to the east. Its latitude is 36° 33' and longitude 139° 51'; and
about six miles to the south-south-east there are two low, black
rocks lying close under the shore.

From Encounter Bay to this slight projection the coast is little
else than a bank of sand, with a few hummocks on the top,
partially covered with small vegetation; nor could anything in
the interior country be distinguished above the bank. The shore
runs waving between east-south-east and south-south-east; but
to form what is called Cape Bernouilli it trends south, and then
curves back south-eastward into a bight. The land then becomes
better clothed with bushes and small trees; and it also differs
from the more northern part in that some little risings of back
land were visible.

During the night we worked up successfully against a south-
south-east wind, for at six in the morning the low, outer extreme
of Cape Jaffa bore N. 15° E., six or seven miles. The shore is
sandy, but rises from the beach to a moderate elevation, and is
then well clothed with small wood. About three leagues to the
south of the cape is a cluster of low rocks, apparently the same
of which captain Baudin had given me information; they do not,

however, lie exactly in the situation expressed in his memorandum, and are not more than two miles from the land. We called them *Baudin's Rocks*.

Four miles beyond the rocks is a point of moderate elevation; sandy, but mostly overspread with bushes. This is their *Cape Lannes;* and on its north side is a small bay, called the *Baye de Rivoli*, with a sandy shore and open to west winds.

Wednesday, 14.—For the last two days there had been a little current in our favour, and notwithstanding that the winds had been mostly adverse, we made some progress along the coast; but on opening out the land beyond Cape Lannes, the current took a northern direction, and at noon of this day we were no further advanced than to have that cape bearing N. 86° E. at the distance of nine or ten miles. In the evening we got sight of a projecting and somewhat elevated part which lies ten leagues to the south-eastward of Cape Lannes, and appears to be the *Cape Buffon* of the French navigators. The intermediate coast is similar to that between Encounter Bay and Cape Bernouilli, with the sole difference that the hummocks upon the sandy bank are somewhat higher: nothing inland appeared above them.

The wind was again favourable in the night for making a long stretch to the southward; and it was prolonged to the next day at noon, when our distance from the coast was judged to be ten leagues; but no part of it was in sight, and we had then got out of soundings, there being no bottom at 200 fathoms.

The eastern wind died away at noon of the 16th, and the ship scarcely had steerage way until after midnight; a breeze then sprung up from the north-westward, and we steered north-east to make the land near Cape Buffon. At half-past seven the cape bore N. 1° W. seven miles, and was ascertained to be in nearly 37° 36' south and 140° 10' east. There is a bight in the coast on its north side where the land was not distinctly seen all round, owing probably to its being a low beach. At nine o'clock we bore away southward, keeping at the distance of two or three miles from the shore. It was the same kind of hummock-topped bank as before described; but a ridge of moderately high hills, terminated to the southward by a bluff, was visible over it, three or four leagues inland; and there was a reef of rocks lying in front of the shore. At noon, two larger rocks were seen at the southern end of the reef, and are those called by the French the *Carpenters*. They lie one or two miles from a sandy projection named by them *Cape Boufflers;* and here a prior title to discovery interferes.

On arriving at Port Jackson I learned, and so did captain Baudin, that this coast had been before visited. Lieutenant (now captain) *James Grant*, commander of His Majesty's brig Lady Nelson, saw the above projection, which he named *Cape Banks*, on Dec. 3, 1800; and followed the coast from thence through Bass Strait. The same principle upon which I had adopted the names applied by the French navigators to the parts discovered by them will now guide me in making use of the appellations bestowed by captain Grant.

The termination *to the west* of that part of the South Coast discovered by captain Baudin in Le Geographe has been pointed out; and it seems proper to specify its commencement *to the east*, that the extent of his *Terre Napoleon* may be properly defined. The beginning of the land which, of all Europeans, was first seen by him, so far as is known, cannot be placed further to the south-east than Cape Buffon; for the land is laid down to the northward of it in captain Grant's chart, though indistinctly. The Terre Napoleon is therefore comprised between the latitudes 37° 36' and 35° 40' south, and the longitudes 140° 10' and 138° 58' east of Greenwich; making, with the windings, about fifty leagues of coast, in which, as captain Baudin truly observed, there is neither river, inlet nor place of shelter, nor does even the worst parts of Nuyts' Land exceed it in sterility.

In the afternoon the wind veered to the southward, and we tacked from the shore, not being able to weather the Carpenters at the south end of the reef. A long swell rolled in at this time, and seemed to announce a gale from the southward, yet the wind died away in the night, and at daybreak a light breeze sprung up at north-west, and enabled us to close in with the land. We passed the Carpenters at the distance of four miles; but at two in the afternoon the wind again died away. A cliffy point, which proved to be the *Cape Northumberland* of captain Grant, was then in sight, as also were two inland mountains lying to the north-east; the nearest is his Mount Schanck, of a flat, table-like form; the further one, Mount Gambier, is peaked.

The long swell from the southward still prevailed, and the barometer was fast falling; but at seven in the evening a breeze sprung up once more from the north-west, and after stretching a little off from the shore, we laid to for the greater part of the night.

Close to Cape Northumberland are two pointed rocks resembling the back fins of sharks; and on its eastern side were heavy breakers, extending more than a mile from the shore. The situation of the cape, as near as it could be ascertained, is in 38° 2′ south and 140° 37½′ east.

Beyond Cape Northumberland the coast was found to trend east-by-north, but curved afterwards to east-by-south; it was higher than we had lately seen and not so barren; nevertheless, the shrubs and small trees did not more than half cover the sandy surface. We pursued the round of the coast at the distance of four or five miles, having three reefs in the top-sails on account of the squally weather. At ten o'clock, in a clear interval, land was seen bearing S. 51° E.; and a thick squall with rain coming on, in which the wind shifted suddenly from north-north-west to south-west, we were forced to haul close up and let out the third reefs in order to weather the coast. A constant succession of rainy squalls prevented us from knowing how the land lay for some time, nor could an observation for the latitude be obtained; but at half-past noon our anxiety was relieved by distinguishing the furthest extreme, a bold, cliffy, cape, bearing S. 72½° E., broad on the lee bow.

This high projection was the *Cape Bridgewater* of captain Grant. A hill upon it slopes to the edge of the cliffs in which the cape is begirt toward the sea; and on the land side it descends so low that the connection of the hill with the main could not be clearly discerned. To the northward, and nearly in a line with the first, are two other hills almost equal to it in elevation. As we passed Cape Bridgewater, a second cliffy head opened at S. 73½° E., and a further round the last at N. 83° E. These are the *Capes Nelson* and *Sir W. Grant*, though differing considerably in relative position from what they are laid down in captain Grant's chart.

At two o'clock, the weather having become somewhat finer, I ventured to bear away along the coast; and presently a small island with two hummocks on it and a rock nearer to the shore were visible: these are *Lawrence's Isles*.

It was seldom that the weather would allow of any thing being distinguished beyond two miles; and when the night came on we were quite uncertain of the trending of the coast. At eight o'clock, by favour of moon light and a short cessation of rain, land was perceived on the lee beam; it seemed to be a head of considerable elevation, and was judged to be from three to six miles off. The fore and mizen top-sails and reefed main-sail were immediately set, notwithstanding the danger to the masts; and there being much sea running, the ship was kept one point from the wind to make her go through the water. We had no chance of clearing the land on the other tack, and therefore our sole hope was that the coast might not trend any further to the southward.

Wednesday, 21.—At two in the morning the strength of the gale obliged us to take in the fore and mizen top sails and main sail; and we had soundings in 45 fathoms, small stones. Our anxiety was great until daylight, when it was dissipated by not finding any land near us; and in the course of the morning the wind moderated, the barometer began to ascend, and the weather became even fine. Our latitude at noon was 39° 10½′ and longitude 144° 22′; the last being 22′ more than given by the log. High land was then visible astern, extending from about N. 50° to 17° W., at the supposed distance of twelve or fifteen leagues.

We were now entered into Bass Strait; and the subsiding of the sea made me suspect that the large island, concerning which I had made inquiry of captain Baudin, was to windward. The south part of this island was discovered by Mr. Reid in a sealing expedition from Port Jackson; and before quitting New South Wales in 1799, I had received an account of its lying to the north-west of Hunter's Isles. It afterwards appeared that the northern part was seen in January 1801 by Mr. John Black, commander of the brig *Harbinger,* who gave to it the name of King's Island. Of this I was ignorant at the time; but since it was so very dangerous to explore the main coast with the present south-west wind, I was desirous of ascertaining the position of this island before going to Port Jackson, more especially as it had escaped the observation of captain Baudin.

We tacked to the south-south-east at three o'clock, working up for King's Island, which was distant about five or six leagues directly to windward. In the night we lay up south, parallel with the east side of the island; but the soundings having diminished to 16 fathoms, I feared we might be approaching a reef of rocks lying off the south-east end, of which Mr. Reid had spoken. We therefore tacked to the northward at eleven o'clock; and after beating until three in the following afternoon, got to an anchor in 9 fathoms, fine sand, under the north-east end of King's Island; the nearest part of the shore being distant a short half mile, and the extremes bearing S. 37° E. and N. 69° W.

A boat was immediately hoisted out, and I landed with the botanical gentlemen. On stepping out of the boat I shot one of those little bear-like quadrupeds called *Womat;* and another was afterwards killed. A seal, of a species different to any yet seen by us, was also procured; its phippers behind were double when compared to the common kinds of seal, and those forward were

smaller, and placed nearer to the head; the hair was much
shorter, and of a blueish, grey colour; the nose flat and broad;
and the fat upon the animal was at least treble the usual quantity.
I never saw the sea elephant, and possibly this might have been
a young female; but there was no appearance of any trunk. A
top-mast studding-sail boom, not much injured, was lying near
the landing-place; and as I afterwards learned that the wreck
of a vessel had been found upon the west side of the island, this
boom had probably drifted from thence.

The north-east part of King's Island extends south-east-by-
east, three or four leagues. The shore is mostly of sand, and
behind the beach it was washed or blown up in great ridges, but
partly overspread with a kind of dog grass which kept the sand
together. In general the land is low; but some little eminences
appeared at a distance, and at the north end of the island there
is a short range of hills, moderately high and covered with wood.
Granite seemed to be the basis of the shore where we landed.
Behind the front ridges of sand was a brush wood, so thick as to be
almost impenetrable; but whilst I was occupied in taking bearings, the botanists found some openings in the brush, and picked
up so many plants as to make them desirous of a further examination. We returned on board at dusk, with our womats, the
seal and a kanguroo; the last being of a middle size between the
small species of the lesser islands and the large kind found at
Kanguroo Island and on the continent. It appeared indeed, all
along the South Coast, that the size of the kanguroo bore some
proportion to the extent of land which it inhabited.

Saturday, 24.—In the morning the wind blew fresh from the
southward. A boat was sent on shore with Mr. Brown and his
party; and at eleven o'clock, when they returned, we got under
way.

A small lake of fresh water was found at a little distance
behind the sandy ridges in front of the shore. This was surrounded by a good vegetable soil; and the number of plants,
collected near it was greater than had before been found upon any
one island. The small lake is too far from the sea side for a ship
to obtain water from it conveniently; but two little streams
which drained from the sand hills made it probable that fresh
water might have been obtained anywhere at this time by digging.
The water of these rills was tinged red, similar to that obtained
at King George's Sound and to the pools I had before seen at
Furneaux's Islands; and as the stone in these places is granite,
and water so discoloured was not found any where else, it seems

very probable that the discolouring arises from the granite and granitic sand.

Two more womats were killed this morning; and a skull was picked up which was thought to be of a small dog, but more probably was that of an opossum.

The time was fast approaching when it would be necessary to proceed to Port Jackson, both on account of the winter season, and from the want of some kinds of provisions. Before this took place I wished to finish as much of the South Coast as possible, and would have recommenced at Cape Bridgewater had the wind been favourable; but it still blew fresh from the southward, and all that part remained a lee shore. I determined, however, to run over to the high land we had seen on the north side of Bass Strait, and to trace as much of the coast from thence eastward as the state of the weather and our remaining provisions could possibly allow.

In steering north-north-west from King's Island, two small isles were seen lying off the north-west side; the first opening from the northern extreme at S. 50°, and the second being clear of it at S. 36° W. These are the same which Mr. Black named New Year's Isles; and his Harbinger's Reefs were seen to extend, in patches, nearly two leagues from the north end of King's Islands; but there is, as I afterwards learned, one or more passages between the reefs, and another between them and the island.

At three in the afternoon the northern land was in sight, and the highest hills of King's Island were sinking below the horizon as seen from the deck. Their distance was twenty-five miles; and consequently the elevation of them is between four and five hundred feet above the level of the sea. At five o'clock a bluff head, the most projecting part of the northern land, was distant three or four leagues; it was Captain Grants' Cape Otway.

We then hauled to the wind and stood off and on; at daylight bore away for the land with a moderate breeze from the southward; and at eight o'clock, when Cape Otway bore N. 69° W. ten miles, we steered north-eastward along the shore. On the west side of Cape Otway the coast falls back somewhat to the north, and projects again at the distance of ten or eleven miles, where it is not, as I think, more than three leagues to the east of the headland seen under the lee at eight in the evening of the 20th. From Cape Otway, eastward, the shore trends east-north-east about three leagues, to a projection called Cape Patton, and according to Captain Grant a bay is formed between them; but at three leagues off nothing worthy of being called a bay could be

perceived. Beyond Cape Patton the coast took a more northern
direction to a point with a flat-topped hill upon it, and further
than this it was not visible.

The whole of this land is high, the elevation of the uppermost
parts being not less than two thousand feet. The rising hills
were covered with wood of a deep green foliage, and without any
vacant spaces of rock or sand; so that I judged this part of the
coast to exceed in fertility all that had yet fallen under
observation.

Cape Otway lies very nearly in latitude 38° 51′ south and
longitude 143° 29′ east. The width of the north-west entrance to
Bass Strait, between this cape on the north and King's Island
to the south is therefore, sixteen leagues; and with the trifling
exception of the Harbinger's Reefs, which occupy not quite two
leagues of the southern part, the passage is free from danger.
In such parts of it as we got soundings the depth was between
38 and 50 fathoms.

Monday, 26.—In the morning we kept close to an east-south-
east wind, steering for the land to the north-eastward; and at
nine o'clock captain Grant's Cape Schanck, the extreme of the
preceding evening, was five leagues distant to the N. 88° E., and a
rocky point towards the head of the bight bore N. 12° E. On
coming within five miles of the shore at eleven o'clock we found
it to be low, and mostly sandy, and that the bluff head which
had been taken for the north-end of an island was part of a
ridge of hills rising at Cape Schanck. We then bore away
westward in order to trace the land round the head of the deep
bight.

On the west side of the rocky point there was a small opening,
with breaking water across it; however, on advancing a little
more westward the opening assumed a more interesting aspect,
and I bore away to have a nearer view. A large extent of water
presently became visible within side; and although the entrance
seemed to be very narrow, and there were in it strong ripplings
like breakers, I was induced to steer in at half-past one, the ship
being close upon a wind and every man ready for tacking at a
moment's warning. The soundings were irregular between 6 and
12 fathoms until we got four miles within the entrance, when they
shoaled quick to 2¾. We then tacked; and having a strong tide
in our favour, worked to the eastward between the shoal and the
rocky point, with 12 fathoms for the deepest water. In making
the last stretch from the shoal the depth diminished from 10
fathoms quickly to 3, and before the ship could come round, the

D D

flood tide set her upon a mud bank and she stuck fast. A boat was lowered down to sound, and finding the deep water lie to the north-west, a kedge anchor was carried out; and having got the ship's head in that direction, the sails were filled and she drew off into 6 and 10 fathoms; and it being then dark, we came to an anchor.

The extensive harbour we had thus unexpectedly found I supposed must be Western Port, although the narrowness of the entrance did by no means correspond with the width given to it by Mr. Bass. It was the information of captain Baudin, who had coasted along from thence with fine weather, and had found no inlet of any kind, which induced this supposition; and the very great extent of the place, agreeing with that of Western Port, was in confirmation of it. This, however, was not Western Port, as we found next morning; and I congratulated myself on having made a new and useful discovery; but here again I was in error. This place, as I afterwards learned at Port Jackson, had been discovered ten weeks before by lieutenant John Murray, who had succeeded captain Grant in the command of the Lady Nelson. He had given it the name of Port Phillip, and to the rocky point on the east side of the entrance that of *Point Nepean*.

Our situation was found in the morning to be near two miles from the south shore, and the extreme towards Point Nepean bore N. 83° W., two leagues. About three miles to the north-by-west were some dry rocks, with bushes on them, surrounded with mud flats; and they appeared to form a part of the same shoal from which we had three times tacked in 2½ and 3 fathoms. The mud bank where the ship had grounded is distinct from the middle shoal; but I am not certain that it is so from the south shore, from which it is one mile distant. The Bluff Mount (named *Arthur's Seat* by Mr. Murray, from a supposed resemblance to the hill of that name near Edinburgh) bore S. 76° E.; but from thence the shore trended northward so far that the land at the head of the port could not be seen even from aloft. Before proceeding any higher with the ship I wished to gain some knowledge of the form and extent of this great piece of water; and Arthur's Seat being more than a thousand feet high and near the water-side, presented a favourable station for that purpose.

After breakfast I went away in a boat, accompanied by Mr. Brown and some other gentlemen, for the Seat. It was seven or eight miles from the ship; and in steering nearly a straight course for it we passed over the northern skirt of the shoal where the ship had touched; but afterwards had from 7 to 5 fathoms nearly to the shore. Having observed the latitude there from an artificial horizon, I ascended the hill; and to my surprise found the port so extensive, that even at this elevation its boundary to the northward could not be distinguished. The western shore extended from the entrance ten or eleven miles in a northern direction to the extremity of what, from its appearance, I called *Indented Head;* beyond it was a wide branch of the port leading to the westward, and I suspected might have a communication with the sea; for it was almost incredible that such a vast piece of water should not have a larger outlet than that through which we had come.

I took an extensive set of bearings from the clearest place to be found on the north-western, bluff part of the hill; and we afterwards walked a little way back upon the ridge. From thence another considerable piece of water was seen, at the distance of three or four leagues; it seemed to be mostly shallow; but as it appeared to have a communication with the sea to the south, I had no doubt of its being Mr. Bass's Western Port.

Arthur's Seat and the hills and vallies in its neighbourhood were generally well covered with wood; and the soil was superior to any upon the borders of the salt water which I have had an opportunity of examining in Terra Australis. There were many marks of natives, such as deserted fire-places and heaps of oyster shells; and upon the peninsula which forms the south side of the port a smoke was rising, but we did not see any of the people. Quantities of fine oysters were lying upon the beaches, between high and low water marks, and appeared to have been washed up by the surf; a circumstance which I do not recollect to have observed in any other part of this country.

Wednesday, 28.—We returned on board at dusk in the evening; and at daylight the anchor was weighed with the intention of coasting round the port with the ship. The wind was at northeast, but the flood tide was in our favour; and having made a stretch toward the middle shoals, we tacked and ran east-south-east along their south side, until past eight, when, the flood having ceased, we came to in 7 fathoms. At slack water in the afternoon we again steered eastward, but were soon obliged to anchor for want of wind; and I found that this slow mode of proceeding was not at all suited to the little time for which we had provisions remaining, besides that there was much probability of getting frequently aground; the plan of examining the port with the ship was therefore abandoned.

Having left orders with Mr. Fowler, the first lieutenant, to take the ship back to the entrance, I went in a boat early next morning with provisions for three days, in order to explore as much of the port as could be done in that time. Round the east end of the middle shoals I carried 6 and 7 fathoms; and keeping north-eastward, had 8 and 9 fathoms at a mile or more from the shore, and 4 close past the second rocky point above Arthur's Seat. The wind being at north-west, I was obliged to land behind some rocks more than two miles short of the third point, but walked to it with my surveying instruments. This was nine miles from the Seat, and the furthest part of the shore seen from thence; further on the shore falls back more eastward, in long sandy beaches, and afterwards curves to the north-west; but it was lost to sight long before joining the land on the west side of the port. After taking angles and observing for the latitude and longtitude, I rowed to windward for Indented Head, five leagues off. At the end of the first mile and a half the depth was 11 fathoms, but afterwards no bottom at 12 until within two miles of the western shore, where it was 9 fathoms. We landed at nine o'clock at night, near the uppermost part which had yet been seen.

Friday, 30.—In the morning a fire was perceived two hundred yards from the tent; and the Indians appeared to have decamped from thence on our landing. Whilst I was taking angles from a low point at the north-easternmost part of Indented Head, a party of the inhabitants showed themselves about a mile from us; and on landing there we found a hut with a fire in it, but the people had disappeared, and carried off their effects. I left some strips of cloth, of their favourite red colour, hanging about the hut, and proceeded westward along the shore to examine the arm of the port running in that direction.

Three natives having made their appearance abreast of the boat, we again landed. They came to us without hesitation, received a shag and some trifling presents with pleasure, and parted with such of their arms as we wished to possess without reluctance. They afterwards followed us along the shore; and when I shot another bird, which hovered over the boat, and held it up to them, they ran down to the water-side and received it without expressing either surprise or distrust. Their knowledge of the effect of fire-arms I then attributed to their having seen me shoot birds when unconscious of being observed; but it had probably been learned from Mr. Murray.

At noon I landed to take an observation of the sun, which gave 38° 7′ 6″ for the latitude; my position being nearly at the

northern extremity of Indented Head. Some bearings were taken
from the brow of a hill a little way back; and after a dinner of
which the natives partook, we left them on friendly terms to
proceed westward in our examination. The water became very
shallow abreast of a sandy point, whence the shore trends nearly
south-west; and there being no appearance of an opening to the
sea this way, I steered across the western arm, as well to ascertain its depth as with the intention of ascending the hills lying
behind the northern shore. Two of the peaks upon these hills had
been set from the ship's deck at sunset of the 25th, at the distance
of thirty-seven miles; and as their elevation must consequently
be a thousand feet, or more, I expected to obtain from thence
such a view of the upper parts of the port as would render the
coasting round it unnecessary.

The width of the western arm was found to be six miles; and
the soundings across augmented regularly to 6 fathoms in mid-
channel, and then decreased in the same way; but there was less
than 3 fathoms at two miles from the northern shore. That side
is indeed very low and marshy, with mud banks lying along it;
and we had difficulty in finding a dry place to pitch the tent, and
still more to procure wood wherewith to cook the ducks I had
shot upon the banks.

May 1st.—At day dawn I set off with three of the boat's crew
for the highest part of the back hills called *Station Peak*. Our
way was over a low plain, where the water appeared frequently
to lodge; it was covered with small-bladed grass, but almost
destitute of wood, and the soil was clayey and shallow. One or
two miles before arriving at the feet of the hills we entered a wood
where an emu and a kanguroo were seen at a distance; and the
top of the peak was reached at ten o'clock. My position was then
21′ of latitude from Point Nepean, in the direction of N. 28° 30′
W., and I saw the water of the port as far as N. 75° E., at the
distance of seven or eight leagues; so that the whole extent of the
port, north and south, is at least thirty miles. The extremity of
the western arm bore S. 15° 45′ W., which makes the extent, east
and west, to be thirty-six miles; but there was no communication
with the sea on that side, nor did the western arm appear to be
navigable beyond seven miles above where I had crossed it.
Towards the interior there was a mountain bearing N. 11° E.,
eleven leagues distant; and so far the country was low, grassy
and very slightly covered with wood, presenting great facility
to a traveller of penetrating inland.

I left the ship's name on a scroll of paper, deposited in a small pile of stones upon the top of the peak; and at three in the afternoon reached the tent, much fatigued, having walked more than twenty miles without finding a drop of water. Mr. Lacy, the midshipman of the boat, had observed the latitude at the tent from an artificial horizon to be 38° 2′ 22″; and Station Peak bore from thence N. 47° W.

In the evening we rowed back to Indented Head, and landed there soon after dark. Fires had been seen moving along the shore, but the people seemed to have fled; though we found two newly erected huts with fires in them, and utensils, which must have belonged to some of the people before seen, since there was boiled rice in one of the baskets. We took up our quarters here for the night, keeping a good watch; but nothing was seen of the Indians till we pushed off from the shore in the morning, when seven showed themselves upon a hill behind the huts. They ran down to examine their habitations, and finding every thing as they had left it, a litte water excepted of which we were in want, they seemed satisfied; and for a short time three of them followed the boat.

Along the north-east and east sides of Indented Head I found the water to be shoal for nearly a mile off; but on approaching the entrance of what Mr. Murray called Swan Harbour, but which I have taken the liberty to converting into *Swan Pond*, it became somewhat deeper. Seeing swans there, I rowed into it after them, but found the place full of mud banks, and seldom more than three or four feet in depth. Three of the birds were caught; and at the south side of the entrance, upon the sandy peninsula, or island as it is when the tide is in, I shot some delicate teal, and found fresh water in small ponds.

The ship was lying about three miles within the mouth of the port, near to the south shore; and after I had taken bearings at two stations on the sandy peninsula, we steered a straight course for her, sounding all the way. It appeared that there was a passage up the port of a mile wide between the middle banks and the western shore, with a depth in it from 3 to 4½ fathoms. On the western extremity of the banks I had 2½ fathoms, and afterwards 5, 7, 4, 7, 8, 9, 9 to the ship.

Lieutenant Fowler had had a good deal of difficulty in getting back to the entrance of the port; owing in part to the western winds, and partly from the shoals, which do not seem to lie in any regular order. He had touched upon one of these, where there was ten feet on one side of the ship, and on the other 5 fathoms. This seems to have been a more eastern part of the same shoal upon which we had before grounded; but no danger is to be feared from these banks to a flat-floored ship.

I find it very difficult to speak in general terms of Port Phillip. On the one hand it is capable of receiving and sheltering a larger fleet of ships than ever yet went to sea; whilst on the other, the entrance, in its whole width, is scarcely two miles, and nearly half of it is occupied by the rocks lying off Point Nepean, and by shoals on the opposite side. The depth in the remaining part varies from 6 to 12 fathoms; and this irregularity causes the strong tides, especially when running against the wind, to make breakers, in which small vessels should be careful of engaging themselves; and when a ship has passed the entrance, the middle shoals are a great obstacle to a free passage up the port. These shoals are met with at four miles directly from the entrance, and extend about ten miles to the east-south-east, parallel with the south shore; they do not seem, however, to be one connected mass, for I believe there are two or three deep openings in them, though we had not time to make an examination.

No runs of fresh water were seen in any excursions; but Mr. Charles Grimes, surveyor-general of New South Wales, afterwards found several, and in particular a small river falling into the northern head of the port. Mr. Grimes was sent by governor King, in 1803, to walk round, and survey the harbour; and from his plan I have completed my chart of Port Phillip. The parts of the coast left unshaded are borrowed from him, and the soundings written at right angles are those of his companion, lieutenant Robbins.

The country surrounding Port Phillip has a pleasing, and in many parts a fertile appearance; and the sides of some of the hills and several of the vallies are fit for agricultural purposes. It is in great measure a grassy country, and capable of supporting much cattle, though better calculated for sheep. To this general description there are probably several exceptions; and the southern peninsula, which is terminated by Point Nepean, forms one, the surface there being mostly sandy, and the vegetation in many places little better than brush wood. Indented Head, at the northern part of the western peninsula, had an appearance particularly agreeable; the grass had been burned not long before, and had sprung up green and tender; the wood was so thinly scattered that one might see to a considerable distance; and the hills rose one over the other to a moderate elevation, but so gently that a plough might every where be used. The vegetable soil is a little mixed with sand, but good, though probably not deep, as I judged by the small size of the trees.

The most common kinds of wood are the *casuarina* and *eucalyptus*, to which Mr. Grimes adds the *banksia, mimosa* and some others; but the timber is rarely sound, and is not large.

Were a settlement to be made at Port Phillip, as doubtless there will be some time hereafter, the entrance could be easily defended; and it would not be difficult to establish a friendly intercourse with the natives, for they are acquainted with the effect of fire-arms and desirous of possessing many of our conveniences. I thought them more muscular than the men of King George's Sound; but, generally speaking, they differ in no essential particular from the other inhabitants of the South and East Coasts except in language, which is dissimilar, if not altogether different to that of Port Jackson, and seemingly of King George's Sound also. I am not certain whether they have canoes, but none were seen.

In the woods are the kanguroo, the emu or cassowary, paroquets, and a variety of small birds; the mud banks are frequented by ducks and some black swans, and the shores by the usual seafowl common in New South Wales. The range of the thermometer was between 61° and 67°; and the climate appeared to be as good and as agreeable as could well be desired in the month answering to November. In 1803, colonel Collins of the marines was sent out from England to make a new settlement in this country; but he quitted Port Phillip for the south end of Van Diemen's Land, probably from not finding fresh water for a colony sufficiently near to the entrance.

The rise of *tide* is inconsiderable in the upper parts of the port; near the entrance it is from three to six feet. By the swinging of the ship, which, however, varied at different anchorages, it appeared to be high water two hours and a half after the moon's passage; but at Point Nepean the time of high water by the shore is said by Mr. Grimes to be only one hour after the moon. At Western Port, Mr. Bass found high water to take place half an hour after the moon's passage, and the tide to rise from ten to fourteen feet. This great increase, in a place so near, seems extraordinary; but may perhaps be accounted for by the meeting of the tides from two entrances, whilst Port Phillip has only one, and that every narrow.

On the 3rd of May at daylight the anchor was weighed to go out of Port Phillip with the last half of the ebb; and the wind being from the westward, we backed, filled and tacked occasionally, dropping out with the tide. When the entrance was cleared, and five miles distant, Mr. Westall took a view of it, which will be an useful assistance in finding this extensive but obscure port; and at eleven o'clock, when we bore away eastward to pass Cape Schanck, he sketched that cape and the ridge of hills terminating at Arthur's Seat. Cape Schanck is a cliffy head, with three rocks lying off, the outermost of which appears at a distance like a ship under sail : the latitude is 38° 29' or 30' south, and longitude 144° 53' east. It will always be desirable for vessels to get sight of this cape before they run far into the great bight for Port Phillip; and if the wind blow strong from the southward it will be unsafe to run without having seen it.

Cape Schanck is also an excellent mark for ships desiring to go into Western Port, of which it forms the west side of the principal entrance; but as there are many breakers and shoals on that side, which extend almost to mid-channel, it will be necessary to give the cape a wide berth by keeping over to Phillip Island on the starboard side.

We steered eastward along the south side of Phillip Island, and passed a needle-like rock lying under the shore. Cape Wollamai is the east end of the island, and forms one side of the small, eastern entrance to the port; and at three o'clock when it bore, N. 14° E., five or six miles, its longitude was ascertained by means of the time-keepers to be 145° 25' east: the latitude deduced from bearings is 38° 33' south. *Wollamai* is the native name for a fish at Port Jackson, called sometimes by the settlers light-horseman, from the bones of the head having some resemblance to a helmet; and the form of this cape bearing a likeness to the head of the fish, induced Mr. Bass to give it the name of Wollamai.

We ran south-eastward along the shore, at the rate of six or seven knots, until sunset; when a steep head, supposed to be the Cape Liptrap of captain Grant, was seen through the haze. We soon afterwards hauled to the wind off shore, under treble-reefed top-sails; and the gale increasing, with much swell from the south-westward, the close reefs were taken in. At midnight, tacked to the northward, and stood off and on till daybreak; the wind being strong at west, and weather squally with rain. We then bore away for the land, which was seen to leeward.

Besides Rodondo, which lies about six miles to the south-by-east of the promontory, I distinguished five or six less conspicuous isles, lying along the south and west sides of this remarkable headland; these are called Glennie's Isles. To the N. 88° E. from Rodondo, and distant about two leagues, was a small island which appears to have been one of Moncur's Isles; and in steering south-eastward we got sight of the Devil's Tower, and of the high island and rocks named Sir Roger Curtis' Isles. These names were given by captain Grant in 1800; but he was not the discoverer of the places to which they are applied. They are all laid down upon my chart of 1799, on the authority of Mr. Bass; and when it is considered that this enterprising man saw them from an open boat, in very bad weather, their relative positions to Wilson's Promontory will be thought surprisingly near the truth. Unfortunately the situation of the promontory itself, owing to some injury done to his quadrant, is considerably in error, being twelve or fourteen miles wrong in latitude. A reef is mentioned by captain Grant as lying to the southward between Rodondo and Moncur's Isles; and a rock, level with the water, was seen in the same situation by the ships Gato and Castle of Good Hope, from which last it received the appropriate name of *Crocodile Rock*. This also was seen by Mr. Bass, and laid down in its relative situation; but in the Investigator I was not sufficiently near to get sight of this important danger.

We continued to steer south-eastward, round all these islands, having a fresh gale at west-south-west with squally weather. Wilson's Promontory was no longer visible.

Not seeing any more islands to the southward from the mast-head, we bore away east soon after noon to make Kent's Groups; and before three o'clock they both came in sight, as did an island to the northward, which seems to have been one of the small cluster discovered by Mr. John Black, and named Hogan's Group.

At five in the evening I thought myself fortunate to get a sight of Furneaux's great island through the haze; and also of a small, craggy isle which had been before fixed relatively to the inner Sister. To obtain the positions of these places by our time-keepers was to me an important object; since they were connected with the former survey of Furneaux's Islands and the north-eastern part of Van Diemen's Land.

At daylight of the 5th the course was altered more northward; and at noon land was seen from the mast head to the north-north-west, probably some of the hills at the back of the Long Beach, and distant not less than twenty leagues: our latitude was 38° 32′ south and longitude 149° 35′ east. The wind had then moderated, and having shifted to north-west we kept close up to make Cape Howe. At four, hove to and sounded, but no bottom could be had with 90 fathoms; the land extended in patches

from west-north-west distant twenty-five or more leagues to
near the Ram Head at north; and consequently the hills at the
back of the Long Beach must be of considerable elevation,
superior to any other land *near the sea* in the southern, or perhaps
any part of New South Wales.

On the wind shifting to the east side of north, next day, I
tacked to get in with the land; being desirous of running near
to as much of the coast, and correcting its longitude in our way
to Port Jackson, as could be done without loss of time; but at
noon the wind veered back, and our north-eastern course was
resumed. The land could not then be further distant than nine or
ten leagues; but no part of it was in sight, nor from the dulness
of the weather could any observation be taken.

After a squally night the wind fixed at west-by-north; and at
daybreak of the 7th the land was visible from west to north-west,
and our course was parallel to it. By four next day the heads of
Port Jackson were in sight. At dusk the flag-staff upon the South
Head bore west-south-west, and our distance from the shore was
seven or eight miles.

I tried to beat up for the port in the night, being sufficiently
well acquainted to have run up in the dark, had the wind permitted; but we were still to leeward in the morning, and Mr.
Westall made a good sketch of the entrance. At one o'clock, we
gained the heads, a pilot came on board, and soon after three the
Investigator was anchored in Sydney Cove.

There was not a single individual on board who was not upon
deck working the ship into harbour; and it may be averred that
the officers and crew were, generally speaking, in better health
than on the day we sailed from Spithead, and not in less good
spirits. I have said nothing of the regulations observed after we
made Cape Leeuwin; they were little different from those
adopted in the commencement of the voyage, and of which a strict
attention to cleanliness and a free circulation of air in the messing
and sleeping-places formed the most essential parts. Several of
the inhabitants of Port Jackson expressed themselves never to
have been so strongly reminded of England as by the fresh colour
of many amongst the Investigator's ship's company.

So soon as the anchor was dropped, I went on shore to wait
upon his Excellency Philip Gidley King, Esq., governor of New
South Wales, and senior naval officer upon the station; to whom
I communicated a general account of our discoveries and
examinations upon the South Coast, and delivered the orders
from the Admiralty and Secretary of State. These orders

directed the governor to place the brig Lady Nelson under my command, and not to employ the Investigator on other service than that which was the object of the voyage; and His Excellency was pleased to assure me that every assistance in the power of the colony to render should be given to forward a service so interesting to his government, and to himself. The Lady Nelson was then lying in Sydney Cove; but her commander, lieutenant Grant, had requested permission to return to England, and had sailed six months before.

Besides the Lady Nelson, there were in the port His Majesty's armed vessel Porpoise, the Speedy, south-whaled, and the Margaret privateer; also the French national ship Le Naturaliste, commanded by captain Hamelin, to whom I communicated captain Baudin's intention of coming to Port Jackson so soon as the bad weather should set in. Le Geographe's boat had been picked up in Bass' Strait by Mr. Campbell of the brig Harrington, and the officers and crew were at this time on board Le Naturaliste.

The duties required to fit the ship for prosecuting the voyage with success being various and extensive, Cattle Point, on the east side of Sydney Cove, was assigned to us by the governor for carrying on some of our employments, whilst others were in progress on board the ship and in the dockyard. On the morning after our arrival we warped to a convenient situation near the point, and sent on shore the tents, the sail-makers and sails, and the cooper with all the empty casks. Next day the observatory was set up, and the time-keepers and other astronomical instruments placed there under the care of lieutenant Flinders, who, with Mr. Franklin, his assistant, was to make the necessary observations and superintend the various duties carrying on at the same place; and a small detachment of marines was landed for the protection of the tents.

PRINTED BY RICHARD CLAY & SONS, LTD.,
AT BUNGAY, SUFFOLK, IN GREAT BRITAIN